ORGANIZATION BEHAVIOR AND CHANGE

Managing Human Resources For Organizational Effectiveness

THOMAS C. HEAD
Assistant Professor
College of Commerce
DePaul University

PETER F. SORENSEN, Jr.
Professor and Chairman of
Management and Organizational Behavior
Illinois Benedictine College

BERNARD H. BAUM
Professor and Director of Health Resources Management
School of Public Health
and
Professor of Management and Sociology
University of Illinois at Chicago

JOANNE C. PRESTON
Professor of Organization Development
School of Business & Management
Pepperdine University

TENTH EDITION

Published by
STIPES PUBLISHING L.L.C.
10–12 Chester Street
Champaign, Illinois 61820

To our families and students.

ISBN 0-87563-645-4

PREFACE

This collection of readings has been drawn together in an effort to facilitate for our students the process of acquiring an introduction and overview of what we feel are the major contemporary perspectives on organizational behavior (OB).

We feel obligated to make our own position and orientation clear. We profess to be "humanistic" in orientation. We believe that organizational effectiveness and the opportunity for human growth and dignity are not incompatible, but rather complementary goals. We recognize, however, that the case for more restrictive or "mechanistic" organizations is not closed or perhaps it is more appropriate to say has just recently been reopened. But even in these more traditional models of organization, there should be no incompatibility between dignity and effectiveness.

Although we anticipate that our students' initial exposure to OB may very well, at times, be confusing, we hope they will take comfort in the knowledge that they are not alone in their confusion, and that to a considerable extent, this is a reflection of the state of development of OB. We hope, however, that in bringing together these readings, our students will have the opportunity of sharing with us more fully the interest, the curiosity, and to some extent, the knowledge which we have acquired concerning organizational behavior.

We have waived royalties or any other form of profit from the sale of this book in order to provide it to students at minimal cost.

Thomas C. Head

Peter F. Sorensen, Jr.

Bernard H. Baum

Joanne C. Preston

TABLE OF CONTENTS

INTRODUCTION

The study of organizational behavior has just entered its adolescent years. On the one hand it is confident that it "knows what it knows", but on the other hand it rebelliously questions the paradigms of the past. It is an outgrowth of the older field of human relations. But unlike the human relations movement, it is more concerned with study, analysis, and understanding than application. The field of OB does, however, provide the basis for extensive behavioral applications and techniques in administration and management. It is interdisciplinary in nature, drawing on the more traditional fields of psychology, sociology, political science, and anthropology. Because of its youth and interdisciplinary nature, it is characterized by a number of approaches to the study of organizations and frequently contradictory findings. Consequently, the student of OB is confronted with a task of considerable magnitude in his/her attempt to "make sense" of the field.

We have chosen for our organizing strategy a scheme which we have found of considerable help in our own attempts at this task. The readings move from an initial micro to a macro orientation. The set of readings following the introductory section is concerned with the smallest unit of behavioral analysis, the individual and problems of motivation. The readings then move to a more macro level of consideration, interpersonal relations, and to the organization as whole. The final section presents articles on specific issues popular among managers today.

The readings include both articles which are written for practicing managers and articles which are written primarily for an academic audience. Both kinds of articles have been included in an attempt to expose the student to the variety of readings which characterize the field.

The collection of readings is divided into six parts: Management and Organizational Behavior, the Individual and Motivation, Interpersonal Behavior, Leadership and Group Dynamics, Organization Structure and Influence, Organization Development and Current Issues, and a seventh section contains a number of surveys frequently used in both research and practice. It is our hope and expectation that these readings in our volume are only the initial phase of the student's exposure to OB and that the material provided in this book can serve as a useful point of departure for further study, both in and out of the classroom.

EXHIBIT 1

ORGANIZATION OF READINGS

INTRODUCTION
HALL
MCGREGOR

MICRO		MACRO		
INDIVIDUAL (MOTIVATION)	INTERPERSONAL (LEADERSHIP AND GROUP DYNAMICS)	ORGANIZATION (STRUCTURE AND INFLUENCE)	ORGANIZATION DEVELOPMENT (CHANGE)	CURRENT ISSUES
HEAD	LUTHANS	LIKERT	LARSEN	HOFSTEDE
HEAD	HUNT	SORENSEN & BAUM	WOODMAN	BLACKBURN
HEAD	HOUSE & MITCHELL	BURNS	BABCOCK	LAWLER
KERR	BLAKE & MOUTON	LAWRENCE & LORSCH	BABUROGLU & GARR	CASCIO
KERR	MOORE	SAYLES	HEAD, SORENSEN & STOTZ	NIELSEN
LAWLER	HOWELL & AVOLIO		SORENSEN, HEAD,	
HAMNER & HAMNER	KEYS		SCOGGINS & LARSEN	
MITCHELL	PRESTON			
	FELDMAN			
	SIMON			
	BERTRAND & MOSIER			

PART I
MANAGEMENT AND ORGANIZATIONAL BEHAVIOR

This section consists of two articles. The first article by Jay Hall discusses how managers learn to manage. The second is by (in many individuals' opinions) the father of organizational behavior, Douglas McGregor. This article sets forth the classic description of Theory X and Theory Y. This discussion is an abridged version of his book *The Human Side of Enterprise,* which is one of the most influential early works in the field.

ON THE CARE AND FEEDING OF MANAGERIAL TALENT

Jay Hall

How do managers learn to manage? Given our lackluster productivity and the generally poor job managers have been doing of late, this question is both timely and legitimate. Any serious attempt to answer it prompts one rather sobering conclusion. Regardless of how they have come to be managers, most people are ill-prepared—educationally, philosophically, and by experience—for the competent practice of management. How can a job of such scope and social importance be so wanting in professionalism? Peculiar notions about the job of management have resulted in even more peculiar approaches to preparing and selecting people for it.

B-School Non Sequiturs

One peculiar avenue to a career in management entails formalized study. Some managers have been trained in schools of business. This is no particular blessing for, while would-be managers are at least exposed to "the logic of the firm," most of their academic hours are spent pondering managerial non sequiturs.

In some instances, students examine antiquated *descriptions* of how practicing managers spend their time. These observations, through some rather convoluted scholarship, then become *prescriptions* for managerial success: "The effective manager is one who knows how to *plan, direct, control,* and *coordinate* the activities of others!" Most b-schools have been at a loss, however, when it comes to teaching *how* a manager should plan, direct, control, etc. In fact, to do so would come perilously close to the issue of *leadership* . . . a topic better left to well-intentioned but naive social scientists who, after all, "never had to make a payroll."

An alternative is the entrepreneurial approach in which students are taught to manage "the whole firm." More pragmatic, bottom-line-oriented b-schools offer large doses of accounting, marketing, finance, and production planning. All well and good, except for the fact that these are *support* functions. Most managers don't do these things; they have specialists who perform such functions for them. So much for the business school route to managerial competence. As author Andrew Hacker has concluded, the main function of business schools seems to be to . . . keep young people on hold until they are old enough to occupy junior-executive desks."

From *Flying Colors*, Vol. 11, No. 4, pp. 59-60. Used by permission of the author.

Unnatural Selection

The vast majority of today's managers follow an even more dubious path to the executive suite. They are "promoted" to management because they have done well in their own specialties. So, outstanding engineers are taken out of engineering and made managers of other engineers. Good teachers become principals or deans. Dependable production workers are made supervisors. It's as if good technical know-how automatically equips a person to manage . . . to organize, coordinate, encourage, and reward the efforts of others. The result, of course, is that by a process of unnatural selection, we have placed in charge people of perhaps outstanding technical talents who, unfortunately, haven't the foggiest idea of what management entails.

So, how *do* managers learn to manage? Well, whether formally prepared in b-school non sequiturs or unnaturally selected, it seems that most managers must actually learn to manage *on the job . . . after* they become managers. Sooner or later, most managers recognize the need for remedial education. This recognition will usually bring them in contact with a multi-billion-dollar industry—the Training and Development business. At this juncture the plot thickens, and the problem of management education is further compounded by greed and ennui.

Any time there is a billion-dollar marketplace, we can expect to find an abundance of suppliers seeking to meet the demand. Training and development of managers is no exception. And, as in other fields, some suppliers will be trustworthy and render valuable service, while others will seek primarily to exploit the situation and make a buck. It is sometimes difficult for the manager-in-training to tell the difference between the two. But this is part of the dilemma.

Science vs. Sophistry

Competent management consists of a mixture of policies, practices, and procedures which somehow enables most of the people to give their best efforts most of the time. Scientific evidence is clear on which policies, practices, and procedures characterize competent management. Forty years of research has converged on the same essential principles, and it ought to be easy to teach these to managers in need of training. But science has a communication problem. It is not always entertaining; it is sometimes boring; and it is always demanding of the student. It is here that we begin to go astray.

Managers are often tempted to follow an easier route. In ancient Greece a group of teachers, notorious for their cleverness and specious arguments, roamed the countryside dispersing beguiling and entertaining lessons for success. Called Sophists, these men specialized in simplistic wisdom and shortcuts to glory. So adept were they at making fallacious arguments sound clever and plausible, that sophistry eventually became synonymous with fallacy.

Sophistry is with us yet, unfortunately, and it flourishes in the billion-dollar marketplace of Training and Development. It collides with the uninspiring veritudes of science, and competes cleverly and speciously for the minds of managers in need of knowledge. The true irony is that managers themselves contribute as much as anyone to the remedial dilemma, because they either place too little value on training and development, on one hand, or insist that their teachers be entertaining and undemanding, on the other.

Second-Class Citizens, Crowd-Pleasers, and Charlatans

The task of educating managers has been a hit-and-miss proposition in most organizations. The lack of a clear plan and established priorities is revealed in the way training itself is managed. We have encouraged sophistry and encouraged mediocrity.

Within many organizations, training and development specialists, educational personnel, are treated as second-class citizens. Training and Development is either used as a dumping ground for lackluster performers from other departments or as part of a job-rotation scheme for broadening junior executives. Average time in training is 18 months. Under-budgeted and under-valued, such training departments have neither the credibility nor expertise to function as effective educators. Theirs is a lip-service function, and they are the first to feel the effects of corporate cutbacks when the crunch comes. Ironically, crunches come often in such organizations, because management is ill-prepared for its tasks and looks with scorn upon the very people who might be able to help.

Where there is a system of second-class citizenry, we can usually expect to find marginal people with a neurotic need to please. Managers tolerate crowd pleasers; and, even if they don't learn much from them, many managers are willing to spend time watching the current version of the Training Department's pony-and-dog show . . . as long as they are not asked to do so too often. The only real cost is that in-house education gets another black eye, and the need for professionalism gives way to indifference.

Enter the professional training vendor. Known by their designer loafers and sound-and-light-show presentations, glib and amiable "knowledge" brokers prey on managers in need of training. On the surface, they look like true Renaissance people—expertly versed in whatever is current. Proponents of MBO in the '60s, zero-based budgeting in the early '70s, coaching and counseling in the mid-'70s, and now in the '80s promoting a mixed bag of time and stress management and quality control circles, they offer easy roads to success. They entertain and charge so much for their services that one can't help but take them seriously . . . for awhile, anyway.

What are managers to do about such confusion in the education marketplace? First off, become more demanding. Ask a couple of very pertinent questions of any who would peddle advice: "Does it work? Where is your proof?" Secondly, be willing to work at the job of management. Managers are developed, not born or selected. Managers themselves must insist on competence in their own ranks.

Toward A New Professionalism

Managers must come to terms with the fact that theirs is a major profession. Affecting the productive and social well-being of hundreds of thousands of people—not to mention the essential health of society's economic organs—management is important. The development of managerial talent must reflect this importance.

Virtually every major profession is based in a core curriculum, a fundamental point of reference around which pertinent ideas and information are organized. For engineering, the foundation is physics; for medicine, the core discipline is physiology and biochemistry; and for the law, jurisprudence is the prime authority. The reason managerial education has been such a hit-and-miss proposition, vulnerable to irrelevancies and sophistry, is that management has yet to recognize its core values.

Like it or not, management is not founded in accounting procedures, principles of financial forecasting, or statistical rules of rational decision-making. Management is the competent exercise of influence on the attitudes and behavior of other people. It is the effective utilization of technical and human resources. And it is the creation of conditions—the provision of a context—according to which people are both willing and able to give their best efforts. Management is a process between human beings, and its core curriculum can be found in applied social science. It is sociology that tells us about work conditions and morale; psychology that tells us about managerial style, motivation and group dynamics; and it is cultural anthropology that can teach us the importance of group mores and value systems. All else, traditional b-school emphasis and entrepreneurial acumen included, is embellishment. Technical and administrative support skills are necessary and important in their own right. But they should not replace the core issue of management—how to accomplish work through the combined efforts of others.

Top management must take the initiative toward a new professionalism. Drawing from social science knowledge, it must clarify its desired model of management and then see to it that this model is actively promulgated. Chief executives must commit themselves and the resources of their organizations to continuing education for managerial and supervisory personnel. Professional training staffs knowledgeable enough in the social sciences both to teach what is valid and to separate science from sophistry, must be recruited and then supported financially and philosophically. From top to bottom, the need for remedial managerial training must be addressed in a responsible and credible fashion. Professionalism demands it.

The price of professionalism is not cheap. But, as Ben Franklin safely observed 200 years ago, the only thing more expensive than education is ignorance.

THE HUMAN SIDE OF ENTERPRISE

Douglas McGregor

It has become trite to say that the most significant developments of the next quarter century will take place not in the physical but in the social sciences, that industry—the economic organ of society—has the fundamental know-how to utilize physical science and technology for the material benefit of mankind, and that we must now learn how to utilize the social sciences to make our human organizations truly effective.

Many people agree in principle with such statements; but so far they represent a pious hope—and little else. Consider with me, if you will, something of what may be involved when we attempt to transform the hope into reality.

I

Let me begin with an analogy. A quarter century ago, basic conceptions of the nature of matter and energy had changed profoundly from what they had been since Newton's time. The physical scientists were persuaded that under proper conditions new and hitherto unimagined sources of energy could be made available to mankind.

We know what has happened since then. First came the bomb. Then, during the past decade, have come many other attempts to exploit these scientific discoveries—some successful, some not.

The point of my analogy, however, is that the application of theory in this field is a slow and costly matter. We expect it always to be thus. No one is impatient with the scientist because he cannot tell industry how to build a simple, cheap, all-purpose source of atomic energy today. That it will take at least another decade and the investment of billions of dollars to achieve results which are economically competitive with present sources of power is understood and accepted.

It is transparently pretentious to suggest any *direct* similarity between the developments in the physical sciences leading to the harnessing of atomic energy and

From *Adventures in Thought and Action: Proceedings of the Fifth Anniversary Convocation of the School of Industrial Management*, M.I.T., Cambridge, Massachusetts, April 9, 1957. Used by Permission of the publisher.

potential developments in the social sciences. Nevertheless, the analogy is not as absurd as it might appear to be at first glance.

To a lesser degree, and in a much more tentative fashion, we are in a position in the social sciences today like that of the physical sciences with respect to atomic energy in the thirties. We know that past conceptions of the nature of man are inadequate and in many ways incorrect. We are becoming quite certain that, under proper conditions, unimagined resources of creative human energy could become available within the organizational setting.

We cannot tell industrial management how to apply this new knowledge in simple, economic ways. We know it will require years of exploration, much costly development research, and a substantial amount of creative imagination on the part of management to discover how to apply this growing knowledge to the organization of human effort in industry.

May I ask that you keep this analogy in mind—overdrawn and pretentious though it may be—as a framework for what I have to say this morning.

Management's Task: Conventional View. The conventional conception of management's task in harnessing human energy to organizational requirements can be stated broadly in terms of three propositions. In order to avoid the complications introduced by a label, I shall call this set of propositions "Theory X":

1. Management is responsible for organizing the elements of productive enterprise—money, materials, equipment, people—in the interest of economic ends.

2. With respect to people, this is a process of directing their efforts, motivating them, controlling their actions, modifying their behavior to fit the needs of the organization.

3. Without this active intervention by management, people would be passive—even resistant—to organizational needs. They must, therefore, be persuaded, rewarded, punished, controlled—their activities must be directed. This is management's task—in managing subordinate managers or workers. We often sum it up by saying that management consists of getting things done through other people.

Behind this conventional theory there are several additional beliefs—less explicit, but widespread:

4.   The average man is by nature indolent—he works as little as possible.

5.   He lacks ambition, dislikes responsibility, prefers to be led.

6.   He is inherently self-centered, indifferent to organizational needs.

7.   He is by nature resistant to change.

8.   He is gullible, not very bright, the ready dupe of the charlatan and the demagogue.

The human side of economic enterprise today is fashioned from propositions and beliefs such as these. Conventional organization structures, managerial policies, practices, and programs reflect these assumptions.

In accomplishing its task—with these assumptions as guides—management has conceived of a range of possibilities between two extremes.

The Hard or the Soft Approach? At one extreme, management can be "hard" or "strong." The methods of directing behavior involve coercion and threat (usually disguised), close supervision, and tight controls over behavior. At the other extreme, management can be "soft" or "weak." The methods for directing behavior involve being permissive, satisfying people's demands, achieving harmony. They will be tractable, accept direction.

This range has been fairly completely explored during the past half century, and management has learned some things from the exploration. There are difficulties in the "hard" approach. Force breeds counterforces: restriction of output, antagonism, militant unionism, subtle but effective sabotage of management objectives. This approach is especially difficult during times of full employment.

There are also difficulties in the "soft" approach. It leads frequently to the abdication of management—to harmony, perhaps, but to indifferent performance. People take advantage of the soft approach. They continually expect more, but they give less and less.

Currently, the popular theme is "firm but fair." This is an attempt to gain the advantages of both the hard and the soft approaches. It is reminiscent of Teddy Roosevelt's "speak softly and carry a big stick."

Is the Conventional View Correct? The findings which are beginning to emerge from the social sciences challenge this whole set of beliefs about man and human nature and about the task of management. The evidence is far from conclusive, certainly, but it is suggestive. It comes from the laboratory, the clinic, the schoolroom, the home, and even to a limited extent from industry itself.

The social scientist does not deny that human behavior in industrial organization today is approximately what management perceives it to be. He has, in fact, observed it and studies it fairly extensively. But he is pretty sure that this behavior is *not* a consequence of man's inherent nature. It is a consequence rather of the nature of industrial organizations, or management philosophy, policy, and practice. The conventional approach of Theory X is based on mistaken notions of what is cause and what is effect.

"Well," you ask, "what then is the *true* nature of man? What evidence leads the social scientist to deny what is obvious?" And, if I am not mistaken, you are also thinking, "Tell me—simply, and without a lot of scientific verbiage—what you think you know that is so unusual. Give me—without a lot of intellectual claptrap and theoretical nonsense—some practical ideas which will enable me to improve the situation in my organization. And remember, I'm faced with increasing costs and narrowing profit margins. I want proof that such ideas won't result simply in new and costly human relations frills. I want practical results, and I want them now."

If these are your wishes, you are going to be disappointed. Such requests can no more be met by the social scientist today than could comparable ones with respect to atomic energy be met by the physicist fifteen years ago. I can, however, indicate a few of the reasons for asserting that conventional assumptions about the human side of enterprise are inadequate. And I can suggest—tentatively—some of the propositions that will comprise a more adequate theory of the management of people. The magnitude of the task that confronts us will then, I think, be apparent.

II

Perhaps the best way to indicate why the conventional approach of management is inadequate is to consider the subject of motivation. In discussing this subject, I will draw heavily on the work of my colleague, Abraham Maslow of Brandeis University. His is the most fruitful approach I know. Naturally, what I have to say will be over-generalized and will ignore important qualifications. In the time at our disposal, this is inevitable.

Physiological and Safety Needs. Man is a wanting animal—as soon as one of his needs is satisfied, another appears in its place. This process is unending. It continues from birth to death.

Man's needs are organized in a series of levels—a hierarchy of importance. At the lowest level, but preeminent in importance when they are thwarted, are his physiological needs. Man lives by bread alone, when there is no bread. Unless the circumstances are unusual, his needs for love, for status, for recognition are inoperative when his stomach has been empty for a while. But when he eats regularly and adequately, hunger ceases to be an important need. The sated man has hunger only in the sense that a full bottle has emptiness. The same is true of the other physiological needs of man—for rest, exercise, shelter, protection from the elements.

A satisfied need is not a motivator of behavior! This is a fact of profound significance. It is a fact which is regularly ignored in the conventional approach to the management of people. I shall return to it later. For the moment, one example will make my point. Consider your own need for air. Except as you are deprived of it, it has no appreciable motivating effect upon your behavior.

When the physiological needs are reasonably satisfied, needs at the next higher level begin to dominate man's behavior—to motivate him. These are called safety needs. They are needs for protection against danger, threat, deprivation. Some people mistakenly refer to these as needs for security. However, unless man is in a dependent relationship where he fears arbitrary deprivation, he does not demand security. The need is for the "fairest possible break." When he is confident of this, he is more than willing to take risks. But when he feels threatened or dependent, his greatest need is for guarantees, for protection, for security.

The fact needs little emphasis that since every industrial employee is in a dependent relationship, safety needs may assume considerable importance. Arbitrary management actions, behavior which arouses uncertainty with respect to continued employment or which reflects favoritism or discrimination, unpredictable administration of policy—these can be powerful motivators of the safety needs in the employment relationship *at every level* from worker to vice president.

Social Needs. When man's physiological needs are satisfied and he is no longer fearful about his physical welfare, his social needs become important motivators of his behavior—for belonging, for association, for acceptance by his fellows, for giving and receiving friendship and love.

Management knows today of the existence of these needs, but it often assumes quite wrongly that they represent a threat to the organization. Many studies have demonstrated that the tightly knit, cohesive work group may, under proper conditions, be far more effective than an equal number of separate individuals in achieving organizational goals.

Yet management, fearing group hostility to its own objectives, often goes to considerable lengths to control and direct human efforts in ways that are inimical to the natural "groupiness" of human beings. When man's social needs—and perhaps his safety needs, too—are thus thwarted, he behaves in ways which tend to defeat organization objectives. He becomes resistant, antagonistic, uncooperative. But this behavior is a consequence, not a cause.

Ego Needs. Above the social needs—in the sense that they do not become motivators until lower needs are reasonably satisfied—are the needs of greatest significance to management and to man himself. They are the egoistic needs, and they are of two kinds:

1. Those needs that relate to one's self-esteem—needs for self-confidence, for independence, for achievement, for competence, for knowledge.

2. Those needs that relate to one's reputation—needs for status, for recognition, for appreciation, for the deserved respect of one's fellows.

Unlike the lower needs, these are rarely satisfied; man seeks indefinitely for more satisfaction of these needs once they have become important to him. But they do not appear in any significant way until physiological, safety, and social needs are all reasonably satisfied.

The typical industrial organization offers few opportunities for the satisfaction of these egoistic needs to people at lower levels in the hierarchy. The conventional methods of organizing work, particularly in mass production industries, give little heed to these aspects of human motivation. If the practices of scientific management were deliberately calculated to thwart these needs—which, of course, they are not—they could hardly accomplish this purpose better than they do.

Self-fulfillment Needs. Finally—a capstone, as it were, on the hierarchy of man's needs—there are what we may call the needs for self-fulfillment. These are the needs for realizing one's own potential, for continued self-development, for being creative in the broadest sense of that term.

It is clear that the conditions of modern life give only limited opportunity for these relatively weak needs to obtain expression. The deprivation most people experience with respect to other lower level needs diverts their energies into the struggle to satisfy *those* needs, and the needs for self-fulfillment remain dormant.

III

Now, briefly, a few general comments about motivations:

We recognize readily enough that a man suffering from a severe dietary deficiency is sick. The deprivation of physiological needs has behavioral consequences. The same is true—although less well recognized—of deprivation of higher-level needs. The man whose needs for safety, association, independence, or status are thwarted is sick just as surely as is he who has rickets. And his sickness will have behavioral consequences. We will be mistaken if we attribute his resultant passivity, his hostility, his refusal to accept responsibility to his inherent "human nature." These forms of behavior are *symptoms* of illness—of deprivation of his social and egoistic needs.

The man whose lower-level needs are satisfied is not motivated to satisfy those needs any longer. For practical purposes, they exist no longer. (Remember my point about your need for air.) Management often asks, "Why aren't people more productive? We pay good wages, provide good working conditions, have excellent fringe benefits and steady employment. Yet people do not seem to be willing to put forth more than minimum effort."

The fact that management has provided for these physiological and safety needs has shifted the motivational emphasis to the social and perhaps to the egoistic needs. Unless there are opportunities *at work* to satisfy these high-level needs, people will be deprived; and their behavior will reflect this deprivation. Under such conditions, if management continues to focus its attention on physiological needs, its efforts are bound to be ineffective.

People *will* make insistent demands for more money under these conditions. It becomes more important than ever to buy the material goods and services which can provide limited satisfaction of the thwarted needs. Although money has only limited value in satisfying many higher-level needs, it can become the focus of interest if it is the *only* means available.

The Carrot and Stick Approach. The carrot and stick theory of motivation (like Newtonian physical theory) works reasonably well under certain circumstances. The means for satisfying man's physiological and (within limits) his safety needs can be provided or withheld by management. Employment itself is such a means, and so are wages, working conditions, and benefits. By these means the individual can be controlled so long as he is struggling for subsistence. Man lives for bread alone when there is no bread.

But the carrot and stick theory does not work at all once man has reached an adequate subsistence level and is motivated primarily by higher needs. Management cannot provide a man with self-respect, or with the respect of his fellows, or with the satisfaction of needs for self-fulfillment. It can create conditions such that he is encouraged and enabled to seek such satisfaction *for himself,* or it can thwart him by failing to create those conditions.

But this creation of conditions is not "control." It is not a good device for directing behavior. And so management finds itself in an odd position. The high standard of living created by our modern technological know-how provides quite adequately for the satisfaction of physiological and safety needs. The only significant exception is where management practices have not created confidence in a "fair break"—and thus where safety needs are thwarted. But by making possible the satisfaction of low-level needs, management has deprived itself of the ability to use as motivators the devices on which conventional theory has taught it to rely—rewards, promises, incentives, or threats and other coercive devices.

Neither Hard nor Soft. The philosophy of management by direction and control—*regardless of whether it is hard or soft*—is inadequate to motivate because the human needs on which this approach relies are today unimportant motivators of behavior. Direction and control are essentially useless in motivating people whose important needs are social and egoistic. Both the hard and the soft approach fail today because they are simply irrelevant to the situation.

People, deprived of opportunities to satisfy at work the needs which are now important to them, behave exactly as we might predict—with indolence, passivity, resistance to change, lack of responsibility, willingness to follow the demagogue, unreasonable demands for economic benefits. It would seem that we are caught in a web of our own weaving.

In summary, then, of these comments about motivation:

Management by direction and control—whether implemented with the hard, the soft, or the firm but fair approach—fails under today's conditions to provide effective motivation of human effort toward organizational objectives. It fails because direction and control are useless methods of motivating people whose physiological and safety needs are reasonably satisfied and whose social, egoistic, and self-fulfillment needs are predominant.

For these and many other reasons, we require a different theory of the task of managing people based on more adequate assumptions about human nature and human motivation. I am going to be so bold as to suggest the broad dimensions of such a theory. Call it "Theory Y," if you will.

1. Management is responsible for organizing the elements of productive enterprise—money, materials, equipment, people—in the interest of economic ends.

2. People are *not* by nature passive or resistant to organizational needs. They have become so as a result of experience in organizations.

3. The motivation, the potential for development, the capacity for assuming responsibility, the readiness to direct behavior toward organizational goals are all present in people. Management does not put them there. It is a responsibility of management to make it possible for people to recognize and develop these human characteristics for themselves.

4. The essential task of management is to arrange organizational conditions and methods of operation so that people can achieve their own goals *best* by directing *their own* efforts toward organizational objectives.

This is a process primarily of creating opportunities, releasing potential, removing obstacles, encouraging growth, providing guidance. It is what Peter Drucker has called "management by objectives" in contrast to "management by control."

And I hasten to add that it does *not* involve the abdication of management, the absence of leadership, the lowering of standards, or the other characteristics usually associated with the "soft" approach under Theory X. Much on the contrary. It is no more possible to create an organization today which will be a fully effective application of this theory than it was to build an atomic plant in 1945. There are many formidable obstacles to overcome.

Some Difficulties. The conditions imposed by conventional organization theory and by the approach of scientific management for the past half century have tied men to limited jobs which do not utilize their capabilities, have discouraged the acceptance of responsibility, have encouraged passivity, have eliminated meaning from work. Man's habits, attitudes, expectations—his whole conception of membership in an industrial organization—have been conditioned by his experience under these circumstances. Change in the direction of Theory Y will be slow, and it will require extensive modification of the attitudes of management and workers alike.

People today are accustomed to being directed, manipulated, controlled in industrial organizations and to finding satisfaction for their social, egoistic, and self-fulfillment needs away from the job. This is true of much of management as well as of workers. Genuine "industrial citizenship"—to borrow again a term from Drucker—is a remote and unrealistic idea, the meaning of which has not even been considered by most members of industrial organizations.

Another way of saying this is that Theory X places exclusive reliance upon external control of human behavior, while Theory Y relies heavily on self-control and self-direction. It is worth noting that this difference is the difference between treating people as children and treating them as mature adults. After generations of the former, we cannot expect to shift to the latter overnight.

V

Before we are overwhelmed by the obstacles, let us remember that the application of theory is always slow. Progress is usually achieved in small steps. Consider with me a few innovative ideas which are entirely consistent with Theory Y and which are today being applied with some success.

Decentralization and Delegation. These are ways of freeing people from the too-close control of conventional organization, giving them a degree of freedom to direct their own activities, to assume responsibility, and, importantly, to satisfy their egoistic needs. In this connection, the flat organization of Sears, Roebuck and Company provides an interesting example. It forces "management by objectives" since it enlarges the number of people reporting to a manager until he cannot direct and control them in the conventional manner.

Job Enlargement. This concept, pioneered by IBM and Detroit Edison, is quite consistent with Theory Y. It encourages the acceptance of responsibility at the bottom of the organization; it provides opportunities for satisfying social and egoistic needs. In fact, the reorganization of work at the factory level offers one of the more challenging opportunities for innovation consistent with Theory Y. The studies by A. T. M. Wilson and his associates of British coal mining and Indian textile manufacture have added appreciably to our understanding of work organization. Moreover, the economic and psychological results achieved by this work have been substantial.

Participation and Consultative Management. Under proper conditions these results provide encouragement to people to direct their creative energies toward organizational objectives, give them some voice in decisions that affect them, provide significant opportunities for the satisfaction of social and egoistic needs. I need only mention the Scanlon Plan as the outstanding embodiment of these ideas in practice.

The not infrequent failure of such ideas as these to work as well as expected is often attributable to the fact that a management has "bought the idea" but applied it within the framework of Theory X and its assumptions.

Delegation is not an effective way of exercising management by control. Participation becomes a farce when it is applied as a sales gimmick or a device for kidding people into thinking they are important. Only the management that has confidence in human capacities and is itself directed toward organizational objectives rather than toward the preservation of personal power can grasp the implications of this emerging theory. Such management will find and apply successfully other innovative ideas as we move slowly toward the full implementation of a theory like Y.

Performance Appraisal. Before I stop, let me mention one other practical application of Theory Y which—while still highly tentative—may well have important consequences. This has to do with performance appraisal within the ranks of management. Even a cursory examination of conventional programs of performance appraisal will reveal how completely consistent they are with Theory X. In fact, most such programs tend to treat the individual as though he were a product under inspection on the assembly line.

Take the typical plan: substitute "product" for "subordinate being appraised," substitute "inspector" for "superior making the appraisal," substitute "rework" for "training or development," and, except for the attributes being judged, the human appraisal process will be virtually indistinguishable from the product inspection process.

A few companies—among them General Mills, Ansul Chemical, and General Electric—have been experimenting with approaches which involve the individual in setting "targets" or objectives *for himself* and in a self-evaluation of performance semi-annually or annually. Of course, the superior plays an important leadership role in this process—one, in fact, which demands substantially more competence than the conventional approach. The role is, however, considerably more congenial to many managers than the role of "judge" or "inspector" which is forced upon them by conventional performance. Above all, the individual is encouraged to take a greater responsibility for planning and appraising his own contribution to organizational objectives; and the accompanying effects on egoistic and self-fulfillment needs are substantial. This approach to performance appraisal represents one more innovative idea being explored by a few managements who are moving toward the implementation of Theory Y.

VI

And now I am back where I began. I share the belief that we could realize substantial improvements in the effectiveness of individual organizations during the next decade or two. Moreover, I believe the social sciences can contribute much to such developments of knowledge in these fields. But if this conviction is to become a reality instead of a pious hope, we will need to view the process much as we view the process of releasing the energy of the atom for constructive human ends—as a slow, costly, sometimes discouraging approach toward a goal which would seem to many to be quite unrealistic.

The ingenuity and the perseverance of industrial management in the pursuit of economic ends have changed many scientific and technological dreams into commonplace realities. It is now becoming clear that the application of these same talents to the human side of enterprise will not only enhance substantially these materialistic achievements but will bring us one step closer to "the good society." Shall we get on with the job?

PART II
THE INDIVIDUAL AND MOTIVATION

This section consists of eight articles which provide a general background for the work being done in the area of motivation. It is not intended to be comprehensive in scope, no single book could discuss all the theories of motivation. Rather, it attempts to acquaint the reader with most of the major theories in the field.

The first article, by Thomas Head, provides a historical picture of motivation research, starting with Phrenology in the mid-1800s and ending with Maslow's Need Hierarchy, circa 1940.

The next article, Contemporary Approaches to Job Redesign, takes the reader through the theory of using the JDS itself to motivate workers. This discussion includes descriptions of both Herzberg's job enrichment and Hackman and Oldham's job redesign. Some later, speculative, material is also described.

The article by Head and the article by Lawler describe the Expectancy Theory. Unlike most of the other theories, no single person developed this approach. Rather, it is a compilation of many theorists' and researchers' works.

The article by Steven Kerr is a classic and so obvious it is hard to imagine that this mistake is still made. You get the behavior that you REWARD! So what do people reward—just the opposite. Even the follow-up survey by the Executive Advisory Panel gives us the clear message. Now—remember it!

The article by Hamner and Hamner describes an alternative approach to job redesign behavior modification, focusing on changing employees' actions rather than cognitive processes.

The final article, by Mitchell, presents a summary of several motivation theories. Some of these theories are not discussed in this book, while others are.

EARLY MOTIVATION THEORIES:
FROM PHRENOLOGY TO FREUD AND BEYOND

Thomas C. Head

Of all the topics studied and written about in management today, the one that clearly dominates is employee motivation. This is most significant when you consider motivation's relative youth. Leadership has been studied since the ancient Greeks, and economics and finance have been around since the 1700s. But motivation was not really considered until the mid 1800s, and then not seriously applied to the work force until the 1940s. But what is motivation? Currently, there are dozens of theories and, consequently, dozens of definitions for motivation. Perhaps the most general, and therefore most accepted, definition is:

> Motivation is the internal force which creates a desire to act, or behave; direct and guide that behavior; and sustain the behavior.

In other words, motivation is what makes us want to work, makes us want to do a good job, and makes us want to keep on doing our best.

Most contemporary theories assume that for the most part motivation is a conscious phenomenon. That is, if we took time to think about it, we could figure out what "motivates" us at any given time. This was not always the case. In fact, the early theorists relied heavily on the unconscious and subconscious, as well as heredity, ignoring the powers of thought and reason in explaining motivation.

PHRENOLOGY

The first attempt to study human personality and motivation began in Germany during the 1840s and '50s, and it was known as phrenology. Phrenology is the pseudo-science of establishing a person's mental and temperamental characteristics through identifying the shape and bumps of the skull.

Phrenology was first proposed by Franz Joseph Gall, but really popularized by a student of his, Johann Caspar Spurzheim. While today we reject the theory as little more than a sideshow event, in its own time it was accepted by the greatest minds in the world as not only valid, but extremely practical as well. In fact, there is actually some truth behind the theory.

The basic principles of phrenology are that all human emotions and thoughts emanate from the brain, and that different parts of the brain control different functions. This much, as we now know, is true. The remainder of the theory is where the theorists were led astray. Phrenologists created a "map" of the brain, somewhat like what is found in Figure 1. They believed that the shape of the skull was determined by the shape of the brain. Therefore if a person had a bump in a certain area of the skull, that meant the brain was over-developed at that location, and consequently, the person will demonstrate the given trait with atypical strength and frequency. Similarly, if the person has a valley, or depression, on the skull, then the given trait is lacking in the individual.

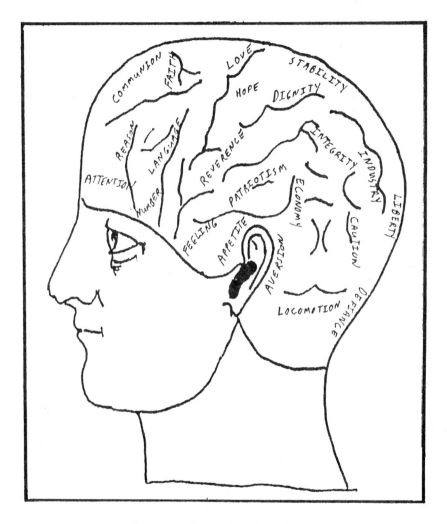

Figure 1. Phrenologist's Brain Map.

As the study of the central nervous system increased, more and more people began to question the validity of phrenology. Most serious scientists stopped believing in it by the 1860s and '70s, and its meteoric climb as the first attempt to predict human motivation was followed by just as fast a drop into obscurity.

CONSTITUTIONAL PSYCHOLOGY

With the passing of phrenology, the study of human motivation drifted for awhile. The next theory which emerged dealt with the connection between a person's body type and his emotional and psychological makeup. While the theory was refined by Sheldon in the 1930s, the earliest writings on the subject were by Lavater in 1804.

While several different researchers devised their own classifications, the following three types of human physique came to be generally accepted:

Endomorphic: This individual is generally soft and round in appearance. The bones and muscles are underdeveloped, and there is a low body surface to mass ratio.

Mesomorphic: This person's body is hard and rectangular in appearance, with well developed muscles. The body is strong and can handle strenuous physical demands.

Ectomorphic: A linear and fragile body with a flat chest and thin and light muscles are characteristic of these individuals.

The driving principle in constitutional psychology is that the structure of the body is the primary determinant of behavior. These researchers maintain that predilections towards certain emotions and behaviors are inherited, exactly as the general physique.

Unlike the phrenologists, the constitutional psychologists conducted rigorous research to support their theories, often utilizing thousands of subjects and highly refined measurements. The end result of all this research was that endomorphics showed viscerotonia characteristics; mesomorphics had somatonia elements; and ectomorphics demonstrated cerebrotonia.

Viscerotonia traits include relaxation, love of comfort, pleasure in digestion, dependence on social approval, deep sleep, and a need for people when troubled. Somatonia is reflected by assertiveness, energetic characteristics, a need for exercise, directness of manner, and a need for action when troubled. Finally, cerebrotonia characteristics include restraint, overly fast reactions, inhibited in social situations, resistance to habit, poor sleep habits, and a need for solitude when troubled.

To this day, there are constitutional psychologists, but they are clearly in the minority. Perhaps the biggest problem with the theory, and therefore its reason for low popularity today, is the fact that it ignores the contribution of the individual's environment in determining behaviors and emotions. It also ignores the fact that as humans age, their physiques often undergo tremendous changes. Even though human emotions and behaviors also change with age, this actually contradicts the constitutional approach, because it proves that behaviors and motivations are not genetic, for if they were, then they would prove impossible to alter.

Sigmund Freud's Developmental Theory

Sigmund Freud is perhaps the most influential psychologist of all time. While very little of what he proposed is used by business persons today, his pioneering efforts in exploring human motivations must be acknowledged. In fact, one of Freud's beliefs, that motivation is in the realm of nonconscious phenomena, was considered as fact in the study of employee motivation until just recently. Freud believed the human mind was like an iceberg. The tip, which is above water, represents conscious thought. But the vast majority of the mass is hidden from sight, the unconscious. Therefore, to understand behavior, one must explore the underlying motives of the person, that which is found in the unconscious.

Freud believed personality is a developmental process. We are born with instincts (related to the id), and our development is a process whereby we learn how to satisfy these instincts and tame them into socially acceptable behaviors (through the ego and superego). The personality is primarily developed in the very early years of life. Afterwards, what occurs is simply refinement of what exists.

Personality develops in response to four major sources of instinctual tensions: physiological growth processes, frustrations, conflicts, and threats. The development occurs when the individual learns new methods of reducing the tension. The learning is typically done through the processes of identification and displacement. Identification is the modeling of behavior after someone else. Typically, we choose role models who are better at satisfying the particular need than we are. Displacement occurs when we must change a method of gratifying our instincts. This is done because either the old method no longer gratifies our needs, or it has become socially unacceptable.

There are different stages in the developmental process, each defined by a particular area of the body which is particularly important to the individual at that point in time. Disturbances and/or problems which occur during the stage can cause fixations, which in turn make for major influences on the person's personality. For example, individuals who are gullible are fixating at the oral stage, while problems in toilet training (anal stage) can cause compulsive neatness.

Freud's theories were, and still are, greatly misunderstood by most individuals. Because of some overreaction to controversial aspects of his work, many seek to dismiss Freud completely. This would be doing him an injustice. However, there are certain complaints concerning his theory which do relegate it to a historical entity when it comes to employee behavior. Freud collected the data from his patients, all of whom were suffering from severe psychological problems. Because of this, his theories tend to be too deterministic in nature. That is, he ignored the importance of choice and conscious thought in explaining behavior. A final problem was not unique to Freud, but applied to all the early theorists. This is the problem of having too broad a theory, one that explains all of human behavior, rather than attempting to explain one aspect, such as work motivation.

Jung's Analytic Theory

Carl Jung, the founder of the Analytic Theory, was a protege of Freud until 1913, when he broke from Freud and proposed his own theory of human behavior and motivation. While Jung still emphasized the unconscious, he felt that the roots of behavior were more than just historical; humans are also affected by their aims and aspirations. Therefore both the past and future influence behavior through unconscious processes.

According to Jung, the personality, or psyche, is comprised of several different facets. The ego is the conscious mind, and the things the person has repressed, forgotten, etc., make up the personal unconscious. But the major determinant of personality is known as the collective unconscious. Jung believed that we not only inherit physical characteristics from our ancestors, but we also retain the cumulative experiences of all the past generations stored in the collective unconscious.

Therefore we are born with predispositions towards items, known as archetypes, which have been established through associations our ancestors have made. One such archetype is love of mother, and another is fear of the dark. Mothers usually represented warmth, affection and caring to our ancestors. In ancient times, dark meant danger from animals, spirits, and the like. Two other archetypes which are so important that they typically are considered as separate determinants of personality are the persona and shadow. The persona represents the roles people adopt to gain social acceptance, while the shadow consists of our animal instincts.

The individual performs the work dictated by the personality by using psychic energy which originates from metabolic processes within the body. The amount of energy we dedicate to expressing a certain personality trait is referred to as its value. We will expend a great deal of energy on the traits for which we place a "high value." Jung also proposed the principle of equivalence which states that if one value weakens, the psychic energy is redirected to another value. In other words, if a person loses interest in one thing, another will crop up to take its place. Another concept of psychic energy is the principle of entropy. Jung believed that we attempt to achieve a balance among all the forces of our psyche, but because humans are not a "closed system," and energy may be added or subtracted, this is a nearly impossible goal to achieve.

Finally, Jung identified two central purposes for the use of psychic energy. The first is to satisfy the instincts for the maintenance of life. Any energy the individual has left after the first goal will be devoted to cultural and spiritual activities. Here the person is striving for self-realization, the fullest most complete harmonious blending of all aspects of the personality.

To this day, Jung has many followers and admirers. Yet he is no longer considered a major influence on motivation and behavior. Perhaps the main reason behind this is that many of the finer points of his theory are in the metaphysical realm. Instead of empirical tests, he based his works on clinical findings and mythical sources. He included in his writings, but did not profess a deep belief in, much from the realm of the occult and mysticism. This was too much for many to take, and Jung has been relegated to a back seat to Freud.

Adler's Individual Psychology

Another protege of Freud who broke with him, around 1911, was Alfred Adler, who founded the Individual Psychology Movement. Adler assumed that everyone has a unique personality in regard to motives, traits, and values. But Adler also assumed that man is a social animal and is motivated by social urges. He did not break entirely from the previous theorists, however. Adler maintained that the social motivation was not acquired through learning, but was biologically inherited, similar to instincts.

While the social elements are major influences of our behavior, there is also the creative self. This is a highly personalized system which searches for experiences that assist in fulfilling the individual's unique style of life. There are two major forces acting on the creative self. The first is a striving for superiority. The second is compensating for a belief of inferiority.

Adler remains extremely well regarded today, particularly in the United States, where he worked in his later years. Many of his concepts, as with Jung and Freud, can still be found in contemporary theories of management. For example, there is a similarity between striving for superiority and McClelland's need for achievement.

Maslow's Need Hierarchy

Abraham Maslow's Need Hierarchy Theory of motivation is doubly important for individuals studying employee motivation. Maslow was the first to propose a theory just on motivation. He did not dwell on the complexities of personality, but concentrated on attempting to explain the force behind behavior. Secondly, Maslow's theory was the first which was used to specifically examine employee motivation. While Maslow used his theory to explain many non-work related behaviors, he happened to propose the model in 1943, just at the time when the study of management was evolving from a natural to a behavioral science. Managers were embracing the concept of motivation and looking to psychologists for answers to their questions.

The basic theory is rather straightforward. Maslow stated that there are five basic human needs arranged in a hierarchical order from low to high.

Physiological: Fulfill basic chemical needs of body, such as food, warmth, and oxygen.

Safety: Freedom from danger and protection from losing gratification of physiological needs.

Social: Affiliation, friendship, love and belongingness.

Esteem: Sense of achievement, confidence, independence, and recognition.

Self-Actualization: Being all you can be, involving full use of creativity, personal and spiritual growth.

The two central premises concerning these needs are: 1) Man is motivated to satisfy the lowest level of unmet need, and 2) a satisfied need cannot serve as a source of motivation.

In other words, a starving man will act to obtain food. However, an individual who has just consumed a seven course gourmet meal is unlikely to be motivated with an offer of a dozen cupcakes.

There are some interesting implications of Maslow's theory for examining employee motivation. Typically, we translate physiological needs into terms of compensation and safety needs to job security. Using Maslow's theory, we can explain away a major management fallacy—that to solve a motivation problem all one has to do is raise a person's pay. This will work if the employee has not been earning enough for a decent living. However, if the person is making enough to live on, then the motives will be focused on higher level needs. Of course, employees will accept a raise in pay, but that will not motivate them to behave any differently. A second application of the theory is found in explaining a recent trend in union contracts. Up until the recession of the 1970s, it was unheard of for unions to make concessions, or give up things, in contract negotiations. But suddenly the employees found that plants were closing left and right. The workers were faced with the possibility of losing their jobs and immediately regressed down the hierarchy to being motivated by a deficiency in safety needs. Unions would agree to pay and benefit cuts and higher productivity rates for merely a guarantee of job security.

Recently, researchers have reexamined Maslow's theory suggesting a refinement of the hierarchy principle. Maslow's theory is usually illustrated by a diagram similar to Figure 2. The figure implies that 100 percent of a need must be gratified before motivation is focused on the next level. Some, however, state that Maslow actually implied (at least in the later years) something resembling Figure 3. In this view, humans can be motivated by various degrees of all five needs simultaneously, with one need being dominant. For example, using the old model at point A an individual will be motivated entirely by social needs. But in the new model, while social needs are responsible for the majority of motivation, the individual is also seeking to gratify three other needs to lesser degrees (the physiological needs are fully satisfied).

Maslow was the first theorist whose work was used to specifically address employee motivation. Through the mid 1960s, researchers attempted to prove and/or disprove the theory with various results. Some confirmed his predictions, others did not. A few suggested that there were only four needs, some, like Alderfer, described three, and a few (Herzberg) advocated two basic needs. Through all this, Maslow's theory has retained its popularity, even with a fundamental flaw. Simply stated, this flaw is that managers have never found a way to really apply the hierarchy to solve actual motivation problems. Maslow gave us an excellent way of thinking about motivation but no tools to use with the theory. Still, almost all contemporary theories of motivation borrow from Maslow while attempting to correct for the lack of applicability.

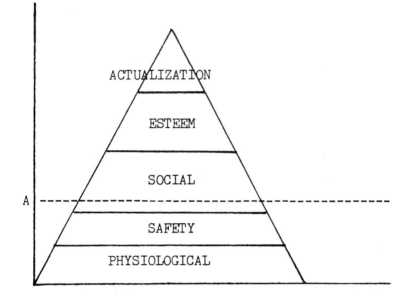

Figure 2. Typical View of Maslow's Theory

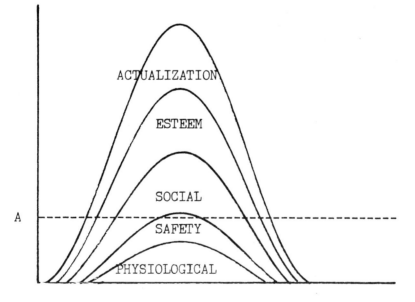
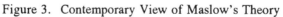

Figure 3. Contemporary View of Maslow's Theory

In 1972, Clayton Alderfer formulated the ERG theory, which was a reworking of Maslow's hierarchy in order to make it consistent with research findings. Alderfer suggests that there are three levels of needs: Existence, Relatedness, and Growth. The existence needs correspond to physiological and safety. Relatedness needs involve social and interpersonal esteem requirements. Finally self-confirmed esteem and self-actualization combine to make up the growth needs.

After creating the three needs, Alderfer proposed several hypotheses regarding the interactions between the three:

1)   The less existence and relatedness needs are fulfilled, the more they will be desired.

2)   The less relatedness needs are fulfilled, the more important the existence needs will become.

3)   The more satisfied the person is with existence, the more the person will focus on relatedness needs.

4)   The less growth needs are satisfied, the more relatedness needs will be desired.

5)   The greater the satisfaction with relatedness needs, the greater the emphasis on growth needs.

6)   The more growth needs are satisfied, the more they will be desired.

As one can see, Alderfer's model is similar to Maslow's when it comes to hypotheses 1, 3, 5, and 6, in that man is motivated by the lowest level of unmet need, and a satisfied need cannot serve to motivate. However, Alderfer contradicts Maslow in hypotheses 2 and 4. Here he states that failure to satisfy one need makes the objects which gratify the lower need all the more important. Therefore, a person who is socially unhappy (lack in relatedness) will strive to satisfy that need but will simultaneously raise in importance things such as pay, benefits, and job security which are used to satisfy the existence needs.

Conclusion

The study of motivation has come a long way since the study of skull bumps. The more contemporary theories which have followed Maslow have tended to focus on motivation as a work-related phenomenon, leaving it to counselors to deal with personality and psychological disorders. Because of this, the theories have also become much more practical by supplying managers with tools to use in correcting motivation problems.

The theories discussed here are all fairly antiquated for management purposes. Even Maslow has gone the way of a historical artifact. But that does not mean that they are not important, for as Santyana said, "Those who cannot remember the past are doomed to repeat it." Motivation, as we know it, developed and grew out of the past research. The contemporary theories all have borrowed what was good from the past and corrected what was bad.

We are probably far from identifying the "ultimate" theory of employee motivation. But as long as the researchers actively revise and develop new models, with a critical eye on what has come before, eventually we may come close to the goal of truly explaining human motivation.

CONTEMPORARY APPROACHES TO JOB REDESIGN

Thomas C. Head, Ph.D., RODC, Department of Management,
DePaul University, Chicago, Illinois 60604

Abstract

Employee motivation, specifically through job design, has become a major topic in Organizational Development today. Companies have become very aware of the indirect costs linked to employee dissatisfaction. Employees must be motivated in a job that they enjoy. This paper examines the various approaches to job design. Several models that relate to this topic are discussed; a new approach is presented that differentiates the concept of role from the job.

From the beginning of the industrial revolution, the art of designing jobs focused on streamlining employees' tasks. During the scientific and classical management movements, specialization became the key; jobs were made as simple and structured as possible. This approach created an efficient system, with minimal waste, perfectly structured for the low cost, assembly line manufacturing of the time. However, this also meant jobs lacked anything that could possibly motivate employees.

During these early management movements, motivation was not really a concern for managers. Wages were poor and profits were simply a function of low costs coupled to high production. Today, organizations face a much different environment. In the United States, wages have never been higher. Profits are closely linked to the quality of the product. Service management, a situation where there are no products per se, has arisen to be dominant in commerce. Demographics are changing; the labor force is becoming older and much better educated. Finally, companies have become aware of indirect costs linked to employee apathy such as turnover, absenteeism, on-the-job accidents, and stress.

Employee motivation, specifically through job design, has become a major topic in Organizational Development today. This paper examines the various approaches to job design starting with Herzberg's classic model. It then discusses the Hackman-Oldham job characteristics theory, Pfeffer and Salancik's social information processing, and a combined model. Finally, the concept of role, as differentiated from the job, is discussed including a new approach for measurement.

© *Organization Development Journal*, Summer 1992, Vol. 10, No. 2.

HERZBERG'S DUAL FACTOR THEORY

Frederick Herzberg's dual factor theory (1964) was the first major model that suggested that the design of the job related to employee motivation. The central premise of his theory is that an employee will be motivated in a job he/she enjoys. Herzberg developed his theory after conducting extensive interviews with professionals. He noted that there was a major difference between the things which were most closely linked to satisfaction and those which were linked to dissatisfaction.

Since the causes of satisfaction and dissatisfaction were distinct, he placed them on two separate continuum, as seen in Figure 1. On one continuum, satisfaction was one anchor; while the lack of any satisfaction was the opposite anchor (the opposite of satisfaction is not dissatisfaction, rather it is a neutral state, the lack of satisfaction). The second continuum was similar in that the anchors consisted of dissatisfaction and the lack of dissatisfaction. Therefore, the most desirable situation was one where the employee was both satisfied *and* lacking satisfaction.

MOTIVATORS	
Absent	Present
No Satisfaction	Satisfaction
HYGIENE	
Absent	Present
Dissatisfaction	No Dissatisfaction

Figure 1. *Herzberg's Dual Factor Theory*

The elements linked to dissatisfaction are referred to as hygiene variables. Simply put, these are anything that are external to the job itself. They include items such as pay and benefits, working conditions, supervision, rules and regulations, coworkers, and structural elements (among many others). Hygiene comes from the concept of community hygiene, such as sewer plants, garbage treatment, etc. These elements will not make the populace physically fit, rather they will only prevent certain diseases from occurring.

Motivators are the variables that cause satisfaction. These include items such as pride, responsibility, personal growth, esteem, autonomy, achievement and self-actualization, among others. Motivators are said to be internal factors, in that they are caused (or eliminated) in the employee's mind through task performance.

In order to "solve" a motivation problem, Herzberg developed a technique called job enrichment (1968). Job enrichment is a two step process. The first step addresses the hygiene factors and removes any source of dissatisfaction. The second step is the key to motivation. It involves redesigning the job to include as many motivator variables as possible. This is accomplished through vertical job loading—including elements of higher job levels (those typically performed by supervisors and managers). Vertical job loading is distinct from horizontal loading, which simply adds similar level duties to the job. This latter approach, known as job enlargement, amounts to giving the worker more of the same thing to do (i.e., turning two screws instead of one) and will result in only temporary improvement, at best.

While the concept of job enrichment proved to be useful, Herzberg's theory has received much criticism (for example, see House & Wigdor, 1967). The first problem was that the model was far too simplistic, especially regarding the minimal role played by hygiene variables. In addition, it is a universalistic theory (applies to all situations), while current management practice requires contingency models. Finally, Herzberg made the mistake of equating satisfaction and motivation as identical concepts.

HACKMAN AND OLDHAM'S JOB CHARACTERISTICS THEORY

Hackman and Oldham developed the job characteristics theory (Hackman & Oldham, 1976; 1980) and corrected many shortcomings in Herzberg's model. They not only hypothesized a solid theoretical base, regarded by many today as the most viable, but they also refined the concept of job enrichment. Finally, they created the Job Diagnostic Survey (Hackman & Oldham, 1975), a noncopyrighted, valid instrument that allows the consultant to analyze exactly which elements of the job need change and monitor improvements as well.

The job characteristics model is illustrated in Figure 2. The central premise is that employees seek to satisfy three psychological states from their jobs: experienced meaningfulness, experienced responsibility, and knowledge of the outcomes. It is impossible to look into a person's brain and measure the satisfaction of these psychological states. Rather, one measures five core job dimensions which, when present, should satisfy these three states. To the extent the five core dimensions are present in the job, the psychological states will be satisfied. Consequently, employees will experience satisfaction and motivation, and performance should increase with absenteeism and turnover decreased.

5 Core Dimensions	3 Psychological States	Outcomes
Skill variety Task identity Task significance	Experienced meaningfulness	Motivation Satisfaction
Autonomy	Experienced responsibility	Performance
Job feedback	Knowledge of the results	Low absenteeism and turnover

Moderating Variables
Individual growth/need/strength
Locus of control
Self esteem

Pay satisfaction
Job security
Coworker satisfaction
Supervision satisfaction

Career stage
Education

Figure 2. *The Hackman-Oldham Job Characteristics Theory*
(adapted from Hackman & Oldham, 1976).

There are three core dimensions related to experienced responsibility. 1) skill variety (the number and complexity of skills required); 2) task identity (the ability to perform an entire task from beginning to end); and 3) task significance (the perceived importance of the task).

There are three core dimensions related to experienced responsibility. They are: 1) skill variety (the number and complexity of skills required); 2) task identity (the ability to perform an entire task from beginning to end); and 3) task significance (the perceived importance of the task). Autonomy, the amount of self control the employee exercises, relates to the psychological state of experienced responsibility. Finally, knowledge of the results links to the feedback received from the job itself (distinct from feedback received from agents, such as supervisors, peers, and subordinates).

Hackman and Oldham base their model upon the assumption that there are objective attributes to a job (core dimensions), and that employees perceive and react to these attributes in terms of motivation and performance.

Hackman and Oldham further suggested that there are several moderator variables present. These variables can (not must) directly increase or decrease the job design/outcome relationships. Individual growth/need/strength is a psychological measure of the degree to which an employee desires complex jobs. Originally considered the most critical moderator, it is based upon the notion that some individuals do not desire complex work, and therefore, will be dissatisfied in enriched jobs. Still, research has proven that despite growth/need/strength, all individuals respond well to complex jobs (it actually is a matter of degree).

Herzberg also identified hygiene factors as moderators. Originally, Hackman and Oldham specifically identified satisfaction with pay, satisfaction with supervision, satisfaction with coworkers, and job security as moderators. While their effect is entirely situational and individual, research does indicate that moderators appear to impact on satisfaction variables more than motivation and performance variables.

Other factors such as social system structure, locus of control, self-esteem, educational level, and organizational type have also been identified as significant moderators. A very interesting moderator variable is career stage. As the employee progresses through his/her career, different aspects of the model become dominant. During the initial period, the "rookie" stage, the individual is just learning the task. The core dimensions of job feedback and task identity are most closely linked to satisfaction and motivation, while other core dimensions tend to be negatively related. After the individual has learned the task, a strong desire for growth characterizes the second stage. Here, the person is most affected by job enrichment. Specifically, the dimensions of skill variety and autonomy are most closely related to satisfaction and motivation. Eventually, the employee will "peak out," and growth is no longer possible. This stage is most often referred to as maintenance. While in this stage, the employee will respond to enrichment, but it is not a major source of satisfaction. Rather, the social aspects of the organization tend to more closely relate to motivation (Katz, 1978; Head, 1981).

Hackman, based upon his work, has developed several guidelines to assist in implementing job redesign projects (Frank & Hackman, 1975). They are:

1. **The use of theory:** Job redesign projects should be undertaken based upon an explicit frame of reference that involves both a theory of job redesign and a theory of change management.

2. **The use of diagnosis:** Diagnosis should be thorough, involving not only the specific jobs considered for change, but the organization's social and technical systems as well.

3. **The development of contingency plans:** As with any change, unforeseen troubles may arise. Plans should be developed ahead of time to deal with these difficulties.

4. **Anticipate setbacks and prepare to modify strategies:** Job redesign is more of an art than a precise science. Therefore, careful monitoring of the change process is essential, and revising plans based on this monitoring information is important to ensure success.

5. **Some suggested techniques to bring about job redesign/job enrichment:** a) forming natural work units; b) combining tasks; c) establishing client relationships; d) vertical loading; and e) opening feedback channels.

Most consider the Hackman-Oldham model to be state-of-the-art in terms of job enrichment and job redesign. It has a well established theoretical base, and proves to be very practical for actual implementation of change. There have been more recent works, which will be discussed next, but the job characteristics theory should serve as the base model for anyone considering job redesign. Other models should be considered for special situations.

PFEFFER AND SALANCIK'S SOCIAL INFORMATION PROCESSING MODEL

Hackman and Oldham base their model upon the assumption that there are objective attributes to a job (core dimensions), and that employees perceive and react to these attributes in terms of motivation and performance. Recently, Salancik and Pfeffer have questioned the validity of this assumption (1977). They argue that motivation and satisfaction are socially constructed phenomena.

What Pfeffer and Salancik suggest, through their social information processing model (1978) is that employees process cues from the social environment to determine which elements of the job are important, how the job ranks on these elements, and how motivated and satisfied he/she should be.

What Pfeffer and Salancik suggest, through their social information processing model (1978) is that employees process cues from the social environment to determine which elements of the job are important, how the job ranks on these elements, and how motivated and satisfied he/she should be. Basically, this boils down to the belief that an employee will evaluate the job and react accordingly, dependent upon what people say about that job. If the employee is told that the job is interesting and desirable, he/she will believe it; and if it is said to be a bad job, the same opinion will follow.

There is much laboratory evidence to support the Pfeffer/Salancik model (see Thomas & Griffin, 1983, for a review), but only one study was conducted in an actual work setting (Griffin, 1983). This study provides useful insights into how this model may be applied. First, the jobs were evaluated using a standard survey instrument. In one plant, the information was used to enrich the jobs. In a second plant, however, a different approach was taken. These supervisors were given intensive communication workshops. Then they were instructed to provide cues to their workers concerning the positive elements of the job. In general, results showed similar improvements in both plants. A fairly inexpensive communications seminar had results comparable to an expensive work enrichment intervention.

It would appear that using social information could replace the need to undergo job enrichment. However, one should be very careful in jumping to this conclusion. First, the technique is still in its infancy, and, for the most part, works best primarily in laboratory settings. It is possible that the use of social cues is similar to behavior modification. The impact of specific cues would have a limited duration, forcing management to revise constantly their communications. Because management can only control a limited amount of the social cues points out another issue making application difficult; an employee will receive cues from coworkers, family members, even perfect strangers. No matter how favorably managers describe a garbage collector's job, the collector in question will always receive statements to the contrary.

GRIFFIN, BATEMAN, WAYNE & HEAD'S INTEGRATED MODEL

Four researchers at Texas A&M University created an experiment to establish which of two models, social information processing or job characteristics, was the most useful for predicting satisfaction and perceptions of the task (Griffin, Bateman, Wayne & Head, 1987). The experiment was very complex, utilizing a $2 \times 2 \times 2 \times 2$ design; the researchers wanted not only to perform a single comparison between cues and job design, but were interested in the effects of change on both models. For instance would the effects of changing social cues from negative to positive be greater than enriching the job? A unique addition, however, was that the change occurred in both directions. In other words, some subjects first performed an enriched task, then were reassigned to a simple task; some received positive cues followed by negative cues.

Perhaps the most important dimension to the research, besides treating the models separately, was that an integrated model was created. Table 1 includes the predictions of this new model.

Table 1. Predictions of the Griffin et al. Model

---

1. Enriched jobs and positive social cues will lead to very high levels of job satisfaction.
2. Enriched jobs and negative social cues or simple jobs and positive social cues will lead to intermediate levels of job satisfaction.
3. Simple jobs and negative social cues will lead to very low levels of job satisfaction.
4. A change from a simple job and negative social cues to an enriched job and positive social cues will lead to a very positive change in job satisfaction.
5. A change from a simple job and positive social cues to an enriched job and positive social cues; or a change from a simple job and negative social cues to an enriched job and negative social cues will lead to a positive change in job satisfaction.
6. A change from a simple job and positive social cues to an enriched job and negative social cues; a change from an enriched job and negative social cues to a simple job and positive social cues, or no change in the combination of an enriched or simple job and positive or negative social cues will lead to no change in job satisfaction.
7. A change from an enriched job and positive social cues to a simple job and positive social cues; or a change from an enriched job and negative social cues to a simple job and negative social cues will lead to a negative change in job satisfaction.
8. A change from an enriched job and positive social cues to a simple job and negative social cues will lead to a very negative change in job satisfaction.

Adapted from Griffin, Bateman, Wayne & Head, 1987

Basically, the premise was that the design of the job and the nature of the cues would combine to dictate the level of satisfaction and task perceptions. For example: 1) The positive attitudes from an enriched job would be enhanced by positive cues, or diminished by negative cues; 2) The negative attitude caused by negative social cues would be somewhat neutralized by an enriched job, or further diminished by a simple job. The same would be true of changes. The most satisfaction would be felt when changing from a simple job with negative cues to an enriched job with positive cues, and the least satisfaction would occur when changing from an enriched job with positive cues to a simple job with negative cues. The other combinations would be interactive—the contradiction between cues and job design partially damping both negative and positive effects.

The results of the experiment indicated that while both social cues and job design did impact satisfaction and perceptions of the task, the level of enrichment was by far the stronger of the two independent models. However, the integrated approach fit the data perfectly; all the predictions were supported at a significance level of $p = .00001$ (the lowest that the software package permitted). This study has significant impact for consultants. It dramatically shows that job enrichment is a better solution to motivation problems than are social cues. However, social cues are also important. If they are not monitored and controlled, negative cues will actually diminish the effect of changing the job, therefore disturbing the cost/benefits of the intervention. In addition, cues supplied by managers (when done in a believable manner) will lead to better results.

THE FORGOTTEN FACTOR: INDIVIDUAL ROLE

Typically, when managers or consultants thank about what people do at work, it is in terms of objective elements of the job. When problems appear, such as motivation or job morale, the first element to be diagnosed is the job. Measured either in terms of objective tasks through any of several job analysis techniques (for example, see Sparks, 1982), or perceptual dimensions with instruments such as the Job Diagnostic Survey.

The social information processing model suggests that these task based approaches may not provide the complete picture. Cues pertaining to the job are obtained. The individual processes this information to establish what is expected of him/her on the job.

Information processing, together with the objective task elements, combine to correlate with the definition of an individual's perceived role in the organization (Katz & Kahn, 1978). The role includes stated and unstated tasks, levels of competence, rules of behavior, criteria, interactions, others' expectations, required attitudes, prohibited activities, and culturally imposed factors.

Therefore, it is not only possible, but probable, different individuals in the same job will have different roles (Roos & Starke, 1981).

The role is very much an individual construct, the summation of all perceived obligations of belonging to a given organization and holding a specific position. Therefore, it is not only possible, but probable, different individuals in the same job will have different roles (Roos & Starke, 1981). Also, the role, as the synergistic view, is certain to impact individual behavior greater than specific measures of the job (for an example, see Warner, 1981).

Many have written on group dynamics and members' roles. For example, Carpenter (1984) has identified requisite roles for group performance. Others have also written much on the impact of problems in roles with organizational behaviors. Role conflict, role ambiguity, role underload and role overload have all been established as potential contributors to stress, resistance to change and group conflicts (Griffin, 1990; Kimberly, 1981).

While most acknowledge the difference between role and task, when obtaining data for problem solving, consultants inevitably revert to the standard data gathering tools, such as the job diagnostic survey. In other words, we acknowledge the difference but choose to ignore it in measurement.

One possible reason for this paradox could be that while the task is somewhat simple to measure, the role (up till now) has proven allusive. At least part of the difficulty is in the individual nature of the role. Another issue is the impossibility to capture, in a standard survey, all the contributors and directions to the role. These two problems force anyone interested in measuring roles to use qualitative methods (for example, see Kimberly, 1981). Traditional qualitative techniques do not lend themselves to analytical comparisons beyond the unit (in this case the individual) for which the data was obtained (VanMaan, Dabbs & Falkner, 1982). Therefore, to obtain useful information on roles for large scale diagnostic purposes a technique is needed to obtain qualitatively comparable information from all affected individuals. Donovan and Head (Donovan, 1991) developed such an instrument.

MEASURING THE ROLE

The instrument, described here, is based upon Stewart's Demands, Constraints, and Choices Model (1982). This model was developed as a framework for understanding managerial tasks, but it is equally relevant for nonmanagerial and professional jobs as well. Stewart suggests that the individual's role can be envisioned through three sets of variables: demands, constraints and choice. Demands are those behaviors which must be performed by the individual or risk formal and informal sanctions. The demands can be imposed by several forces, including (but not limited to) objective job requirements, superiors' expectations, and cultural (corporate, professional, and society) norms and values. The second variable, constraints, represents the elements which impose limits to the employee's behavior. As with the demands, constraints may be derived from both organizational and environmental factors. Government laws, regulations and policies, availability of resources, and prevailing sociocultural morals, etc., are all possible sources of environmentally imposed constraints. Bureaucratic considerations, internal resources, corporate culture and taboos, and managerial limitations are examples of some of the internal sources for constraints. Choice, as the degree of freedom in behavior, is the final element to the model. This reflects the employee's ability to select behaviors that meet the demands of the position while acting within the constraints. Another element of choice reflects those aspects of the job that are optional opportunities, behaviors that are not required but that the individual may choose to perform.

The process begins by having each individual carefully identify, on paper, all the constraints and demands pertaining to that person's own role. Next, the person is presented with a sheet of paper that has a large square printed on it. It is explained that the space inside the square represents all possible employee behaviors. The individual is instructed to demonstrate graphically the amount of demands he/she experiences by drawing a square within the original square, starting at the lower left corner. The greater the demands, the larger the internal square (see Figure 3 for an example). Next, the individual should graph the level of constraints experienced by drawing a diagonal line in the original square, from the upper left to the lower right. Anything above this line represents behaviors not permitted by the constraints, any below are feasible behaviors. The greater the perceived constraints, the greater the illegitimate area above the line becomes (see Figure 4 for an example).

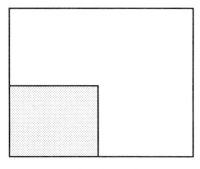

a. few demands   b. many demands

Figure 3. Diagraming the role demands

What each individual has created is a graphical representation of his/her role. This information may be used by managers and consultants to compare, diagnose, and plan interventions based upon individual role, not just task, perceptions.

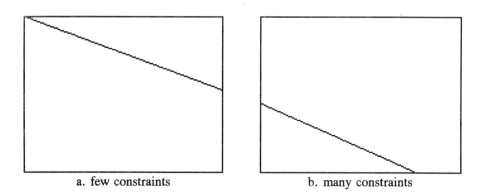

a. few constraints   b. many constraints

Figure 4. Diagramming the role constraints

What each individual has created is a graphical representation of his/her role. This information may be used by managers and consultants to compare, diagnose, and plan interventions based upon individual role, not just task, perceptions. Figure 5 is a representative graph, clearly breaking the role up into easily identifiable sections of demands, constraints, and choice. These figures can be compared to each other, to "ideals," to management perceptions, or simply used as a survey feedback device. Questions such as: Are these really constraints?, Demands?, Is there enough choice?, Too much choice?, Are the demands realistic?, and others can all be discussed. In addition, several potential problems can be identified, such as role ambiguity (Figure 6), some types of role conflict (Figure 7), role overload (Figure 8), and role underload (Figure 9).

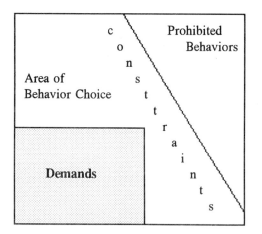

Figure 5. Prototypical depiction of role

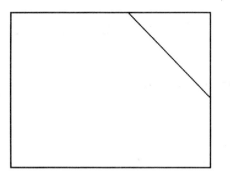

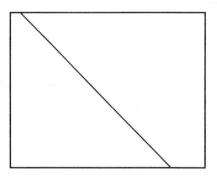

Figure 6. Graph depicting potential
role ambiguity

Figure 7. Graph depicting potential
role conflict

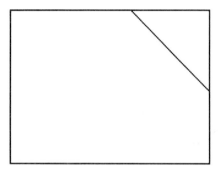

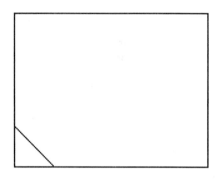

Figure 8. Graph depicting potential
role overload

Figure 9. Graph depicting potential
role underload

While this instrument can be of great diagnostic use, it is not intended to replace totally other methods of measurement, rather, to complement them. The change agent can use instruments such as the job diagnostic survey, to obtain data on the task and its environment in general. Then, the use of this role conceptualization instrument would prove beneficial as a means to collect information critical to interventions at the individual level.

CONCLUSION

Job redesign/enrichment has proven to be a very effective tool for organization development consultants. It is interesting to note that many of the problems job redesign has been called upon to correct are the direct result of the earlier approaches to designing jobs: standardization and simplification.

Table 2. Job Enrichment Has Been Used To Solve These Problems

1. Poor morale/satisfaction
2. Poor motivation
3. Poor performance: Quality and quantity
4. High turnover
5. High absenteeism
6. Alienation from work
7. Poor quality of work life
8. Low work force commitment
9. Need for culture change
10. Introduction of new technology
11. Lack of group cohesion
12. Reduce job monotony
13. Assist in quality circles
14. Reduce costs
15. Reduce stress

In a recent review of case studies (Head, 1990), it was found that organizations used job enrichment to solve a wide variety of problems (listed in Table 2) from increasing motivation to reducing employee stress. Job enrichment/redesign has also been implemented in at last 29 countries (listed in Table 3).

Table 3. Countries Where Job Enrichment Has Been Implemented

USA	Poland	New Zealand
Canada	Yugoslavia	Greece
China	Norway	Mexico
Taiwan	Sweden	Austria
Japan	Denmark	India
Great Britain	Germany	Spain
Australia	Belgium	Switzerland
Scotland	France	Turkey
Ireland	Venezuela	Finland
USSR		Brazil

The critical question, of course, must be how effective is job redesign? In his review, Head found that in 85% of the cases that specifically addressed the issue, job enrichment had a positive impact upon employee morale and satisfaction.

The critical question, of course, must be how effective is job redesign? In his review, Head found that in 85% of the cases that specifically addressed the issue, job enrichment had a positive impact upon employee morale and satisfaction. Motivation improved in 81% of the organizations that studied that outcome. Sixty-nine percent of the users who measured results reported reduced costs—77% showed better work quality, but only 53% reported higher productivity (quantity). Turnover, when studied, showed a decrease 50% of the time and absenteeism was successfully reduced in 42% of the relevant cases.

Therefore, it can be concluded that job redesign/enrichment is a practical and successful intervention used by consultants for a variety of problems. It has had an interesting and steady development, one that is by no means over. What changes will the future bring? Learning more about the role and social cues are two areas bound to be the bases of much future investigation. Other dimensions and theories also will be developed. Some will prove useful, others will flop. But as long as the consultant follows Hackman's principles which include complete diagnosis, theory based intervention, and careful monitoring, job redesign will remain on the forefront of organization development.

References

Carpenter, N. (1984). The seven pieces: Identifying group roles. In Pfeiffer & Goodstein (Eds.), *The 1984 annual: Developing human resources.* San Diego, CA: University Associates, Inc.

Donovan, C. (1991, May). Examining the value of role in job satisfaction. Paper presented at the 21st Annual Information Exchange of the Organization Development Institute, Williams Bay, Wisconsin.

Frank, L. L., & Hackman, J. R. (1975). A failure of job enrichment: The case of the change that wasn't. *Journal of Applied Behavioral Science,* 11, 413–436.

Griffin, R. W. (1982). *Task redesign.* Glenview, IL: Scott Foresman.

Griffin, R. W. (1983). Objective and social sources of information in task redesign: A field experiment. *Administrative Science Quarterly,* 28, 184–200.

Griffin, R. W. (1990). *Management.* Boston: Houghton-Mifflin.

Griffin, R. W., Bateman, T. S., Wayne S. J., & Head, T. C. (1987). Objective and social factors as determinants of task perceptions and responses: An integrated perspective and empirical investigation. *Academy of Management Journal,* 30, 501–523.

Hackman, J. R., & Oldham, G. R. (1975). Development of the Job Diagnostic Survey. *Journal of Applied Psychology*, 60, 159–170.

Hackman, J. R., & Oldham, G. R. (1976). Motivation through the design of work: Test of a theory. *Organizational Behavior and Human Performance*, 16, 250–279.

Hackman, J. R., & Oldham, G. R. (1980). *Work Redesign*. Reading, MA: Addison-Wesley.

Head, T. C. (1981). The relationship of employee tenure and job satisfaction in police work. *Midwest Academy of Management Proceedings*, 195–202.

Head, T. C. (1990). The rules of job enrichment: A review and reexamination. *Proceedings of the 20th annual information exchange of the Organization Development Institute*, 286–290.

Herzberg, F. (1964). The motivation-hygiene concept and problems of manpower. *Personnel Administration*, 27(1), 3–7.

Herzberg, F. (1968). One more time: How do you motivate employees? *Harvard Business Review*, 46(1), 53–62.

House, R. J., & Wigdor, L. A. (1967). Herzberg's dual-factor theory of job satisfaction and motivation: A review of the evidence and a criticism. *Personnel Psychology*, 20, 369–389.

Katz, D., & Kahn, R. L. (1978). *The social psychology of organizations* (2nd ed.). New York: John Wiley and Sons.

Katz, R. (1978). Job longevity as a situational factor in job satisfaction. *Administrative Science Quarterly*, 204–223.

Kimberly, J. R. (1981). Managerial innovation. In Nystrom & Starbuck (Eds.), *Handbook of Organizational Design, Vol. 1* (pp. 84–104). London: Oxford University Press.

Roos, L. L., & Starke, F. A. (1981). Organizational roles. In Nystrom & Starbuck (Eds.), *Handbook of Organizational Design, Vol. 1* (pp. 290–308). London: Oxford University Press.

Salancik, G. R., & Pfeffer, J. (1977). An examination of need satisfaction models of job attitudes. *Administrative Science Quarterly*, 23, 224–253.

Salancik, G. R., & Pfeffer, J. (1978). A social information processing approach to job attitudes and task design. *Administrative Science Quarterly, 23,* 224–253.

Sparks, C. P. (1982). Job analysis. In Rowland & Ferris (Eds.), *Personnel Management.* Boston: Allyn & Bacon.

Stewart, R. (1982). *Choices for the manager: A guide to understanding managerial work.* Englewood Cliffs, NJ: Prentice-Hall.

Thomas, J., & Griffin, R. W. (1983). The social information processing model of task design: A review of the literature. *Academy of Management Review, 8,* 672–682.

VanMaan, J., Dabbs, J. M., & Falkner, R. R. (1982). *Varieties of qualitative research.* Beverly Hills: Sage.

Warner, M. (1981). Organizational experiments and social innovations. In Nystrom & Starbuck (Eds.), *Handbook of Organizational Design, Vol. 1* (pp. 165–185). London: Oxford University Press.

EXPECTANCY THEORY AND EMPLOYEE MOTIVATION:
A CONGLOMERATION

Thomas C. Head

It is customary to start the discussion of a specific theory with a long-winded thesis concerning its author's history and perspective on life (as most theories reflect this data in the assumptions). Such will not be the case here for reasons which will soon become clear.

Rather, when discussing the Expectancy Theory of motivation it is best to begin with a discussion of how it greatly differs from most other motivation theories.

HOW IS EXPECTANCY THEORY UNIQUE?

The most obvious, and most confusing, unique attribute is that the theory is actually known by several different names. While Expectancy is probably the most frequently used (as it is the simplest), the following is a list (in no way exhaustive except for having to read it) of common aliases:

Valence-Instrumentality-Expectancy
Instrumentality-Expectancy
Expectancy-Instrumentality
Expectancy-Valence
Instrumentality
Expectancy-Instrumentality-Valence
Path-Goal

The reason for the great diversity in titles leads us to the second difference in the Expectancy Theory. No one single individual actually developed it. Unlike Maslow's Hierarchy, Adam's Equity, Herzberg's Dual Factor, Hackman & Oldham's Job Characteristics, etc., the Expectancy Theory has been formulated by bringing together diverse research into one conglomeration. Most attribute Victor Vroom (1964) as the first to coalesce the theory, but in fact one could actually trace its roots to Tolman's (1932) work in the 1920s.

Credit is not the issue here, rather it is in trying to understand the literature. With such a diverse background and so many contributors, a standard literature review becomes quite difficult. The principle thorn in the side is that different writers use different labels to identify the same concept. A more hidden difficulty is that the various authors hold a wide range of assumptions which are at the core of the writings. So even if one wades through the different labels, trying to establish if in fact they represent identical constructs can be even more difficult.

What all this means is that the rest of this article presents a discussion of what one author believes are the generally, but not universally, accepted aspects of the theory.

While Expectancy is no longer the only conscious theory of motivation (Job Characteristics also maintains this assumption) it was the first. This means motivation is generally in the realm of the conscious, as opposed to the subconscious. This takes much of the mystery out of motivation, for it is assumed that employees can generally know, and tell, why they are "motivated" or what will "motivate" their behavior. This makes researching, measuring, and resolving problems much easier.

An interesting side issue to this consciousness is the fact that what motivates employees can, and will change, and that employees are aware of this. These changes will occur for various reasons based upon a variety of intrinsic and extrinsic factors. For example, overtime pay in the dead of winter might prove effective in having a person work through the weekend. Making the same offer, to the same individual, for the first warm, sunny weekend in May probably will not work. One incentive organizations use in the motivation battle is life insurance. Generally it can be assumed that this is one benefit most would prefer not to make use of, and in fact for single, childless, unencumbered employees life insurance is typically of little concern. However when the same employee gets married and has children, the security life insurance can provide might be of major importance.

While this article will not address the issue, a fascinating difference between Expectancy and other motivation approaches is the fact that Expectancy gave birth to a leadership theory, known as Path-Goal (Evans, 1970; House, 1971). Path-Goal assumes that the central duty for a leader is to ensure employee motivation. This is accomplished by using principles logically derived from the Expectancy theory.

Almost all motivation theories assume that satisfaction (typically a satisfying of a need or needs) causes performance. But if one looks closely at the description of the model in a later section, the Expectancy theory maintains that performance will cause satisfaction. Through successfully completing an assigned task, the employee knows that a highly desired reward will be forthcoming which results in satisfaction. This is similar in many ways to the goal setting, and in fact much of the research for both is highly complementary.

PERFORMANCE

Possibly the most critical, for the practitioner, difference between Expectancy and other motivation theories lies in the motivation/performance link. Most theories, like the Need Hierarchy, Equity, Dual Factor, Goal Setting, Manifest Needs, and Organizational Behavior Modification assume motivation and performance are synonymous. This is not true of Expectancy. The Expectancy model assumes that motivation in the guise of effort is essential for performance; however, it is by no means all that is required. In addition to the drive, employees must have the following in order to perform:

Ability: It is hard to believe, yet seldom do motivation theorists include the employee's ability to perform the job into their models. Common sense dictates that if an individual is lacking in critical skills, knowledge, aptitudes, and/or experience that no matter how much desire there is, performance will be impossible. Actually possessing the ability is also not enough. Like the "little engine that could," one must believe she has the ability. External locus of control, low self esteem and past failures are all things which can destroy one's personal assessment of ability.

Role Clarity: Effort and ability are still not enough to assure performance. Employees must also know what the jobs entail. For those who can't comprehend how an employee wouldn't know the job, might I suggest that you take a breather now and read your job description. Welcome back. Did your description actually identify what you do? Okay, but what if you eliminated the last line " . . . and other duties to be assigned later," which covers 90% of the job? And, of course, jobs are always changing, along with management's expectations. Then ask most managers about what level of performance is desirable, and you receive "Just do your best." If the manager has taken an organization behavior course, you receive "I have full confidence in you, and I know you will do your best." Given all of this, is it no wonder that ambiguity is one of the top three causes of stress in today's workplace?

Role Acceptance: Even when the employee comprehends the job duties and expectancies, something else is still required: role acceptance. The individual must agree to perform the duties. If a person does not believe that a task or a management request falls into the legitimate job requirements, the likelihood for performance is very slim. This could occur for many reasons, such as personal ethics, pride, tunnel vision, rigid thinking, or even laziness. One commonly rejected request managers make is asking secretaries to run personal errands. Another is assuming that the clerical staff will always make the coffee. If you don't believe me, just try this once.

Opportunity To Perform: Have you ever been given an assignment, but not adequate time to finish it well? Or maybe the authority? Has your department been given additional responsibilities without additional manpower? Possibly you have found yourself with a major report to complete and you know a computer program that would do the work in the time required, but your company won't purchase it? Or you have been given a new software program to use, but no training on how to use it? All of the following were examples of the final requirement for performance—that the individual be given the opportunity to perform. This means that the organization provides the tools, time, authority, and resources (financial and human) needed to do the assigned task.

THE EXPECTANCY MODEL
(IN ITS SIMPLIFIED GLORY)

There is no single model which encompasses all the dimensions of the Expectancy Model. But, with the idea that nothing is easier to add onto than a good simple framework, often the theory can be described in terms of the following equation (for those with math anxiety, please take a deep breath before continuing):

$$M = (E {\rightarrow} P)(P {\rightarrow} O) V$$

where M is motivation, E is effort, P is performance, O is outcome, and V is valence.

(You may now exhale the breath).

This formula breaks motivation into three conscious components, which combined determines the level of effort (motivation) an individual will put forth.

$(E {\rightarrow} P)$ = Effort to Performance. The first assessment an individual makes when confronted with a task is whether or not he can accomplish the task, and if so, how much effort it will require. $E {\rightarrow} P$ is measured using a 0 to 1 scale. If the employee believes that the task is impossible to perform, no matter how much effort is extended, the score will be 0. But if the person believes that she can easily do the task the score will be 1. The more difficult the task (meaning the more effort will have to be exerted for successful performance) the closer the score will be to 0.

$(P \rightarrow O)$ = Performance to Outcome. The second assessment the employee will make is whether or not an outcome will be received if the task is completed satisfactorily. Once again this is measured with a scale of 0 to 1. The score of 1 will be assigned if the employee is sure that an outcome will be received. Asking a nonexempt employee to work overtime is a good example. If the worker puts in the time the company will pay time and a half. But what about the following case? Manager to subordinate: "I'd like you to take a crack at this project. It's a really high visibility item, and if you do well the big wigs will remember it the next promotion." The outcome being used here is a promotion. If the subordinate believes the manager, a score close to 1 will be assigned. However, what if the subordinate has heard this line time and time again? Doubt will have set in, and the greater the doubt, the closer the score will approach 0.

V = Valence. The final element of the motivation equation is the perceived valence. Valence is the value the individual places on the outcome to be received, and is measured on a scale of -1 to $+1$. The more the employee likes the promised outcome, the greater the score. A very desirable outcome will receive a 1. What type of an outcome would receive a negative (demotivating) value? Offering a person time and a half for working over the weekend that he was taking a trip with the family could be an example. The individual equates the extra money with the disappointment, frustration and anger of not being able to take the trip, and the money becomes a symbol of all evil in the organization. If the employee is apathetic towards the proposed outcome he will assign the 0 value.

With the assigned values of the three elements conceptually the level of motivation becomes very easy to ascertain. If the employee believes she can do the job, will definitely receive an outcome, and the outcome is highly desired $(1 \times 1 \times 1 = 1)$ she will be highly motivated. However if the same employee does not believe she could do the job (0), or that an outcome will not be forthcoming (0), or is apathetic towards the outcome (0), then there will be no motivation, for a 0 times any number equals 0. If the promised outcome has a negative evaluation, then since a negative times any number (other than 0) is a negative, motivation will be negative. Negative motivation means that the individual is most likely to do the opposite of the requested task.

TWO NOTEWORTHY EXTENSIONS

While there have been countless alterations to the model described in the previous section, there are two extensions which merit special notice.

The first is the work of Galbraith and Cummins (1967). They proposed a two-tiered structure of outcomes: primary and secondary. Primary outcomes are those which involve intrinsic rewards, such as pride, self esteem, sense of achievement, etcetera. These are derived from within the individual as a result of task performance. Secondary outcomes involve extrinsic rewards, those typically supplied by the organization. These can include pay, benefits, promotions, improved tasks, and the like.

This extension has created a wealth of research on its own. One of the most significant findings from this body of knowledge is a danger of using extrinsic rewards. Take an individual who is intrinsically motivated and thereby performs well on the job. The company may make a grave mistake if it stresses extrinsic rewards. By the constant emphasis of pay raises, promotions, etcetera, doubt as to motives can arise. The intrinsically motivated employee will begin to wonder whether she is performing because of the enjoyment, or because of the pay. Eventually this doubt will lead to the destruction of intrinsic motivation. The moral is that out of fairness organizations should provide extrinsic rewards, but emphasis should be placed on intrinsic outcomes.

Porter & Lawler Extension

The Porter and Lawler (1968) extension is discussed in detail in the Lawler article which appears elsewhere in this book. Therefore it won't be dwelled upon here. The significant contributions are in the incorporation of role perceptions and equity issues into the model. In addition they designed feedback loops into the model. This, in essence, means that the $E{\rightarrow}P$ and $P{\rightarrow}O$ relationships will be strengthened if the employee has experienced them in the past, and satisfaction with a received outcome will influence future assessments of its valence.

APPLYING THE EXPECTANCY MODEL

Miner (1980) conducted an extensive review of the Expectancy model. From this he developed three suggestions for using the model to improve employee motivation:

1. Companies should identify which rewards the employees truly desire, and use this information when designing the reward systems.

2. Managers should take great care to insure that the employees have role clarity, understanding, and acceptance. Of particular importance is that supervisors make sure their subordinates realize they can do the job $(E{\to}P)$ and that rewards will be forthcoming $(P{\to}O)$.

3. Finally, the organization should truly link the rewards with performance by: giving employees what they want; not rewarding poor performance (even with cost of living increases); and publicizing the linkages between performance and rewards. This last suggestions includes eliminating the secrecy which surrounds most organizational reward systems.

CONCLUSION

The purpose of this article was to acquaint the reader with the basic premises behind the Expectancy Theory of motivation. It is no way intended to be comprehensive, just informative. If I have accomplished this, you are now prepared to read the much more thorough Lawler article. If I have not, you should ask the instructor a great deal of questions, as most likely you will be required to read the Lawler article anyway.

References

Evans, Martin G.   "The Effects of Supervisory Behavior On The Path Goal Relationship," *Organizational Behavior And Human Performance*, *5*, 1970, pp. 279-282.

Galbraith, Jay & Cummins, Larry L.   "An Empirical Investigation Of The Task Performance: Interactive Effects Between Instrumentality-Valence And Motivation-Ability," *Organizational Behavior And Human Performance*, *2*, 1967, 237-257.

House, Robert J.   "A Path-Goal Theory Of Leader Effectiveness," *Administrative Science Quarterly*, *16,* 1971, pp. 321-338.

Miner, John B.   *Theories Of Organizational Behavior*. Hinsdale, IL: Dryden Press, 1980.

Porter, Lyman W. & Lawler, Edward E.   *Managerial Attitudes And Performance*. Homewood, IL: Irwin, 1968.

Tolman, Edward C. *Purposive Behavior In Animals And Men*. New York: Appleton-Century-Crofts, 1932.

Vroom, Victor H. *Work And Motivation*. New York: Wiley, 1964.

ON THE FOLLY OF REWARDING A, WHILE HOPING FOR B

Steven Kerr

Executive Overview

This article, updated for AME, needs no introduction.[1] Even today, the original article is still widely reprinted. Now part of the lexicon, it truly qualifies as an Academy of Management Classic. For almost twenty years, its title has reminded executives and scholars alike—"it's the reward system, stupid!" We hope you enjoy the update!   *Editor*

Whether dealing with monkeys, rats, or human beings, it is hardly controversial to state that most organisms seek information concerning what activities are rewarded, and then seek to do (or at least pretend to do) those things, often to the virtual exclusion of activities not rewarded. The extent to which this occurs of course will depend on the perceived attractiveness of the rewards offered, but neither operant nor expectancy theorists would quarrel with the essence of this notion.

Nevertheless, numerous examples exist of reward systems that are fouled up in that the types of behavior rewarded are those which the rewarder is trying to discourage, while the behavior desired is not being rewarded at all.

FOULED UP SYSTEMS

In Politics

Official goals are "purposely vague and general and do not indicate . . . the host of decisions that must be made among alternative ways of achieving official goals and the priority of multiple goals . . ."[2] They usually may be relied on to offend absolutely no one, and in this sense can be considered high acceptance, low quality goals. An example might be "All Americans are entitled to health care."

© *Academy of Management Executive,* 1995, Vol. 9, No. 1.

[1] Originally published in 1975, *Academy of Management Journal,* 18, 769–783.

[2] Charles Perrow, "The Analysis of Goals in Complex Organizations," in A. Etzioni (ed.), *Readings on Modern Organizations* (Englewood Cliffs, NJ: Prentice-Hall, 1969), 66.

Operative goals are higher in quality but lower in acceptance, since they specify where the money will come from, and what alternative goals will be ignored.

The American citizenry supposedly wants its candidates for public office to set forth operative goals, making their proposed programs clear, and specifying sources and uses of funds. However, since operative goals are lower in acceptance, and since aspirants to public office need acceptance (from at least 50.1 percent of the people), most politicians prefer to speak only of official goals, at least until after the election. They of course would agree to speak at the operative level if "punished" for not doing so. The electorate could do this by refusing to support candidates who do not speak at the operative level. Instead, however, the American voter typically punishes (withholds support from) candidates who frankly discuss where the money will come from, rewards politicians who speak only of official goals, but hopes that candidates (despite the reward system) will discuss the issues operatively.

In War

If some oversimplification may be permitted, let it be assumed that the primary goal of the organization (Pentagon, Luftwaffe, or whatever) is to win. Let it be assumed further that the primary goal of most individuals on the front lines is to get home alive. Then there appears to be an important conflict in goals—personally rational behavior by those at the bottom will endanger goal attainment by those at the top.

But not necessarily! It depends on how the reward system is set up. The Vietnam war was indeed a study of disobedience and rebellion, with terms such as "fragging" (killing one's own commanding officer) and "search and evade" becoming part of the military vocabulary. The difference in subordinates' acceptance of authority between World War II and Vietnam is reported to be considerable, and veterans of the Second World War were often quoted as being outraged at the mutinous actions of many American soldiers in Vietnam.

Consider, however, some critical differences in the reward system in use during the two conflicts. What did the GI in World War II want? To go home. And when did he get to go home? When the war was won! If he disobeyed the orders to clean out the trenches and take the hills, the war would not be won and he would not go home. Furthermore, what were his chances of attaining his goal (getting home alive) if he obeyed the orders compared to his chances if he did not? What is being suggested is that the rational soldier in World War II, whether patriotic or not, probably found it expedient to obey.

Consider the reward system in use in Vietnam. What did the soldier at the bottom want? To go home. And when did he get to go home? When his tour of duty was over! This was the case whether or not the war was won. Furthermore, concerning the relative chance of getting home alive by obeying orders compared to the chance if they were disobeyed, it is worth noting that a mutineer in Vietnam was far more likely to be assigned rest and rehabilitation (on the assumption that fatigue was the cause) than he was to suffer any negative consequence.

In his description of the "zone of indifference," Barnard stated that "a person can and will accept a communication as authoritative only when . . . at the time of his decision, he believes it to be compatible with his personal interests as a whole."[3] In light of the reward system used in Vietnam, wouldn't it have been personally irrational for some orders to have been obeyed? Was not the military implementing a system which rewarded disobedience, while hoping that soldiers (despite the reward system) would obey orders?

In Medicine

Theoretically, physicians can make either of two types of error, and intuitively one seems as bad as the other. Doctors can pronounce patients sick when they are actually well (a type 1 error), thus causing them needless anxiety and expense, curtailment of enjoyable foods and activities, and even physical danger by subjecting them to needless medication and surgery. Alternately, a doctor can label a sick person well (a type 2 error), and thus avoid treating what may be a serious, even fatal ailment. It might be natural to conclude that physicians seek to minimize both types of error.

Such a conclusion would be wrong. It has been estimated that numerous Americans have been afflicted with iatrogenic (physician *caused*) illnesses.[4] This occurs when the doctor is approached by someone complaining of a few stray symptoms. The doctor classifies and organizes these symptoms, gives them a name, and obligingly tells the patient what further symptoms may be expected. This

---

[3] Chester I. Barnard, *The Functions of the Executive* (Cambridge, MA: Harvard University Press, 1964), 165.

[4] L. H. Garland, "Studies of the Accuracy of Diagnostic Procedures," *American Journal Roentgenological, Radium Therapy Nuclear Medicine,* Vol. 82, 1959, 25–38; and Thomas J. Scheff, "Decision Rules, Types of Error, and Their Consequences in Medical Diagnosis," in F. Massarik and P. Ratoosh (eds.), *Mathematical Explorations in Behavioral Science* (Homewood, IL: Irwin, 1965).

information often acts as a self-fulfilling prophecy, with the result that from that day on the patient for all practical purposes is sick.

Why does this happen? Why are physicians so reluctant to sustain a type 2 error (pronouncing a sick person well) that they will tolerate many type 1 errors? Again, a look at the reward system is needed. The punishments for a type 2 error are real: guilt, embarrassment, and the threat of a malpractice suit. On the other hand, a type 1 error (labeling a well person sick) is a much safer and conservative approach to medicine in today's litigious society. Type 1 errors also are likely to generate increased income and a stream of steady customers who, being well in a limited physiological sense, will not embarrass the doctor by dying abruptly. Fellow physicians and the general public therefore are really *rewarding* type 1 errors while *hoping* fervently that doctors will try not to make them.

A current example of rewarding type 1 errors is provided by Broward County, Florida, where an elderly or disabled person facing a competency hearing is evaluated by three court-appointed experts who get paid much more *for the same examination* if the person is ruled to be incompetent. For example, psychiatrists are paid $325 if they judge someone to be incapacitated, but earn only $125 if the person is judged competent. Court-appointed attorneys in Broward also earn more—$325 as opposed to $175—if their clients lose than if they win. Are you surprised to learn that, of 598 incapacity proceedings initiated and completed in the county in 1993, 570 ended with a verdict of incapacitation?[5]

In Universities

Society *hopes* that professors will not neglect their teaching responsibilities but *rewards* them almost entirely for research and publications. This is most true at the large and prestigious universities. Clichés such as "good research and good teaching go together" notwithstanding, professors often find that they must choose between teaching and research-oriented activities when allocating their time. Rewards for good teaching are usually limited to outstanding teacher awards, which are given to only a small percentage of good teachers and usually bestow little money and fleeting prestige. Punishments for poor teaching are also rare.

Rewards for research and publications, on the other hand, and punishments for failure to accomplish these, are common. Furthermore, publication-oriented résumés usually will be well-received at other universities, whereas teaching credentials, harder to document and quantify, are much less transferable.

---

[5] *Miami Herald,* May 8, 1994, 1a, 10a.

Consequently it is rational for university professors to concentrate on research, even to the detriment of teaching and at the expense of their students.

By the same token, it is rational for students to act based upon the goal displacement[6] which has occurred within universities concerning what they are rewarded for. If it is assumed that a primary goal of a university is to transfer knowledge from teacher to student, then grades become identifiable as a means toward that goal, serving as motivational, control, and feedback devices to expedite the knowledge transfer. Instead, however, the grades themselves have become much more important for entrance to graduate school, successful employment, tuition refunds, and parental respect, than the knowledge or lack of knowledge they are supposed to signify.

It therefore should come as no surprise that we find fraternity files for examinations, term paper writing services, and plagiarism. Such activities constitute a personally rational response to a reward system which pays off for grades rather than knowledge. These days, reward systems—specifically, the growing threat of lawsuits—encourage teachers to award students high grades, even if they aren't earned. For example:

> When Andy Hansen brought home a report card with a disappointing C in math, his parents . . . sued his teacher. . . . After a year and six different appeals within the school district, another year's worth of court proceedings, $4000 in legal fees paid by the Hansens, and another $8500 by the district . . . the C stands. Now the student's father, auto dealer Mike Hansen, says he plans to take the case to the State Court of Appeals. . . . "We went in and tried to make a deal: They wanted a C, we wanted an A, so why not compromise on a B?" Mike Hansen said. "But they dug in their heels, and here we are."[7]

In Consulting

It is axiomatic that those who care about a firm's well-being should insist that the organization get fair value for its expenditures. Yet it is commonly known that firms seldom bother to evaluate a new TQM, employee empowerment program, or whatever, to see if the company is getting its money's worth. Why? Certainly it

---

[6] Goal displacement results when means become ends in themselves and displace the original goals. See Peter M. Blau and W. Richard Scott, *Formal Organizations* (San Francisco, CA: Chandler, 1962).

[7] *San Francisco Examiner,* reported in *Fortune,* February 7, 1994, 161.

is not because people have not pointed out that this situation exists; numerous practitioner-oriented articles are written each year on just this point.

One major reason is that the individuals (in human resources, or organization development) who would normally be responsible for conducting such evaluations are the same ones often charged with introducing the change effort in the first place. Having convinced top management to spend money, say, on outside consultants, they usually are quite animated afterwards in collecting rigorous vignettes and anecdotes about how successful the program was. The last thing many desire is a formal, revealing evaluation. Although members of top management may actually *hope* for such systematic evaluation, their reward systems continue to *reward* ignorance in this area. And if the HR department abdicates its responsibility, who is to step into the breach? The consultants themselves? Hardly! They are likely to be too busy collecting anecdotal "evidence" of their own, for use on their next client.

In Sports

Most coaches disdain to discuss individual accomplishments, preferring to speak of teamwork, proper attitude, and one-for-all spirit. Usually, however, rewards are distributed according to individual performance. The college basketball player who passes the ball to teammates instead of shooting will not compile impressive scoring statistics and is less likely to be drafted by the pros. The ballplayer who hits to right field to advance the runners will win neither the batting nor home run titles, and will be offered smaller raises. It therefore is rational for players to think of themselves first, and the team second.

In Government

Consider the cost-plus contract or its next of kin, the allocation of next year's budget as a direct function of this year's expenditures—a clear-cut example of a fouled up reward system. It probably is conceivable that those who award such budgets and contracts really hope for economy and prudence in spending. It is obvious, however, that adopting the proverb "to those who spend shall more be given," rewards not economy, but spending itself.

In Business

The past reward practices of a group health claims division of a large eastern insurance company provides another rich illustration. Attempting to measure and reward accuracy in paying surgical claims, the firm systematically kept track of the number of returned checks and letters of complaint received from policyholders. However, underpayments were likely to provoke cries of outrage from the insured, while overpayments often were accepted in courteous silence. Since it was often impossible to tell from the physician's statement which of two surgical procedures, with different allowable benefits, was performed, and since writing for clarifications would have interfered with other standards used by the firm concerning percentage of claims paid within two days of receipt, the new hire in more than one claims section was soon acquainted with the informal norm: "When in doubt, pay it out!"

This situation was made even worse by the firm's reward system. The reward system called for annual merit increases to be given to all employees, in one of the following three amounts:

1. If the worker was "outstanding" (a select category, into which no more than two employees per section could be placed): 5 percent
2. If the worker was "above average" (normally all workers not "outstanding" were so rated): 4 percent
3. If the worker committed gross acts of negligence and irresponsibility for which he or she might be discharged in many other companies: 3 percent.

Now, since the difference between the five percent theoretically attainable through hard work and the four percent attainable merely by living until the review date is small, many employees were rather indifferent to the possibility of obtaining the extra one percent reward. In addition, since the penalty for error was a loss of only one percent, employees tended to ignore the norm concerning indiscriminant payments.

However, most employees were not indifferent to a rule which stated that, should absences or latenesses total three or more in any six-month period, the entire four or five percent due at the next merit review must be forfeited. In this sense, the firm was *hoping* for performance, while *rewarding* attendance. What it got, of course, was attendance. (If the absence/lateness rule appears to the reader to be stringent, it really wasn't. The company counted "times" rather than "days" absent, and a ten-day absence therefore counted the same as one lasting two days. A worker in danger of accumulating a third absence within six months merely had to remain ill—away from work—during a second absence until the first absence was more than six months old. The limiting factor was that at some point salary ceases, and sickness benefits take over. This was usually sufficient to get the younger workers to return, but for those with 20 or more years' service, the company provided sickness benefits of 90 percent of normal salary, tax-free! Therefore. . . .).

Thanks to the U.S. government, even the reporting of wrongdoing has been corrupted by an incredibly incompetent reward system that calls for whistleblowing employees to collect up to thirty percent *of the amount of a fraud* without a stated limit. Thus prospective whistleblowers are encouraged to delay reporting a fraud, even to actively participate in its continuance, in order to run up the total and, thus, their percentage of the take.

I'm quite sure that by now the reader has thought of numerous examples in his or her own experience which qualify as "folly." However, just in case, Table 1 presents some additional examples well worth pondering.

Table 1
Common Management Reward Follies

We hope for . . .	*But we often reward . . .*
• long-term growth; environmental responsibility	• quarterly earnings
• teamwork	• individual effort
• setting challenging "stretch" objectives	• achieving goals; "making the numbers"
• downsizing; rightsizing; delayering; restructuring	• adding staff; adding budget; adding Hay points
• commitment to total quality	• shipping on schedule, even with defects
• candor; surfacing bad news early	• reporting good news, whether it's true or not; agreeing with the boss, whether or not (s)he's right

CAUSES

Extremely diverse instances of systems which reward behavior A although the rewarder apparently hopes for behavior B have been given. These are useful to illustrate the breadth and magnitude of the phenomenon, but the diversity increases the difficulty of determining commonalities and establishing causes. However, the following four general factors may be pertinent to an explanation of why fouled-up reward systems seem to be so prevalent.

1. Fascination with an "Objective" Criterion

Many managers seek to establish simple, quantifiable standards against which to measure and reward performance. Such efforts may be successful in highly predictable areas within an organization, but are likely to cause goal displacement when applied anywhere else.

2. Overemphasis on Highly Visible Behaviors

Difficulties often stem from the fact that some parts of the task are highly visible while other parts are not. For example, publications are easier to demonstrate than teaching, and scoring baskets and hitting home runs are more readily observable than feeding teammates and advancing base runners. Similarly, the adverse consequences of pronouncing a sick person well are more visible than those sustained by labeling a well person sick. Team-building and creativity are other examples of behaviors which may not be rewarded simply because they are hard to observe.

3. Hypocrisy

In some of the instances described the rewarder may have been getting the desired behavior, notwithstanding claims that the behavior was not desired. For example, in many jurisdictions within the U.S. judges' campaigns are funded largely by defense attorneys, while prosecutors are legally barred from making contributions. This doesn't do a whole lot to help judges to be "tough on crime" though, ironically, that's what their campaigns inevitably promise.

4. Emphasis on Morality or Equity Rather than Efficiency

Sometimes consideration of other factors prevents the establishment of a system which rewards behavior desired by the rewarder. The felt obligation of many Americans to vote for one candidate or another, for example, may impair their ability to withhold support from politicians who refuse to discuss the issues. Similarly, the concern for spreading the risks and costs of wartime military service may outweigh the advantage to be obtained by committing personnel to combat until the war is over. The 1994 Clinton health plan, the Americans with Disabilities Act, and many other instances of proposed or recent governmental intervention provide outstanding examples of systems that reward inefficiency, presumably in support of some higher objective.

MORE ON THE FOLLY [1]

Steven Kerr

Executive Overview

Periodically, we conduct an informal poll of our Executive Advisory Panel for their views on topics that appear in AME articles. In this issue, we have published an updated version of Steven Kerr's "On the Folly of Rewarding A, While Hoping for B." Since this article was first published twenty years ago, we wondered how much progress corporate America has made in addressing Kerr's "folly." Here's what our Panel members told us. See if it rings true for you.

The Editors

Ninety percent of our respondents told us that Kerr's folly is still prevalent in corporate America today. Over half concluded that the folly is widespread in their companies. What was true two decades ago remains so today—managers still cling to quantifiable standards when they reward others and as their primary explanation for the folly's perniciousness.

While the historical fundamentals of the folly are still intact, some of the examples our panel members provided are of recent vintage. Here are what a few of them reported:

We hope for . . .	But we reward . . .
⇒ Teamwork and collaboration	⇒ The best team members
⇒ Innovative thinking and risk taking	⇒ Proven methods and not making mistakes
⇒ Development of people skills	⇒ Technical achievements and accomplishments
⇒ Employee involvement and empowerment	⇒ Tight control over operations and resources
⇒ High achievement	⇒ Another year's effort

Academy of Management Executive

[1] The poll was conducted by Kathy Dechant and Jack Veiga in November 1994.

Finally, we asked our panel members to tell us what they believed was the most formidable obstacle in dealing with the folly. While the responses were varied, three themes emerged:

1. *The inability to break out of the old ways of thinking about reward and recognition practices.* In particular, there appears to be a need for new goal and target behavior definition, including non-quantifiable behavior and that which is system focused rather than job or functionally dependent. Among the deterrents to change are the entitlement mentality of workers and the reluctance of management to commit to revamping or revitalizing performance management processes and systems.

2. *Lack of a holistic or overall system view of performance factors and results.* To a great extent, this is still caused by organizational structures that promote optimization of sub-unit results at the expense of the total organization.

3. *Continuing focus on short-term results by management and shareholders.*

To say that Kerr's folly is alive and well is an understatement. Hopefully, some future managers will hear this wake up call. Just in case they're not listening, we'll say it again—IT'S THE REWARD SYSTEM, STUPID!

JOB ATTITUDES AND EMPLOYEE MOTIVATION: THEORY, RESEARCH, AND PRACTICE

Edward E. Lawler, III

Industrial psychologists have been seriously concerned with the measurement, interpretation and implications of job attitudes ever since the Western Electric Studies (Roethlisberger & Dickson, 1939). When Herzberg, Mausner, Peterson and Capwell (1957) reviewed the literature as of 1955, they pointed out that there were several thousand studies in the psychological literature that were concerned with job attitudes. At the present time there must be at least five thousand studies in the literature. Most of these job attitude studies have had as their major focus job satisfaction.

Industrial psychology more than any other area in psychology, has been concerned with the study of satisfaction. It is one of the few significant areas of research in psychology where industrial psychologists have contributed much of the important research work. In most of its work, industrial psychology has been parasitic. It has borrowed basic findings and concepts from other areas of psychology and has contributed little that is new to the understanding of human behavior. This is not true for the study of satisfaction or for the study of some other kinds of attitudes toward tasks and jobs, however. In this area industrial psychology has been in the forefront of knowledge. It is also an area that is clearly identified with industrial psychology. Some may regard this as an albatross around the neck of industrial psychology and clearly prefer that industrial psychology not be identified with this research. This view certainly is easy to understand given the many problems that are present in this body of research. For a long time, much of this work has been atheoretical, full of contradictory findings, and full of poorly designed and poorly executed studies. Recently there has been the great Herzberg controversy which certainly has tended at times to degenerate to nothing but a name calling battle (see e.g., Viteles, 1969) and some rather irrational defenses of a theory that is more in need of growth and development than of a rigid defense of the status quo (Whitsett & Winslow, 1967; Winslow & Whitsett, 1968). Work on this theory has hardly been exemplary of the kind of theory-research interplay that one expects to find in a mature field of scientific research, but then this field is not a mature one. it is suffering growing pains. The very fact that it is suffering these growing pains is at least evidence that it is alive and that growth is taking place.

From *Personnel Psychology,* Vol. 23, 1970, pp. 223-227. Used by permission of the publisher.

Theories are being expounded, some ingenious attempts are being made to test them, and knowledge is being accumulated. Admittedly, some of the knowledge that is being accumulated is negative knowledge in the sense that it says certain theories or ways of thinking are not correct. But, this is progress. It is all too easy to look at a few years of research in a field and conclude that no progress is being made and that a lot of energy has been wasted running down blind alleys. It certainly is possible to get this feeling when looking at the research on job attitudes. and many have gotten it (e.g., Viteles, 1969). But, by standing back and taking a little longer term perspective, a quite different picture presents itself as far as the work on job attitudes is concerned. Looking at the research in this area during the last fifteen years there are signs of growth and development so clear that even the most vociferous singer of songs of despair has to admit progress has been made.

SATISFACTION AND PERFORMANCE

As an example of an area where significant progress has been made, consider the issue of how job attitudes are related to motivation. In 1955, Brayfield and Crockett's article on the relationship between satisfaction and performance appeared. At that point in time, many psychologists apparently believed that satisfaction caused performance and the research evidence that existed in 1955 could have been interpreted as either supporting or disproving the view that satisfaction causes performance. In fact, one review done in that year concluded that satisfaction was related to performance (Herzberg et al., 1957) while Brayfield and Crockett concluded it was not. At this time, it is hard for me to imagine that anyone could argue that satisfaction can best be thought of as only a cause of performance. It probably is true that under certain conditions satisfaction may be related to performance, but this does not mean that it is a cause of performance.

The recent research on the relationship between satisfaction and performance has not focused on the simple yes or no question; is satisfaction related to performance? Differential studies that are concerned with specifying the causal basis for any relationships that are found between satisfaction and performance have been done. Admittedly, there are not too many of these new look studies, but a brief summary of what they and other studies show about the relationship between satisfaction and performance is warranted.

1. Satisfaction is an indicator of an employee's motivation to come to work. Research studies have consistently found relationships between satisfaction and absenteeism and turnover (Brayfield & Crockett, 1955; Herzberg et al., 1957; Schuh, 1967; Vroom, 1964). This relationship can be explained by using an expectancy theory approach to motivation (Lawler, 1967). According to this view a person's motivation to attend his job is strongly influenced by the relative attractiveness of attending the job (Vroom, 1964).

People will be motivated to come to work only if it is the most positively valent behavior that is open to them. The person who says he is satisfied with his job is in effect saying that his job somehow is instrumental for satisfying his needs, while the person who says he is not satisfied with his job is saying that his job is not instrumental for satisfying his needs (Lawler, 1967). Thus, the person who is dissatisfied with his job is likely to see attending his job as a less positively valent behavior than is the person who is satisfied with his job (Graen, 1969). Because of this, the dissatisfied person is likely to come to work less often.

2. Satisfaction influences the motivation to perform a job effectively only very indirectly. It influences the motivation to perform because it has the power to influence the valence or attractiveness of certain kinds of rewards, and valence of rewards does influence motivation directly. There is evidence, for example, that as employees become more satisfied with their pay, it becomes less important to them (Lawler & Porter, 1963). There is also evidence that the less important pay is, the less it can serve as a motivator (Schneider & Olson, in press). A similar relationship seems to exist for most rewards, with the possible exception of rewards or outcomes that fulfill self-actualization needs. These may become more important as they become better satisfied (Alderfer, 1969). Still, for most rewards, the relationship is a negative one, suggesting that if only this influence operated, satisfaction should be negatively related to performance. Thus, high satisfaction should lead to lower motivation, not higher motivation as was once argued. This is, of course, not the only process operating that influences the relationship between satisfaction and motivation, and thus it is rare to find a negative relationship between satisfaction and motivation among people who are working in organizations. However, much of the research on animal behavior shows this relationship does exist where subjects are motivated by rewards like food and water (Cofer & Appley, 1964). Animal researchers frequently point out that a satisfied need is not a motivator.

3. Performance can, under certain conditions, influence satisfaction rather directly. It can influence satisfaction where it leads to rewards like pay and promotion, which influence satisfaction (Lawler & Porter, 1967b; Porter & Lawler, 1968a). It probably is important to talk separately here about extrinsic rewards and intrinsic rewards because of the differences in their relationship to performance. Extrinsic rewards, like pay, have to be given by someone else, and for this reason they might not be given in close accord with the person's performance. If they are not, then there are some reasons to expect a zero or negative relationship between satisfaction and performance. This statement is based on two findings. First, that as the amount of reward received increases, so does satisfaction (Lawler & Porter, 1963). Second, that as people feel they are performing better, they expect greater

amounts of reward (Porter & Lawler, 1968a). Thus, in a situation where the good performing employees are rewarded the same as poor performing employees, a negative relationship should exist between satisfaction and performance because the better performers will be experiencing the same level of rewards as the poor performers, but will feel they should be rewarded more highly. In short, the good performers will have a greater discrepancy between what they receive and what they feel they should receive. In a situation where rewards are tied to performance, a positive relationship between satisfaction and performance should exist (Lawler & Porter, 1967b). This should come about because the good performers will be getting more rewards and should be more satisfied. The one qualification that is necessary here concerns just how large the differences are in the rewards received by the good and poor performers. If they are small, then it is not likely that a substantial positive relationship will exist, because good performers have higher aspirations than do poor performers and it will take more than a small difference in reward level to make them more satisfied than the poor performers.

The situation is somewhat different for intrinsic rewards, because they are given by the person to himself when he performs well. Thus, they are closely tied to performance, and because of this, satisfaction with them typically should be more closely tied to performance than is satisfaction with other kinds of rewards. The one qualification that is necessary here centers around the kind of job the people hold. There is some evidence (e.g., Blauner, 1964) that good performance on certain kinds of jobs simply is not intrinsically satisfying. On these types of jobs, no relationship would be expected between intrinsic satisfaction and performance (Lawler & porter, 1967b). Basically, jobs that allow the holder low control, that are not challenging, and that provide little feedback, would seem to fall into this category.

At this point it should be obvious that the relationship between satisfaction and motivation is a very complex one. Satisfaction can be both a cause and a consequence of performance. In some situations it is possible that a strong negative relationship between the two will exist, while in others a strong positive relationship will exist. There is one process operating which leads to a negative relationship between the two and that is the tendency of satisfaction to decrease the importance of most rewards. But this tendency toward a negative relationship may be neutralized or even reversed by the ability of performance to influence satisfaction if performance leads to rewards. If a strong performance-reward link exists, a strong positive relationship can exist because of the good performers' feelings that they are better rewarded.

Despite the complexity of the relationship between satisfaction and performance, there are some interesting implications for practice that can be drawn from it.

1. The data do suggest that the actual level of satisfaction which exists in an organization is important and should be monitored because it is so strongly related to absenteeism and turnover. Regular monitoring of satisfaction should allow organizations to measure the impact of their reward policies and to predict the levels of absenteeism and turnover that are likely in the future. The higher the satisfaction the less the absenteeism and turnover. In short, high levels of satisfaction are generally desirable because they can increase an employee's motivation to come to work. Economically, it pays to have a general high satisfaction level because turnover and absenteeism are very costly.

2. It is important for organizations to look at the variance in satisfaction that is reported and at the relationship between satisfaction and performance (Porter & Lawler, 1968b). A general high level of satisfaction can come about in an organization in several ways. It can come about because everyone experiences that level of satisfaction or because some people are very satisfied and others are dissatisfied. Variance in job satisfaction is not good per se, but it is desirable if it is positively correlated with performance. There are several reasons why it is advantageous for a positive relationship between satisfaction and performance to exist. First, since turnover and absenteeism are related to satisfaction it should lead to turnover and absenteeism being greatest among poor performers, because they are the employees who are dissatisfied. This kind of turnover is, of course, precisely the kind that organizations not only can stand, but should seek. Secondly, a positive relationship between satisfaction and performance indicates that rewards are being distributed according to performance. This is desirable since it can lead to increased motivation. All this suggests that organizations ought to monitor both the satisfaction levels that exist and systematically try to determine who the satisfied employees are. The answer to the question, "Who are the satisfied employees?" should be, "The good performers." It if isn't, then the organizational reward system probably isn't functioning well. It bears repeating that in this view, the relationship between satisfaction and performance is important and should be monitored not to determine if satisfaction leads to performance, but because it tells something about how rewards are being given out in an organization. In short, we have come a long way from the time when we were worried about whether satisfaction leads to performance, and when many urged that workers be kept happy because it would make them work harder.

ATTITUDES AND MOTIVATION

Probably the most significant recent advances in understanding the relationship between attitudes and motivation have come from the research that has been concerned with attitudes other than satisfaction attitudes. Prior to 1957, almost all job attitude studies focused only on people's feelings of satisfaction and on what aspects of jobs (e.g., pay, supervision) are important to them. This is no longer true, and it is my view that this recent research on other job attitudes has contributed a great deal more to our understanding of motivation than all the research on satisfaction. Particularly impressive is the research which has been concerned with path-goal attitudes, instrumentalities, expectancies, role perceptions and intentions. Let me summarize this group of research studies and then consider the implications of the results for motivation in organizations.

People's statements about how they intend to perform and of their goals in a situation are good predictors of their actual performance in the situation (Lock & Bryan, 1967). This suggests that people set performance goals for themselves when they are in a given situation and that they are motivated to perform in accord with the goals they set. Thus, conscious thought processes are related to motivation and, therefore, motivation presumably can be influenced by affecting the kind of goals people set for themselves.

Figure 1 presents a model that is based upon an earlier model suggested by Porter and Lawler (1968a) which may help explain what influences the goals and intentions of people. It shows the relationship that exists between expectancy, instrumentality, and importance attitudes and extrinsic motivation. The first term in the model $E{\rightarrow}P$ refers to a person's subjective probability about the likelihood that he can perform at a given level, or in other words, that effort on his part will lead to successful performance. This term can be thought of as varying from 0 to 1. As a general rule, the less likely a person feels it is that he can perform at a given level, the less likely he will be to try to perform at that level (Vroom, 1964). In short, people do not try to perform at levels that they do not feel they can achieve. Thus, when this probability is 0, no motivation is present. The model also shows that this $E{\rightarrow}P$ probability is directly influenced by self-esteem. The higher the person's self-esteem, the more realistic will be his $E{\rightarrow}P$ subjective probabilities. A person's $E{\rightarrow}P$ probabilities are also, of course, strongly influenced by the situation he finds himself in and by his previous experience in that and similar situations.

The second factor that influences motivation is made up of a combination of a number of beliefs about what the outcomes of successful performance will be and the valence of these outcomes (Box 2). Figure 1 shows that the person's subjective probability that performance will lead to an outcome $[P{\rightarrow}O]$ should be multiplied by the valence of that outcome $[V]$. Finally, it is suggested that the products of all probability times valence combinations should be added together for all outcomes

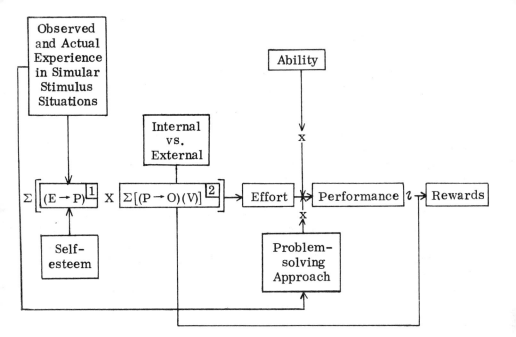

Figure 1. Extrinsic motivation model.

that are seen to be related to performance. Valence is considered to vary from $+1$ (very desirable) to -1 (very undesirable) and the performance to outcomes probabilities to vary from $+1$ (performance sure to lead to outcome) to 0 (performance not related to outcome). Hence, this second factor will be larger, the more positively valent rewards are seen to be obtained as a result of good performance and the less negatively valent outcomes are seen to result from performance.

A person's performance outcome subjective probability beliefs are shown to be influenced by two factors. One is an individual difference factor that Rotter (1967) has referred to as a belief in internal vs. external control. According to this view, some see things in terms of internal control (that is, they act on world) while others see the world in terms of external control (the world acts on them). It would seem that the more a person is oriented toward internal control, the more he is likely to feel that performance will lead to outcomes while the more he is oriented toward external control, the less likely he would be to have high performance outcome subjective probabilities. Some evidence for this has been found in data recently collected by the author. It shows that high internal control managers do seem to see stronger performance outcome association for outcomes like pay and promotion than do high externalizers. Figure 1 also shows that a feedback loop from the strength of the connection between performance and outcomes to the $P \rightarrow O$ probability exists. This is included to illustrate the importance of learning in determining what a person's performance outcome probabilities will be in a given situation (Graen,

1969). Clearly, the degree to which performance, in similar situations, has been closely followed by outcomes in the past will influence the person's beliefs about what outcomes performance will lead to.

The two factors that so far have been said to influence the strength of a person's extrinsic motivation to perform effectively, briefly, are (1) the person's belief that his effort can be converted into performance, and (2) the net attractiveness of the events that are felt to stem from good performance. These two factors are shown to combine multiplicatively, because if the first is zero or if the second is zero or negative, there will be no motivation to perform effectively. On the other hand, the greater the product of these two factors, the greater will be the motivation to perform effectively. Thus, if a person doesn't believe that good performance will follow from his effort, he will not be motivated to perform well even though he feels good performance will lead to a number of desirable outcomes. Similarly, unless good performance is seen to lead to positive outcomes, the person will not be motivated to perform well even if he is sure he can perform well by putting forth effort.

When consideration is being given to the strength of a person's motivation to perform at a given level, in some cases it is necessary to consider more than just the $E{\rightarrow}P$ probability and the $P{\rightarrow}O$ probabilities that are associated with the person achieving that level of performance. When the $E{\rightarrow}P$ probability is less than 1, that is, when a person is not sure he can convert his effort into the level of performance which he is considering, then it may be necessary to consider the subjective probability that trying to perform at a given level will actually lead to performance at a different level. In the case where a person is trying to perform at a high level, this may mean considering the possibility that he will be unsuccessful and perform at a low level. Figure 2 gives an illustration of this point. It shows an example where the person considers the probability of successful performance to be .8 and of unsuccessful performance to be .2. In this case it is important to consider the two $E{\rightarrow}P$ probabilities and the outcomes that are seen to be associated with them. Normally the $E{\rightarrow}P$ probabilities should sum to approximately 1 while the $P{\rightarrow}O$ probabilities will not. If other $E{\rightarrow}P$ probabilities are considered, they should be combined with the appropriate $(P{\rightarrow}O(V)$ combinations for that level of performance. The results of such additional $(E{\rightarrow}P[(P{\rightarrow}O)(V)]$ combinations as are appropriate should be summed with the original one for the probability that trying to perform at a given level will actually lead to performing at that level. This is shown in the model by the Σ sign that precedes the first term.

The strength of a person's motivation to perform correctly is most directly reflected in his effort. That is, in how hard he works. This effort expenditure may or may not result in good performance (Lawler & Porter, 1967a) since at least two factors must be right if effort is to be converted into performance. First, the person must possess the necessary abilities in order to perform the job well. A number of

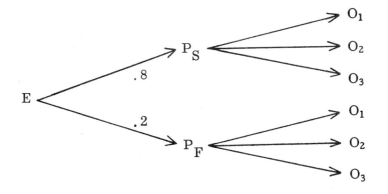

Figure 2. Illustration of model.

authors (e.g., Lawler, 1966; Maier, 1955; Vroom, 1964) have argued that motivation and ability combine multiplicatively in order to determine performance. A similar view is presented in Figure 1. Ability is shown to combine multiplicatively with effort in order to stress the point that if ability is zero so will performance be zero. In other words, unless both ability and effort are high, there cannot be good performance. Great amounts of effort cannot completely take the place of ability.

A second factor also is seen to intervene between effort and performance. This is the person's perception of how his effort can best be converted into performance. It is assumed that this perception is learned by the subject on the basis of previous experience in similar situations. This "how to do it" perception can obviously vary widely in accuracy. It is shown to combine multiplicatively with effort in order to stress the point that unless it is accurate, performance will be zero just as in the case of ability being low. Some evidence to support the importance of this point has been provided by several studies which have shown that where erroneous "how to do it" perceptions exist, the performance of managers is low even though their effort or motivation may be high (Lawler & Porter, 1967a). The particular perceptions focused upon have been people's perceptions of the degree to which successful performance on their job demands inner directed behavior.

Although it is not shown in the model, it is obvious that situational blocks can often prevent performance from being high even when ability and motivation are high and the person correctly directs his effort. This could be shown in the model as an additional box intervening between effort and performance. The final link in the model is represented by the wavy line that connects performance to rewards. It is drawn as a wavy line to indicate that extrinsic rewards do not always follow directly from performance. If Locke's concept of intention were to be placed in the model, it would appear just before effort, showing that it is determined by the first two factors and that it is the immediate determinant of effort.

Figure 3 presents a model for intrinsic motivation. It is similar to the one presented for extrinsic motivation with but two exceptions. The first is that it shows the $E{\to}P$ probability as influencing the $P{\to}O$ probabilities. This is included because much of the research on achievement motivation has shown that achievement motivation comes into play only when certain $E{\to}P$ probabilities exist. Because of this connection, the greatest intrinsic motivation may not be generated when the $E{\to}P$ probability is very high. Both Atkinson (1964) and McClelland (1961) have suggested that under some conditions the highest intrinsic motivation may result when effort is seen to have only a 50-50 chance of leading to good performance.

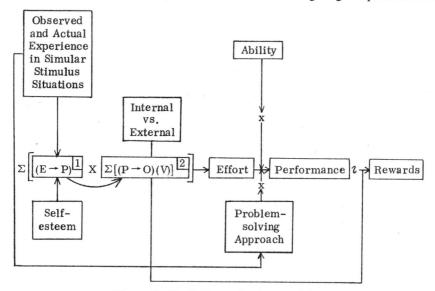

Figure 3. Intrinsic motivation model.

Under this condition, a whole set of intrinsic rewards get tied to performance that are not involved when there is certainty that effort will lead to good performance. Specifically, feelings of achievement, accomplishment and growth are seen to result from successful performance when there is less than a perfect relationship between effort and performance. Thus, in some instances, motivation may be highest when the effort to performance probability is not perfect because of the potential influence of this first factor on the second factor. In other words, the perceived consequence of good performance may be greatest when the first term is less than 1 despite the fact that 1 represents the greatest value that can be multiplied by the second term. Apparently, once the first term exceeds .5, further increase in it only serves to decrease the value of the second term, thus negating any increase in the first term. Because of this effect the highest motivation may well come when the first term is around .5.

The intrinsic reward model also differs from the extrinsic one in that it shows a more direct connection between performance and rewards. This comes about because the rewards are given by the individual to himself and thus are closely related to behavior. It is because of this close connection and the strong $P{\rightarrow}O$ connections it causes, that intrinsic rewards can be such significant motivators.

Although both of these models go beyond the data that currently exists, there is evidence to support much of the thinking in the model. The model suggests that $E{\rightarrow}P$ beliefs and $P{\rightarrow}O$ beliefs should be related to performance, and a number of studies have shown that they are (Galbraith & Cummings, 1967; Georgopoulos, Mahoney & Jones, 1957; Hackman & Porter, 1968; Lawler & Porter, 1967a; Porter & Lawler, 1968a; Spitzer, 1964). They also lead to the prediction that these beliefs should be more highly correlated with future performance than with present or past performance, and one study has suggested that this is true (Lawler, 1968). They suggest that attitudes about the value of rewards should be related to performance only where those rewards are related to performance, and one study has found evidence to show just this (Schneider & Olson, in press). Data also exists to support the point that ability combines multiplicatively with motivation to determine performance, and that role perceptions combine similarity with motivation.

The approach suggested by the models is particularly interesting since it leads to a number of important, immediately useful implications for practice. Let me enumerate a few of them.

1. Instead of focusing on satisfaction and trying to increase it in order to increase performance, the emphasis should be on $E{\rightarrow}P$, $P{\rightarrow}O$ and V attitudes. Attempts should be made to provide jobs that are challenging enough so that $E{\rightarrow}P$ probabilities will be generated that will lead to feelings of achievement and other intrinsic outcomes being tied to performance. Extrinsic rewards like pay and promotion should be closely tied to performance so that high $P{\rightarrow}O$ probabilities exist for them.

2. Attitude surveys should focus on $E{\rightarrow}P$ and $P{\rightarrow}O$ and V types of attitudes in order to assess the level of motivation that exists in an organization. (Porter & Lawler, 1968b). Indexes of the motivation levels operating in subparts of an organization or in a total organization could be developed. This would make it possible to compare the levels of motivation that exist in different parts of the same organization and in different organizations. This has not been done since most attitude surveys have focused only on satisfaction and as has been pointed out, satisfaction levels tell little about motivation. Satisfaction measures, however, when collected along with the kind of motivational measures discussed here should enable an organization to predict what the future holds not only in terms of absenteeism and turnover, but also in terms of motivation. Thus, collecting expectancy attitude data should not

be regarded as a substitute for collecting satisfaction data but as a long needed compliment to it.

3. Organizations should make an effort to regularly measure the kinds of $E{\to}P$, $P{\to}O$ and V attitudes that exist. If the levels of the attitudes are monitored over time, then it should be possible to measure and predict changes in the motivation level in an organization. It should also be possible to gauge the impact of changes in pay and promotion policies on the degree to which these rewards operate as motivators. In short, by measuring the right kind of attitudes, the potential exists for monitoring the motivation levels that exist in an organization over time.

4. Superiors and subordinates should work toward developing shared perceptions of how the subordinate's job should be done. It is important that they have common perceptions, otherwise the situation can develop where a subordinate may be very motivated and yet be performing incorrectly because he perceives his role incorrectly. One way of decreasing the chance that this might occur is by structuring performance appraisal sessions in such a way that specific objectives and goals are decided on. Another approach is to have both superiors and subordinates develop job descriptions for the subordinates' job. The elements of these descriptions could then be ranked for importance by each independently and these ranks compared as a way of getting the superior and subordinate to talk about the differences in their perceptions of the job.

5. Superiors should be aware of what type of outcomes their subordinates value so that these outcomes can be tied to their performance. That is, superiors should try to individualize the rewards system to capitalize on the individual differences among people in how they value different outcomes.

6. Organizations that wish to use pay or other rewards as a motivator should select people on the basis of how important these rewards are to them. If pay is to be used, for example, people who value pay should be selected. Similarly, if pay is to be used, people high on internal control and self-esteem should be selected.

These suggestions for practice that have been listed are but a few of the many that could be drawn from the recent research and theorizing on attitudes and motivation. They represent significant advances over what was in the literature just a few years ago. We have come a long way in the last fifteen years. This progress has led to significant dividends and it is about to begin to pay even greater dividends, dividends that will appear in terms of improved practices within organizations and in terms of better research. Many aspects of the thinking represented in the models is untested, but potentially testable. Hopefully, the next ten years will see many of the links in the models subjected to empirical tests so that ten years from now someone will be able to say that considerable progress has been made since 1969.

References

Alderfer, C. P. "An Empirical Test of a New Theory of Human Needs." *Organizational Behavior and Human Performance,* IV (1969), 142–175.

Atkinson, J. W. *An Introduction to Motivation.* Princeton: Van Nostrand, 1964.

Blauner, R. *Alienation and Freedom.* Chicago: University of Chicago, 1964.

Brayfield, A. H., and Crockett, W. H. "Employee Attitudes and Employee Performance." *Psychology Bulletin,* LII (1955), 396–424.

Cofer, C. N., and Appley, M. H. *Motivation: Theory and Research.* New York: Wiley, 1964.

Galbraith, J., and Cummings, L. L. "An Empirical Investigation of the Motivational Determinants of Task Performance: Interactive Effects Between Instrumentality—Valence and Motivation—Ability." *Organizational Behavior and Human Performance,* II (1967), 237–257.

Georgopoulos, B. S., Mahoney, G. M., and Jones, N. W. "A Path-Goal Approach to Productivity." *Journal of Applied Psychology,* XLI (1957), 345–353.

Graen, G. "Instrumentality Theory of Work Motivation: Some Experimental Results and Suggested Modifications." *Journal of Applied Psychology Monograph,* LIII (2) (1969), 1–25.

Hackman, J. R., and Porter, L. W. "Expectancy Theory Predictions of Work Effectiveness." *Organizational Behavior and Human Performance,* III (1968), 417–426.

Herzberg, F., Mausner, G., Peterson, R. O., and Capwell, D. R. *Job Attitudes: Review of Research and Opinion.* Pittsburgh: Psychological Service of Pittsburgh, 1957.

Lawler, E. E. III. "Ability as a Moderator of the Relationship Between Job Attitudes and Job Performance." *Personnel Psychology,* XIX (1966), 153–164.

Lawler, E. E. III. "A Correlational—Causal Analysis of the Relationship Between Expectancy Attitudes and Job Performance." *Journal of Applied Psychology,* LII (1968), 462–468.

Lawler, E. E. III. "Attitude Surveys and Job Performance." *Personnel Administration,* XXX (5) (1967), 3–5, 22–24.

Lawler, E. E. III, and Porter, L. W. "Antecedent Attitudes of Effective Managerial Performance." *Organizational Behavior and Human Performance,* II (1967), 122–142(a).

Lawler, E. E. III, and Porter, L. W. "The Effect of Performance on Job Satisfaction." *Industrial Relation,* VII (1967), 20–28(b).

Lawler, E. E. III, and Porter, L. W. "Perceptions Regarding Management Compensation." *Industrial Relations,* III (1963), 41–49.

Locke, E. A., and Bryan, J. F. *Goals and Intentions as Determinants of Performance Level, Task Choice and Attitudes.* Washington: American Institute for Research, 1967.

Maier, N. R. F. *Psychology in Industry* (2nd Ed.). Boston: Houghton-Mifflin, 1955.

McClelland, D. C. *The Achieving Society.* Princeton: Van Nostrand, 1961.

Porter, L. W., and Lawler, E. E. III. *Managerial Attitudes and Performance.* Homewood, Illinois: Irwin-Dorsey, 1968(a)

Porter, L. W., and Lawler, E. E. III. "What Job Attitudes Tell About Motivation." *Harvard Business Review,* XLVI(1) (1968), 118–126(b).

Roethlisberger, E. J., and Dickson, W. J. *Management and the Worker.* Cambridge: Harvard University Press, 1939.

Rotter, J. B. "Generalized Expectancies for Internal Versus External Control of Reinforcement." *Psychological Monographs,* LXXX(1) (1966), 1–28.

Schneider, B., and Olson, L. "Effort as a Correlate of Organization Reward System and Individual Values." *Personnel Psychology,* in press.

Schuh, A. J. "The Predictability of Employee Tenure: A Review of the Literature." *Personnel Psychology,* XX (1967), 133–152.

Spitzer, M. E. *Goal-attainment, Job Satisfaction and Behavior.* (Doctoral Dissertation, New York University). Ann Arbor, Michigan: University Microfilms, 1964. No. 64-10,048.

Viteles, M. S. "The Two Faces of Applied Psychology." *International Review of Applied Psychology,* XVIII (1969), 5-10.

Vroom, V. H. *Work and Motivation.* New York: Wiley, 1964.

Whitsett, D., and Winslow, E. K. "Analysis of Studies of the Motivation-Hygiene Theory." *Personnel Psychology,* XX (1967), 391-415.

Winslow, E. K., and Whitsett, D. "Dual-Factor Theory: A Reply to House and Wigdor." *Personnel Psychology,* XXI (1968), 55-58.

BEHAVIOR MODIFICATION ON THE BOTTOM LINE

W. Clay Hamner and Ellen P. Hamner

It may be easy to say *what* a manager does. Telling *how* he influences the behavior of the employee in the direction of task accomplishment is far more difficult to comprehend and describe. The purpose of this article is to describe and spell out the determinants of employee productivity or performance from a reinforcement theory point of view, and to show how managing the contingencies of positive reinforcement in organization settings leads to successful management. We hope these descriptions will enable the manager to understand how his or her behavior affects the behavior of subordinates and to see that, in many cases, a worker's failure to perform a task properly is a direct outcome of the manager's own behavior. The employee has failed to perform because the manager has failed to motivate.

MANAGING THE CONTINGENCIES OF REINFORCEMENT

The interrelationship among three components—work environment, task performance, and consequences of reinforcements—are known as the contingencies of reinforcement. The reward that is contingent upon good performance in a given work situation (environment) acts as a motivator for future performance. The manager controls the *work environment* (Where am I going? What are the goals? Is the leader supportive? Is this a pleasant place to work?), the *task assignment* (How will I get there? What behavior is desired? What is considered appropriate performance?), and the *consequences* of job performance (How will I know when I've reached the desired goal? Is the feedback relevant and timely? Is my pay based upon my performance?). By shaping these three components of behavior so that all are positive, the manager can go a long way toward creating a work climate that supports high productivity.

ARRANGING THE CONTINGENCIES OF REINFORCEMENT

Someone who expects to influence behavior must be able to manipulate the consequences of behavior. Whether managers realize it or not, they constantly shape the behavior of their subordinates by the way they utilize the rewards at their

---

disposal. Employers intuitively use rewards all the time—but their efforts often produce limited results because the methods are used improperly, inconsistently, or inefficiently. In many instances, employees are given rewards that are promote. Even when they are, long delays often intervene between the occurrence of the desired behavior and its intended consequences. Special privileges, activities, and rewards are often furnished according to length of service rather than performance requirements. In many cases, positive reinforcers are inadvertently made contingent upon the wrong kind of behavior. In short, intuition provides a poor guide to motivation.

A primary reason managers fail to "motivate" workers to perform in the desired manner is their failure to understand the power of the contingencies of reinforcement over the employee. The laws or principles for arranging the contingencies to condition behavior are not hard to understand; if properly applied, they constitute powerful managerial tools that can be used for increasing supervisory effectiveness.

Conditioning is the process by which behavior is modified through manipulation of the contingencies of behavior. To understand how this works, we will first look at various kinds of arrangements of the contingencies: *positive reinforcement* conditioning, *escape* conditioning, *extinction* conditioning, and *punishment* conditioning. The differences among these kinds of contingencies depend on the consequences that result from the behavioral act. Positive reinforcement and avoidance learning are methods of strengthening desired behavior, while extinction and punishment are methods of weakening undesired behavior.

Positive Reinforcement

According to B. F. Skinner, a positive reinforcer or reward is a stimulus that, when added to a situation, strengthens the probability of the responses in that situation. Behavior that appears to lead to a positive consequence tends to be repeated, while behavior that appears to lead to a negative consequence tends not to be repeated.

Once it has been determined that a specific consequence has reward value to a work group, we can use it to increase that group's performance. Thus, the first step in the successful application of reinforcement procedures is to select reinforcers that are sufficiently powerful and durable to establish and strengthen desired behavior. These could include such things as an interesting work assignment, the chance to use one's mind, seeing the results of one's work, good pay, recognition for a job well done, promotion, freedom to decide how to do a job, and so on.

The second step is to design the contingencies in such a way that the reinforcing events are made contingent on the desired level of performance. This is the rule of reinforcement most often violated. Rewards *must* result from performance—and the better an employee's performance is, the greater his or her rewards should be.

Unless a manager is willing to discriminate among employees on the basis of their performance levels, the effectiveness of his or her power over the employee is nil. For example, Edward E. Lawler III, a leading researcher on pay and performance, has noted that one of the major reasons managers are unhappy with their salary system is that they do not perceive the relationship between how hard they work (productivity) and how much they earn. In a survey of 600 managers, Lawler found virtually no relationship between their pay and their rated level of performance.

The third step is to design the contingencies in such a way that a reliable procedure for eliciting or inducing the desired response patterns is established; when desired responses rarely occur, there are few opportunities to influence behavior through contingency management. Training programs, goal-setting programs and similar efforts should be undertaken to let workers know what is expected of them. If the criterion for reinforcement is unclear, unspecified or set too high, most—if not all—of the worker's responses go unrewarded; eventually his or her efforts will be extinguished.

Escape Conditioning

The second kind of contingency arrangement available to the manager is called escape or avoidance conditioning. Just as with positive reinforcement, this is a method of strengthening desired behavior. A contingency arrangement in which an individual's performance can terminate a noxious environment is called escape learning. When behavior can prevent the onset of a noxious stimulus, the procedure is called avoidance learning.

An employee is given an unpleasant task assignment, for example, with the promise that when he completes it, he can move on (escape) to a more pleasant job. Or a manager is such an unpleasant person to be around that the employees work when he is present in order to "avoid" him.

Let's note the distinction between strengthening behavior through positive reinforcement techniques and doing so through avoidance learning techniques. In one case, the individual works hard to gain the consequences from the environment (provided by the manager in most cases) that result from good work, and in the second case, the individual works hard to avoid the negative aspects of the environment itself (again, the manager is the source). In both cases the same behavior is strengthened over the short run. In escape learning, however, the manager is more process-oriented; he or she must be present in order to elicit the desired level of performance. Under positive reinforcement, however, the manager is outcome-oriented and does not have to be physically present at all times in order to maintain the desired level of performance.

Extinction

When positive reinforcement for a learned or previously conditioned response is withheld, individuals will still continue to exhibit that behavior for an extended period of time. With repeated non-reinforcement, however, the behavior decreases and eventually disappears. This decline in response rate as a result of non-rewarded repetition of a task is defined as *extinction.*

This method, when combined with a positive reinforcement method, is the procedure of behavior modification recommended by Skinner. It leads to the fewest negative side effects. Using the two methods together allows employees to get the rewards they desire and allows the organization to eliminate the undesired behavior.

Punishment

Punishment is the most controversial method of behavior modification. Punishment is defined as presenting an aversive or noxious consequence contingent upon a response. The Law of Effect operates here, too: As rewards strengthen behavior, punishment weakens it. Notice carefully the difference between withholding rewards in the punishment process and withholding rewards in the extinction process. In the extinction process, we withhold rewards for behavior that has previously been rewarded because the behavior was previously desired. In punishment, we withhold a reward because the behavior is undesired, has never been associated with the reward before, and is plainly un undesirable consequence.

RULES FOR USING OPERANT CONDITIONING TECHNIQUES

Rule 1. Don't Give the Same Level of Reward to All

Differentiate rewards based on performance in relation to defined objectives or standards. We know that people compare their performance with the performance of their peers to determine how well they are doing and that they compare their rewards with peer rewards to determine how to evaluate theirs. Some managers may think that the fairest compensation system is one in which everyone in the same job classification gets the same pay, but employees want differentiation as evidence of how important their services are to the organization. Managers who reward all people at the same level are simply encouraging, at most, only average performance. Behavior leading to high performance is being extinguished (ignored), while average and poor performance are being strengthened by means of positive reinforcement.

Rule 2. *Failure to Respond to Behavior Has Reinforcing Consequences*

Managers who find the job of differentiating between workers so unpleasant or so difficult that they fail to respond to their behavior must recognize that failure to respond is itself a form of response that, in turn, modifies behavior. Superiors are bound to shape the behavior of their subordinates by the way in which they utilize the rewards at their disposal. Therefore, managers must be careful that they examine the consequences on performance of their non-actions as well as their actions.

Rule 3. *Tell a Person What Behavior Gets Reinforced*

By making clear to a worker the contingencies of reinforcement, a manager may actually be increasing his individual freedom. The employee who has a standard against which to measure his job will have a built-in feedback system that allows him or her to make judgments about his or her own level of performance. The awarding of reinforcements in an organization where workers' goals are specified will be associated with worker performance, not supervisory bias. The assumption is, of course, that the supervisor rates the employee accurately and then reinforces the employee according to his ratings. If the supervisor fails to rate accurately or administer rewards based on performance, then the worker will be forced to search for the "true" contingencies—that is, what behavior he or she should display in order to get rewarded (ingratiation? loyalty? positive attitude?).

Rule 4. *Tell a Person What He or She Is Doing Wrong*

As a general rule, very few people find failure rewarding. One assumption of behavior conditioning, therefore, is that a worker wants to be rewarded for positive accomplishments. A supervisor should never use extinction or punishment as the sole method for modifying behavior—but if one of these is used judiciously in conjunction with positive reinforcement techniques, such combined procedures can hasten the change process. If the supervisor fails to specify why a reward is being withheld, the employee may associate the withholding of the reward with past desired behavior instead of the behavior that the supervisor is trying to extinguish.

Thus the supervisor extinguishes good performance while having no effect on the undesired behavior.

Rule 5. *Don't Punish in Front of Others*

The reason for this rule is quite simple. The punishment (for example, a reprimand) should be enough to extinguish the undesired behavior. By administering the punishment in front of the work group, the worker is doubly punished; he also "loses face." This additional punishment may lead to negative side-effects in three ways. First, the worker whose self-image is damaged may feel that he must retaliate in order to protect himself. Therefore, the supervisor has actually increased undesired responses. Second, the work group may associate the punishment with another behavior of the worker and, through "avoidance learning" techniques, may modify their own behavior in ways not intended by the supervisor. Third, the work group is also being punished—in the sense that observing a member of their team being reprimanded is unpleasant to most people. This may result in lowered performance of the total work group.

Rule 6. *Make the Consequences Equal to the Behavior*

In other words, don't cheat the worker out of his just rewards. If he is a good worker, tell him. Many supervisors find it very difficult to praise an employee. Others find it very difficult to counsel an employee about what he is doing wrong. When a manager fails to use these reinforcement tools, he is actually reducing his effectiveness. Over-rewarding a worker my make him feel guilty and certainly reinforces his current performance level. If the performance level is lower than that of others who get the same reward, he has no reason to increase his output. When a worker is under-rewarded, he becomes angry with the system. His behavior is being extinguished and the company may be forcing the good employee (under-rewarded) to seek employment elsewhere while encouraging the poor employee (over-rewarded) to stay on.

SETTING UP A POSITIVE REINFORCEMENT PROGRAM IN INDUSTRY

Many organizations are setting up formal motivational programs in an attempt to use the principles of positive reinforcement to increase employee productivity.

A positive reinforcement approach to management differs from traditional motivational theories in two basic ways. First, as noted above, a positive reinforcement program calls for the maximum use of reinforcement and the minimum use of punishment. Punishment tends to leave the individual feeling controlled and coerced. Second, a positive reinforcement program avoids psychological probing into the worker's attitudes as a possible cause of behavior. Instead, the work situation itself is analyzed, with the focus on the reward contingencies that cause a worker to act the way in which he does.

A positive reinforcement program, therefore, is result-oriented rather than process-oriented. Geary A. Rummler, president of Praxis Corporation, a management consultant firm, claims that the motivational theories of such behavioral scientists as Herzberg and Maslow, which stress workers' psychological needs, are impractical. "They can't be made operative. While they help classify a problem, a positive reinforcement program leads to solutions."

Stages in Program Development

Positive reinforcement programs currently used in industry generally involve at least four stages. The *first stage,* according to Edward J. Feeney, formerly vice-president systems, of Emery Air Freight Corporation, is to define the behavioral aspects of performance and do a performance audit. This step is potentially one of the most difficult, since some companies do not have a formal performance evaluation program especially for non-managerial employees, and those that do have a program often rate the employee's behavior on non-job related measures (such as friendliness, loyalty, cooperation, overall attitude, and so on). But once these behavioral aspects are defined, the task of convincing managers that improvement is needed and of persuading them to cooperate with such a program is simplified. Feeney asserts, "Most managers genuinely think that operations in their bailiwick are doing well; a performance audit that proves they're not comes as a real and unpleasant surprise."

The *second stage* in developing a working positive reinforcement program is to develop and set specific goals for each worker. Failure to specify concrete behavioral goals is a major reason many programs do not work. Goals should be expressed in such terms as "decreased employee turnover" or "schedules met" rather than only in terms of "better identification with the company" or "increased job satisfaction." The goals set, therefore, should be in the same terms as those defined in the performance audit, goals that specifically relate to the task at hand. Goals should be reasonable—that is, set somewhere between "where you are" (as spelled out in the performance audit) and some ideal.

While it is important for the manager to set goals, it is also important for the employee to accept them. An approach that tends to build in goal acceptance is to allow employees to work with management in setting work goals. According to John C. Emery, president of Emery Air Freight Corporation, the use of a participatory management technique to enlist the ideas of those performing the job not only results in their acceptance of goals, but also stimulates them to come up with goals.

The *third stage* in a positive reinforcement program is to allow the employee to keep a record of his or her own work. The process of self-feedback maintains a continuous schedule of reinforcement for the worker and helps him obtain intrinsic reinforcement from the task itself. There employees can total their own results, they can see whether they are meeting their goals and whether they are improving over their previous performance level (as measured in the performance audit stage). In other words, the worker has two chances of being successful—either by beating his previous record or by beating both his previous record and his established goal. E. D. Grady, general manager—operator services for Michigan Bell, maintains that the manager should set up the work environment in such a way that people have a chance to succeed. One way to do this, he says, is to "shorten the success interval." Grady says, "If you're looking for success, keep shortening the interval of measurement so you can get a greater chance of success which you can latch on to for positive reinforcements." Instead of setting monthly or quarterly goals, for example, set weekly or daily goals.

The *fourth stage*—the most important step in a positive reinforcement program—is one that separates it from all other motivation plans. The supervisor looks at the self-feedback report of the employee and/or other indications of performance (sales records, for example) and then praises the positive aspects of the employee's performance (as determined by the performance audit and subsequent goal setting). This extrinsic reinforcement should strengthen the desired performance, while the withholding of praise for substandard performance should give the employee incentive to improve that performance level. Since the worker already knows the areas of his or her deficiencies, there is no reason for the supervisor to criticize the employee. In other words, negative feedback is self-induced, whereas positive feedback comes from both internal and external sources.

As noted previously, this approach to feedback follows the teachings of B. F. Skinner, who believes that use of positive reinforcement leads to a greater feeling of self-control, while the avoidance of negative reinforcement keeps the individual from feeling controlled or coerced. Skinner says, "You can get the same effect if the supervisor simply discovers things being done right and says something like 'Good, I see you're doing it the way that works best.'"

While the feedback initially used in step four of the positive reinforcement program is praise, it is important to note that other forms of reinforcement can have the same effect. M. W. Warren, the director of organization and management development at the Questor Corporation, says that the five "reinforcers" he finds most effective are (1) money (but only when it is a consequence of a specific performance and when the relation to the performance is known); (2) praise or recognition; (3) freedom to choose one's own activity; (4) opportunity to see oneself become better, more important, or more useful; and (5) power to influence both co-workers and management. Warren states, "By building these reinforcers into programs at various facilities, Questor is getting results." The need for using more than praise after the positive reinforcement program has proved effective is discussed by Skinner.

> It does not cost the company anything to use praise rather than blame, but if the company then makes a great deal more money that way, the worker may seem to be getting gypped. However, the welfare of the worker depends on the welfare of the company, and if the company is smart enough to distribute some of the fruits of positive reinforcement in the form of higher wages and better fringe benefits, everybody gains from the supervisor's use of positive reinforcements. (*Organizational Dynamics,* Winter, 1973, p. 35.)

EARLY RESULTS OF POSITIVE REINFORCEMENT PROGRAMS IN ORGANIZATIONS, 1969–1973

Companies that claimed to be implementing and using positive reinforcement programs such as the one described above include Emery Air Freight, Michigan Bell Telephone, Questor Corporation, Cole National Company in Cleveland, Ford Motor Company, American Can, Upjohn, United Air Lines, Warner-Lambert, Addressograph-Multigraph, Allis-Chalmers, Bethlehem Steel, Chase Manhattan Bank, IBM, IT&T, Proctor and Gamble, PPG Industries, Standard Oil of Ohio, Westinghouse, and Wheeling-Pittsburgh Steel Corporation (see *Business Week,* December 18, 1971 and December 2, 1972). Because such programs are relatively new in industrial settings (most have begun since 1968), few statements of their relative effectiveness have been reported. In the Winter 1973 issue of *Organizational Dynamics* (p. 49), it was stated that "there's little objective evidence available, and what evidence there is abounds in caveats—the technique will work under the proper circumstances, the parameters of which are usually not easily apparent."

In the sea of employee training, Northern Systems Company, General Electric Corporation, and Emery Air Freight claim that positive reinforcement has improved the speed and efficiency of their training program. In the programmed learning program, the Northern Systems Company structures the feedback system in such a way that the trainee receives positive feedback only when he demonstrates correct performance at the tool station. The absence of feedback is experienced by the trainee when he fails to perform correctly. Therefore, through positive reinforcements, he quickly perceives that correct behaviors obtain for him the satisfaction of his needs, and that incorrect behaviors do not. Emery has designed a similar program for sales trainees. *Business Week* reported the success of the program by saying:

> It is a carefully engineered, step-by-step program, with frequent feedback questions and answers to let the salesman know how he is doing. The course contrasts with movies and lectures in which, Feeney says, the salesman is unable to gauge what he has learned. The aim is to get the customer on each sales call to take some kind of action indicating that he will use Emery services. Significantly, in 1968, the first full year after the new course was launched, sales jumped from $62.4 million to $79.8 million, a gain of 27.8 percent compared with an 11.3 percent rise the year before.

Since 1969, Emery has instituted a positive reinforcement program for all of its employees and credits the program with direct savings to the company of over $3 million in the first three years and indirectly with pushing 1973 sales over the $150 million mark. While Emery Air Freight is and remains the biggest success story for a positive reinforcement program to date, other companies also claim improvements as a result of initiating similar programs. At Michigan Bell's Detroit office, 2,000 employees in 1973 participated in a positive reinforcement program. Michigan Bell credits the program with reducing absenteeism from 11 percent to 6.5 percent in one group, from 7.5 percent to 4.5 percent in another group, and from 3.3 percent to 2.6 percent for all employees. In addition, the program has resulted in the correct completion of reports on time 90 percent of the time as compared with 20 percent of the time before the program's implementation. The Wheeling-Pittsburgh Steel Corporation credits its feedback program with saving $200,000 a month in scrap costs.

In an attempt to reduce the number of employees who constantly violated plant rules, General Motors implemented a plan in one plant that gave employees opportunities to improve or clear their records by going through varying periods of time without committing further shop violations. They credit this positive reinforcement plan with reducing the number of punitive actions for shop-rule infractions by two-thirds from 1969 to 1972 and the number of production-standard grievances by 70 percent during the same period.

While there was a great deal of interest in applying behavior modification in industrial settings after the successes of Emery Air Freight and others who followed suit were made known in 1971, the critics of this approach to worker motivation predicted that it would be short-lived. Any success would owe more to a "Hawthorne Effect" (the positive consequences of paying special attention to employees) than to any real long-term increase in productivity and/or worker satisfaction. The critics pointed out—quite legitimately, we might add—that most of the claims were testimonial in nature and that the length of experience between

1969-1973 was too short to allow enough data to accumulate to determine the true successes of positive reinforcement in improving morale and productivity. With this in mind, we surveyed ten organizations, all of which currently use a behavior modification approach, to see if the "fad" created by Emery Air Freight had died or had persisted and extended its gains.

Specifically, we were interested in knowing (1) how many employees were covered; (2) the kinds of employees covered; (3) specific goals (stages 1 & 2); (4) frequency of self-feedback (stage 3); (5) the kinds of reinforcers used (stage 4); and (6) results of the program.

CURRENT RESULTS OF POSITIVE REINFORCEMENT PROGRAMS IN ORGANIZATIONS

The ten organizations surveyed included Emery Air Freight, Michigan Bell—Operator Services, Michigan Bell—Maintenance Services, Connecticut General Life Insurance Company, General Electric, Standard Oil of Ohio, Weyerhaeuser, City of Detroit, B. F. Goodrich Chemical Company, and ACDC Electronics. In our interviews with each of the managers, we tried to determine both the success and the failures they attributed to the use of behavior modification or positive reinforcement techniques. We were also interested in whether the managers saw this as a fad or as a legitimate management technique for improving the productivity and quality of work life among employees.

Emery Air Freight

. . . Emery Air Freight still [uses] positive reinforcement as a motivational tool. John C. Emery commented: "Positive reinforcement, always linked to feedback systems, plays a central role in performance improvement at Emery Air Freight. All managers and supervisors are being trained via self-instructional, programmed instruction texts—one on reinforcement and one on feedback. No formal off-the-job training is needed. Once he has studied the texts, the supervisor is encouraged immediately to apply the learning to the performance area for which he is responsible."

Paul F. Hammond, Emery's manager of system performance and the person currently in charge of the positive reinforcement program, said that there are a considerable number of company areas in which quantifiable success has been attained over the last six or seven years. Apart from the well-publicized container savings illustration (results of which stood at $600,000 gross savings in 1970 and over $2,000,000 in 1975), several other recent success stories were noted by Emery and Hammond. They include:

- Standards for customer service on the telephone had been set up, and service was running 60 to 70 percent of standard. A program very heavily involved with feedback and reinforcement was introduced a few years ago and increased performance to 90 percent of objectives within three months—a level that has been maintained ever since.

- Several offices have installed a program in which specified planned reinforcements are provided when targeted levels of shipment volume are requested by Emery customers. All offices have increased revenue substantially; one office doubled the number of export shipments handled, and another averages an additional $60,000 of revenue per month.

- A program of measuring dimensions of certain lightweight shipments to rate them by volume rather than weight uses reinforcement and feedback extensively. All measures have increased dramatically since its inception five years ago, not the least of which is an increase in revenue from $400,000 per year to well over $2,000,000 per year.

While this latest information indicates that positive reinforcement is more than a fad at Emery Air Freight, Emery pointed out that a major flaw in the program had to be overcome. He said, "In as much as praise is the most readily available no-cost reinforcer, it tends to be the reinforcer used most frequently. However, the result has been to *dull* its effect as a reinforcer through its sheer repetition, even to risk making praise an *irritant* to the receiver." To counter this potential difficulty, Emery managers and supervisors have been taught and encouraged to expand their reinforcers beyond praise. Among the recommended reinforcers have been formal recognition such as a public letter or a letter home, being given a more enjoyable task after completing a less enjoyable one, invitations to business luncheons or meetings, delegating responsibility and decision-making, and tying such requests as special time off or any other deviation from normal procedure to performance. Thus, it seems that Skinner's prediction made in 1973 about the need for using more than praise after the reinforcement program has been around for a while has been vindicated at Emery Air Freight.

Michigan Bell—Operator Services

The operator services division is still actively using positive reinforcement feedback as a motivational tool. E. D. Grady, general manager for Operator Services said, "We have found through experience that when standards and feedback are not provided, workers generally feel their performance is at about the 95 percent level. When the performance is then compared with clearly defined standards, it is usually found to meet only the 50th percentile in performance. It has been our experience, over the past ten years, that when standards are set and feedback provided in a positive manner, performance will reach very high levels—perhaps in the upper 90th percentile in a very short period of time. . . . We have also found that when positive reinforcement is discontinued, performance returns to levels that existed prior to the establishment of feedback." Grady said that while he was not able at this time to put a specific dollar appraisal on the cost savings from using a positive reinforcement program, the savings were continuing to increase and the program was being expanded.

In one recent experiment, Michigan Bell found that when goal setting and positive reinforcement were used in a low-productivity inner-city operator group, service promptness (time to answer call) went from 94 to 99 percent of standard, average work time per call (time taken to give information) decreased from 60 units of work time to 43 units of work time, the percentage of work time completed within ideal limits went from 50 to 93 percent of ideal time (standard was 80 percent of ideal, and the percentage of time operators made proper use of references went from 80 to 94 percent. This led to an overall productivity index score for these operators that was significantly higher than that found in the control group where positive reinforcement was not being used, even though the control group of operators had previously (six months earlier) been one of the highest producing units.

Michigan Bell—Maintenance Services

Donald E. Burwell, Division Superintendent of Maintenance and Services at Michigan Bell, established a goal-setting and positive reinforcement program in early 1975. He said, "After assignment to my present area of responsibility in January, I found that my new department of 220 employees (maintenance, mechanics, and janitorial services), including managers, possessed generally good morale. However, I soon became aware that 1973 performances were generally lower than the 1973 objectives. In some cases, objectives were either ambiguous or non-existent."

With the help of a consultant, Burwell overcame the problem by establishing a four-step positive reinforcement program similar to the one described earlier in this article. As a result, the 1974 year-end results showed significant improvements over the 1973 base year averages in all areas, including safety (from 75.6 to 89.0), service (from 76.4 to 83.0), cost performance/hour (from 27.9 to 21.2, indexed), attendance (from 4.7 to 4.0) and worker satisfaction and cooperation (3.01 to 3.51 on a scale of 5), and worker satisfaction with the supervisors (2.88 to 3.70, also on a scale of 5). 1975 figures reflect continuing success.

While Burwell is extremely pleased with the results of this program to date, he adds a word of caution to other managers thinking of implementing such a program. "I would advise against accepting any one method, including positive reinforcement, as a panacea for all the negative performance trends that confront managers. On the other hand, positive reinforcement has aided substantially in performing improvement for marketing, production, and service operators. Nevertheless, the manager needs to know when the positive effects of the reinforcement program have begun to plateau and what steps he should consider taking to maintain his positive performance trends."

Connecticut General Life Insurance Company

The Director of Personnel Administration at Connecticut General Life Insurance Company, Donald D. Illig, stated that Connecticut General has been using positive reinforcement in the form of an attendance bonus system for 25 years with over 3,200 clerical employees. Employees receive one extra day off for each ten weeks of perfect attendance. The results have been outstanding. Chronic absenteeism and lateness have been drastically reduced, and the employees are very happy with the system. Illig noted, however, that "Our property and casualty company, with less than half the number of clerical employees countrywide, has not had an attendance-bonus system . . . and wants no part of it. At the crux of the problem is an anti-Skinnerian feeling, which looks at positive reinforcement—and thus an attendance-bonus system—as being overly manipulative and old-fashioned in light of current theories of motivation."

General Electric

A unique program of behavior modification has been introduced quite successfully at General Electric as well as several other organizations by Melvin Sorcher, formerly director of personnel research at G.E. The behavior modification program used at G. E. involves using positive reinforcement and feedback in training employees. While the first program centered primarily on teaching male supervisors how to interact and communicate with minority and female employees and on teaching minority and female employees how to become successful by improving their self-images, subsequent programs focused on the relationship between supervisors and employees in general. By using a reinforcement technique known as behavior modeling, Sorcher goes beyond the traditional positive reinforcement ("PR") program. The employee is shown a videotape of a model (someone with his own characteristics—that is, male or female, black or white, subordinate or superior) who is performing in a correct or desired manner. Then, through the process of role playing, the employee is encouraged to act in the successful or desired manner shown on the film (that is, he is asked to model the behavior). Positive reinforcement is given when the goal of successful display of this behavior is made in the role-playing session.

Sorcher notes that this method has been successfully used with over 1,000 G. E. supervisors. As a result, productivity has increased, the self-esteem of hard-core employees has increased, and EEO objectives are being met. He says, "The positive results have been the gratifying changes or improvements that have occurred, especially improvements that increase over time as opposed to the usual erosion of effort after most training programs have passed their peak. . . . On the negative side, some people and organizations are calling their training 'behavior modeling' when it does not fit the criteria originally defined for such a program. For example, some programs not only neglect self-esteem as a component, but show little evidence of how to shape new behaviors. . . . Regarding the more general area of behavior modification and positive reinforcement, there is still a need for better research. There's not a lot taking place at present, which is unfortunate because on the surface these processes seem to have a lot of validity.

Standard Oil of Ohio

T. E. Standings, manager of psychological services at SOHIO, tried a training program similar to the one used by Sorcher at General Electric. After 28 supervisors had completed five weeks of training, Standings disbanded the program even though there were some short-term successes. He said, "My feelings at this point are that reinforcement cannot be taught at a conceptual level in a brief period of time. (Of course, the same comments can no doubt be made about Theory Y, MBO, and TA.) I see two alternatives: (1) Identify common problem situations, structure an appropriate reinforcement response for the supervisor, and teach the response through the behavioral model, or (2) alter reinforcement contingencies affecting defined behaviors through direct alternatives in procedural and/or informational systems without going through the supervisor directly."

Weyerhaeuser Company

Whereas Emery Air Freight has the longest history with applied reinforcement theory, Weyerhaeuser probably has the most experience with controlled experiments using goal setting and PR techniques. The Human Resource Research Center at Weyerhaeuser, under the direction of G. P. Latham, is actively seeking ways to improve the productivity of all levels of employees using the goal-setting, PR feedback technique.

According to Dr. Latham, "The purpose of our positive reinforcement program is threefold: (1) To teach managers to embrace the philosophy that 'the glass is half-full rather than half-empty.' In other words, our objective is to teach managers to minimize criticism (which is often self-defeating since it can fixate the employee's attention on ineffective job behavior and thus reinforce it) and to maximize praise and hence fixate both theirs and the employee's attention on effective job behavior. (2) To teach managers that praise by itself may increase job satisfaction, but that it will have little or no effect on productivity unless it is made contingent upon specified job behaviors. Telling an employee that he is doing a good job in no way conveys to him what he is doing correctly. Such blanket praise can inadvertently reinforce the very things that the employee is doing in a mediocre way. (3) To teach managers to determine the optimum schedule for administering a reinforcer—be it praise, a smile, or money in the employee's pocket."

Weyerhaeuser has found that by using money as a reinforcer (that is, as a bonus over and above the worker's hourly rate), they obtained a 33 percent increase in productivity with one group of workers, an 18 percent increase in productivity with a second group of workers, and an 8 percent decrease in productivity with a third group of workers. Latham says, "These findings point out the need to measure and document the effectiveness of any human resource program. The results obtained in one industrial setting cannot necessarily be expected in another setting."

Latham notes that because of its current success with PR, Weyerhaeuser is currently applying reinforcement principles with tree planters in the rural South as well as with engineers and scientists at their corporate headquarters. In the latter case, they are comparing different forms of goal-setting (assigned, participative, and a generalized goal of "do your best") with three different forms of reinforcement (praise or private recognition from a supervisor, public recognition from a supervisor, public recognition in terms of a citation for excellence, and a monetary reward). Latham adds, "The purpose of the program is to motivate scientists to attain excellence. Excellence is defined in terms of the frequency with which an individual displays specific behaviors that have been identified by the engineers/scientists themselves as making the difference between success and failure in fulfilling the requirements of their job."

City of Detroit, Garbage Collectors

In December 1972, the City of Detroit instituted a unique productivity bonus system for sanitation workers engaged in refuse collection. The plan, which provides for sharing the savings for productivity improvement efforts, was designed to save money for the city while rewarding workers for increased efficiency. The city's Labor Relations Bureau negotiated the productivity contract with the two unions concerned with refuse collection. The American Federation of State, County, and Municipal Employees (AFSCME), representing sanitation laborers (loaders), and the Teamsters Union, representing drivers. The two agreements took effect on July 1, 1973.

The bonus system was based on savings gained in productivity (reductions in paid man-hours per ton of refuse collected, reduction in the total hours of overtime, percentage of routes completed on schedule, and effectiveness or cleanliness). A bonus pool was established and the sanitation laborers share 50-50 in the pool with the city—each worker's portion being determined by the number of hours worked under the productivity bonus pool, exclusive of overtime.

By any measure, this program was a success. Citizen complaints decreased dramatically. During 1974, the city saved $1,654,000 after the bonus of $307,000 ($350 per man) was paid. The bonus system is still in effect, but the unions are currently disputing with the city the question of what constitutes a fair day's work. Both unions involved have expressed doubts about the accuracy of the data used to compute the productivity index or, to be more precise, how the data are gathered and the index and bonus computed. Given this expected prenegotiation tactic by the unions, the city and the customers both agree that the plan has worked.

B. F. Goodrich Chemical Company

In 1972, one of the production sections in the B. F. Goodrich Chemical plant in Avon Lake, Ohio, as measured by standard accounting procedures, was failing. At that time, Donald J. Barnicki, the production manager, introduced a positive reinforcement program that included goal-setting and feedback about scheduling, targets, costs, and problem areas. This program gave the information directly to the foreman on a once-a-week basis. In addition, daily meetings were held to discuss problems and describe how each group was doing. For the first time, the foremen and their employees were told about costs that were incurred by their group. Charts were published that showed area achievements in terms of sales, cost, and productivity as compared with targets. Films were made that showed top management what the employees were doing, and these films were shown to the workers so they would know what management was being told.

According to Barnicki, this program of positive reinforcement turned the plant around. "Our productivity has increased 300 percent over the past five years. Costs are down. We had our best starting time in 1976 and passed our daily production level from last year the second day after we returned from the holidays."

Edward J. Feeney, of Emery Air Freight fame, now heads a consulting firm that works with such firms as General Electric, Xerox, Braniff Airways, and General Atomic in the area of positive reinforcement programs. One of Mr. Feeney's current clients is the ACDC Electronics Company (a division of Emerson Electronics). After establishing a program that incorporated the four-step approach outlined earlier in this article, the ACDC Company experienced a profit increase of 25 percent over the forecast; a $550,000 cost reduction on $10 million in sales; a return of 1,900 percent on investment, including consultant fees; a reduction in turnaround time on repairs from 30 to 10 days; and a significant increase in attendance.

According to Ken Kilpatrick, ACDC President, "The results were as dramatic as those that Feeney had described. We found our output increased 30–40 percent almost immediately and has stayed at that high level for well over a year." The results were not accomplished, however, without initial problems, according to Feeney. "With some managers there were problems of inertia, disbelief, lack of time to implement, interest, difficulty in defining output for hard-to-measure areas, setting standards, measuring past performance, estimating economic payoffs, and failure to apply all feedback or reinforcement principles." Nevertheless, after positive results began to surface and initial problems were overcome, the ACDC management became enthused about the program.

CONCLUSION

This article has attempted to explain how reinforcement theory can be applied in organizational settings. We have argued that the arrangement of the contingencies of reinforcement is crucial in influencing behavior. Different ways of arranging these contingencies were explained, followed by a recommendation that the use of positive reinforcement combined with oral explanations of incorrect behaviors, when applied correctly, is an underestimated and powerful tool of management. The correct application includes three conditions: *First,* reinforcers must be selected that are sufficiently powerful and durable to establish and strengthen behavior; *second,* the manager must design the contingencies in such a way that the reinforcing events are made contingent on the desired level of performance; *third,* the program must be designed in such a way that it is possible to establish a reliable training procedure for inducing the desired response patterns.

To meet these three conditions for effective contingency management, many firms have set up a formal positive reinforcement motivational program. These include firms such as Emery Air Freight, Michigan Bell, Standard Oil of Ohio, General Electric, and B. F. Goodrich, among others. Typically, these firms employ a four-stage approach in designing their programs: (1) A performance audit is conducted in order to determine what performance patterns are desired and to measure the current levels of that performance; (2) specific and reasonable goals are set for each worker; (3) each employee is generally instructed to keep a record of his or her own work; and (4) positive aspects of the employee's performance are positively reinforced by the supervisor. Under this four-stage program, the employee has two chances of being successful—he can beat his previous level of performance or he can beat that plus his own goal. Also under this system, negative feedback routinely comes only from the employee (since he knows when he failed to meet the objective), whereas positive feedback comes from both the employer and his supervisor.

While we noted that many firms have credited this approach with improving morale and increasing profits, several points of concern and potential shortcomings of this approach should also be cited. Many people claim that you cannot teach reinforcement principles to lower-level managers very easily, and unless you get managers to understand the principles, you certainly risk misusing these tools. Poorly designed reward systems can interfere with the development of spontaneity and creativity. Reinforcement systems that are deceptive and manipulative are an insult to employees.

One way in which a positive reinforcement program based solely on praise can be deceptive and manipulative occurs when productivity continues to increase month after month and year after year, and the company's profits increase as well, but employee salaries do not reflect their contributions. This seems obviously unethical and contradictory. It is unethical because the workers are being exploited, and praise by itself will not have any long-term effect on performance. Emery Air Freight, for example, has begun to experience this backlash effect. It is contradictory because the manager is saying he believes in the principle of making intangible rewards contingent on performance but at the same time refuses to make the tangible monetary reward contingent on performance. Often the excuse given is that "our employees are unionized." Well, this is not always the case. Many firms that are without unions, such as Emery, refuse to pay on performance. Many other firms with unions have a contingent bonus plan. Skinner in 1969 warned managers that a poorly designed monetary reward system may actually reduce performance. The employee should be a willing party to the influence attempt, with both parties benefitting from the relationship.

Peter Drucker's concern is different. He worries that perhaps positive reinforcers may be misused by management to the detriment of the economy. He says, "The carrot of material rewards has not, like the stick of fear, lost its potency. On the contrary, it has become so potent that it threatens to destroy the earth's finite resources if it does not first destroy more economies through inflation that reflects rising expectations." In other words, positive reinforcement can be too effective as used by firms concerned solely with their own personal gains.

Skinner, in an interview in *Organizational Dynamics,* stated that a feedback system alone may not be enough. He recommended that the organization should design feedback and incentive systems in such a way that the dual objective of getting things done and making work enjoyable is met. He says what must be accomplished, and what he believes is currently lacking, is an effective training program for managers. "In the not-too-distant future, however, a new breed of industrial managers may be able to apply the principles of operant conditioning effectively."

We have evidence in at least a few organizational settings that Skinner's hopes are on the way to realization, that a new breed of industrial managers are indeed applying the principles of operant conditioning effectively.

Selected Bibliography

For an understandable view of Skinner's basic ideas in his own words, see B. F. Skinner's *Contingencies of Reinforcement* (Appleton-Century-Crofts, 1969) and Carl R. Rogers and B. F. Skinner's "Some Issues Concerning the Control of Human Behavior" (*Science,* 1965, Vol. 24, pp. 1057-1066). For Skinner's views on the applications of his ideas in industry, see "An Interview with B. F. Skinner (*Organizational Dynamics,* Winter 1973, pp. 31-40).

For an account of Skinner's ideas in action, see the same issue of *Organizational Dynamics* (pp. 41–50) and "Where Skinner's Theories Work" (*Business Week,* December 2, 1972, pp. 64–69)

An article highly critical of the application of Skinner's ideas in industry is W. F. Whyte's "Pigeons, Persons, and Piece Rates" *Psychology Today,* April 1972, pp. 67–68). For a more sympathetic and more systematic treatment see W. R. Nord's "Beyond the Teaching Machine: The Negative Area of Operant Conditioning" in *The Theory and Practice of Management, Organizational Behavior and Human Performance* (1969, No. 4, pp. 375-301).

For previous comments on behavior modification by the author, see W. Clay Hamner's "Reinforcement Theory and Contingency Management" in L. Tosi and W. Clay Hamner, eds., *Organizational Behavior and Management: A Contingency Approach* (St. Clair Press, 1974, pp. 188-204) and W. Clay Hamner's "Worker Motivation Programs:

Importance of Climate Structure and Performance Consequences" in W. Clay Hamner and Frank L. Schmidt's *Contemporary Problems in Personnel* (St. Clair Press, 1974, pp. 280–308).

Last, the best discussion of the general subject of pay and performance is Edward E. Lawler III's *Pay and Organizational Effectiveness* (McGraw-Hill, 1971).

MOTIVATION: NEW DIRECTIONS FOR THEORY, RESEARCH, AND PRACTICE

Terence R. Mitchell

The current state of motivation theory is reviewed. Emphasis is placed on the internal, unobservable aspects of motivation and the distinction between motivation and behavior and performance. Major theories of motivation concerned with the arousal and choice of behavior are examined, problems of implementation are discussed, and directions for future research are suggested. They include study of the circumstances under which any given motivational theory is most effective. The long-run objective should be a contingency type model of motivation.

Over the last five years various professional commitments have led this author to look at the field of motivation from both a theory-research perspective as well as a practical or applied perspective. The analysis of the theoretical and research literature has resulted in detailed and comprehensive review papers (Mitchell, 1979; Mitchell, in press). The attempts to deal with applications and implications were prompted by field research endeavors (Latham, Mitchell, and Dossett, 1978) and the writing and revision of a textbook (Mitchell, 1978). Several ideas have emerged from these activities.

First, from the reviews of motivation theory and research (Campbell & Pritchard, 1976; Korman, Greenhaus, and Badin, 1977; Locke, 1975; Staw, 1977), it became clear that some shifts in the field were occurring. The overwhelming percentage of current papers are concerned with information processing or social-environmental explanations of motivation (Salancik & Pfeffer, 1977, 1978) rather than need-based approaches or approaches that focus on individual differences. These latter approaches, represented by people like Maslow, have almost disappeared in the literature.

The information processing approaches are illustrated by the large amount of work on expectancy theory, goal setting, and equity theory. Theories focusing on the job environment, such as operant conditioning or job enrichment, and theories emphasizing social cues and social evaluations also have been important. These approaches have all been helpful in increasing the understanding of motivation.

Reprinted with permission of publisher from *Academy of Management Review*, 1982, Vol. 7, No. 1, pp. 80–88.

A second trend, however, has not been so widely recognized. More specifically, when one reviews this research, it becomes readily apparent that most of the studies investigate only one theory in depth. Many studies set out to demonstrate that goal setting, operant conditioning, or expectancy theory work. In other cases, the research is concerned with fine tuning the theory (e.g., Is participative or assigned goal setting better? Should expectancies be added to or multiplied by valences? Is a variable or continuous schedule of reinforcement best?). These questions are important, but few studies have been designed to integrate theories, to test them competitively, or to analyze the settings in which different theories work best.

Several issues also emerged from the practical experiences and attempts to summarize applied principles. First, there are some preliminary questions that must be answered and requirements that need to be met before implementing any motivational system. These questions and requirements revolve around (1) how people are evaluated and (2) the demands of the task. In other words, to apply motivational principles, one must do some preliminary work involving other organizational factors.

Second, in attempting to apply motivational principles in an organization, one often runs into mitigating circumstances. There are situations and settings that make it exceptionally difficult for a motivational system to work. These circumstances may involve the kinds of jobs or people present, the technology, the presence of a union, and so on. The factors that hinder the application of motivational theory have not been articulated either frequently or systematically. The purpose of this paper is to review what is currently known about motivation, describe some theoretical areas in which ambiguity exists, and identify some situational constraints on the utilization of this knowledge.

The goal of this paper is not to provide a comprehensive source of references on the topic of motivation. Vast resources are already available for that purpose. There are whole books devoted to the topic (Korman, 1974; Lawler, 1973; Ryan, 1970; Vroom, 1964; Weiner, 1972), books of readings (McClelland and Steele, 1973; Steers & Porter, 1979; Tosi, House, & Dunnette, 1972), and many review articles (Campbell & Pritchard, 1976; Korman et al., 1977; Locke, 1975; Mitchell, 1979; Staw, 1977). The material and principles discussed in this paper will be dealt with at a fairly global level. This is not to say that the ideas are not supportable or that a detailed level of analysis is not important. In most cases, at least one representative citation will be provided. However, the objective of the paper is to stimulate debate and interest in some issues about motivation that (1) have been said infrequently or (2) have recently emerged and need to be highlighted.

BACKGROUND

Many nonacademics would probably describe motivation as the degree to which an individual wants and tries hard to do well at a particular task or job. Dictionary definitions describe motivation as the goad to action. The more technical definitions given by social scientists suggest that motivation is the psychological processes that cause the arousal, direction, and persistence of behavior (Atkinson, 1964; Campbell, Dunnette, Lawler, & Weick, 1970; Huse & Bowditch, 1977; Kast & Rosenzweig, 1979; Korman, 1974; Luthans, 1977). Many authors add a voluntary component or goal directed emphasis to that definition (Hellriegel & Slocum, 1976; Lawler, 1973; Ryan, 1970; Vroom, 1964). Thus motivation becomes those psychological processes that cause the arousal, direction, and persistence of voluntary actions that are goal directed.

Although there is some disagreement about the importance of different aspects of this definition (e.g., whether arousal or choice is more important), there is consensus about some underlying properties of this definition. First, motivation traditionally has been cast as an *individual* phenomenon. Each individual is unique and all of the major motivational theories allow in one way or another for this uniqueness to be demonstrated (e.g., different people have different needs, expectation, values, attitudes, reinforcement histories, and goals). Second, motivation usually is described as *intentional*. That is, motivation supposedly is under the employee's control. Most behaviors that are seen as influenced by motivation (e.g., effort on the job) typically are viewed as actions the individual has chosen to do.

A third point is that motivation is *multifaceted*. The two factors of general importance have been the arousal (activation, energizers) and direction (choice) of behavior. The question of persistence has been of minor importance, partly because the issue of maintenance of behavior (once it is started and directed) has received less attention, and partly because some authors have defined persistence simply as the reaffirmation of the initial choice of action (March & Simon, 1958).

The arousal question has focused on what gets people activated. What are the circumstances that arouse people so they want to do well? The second question, that of choice, deals with the force on the individual to engage in desired behaviors. Given that the person is aroused, what gets them going in a particular direction? These distinctions are reflected in much of the writing on motivation.

The fourth point to make is that the purpose of motivational theories is to predict *behavior*. Motivation is concerned with action and the internal and external forces that influence one's choice of action. Motivation is not the behavior itself, and it is not performance. The behavior is the criterion—that which is chosen. And in some cases, the chosen action will be a good reflection of performance. But the psychological process, the actual behavior, and performance are all different things, and the confusion of the three frequently has caused problems in analysis, interpretation, and application.

So, given these elaborations, a definition of motivation becomes somewhat more detailed. Motivation becomes the degree to which an individual wants and chooses to engage in certain specified behaviors. Different theories propose different reasons, but almost all of them emphasize an individual, international choice of behavior analysis.

PRELIMINARY QUESTIONS

Given that one understands what motivation is, the next question concerns why it is important to management. Most organizations function under the principle of rationality (Scott & Hart, 1979). That is, the primary goal of management is to increase efficiency by getting the greatest output at the lowest cost. Therefore, any behaviors that contribute to greater efficiency will be actions that management will want to encourage. These actions might be coming to work, being punctual, or exerting a lot of effort. Because these behaviors often are assumed by management to be motivated—voluntary choices controlled by the individual—management often establishes what it calls a motivational system. This system is intended to influence the factors that cause the behavior in question.

The important point to make is that one must be clear in distinguishing between this motivation system and the definition of motivation as a cognitive, individual, intentional phenomenon. The motivational system is imposed from the outside. It is constructed according to the assumptions held by management about (1) what behaviors are important for effectiveness and (2) the factors that influence these behaviors. To make sure these assumptions are correct, some preliminary work should be done before any system is tried.

Performance Appraisal

Although many organizational factors contribute to effectiveness, such as turnover, absenteeism, and technology, probably the factor that is described as most important—and one that management feels it can influence—is job performance. Job performance typically is viewed as partially determined by the motivation to work hard and, therefore, increases in motivation should result in greater effort and higher performance. However, to have any idea about the effects of a motivational system, one must have a good performance appraisal instrument. Changes in performance must be detectable and demonstrable. There is not enough space to go into the merits of various appraisal procedures (Kane & Lawler, 1979; Kavanaugh, 1981;

Landy & Farr, 1980), but there are some generalizations that can be made about appraisal and its relationship to motivation.

First, it goes without question that a both reliable and valid system is needed—not only for issues of motivation but for issues of selection, promotion, counseling, and adherence to legal guidelines. In short, a sound appraisal device is necessary for many personnel functions.

But besides the methodological properties of the device, there are some substantive issues as well. The more closely a performance appraisal device fits with the definition of motivation, the easier it will be to assess the effects of motivational interventions or strategies. More specifically, if performance is defined in behavioral and individual terms and so is motivation, then the concepts and their measures show correspondence. They are less likely to be confounded by other factors.

The distinction is very important. Some appraisals use group or team goals as performance criteria as opposed to individual performance. Also, some appraisals emphasize outcomes (policies sold) as opposed to behavior (clients visited). The further away one gets from individual behavior, the more difficult it is to infer directly and unambiguously a change in motivation rather than a change in performance.

To some extent, however, the type of appraisal may be dictated by the technology or task with which people are engaged. In some cases group performance or outcomes may be the best one can do. This is a point that will be covered later, but at this juncture, it is sufficient to mention that (1) a good performance appraisal device is necessary and (2) the closer this device is to measuring individual behavior, the easier it is to evaluate the effects of motivational systems or technologies introduced by management.

Factors Influencing Performance

Given that a good performance appraisal system is in place and that it measures individual behavior, the next question is: Does motivation make a difference for performance? Many years ago, Vroom suggested the equation: performance = ability × motivation; and somewhat later, the term role perceptions was added to the right side of that equation (Porter & Lawler, 1968). More recently, Campbell and Pritchard (1976) expanded that definition to performance $= f$ (aptitude level × skill level × understanding of the task × choice to expend effort × choice of degree of effort × choice to persist × facilitation and inhibiting conditions not under the control of the individual). These authors recognized that performance is caused by at least four and maybe more factors. In order to do well, one must (1) know what is required (role expectations), (2) have the ability to do what is required, (3) be motivated to do what is required, and (4) work in an environment in which intended actions can be translated into behavior.

The implication is that there probably are some jobs for which trying to influence motivation will be irrelevant for performance. These circumstances can occur a variety of ways. There may be situations in which ability factors or role expectation factors are simply more important than motivation. For example, the best predictor of high school grades typically is intellectual endowment, not hours spent studying. In a paper entitled "Performance Equals Ability and What," Dunnette concluded that "ability differences still are empirically the most important determiners of differences in job performance" (1973, p. 22). Some of the problems referred to in this quote pertain to inadequate performance measures or poorly articulated theories of motivation, but part of the problem is that performance on some tasks simply is controlled more by ability than by motivation.

Another circumstance may occur in which performance is controlled by technological factors. For example, on an assembly line, given that minimally competent and attentive people are there to do the job, performance may not vary from individual to individual. Exerting effort may be irrelevant for performance.

One way to gain information about these issues is through a thorough job analysis. The type of analysis can help to determine what behaviors contribute to performance and the extent to which these behaviors are controlled voluntarily (motivated) or controlled by ability factors, social factors, or technology. Except for some recent work by Hackman (Hackman & Morris, 1975; Hackman & Oldham, 1980), this is infrequently discussed.

The implications of the points about job analysis, performance appraisal, the factors that contribute to performance appraisal, and the factors that contribute to performance boil down to one crucial point: *Performance is not the same as motivation.* If one wants to assess changes in motivation or the influence of interventions on motivation, then one must measure motivation and its contribution to behavior. If performance is assessed globally or non-behaviorally, then performance is not a good indicator of motivation. Even when performance is individually and behaviorally assessed, motivation may control substantially less than 100 percent of the variance in performance. That is, behaviors may be jointly determined by ability and motivation or some other combination of factors. When either of these two circumstances is true, the researcher or practitioner should seek to define and assess motivation separately. This point is infrequently recognized (Lawler, 1974) and almost never practiced.

In summary, before any motivation system is installed, one must be sure (a) that there is a good performance appraisal system available, (b) that motivation is an important contributor to performance, and (c) that where motivation clearly is not the major contributor to performance, a separate measure of motivation or of behaviors clearly caused by motivation is developed. When these three conditions are not being met, there is little point in pursuing the topic further. If they do exist, then one has the opportunity to put into practice what has been learned from previous research on motivation.

RESEARCH REVIEW

As mentioned earlier, theories of motivation typically are concerned with the questions of arousal and behavioral choice. The purpose of a review of these topics is not to criticize the different motivational theories. All of them have revealed some aspects of motivation that have empirical support. But some of the *factors controlling behavior* that they emphasize are more or less applicable in various situations. It is hoped that an understanding of these mitigating circumstances can serve as an initial step in developing contingency models of motivation: models that describe when and where certain motivational systems will be most effective.

Theories of Arousal

The most popular theories of arousal for many years have been those that emphasize needs. Theories that emphasize individual needs (e.g., need achievement) or group needs (e.g., need hierarchies) all postulate that the arousal process is due to need deficiencies. That is, people want certain things in their jobs and they will work to fulfill those needs.

The major implications of this research have been two-fold. First, these theories clearly recognize and make central the ideal of individual differences (Alderfer, 1977). Different people are motivated by different things. The second widely accepted point is that organizations generally have overlooked upper level needs. The works of such people as Maslow, McGregor, Herzberg, and Alderfer all suggest that, in general, organizations spend much more time being concerned with the fulfillment of lower level needs (e.g., through motivational systems emphasizing pay, hours of work, and the physical setting) than with the fulfillment of upper level needs (e.g., through systems emphasizing autonomy, recognition, creativity, and variety).

In recent years there has been a shift away from these need-based theories of arousal (Salancik & Pfeffer, 1977, 1978; Weiner, 1972) to approaches that emphasize processes such as social facilitation or evaluation apprehension (Ferris, Beehr, & Gilmore, 1978). These theories suggest that people are aroused by the presence of others and the knowledge that other people are evaluating them. The social cues in the form of expectations given off by subordinates, co-workers, and supervisors become important causes of arousal.

Other current approaches emphasize some ideas of cognitive inconsistency—for example, Korman's (1976) work on self-esteem—or the match between task related needs and the characteristics of the job. An example of this latter approach is Hackman and Oldham's (1980) theory of job enrichment suggesting that an enriched job is motivating only for those who have high needs for growth.

What almost all of these theories emphasize in one way or another is that arousal is seen as (1) current and (2) highly related to the social or task environment. Thus, instead of deep-seated needs developed a long time ago that reside solely within the individual, a much more external and present frame of reference is emerging. Central to almost all of the new approaches is the idea that the individual cognitively processes and evaluates a lot of information and that motivation is linked strongly to this information processing activity.

In summary, the arousal theories say (1) attend to individual differences, (2) try to attend to upper level (intrinsic) needs, (3) note that social expectations have powerful effects, and (4) note that current information is extremely important. In attempting to implement these ideas, however, difficulties often arise. Some of these obstructions are as follows:

First, there is a whole set of organizational factors that make it difficult to individualize rewards and emphasize upper level intrinsic needs. The larger the organization and the more heterogeneous the work force, the more difficult it becomes. Ideally one would like to let employees have some choice in their compensation—for example, cafeteria style plans (Lawler, 1976)—and let managers have greater flexibility in the administration of rewards. But in practice, these strategies are hard to implement. Dealing with unions also tends to restrict this flexibility because their striving for equity often leads to solidifying reward systems rather than increasing the latitude of management.

The theories that focus on social cues and expectations require that people be observed and that management have some influence on social norms. One idea that strives to let evaluation apprehension operate at the appropriate level is to match the level of appraisal with those people who most frequently observe the work of the individual. So, for example, if supervisors do not directly observe the work of subordinates, but co-workers or their subordinates do observe this individual, then have peer or subordinate evaluations be part of the appraisal process.

Influencing social norms is more problematical. Factors like organizational climate are known to be important, and processes such as team building may help to instill norms or expectations for hard work. However, very little theory or research exists that uses these norms as dependent variables. This is an area for further work.

In summary, some important things have been learned about arousal as an individualized process and one that is frequently related to current social cues. However, practical limitations, such as organization size, unions, or heterogeneity of personnel, may limit attempts to implement the knowledge. Also, further work is needed on understanding how one can influence social norms and expectations.

Theories of Choice

The major theories of behavioral choice are goal setting, expectancy theory, operant conditioning, and equity theory. The research on goal setting is quite clear. People work harder with goals than without goals. This is especially true if the goals are specific and difficult and if feedback exists (Locke, 1978; Steers & Porter, 1974; Yukl & Latham, 1978). The areas of ongoing research emphasize such issues as whether participative or assigned goal setting works best, whether rewards directly influence motivation, or whether they influence motivation by changing the level of the goal.

Expectancy theory and operant conditioning are very different in underlying philosophy (cognitive versus non-cognitive), but they generate similar principles of application. Both approaches argue that (1) rewards should be closely tied to behavior, (2) reward administration should be frequent and consistent, and (3) people are motivated by outcomes (expected or past).

Reviews of expectancy theory (Connolly, 1976; Mitchell, 1980; Schwab, Olian-Gottlieb, & Heneman, 1979) and operant conditioning or social learning (Babb & Kopp, 1978; Davis & Luthans, 1980) are available. People doing research on both theories are concerned with issues that have to do with how to tie rewards to behavior, what sorts of schedules to use, how to measure various theoretical components, and so on. But except for some minor disagreements (Mawhinney & Behling, 1973), the approaches are in agreement about principles of application.

Equity theory (Carrell & Dittrich, 1978; Goodman, 1977) suggests that people are motivated by a desire for fairness. When they believe they are being treated unfairly, they will behave in ways that they believe will restore their sense of equity. Although over-reward (getting more than one should) and under-reward (getting less than one should) are similar from a theoretical perspective, the research suggests otherwise. People are more comfortable (less likely to change their behavior) with over-reward than with under-reward. If people feel that they are under-rewarded and can do little about directly influencing their rewards, they are liable to be dissatisfied, work less, and be absent more frequently than when they feel that they are being treated equitably.

Without getting into detailed analyses, one can point out some important differences and similarities between these approaches. The most striking difference is the basic underlying motivational mechanism postulated as the cause of behavior. There are (1) intentions to reach a goal, (2) expectations of maximum payoff, (3) past reinforcement histories, and (4) a desire for fairness. The similarities are that all four approaches define motivation as an individual, intentional process. Also, except for the operant approach, all three of the others focus on relatively current information processing. In this respect, the arousal and choice models seem to be headed in a similar direction. Finally, three of the models define motivation as directly influenced by outcomes (expectancy, operant, and equity approaches); goal setting sees outcomes as indirectly influencing motivation through goal level and intentions.

In order to utilize the information generated from these approaches, one must be able to set specific individual goals, tie rewards to individual behavior, and treat people fairly and equitably. As usual, this is easier said than done. A number of circumstances or situations make it difficult to implement these ideas.

One major problem is that many jobs involve considerable interdependence (Lawler, 1973). People frequently must work with others in order for the job to be accomplished successfully. This interdependence often makes it difficult to specify or tease out individual contributions. To the extent to which there is failure to assess individual behavioral contributions accurately, there will be trouble with individual goal setting and reward administration. Either group goals or rewards may be used.

A second important factor is observability. Individual feedback and reward administration both depend on the extent to which one knows what employees are doing. In many cases, people work alone, or in relatively isolated situations (e.g., within offices, on the road). To the extent that there is poor information about what people actually do, there will be difficulty with implementation.

A third problem has to do with change. In certain situations, jobs and people change fairly rapidly. The changes in jobs may be due to changes in technology, and the changes in people may be due to turnover. Note, again, that motivation emphasizes an individualized behavioral approach. Changes in jobs and people necessitate changes in the motivation system in the form of different behaviors to observe and different rewards to administer.

Finally, the heterogeneity of jobs causes difficulty as well. Each different type of job ideally should require a different job description, different behaviors, and therefore, different reward systems. These last two points focus on the compromise often required in implementing motivational principles. In many cases, people or jobs must be lumped together. However, it should be recognized that, to the extent to which there is deviation from the individual behavioral conceptualization of motivation, there probably will be a reduction in the effectiveness of the motivational program and the ability to measure its impact.

DISCUSSION

An analysis of both the theory and practice described above results in some important statements about where research on the topic of motivation should go from here. In terms of theoretical development, it appears as if three things are needed.

First, more integration is needed. Except for a few papers—for example, Lock (1978) and Wofford (1979)—very little theoretical work has been done to suggest the additive or interactive effects of the various approaches. The empirical studies that do compare to combine approaches suggest that combining various factors can lead to an increase in motivation. For example, a paper by White, Mitchell, and Bell (1977) demonstrates that evaluation apprehension, goal setting, and social pressure all have significant effects on motivation and that these effects might be additive.

A second implication that follows the above line of reasoning is that contingency type models of motivation need to be developed and tested. More specifically, the question is no longer whether goal setting or operant approaches work; it is where and when they work best. The mitigating circumstances that were described make it more difficult for one theory to work than another. For example, social cues and evaluation apprehension may increase in importance with interdependence, and goal setting and expectancy or operant approaches may become less feasible. With interdependence comes more social interaction and the chance to observe the behavior of others. Social cues and evaluation apprehension should be more salient. On the other hand, interdependence may make it more difficult to specify individual contributions and reward them. At this point, there is almost nothing in the literature that suggests when and where different motivational strategies will be most appropriate.

The third issue complements the other two. Because many jobs are, in fact, interdependent, social, and subject to change, more theory and research needs to be generated on how group processes effect motivation. Strategies such as team building or other interventions designed to increase commitment and motivation need to be studied as motivational models. An understanding is needed of the effects of such interventions on motivated behaviors and how these behaviors contribute to performance. It is hoped that more attention to the above issues will result in a more comprehensive understanding of not only the causes of motivation, but how and when and where different strategies should be used.

Hand in hand with these changes in theory and research should come changes in practice. One of the first things that should be developed is a set of diagnostic questions that any manager should ask about the motivational process. A flow chart or decision tree could be developed, such as the one presented in Exhibit 1. To some extent, this looks like the Vroom and Yetton (1973) model. Unfortunately, the Vroom and Yetton model is vastly superior in its level of detail, analysis, and support. For example, the weighting of factors 3 through 7 in Exhibit 1 is still unknown. There is little to guide one as to the order in which to ask the questions. But, more importantly, there is little guidance about what to do if the answers to 3 through 7 are yes. If what people do can be observed, if various rewards can be utilized, and if rewards can be tied to individual behavior without concern for social pressures or changes in the job, then systems are available that are ready to go. However, the situation is more ambiguous if the reverse of these conditions holds. The knowledge about how to influence motivation when correct behaviors are hard to define and observe, constantly changing, and under the control of interdependence or social pressures is severely limited.

Exhibit 1
A Flow Diagram of Questions About Motivation

1. Can performance be defined in individual, behavioral terms? If not, develop a separate measure of motivation.
2. Is motivation important for performance, or are abilities and situational factors more important? If motivation is important, but not the same as performance, develop a separate measure of motivation.

If one cannot meet the requirements of questions 1 and 2, it may not be worth it to proceed further. If, however, motivation is important for performance and performance is a good reflection of motivation and a good measure of motivation exists, then proceed with the analysis.

3. Is the reward system rigid and inflexible? In other words, are people and tasks grouped into large categories for reward purposes?
4. Is it difficult to observe what people are actually doing on the job?
5. Is an individual's behavior dependent heavily on the actions of others?
6. Are there lots of changes in people, jobs, or expected behavior?
7. Are social pressures the major determinants of what people are doing on the job?

If questions 3 through 7 are answered with a no, then some system combining a needs analysis with goal setting, operant, expectancy, and equity ideas should be effective.

The obvious implication for the practitioner is that the cost of implementing one of the more traditional motivation systems (e.g., MBO, behavior modification) might outweigh the benefit under these latter conditions. Until there are better answers to the question of how to influence motivation when these conditions exist, it will be difficult to develop any sort of comprehensive strategy for enhancing motivation. Thus, although the focus of current research is coming to recognize the importance of social processes, changes in jobs or people (Katz, 1980), and problems in flexibility and ability to give feedback (Ilgen, Fisher, & Taylor, 1979; Nadler, 1979), few remedies for these problems have been developed. Until this is done, a substantial inadequacy will remain in the ability to understand and influence motivation of the job.

References

Alderfer, C. P. A critique of Salancik and Pfeffer's examination of need satisfaction theories. *Administrative Science Quarterly*, 1977, 22, 658–669.

Atkinson, J. W. *An introduction to motivation.* Princeton, N. J.: Van Nostran 1964.

Babb, H. W., and Kopp, D. G. Applications of behavior modifications in organi tions: A review and critique. *Academy of Management Review*, 1978 281–290.

Campbell, J. P., Dunnette, M. D., Lawler, E. E., III, and Weick, K. E. *Managerial behavior, performance, and effectiveness.* New York: McG Hill, 1970.

Carrell, M. R., and Dittrich, J. E. Equity theory: The recent literature, me ological considerations, and new directions. *Academy of Manag Review*, 1978, 3, 202–210.

Connolly, T. Some conceptual and methodological issues in expectancy mc of work performance motivation. *Academy of Management Review*, 197(4), 37–47.

Davis, T. R. V., and Luthans, F. A social learning approach to organ onal behavior. *Academy of Management Review*, 1980, 5, 281–290.

Dunnette, M. D. Performance equals ability and what? Center for the udy of Organizational Performance and Human Effectiveness, Univ ity of Minnesota, Technical Report No. 4009, Minneapolis, 1973.

Ferris, G. R., Beehr, T. A., and Gilmore, D. C. Social facilitation: A review and alternative conceptual model, *Academy of Management Review,* 1978, 3, 338–347.

Goodman, P. S. Social comparison process in organizations. In B. M. Staw and G. R. Salancik (Eds.), *New directions in organizational behavior* (Vol. 1). Chicago: St. Clair Press, 1977, 97–132.

Hackman, J. R., and Morris, G. G. Group tasks, group interaction process, and group performance effectiveness. In L. Berkowitz (Ed.), *Advances in experimental social psychology.* (Vol 7). New York: Academic Press, 1975.

Hackman, J. R., and Oldham, G. R. *Work redesign.* Reading Mass.: Addison-Wesley, 1980.

Hellriegel, D., and Slocum, J. W., Jr. *Organizational behavior: Contingency views.* St. Paul, Minn.: West Publishing, 1976.

Huse, E. F., and Bowditch, J. L. *Behavior in organizations: A systems approach to managing.* Reading, Mass.: Addison-Wesley, 1977.

Ilgen, D. R., Fisher, C. D., and Taylor, M. S. Consequences of individual feedback on behavior in organizations. *Journal of Applied Psychology,* 1979, 64, 349–371.

Kane, J. S., and Lawler, E. E. Performance appraisal effectiveness: Its assessment and determinants. In B. Staw (Ed.), *Research in organizational behavior.* (Vol. 1). Greenwich, Conn.: JAI Press, 1979, 425–478.

Kast, F. E., and Rosenzweig, J. E. *Organization and management: A systems approach.* New York: McGraw-Hill, 1979.

Katz, R. Time and work: Toward an integrative perspective. In B. M. Staw and L. L. Cummings (Eds.), *Research in organizational behavior* (Vol. 2). Greenwich, Conn.: JAI Press, 1980, 81–128.

Kavanagh, M. J. Performance appraisal. In K. Rowland and G. Ferris (Eds.), *Personnel management.* Boston, Mass.: Allyn and Bacon, 1981.

Korman, A. K. *The psychology of motivation.* Englewood Cliffs, N. J.: Prentice-Hall, 1974.

Korman A. K. Hypothesis of work behavior revisited and an extension. *Academy of Management Review,* 1976, 1 (1), 50–63.

Korman, A. K., Greenhause, J. H., and Badin, I. J. Personnel attitudes and motivation. *Annual Review of Psychology*, 1977, 28, 175–196.

Landy, F. J., and Farr, J. L. Performance rating. *Psychological Bulletin*, 1980, 87, 72–107.

Latham, G. P., Mitchell, T. R., and Dossett, D. L. The importance of participative goal setting and anticipated rewards of goal difficulty and job performance. *Journal of Applied Psychology*, 1978, 63, 163–171.

Lawler, E. E., III. *Motivation in work organizations.* Monterey, Cal.: Brooks/Cole, 1973.

Lawler, E. E., III. New approaches to pay administration. *Personnel*, 1976, 53, 11–23.

Locke, E. A. Personnel attitudes and motivation. *Annual Review of Psychology*, 1975, 26, 457–480.

Locke, E. A. The ubiquity of the techniques of goal setting in theories and approaches to employee motivation. *Academy of Management Review*, 1978, 3, 594–601.

Luthans, F. *Organizational behavior.* New York: McGraw-Hill, 1977.

March, J. G., and Simon, H. A. *Organizations.* New York: Wiley, 1958.

Mawhinney, T. C., and Behling, O. Differences in predictions of work behavior from expectancy and operant models of individual motivation. *Proceedings of the Academy of Management*, 1973, 383–388.

McClelland, D. C., and Steele, R. S. *Human motivation: A book of readings.* Morristown, N. J.: General Learning Press, 1973.

Mitchell, T. R. Organizational behavior. *Annual Review of Psychology*, 1979, 30, 243–281.

Mitchell, T. R. Expectancy-value models in organizational psychology. In N. Feather (Ed.), *Expectancy, incentive and action.* Hillsdale, N. J.: Erlbaum and Associates, 1980.

Mitchell, T. R. Motivational strategies. In K. Rowland and G. Ferris (Eds.), *Personnel management.* Boston, Mass.: Allyn and Bacon, in press.

Mitchell, T. R. *People in organizations: Understanding their behavior.* New York: McGraw-Hill, 1978.

Nadler, D. A. The effects of feedback on task group behavior: A review of the experimental research. *Organizational Behavior and Human Performance,* 1979, 23, 309–338.

Porter, L. W., and Lawler, E. E., III. *Managerial attitudes and performance.* Homewood, Ill.: Dorsey, 1968.

Ryan, T. A. *Intentional behavior: an approach to human motivation.* New York: Ronald Press, 1970.

Salancik, G. R., and Pfeffer, J. An examination of need satisfaction models of job attitudes. *Administrative Science Quarterly,* 1977, 22, 427–456.

Salancik, G. R., and Pfeffer, J. A social information processing approach to job attitudes and task design. *Administrative Science Quarterly,* 1978, 23, 224–253.

Schwab, D. P., Olian-Gottlieb, J. D., and Heneman, H. G., III. Between subjects expectancy theory research: A statistical review of studies predicting effort and performance. *Psychological Bulletin,* 1979, 86, 139–147.

Scott, W. G., and Hart, D. K. *Organizational America.* Boston: Houghton-Mifflin.

Staw, B. M. Motivation in organizations: Toward synthesis and redirection. In B. M. Staw and G. R. Salancik (Eds.), *New directions in organizational behavior* (Vol. 1). Chicago: St. Clair Press, 1977, 54–95.

Steers, R. M., and Porter, L. W. The role of task-goal attributes in employee performance. *Psychological Bulletin,* 1974, 81, 434–452.

Steers, R. M., and Porter, L. W. *Motivation and work behavior.* New York: McGraw-Hill, 1979.

Tosi, H. L., House, R. J., and Dunnette, M. D. *Managerial motivation and compensation: A selection of readings.* East Lansing, Mich.: MSU Business Studies. 1972.

Vroom, V. H. *Work and motivation.* New York: Wiley, 1964.

Vroom, V. H., and Yetton, P. W. *Leadership and decision making.* Pittsburgh: University of Pittsburgh Press, 1973.

Weiner, B. *Theories of motivation: From mechanism to cognition.* Chicago: Rand McNally, 1972.

White, S., Mitchell, T. R., and Bell, C. H. Goal setting, evaluation apprehension and social cues as determinants of job performance and job satisfaction in a simulated organization. *Journal of Applied Psychology,* 1977, 62, 665–673.

Wofford, J. C. A goal-energy-effort requirement model (GEER) of work motivation. *Academy of management Review,* 1979, 4, 193–201.

Yuki, G. A., and Latham, G. P. Interrelationships among employee participation, individual differences, goal difficulty, goal acceptance, instrumentality and performance. *Personnel Psychology,* 1978, 31, 305–324.

PART III
INTERPERSONAL BEHAVIOR
LEADERSHIP AND GROUP DYNAMICS

This part includes readings at a more macro level of analysis, the interpersonal relations of leadership, and group dynamics. There are readings on leadership, one on the topic of group norms, and a final one related to decision making in organizational contexts.

The first article, by Fred Luthans, examines the difference between managers who have had quick promotions (successful) and those with highly motivated subordinates (effective). The next reading presents review of one of the most researched theories of leadership, Fiedler's Contingency model. In his discussion, Hunt presents the basics as well as how to best use the theory.

The House and Mitchell article discusses the Path-Goal Theory of Leadership. This is another contingency theory and is closely linked to the Expectancy theory of motivation discussed in the previous section.

The next two articles discuss theories more popular among managers than academics. The first article discusses the Managerial Grid concept of Blake and Mouton. While universalistic in nature (one best way), it has been shown to be useful in conflict reduction activities. The Moore article presents the Life Cycle theory of leadership, more recently known as situational leadership. The next two articles on leadership present discussions on specific aspects of leadership. Howell and Avolio examine the ethical use of charisma in turnaround situations. Then Keys and Case present research findings on successful techniques to acquit and use influence and the tactics which are used most frequently and most effective.

The article by Joanne Preston reviews building trust in relationships through communication. The behaviors for building a positive climate of trust for the consultant and manager will be examined.

Feldman discusses the issues surrounding group norms, the unwritten rules which guide and structure behaviors and activities in group situations. The article in this section, by Herbert Simon, talks about managerial decision-making. The final article by Bertrand and Mosier discuss the technological and psychological requirements of group performance, an approach often referred to as socio-technical.

SUCCESSFUL VS. EFFECTIVE REAL MANAGERS

Fred Luthans

What do *successful* managers—those who have been promoted relatively quickly—have in common with *effective* managers—those who have satisfied, committed subordinates and high performing units? Surprisingly, the answer seems to be that they have little in common. Successful managers in what we define as "real organizations"—large and small mainstream organizations, mostly in the mushrooming service industry in middle America—are not engaged in the same day-to-day activities as effective managers in these organizations. This is probably the most important, and certainly the most intriguing, finding of a comprehensive four-year observational study of managerial work that is reported in a recent book by myself and two colleagues, titled *Real Managers.*[1]

The startling find that there is a difference between successful and effective managers may merely confirm for many cynics and "passed over" managers something they have suspected for years. They believe that although managers who are successful (that is, rapidly promoted) may be astute politicians, they are not necessarily effective. Indeed, the so-called successful managers may be the ones who do not in fact take care of people and get high performance from their units.

Could this finding explain some of the performance problems facing American organizations today? Could it be that the successful managers, the politically savvy ones who are being rapidly promoted into responsible positions, may not be the effective managers, the ones with satisfied, committed subordinates turning out quantity and quality performance in their units?

This article explores the heretofore assumed equivalence of "successful managers" and "effective managers." Instead of looking for sophisticated technical or governmental approaches to the performance problems facing today's organizations, the solution may be as simple as promoting effective managers and learning how they carry out their jobs. Maybe it is time to turn to the real managers themselves for some answers.

And who are these managers? They are found at all levels and in all types of organizations with titles such as department head, general manager, store manager, marketing manager, office manager, agency chief, or district manager. In other words, maybe the answers to the performance problems facing organiza-

Reprinted with permission of Publisher from the *Academy of Management Executive,* 1988, Vol. 2, pp. 127–132.

tions today can be found in their own backyards, in the managers themselves in their day-to-day activities.

The Current View of Managerial Work

Through the years, management has been defined, as the famous French administrator and writer Henri Fayol said, by the functions of planning, organizing, commanding, coordinating, and controlling. Only recently has this classical view of managers been challenged.[2] Starting with the landmark work of Henry Mintzberg, observational studies of managerial work have found that the normative functions do not hold up. Mintzberg charged that Fayol and others' classical view of what managers do was merely "folklore."[3]

On the basis of his observations of five CEOs and their mail, Mintzberg concluded that the manager's job consisted of many brief and disjointed episodes with people inside and outside the organization. He discounted notions such as reflective planning. Instead of the five Fayolian functions of management, Mintzberg portrayed managers in terms of a typology of roles. He formulated three interpersonal roles (figurehead, leader, and liaison); three informational roles (monitor or nerve center, disseminator, and spokesman), and four decision-making roles (entrepreneur, disturbance handler, resource allocator, and negotiator). Although Mintzberg based this view of managers on only the five managers he observed and his search of the literature, he did ask, and at least gave the beginning of an answer to, the question of what managers really do.

The best known other modern view of managerial work is provided by John Kotter. His description of managers is based on his study of 15 successful general managers. Like Mintzberg, Kotter challenged the traditional view by concluding that managers do not so simply perform the Fayolian functions, but rather spend most of their time interacting with others. In particular, he found his general managers spent considerable time in meetings getting and giving information. Kotter refers to these get-togethers as "network building." Networking accomplishes what Kotter calls a manager's "agenda"—the loosely connected goals and plans addressing the manager's responsibilities. By obtaining relevant and needed information from his or her networks, the effective general manager is able to implement his or her agenda. Like Mintzberg, Kotter's conclusions are based on managerial work from a small sample of elite managers. Nevertheless, his work represents a progressive step in answering the question of what managers do.

The next step in discovering the true nature of managerial work called for a larger sample that would allow more meaningful generalizations. With a grant from the Office of Naval Research, we embarked on such an effort.[4] We used trained observers to freely observe and record in detail the behaviors and activities of 44 "real" managers.[5] Unlike Mintzberg's and Kotter's managers, these managers came from all levels and many types of organizations (mostly in the service sector—such as retail stores, hospitals, corporate headquarters, a railroad, government agencies, insurance companies, a newspaper office, financial institutions, and a few manufacturing companies).

We reduced the voluminous data gathered from the free observation logs into managerial activity categories using the Delphi technique. Delphi was developed and used during the heyday of Rand Corporation's "Think Tank." A panel offers independent input and then the panel members are given composite feedback. After several iterations of this process, the data were reduced into the 12 descriptive behavioral categories shown in Exhibit 1. These empirically derived behavioral descriptors were then conceptually collapsed into the four managerial activities of real managers:

Exhibit 1
The Activities of Real Managers

Descriptive Categories
Derived From Free Observation

Real Managers'
Activities

Exchanging Information

Communication

Paperwork

Planning

Decision Making

Traditional Management

Controlling

Interacting with Outsiders

Networking

Socializing/Politicking

Motivating/Reinforcing

Disciplining/Punishing

Managing Conflict

Human Resource Management

Staffing

Training/Developing

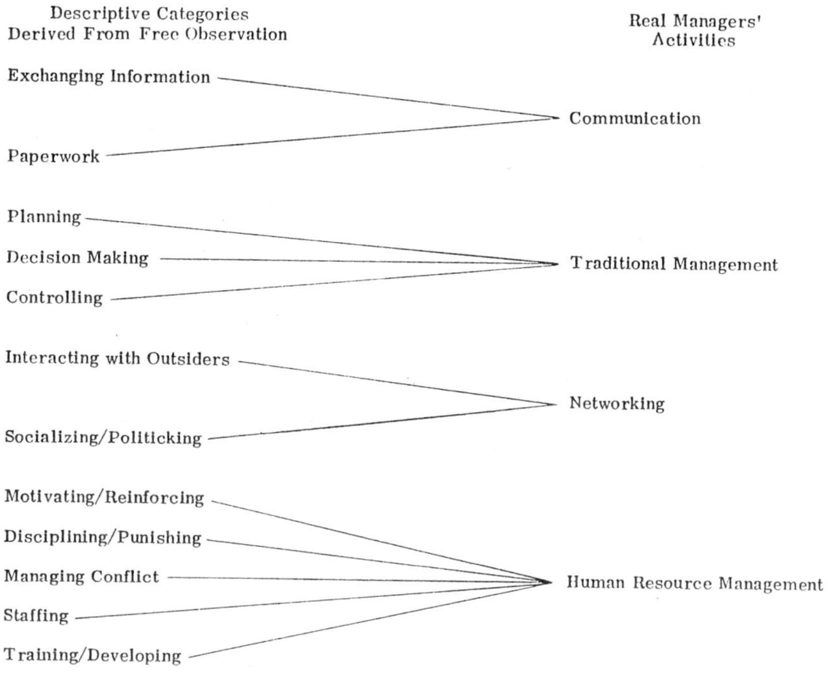

1.   *Communication.*   This activity consists of exchanging routine information and processing paperwork.   Its observed behaviors include answering procedural questions, receiving and disseminating requested information, conveying the results of meetings, giving or receiving routine information over the phone, processing mail, reading reports, writing reports/memos/letters, routine financial reporting and bookkeeping, and general desk work.

2.   *Traditional Management.* This activity consists of planning, decision making, and controlling.   Its observed behaviors include setting goals and objectives, defining tasks needed to accomplish goals, scheduling employees, assigning tasks, providing routing instructions, defining problems, handling day-to-day operational crises, deciding what to do, developing new procedures, inspecting work, walking around inspecting the work, monitoring performance data, and doing preventive maintenance.

3.   *Human Resource Management.*   This activity contains the most behavioral categories: motivating/reinforcing, disciplining/punishing, managing conflict, staffing, and training/developing.   The disciplining/punishing category was subsequently dropped from the analysis because it was not generally permitted to be observed.   The observed behaviors for this activity include allocating formal rewards, asking for input, conveying appreciation, giving credit where due, listening to suggestions, giving positive feedback, group support, resolving conflict between subordinates, appealing to higher authorities or third parties to resolve a dispute, developing job descriptions, reviewing applications, interviewing applicants, filling in where needed, orienting employees, arranging for training, clarifying roles, coaching, mentoring, and walking subordinates through a task.

4.   *Networking.*   This activity consists of socializing/politicking and interacting with outsiders.   The observed behaviors associated with this activity include non-work-related "chit chat"; informal joking around; discussing rumors, hearsay and the grapevine; complaining, griping, and putting others down; politicking and gamesmanship; dealing with customers, suppliers, and vendors; attending external meetings; and doing/attending community service events.

These four activities are what real managers do.   They include some of the classic notions of Fayol (the traditional management activities) as well as the more recent views of Mintzberg (the communication activities) and Kotter (the networking activities).   As a whole, however, especially with the inclusion of human resource management activities, this view of real managers' activities is more comprehensive than previous sets of managerial work.

After the nature of managerial activity was determined through the free observation of the 44 managers, the next phase of the study was to document the relative frequency of these activities. Data on another set of 248 real managers (not the 44 used in the initial portion of this study) were gathered. Trained participation observers filled out a checklist based on the managerial activities at a random time once every hour over a two-week period. We found that the real managers spend not quite a third of their time and effort in communication activities, about a third in traditional management activities, a fifth in human resource management activities, and about a fifth in networking activities. This relative frequency analysis based on observational data of a large sample provides a more definitive answer to the question of what real managers do than the normative classical functions and the limited sample of elite managers used by Mintzberg and Kotter.

How the Difference Between Successful and Effective Real Managers Was Determined

Discovering the true nature of managerial work by exploding some of the myths of the past and extending the work of Mintzberg and Kotter undoubtedly contributes to our knowledge of management. However, of more critical importance in trying to understand and find solutions to our current performance problems is singling out successful and effective managers to see what they really do in their day-to-day activities. The successful-versus-effective phase of our real managers study consisted of analyzing the existing data based on the frequencies of the observed activities of the real managers. We did not start off with any preconceived notions or hypotheses concerning the relationships between successful and effective managers. In fact, making such a distinction seemed like "splitting hairs" because the two words are so often used interchangeably. Nevertheless, we decided to define success operationally in terms of the speed of promotion within an organization. We determined a success index on a sample of the real managers in our study. It was calculated by dividing a manager's level in his or her organization by his or her tenure (length of service) there.[6] Thus, a manager at the fourth level of management, who has been with his or her organization for five years would be rated more successful than a manager at the third level who has been there for 25 years. Obviously, there are some potential problems with such a measure of success, but for our large sample of managers this was an objective measure that could be obtained.

The definition and measurement of effectiveness is even more elusive. The vast literature on managerial effectiveness offered little agreement on criteria or measures. To overcome as many of the obstacles and disagreements as possible, we used a combined effectiveness index for a sample of the real managers in our study that represented the two major—and generally agreed upon—criteria of both management theory/research and practice: (1) getting the job done through high quantity and quality standards of performance, and (2) getting the job done through people, which requires their satisfaction and commitment.[7]

We obviously would have liked to use "hard measures" of effectiveness such as profits and quantity/quality of output or service, but again, because we were working with large samples of real managers from widely diverse jobs and organizations, this was not possible.

What Do Successful Real Managers Do?

To answer the question of what successful real managers do, we conducted several types of analyses—statistical (using multiple regression techniques), simple descriptive comparisons (for example, top third of managers as measured by the success index vs. bottom third), and relative strength of correlational relationships.[8] In all of these analyses, the importance that networking played in real manager success was very apparent. Of the four real manager activities, only networking had a statistically significant relationship with success. In the comparative analysis, we found that the most successful (top third) real managers were doing considerably more networking and slightly more routine communication than their least successful (bottom third) counterparts. From the relative strength of relationship analysis, we found that networking makes the biggest relative contribution to manager success and, importantly, human resource management activities makes the least relative contribution.

What does this mean? It means that in this study of real managers, using speed of promotion as the measure of success, it was found that successful real managers spent relatively more time and effort socializing, politicking, and interacting with outsiders than did their less successful counterparts. Perhaps equally important, the successful real managers did not give much time or attention to the traditional management activities of planning, decision making, and controlling or to the human resource management activities of motivating/reinforcing, staffing, training/developing, and managing conflict. A representative example of this profile would be the following manager's prescription for success:

> "I find that the way to get ahead around here is to be friendly with the right people, both inside and outside the firm. They get tired of always talking shop, so I find a common interest—with some it's sports, with others it's our kids—and interact with them on that level. The other formal stuff around the office is important, but I really work

at this informal side and have found it pays off when promotion time rolls around."

In other words, for this manager and for a significant number of these real managers we studied, networking seems to be the key to success.

What Do Effective Real Managers Do?

Once we answered the question of what successful managers do, we turned to the even more important question of what effective managers do. It should be emphasized once again that, in gathering our observational data for the study, we made no assumptions that the successful real managers were (or were not) the effective managers. Our participant observers were blind to the research questions and we had no hypothesis concerning the relationship between successful and effective managers.

We used the relative strength of correlational relationship between the real managers' effectiveness index and their directly observed day-to-day activities and found that communication and human resource management activities made by far the largest relative contribution to real managers' effectiveness and that traditional management and—especially—networking made by far the least relative contribution.[9]

These results mean that if effectiveness is defined as the perceived quantity and quality of the performance of a manager's unit and his or her subordinates' satisfaction and commitment, then the biggest relative contribution to real manager effectiveness comes from the human oriented activities—communication and human resource management. A representative example of this effectiveness profile is found in the following manager's comments:

"Both how much and how well things get done around here, as well as keeping my people loyal and happy, has to do with keeping them informed and involved. If I make a change in procedure or the guys upstairs gave us a new process or piece of equipment to work with, I get my people's input and give them the full story before I lay it on them. Then I make sure they have the proper training and give them feedback on how they are doing. When they screw up, I let them know it, but when they do a good job, I let them know about that too."

This manager, like our study of real managers in general, found that the biggest contribution to effectiveness came from communicating and human resource management activities.

Equally important, however, was the finding that the least relative contribution to real managers' effectiveness came from the networking activity. This, of course, is in stark contrast to our results of the successful real manager analysis. Networking activity had by far the strongest relative relationship to success, but the weakest with effectiveness. On the other hand, human resource management activity had a strong relationship to effectiveness (second only to communication activity), but had the weakest relative relationship to success. In other words, the successful real managers do not do the same activities as the effective real managers (in fact, they do almost the opposite). These contrasting profiles may have significant implications for understanding the current performance problems facing American organizations. However, before we look at these implications and suggest some solutions, let's take a look at those real managers who are both successful and effective.

What Do Managers Who Are Both Successful and Effective Do?

The most obvious concluding question is what those who were found to be both successful and effective really do. This "combination" real manager, of course, is the ideal—and has been assumed to exist in American management over the years.

Since there was such a difference between successful and effective managers in our study, we naturally found relatively few (less than 10% of our sample) that were both among the top third of successful managers and the top third of effective managers. Not surprisingly, upon examining this special group, we found that their activities were very similar to real managers as a whole. They were not like either the successful or effective real managers. Rather, it seems that real managers who are both successful and effective use a fairly balanced approach in terms of their activities. In other words, real managers who can strike the delicate balance between all four managerial activities may be able to get ahead as well as get the job done.

Important is the fact that we found so few real managers that were both successful and effective. This supports our findings on the difference between successful and effective real managers, but limits any generalizations that can be made about successful and effective managers. It seems that more important in explaining our organizations' present performance problems, and what to do about them, are the implications of the wide disparity between successful and effective real managers.

Implications of the Successful versus Effective Real Managers Findings

If, as our study indicates, there is indeed a difference between successful and effective real managers, what does it mean and what should we do about it? First of all, we need to pay more attention to formal reward systems to ensure that effective managers are promoted. Second, we must learn how effective managers do their day-to-day jobs.

The traditional assumption holds that promotions are based on performance. This is what the formal personnel policies say, this is what new management trainees are told and this is what every management textbook states *should* happen. On the other hand, more "hardened" (or perhaps more realistic) members and observers of *real* organizations (not textbook organizations or those featured in the latest best sellers or videotapes) have long suspected that social and political skills are the real key to getting ahead, to being *successful*. Our study lends support to the latter view.

The solution is obvious, but may be virtually impossible to implement, at least in the short run. Tying formal rewards—and especially promotions—to performance is a must if organizations are going to move ahead and become more productive. At a minimum, and most pragmatically in the short run, organizations must move to a performance-based appraisal system. Managers that are *effective* should be *promoted.* In the long run organizations must develop cultural values that support and reward effective performance, not just successful socializing and politicking. This goes hand-in-hand with the current attention given to corporate culture and how to change it. An appropriate goal for cultural change in today's organizations might simply be to make effective managers successful.

Besides the implications for performance-based appraisals and organizational culture that came out of the findings of our study is a lesson that we can learn from the effective real managers themselves. This lesson is the importance they give and effort they devote to the human-oriented activities of communicating and human resource management. How human resources are managed—keeping them informed, communicating with them, paying attention to them, reinforcing them, resolving their conflicts, training/developing them—all contribute directly to managerial effectiveness.

The disparity our study found between successful and effective real managers has important implications for the performance problems facing today's organizations. While we must move ahead on all fronts in our search for solutions to these problems, we believe the activities basic to the effective real managers in our study—communication and human resource management—deserve special attention.

End Notes

1.   The full reference for the book is Fred Luthans, Richard M. Hodgetts, and Stuart Rosenkrantz, *Real Managers* (Cambridge, MA: Ballinger, 1988). Some of the preliminary material from the real managers study was also included in the presidential speech given by Fred Luthans at the 1986 Academy of Management meeting. Appreciation is extended to the co-authors of the book, Stu Rosenkrantz and Dick Hodgetts, to Diane Lee Lockwood on the first phase of the study, and to Avis Johnson, Hank Hennessey and Lew Taylor on later phases. These individuals, especially Stu Rosenkrantz, contributed ideas and work on the backup for this article.

2.   The two most widely recognized challenges to the traditional view of management have come from Henry Mintzberg, *The Nature of Managerial Work* (New York: Harper & Row, 1973) and John Kotter, *The General Managers* (New York: Free Press, 1982). In addition, two recent comprehensive reviews of the nature of managerial work can be found in the following references: Colin P. Hales, "What Do Managers Do? A Critical Review of the Evidence," *Journal of Management Studies* (1986, 23, pp. 88–115) and Stephen J. Carroll and Dennis J. Gillen, "Are the Classical Management Functions Useful in Describing Managerial Work?" *Academy of Management Review* (1987, 12, pp. 38–52).

3.   See Henry Mintzberg's article, "The Manager's Job: Folklore and Fact," *Harvard Business Review* (July–August, 1975, 53, pp. 49–61).

4.   For those interested in the specific details of the background study, see Luthans, Hodgetts and Rosenkrantz (End note 1 above).

5.   The source that details the derivation, training of observers, procedures, and reliability and validity analysis of the observation system used in the real managers study is Fred Luthans and Diane L. Lockwood's "Toward an Observation System for Measuring Leader Behavior in Natural Settings," in J. Hunt, D. Hosking, C. Schriesheim, and R. Stewart (Eds.), *Leaders and Managers: International Perspectives of Managerial Behavior and Leadership* (New York: Pergamon Press, 1986, pp. 117–141).

6.   For more background on the success portion of the study and the formula used to calculate the success index see Fred Luthans, Stuart Rosenkrantz, and Harry Hennessey, "What Do Successful Managers Really Do? An Observational Study of Managerial Activities," *Journal of Applied Behavioral Science* (1985, 21, pp. 255–270).

7. The questionnaire used to measure the real managers' unit quantity and quality of performance was drawn from Paul E. Mott, *The Characteristics of Effective Organizations* (New York: Harper & Row, 1972). Subordinate satisfaction was measured by the Job Diagnostic Index found in P. C. Smith, L. M. Kendall, and C. L. Hulin, *The Measurement of Satisfaction in Work and Retirement* (Chicago: Rand-McNally, 1969). Subordinate commitment is measured by the questionnaire in Richard T. Mowday, L. W. Porter, and Richard M. Steers, *Employee-Organizational Linkages: The Psychology of Commitment, Absenteeism, and Turnover* (New York: Academic Press, 1982). These three standardized questionnaires are widely used research instruments with considerable psychometric back-up and high reliability in the sample used in our study.

8. For the details of the multiple regression analysis and simple descriptive comparisons of successful versus unsuccessful managers, see End note 6 above. To determine the relative contribution the activities identified in Exhibit 1 made to success, we calculated the mean of the squared correlations (to approximate variance explained) between the observed activities of the real managers and the success index calculated for each target manager. These correlation squared means were then rank ordered to obtain the relative strengths of the managerial activities' contribution to success.

9. The calculation for the relative contribution the activities made to effectiveness was done as described for success in End note 8. The statistical and top third-bottom third comparison that was done in the success analysis was not done in the effectiveness analysis. For comparison of successful managers and effective managers, the relative strength of relationship was used; see *Real Managers* (End note 1 above) for details.

BREAKTHROUGH IN LEADERSHIP RESEARCH

J. G. Hunt

Much research has been conducted concerning the kind of leadership style needed to promote effective work performance. However, research results have not been consistent. Some studies have shown that a directive, task-oriented leadership style promotes effective group performance while others have shown that a non-directive human relations-oriented style is best.

These inconsistent results have led some people to consider the situation in which the leader and his subordinates operate. Progressive managers have recognized for some time that the kind of leadership style which is best in one situation may not be most effective in another situation. The problem has been to develop a model for classifying situations so that the most effective style of leadership to use in a given situation can be predicted successfully.

This paper describes a model developed by Professor F. E. Fiedler at the University of Illinois that allows the kind of classification discussed above.[1] A recent test of this model in three business organizations is also discussed.

Research Background

Before describing this model, it would be useful to briefly examine Fiedler's measure of leadership style and some of the research which led to the model. The leadership style measure is based on a simple scale indicating the extent to which a leader describes favorably or unfavorably the individual with whom he has been able to work least well. This "least preferred" person does not need to be someone with whom the leader is presently working, but can be (and usually is) someone with whom he has worked in the past. Such a person will usually be a worker rather than another leader.

After a great deal of research, Fiedler has concluded that the leader who favorably describes the person with whom he has been able to work least well tends

---

From *Personnel Administration,* September-October, 1967, Used by permission of the publisher.

[1]F. E. Fiedler, "A Contingency Model of Leadership Effectiveness," in L. Berkowitz (Ed.), *Advances in Experimental Social Psychology.* New York: Academic Press, 1964.

to show "human relations-oriented" leader behavior. In oversimplified terms, he wants to be a "nice guy." On the other hand, a leader who unfavorably describes the individual with whom he has been able to work least well tends to be "task-oriented." He primarily wants to get the job done.[2]

Fiedler and his associates examined the relationship between leadership style and group performance in the following kinds of work groups: basketball teams, fraternity houses, surveying teams, bomber crews, infantry squads, open-hearth steel shops, farm supply service companies, and many samples of artificial laboratory groups performing a variety of creative type tasks.[3] The relationship between leadership style and performance in these groups was far from simple. Results were difficult to predict and interpret because leader-member relations, stress, and job type influenced this relationship. This problem, together with inconsistent results obtained by other researchers, led Fiedler to develop the model described.

Dimensions of Leadership Influence

The model is built around the idea of "favorableness for the leader." The important question is: "What dimensions of the group or task situation make it easy or hard for the leader to exert influence on group performance?" From his earlier research, Fiedler concluded that three dimensions seemed to be important. These dimensions are sorted into different combinations in terms of a "favorableness for the leader" axis so that the leader's opportunity to influence group performance ranges from very favorable to very unfavorable. The three dimensions are: (1) *leader-member relations;* (2) *task structure;* and (3) *leader position power.* *Leader-member relations* refer to the leader's feeling of acceptance by his sub-ordinates. *Task structure* refers to the degree to which the subordinates' jobs are routine and spelled out "by the numbers" versus being vague and undefined. For instance, an assembly line worker's job would fall into the first category, while a superintendent's job would generally be relatively low in structure. *Position power* refers to the power of the leadership position as distinct from any personal power the leader might have.

Figure 1 shows these three dimensions ordered into eight different combinations along the horizontal axis according to their favorableness for the leader.

---

[2]F. E. Fiedler, "A Review of Research on ASo and LPC Scores as Measures of Leadership Style," Technical Report No. 33, Urbana, Ill.: Group Effectiveness Research Laboratory, University of Illinois, 1966.

[3]These are usually groups of college students which are set up to test a specific idea.

- 138 -

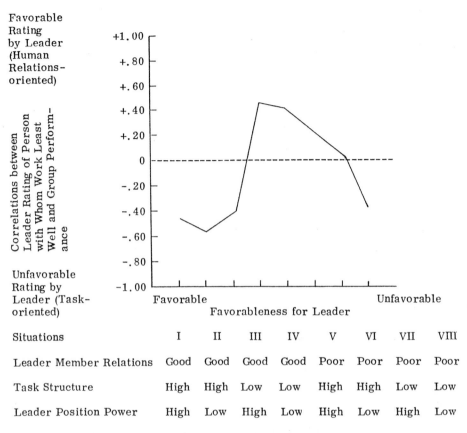

Situations	I	II	III	IV	V	VI	VII	VIII
Leader Member Relations	Good	Good	Good	Good	Poor	Poor	Poor	Poor
Task Structure	High	High	Low	Low	High	High	Low	Low
Leader Position Power	High	Low	High	Low	High	Low	High	Low

Figure 1. A model which shows the relationship between Fiedler's leadership style measure and performance for different situations.

Situation I is the most favorable while Situation VIII is the least favorable. In sorting these dimensions, Fiedler has assumed leader-member relations to be most important and power least important. He argues that a leader who is or feels himself to be accepted can often compensate for inadequacies in the other dimensions, and a leader with relatively little power can often be successful if he has a highly structured task.

Once the dimensions are arranged into these eight situations, it is possible to plot the numerical relationship or correlation between leadership style and group performance for each of these situations and obtain the curve in Figure 1.[4]

We can interpret this curve as follows: All the points below the horizontal dividing line indicate a negative relationship (correlation) between leadership style and work performance. This means that a leader who unfavorably evaluates the person with whom he has been able to work least well obtains better performance than a leader who favorably evaluates such a person. In other words, a task-oriented leader is here more effective than a human relations-oriented leader. The opposite is true for all points above the mid-line; that is, a human relations-oriented leader is here more effective than a task-oriented leader.

Figure 1 tells us that under very favorable (Situations I through III) and very unfavorable (Situation VIII) conditions, the task-oriented leader is most effective. On the other hand, under conditions intermediate in favorableness (Situations IV through VI) the human relations-oriented leader performs best. (Situation VII is apparently a special case in which the nearly zero correlation shows that leadership style apparently makes little difference.) Thus, the model shows some of the conditions under which a given style of leadership is most appropriate.

Testing the Model in Organizations

The model was tested in industrial and business organizations. It was assumed that if it predicted successfully in these organizations it would have important implications for manager selection, placement and training.

Five samples were secured from three organizations. In Company X there were 18 groups of research chemists and 11 groups of skilled craftsmen. Company Y was a grocery chain where 24 grocery departments and 21 meat departments were sampled. In Company Z, a farm implement manufacturing firm, the model was tested one step higher in the organization, and 15 management teams consisting of a general foreman and his subordinate foremen were considered.

---

[4]Technical note: This survey was obtained from Fiedler's studies by plotting the average correlation between leadership style and performance obtained for each of the situations. Twelve years' worth of data from 15 studies using over 800 groups were used to plot the curve. Every point is an average correlation based on several samples, each of which consists of a number of leaders and work groups. The numbers on the vertical axis indicate the strength of the relationship with plus or minus 1.00 being a perfect positive or negative correlation and 0 indicating no relationship between leadership style and performance.

The work group supervisors' leadership style was measured by having these supervisors use Fiedler's scale to evaluate the person with whom they had been able to work least well. *Leader-member relations* were measured by asking each supervisor to rate the atmosphere of his group, using a number of eight-point scales. Fiedler used this measure in many of his studies and showed that a leader's rating of *group atmosphere* indicates the degree to which he feels accepted by his group members.[5]

Task Structure was measured by having at least three raters in each company rate the structure of the jobs of the group members in the samples. The jobs were rated in terms of the following dimensions:

1. Clearness of job goals;

2. The number of ways in which a job can be performed;

3. The degree to which job decisions can be shown to be correct;

4. The degree to which there is more than one "correct solution" to job problems.[6]

These ratings were cross-checked by giving 13 business school graduate students and faculty members short descriptions of the jobs and having them rate the jobs on the same scale as the company raters. A high agreement was found between the two sets of raters, so the average of both was used to get the final rating. Finally, the scores for each *type* of job in a group (excluding the supervisor) were averaged to obtain a group *task structure* score.

Position power in each sample was measured by asking an official familiar with company policy to consider 13 questions and answer them "yes" and "no" according to this policy. The questions referred to *expert* and *reward and punishment* power granted by the organization to the sampled supervisors.

Performance of the research chemists and shop craftsmen was measured by using ratings of three officials familiar with their work. In the supermarket meat

---

[5]F. E. Fiedler, "A Contingency Model for the Prediction of Leadership Effectiveness," Technical Report No. 10, Urbana, Ill.: Group Effectiveness Research Laboratory, University of Illinois, 1963, pp. 3-4.

[6]These are adapted from M. E. Shaw, "Scaling Group Tasks: A Method for Dimensional Analysis," Technical Report No. 1, Gainesville, Florida: University of Florida, 1963.

and grocery departments, productivity figures in terms of sales per man hour were available. Finally, a ratio of actual to expected departmental productivity was used to measure the performance of the production foremen sample.

Classifying the Group

The samples were first classified on the basis of *position power* and *task structure*. All the samples were found to have leaders with "high" position power. This, of course, is what would be expected in most kinds of business and industrial organizations. *Task structure* was classified as "high" for all the samples except the production foremen and part of the research chemists.

After classification of the samples by *power* and *task structure, group atmosphere* was considered. The *group atmosphere* scores for the groups in each subsample were arranged in descending order and the mid-point was used to divide the groups into those with "good" and those with "poor" *group atmosphere*. Thus, it was possible to sample groups in Situations I, III, V, and VII of the model. These are probably the most important situations to test in industrial organizations because of the supervisor's high *position power* in most organizations of this type. Hence it is argued that this is a comprehensive test of the model in these kinds of samples.

A summary of the average correlations for each of these samples is shown in Figure 2. These average correlations lie quite close to Fiedler's curve based on the average correlations of his studies.[7] It was, therefore, concluded that the model predicts performance successfully in organizations of the kind tested here.

Importance to Management

The model provides knowledge about some of the group-task variables which apparently make a difference in the kind of leadership style that will get best results. This knowledge can be used in a number of ways. Some of these are discussed here.

---

[7]Technical note: Where appropriate, statistical tests were applied to the individual correlations from which these average correlations were obtained. These tests showed that there was only about one chance in one hundred that these results could have been obtained by chance.

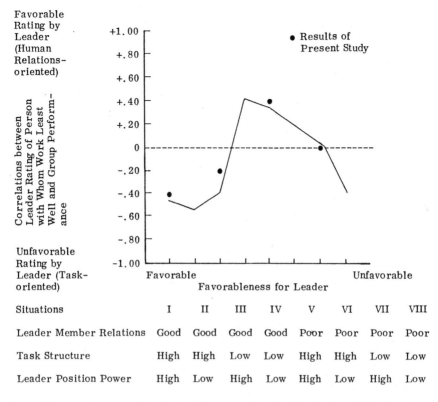

Situations	I	II	III	IV	V	VI	VII	VIII
Leader Member Relations	Good	Good	Good	Good	Poor	Poor	Poor	Poor
Task Structure	High	High	Low	Low	High	High	Low	Low
Leader Position Power	High	Low	High	Low	High	Low	High	Low

Figure 2. Average Correlations Between Leadership Style and Performance of Present Study Compared with Those Predicted by Model.

Human Relations Training[8]

Available evidence indicates that human relations training given to supervisors "across the board" has typically not been very carefully evaluated, or where it has, results are disappointing.

If it is assumed that such training can effectively change the supervisor's behavior (an assumption which some people question but which is not discussed here), then Fiedler's model suggests the following:

---

[8]For a more detailed discussion of this topic, see J. C. Hunt, "Another Look at Human Relations Training," *Training and Development Journal,* in press.

1.   Give training only to those supervisors in situations calling for this kind of behavior rather than "across the board" as has typically been done.

2.   Train the supervisor to diagnose group-task situations so that he can modify his leadership style accordingly.

Alternatives to Human Relations Training

Let's consider first what Fiedler has termed "organization engineering." Here one or more group-task dimensions are modified to fit the leadership style of a given manager. The primary interest is in concentrating on groups with human relations-oriented managers in Situations I and III, and groups with task-oriented managers in Situation V.[9] According to Figure 2, these groups would have managers with the wrong style for their particular situation.

Now, according to the model, productivity could be improved by modifying dimensions as shown in Table 1. The effect of this modification is to change the situation in which a leader is operating to one more appropriate for his leadership style. This table shows, for example, that where there is a human relations-oriented leader in Situation I we can modify *task structure* and *position power* and place him in Situation IV, where his particular leadership style is called for. The rest of the table can be interpreted in a similar manner.

An assumption in Table 1 was made that *task structure* and *position power* can be lowered, and that it was not desirable to lower *group atmosphere* from good to poor. This is why it was suggested that Situations I and III with human relations-oriented leaders be changed only to Situation IV rather than to V as well. On a common sense basis, it does not seem that *group atmosphere* should be made less favorable.

A related possibility concerns transfer or initial placement of supervisors so that their leadership style will be congruent with the group-task situation to which they are assigned. The objective is the same as the organization engineering approach but it is accomplished by moving the supervisor rather than modifying the situation. Most of the previous arguments also hold here so that little more needs to be said about this approach.

---

[9]Situation VII is not considered since the model shows an approximately zero correlation between leadership style and performance in that situation.

Table 1. Changes in Group-task Dimensions Required to Improve Productivity in Situations Where Leadership Style and Dimensions are Mismatched.

| | For Human Relations-oriented Leader | | | | For Task-oriented Leader | | | | | |
| | Change: | | | | Change: | | | | | |
Situation	From I	To IV	From IIII	To IV	From V	To I	From V	To II	From V	To III
Group-task Dimensions:										
Group Atmosphere	Good	NC*	Good	NC	Poor	Good	Poor	Good	Poor	Good
Task Structure	High	Low	Low	NC	High	NC	High	NC	High	Low
Position Power	High	Low	High	Low	High	NC	High	Low	High	NC

* NC = No Change.

PATH-GOAL THEORY OF LEADERSHIP

Robert J. House and Terence R. Mitchell

An integrated body of conjecture by students of leadership, referred to as the "Path-Goal Theory of Leadership," is currently emerging. According to this theory, leaders are effective because of their impact on subordinates' motivation, ability to perform effectively, and satisfactions. The theory is called Path-Goal because its major concern is how the leader influences the subordinates' perceptions of their work goals, personal goals and paths to goal attainment. The theory suggests that a leader's behavior is motivating or satisfying to the degree that the behavior increases subordinate goal attainment and clarifies the paths to these goals.

Historical Foundations

The path-goal approach has its roots in a more general motivational theory called expectancy theory.[1] Briefly, expectancy theory states that an individual's attitudes (e.g., satisfactions with supervision or job satisfaction) or behavior (e.g., leader behavior or job effort) can be predicted from: (1) the degree to which the job, or behavior, is seen as leading to various outcomes (expectancy) and (2) the evaluation of these outcomes (valences). Thus, people are satisfied with their job if they think it leads to things that are highly valued, and they work hard if they believe that effort leads to things that are highly valued. This type of theoretical rationale can be used to predict a variety of phenomena related to leadership, such as why leaders behave the way they do, or how leader behavior influences subordinate motivation.[2]

This latter approach is the primary concern of this article. The implication for leadership is that subordinates are motivated by leader behavior to the extent that this behavior influences expectancies, e.g., goal paths and valences, e.g., goal attractiveness.

Several writers have advanced specific hypotheses concerning how the leader affects the paths and the goals of subordinates.[3] These writers focused on two issues: (1) how the leader affects subordinates' expectations that effort will lead to effective performance and valued rewards, and (2) how this expectation affects motivation to work hard and perform well.

From *Journal of Business,* Autumn, 1974, pp. 81-97. Used by permission of the publisher.

While the state of theorizing about leadership in terms of subordinates' paths and goals is in its infancy, we believe it is promising for two reasons. First, it suggests effects of leader behavior that have not yet been investigated but which appear to be fruitful areas of inquiry. And, second, it suggests with some precision the situational factors on which the effects of leader behavior are contingent.

The initial theoretical work by Evans asserts that leaders will be effective by making rewards available to subordinates and by making these rewards contingent on the subordinate's accomplishment of specific goals.[4] Evans argued that one of the strategic functions of the leader is to clarify for subordinates the kind of behavior that leads to goal accomplishment and valued rewards. This function might be referred to as path clarification. Evans also argued that the leader increases the rewards available to subordinates by being supportive toward subordinates, i.e., by being concerned about their status, welfare and comfort. Leader supportiveness is in itself a reward that the leader has at his or her disposal, and the judicious use of this reward increases the motivation of subordinates.

Evans studied the relationship between the behavior of leaders and the subordinates' expectations that effort leads to rewards and also studied the resulting impact on ratings of the subordinates' performance. He found that when subordinates viewed leaders as being supportive (considerate of their needs) and when these superiors provided directions and guidance to the subordinates, there was a positive relationship between leader behavior and subordinates' performance ratings.

However, leader behavior was only related to subordinates' performance when the leader's behavior also was related to the subordinates' expectations that their effort would result in desired rewards. Thus, Evans' findings suggest that the major impact of a leader on the performance of subordinates is clarifying the path to desired rewards and making such rewards contingent on effective performance.

Stimulated by this line of reasoning, House and Dessler advanced a more complex theory of the effects of leader behavior on the motivation of subordinates.[6] The Theory intends to explain the effects of four specific kinds of leader behavior on the following three subordinate attitudes or expectations: (1) the satisfaction of subordinates, (2) the subordinates' acceptance of the leader and (3) the expectations of subordinates that effort will result in effective performance and that effective performance is the path to rewards. The four kinds of leader behavior included in the theory are: (1) directive leadership, (2) supportive leadership, (3) participative leadership and (4) achievement-oriented leadership. Directive leadership is characterized by a leader who lets subordinates know what is expected of them, given specific guidance as to what should be done and how it should be done, makes his or her part in the group understood, schedules work to be done, maintains definite standards of performance and asks that group members follow standard rules and regulations. Supportive leadership is characterized by a friendly and approachable leader who shows concern for the status, well-being and needs of subordinates. Such a leader does little things to make the work more pleasant, treats members as equals and is friendly and approachable. Participative leadership is characterized by a leader who consults with subordinates, solicits their suggestions and takes these suggestions seriously into consideration before making a decision. An achievement-oriented leader sets challenging goals, expects subordinates to perform at their highest level, continuously seeks improvement in performance *and* shows a high degree of confidence that the subordinates will assume responsibility, put forth effort and accomplish challenging goals. This kind of leader constantly emphasizes excellence in performance and simultaneously displays confidence that subordinates will meet high standards of excellence.

A number of studies suggest that these different leadership styles can be shown by the same leader in various situations.[6] For example, a leader may show directiveness toward subordinates in some instances and be participative or supportive in other instances.[7] Thus, the traditional method of characterizing a leader as either highly participative and supportive *or* highly directive is invalid; rather, it can be concluded that leaders vary in the particular fashion employed for supervising their subordinates. Also, the theory, in its present stages, is a tentative explanation of the effects of leader behavior—it is incomplete because it does not explain other kinds of leader behavior and does not explain the effects of the leader on factors other than subordinate acceptance, satisfaction and expectations. However, the theory is stated so that additional variables may be included in it as new knowledge is made available.

Path-Goal Theory

General Propositions

The first proposition of path-goal theory is that leader behavior is acceptable and satisfying to subordinates to the extent that the subordinates see such behavior as either an immediate source of satisfaction or as instrumental to future satisfaction.

The second proposition of this theory is that the leader's behavior will be motivational, i.e., increase effort, to the extent that (1) such behavior makes satisfaction of subordinate's needs contingent on effective performance and (2) such behavior complements the environment of subordinates by providing the coaching, guidance, support and rewards necessary for effective performance.

These two propositions suggest that the leader's strategic functions are to enhance subordinates' motivation to perform, satisfaction with the job and acceptance of the leader. From previous research on expectancy theory of motivation, it can be inferred that the strategic functions of the leader consist of:

(1) recognizing and/or arousing subordinates' needs for outcomes over which the leader has some control, (2) increasing personal payoffs to subordinates for work-goal attainment, (3) making the path to those payoffs easier to travel by coaching and direction, (4) helping subordinates clarify expectancies, (5) reducing frustrating barriers and (6) increasing the opportunities for personal satisfaction contingent on effective performance.

Stated less formally, the motivational functions of the leader consist of increasing the number and kinds of personal payoffs to subordinates for work-goal attainment and making paths to these payoffs easier to travel by clarifying the paths, reducing road blocks and pitfalls and increasing the opportunities for personal satisfaction en route.

Contingency Factors

Two classes of situational variables are asserted to be contingency factors. A contingency factor is a variable which moderates the relationship between two other variables such as leader behavior and subordinate satisfaction. For example, we might suggest that the degree of structure in the task moderates the relationship between leaders' directive behavior and subordinates' job satisfaction. Figure 1 shows how such a relationship might look. Thus, subordinates are satisfied with directive behavior in an unstructured task and are satisfied with nondirective behavior in a structured task. Therefore, we say that the relationship between leader directiveness and subordinate satisfaction is contingent upon the structure of the task.

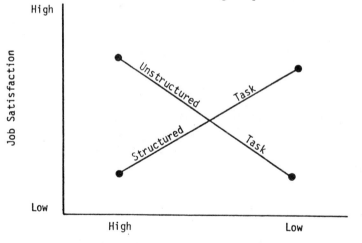

Figure 1. Hypothetical Relationship Between Directive Leadership and Subordinate Satisfaction with Task Structure as a Contingency Factor.

The two contingency variables are (a) personal characteristics of the subordinates and (b) the environmental pressures and demands with which subordinates must cope in order to accomplish the work goals and to satisfy their needs. While other situational factors also may operate to determine the effects of leader behavior, they are not presently known.

With respect to the first class of contingency factors, the characteristics of subordinates, path-goal theory asserts that leader behavior will be acceptable to subordinates to the extent that the subordinates see such behavior as either an immediate source of satisfaction or as instrumental to future satisfaction. Subordinates' characteristics are hypothesized to partially determine this perception. For example, Runyon[8] and Mitchell[9] show that the subordinate's score on a measure called Locus of Control moderates the relationship between participative leadership style and subordinate satisfaction. The Locus-of-Control measure reflects the degree to which an individual sees the environment as systematically responding to his or her behavior. People who believe that what happens to them occurs because of their behavior are called internals; people who believe that what happens to them occurs because of luck or chance are called externals. Mitchell's findings suggest that internals are more satisfied with a participative leadership style and externals are more satisfied with a directive style.

A second characteristic of subordinates on which the effects of leader behavior are contingent is subordinates' perception of their own ability with respect to their assigned tasks. The higher the degree of perceived ability relative to task demands, the less the subordinate will view leader directiveness and coaching behavior as acceptable. Where the subordinate's perceived ability is high, such behavior is likely to have little positive effect on the motivation of the subordinate and to be perceived as excessively close control. Thus, the acceptability of the leader's behavior is determined in part by the characteristics of the subordinates.

The second aspect of the situation, the environment of the subordinate, consists of those factors that are not within the control of the subordinate but which are important to need satisfaction or to ability to perform effectively. The theory asserts that effects of the leader's behavior on the psychological states of subordinates are contingent on other parts of the subordinates' environment that are relevant to subordinate motivation. Three broad classifications of contingency factors in the environment are:

- The subordinates' task

- The formal authority system of the organization

- The primary work group

Assessment of the environmental conditions makes it possible to predict the kind and amount of influence that specific leader behaviors will have on the motivation of subordinates. Any of the three environmental factors could act upon the subordinate in any of three ways: first, to serve as stimuli that motivate and direct the subordinate to perform necessary task operations; second, to constrain variability in behavior. Constraints may help the subordinate by clarifying expectancies that effort leads to rewards or by preventing the subordinate from experiencing conflict and confusion. Constraints also may be counterproductive to the extent that they restrict initiative or prevent increases in effort from being associated positively with rewards. Third, environmental factors may serve as rewards for achieving desired performance, e.g., it is possible for the subordinate to receive the necessary cues to do the job and the needed rewards for satisfaction from sources other than the leader, e.g., coworkers in the primary work group. Thus, the effect of the leader on subordinates' motivation will be a function of how deficient the environment is with respect to motivational stimuli, constraints or rewards.

With respect to the environment, path-goal theory asserts that when goals and paths to desired goals are apparent because of the routine nature of the task, clear group norms or objective controls of the formal authority systems, attempts by the leader to clarify paths and goals will be both redundant and seen by subordinates as imposing unnecessary, close control. Although such control may increase performance by preventing soldiering or malingering, it also will result in decreased satisfaction (see Figure 1). Also with respect to the work environment, the theory asserts that the more dissatisfying the task, the more the subordinates will resent leader behavior directed at increasing productivity or enforcing compliance to organizational rules and procedures.

Finally, with respect to environmental variables the theory states that leader behavior will be motivational to the extent that it helps subordinates cope with environmental uncertainties, threats from others or sources of frustration. Such leader behavior is predicted to increase subordinates' satisfaction with the job context and to be motivational to the extent that it increases the subordinates' expectations that their effort will lead to valued rewards.

These propositions and specification of situational contingencies provide a heuristic framework on which to base future research. Hopefully, this will lead to a more fully developed, explicitly formal theory of leadership.

Figure 2 presents a summary of the theory. It is hoped that these propositions, while admittedly tentative, will provide managers with some insights concerning the effects of their own leader behavior and that of others.

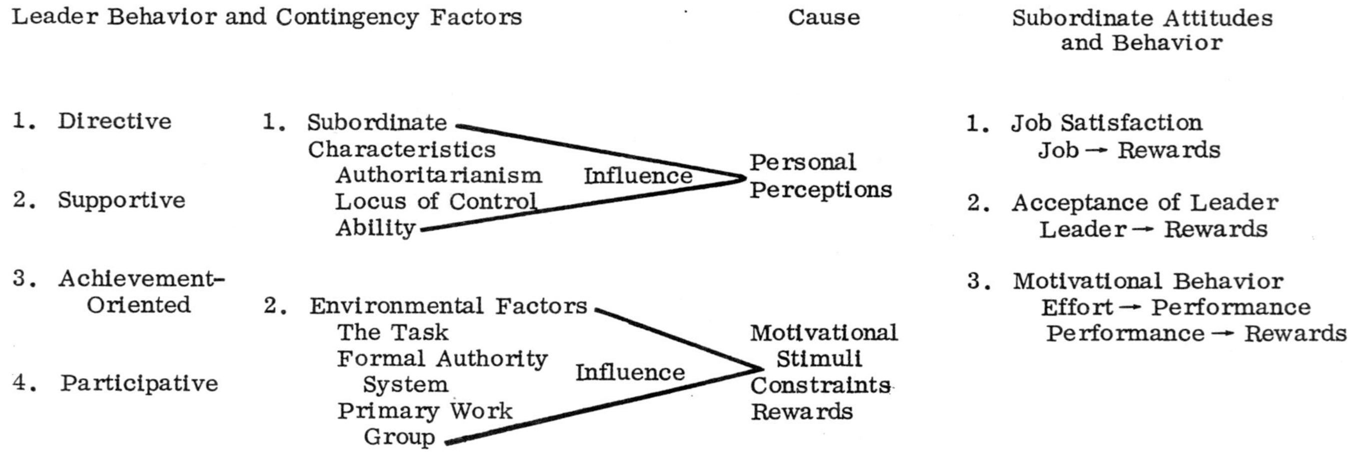

Leader Behavior and Contingency Factors   Cause   Subordinate Attitudes and Behavior

1. Directive   1. Subordinate   1. Job Satisfaction
                       Characteristics   Personal   Job → Rewards
                       Authoritarianism   Influence Perceptions
2. Supportive   Locus of Control   2. Acceptance of Leader
                       Ability   Leader → Rewards

3. Achievement-   2. Environmental Factors   Motivational   3. Motivational Behavior
   Oriented   The Task   Stimuli   Effort → Performance
                       Formal Authority   Influence Constraints   Performance → Rewards
4. Participative   System   Rewards
                       Primary Work
                       Group

Figure 2. Summary of Path-Goal Relationships.

Empirical Support

The theory has been tested in a limited number of studies which have generated considerable empirical support for our ideas and also suggest areas in which the theory requires revision. A brief review of these studies follows.

Leader Directiveness

Leader directiveness has a positive correlation with satisfaction and expectancies of subordinates who are engaged in ambiguous tasks and has a negative correlation with satisfaction and expectancies of subordinates engaged in clear tasks. These findings were predicted by the theory and have been replicated in seven organizations. They suggest that when task demands are ambiguous or when the organization procedures, rules and policies are not clear, a leader behaving in a directive manner complements the tasks and the organization by providing the necessary guidance and psychological structure for subordinates.[10] However, when task demands are clear to subordinates, leader directiveness is seen more as a hindrance.

However, other studies have failed to confirm these findings.[11] A study by Dessler[12] suggests a resolution to these conflicting findings—he found that for subordinates at the lower organizational levels of a manufacturing firm who were doing routine, repetitive, unambiguous tasks, directive leadership was preferred by closed-minded, dogmatic, authoritarian subordinates and nondirective leadership was preferred by non-authoritarian, open-minded subordinates. However, for subordinates at higher organizational levels doing non-routine, ambiguous tasks, directive leadership was preferred for both authoritarian and non-authoritarian subordinates. Thus, Dessler found that two contingency factors appear to operate simultaneously: subordinate task ambiguity and degree of subordinate authoritarianism. When measured in combination, the findings are as predicted by the theory; however, when the subordinate's personality is not taken into account, task ambiguity does not always operate as a contingency variable as predicted by the theory. House, Burill and Dessler recently found a similar interaction between subordinate authoritarianism and task ambiguity in a second manufacturing firm, thus adding confidence in Dessler's original findings.[13]

Supportive Leadership

The theory hypothesizes that supportive leadership will have its most positive effect on subordinate satisfaction for subordinates who work on stressful, frustrating or dissatisfying tasks. This hypothesis has been tested in 10 samples of employees,[14] and in only one of these studies was the hypothesis disconfirmed.[15] Despite some inconsistency in research on supportive leadership, the evidence is sufficiently positive to suggest that managers should be alert to the critical need for supportive leadership under conditions where tasks are dissatisfying, frustrating or stressful to subordinates.

Achievement-Oriented Leadership

The theory hypothesizes that achievement-oriented leadership will cause subordinates to strive for high standards of performance and to have more confidence in the ability to meet challenging goals. A recent study by House, Valency and Van der Krabben provides a partial test of this hypothesis among white collar employees in service organizations.[16] For subordinates performing ambiguous, repetitive tasks, they found a positive relationship between the amount of achievement orientation of the leader and subordinates' expectancy that their effort would result in effective performance. Stated less technically, for subordinates performing ambiguous, non-repetitive tasks, the higher the achievement orientation of the leader, the more the subordinates were confident that their efforts would pay off in effective performance. For subordinates performing moderately unambiguous, repetitive tasks, there was no significant relationship between achievement-oriented leadership and subordinate expectancies that their effort would lead to effective performance. This finding held in four separate organizations.

Two plausible interpretations may be used to explain these data. First, people who select ambiguous, nonrepetitive tasks may be different in personality from those who select a repetitive job and may, therefore, be more responsive to an achievement-oriented leader. A second explanation is that achievement orientation only affects expectancies in ambiguous situations because there is more flexibility and autonomy in such tasks. Therefore, subordinates in such tasks are more likely to be able to change in response to such leadership style. Neither of the above interpretations have been tested to date; however, additional research is currently under way to investigate these relationships.

Participative Leadership

In theorizing about the effects of participative leadership, it is necessary to ask about the specific characteristics of both the subordinates and their situation that would cause participative leadership to be viewed as satisfying and instrumental to effective performance.

Mitchell recently described at least four ways in which a participative leadership style would impact on subordinate attitudes and behavior as predicted by expectancy theory.[17] First, a participative climate should increase the clarity of organizational contingencies. Through participation in decision making, subordinates should learn what leads to what. From a path-goal viewpoint participation would lead to greater clarity of the paths to various goals. A second impact of participation would be that subordinates, hopefully, should select goals they highly value. If one participates in decisions about various goals, it makes sense that this individual would select goals he or she wants. Thus, participation would increase the correspondence between organization and subordinate goals. Third, we can see how participation would increase the control the individual has over what happens on the job. If our motivation is higher (based on the preceding two points), then having greater autonomy and ability to carry out our intentions should lead to increased effort and performance. Finally, under a participative system, pressure towards high performance should come from sources other than the leader or the organization. More specifically, when people participate in the decision process they become more ego-involved; the decisions made are in some part their own. Also, their peers know that is expected and the social pressure has a greater impact. Thus, motivation to perform well stems from internal and social factors as well as formal external ones.

A number of investigations prior to the above formulation supported the idea that participation appears to be helpful,[18] and Mitchell presents a number of recent studies that support the above four points.[19] However, it is also true that we would expect the relationship between a participative style and subordinate behavior to be moderated by both the personality characteristics of the subordinate and the situational demands. Studies by Tannenbaum and Alport and Vroom have shown that subordinates who prefer autonomy and self-control respond more positively to participative leadership in terms of both satisfaction and performance than subordinates who do not have such preferences.[20] Also, the studies mentioned by Runyon[21] and Mitchell[22] showed that subordinates who were external in orientation were less satisfied with a participative style of leadership than were internal subordinates.

House also has reviewed these studies in an attempt to explain the ways in which the situation or environment moderates the relationship between participation and subordinate attitudes and behavior.[23] His analysis suggests that where participative leadership is positively related to satisfaction, regardless of the predispositions of subordinates, the tasks of the subjects appear to be ambiguous and ego-involving. In the studies in which the subjects' personalities or predispositions moderate the effect of participative leadership, the tasks of the subjects are inferred to be highly routine and/or non-involving.

House reasoned from this analysis that the task may have an overriding effect on the relationship between leader participation and subordinate responses, and that individual predispositions or personality characteristics of subordinates may have an effect only under some tasks. It was assumed that when task demands are ambiguous, subordinates will have a need to reduce the ambiguity. Further, it was assumed that when task demands are ambiguous, participative problem solving between the leader and the subordinate will result in more effective decisions than when the task demands are unambiguous. Finally, it was assumed that when the subordinates are ego-involved in their tasks they are more likely to want to have a say in the decisions that affect them. Given these assumptions, the following hypotheses were formulated to account for the conflicting findings reviewed above:

- When subjects are highly ego-involved in a decision or a task and the decision or task demands are ambiguous, participative leadership will have a positive effect on the satisfaction and motivation of the subordinate, *regardless* of the subordinate's predisposition toward self-control, authoritarianism or need for independence.

- When subordinates are not ego-involved in their tasks and when task demands are clear, subordinates who are not authoritarian and who have high needs for independence and self-control will respond favorably to leader participation and their opposite personality types will respond less favorably.

These hypotheses were derived on the basis of path-goal theorizing; i.e., the rationale guiding the analysis of prior studies was that both task characteristics and characteristics of subordinates interact to determine the effect of a specific kind of leader behavior on the satisfaction, expectancies and performance of subordinates. To date, one major investigation has supported some of these predictions[24] in which personality variables, amount of participative leadership, task ambiguity and job satisfaction were assessed for 324 employees of an industrial manufacturing organization. As expected, in non-repetitive, ego-involving tasks, employees (regardless of their personality) were more satisfied under a participative style than a non-participative style. However, in repetitive tasks which were less ego-involving, the amount of authoritarianism of subordinates moderated the relationship between leadership style and satisfaction. Specifically, low authoritarian subordinates were *more satisfied* under a participative style. These findings are exactly as the theory would predict, thus, it has promise in reconciling a set of confusing and contradictory findings with respect to participative leadership.

Summary and Conclusions

We have attempted to describe what we believe is a useful theoretical framework for understanding the effect of leadership behavior on subordinate satisfaction and motivation. Most theorists today have moved away from the simplistic notions that all effective leaders have a certain set of personality traits or that the situation completely determines performance. Some researchers have presented rather complex attempts at matching certain types of leaders with certain types of situations, e.g., the articles written by Vroom and Fiedler in this issue. But, we believe that a path-goal approach goes one step further. It not only suggests what type of style may be most effective in a given situation—it also attempts to explain *why* it is most effective.

We are optimistic about the future outlook of leadership research. With the guidance of path-goal theorizing, future research is expected to unravel many confusing puzzles about the reasons for and effects of leader behavior that have, heretofore, not been solved. However, we add a word of caution: the theory, and the research on it, are relatively new to the literature of organizational behavior. Consequently, path-goal theory is offered more as a tool for directing research and stimulating insight than as a proven guide for managerial action.

Footnotes

* This article is also to be reprinted in *Readings in Organizational and Industrial Psychology* by G. A. Yukl and K. N. Wexley, 2nd edition (1975). The research by House and his associates was partially supported by a grant from the Shell Oil Company of Canada. The research by Mitchell and his associates was partially supported by the Office of Naval Research Contract NR-170-761, N00014-67-A-0103-0032 (Terence R. Mitchell, Principal Investigator)

1. T. R. Mitchell, "Expectancy Model of Job Satisfaction, Occupational Preference and Effort: A Theoretical, Methodological and Empirical Appraisal," *Psychological Bulletin* (1974, in press).

2. D. M. Nebeker and T. R. Mitchell, "Leader Behavior: An Expectancy Theory Approach," *Organization Behavior and Human Performance,* 11(1974), pp. 355–367.

3. M. G. Evans, "The Effects of Supervisory Behavior on the Path-Goal Relationship," *Organization Behavior and Human Performance,* 55(1970), pp. 277–298; T. H. Hammer and H. T. Dachler, "The Process of Supervision in the Context of Motivation Theory," Research Report No. 3 (University of Maryland, 1973); F. Dansereau, Jr., J. Cashman and G. Graen, "Instrumentality Theory and Equity Theory As Complementary Approaches in Predicting the Relationship of Leadership and Turnover Among Managers," *Organization Behavior and Human Performance,* 10(1973), pp. 184–200; R. J. House, "A Path-Goal Theory of Leader Effectiveness," *Adminis-*

trative Science Quarterly, 16, 3(September 1971), pp. 321–338; T. R. Mitchell, "Motivation and Participation: An Integration," *Academy of Management Journal,* 16, 4(1973), pp. 160–179; G. Graen, F. Dansereau, Jr. and T. Minami, Dysfunctional Leadership Styles," *Organization Behavior and Human Performance,* 7(1972), pp. 216–236;_____, "An Empirical Test of the Man-in-the-Middle Hypothesis Among Executives in a Hierarchical Organization Employing a Unit Analysis," *Organization Behavior and Human Performance,* 8(1972), pp. 262–285; R. J. House and G. Dessler, "The Path-Goal Theory of Leadership: Some Post Hoc and A Priori Tests," to appear in J. G. Hunt, ed., *Contingency Approaches to Leadership* (Carbondale, Ill.: Southern Illinois University Press, 1974).

4. M. G. Evans, "Effects of Supervisory Behavior";_____, "Extensions of a Path-Goal Theory of Motivation," *Journal of Applied Psychology,* 59 (1974), pp. 172–178.

5. R. J. House, "A Path-Goal Theory"; R. J. House and G. Dessler, "Path-Goal Theory of Leadership."

6. R. J. House and G. Dessler, "Path-Goal Theory of Leadership"; R. M. Stogdill, *Managers, Employees, Organization* (Ohio State University, Bureau of Business Research, 1965); R. J. House, A. Valency and R. Van der Krabben, "Some Tests and Extensions of the Path-Goal Theory of Leadership" (in preparation)

7. W. A. Hill and D. Hughes, "Variations in Leader Behavior As a Function of Task Type," *Organization Behavior and Human Performance* (1974, in press).

8. K. E. Runyon, "Some Interactions Between Personality Variables and Management Styles," *Journal of Applied Psychology,* 57, 3(1973), pp. 288–294; T. R. Mitchell, C. R. Smyser and S. E. Weed, "Locus of Control: Supervision and Work Satisfaction," *Academy of Management Journal* (in press).

9. T. R. Mitchell, "Locus of Control."

10. R. J. House, "A Path-Goal Theory"; _____ and G. Dessler, "Path-Goal Theory of Leadership"; A. D. Szalagyi and H. P. Sims, "An Exploration of the Path-Goal Theory of Leadership in a Health Care Environment," *Academy of Management Journal* (in press); J. D. Dermer, "Supervisory Behavior and Budget Motivation" (Cambridge, Mass.: unpublished, MIT, Sloan School of Management, 1974); R. W. Smetana," The Relationship Between Managerial Behavior and

Subordinate Attitudes and Motivation: A Contribution to a Behavioral Theory of Leadership" (Ph.D. diss., Wayne State University, 1974).

11. S. E. Weed, T. R. Mitchell and C. R. Smyser, "A Test of House's Path-Goal Theory of Leadership in an Organizational Setting" (paper presented at Western Psychological Association, 1974); J. D. Dermer and J. P. Siege, "A Test of Path-Goal Theory: Disconfirming Evidence and a Critique" (unpublished, University of Toronto, Faculty of Management Studies, 1973); R. S. Schuler, "A Path-Goal Theory of Leadership: An Empirical Investigation" (Ph.D. diss., Michigan State University, 1973); H. K. Downer, J. E. Sheridan and J. W. Slocum, Jr., "Analysis of Relationships Among Leader Behavior, Subordinate Job Performance and Satisfaction: A Path-Goal Approach" (unpublished mimeograph, 1974); J. E. Stinson and T. W. Johnson, "The Path-Goal Theory of Leadership: A Partial Test and Suggested Refinement," *Proceedings* (Kent, Ohio: 7th Annual Conference of the Midwest Academy of Management, April 1974), pp. 18–36.

12. G. Dessler, "An Investigation of the Path-Goal Theory of Leadership" (Ph.D. diss., City University of New York, Bernard M. Baruch College, 1973).

13. R. J. House, D. Burrill and G. Dessler, "Tests and Extensions of Path-Goal Theory of Leadership, I" (unpublished, in process).

14. R. J. House, "A Path-Goal Theory"; _____ and G. Dessler, "Path-Goal Theory of Leadership"; A. D. Szalagyi and H. P. Sims, "Exploration of Path-Goal"; J. E. Stinson and T. W. Johnson, Proceedings; R. S. Schuler, "Path-Goal: Investigation"; H. K. Downer, J. E. Sheridan and J. W. Slocum, Jr., "Analysis of Relationships"; S. E. Weed, T. R. Mitchell and C. R. Smyser, "Test of House's Path-Goal."

15. A. D. Szalagyi and H. P. Sims, "Exploration of Path Goal."

16. R. J. House, A. Valency and R. Van der Krabben, "Tests and Extensions of Path-Goal Theory of Leadership, II" (unpublished, in process).

17. T. R. Mitchell, "Motivation and Participation."

18. H. Tosi, "A Reexamination of Personality As a Determinant of the Effects of Participation," *Personnel Psychology,* 23(1970), pp. 91–99; J. Sadler "Leadership Style, Confidence in Management and Job Satisfaction," *Journal of Applied Behavioral Sciences,* 6(1970), pp. 3–19; K. N. Wexley, J. P. Singh and J. A. Yukl, "Subordinate Personality As a Moderator of the Effects of Participation in Three Types of Appraisal Interviews," *Journal of Applied Psychology,* 83 1(1973), pp. 54–59.

19. T. R. Mitchell, "Motivation and Participation."

20. A. S. Tannenbaum and F. H. Allport, "Personality Structure and Group Structure: An Interpretive Study of Their Relationship Through an Event-Structure Hypothesis," *Journal of Abnormal and Social Psychology,* 53(1956), pp. 272–280; V. H. Vroom, "Some Personality Determinants of the Effects of Participation," *Journal of Abnormal and Social Psychology,* 59(1959), pp. 322–327.

21. K. E. Runyon, "Some Interactions Between Personality Variables and Management Styles," *Journal of Applied Psychology,* 57, 3(1973), pp. 288–294.

22. T. R. Mitchell, C. R. Smyser and S. E. Weed, "Locus of Control."

23. R. J. House, "Notes on the Path-Goal Theory of Leadership" (University of Toronto, Faculty of Management Studies, May 1974).

24. R. S. Schuler, "Leader Participation, Task Structure and Subordinate Authoritarianism." (unpublished mimeograph, Cleveland State University, 1974).

AN OVERVIEW OF THE GRID

Robert R. Blake and Jane Srygley Mouton

Organizations can change but, will they?

Dramatic changes are occurring in the way Americans handle their affairs. This is true across the spectrum, from commercial firms to government agencies, to schools and universities. What these are, and how they can be met and brought under management is discussed below.

Breakdown of Authority and Obedience

In the past, bosses could exercise work-or-starve authority over their subordinates. They expected and got obedience from them. Authority-obedience was the basis for supervision that built pyramids, big ships, great armies, and that made Prussia famous.

But authority-obedience as a way of life has been under greater and greater attack for the past hundred years. Though wars tended to bring it back, during peacetime it became more and more objectionable as a basis for getting people to cooperate. But today, in an environment of vastly improved education and of relative affluence, many are rejecting traditional authority and trying to set up and act upon their own.

The year 1968 might be taken as the beginning of the end for authority-obedience as the control mechanism of American society. That was the year when Detroit and Watts burned. It was when young people were burning their draft cards and dodging the draft by heading for Canada, Sweden and elsewhere. And it was when several universities' presidents were held as hostages in their offices. Furthermore, truancy, runaways and drug problems tell us that the old family pattern where father was boss and the children complied with his authority has crumbled too.

The 1964 Civil Rights Act put society on notice that equality, not authority and obedience, was to be the basis for race relations in the future. Other federal legislation established standards for organizations to be more responsible for the safety of their employees, for their customers and for the everyday citizen as well.

Understanding all this new found and partly enforced equality and social justice and the motivations that underlie it is important for comprehending the new day that is emerging.

These many influences tell us as far as bosses and subordinates are concerned that authority and obedience is no longer the name of the game.

The new relationship between a "boss" and a "subordinate" is such that they seek to reach mutual understanding and agreement as to the course of action to be taken, as well as how to go about it. Before coming to any conclusion on the "how," though, the *main* alternative ways of managing will be presented. First examined is how management occurs under an authority-obedience system and its strengths and weaknesses. Then the "love conquers all" proposition will be considered. This is where the boss says, "If my subordinates love me, they'll do what I want without me having to tell them."

Then those hard-to-notice managers who are doing the least amount to get by on a "see no evil, speak no evil, hear no evil" basis will be viewed. Next to be described is the "halfway is far enough" manager who deals with problems by compromise, adjustment, and accommodation of differences, by being willing to do what's "practical." Finally the possibility already introduced, seeking for excellence through getting the highest possible involvement-participation-commitment to organization purpose, up and down the line, is evaluated.

The Grid

The Grid is a way of sorting out all these possibilities and seeing how each compares with the others. What is involved is this:

The Grid, shown in Figure 1, clarifies and crystallizes many of the different possible ways of supervision. Here is the basis of it. Any person who is working has some assigned responsibilities. This is true whether he or she works very low on the job ladder or high up in the organization. There are two matters on his or her mind whenever acting as a manager. One is *production*—getting results or accomplishing the mission. How intensely he or she thinks about results can be described as a degree of concern for production. On the Grid, the horizontal axis stands for concern for production. It is a nine-point scale where 9 shows high concern for production and 1, low concern.

A manager is also thinking about those whose work he or she directs, because he or she has to get results through people. The Grid's vertical axis represents this concern for people. This, too, is on a nine-point scale with 9 a high degree and 1 a low degree.

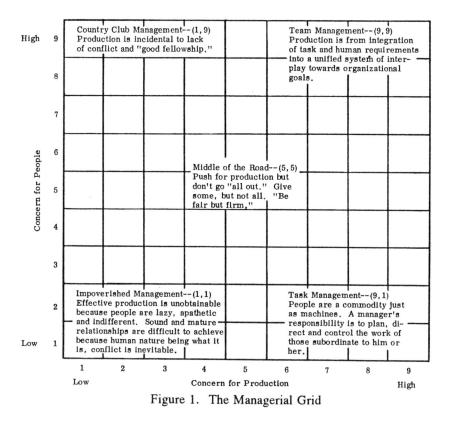

Figure 1. The Managerial Grid

The Grid identifies these two concerns. It does so in a way that enables a person to see how the two concerns interact. Various "theories" are found at points of intersection of the two scales. Whether he or she realizes it or not, these are theories that different managers use when they think about how to get results through people. Five of the many possible theories or styles of management mentioned earlier stand out clearly. They appear in the four corners and in the center of the Grid.

Going Around the Grid

As can be seen from the Grid figure, in the lower right corner, 9,1 represents a great deal of concern for output but little for the people who are expected to produce. 9,1 is the authority-obedience theory. At the opposite corner of the Grid, the top left, is the 1,9 theory. It's the "love conquers all" approach. In the lower left Grid corner is 1,1. It might seem odd that a manager could have almost no concern for either production or people. He or she goes through the motions of being part of the organization but is not really contributing to it. But such managers do exist, even though they may not be easy to notice until you know their theory. They are not doers but freeloaders, getting by on a "speak no, hear no, see no evil" basis. They have not physically quit the firm, but they walked out mentally, perhaps many years ago.

In the center is the 5,5 style. The manager with this approach is going up the middle of the road. His or her attitude is, "Get results but don't kill yourself! Don't push too much or you will be seen as a 'hard nose.' Don't let people off too easily or they will think you are soft. Be fair but firm. Do the job but find a comfortable tempo." The 5,5 manager is an "organization man."

The upper right corner, the 9,9 position, is high concern for production united with high concern for people. A person who manages according to this theory stresses understanding and agreement through involvement-participation-commitment as the key to solving boss-subordinate problems. Whenever disagreements arise, he or she sees to it that facts are examined. The problem is thrashed through to solution in an open and aboveboard way that can result in mutual understanding with full commitment to conclusions reached. People working together in a 9,9 manner know that they have a common stake in the outcome of their endeavors. They mesh effort in an interdependent way. The 9,9 theory doesn't abide by the laws of simple arithmetic. On the joining of contributions, "one" plus "one" can add up to "three."

You may have figured out that there are 81 combinations of concerns represented on the Grid. Adjacent to 9,1 are 8,2 and 7,3. And 1,9 has 2,8 and 3,7 near it. There are 3,3 4,4 6,6, 7,7 along the diagonal between 1,1 and 9,9 and so on. But our main emphasis are the most distinct styles. They're the ones you see most often. But you might think of a Grid style as you do shades of hair—black, brown, red, blond and white.

Within each hair shade there's a variety—for example, twenty-seven different ways to be blond—yet on your driver's license the outstanding feature is enough for identification. The five main Grid styles, too, are broadly descriptive. We'll use them in much the same way. While talking about 9,1, remember it's just a tinge away to 8,2 or 7,3, or a halftone or so to 6,4, but all these neighboring combinations describe behavior in broadly similar ways.

Basic Assumptions

Grid theories describe sets of basic assumptions under which people deal with one another. An *assumption* is what you take for granted as being true or reliable. Maybe you learned most of your present-day assumptions as you grew up. "I have to be . . . (a tough character or nice person) . . . to get what I want," illustrates some assumptions from childhood that persist. In supervision they lay down the pathway of the boss's everyday approach. Managers act on the assumptions they hold even though it may be rare for you to put them into words. The same set of assumptions usually underlies a whole range of attitudes and activities.

For example, a 1,9-oriented boss who wants to please subordinates may be quite inventive in finding all sorts of ways to show personal warmth. His or her behavior may not be so simple as to say "I appreciate you and everything you do" 25 times a day, but, nonetheless, the subordinate dominates his or her thoughts and concerns. His or her subordinate might say, "I never know what nice surprise the boss will think up next," and yet the manager's core assumptions are remarkably consistent—to please his or her subordinate and win their appreciation.

Were persons to act without assumptions, their behavior would be random, purposeless; it would make no sense in any predictable way. Even so, it is not enough just to have a set of assumptions—an old set. Faulty assumptions can ruin a manger. More reliable ones can enhance his or her work and enrich his or her life on the job, not to mention elsewhere. When a person acting under any set of assumptions understands them, that Grid knowledge can aid him or her to predict what the impact of his or her behavior will be on colleagues and subordinates. Thus, learning the Grid framework will help you understand what kinds of actions are likely to lead to what kind of results.

"Dominants" and "Backups"

Does a manager have just one Grid style strategy or does he or she skip over the surface of the Grid, shifting and adapting according to how he or she sees the situation?

All but a very few do have characteristic styles which, presently they are using most of the time. Let's call this the manager's *dominant* style. Each boss's basic approach resembles one that is founded on either 9,1; 1,9; 5,5; 1,1 or 9,9 assumptions. How can the idea that a person has a dominant Grid style be squared with the fact that people observably do shift and change? It can be understood in the following way. Not only does a supervisor have a dominant style, he or she also has a back-up strategy and sometimes a third strategy to fall back on even beyond the second way of operating.

The back-up strategy is likely to show when a manager runs up against difficulty in using the dominant strategy. A back-up Grid strategy is the one he or she falls back on, particularly when feeling the strain of tension, frustration or conflict. This can happen when initial efforts meet nothing but resistance or when, at the point of getting down to working on a project, the subordinate's enthusiasm turns to stubborn reluctance.

Apparent complexity, when you first encounter it, can be confusing. Maybe you have played with a kaleidoscope. It contains bits of glass, not many, of different shapes and colors, and these can arrange themselves in an endless variety of patterns that you see reflected from its mirrors. Children are fascinated yet bewildered by this. When the key to understanding has been found, however, what previously appeared bewildering now makes sense.

Any Grid style can be a back-up to any other. For example, even a 1,9-oriented manager, when sharply challenged, might turn stubborn and go 9,1. Again, a person who normally deals in a 9,9 way may meet continued resistance from a subordinate. Unable to find a way of getting on to an action basis with him or her, he or she may shift to a 5,5 approach, negotiating for some kind of compromise where both boss and subordinate will be partially satisfied.

There are no natural links between one particular Grid style and another in terms of dominant-to-back-up. It all depends on the individual and his or her situation. You may sometimes see a person who habitually comes on in a 9,1 way, pressing hard for a time, then breaking off, crestfallen. He or she has switched to a different set of assumptions and moved back to a 1,1 state of resignation, feeling a sense of powerlessness, feeling that he or she is a victim of hostile fate. Who knows, had he or she used a different style from the beginning, or another set of back-up assumptions, and continued talking with the subordinate, he or she might have gotten the reaction desired.

The 9,9 approach is acknowledged by managers as the soundest way to achieve excellence. This conclusion has been verified from studies throughout the U.S. and around the world. The 9,9 theory defines a model that people say with conviction they want, not only for a guide to their own conduct, but also as a model of what they want their organization and agencies to become.

That's what the Grid is. The Grid can be used to investigate how a boss supervises in everyday work. There are many boss-subordinate issues that can be looked at in this way. How boss and subordinate communicate is one. Another is the manner in which the boss gives work directions. Others involve managing mistakes, dealing with complaints, and how the boss reacts to hostile feelings.

Change

There are many approaches to change and development, but two are of particular importance in business, industry and government. One critical development step involves the matter of performance evaluation, i.e., how the boss talks with a subordinate to help him or her increase effectiveness. This is individual development. The other, to be treated later, involves *organizational development.*

Individual Development

A special word needs to be said about person-to-person individual development. One of the major approaches used today to help people develop involves having bosses interview their subordinates, usually once a year but with the option of doing so more frequently, to help each subordinate see how he or she is performing and how he or she might do better.

This performance review and evaluation involves a more or less prescribed procedure. It starts with the boss and (in principle) the subordinate mutually setting up performance standards and measures of results. The second step, perhaps a year later, or at the end of a briefer period, is for the boss and subordinate to hold another session to review how well the subordinate did in meeting specific and agreed performance standards.

Then, whether simultaneously at annual performance rating time or not, the boss, working alone, also calibrates subordinate performance in terms of standard categories on a rating for such as "responsibility" and "initiative," which apply to all jobs. These evaluations are intended to be used for several purposes. One is for aiding a subordinate to see how he or she can improve performance. Another is to identify special training and development opportunities. Most generally they are used as the basis for pay raises, promotion and termination.

A boss can do any one of these things in a 9,1; 1,9; 1,1; 5,5 or 9,9 way, and, as you can well appreciate, the quality of individual development, if any, hangs in the balance.

Organization Development

Sound management can only meet the challenge of change by seeing the deeper issue: organization development. But a blueprint of an excellent organization is needed to describe an organization so well managed that it can grasp opportunity from the challenge of change. What would such an organization be like?

1. *Its objectives would be sound, strong, and clear.* Its leaders would know where it was headed and how to get there. Its objectives would also be understood and embraced by all members of the management body. These persons would strive to contribute because the organization's objectives and their own goals would be consistent. There would be a high level of commitment to organization goals as well as to personal goals. Commitment would be based on understanding. To be understood, goals would be quite specific.

Every business has an objective, "profit." But this is too vague to motivate persons to greater effectiveness. Profit needs to be converted into concrete objectives. One might be, "To develop a position in the plastic industry which will service 20 percent of this market within the next five years." In a government organization, a specific objective might be "To establish six urban renewal demonstration projects distributed by regions and by city size within 10 months." Government objectives would be implemented through program planning and budgeting rather than the profit motive.

2. *Standards of excellence would be high.* Managers would be thoroughly acquainted with their areas of operation. A premium would be placed on knowledge and thorough analysis rather than on opinion and casual thought.

3. *The work culture would support the work.* It would be an organization culture in which the members would be highly committed to achieving the goals of the organization, with accomplishment the source of individual gratification.

4. *Teamwork would increase individual initiative.* There would be close cooperation within a work team, each supporting the others to get a job done. Teamwork would cut across department lines.

5. *Technical business knowledge is needed.* This is critical for valid decision-making and problem-solving and would come through coaching, developmental assignments, on-the-job training and special courses.

6. *Leadership would be evident.* With sound objectives, high standards of excellence, and a culture characterized by high commitment, sound teamwork and technical know-how, productivity would increase.

The way of life or culture of an organization can be a barrier to effectiveness. Barriers may stem from such elements of culture as the attitudes or traditions present in any unit of the organization. Culture both limits and guides the actions of the persons in the organization. Because of traditional ways and fear of change, an organization's leaders may be reluctant to apply modern management science. Yet, the need for change may be quite evident.

Criteria for Change

A sound approach to introducing change and improvement is a *Grid Organization Development* effort. It should:

1. *Involve the widest possible participation of executives, managers and supervisors* to obtain a common set of concepts about how management can be improved.

2. *Be carried out by the organization itself.* The development of subordinates is recognized as part of the manager's job. When organization members from the line become the instructors, higher management's commitment, understanding and support for on-the-job application and change are ensured.

3. *Aim to improve the skills of executives and supervisors who must work together to improve management.* This means the skills of drawing on each other's knowledge and capacities, of making constructive use of disagreement and of making sound decisions to which members become committed.

4. *Aim to improve the ability of all managers to communicate better* so that genuine understanding can prevail.

5. *Clarify styles of management* so that managers learn how the elements of a formal management program (e.g., planned objectives, defined responsibilities, established policies) can be used without the organization's becoming overly formal and complex or unduly restricting personal freedom and needed individual initiative.

6. *Aid each manager to investigate managerial style* to understand its impact and learn to make changes to improve it.

7. *Provide for examination of the organization's culture* to develop managers' understanding of the cultural barriers to effectiveness and how to eliminate them.

8. *Constantly encourage managers to plan and introduce improvements* based on their learning and analysis of the organization.

How to Get There

Grid Organization Development is one way of increasing the effectiveness of an organization, whether it is a company, a public institution or a government agency. The behavioral science concepts on which organization development is based reach back more than 50 years. Because organization development itself is only a decade or so old, those unfamiliar with its rationale may look upon it with doubt or skepticism, see it as a mystery or a package, a gimmick or a fad. Experience pin-points which behavioral science concepts are tied to the struggle for a more effective organization. This has done much to help managers apply the pertinent concepts to everyday work.

There are several questions preceding the definition of organization development as it is applied to raise an organization's capacity to operate by using behavioral science concepts. One question is, "What is an organization?" Another is, "What is meant by development?" Finally, "What is it that organization development adds to the organization, that it lacks without it?" The goal of organization development is to increase operational effectiveness by increasing the degree of integration of the organization around its profit/production/or service purpose.

It seems almost self-evident that everyone in an organization would have a clear idea of the *purpose* toward which its efforts were being directed. Yet this is seldom true. For many persons, an organization's purpose is fuzzy, unrealistic and with little force as a motivator. A major organization development contribution is to clarify organization purposes and identify individual goals with them to increase efforts toward their attainment.

As for the *human interaction* process, some styles of managing may decrease a person's desire to contribute to the organization's purpose. The kind of supervision exercised not only fails to make a subordinate feel "in" but even serves to make him or her feel "out." His or her efforts are alienated rather than integrated. This may hold true in the coordination of efforts between organized units. Relationships between divisions, for example, may deteriorate into the kind of disputes that can be reconciled only through arbitration by higher levels of management. At best, they are likely to encourage attitudes of appeasement and compromise.

The organization's culture, its history, its traditions, its customs and habits which have evolved from earlier interaction and have become norms regulating human actions and conduct may be responsible for many of the organization's difficulties and a low degree of integration within it.

Organization development deliberately shifts the emphasis away from the organization's structure, from human technical skill, from wherewithal and results per se as it diagnoses the organization's ills. Focusing on organization purpose, the human interaction process and organization culture, it accepts these as the areas in which problems are preventing the fullest possible integration within the organization. Once an organization has moved to the point of which the three key properties are fully developed, the problems that originally seemed to be related to the others are more easily corrected.

Six Phase Approach

How, specifically, does one go about organization development? The Managerial Grid is one way of achieving it. The six-phase approach provides the various methods and activities for doing so.

Phase 1 of the six-phase approach involves study of *The Managerial Grid*. Managers learn the Grid concepts in seminars of a week's length.

These seminars are conducted both on a "public" and on an internal basis. They involve hard work. The program requires 30 or more hours of guided study before the beginning of the seminar week. A seminar usually begins Sunday evening, and participants work morning, afternoon and evening through the following Friday.

The sessions include investigation by each person of his or her own managerial approach and alternative ways of managing which he or she is able to learn, experiment with and apply. He or she measures and evaluates team effectiveness in solving problems with others. He or she also studies methods of team action. A high point of Grid Seminar learning is when he or she receives a critique of his or her team. The emphasis is on personal style of managing, not on character or personality traits. Another high point of the Grid Seminar is when the manager critiques the style of his or her organization's culture, its traditions, precedents and past practices, and begins to consider steps for increasing the effectiveness of the whole organization.

Participants in a Grid Seminar can expect to gain insight into their own and other managerial approaches and develop new ways to solve managerial problems. They can expect to improve team effectiveness skills. They will on completion of Phase 1 have new standards of candor to bring to work activities and a greater awareness of the effects of their company's culture upon the regulation of work.

Comments are often heard to the effect, "The Grid has helped me to a better understanding and is useful in many aspects of my life." But the vital question is in the use made of Phase 1 learning. The test for the manager is usefulness on the job. To direct this usefulness to the work situation, and incidentally enhance it from a personal point of view, one proceeds to Phase 2.

Work Team Development

Phase 2 is Work Team Development. As the title suggests, work team development is concerned with development of the individual and the work team. Phases 1 and 2 are often viewed as *management* development. The purpose of Phase 2 is to aid work team members to apply their Phase 1 learning directly to the operation of their team.

Individual effort is the raw material out of which sound teamwork is built! It cannot be had just for the asking. Barriers that prevent people from talking out their problems need to be overcome before their full potential can be realized.

Work team development starts with the key executive and those who report to him or her. It then moves down through the organization. Each supervisor sits down with subordinates as a team. They study their barriers to work effectiveness and plan ways to overcome them. An important result to be expected from the Phase 2 effort is teamwide agreement on ground rules for team operation. The team may also be expected to learn to use critique to improve teamwork on the job. Teamwork is increased through improving communication, control and problem-solving. Getting greater objectivity into work behavior is vital to improved teamwork.

A team analysis of the team culture and operating practices precedes the setting of goals for improvement of the team operation along with a time schedule for achieving these goals. Tied into the goal-setting for the team is personal goal-setting by team members. This might be a goal for trying to change aspects of behavior so as to increase a member's contribution to teamwork. Setting standards for achieving excellence are involved throughout the process.

Intergroup Development

Phase 3 is Intergroup Development. It represents the first step in Grid OD that is applied to organization components rather than to individuals. Its purpose is to achieve *better problem-solving between groups through a closer integration of units that have working interrelationships!*

Managers examine and analyze these working relationships to strengthen and unify the organization across the board. Some dramatic examples of successful

Phase 3 applications between labor and management groups are on record. Other units that might appropriately be involved in Phase 3 would be a field unit and the headquarters group to whom it reports, or two sections within a division, or a region and its reporting parent group. It is the matter of coordination between such units that is the target of Phase 3. Problems of integration may be problems of function or merely problems in terms of level.

Management is inclined to solve the problem of functional coordination by setting up systems of reporting and centralized planning. Misunderstandings or disagreements between levels are often viewed as "a communications problem." Phase 3, in recognition that many problems are relationship problems, seeks closer integration of units through the exchange and comparison of group images as set forth by the members of two groups.

Areas of misunderstanding are identified while conditions are created to reduce such intergroup problems and plan steps of operational coordination between the groups. Only groups that stand in a direct, problem-solving relationship with one another and share a need for improved coordination participate in Phase 3 intergroup development. And only those members with key responsibilities for solving the coordination problem are participants.

The activities of Phase 3 naturally follow Phase 2 because when there is conflict between working teams, if the teams themselves have already had the opportunity to solve their internal problems, they are prepared to engage in activities designed to solve their problem of working together. Phase 3 also can be expected to clear the decks for Phases 4 and 5. Any past intergroup problems that were barriers to coordinated effort are solved before the total organization development effort is launched in the latter phases.

A successful Phase 3 will link groups vertically and horizontally and reduce intergroup blockages. This increases the problem-solving between departments, divisions and other segments wherever coordination of effort is a vital necessity. Persons who have participated in Phase 3 report improved intergroup relationships and express appreciation of the team management concept, pointing out that it reverses the traditional procedure in which criticism flows from one level of management down to the next.

Organization Blueprint

Phase 4 calls for the Production of an Organization Blueprint. Phases 1, 2 and 3 represent pruning the branches. Phase 4 gets at the root structure. A long-range blueprint is developed to ensure that the basic strategies of the organization are "right." The immediate goal is to set up a model that is both realistic and obtainable for an organization's system for the future. How is this done? The existing corporate entity is momentarily set aside while an ideal concept is drawn up representing how it would be organized and operated if it were truly effective. The optimal organization blueprint is produced as a result of a policy diagnosis based on study of a model organization culture. The blueprint is drawn up by the top team and moves down through lower levels. The outcome is organization-wide understanding of the blueprint for the future.

It can be expected that as a result of Phase 4, the top team will have set a direction of performance goals to be achieved. Individuals and work teams will have developed understanding and commitment to both general and specific goals to be achieved.

Blueprint Implementation

Phase 5 is Blueprint Implementation. That is, Phase 5 is designed for the carrying out of the organizational plan through activities that change the organization from what it "is" to what it "should be." A Phase 5 may spread over several years, but as a result there comes about the effective realization of the goals that have been set in Phase 4 and specific accomplishments, depending on concrete issues facing the organization. During Phase 5, the members who are responsible for the organization achieve agreement and commitment to courses of action that represent steps to implement the Phase 4 blueprint for the future.

Stabilization

Phase 6 is Stabilization. It is for reinforcing and making habitual the new patterns of management achieved in Phases 1 through 5. Organization members identify tendencies to slip back into the older and less effective patterns of work and take corrective action. Phase 6 involves an overall critique of the state of the OD effort for the purpose of replanning for even greater effectiveness. It is not only to support and strengthen the changes achieved through earlier activities, but also to identify weaknesses and plan ways of eliminating them.

By the time Phase 6 is under way, the stabilization of new communication, control and problem-solving approaches should be evident. Moveover, there should be complete managerial confidence and competence in resisting the pressures to revert to old managerial habits.

As we see our business, government and educational institutions facing crisis after crisis, we realize the need for change becomes more imperative with each passing day. Behavioral science ideas and technology now provide a way through which need can become actuality.

"Organizations *can* change!" This issue is *will* they? Problems are inherent in every organization. What is needed is the will, determination and effort to solve them.

Reference

1.   Robert R. Blake and Jane Srygley Mouton, The Managerial Grid Laboratory-Seminar Materials. Austin, Texas: Scientific Methods, Inc., 1972.

THE FMI: DIMENSIONS OF FOLLOWER MATURITY

Loren I. Moore

Leaders cannot lead without followers. In any group task situation, followers are vital. As individuals, they can accept or reject a leader; as a group, they determine whatever personal effectiveness a leader may have. While most leadership theories hold that leader effectiveness is a function of the group's cooperation, receptivity, etc., no current strategies are available to categorize and quantify the dimensions of follower maturity. The Follower Maturity Index (FMI), an instrument derived, in part, from life-cycle leadership theory (Hersey & Blanchard, 1972) and based on observations of verbal and nonverbal behavior in a variety of task groups, constitutes a first step toward a description of maturity in follower behavior.

This article briefly outlines the theory on which the instrument is based and definitively outlines the specifics of the instrument.

LIFE-CYCLE THEORY

Life-cycle leadership theory (Hersey & Blanchard, 1972) posits a curvilinear relationship between the leader's task- and relationship-oriented behavior and follower maturity over a period of time.

Beginning with structured task behavior, the appropriate behavior for working with immature followers or groups, the life-cycle theory of leadership suggests that the leader's behavior should move through (1) high task-low relationship behavior to (2) high task-high relationship and (3) from high relationship-low task to (4) low task-low relationship behavior as (and if) the followers progress from immaturity to maturity (Figure 1).

The life-cycle theory of leadership focuses on the appropriateness or effectiveness of leadership styles, according to the level of maturity of the followers at any given time for any specific task. Some bench marks of maturity have been provided (Figure 1) for determining appropriate leadership style by dividing the maturity continuum into three categories: low, average, and high maturity. The theory states that when working with followers who are of low maturity in terms of accomplishing a specific task, a highly task-oriented style (quadrant 1) has the

---

From *Group & Organizational Studies,* June 1976, pp. 203–222. Used by permission of the publisher.

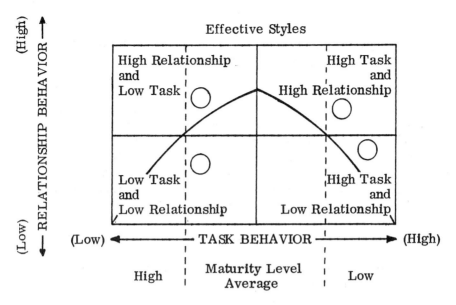

Figure 1.   The Life-Cycle Theory of Leadership, Task and Relationship Dimension of Leader Behavior, Maturity Level with Low, Average, and
High Bench Marks (Hersey & Blanchard, 1972).

highest probability of success; in dealing with followers who are of average maturity
on a task, moderate structure and a moderate-to-high relationship-oriented style
(quadrants 2 and 3) appear to be most appropriate; and a low-task and low-
relationship orientation (quadrant 4) has the highest probability of success working
with followers who rank high in maturity.

The life-cycle theory of leadership is based on a relationship between the
amount of direction (task behavior) and the amount of socio-emotional support
(relationship behavior) a leader provides and the followers' observable level of
"maturity."

Maturity is defined as the level of achievement motivation, willingness and
ability to take responsibility, and task-relevant education and experience of an
individual or a group (Hersey & Blanchard, 1972). Additionally, maturity is
congruent with changes in behavior from passive to active, from dependent to
independent, from the ability to behave in few ways to the ability to behave in many
ways, from shallow and erratic to deeper and stronger interests, from short-time
perspectives to long-time perspectives, from subordinate to equal or superordinate
positions, and from lack of awareness and control to awareness and control over self
or the actions of followers (Argyris, 1957).

In *Personality and Organization,* Argyris (1957) discussed basic self-actualization trends of the human personality:

> One can then logically assume that, at any given moment in time, the human personality will be predisposed to find expression for these developmental trends. Such an assumption implies another, namely, that there are basic development trends characteristic of a relatively large majority of the population being considered. . . . This does not preclude the possibility that each individual can express these basic characteristics in his own idiosyncratic manner. Thus the concept of individual differences is still held. (p. 49)

He assumes that beings in our culture:

1. Tend to develop from a state of passivity as infants to a state of increasing activity as adults.

2. Tend to develop from a state of dependence upon others as infants to a state of relative independence as adults. Relative independence is the ability to "stand on one's own two feet" and simultaneously to acknowledge health dependencies. It is characterized by the liberation of the individual from his childhood determiners of behavior (e.g., family) and developing his own set of behavioral determiners.

3. Tend to develop from being capable of behaving only in a few ways as an infant to being capable of behaving in many different ways as an adult.

4. Tend to develop from having erratic, casual, shallow, quickly dropped interests as an infant to having deeper interests as an adult.

5. Tend to develop from having a short-time perspective (i.e., the present largely determines behavior) as an infant to a much longer time perspective as an adult (i.e., where behavior is more affected by the past and the future).

6. Tend to develop from being in a subordinate position in the family and society as an infant to aspiring to occupy an equal and/or superordinate position relative to their peers.

7. Tend to develop from a lack of awareness of self as an infant to an awareness of and control over self as an adult. (pp. 50–51)

Using the assumptions made by Argyris and the theoretical definition of maturity outlined by Hersey and Blanchard, the author has developed the Follower Maturity Index to illustrate ten dimensions of behavior.

THE FOLLOWER MATURITY INDEX

Each dimension has been placed on a continuum (see Figure 2), assuming, for follower behavior purposes, that the attributes and aspects of individual personality are applicable to the followers as a group, a practice noted in group theory (Likert, 1971). A further generalization can be made that Hersey and Blanchard's and Argyris's dimensions are descriptive of basic multidimensional developmental processes through which the maturity of followers may be observed. At any time, any group can have its degree of maturity plotted within these dimensions. Maturity may now be defined more precisely as the followers' plotted profile along the developed dimensions.

Maturity level, then, is the degree of follower behavior observed in verbal and nonverbal manifestations of these dimensions.

Observational Base

Seven hundred eighty-eight people who worked in a variety of task groups in thirty-two leadership seminars conducted by the author completed the FMI to determine the maturity level of their groups. The analysis of data was conducted by discussions following group tasks and by post hoc review of videotapes. Followers rated their own behavior and their own groups' maturity levels. The instrument was used primarily as a teaching device; no statistical tests were run because the purpose of the study was to provide a field test of the instrument's utility.

DIMENSIONS OF FOLLOWER MATURITY

Dimension of Behavior: Achievement

The primacy of goal achievement is evident. Without goal achievement, there is no leadership and, by definition, the group that does not exist for a purpose is not a group of followers. The major problem with using achievement as the basis for maturity determination is the absence of measures of achievement in most field situations and the conflict between long- and short-range goals. The problem is one of optimal goal achievement by followers without empirical, agreed-upon measures of achievement.

Verbal and Nonverbal Behavior

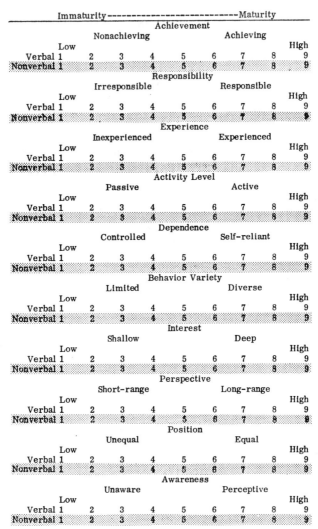

Figure 2. Follower Maturity Index

For each of the Immaturity-Maturity continua that appear above, indicate on a scale from 1 (low) to 9 (high) where you perceive your group being with respect to each dimension, both verbally and non-verbally.

Verbal Maturity-Level Indicators

Low. Typical responses: "This is what the paper said"; "This is the goal"; "I don't care what you think the goal is"; "Scores or points are the important thing"; "Before we can do anything we have to get to know each other"; "Well, let's ask what we are supposed to do"; "We decided once"; "Keep going"; "If we take time for that now, we won't finish."

Average. Typical responses: "Let's see where we are"; "I think we can change"; "We may be working toward the same goal"; "Keep going; we can't change now"; "It's a good way to beat the other teams"; "I think this may be the goal"; "What do you see as the goal?"; "What do you think is best for scores?"; "Our goal is this; I don't care what the organization wants"; "I am interested in your goal and how you feel, but only as it affects what we are doing."

High. Typical responses: "Here's how I see it"; "We can consider anything"; "It's time to review where we are and where we are going"; "We need to continually review progress"; "Let's review or reaffirm our goals"; "That's a wild idea, but I like it"; "Let's negotiate our goals with the institution"; "What do we want as our goal?"; "I think our goal is more important than what they say, but we have a responsibility to their goal, too."

Nonverbal Maturity-Level Indicators

Low. Followers: keep at task; don't listen to new ideas; commence working immediately; subgroup on irrelevant task; are unresponsive to others; are inattentive; are sealed off; exhibit incongruent behaviors; and do not start task.

Average. Followers: exhibit generally congruent behavior; commence working on some set of goals; subgroup on tangential tasks; encourage each other, smile, wink, have some new ideas, but stay mostly with original plan; have coats open; and listen to others' ideas.

High. Followers: put hands on hips; lean forward; have coats off, shoes off, "stripped for action"; pitch in and help; do not laugh at "way out" suggestions or ideas; subgroup on primary tasks; are open to new ideas, new goals; and exhibit congruent behavior.

Comments

Achievement appears to be the keystone for maturity behavior. McBer (1970) listed an achievement process that could include setting initial goals, anticipating problems and risks, planning and taking moderate-risk actions, obtaining necessary information for task completion, reviewing programs, and revising. There should be a system of evaluation for achievement.

The quality of task achievement appears to increase, or at least remain the same, as followers mature. The observer is looking for behaviors, either verbal or nonverbal, in which the followers take individual and group responsibility; seek concrete feedback; attempt creative or innovative solutions; attempt to outperform other groups; attempt to set and meet self-imposed standards; and use power or affiliation to accomplish the assigned task (McClelland, 1961; McClelland, Atkinson, Clark, & Lowell, 1953). Only in rare cases could followers be considered mature if they did not accomplish the assigned task and did not first negotiate that fact with the organization. In such a case, the followers, on the basis of information available only to them and not to the leader or parent organization, chose an alternate task. In field situations where this is likely to happen, the followers are generally given only the broadest tasks. There is often a conflict between short-range goals and long-range goals. As Forrester (1971) pointed out, the short-range goal may be in direct opposition to the long-range goal, which complicates the problem of making a maturity judgment. One good indicator of average to high maturity appears to be when the followers recognize the difference between their short- and long-range goals.

Probably the most difficult problem of all when using achievement as a basis for determining maturity is that in the majority of field situations, there is no correct answer, although there may be correct answers in training situations. Organization development programs try to solve this problem by having everyone share a "common vision" of where the enterprise should be going. Another effective way is to create a good strategy and goal and then to build a series of guidelines or steps along the way. The followers can determine how well they are proceeding toward the goal. If the group members are mature enough, they may offer considerable input as to what the grand strategy and the steps could be. To attempt the same activity with an immature group will only increase the group's confusion and immaturity.

Mature followers will be effective and efficient. They will expend effort and resources in comparable measure to the goal to be attained and will recognize the time limitations that are placed upon tasks.

It appears that most groups achieve at levels below their potential but high enough for survival. A movement toward more fully accomplishing long- and short-range goals (in terms of potential) could help determine the effectiveness of leader behavior.

Dimension of Behavior: Responsibility

The willingness and ability to take responsibility is another key to maturity level. Willingness requires the group to "take ownership" for what is happening. Ability to take responsibility may be limited by law, experience, or education. Thus, the mutual exclusivity desired in a taxonomy is not present. Responsibility appears frequently in other dimensions of maturity.

Verbal Maturity-Level Indicators

Low. Typical responses: "May we do this?"; "I don't think I can do this"; "Whose idea is this?"; "What should we do?"; "Who wants us to do this?"; "It's George's idea, not mine"; "Can we get hurt doing that?"; "You choose!"; "It's not my fault"; "You made me do it"; "Why me?"

Average. Typical responses: "I think we can do it"; "Who can do this?"; "What is the talent of our team?"; "Here's an idea"; "How about doing this?"; "Can we do this?"; "Let's think about George's idea"; "We might get hurt doing that"; "Let's talk about this or vote on it"; "We could have tried another way"; "Nobody made me do it"; "I'm used to being misunderstood."

High. Typical responses: "We can do it"; "I am not good at that, but I can do this"; "These are the skills of our group"; "I like this idea"; "Let's do this"; "We can do this"; "I want to do George's idea"; "I don't care if we get hurt or not"; "Let's talk it out"; "It was a good choice. We stand by it"; "We wanted to."

Nonverbal Maturity-Level Indicators

Low. Followers: draw back from group; are fragmented; do not participate; hide; sneer; one member speaks for group; say "I am not mad" (though red-faced); exhibit closed arm and hand movement; and hold back.

Average. Followers: some in/some out; subgroup; one or two members speak; exhibit pats, strokes of encouragement, and agreement; and exhibit support of choice.

High. Followers: are into group; move in general as a group; reinforce each other; and exhibit spontaneous support of members.

Comments

The willingness and ability to take responsibility is the second of Hersey and Blanchard's (1972) concepts of maturity behavior. The leader will note in other dimensions of behavior that "responsibility" appears frequently in the definition or in the comments.

Willingness to take responsibility is frequently expressed in here-and-now or "I" statements in which followers, accepting ownership of group problems, are supportive of other members verbally (by such statements as "right on") and physically remain with the other followers. One or more members of a group may dissociate themselves from what is happening in the group by subgrouping, by speaking of other things, and frequently, by using humor to avoid taking responsibility for what is happening.

Dimension of Behavior: Experience

Task-relevant experience, with or without education in a fundamental sense, may determine the ability of followers in task achievement. However, experience relevant to the task is usually not lacking. There is more often a misuse of the experiences of followers by followers.

Verbal Maturity-Level Indicators

Low. Typical responses: "What does this mean?"; "I don't understand this"; "This task isn't clear"; "What are we supposed to do here?"; "We don't have nearly enough time to do this"; "This is too big a job for us"; "We don't have the resources to start on this"; "This isn't a routine item. What is this?"; "I know what this is" (when I don't); "That's your job" (stereotyping).

Average. Typical responses: "There are a couple of interpretations of this task"; "Here's what I think it means"; "I've never seen anything like this before"; "We haven't been taught to do this kind of thing"; "We don't have time to do it the way I know how"; "This is almost a routine procedure"; "Do you know?"; "I've seen things like this before"; "Who knows about this?"; "I know a little about this"; "You have done this before in your job; can you help any?"; "Here are some ideas."

High. Typical responses: "We have done this before"; "We learned that in the first task"; "You were wrong before, but I think you are right now"; "I don't know anything about this; I don't know what I can contribute"; "Let's do this"; "We can plan our time and get the job done"; "I know something about this"; "We can figure out what has to be done with what we know"; "Let's review the problem"; "I don't know about this" (when I don't).

Nonverbal Maturity-Level Indicators

Low. Followers: have no comments; are defensive (folded arms); have little or no eye contact; give a pretense of working at task; are busy working on unrelated task; do not pay attention to ideas; exhibit actions to reject; frown; exhibit incongruent behavior between the verbal message and the content, e.g., "We want to hear what you can offer" (while turning away); and have restricted body movement.

Average. Followers: show appropriate bodily movement; work at a similar task; have minimum eye contact; do fewer non-task-related activities; listen (bodily) to others' ideas; exhibit some smiles, encouragement; question, raise eyebrows; show more reasonable congruity between nonverbals and message content; and draw or make gestures freely to express ideas.

High. Followers: are physically present, are reflective of others' content; are acceptant of ideas and knowledge, whatever the source; focus inside of group for resources; and respond appropriately to others.

Comments

Task-relevant education and experience is the third of Hersey and Blanchard's (1972) concepts of maturity. The task-relevant education and/or experience frequently determines the ability of a group to accept responsibility. In a fundamental sense, it may control the ability or potential of the follower in terms of achievement of tasks. To assemble a computer may be beyond the capabilities of a group of followers. The hiring of a person to assemble a computer may not be.

Followers rarely make any inventory or search of task-relevant education and experience of the members. The degree to which a group does this consciously may be an excellent indicator of its maturity. In his research on highly effective teams or groups, Likert (1971) based much of his discussion on the ability of a group to be supportive, an ability that appears to be a learned skill. Experience and education may be thought of in terms of membership skills (Berlew, 1972) or follower skills. In the field situation, the followers usually have the experience and education necessary to accomplish the task; if they do not, a mature group of followers is aware of the fact and takes steps to correct it. Usually, ideas, knowledge, and insights that emerge in a group are judged not on merit, but on source. A measure of follower maturity is the degree to which the education and experience of all the group's members are utilized.

Dimension of Behavior: Activity

The level of activity of followers on an active-passive continuum was difficult to determine. A true measure of the activity level of followers may be more a climate measurement over a period of time than discretely measurable units. There appeared to be a pseudo-activity, so-called because the behavior of the followers was not task-relevant. The most common phenomenon was that one or two members of a group assumed an internal (to the followers) leader position. The remainder of the group was then quite passive. There also appeared to be a more mature behavior that was actively passive, that is, an active choice on the part of the followers to be passive and limit their activity.

Verbal Maturity-Level Indicators

Low. Typical responses: "What does the instructor say?"; "I don't care"; "It doesn't matter to me"; "Who's the leader?"; "That's your job"; "What do you want?"

Average. Typical responses: "What do you think we should do?"; "Here are some things we could try"; "Whatever you say"; "I'm ready if you are"; "I don't care about that part"; "You two have a good idea; let's try that"; "Let's check with the instructor"; "I don't think we can do that; let's ask"; "We need you on this."

High. Typical responses: "This is what we want to do"; "We want to . . . "; "Let's work something out with the institution so we can both be happy"; "We are going to do that"; "This time we will do it this way."

Nonverbal Maturity-Level Indicators

Low. Followers: exhibit incongruent behavior between verbal and nonverbal; are quiet—little or no task-related noise; stay where put; are silent, show defensive measures, lean back, and listen; one or two members of group dominate conversation, give orders, etc.; point or direct with hands or arms; shout; and are unresponsive to others.

Average. Followers: show more congruent nonverbals; subgroup about task or away from task; show moderate participation by all of group; move (physically) to join or link; gather around; and show some responsiveness.

High. Followers: are very congruent; show movement appropriate to group's purpose; show individual body movement appropriate to task; and are completely responsive to others in group.

Comments

The active-passive continuum is not simple to evaluate. Usually groups will be pseudo-active with much activity that has little to do with the task. Next, one or two members will assume internal (to the group) leadership. These members will be quite active and the remainder of the group will be passive. The group is still at a low level of group maturity. In field work, because the task is being accomplished, the tendency is to treat the group as if it is as mature as these one or two individuals. The maturity level appears high, as the task continues to be accomplished. The danger is that the one or two individuals may leave the group, or the group may be assigned tasks for which these individuals do not have the necessary education or experience (though someone else in the group may) to accomplish the task.

In the training situation, this can become quite evident with changing groups and tasks. In field work, major or minor disasters can follow an inappropriate maturity determination. It is group maturity, not individual maturity, that is the basis of life-cycle leadership theory. Further, there is such a behavior as being "actively passive," as in active listening. The key appears to be an active choice on the part of the members of the group to be passive. One instant of observation is not sufficient to determine active-passive dimensions. Active-passive is more a climate over a period of time. Unfortunately, when there is no set time period for a "climate" to be observed, numerous observations need to be made.

Dimension of Behavior: Dependence

Dependence is the characteristic of being influenced or subject to another. The more mature followers appeared to be operating at the full limits of their independence within the particular structure while simultaneously attempting to expand their independence through responsible negotiation with the system. Low- and average-maturity followers appeared to have self-imposed, unrealistic dependencies. The dependence dimension also is vital in a variety of linking roles in our complex organizations, in which a person is a leader in one group, a follower in another.

Verbal Maturity-Level Indicators

Low. Typical responses: "What's required?"; "Is this what we are supposed to do? What are we supposed to do?"; "May we do that?"; "We can't do that; it doesn't say to do it."; "What?"; "Why this?"; "We must do this."

Average. Typical responses: "Can we do that?"; "Do it if you want to"; "We changed our minds"; "What are we doing?"; "Are we doing it right?"; "Why are we doing this?"; "What are the options?"; "Can we change that?"; "Is this an option?"

High. Typical responses: "This is what we will do"; "We can do it"; "You can do it if you want to"; "Here's the plan, and this is the product."

Nonverbal Maturity-Level Indicators

Low. Followers: show automatic execution of orders; remain where seated, placed, or put; link with loudest talker or most powerful person in group; follow physically whoever leads; withdraw from activity; and ignore others.

Average. Followers: show moderately congruent behavior; go get required materials; bodily refuse to carry out leader's orders; move to link with others; participate in activity for participation's sake; move away from one who has dominated in the past; and are supportive of others, smile, nod.

High. Followers: exhibit movement appropriate to task accomplishment; and stand on own two feet, defend ideas.

Comments

This dimension of dependence is one of the more difficult to describe because it appears on so many levels within the follower's interpersonal relationships with the leader and with each other. The emphasis is on dependence on or independence from the appointed leader, with only tangential interest in those followers who attempt to displace the appointed leader.

The very nature of the dependence dimension also causes difficulty. The act of being influenced by or subject to another is almost the definition of being a follower. Much dependency seems to be self-imposed and does not truly originate from the leader or the situation. For example, some of the most disciplined institutions, such as the church or the military, have used a very structured dependency to promote a fuller freedom or independence.

Mature followers seem to be operating to the full limits of their independence within the organization or institution, while simultaneously seeking to expand their independence with a responsible negotiation with the system. Most followers, when seeking independence, do not consider the other elements of maturity behavior.

Dimension of Behavior: Variety

More mature followers capable of exhibiting a variety of behaviors could accept, proact, and react to changes. They were flexible and capable of adapting. Such followers were an asset both to themselves and to their leader, as they were able to compensate properly for leader and situation influences that prevented less mature followers from optimum task achievement.

Verbal Maturity-Level Indicators

Low. Typical responses: "Let's do it the way we did it last time"; "There is only one way to do this"; "You count up—you're good at that"; "Here's the way"; "This is the same"; "Here we go again"; "The same old thing"; "I know what's going to happen"; "What difference does it make? We can't change anything."

Average. Typical responses: "Here's a way for consideration"; "What are some other ways?"; "Let's list the ways"; "What's the real problem this time?"; "Who knows about this?"; "Let's change what we did before"; "Here's what is expected"; "There are a lot of ways to go about this."

High. Typical responses: "Let's start this way; we can change later"; "This just doesn't look like the other problem; this is different"; "I know what I said last time. I want to change my mind"; "We are not locked into one way"; "That's fine, but let's do it another way now"; "We can blend everyone's ideas into this."

Nonverbal Maturity-Level Indicators

Low. Followers: show restricted movement; act the same as the first time, i.e., as if no time had passed; have very general comments; exhibit incongruent behaviors; treat major and minor issues the same; are oblivious to others' emotions or content; are tired or fatigued; and show perfunctory actions.

Average. Followers: show a change toward more appropriate behavior, i.e., laugh if the topic is humorous, are serious if the topic is serious; have varied eye contact; do fewer nonrelated activities; open up more; and display more types of nonverbals.

High. Followers: exhibit behavior that is generally unpredictable, but highly relevant to the task; and are physically present and involved.

Comments

The variety of behaviors that a group of followers exhibits and is capable of can be a crucial item. A mature group capable of behaving in a variety of ways can make up for the leader's mistakes in maturity diagnosis and leadership actions or inactions. The mature followers can react in a variety of ways. They are capable of change; they are capable of different responses; they are not locked into one solution (although that solution may have been a good one). Immature groups of followers present a stereotyped behavior in the field situations. They are socialized (Schien, 1971) into their response. Much of their behavior is not based on the present facts and present situations, but on the past. Their responses are predictable—one set of immature followers is interchangeable with another set.

Dimension of Behavior: Interests

A continuum of interests from few and weak to varied and strong was difficult to chart; yet, there did appear to be manifestations of such levels of interests in follower behavior. Most often the words "I am interested in this" or "I am not interested in the task" were used in verbal communications. Indifference, reflected in closed-body positions (sometimes even closed eyes) and physical inattention, was the most common nonverbal manifestation.

Verbal Maturity-Level Indicators

Low. Typical responses: "This is foolish"; "I'm not interested in this"; "What is this about?"; "I don't see the point"; "This doesn't appeal to me"; "This doesn't interest me."

Average. Typical responses: "Let's give this a try"; "This might be important"; "There must be some reason for this"; "I can see some value"; "Let's see if we can find out"; "Let's talk it out."

High. Typical responses: "I feel strongly about this"; "This is an important part"; "We should try to give this a chance"; "I learned something last time"; "We can decide its value to us"; "I'm interested in this."

Nonverbal Maturity-Level Indicators

Low. Followers: are aloof; pay no attention to task; show incongruent behaviors; question for the sake of questioning; and exhibit closed-body posture, folded arms, etc.

Average. Followers: pay some attention to task; show some attention to others; generally attend to task, leaning into group; are responsive to others' comments with smiles, nods; and ask relevant questions.

High. Followers: exhibit appropriate body movement for task; and physically move to points of interest.

Comments

The leadership literature supports the fact that people change only as they are interested or see a reason to do so (Beckhard, 1969; Schien, 1971; Fiedler, 1971) or if there is more reason to change than not to change.

One common phenomenon with a group of followers in leadership studies is the followers' demonstrated lack of interest in the topic. For example, they supposedly are interested in maturity determination, yet they talk of other things. They are really interested in doing what they were told to do by "attending" that session. The most obvious trait of immature people is that they are "not interested in anything." One determination of maturity is the degree to which the group moves from erratic and shallow interests to deep, strong interests.

Dimension of Behavior: Perspective

A follower's perspective continuum from short- to long-term was the most questionable dimension. Perspective appeared to be an attitudinal dimension of maturity. (Although perspective and interests offered the weakest cases as separate dimensions of maturity, they remained as dimensions because further research was required for all dimensions, and to discard them was felt to be premature.)

Verbal Maturity-Level Indicators

Low. Typical responses: "Start!"; "Let's get it over with"; "Let's get going on this"; "Don't spend a lot of time talking about it; let's go!"; "I don't care about that; I want to start"; "This doesn't fit here"; "This is too petty for me to do"; "I don't like this"; "Let's talk it over."

Average. Typical responses: "We aren't prepared enough to do it"; "Where does this fit?"; "We have enough preparation to *try* to do it"; "Here is a plan"; "Does this fit into the big picture?"; "This might fit"; "I don't see how it is supposed to help, but I am willing"; "We can accept that."

High. Typical responses: "What's the payoff for us in the long run?"; "This is what we can do"; "Here's how this fits into the big picture."

Nonverbal Maturity-Level Indicators

Low. Followers: show inertia; leave (actual or preparatory); are on edge of chair; start automatically on the task; show incongruent behavior; have brief curt comments; and are insensitive to others.

Average. Followers: remain awhile to work on task; show moderately congruent behavior; pay some attention to others; and have moderate-length discussions with others (longer than perfunctory, curt comments).

High. Followers: remain after required time to complete task; are comfortable in surroundings; and show congruent behavior.

Comments

Time perspective may be most closely related to long- or short-range goals. But whereas goals imply accomplishing something, time perspective is the way that the activity is approached. Followers can approach something from a "this is a one-time shot; let's get it over with" attitude to a more long-range "there is something in this that is part of something bigger; this all fits in or can be made to fit in" attitude.

It appears that the short-time perspective, called the "quick fix," can in the long run be quite harmful. A series of short-time, quick fixes can, in fact, destroy the possibility of a long run. The long-range time perspective seems to give more leniency and flexibility to follower behavior. The case for time perspectives as a completely distinct dimension of follower behavior is not strong.

Dimension of Behavior: Position

The position (rank, status, situation, or placement) of followers appeared to be a powerful dimension of maturity. The ability of a group of followers to utilize internal resources on the basis of merit and task achievement, rather than on social or other position of the originators, appeared to be a measure of higher levels of maturity.

The reward and punishment systems of organizations have entangled position, power, and influence in behaviors that are extremely difficult to separate. The issues of positional and personal power are involved in this dimension. Position ranks with achievement, responsibility, and experience as a consistent, understandable dimension of maturity.

Verbal Maturity-Level Indicators

Low. Typical responses: "May I?"; "I'm the leader and I say so"; "You shut up"; "It's not your place"; "May we?"; "You be the boss"; "Do it my way or pay the penalty"; "I couldn't care less"; "You do that, you do that, and I do this."

Average. Typical responses: "Could I?"; "Could we?"; "You're not my boss"; "Let's discuss the issue"; "Let's vote"; "Just tally up the scores"; "Majority rules"; "That's O.K. for in here, but what about outside?"; "I'm interested in what you say."

High. Typical responses: "We will"; "I don't care if you are the boss; you are wrong about this"; "Everyone's ideas are being considered"; "I'll step aside if there is a better way"; "It's agreed that we split up and work separately"; "I trust what you say. I don't need to go over it."

Nonverbal Maturity-Level Indicators

Low. Followers: speak only when spoken to; dominate conversation; yell someone down; do not share equal "air time"; step on or interrupt; stand over one another; have a self-appointed leader or spokesperson; show incongruent behavior; frown, scowl, or exhibit threatening glances; are inattentive, do not watch others, glance away, and point or direct others.

Average. Followers: show parity of position (not one over others); use voting process, share equal air time; pick spokesperson, then abandon him or her; have humorous exchange of roles; have some encouragement or praise of others; exhibit relatively few threatening glances and comments; and look quizzical.

High. Followers: divide air time appropriately; subdivide to accomplish task; pick leader and back up choice; rotate roles; have leadership roles and positions appropriate to the task; exhibit congruent behavior; show cheerful enthusiasm; and display liking and acceptance with hugs, pats, touching, handshakes.

Comments

By definition, followers are those who are not the designated leader. In theory, all should be equal as followers, but obviously this is not the case. Followers bring with them and have attributed to them positional and personal power by other followers. Projections by some writers indicate the most prevalent type of leadership and decision making of the future will be collegial (Schmidt, 1970; Delaney, 1972).

The life-cycle theory of leadership also requires that as the maturity level of followers increases, they will display the task and relationship behavior necessary for task accomplishment (up to that point it had been leader behavior).

The most important measurement of maturity level is the follower's abilities to base position and leadership action on the specific task at hand. The best idea should be used, no matter who originated it; that is, rank structure or placement of the followers is based on the task. This does not mean that the president of the company is not the president, although for a specific task his most appropriate behavior might be to answer the question of a very junior computer programmer.

In times of crisis, the leader is maturely given almost dictatorial powers (e.g., Winston Churchill) because of the need for rapid, consistent decision making. When the crisis has passed, the mature followers restore their own peer position.

Dimension of Behavior: Awareness

Followers appeared to exhibit behavior ranging on a continuum from lack of awareness and control to awareness of their behavior and its consequences. Follower awareness appeared to parallel or be similar to individual awareness and control of internal and external influences on behavior.

Verbal Maturity-Level Indicators

Low. Typical responses: "What's happening?"; "What are you doing?"; "What am I doing?"

Average. Typical responses: "Why are we doing this?"; "I think I see what you mean"; "Let's look at what is happening"; "Who knows something about this?"; "I would like to . . . "; "Have you thought about . . . "; "I would like to hear how you feel about this"; "I thought this is what we did before."

High. Typical responses: "What we are doing is . . . "; "I understand; I want to . . . "; "This applies to what we did before"; "We are ready for this"; "We are not ready for this"; "I see what you mean."

Nonverbal Maturity-Level Indicators

Low. Followers: leave group; show no reaction to others' or own feelings; place hands over mouth or ears; turn away; and utter terse comments.

Average. Followers: are somewhat congruent; actively watch others; express own feelings; show moderate reaction to others; and have general eye contact.

High. Followers: are congruent; express feelings; and exhibit appropriate movement.

Comments

The lack of awareness followers have of their own activities parallels the general lack of awareness and sense of control most individuals exhibit in their behavior. Gestalt psychology (Perls, Hefferline, & Goodman, 1951) and education of the self (Weinstein & Fantini, 1970) have specifically tried to address this lack of awareness of individuals and groups.

The psychological expression "here and now" is most appropriate to the behaviors of followers. Immature followers do not see themselves in a here-and-now situation. In truth, they usually have had little training in awareness of how they feel as individuals and how they are affecting each other as members of the group. Average-maturity followers have a general awareness of themselves as a group and of the degree of control that they are able to exercise.

General Implications

1. The observable maturity level of a newly formed group is usually low. Therefore, the most consistently appropriate leadership behavior is initially quadrant 1 (high task-low relationship). Task emphasis for newly formed groups would greatly facilitate an initial solution to many leadership problems. In training and field situation, groups with an observable low level of follower maturity consistently failed to accomplish tasks if the appointed leader or another member of the group did not exercise leadership behavior in quadrant 1.

2. The determination of follower-behavior level in even the most general terms was consistently commented upon by participants in training and field situations as a practical basis for leader and follower actions. Participants demonstrated changed behavior (i.e., attempting to exhibit appropriate leader behavior) on the basis of observable follower behavior in specific cases.

3. The most common mistake made in the determination of follower-maturity level was to assume that follower maturity is the sum of individual maturity—that a group of mature individuals automatically equals a mature group. The leader then uses a style of leadership he considers appropriate for a high-maturity level. Because his diagnosis is incorrect, however, the results are less than optimal. There is failure to complete the task, inappropriate use of resources, and follower confusion. It has been suggested that the leader should use quadrant 1 with newly formed groups, changing as rapidly as possible to quadrant 2 (high task-high relationship behavior) based on observable follower behavior.

4. Quadrant 2 (proportionally 85 percent) covers the majority of follower-maturity cases—low and average. High-maturity followers will understand what the leader is doing and will be able to modify their behavior accordingly (by reason of maturity). This does not mean that quadrant 2 leader behavior would be the leader's only style. With definite *observable* indications of high follower maturity, the leader would use quadrant 3 or 4 leadership styles. The least risk to task accomplishment would be to emphasize quadrant 2 leader behavior.

5. Hierarchical organizations and models, particularly the church, the military, schools, and business, tend to predispose people to think of influence as possessed and exercised only by those in a superior position. This study, with its emphasis on followers, indicates that all the elements of leadership (leader, followers, and situation) possess influence. The determination of follower maturity allows the leader (and followers) to utilize more fully the influence of the followers for optimum task accomplishment.

Implications for Organization Development and Consulting

1. At the present time, organization development (OD) is really the development of influence to achieve goals in a given situation—i.e., leadership. If OD is, in fact, leadership attempting to use all the elements of leadership, then the determination of follower maturity is an even more vital, useful concept and skill.

2. The ability to diagnose organizational behavior in terms of follower maturity would provide an appropriate basis for an OD consultant's personal behavior within the system or for a recommended intervention.

3. Organizations may be viewed as a linking of followers and leaders in various arrays and positions. By systematically establishing the leader and followers in each specific submodule, a determination of follower maturity can be made in order that appropriate leader behavior may be used. The submodules can then be viewed as a whole.

Research Implications

1. The dimensions of maturity have been tentatively established. However, the technical problems of taxonomies, mutual exclusiveness, discrete units of measurement and techniques of measuring, observing, or determining a group's maturity level remain to be solved.

2. The maturity instrument used in the study was designed for use in leadership-learning experiences. The validity and reliability of a maturity instrument based on these or other dimensions must be established.

3. Videotaping follower maturity behavior offers great promise for systematic observation and analysis of complex maturity concepts. Such a system would require simultaneous taping of all followers and participants, limiting the initial observation to small groups. Systematic observation would be necessary to study follower maturity. A set of procedures to organize follower activity (such as a seminar) would allow follower maturity to be observed, recorded, and analyzed. To accomplish these ends, the dimensions of maturity have been developed. These can then be used to identify, record, and measure the events that take place in any leader-follower situation.

References

Argyris, C. *Personality and Organization.* New York: Harper & Row, 1957.

Beckhard, R. *Organizational Development: Strategies and Models.* Reading, Mass.: Addison-Wesley, 1969.

Berlew, D. E. *The Group Membership Game.* Newport, R. I.: Human Resource Management Consultant Training, 1972.

Delaney, R. F. The long-range future of the Navy, 1972-1985. *Phase II Report, Volume I, Group Research Project Report.* Newport, R. I.: U.S. Naval War College, 1972.

Fiedler, F. E. *Leadership.* New York: General Learning Corp., 1971.

Forrester, J. W. *World Dynamics.* Cambridge, Mass.: Wright Allen Press, 1971.

Hersey, P. and Blanchard, K. H. *Management of Organizational Behavior.* Englewood Cliffs, N. J.: Prentice-Hall, 1972.

Likert, R. The nature of highly effective groups. In D. A. Kolb, I. M. Rubin and J. M. McIntyre (Eds.), *Organization Psychology: A Book of Readings* (2nd ed.). Englewood Cliffs, N. J.: Prentice-Hall, 1971.

McBer & Company. *Measuring Motivation.* Cambridge, Mass.: Sterling Institute, 1970.

McClelland, D. C. *The Achieving Society.* Princeton, N. J.: D. Van Nostrand, 1961.

McClelland, D. C., Atkinson, J. W., Clark, R. A. and Lowell, E. L. *The Achievement Motive.* New York: Appleton-Century-Crofts, 1953.

Perls, F., Hefferline, R. and Goodman, P. *Gestalt Therapy.* New York: Julian Press, 1951.

Schien, E. H. Organizational socialization of the profession of management. In D. A. Kolb, I. M. Rubin and J. M. McIntyre (Eds.), *Organization Psychology: A Book of Readings* (2nd ed.). Englewood Cliffs, N. J.: Prentice-Hall, 1971.

Schmidt, W. *Organizational Frontiers and Human Values.* Belmont, Calif.: Wadsworth, 1970.

Weinstein, G. and Fantini, M. (Eds.), *Toward Humanistic Education: A Curriculum of Affect.* New York: Praeger, 1970.

THE ETHICS OF CHARISMATIC LEADERSHIP: SUBMISSION OR LIBERATION?

Jane M. Howell, The University of Western Ontario
Bruce J. Avolio, State University of New York at Binghamton

Executive Overview

Charismatic business leaders are often heralded as corporate heroes by orchestrating turnarounds, launching new enterprises, engaging in organizational renewal or change, and obtaining extraordinary performance from individuals. The effectiveness of these leaders may be interpreted by executives as an unqualified recommendation for such leadership in their organizations. However the risks involved in charismatic leadership are at least as large as the promises. What is missing from current discussions about charisma is consideration of its darker side.

In this article we focus on a paradox that emerges whenever one discusses leaders such as Robert Campeau, Max DePree, Lee Iacocca, Ross Johnson, Ralph Larsen, and Michael Milken: why are some charismatic leaders destructive, while others are beneficial to followers, organizations, and even entire societies? Drawing on the results from an interview study as well as the popular management literature, we describe the qualities and values that differentiate ethical and unethical charismatic leaders. We also examine the impact ethical and unethical charismatic leaders have on followers and how organizations can develop ethical charismatic leaders.

ARTICLE

"Wanted: Corporate Leaders. Must have vision and ability to build corporate culture. Mere managers need not apply."[1]

Charismatic leaders are celebrated as the heroes of management. By turning around ailing corporations, revitalizing aging bureaucracies, or launching new enterprises, these leaders are viewed as the magic elixir to cure organizational woes and change the course of organizational events. Charismatic leaders achieve these

---

© *Academy of Management Executive*, 1992, Vol. 6, No. 2.

[1]Quote from W. Kiechel III, "Wanted: Corporate Leaders," *Fortune*, May 30, 1983, 135.

heroic feats by powerfully communicating a compelling vision of the future, passionately believing in their vision, relentlessly promoting their beliefs with boundless energy, propounding creative ideas, and expressing confidence in followers' abilities to achieve high standards. Charismatic leaders are typically viewed as effective leaders: leaders who inspire extraordinary performance in followers as well as build their trust, faith, and belief in the leader.[2] But is charisma a desirable force for leading an organization? While the virtues of charismatic leaders are extolled in the popular management press, and in a growing number of studies, the potential dark side of these leaders is often ignored.

Charismatics can be very effective leaders, yet they may vary in their ethical standards. The label charismatic has been applied to very diverse leaders in politics (Adolf Hitler, Benito Mussolini, Franklin Delano Roosevelt), in religious spheres (Jesus Christ, Jim Jones), in social movement organizations (Mahatma Gandhi, Martin Luther King, Jr., Malcolm X) and in business (Lee Iacocca, Mary Kay Ash, John DeLorean). This list underscores that the term "charisma" is value neutral: it does not distinguish between good or moral and evil or immoral charismatic leadership. This means the risks involved in charismatic leadership are at least as large as the promises. Charisma can lead to blind fanaticism in the service of megalomaniacs and dangerous values, or to heroic self-sacrifice in the service of a beneficial cause.[3] An awareness of this risk is missing from most of the current

---

[2]For nontechnical reading about charismatic leadership, the following are suggested: B. M. Bass's *Leadership and Performance Beyond Expectations* (New York: Free Press, 1985); and "Leadership: Good, Better, Best," *Organizational Dynamics*, 1985; W. G. Bennis and B. Nanus's *Leaders: The Strategies for Taking Charge* (New York: Harper & Row, 1985); J. M. Kouzes and B. Z. Posner's *The Leadership Challenge: How to Get Extraordinary Things Done in Organizations* (San Francisco: Jossey-Bass, 1987). Early writings on charisma include M. Weber, *The Theory of Social and Economic Organizations* (R. A. Henderson and T. Parsons, Trans.), (New York: Free Press, 1947); P. Selznick, *Leadership in Administration* (Evanston: Row, Peterson, 1957); and A. Etzioni, *A Comparative Analysis of Complex Organizations*, (New York: Free Press). More recent literature on charismatic leadership in organizations includes a chapter by R. J. House in "A 1976 Theory of Charismatic Leadership," *Leadership: The Cutting Edge*, edited by J. G. Hunt & L. L. Larson, (Carbondale, IL: Southern Illinois University Press, 1977), 189–204, which traces the historical significance of the topic as well as describes the personality characteristics, behaviors, and effects of such leaders.

[3]For more on charismatic leadership that is prosocial or antisocial, see J. M. Howell's "Two Faces of Charisma: Socialized and Personalized Leadership in Organizations" in *Charismatic Leadership: The Elusive Factor in Organizational Effectiveness* (San Francisco: Jossey-Bass, 1988), edited by J. A. Conger and R. N.

popular writings on charismatic leadership, which may be interpreted by executives and managers as an unqualified recommendation of such leadership. In this article, we argue that rather than dismiss charisma on the grounds of its associated risks, we need to understand the differences between ethical and unethical charismatic leaders so managers can make informed decisions about recruiting, selecting, and promoting their future organizational leaders who will pursue visions that benefit their organizations rather than simply building their own power base at the expense of the organization.

Charisma can lead to blind fanaticism in the service of megalomaniacs and dangerous values, or to heroic self-sacrifice in the service of a beneficial cause.

To understand the ethics of charismatic leadership, we interviewed and surveyed more than 150 managers in 25 large Canadian organizations.[4] Based on these managers' descriptions of their bosses, we identified twenty-five charismatic leaders for in-depth study. Each leader was interviewed for two hours about his or her philosophy, values, and attitudes towards followers and completed a questionnaire measuring various personality characteristics and leadership behaviors. To determine whether a charismatic leader was ethical or unethical, interview transcripts were content analyzed for the presence of themes related to whether the leader attacked moral abuses, confronted and resolved dilemmas, encouraged pursuits of ideals, cultivated an ethically responsible culture, and fostered and rewarded those with moral integrity.[5] We draw on these interviews and questionnaire responses, as well as popular accounts of well-known charismatic leaders, to highlight the key characteristics and behaviors of ethical and unethical charismatic leaders.

We first describe the key behaviors and moral standards that differentiate ethical from unethical charismatic leaders. The impact of ethical and unethical

---

Kanungo; B. M. Bass "The Two Faces of Charismatic Leadership," *Leaders Magazine*, *12*, 4, 44–45; R. J. House, J. M. Howell, B. Shamir, B. J. Smith, and W. D. Spangler's "Charismatic Leadership: A 1990 Theory and Five Empirical Tests," Unpublished Manuscript, The Wharton School, University of Pennsylvania; and J. M. Howell and R. J. House's "Socialized and Personalized Charisma: An Essay on the Bright and Dark Sides of Leadership," Unpublished manuscript, School of Business Administration, University of Western Ontario.

[4]For more information about the method and findings of this study, see J. M. Howell and C. A. Higgins "Champions of Technological Innovation," *Administrative Science Quarterly*, 1990, *35*, 317–341.

[5]In their recent book *Good Management: Business Ethics in Action* (Toronto, Prentice-Hall, 1991), F. Bird and J. Gandz discuss in detail ethical leadership.

charismatic leaders on their followers' development is discussed next. Finally, we outline how managers can nurture ethical charismatic leadership in their organizations.

CHARISMATIC LEADERS: SOME UNCOMMON DENOMINATORS

Many charismatic leaders incorporate their followers' hopes, dreams, and aspirations in their vision. These leaders develop creative, critical thinking in their followers, provide opportunities for them to develop, welcome positive and negative feedback, recognize the contributions of others, share information with followers, and have moral standards that emphasize collective interests of the group, organization, or society. We call these leaders "ethical charismatics." Other charismatic leaders are interested in pursuing their own personal vision. These charismatic leaders control and manipulate their followers, promote what is best for themselves rather than their organizations, and have moral standards that promote self-interests. We call these leaders "unethical charismatics."

Ethical charismatic leaders use power in socially constructive ways to serve others. They are genuinely concerned about contributing to the welfare of followers.

We now examine the marks of ethical and unethical charismatic leaders to see how those who seek to be leaders might avoid the often attractive traps associated with unethical leadership, while cultivating the characteristics of genuinely ethical leadership. As illustrated in Exhibit 1 and described below, ethical and unethical charismatic leaders are distinguished by five key behaviors: exercising power, creating visions, communicating with followers, intellectually stimulating followers, developing followers, and moral standards.

Exercising Power

Exercising power or influence varies among ethical and unethical charismatic leaders. Ethical charismatic leaders use power in socially constructive ways to serve others. They are genuinely concerned about contributing to the welfare of followers. Leadership that stresses serving rather than dominance, status or prestige is reflected in the construction services company Townsend and Bottum, Inc.'s Plan for Continuity:

> *"It shall be an organization operating with the highest principles of integrity, service to society and clients, in an environment of trust which will nurture growth and development of employees so that they become stronger, more autonomous, and more serving of their fellow men and women."* [6]

---

[6]Quote from J. E. Liebig, *Business Ethics: Profiles in Civic Virtue* (Golden, CO: Fulcrum, 1990), 174.

Unethical Charismatic Leader	Ethical Charismatic Leader
• uses power only for personal gain or impact	• uses power to serve others
• promotes own personal vision	• aligns vision with followers' needs and aspirations
• censures critical or opposing views	• considers and learns from criticism
• demands own decisions be accepted without question	• stimulates followers to think independently and to question the leader's view
• one-way communication	• open, two-way communication
• insensitive to followers' needs	• coaches, develops, and supports followers; shares recognition with others
• relies on convenient external moral standards to satisfy self-interests	• relies on internal moral standards to satisfy organizational and societal interests

Exhibit 1. Individual Qualities of Ethical and
Unethical Charismatic Leaders

In contrast, unethical charismatics exercise power in dominant and authoritarian ways to serve their self-interests, to manipulate others for their own purposes, and to win at all costs. Power is used for personal gain or impact. Exercising power in a dominant and controlling manner was captured in the words of an invited speaker at an American Management Association Conference for presidents: "I want men that are vicious, grasping, and lusting for power. He who has the gold makes the rules."[7]

---

[7]Quote from M. DePree, *Leadership is an Art* (New York: Dell, 1989), 68.

Ethical and unethical charismatic leaders differ in how they create and express their vision. Ethical charismatic leaders express goals that are follower driven; their visions are ultimately responsive to the interests and desires of their followers. Followers actively contribute to and develop the vision further so that it is shared. In the words of one of the charismatic leaders we interviewed:

"My job is to transfer some of the dream so others think it's as neat as I think it's neat. I use all of the emotional trigger words to get people to buy into the concept. You don't want manipulation because you really do want their best creative efforts on it. So it's really exciting them with the potential to get them to buy in. So you have to spend a lot of time talking and transferring the potential notions so that they own a piece of it."

President and CEO Bill O'Brien of The Hanover Insurance Companies strongly believes in the power of a shared vision:

"In my first year as president, I went across the country and I talked to every single employee in every branch of the company. I told them what my vision was for The Hanover Insurance Company. Now a vision is an intensely personal thing. Your vision gets you out of bed to go to work in the morning. My vision gets me working. My vision doesn't do a lot for you. So, we don't have a lot of meetings on what should be the vision of the company or what should be the vision of a department. We encourage our people if they run an operation to have a vision for it. And then, when they are facing live, real situations, act in a visionary way. I have never seen a vision come out of a committee. I have heard people say, 'Here is what I believe and here is what I think we can do. What do you think?' That kind of process will build some visions. We encourage every single department to build its own vision of what it wants to become. When we first did it, everybody thought we were going to have chaos. But there is remarkable harmony between what a branch or department envisions and what a company sees." [8]

While ethical charismatic leaders develop their visions partly through interaction with followers, unethical charismatic leaders derive their visions solely from within themselves. Unethical charismatic leaders communicate goals that promote their own personal agenda often to the disadvantage of others. In the

---

[8]Quote from J. E. Liebig, *Business Ethics: Profiles in Civic Virtue*, 134–135.

extreme, the leader's goals are pursued without question. As one leader remarked to us: "The key thing is that it is my idea; and I am going to win with it at all costs."

Communicating with Followers

To set agendas that represent the interests of their followers, ethical charismatic leaders continuously seek out their viewpoints on critical issues. Such leaders listen to the ideas, needs, aspirations, and wishes of followers and then, within the context of their own well-developed system of beliefs, respond to these in an appropriate way. They invite two-way communication with subordinates, while still promoting a sense of knowing what they are doing. This sense of mutual interaction is captured in one charismatic leader's comment: "If you don't walk the plant, you don't know what's going on. You have to work at it."

Open communication with employees is a key principle at Wal-Mart Stores, the highly successful retailing giant.[9] To stay in touch with employees, or "associates" in Wal-Mart's language, the charismatic founder Sam Walton relies on a highly elaborate communication system ranging from a six-channel satellite system to a private airforce of eleven planes. Says CEO David Glass, "We believe nothing constructive happens in Bentonville [the company's headquarters]. Our grass-roots philosophy is that the best ideas come from people on the firing line."

Similarly, Bill O'Brien of The Hanover Insurance Companies promotes the values of openness and localness. Within Hanover, information is widely disseminated. In Bill O'Brien's words: "My reports to the board, for instance, go right down into the middle management of our branches. They are available to anyone."[10] Localness means that a decision is made or an action taken at the lowest level of the organization that is competent to do so. Interference by higher levels is inappropriate and demoralizing according to this Hanover value.

What do unethical charismatics do in contrast? They are one-way communicators, close-minded to input and suggestions from others. For a time, Ken Olsen at Digital Equipment Corporation created a culture that completely discouraged a reexamination of old strategies. Telling the founder of a successful organization that the nature of the game had changed and that his vision must be updated was very

---

[9]The description of the excellent quality of management at Wal-Mart Stores is drawn from S. Smith "Leaders of the Most Admired," *Fortune*, January 29, 1990, 46.

[10]Quote from J. E. Liebig, *Business Ethics: Profiles in Civic Virtue*, 136.

difficult. How do you tell the creator to reevaluate his creation, particularly when you have a very strong and outspoken leader? Many of his key advisors avoided discussions about changes that were necessary to Digital's marketing strategy, because of the negative reaction they anticipated from him. [11]

Accepting Feedback

Ethical charismatic leaders are realistic in their appraisal of their own abilities and limitations. They learn from criticism, rather than being fearful of it. This requires them to be open to advice and willing to have their initial judgements challenged. In his discussion of the art of leadership, Max DePree, CEO of Herman Miller, a highly profitable furniture design and manufacturing company, asserts that leaders who are clear about their own beliefs (assumptions about human nature, the role of the organization, and the measurement of performance, for example) have the self-confidence to encourage contrary opinions, and can enhance themselves through the strengths of others.

Unethical charismatic leaders have an inflated sense of self-importance, thriving on attention and admiration from others and shunning contrary opinions. Such leaders attract and gravitate towards loyal and uncritical followers. As one former disciple of Michael Milken, the junk bond king, said, "If he walked off the cliff, everyone in that group would have followed him." [12] Successful followers quickly learn to offer the leader information that he or she wants to hear, whether that information is correct or not.

Creating loyal supporters and eliminating dissenters were characteristic of Texas Instruments (TI) President J. Fred Bucy and CEO Mark Shepard, Jr.'s leadership style. Both men turned TI's low-cost policy into a fanatical obsession by building in control mechanisms that completely squashed any opportunity for individual initiative, thought, or innovation. Both were unwilling to have their strategies questioned no matter how disastrous the results. Both were intolerant and intimidating bosses.

Over time, TI employees spent more time telling Shepard and Bucy what they wanted to hear, rather than what was important or even critical to operations. This

---

[11]For a discussion of controlling leadership see D. Miller, *The Icharus Paradox: How Exceptional Companies Brag About Their Own Down Fall* (New York: Harpur Business, 1990).

[12]For more information on Milken's life, refer to *The Predator's Ball* by Connie Bruck.

destructive behavior was exemplified by TI employees who withheld critical information from Bucy and Shepard about the disastrous slump in the home computer division until inventory had piled up in the aisles.[13]

Lee Avery at Montgomery Ward practiced a similar brand of leadership. If anyone was foolish enough to differ with Avery he vowed to throw them out the window. After a major purge of his corporate executives he remarked, "I have never lost anyone I wanted to keep."[14]

Stimulating Followers Intellectually

Another important characteristic that differentiates ethical and unethical charismatic leaders is the intellectual development of their followers. Unethical charismatic leaders expect and even demand that their decisions be accepted without question. Ethical charismatic leaders encourage their followers to view the world from different perspectives which they themselves may not have previously considered. They ask their followers to question the "tried and true" ways to solving problems by re-evaluating the assumptions they used to understand and analyze the problem. As one leader commented: "You want the best creativity, the best ideas to give you the biggest success."

Developing Followers

Ethical and unethical charismatic leaders differ in the strategies they use to develop followers. Unethical charismatic leaders are insensitive and unresponsive to followers' needs and aspirations, while ethical charismatic leaders focus on developing people with whom they interact to higher levels of ability, motivation, and morality. "I enjoy developing people from the standpoint of seeing more potential in them than they see in themselves. I try to bring that potential out in people," said one leader in our study. They also express confidence in followers' capabilities to achieve the vision. And when the vision is met, ethical charismatic leaders share recognition with others. "I'd rather transfer the recognition to my people and make them feel that it's their project, it's their contribution, and it's their result," stated one leader. According to another leader: "You certainly share the

---

[13]For a review of Texas Instruments downward slide refer to Brian O'Reilly, "Texas Instruments: New Boss, Big Job," *Fortune*, July 8, 1985.

[14]For a discussion of Lee Avery's leadership style see D. Miller, *The Icharus Paradox: How Exceptional Companies Brag About Their Own Down Fall* (New York: Harpur Business, 1990).

center of applause. You make sure you share as much of the success and excitement as you can."

Moral Standards

Charismatic leaders differ widely in their moral standards which influences their decisions of what's right or wrong. Ethical charismatic leaders follow self-guided principles which may go against the majority opinion. Such leaders are not swayed by popular opinion unless it is in line with their principles. They promote a vision that inspires followers to accomplish objectives that are constructive for *both* the organization and society. Their vision is driven by "doing what's right" as opposed to "doing the right thing." Through the personal values they espouse, ethical charismatic leaders develop the moral principles, standards, and conduct of their followers.[15]

Ethical charismatic leaders possess three primary virtues: courage, a sense of fairness or justice, and integrity. Courage enables leaders to assume reasonable risks. When they believe something is wrong they speak up. Considering and balancing stakeholder claims underlies the virtue of justice. Just leaders respect others' rights and interests and honor principles. Leaders with strong integrity are characterized by internal consistency, acting in concert with their values and beliefs.

Jeff Furnam, chief financial officer of Ben and Jerry's Ice Cream, described Ben and Jerry as leaders who were using their success in business to show other leaders that they could maximize profit, while still having a positive social impact on society. Their attempt to get other U.S. companies to donate pretax profits for social programs is just one example of their overall strategy to create a higher moral standard for other business leaders to follow.

Integrity is a key value at Herman Miller. While executives at other companies were preoccupied with "looking out for number one" by arranging golden parachutes for themselves, in 1986 Herman Miller introduced silver parachutes for all its employees with more than two years of service.[16] In the event of a hostile takeover of Herman Miller that led to termination of employment, the silver

---

[15]For more on values and ethics of leaders, see K. Andrews, "Ethics in Practice," *Harvard Business Review*, September–October 1989, 99–104, and F. Bird and J. Gadz, *Good Management: Business Ethics in Action* (Toronto, Prentice-Hall, 1991).

[16]See M. DePree, *Leadership is an Art* (New York, Dell, 1989), xviii.

parachute plan would offer a soft landing for employees whose welfare is often ignored in corporations.

Adherence to ethical principles is also accorded a high profile at Johnson & Johnson.[17] CEO Ralph Larsen enjoys telling employees at Johnson & Johnson about his days as a trainee in one of the company's baby shampoo factories. He recalls attending a management meeting where a great debate ensued about whether to ship a large batch of shampoo that was safe but did not meet Johnson & Johnson's "no tears" standard. The ultimate decision was to absorb the loss. Similarly, in the tragic Tylenol case in which eight people died by swallowing poisoned capsules, the product was quickly recalled, mistakes were admitted, and the company lost $240 million in earnings. Says Larsen: "If we keep trying to do what's right, at the end of the day we believe the marketplace will reward us."

Behind these ethical decisions at Johnson & Johnson lies the Credo, a forty-four year old statement created by Robert Wood Johnson, son of the founder. The Credo emphasizes honesty, integrity, and respect for people—phrases common to most such statements. The difference is that senior executives at Johnson & Johnson devote considerable time and energy to ensuring that employees live by those words. Every few years, senior managers gather to debate the Credo's contents, a process used to keep ideas current. On his tours Larsen always mentions the document. "I tell employees they have to be prepared to take the short hit. In the end they'll prosper." In symbol and deeds the ethical standards of the leader and company are clearly articulated.

Unethical charismatic leaders follow standards if they satisfy their immediate self-interests. They are adept at managing an impression, that what they are doing conforms to what others consider "the right thing to do." By applying their enormous skills of communication, they can manipulate others to support their personal agenda.

A striking example of the values espoused by unethical charismatic leaders is Ross Johnson, the former chief executive officer and president of RJR Nabisco.[18] Over his career, Johnson gained the reputation as a glib, self-serving "win at all costs" executive with "a patina of charisma." He would fire executives with

---

[17]The description of the outstanding corporate citizenship of Johnson & Johnson is drawn from B. Dumaine, "Leaders of the Most Admired," *Fortune*, January 29, 1990, 50, 54.

[18]The best selling book *Barbarians At The Gate* by B. Burrough and J. Helyar (New York: Harper & Row, 1990) documents the fight to control RJR Nabisco and the central role played by CEO Ross Johnson.

no remorse, especially those who fell from his favor. Responsible for scattering one of America's largest, most venerable corporations to the winds through a massive leveraged buyout, Johnson was renown for his notoriously bloated expense accounts and lavish perks. He failed to investigate, and even protected, flagrant violations of spending by senior company executives. In one instance, he condoned payments from the company's international operations to a dummy corporation, which appeared to be billing the company for thousands of dollars of a senior executive's personal expenses. Johnson's reaction was to fire the people who uncovered the unethical activities and to promote the executive to president, despite an internal investigation which revealed that the executive had exercised poor judgment.

In this section, we have examined how two very different leaders who have been labelled charismatic, can differ markedly in their use of power, creation of visions, communication style, tolerance of opposing views, sensitivity to the needs of others and moral standards. We now discuss how the distinctive qualities of ethical and unethical charismatic leaders impact on followers.

THE IMPACT OF CHARISMATIC LEADERS: DEVELOPING OR ENSLAVING FOLLOWERS?

The double-edged sword of charismatic leadership is readily seen in the impact on followers. Ethical charismatic leaders convert followers into leaders. By expressing confidence in followers' abilities to accomplish collective goals, and by encouraging followers to think on their own and to question the established ways of doing things, they create followers who are more capable of leading themselves. According to Max DePree, this is the essence of leadership: "liberating people to do what is required of them in the most effective and humane way possible."[19] Followers feel independent, confident, powerful, and capable. They eventually take responsibility for their own actions, gain rewards through self-reinforcement, and like their leader, establish a set of internal standards to guide their actions and behavior.[20]

The magnitude of impact that charismatic leaders can have on followers was shown many years after the death of Walt Disney. Almost two decades after his

---

[19]Quote from M. DePree, *Leadership is an Art*, 1.

[20]For more information on the impact of leadership on follower development refer to B. J. Avolio and T. Gibbons, "Developing transformational leaders: A lifespan approach" in *Charismatic Leadership: The Elusive Factor in Organizational Effectiveness*, edited by J. A. Conger and R. N. Kanungo (San Francisco: Jossey-Bass, 1988).

death, managers would continually quote Disney to justify their decisions. Disney's strategy and policies were seen as unalterable and God help anyone who tried to change them![21]

Unethical charismatic leaders select or produce obedient, dependent, and compliant followers. They undermine followers' motivation and ability to challenge existing views, to engage in self-development, and to develop independent perspectives. Ultimately, followers' self-worth becomes inextricably linked to supporting the achievement of the leader's vision. If the leader deviates into unethical means for achieving his or her vision, followers are unlikely to question the leader's action. Since the leader is the moral standard bearer, followers can rationalize even the most destructive actions and behaviors. Michael Milken is a recent example of an unethical charismatic leader who abused power. Milken was terribly arrogant. He rarely had the patience to listen to other view points. As one Drexel executive declared, "What he wanted was bodies—but loyal bodies. Disciples."[22]

The impact of charismatic leaders on followers is often more extreme during periods of crisis. For the unethical charismatic leader, a crisis situation is often ripe for gaining or solidifying his or her power base. This power base can then be used to secure the leader's personal vision and to minimize dissent among followers. Followers easily become dependent on the leader who provides a clear action plan to pursue. "So strong is the belief in the leader's charismatic powers that the followers place their destinies in his or her hands. It is as if they have fallen under a magical spell; they become submissive, obedient, enraptured, and blind in their absolute loyalty."[23] The leader's authority over them seems boundless.

After the crisis subsides, followers increasingly rely on the leader for direction. Over time, they lose their self-confidence to question the leader's thinking and decisions, magnifying their dependence on the leader.

Followers of the ethical charismatic leader enter crises with a greater willingness to analyze the problem and offer solutions to the leader. The ethical charismatic leader works assiduously to develop followers' self-esteem, so that

---

[21]See I. Ross, "Disney Gambles on Tomorrow," *Fortune*, October 4, 1982.

[22]See *The Predators' Ball* by Connie Bruck for further details about Michael Milken.

[23]Quote from N. C. Roberts and R. T. Bradley's "Limits of Charisma" in *Charismatic Leadership: The Elusive Factor in Organizational Effectiveness* (San Francisco: Jossey-Bass, 1988), edited by J. A. Conger and R. N. Kanungo.

during a crisis followers are able to offer counsel to the leader to help resolve problems. They provide the needed checks and balances concerning the leader's decisions. Since followers have trust and faith in their leader, they will rally behind the leader's decision when there is no longer time to deliberate. Crises are not used by ethical charismatic leaders to blame followers for their inadequacies. Rather, crises are used to develop strength and a sense of purpose in the mission and vision. Crises often underscore the leader's intention to do what's right.

Ethical charismatic leaders use the crisis as a learning experience, once the crisis has passed. They point to the need for followers to develop their own capabilities so that future crises can be avoided, dealt with more effectively, or handled by followers themselves, when the leader is unavailable.

THE FAILURE OF SUCCESS

First suggested by Camille Cavour, then articulated by Lord Acton, absolute power corrupts absolutely. The trap that awaits charismatic leaders who have a successful track record partially lies in the accolades that accompany their accomplishments. If they readily believe the praises heaped upon them, they can be seduced by delusions of invincibility and greatness. Rather than focusing on the next challenge, they become preoccupied with maintaining an aura of greatness. Image management replaces active, meaningful contribution to the organization.

The trap that awaits charismatic leaders who have a successful track record partially lies in the accolades that accompany their accomplishments.

Ethical charismatic leaders have developed a value system that will help avoid the trappings of success. Moreover, the promotion of followers to higher stages of development provides the ethical charismatic leader with critical input that may keep them from straying down the wrong path.

Don Burr, founder, president, and CEO of the now defunct People Express Airline, exemplifies a recent example of the corruptive influence of success.[24] During the airline's formative years, Burr was heralded as an invincible charismatic leader. His accomplishments were widely praised in boardrooms, in the airline industry, and the management press. Touted as an entrepreneurial legend, Burr brought his company from a standing start in 1981 to $1 billion in revenues by 1984. The rapid growth was largely attributed to Burr's innovative management policies, hinging on employees being major stockholders in the company, opportunities for personal and professional growth through continuing education,

---

[24]Accounts tracing the rise and fall of Donald Burr's People Express Airline include J. A. Byrne "Up, Up and Away?" *Business Week*, November 25, 1985, 80–94; J. R. Norman "People is Plunging, but Burr is Staying Cool," *Business Week*, July 7, 1986, 31–32; E. M. Garrett, "The Troops are Restless at People Express," *Venture*, 1986, *8*, 102–104.

cross-utilization and job rotation, promotion from within the company, security of lifetime employment, and compensation higher than other companies paid for similar skills and experience. However, after achieving their market niche, rather than nurturing the growth of People Express, Burr went on a spending spree, acquiring other airlines. As the airline's growth failed to keep up with Burr's rapid expansion of routes and schedules, he shifted his consultative leadership style to an executive who fired anyone who challenged his views. Burr became a masterful manipulator and dictator, unreceptive to criticism or challenges. Employees lost their sense of family and gained a sense of alienation. Key management people left the company and fear pervaded the organization, ultimately resulting in its demise.

It is unclear whether Don Burr had the seeds of unethical charismatic leadership, or if he changed as a consequence of the crisis confronting his organization. What is apparent from this example is that he failed to take advantage of followers' input and the input of others outside the organization during a critical stage in the company's life cycle, unfortunately resulting in its demise.

A charismatic leader from our interview study, who had established a highly successful track record, was also keenly aware of the corruption of multiple successes. He was determined to avoid it.

> *"Over the course of my career I've become more concerned with getting my people to buy-in and let them have a large piece of success than I might have done as a young Turk. You use less brute strength and more intelligence. But then that's just a function of living. You have to stay humble. If you think what you are doing today is important, all you have to do is put it in context of how it will be in 500 million years. I keep a 'humble-izer' in my pocket—an acropod—a little sea urchin that lived in Arcona that's 500 million years old. It reminds me to stay humble."*

Thomas J. Watson, Sr. was keenly aware of the trap of success as exemplified in a speech delivered to a group of IBM managers in Paris during the height of the Great Depression.[25] "People often speak to me about our successful business. I always correct them. We have not made a success, but I do feel IBM is succeeding. We want you to also feel that you have not succeeded. We want you to feel that you are aiming for success but you are never going to catch up with it, for if you do, you are finished." Perhaps, the key distinction is to encourage all members of the organization to think more about what they can do to continuously improve the organization, always questioning the reasons for success. Leaders who fear changes might disrupt their strategies used to achieve success, are showing the early sign of leadership paralysis. Often such leaders abuse their power in the spirit of maintaining the status quo.

---

[25]Quote was taken from a speech delivered by Thomas J. Watson, Sr. on July 29, 1930 entitled, "Growing Man" in *As a Man Thinks,* by Thomas J. Watson, Sr.

CREATING AND MAINTAINING ETHICAL
CHARISMATIC LEADERSHIP

"Beware charisma! . . . But to beware does not necessarily mean or entail 'Avoid!' . . . Be aware! Then choose. "[26]

"As a transforming force, charisma is charged with explosive, unpredictable potential that, like the genie when released from the bottle, is beyond our control."[27] Executives and managers need to be aware of the risks of unleashing its darker side as well as the promises of cultivating its brighter side. Without awareness of the key behaviors, moral standards, and effects distinguishing ethical and unethical charismatic leaders, appointing a charismatic to a leadership position can be dangerous. The attributes which contribute to the unethical charismatic leader's success in aggressively ascending the corporate ladder may contribute to his or her ultimate failure as a leader.

How can the risks associated with charismatic leadership be diminished and the promises be enhanced? Clearly, managers and executives need to carefully select and promote their charismatic leaders. While the bright charismatic stars can be readily identified in organizations, should they be promoted to senior positions? We believe that the acid test for promotion is whether the candidate meets each of the key ethical charismatic behaviors outlined in Exhibit 1. If the candidate fails to meet any of these dimensions, he or she should not be promoted.

In fact, our ethical charismatic leaders reported that the most significant factor influencing their development of values and priorities was role models with whom they had very direct personal contact.

More generally, given the importance of ethical charismatic leaders for developing future leadership potential within organizations, how can ethical charismatic leaders themselves be created and sustained in organizations? What kinds of organizational policies, procedures, and processes can increase ethical charismatic leaders' probability of emergence and ultimate success? To answer these questions we asked our ethical charismatic leaders what top management needs to do to support their behavior. Six key factors were identified.

---

[26]Quote from C. Hodgkinson, *The Philosophy of Leadership* (New York: St. Martin's Press, 1983), 187.

[27]Quote from N. C. Roberts and R. T. Bradley's "Limits of Charisma," 273.

- Top management commitment to a clearly stated code of ethical conduct that is continually enforced helps establish acceptable standards or boundaries for employee conduct.[28]

- Recruiting, selecting, and promoting managers with high moral standards are ways of creating a culture of ethical responsibility.

- Developing performance standards and rewards that emphasize, for example, respect for people as individuals.

- Providing leaders with education and training that teaches them how to integrate diverse points of view. Being able to see the interrelationships among new perspectives and old, lies at the source of moral development.[29]

- Training individuals with the necessary personality characteristics, social skills, and motivation to acquire ethical charismatic leader behaviors.[30] Training in ethical leadership skills must be consistent with the philosophy of the top leadership in the company and the company culture.

- Identifying heroes or heroines who exemplify high moral conduct. Such heroes or heroines need to be heralded by top management as essential to the long-term success of the organization.[31]

---

[28]The value of an organizational ethics policy for reducing unethical decision behavior was reported by W. H. Hegarty and H. P. Sims, Jr. "Organizational Philosophy, Policies, and Objectives Related to Unethical Decision Behavior: A Laboratory Experiment," *Journal of Applied Psychology*, 1979, *64*, 331–338.

[29]Ways of enhancing ethical decision making in organizations are discussed by L. K. Trevino "Ethical Decision Making in Organizations: A Person-Situation Interactionist Model," *Academy of Management Review*, 1986, *11*, 601–617. The impact of education and training on moral development is discussed by G. D. Baxter and C. A. Rarick in, "Education for the Moral Development of Managers: Kohlberg's Stages of Moral Development and Integrative Education," *Journal of Business Ethics*, 1987, *6*, 243–248.

[30]Charismatic leadership training and its related caveats are described in J. M. Howell and P. J. Frost's "A Laboratory Study of Charismatic Leadership," *Organizational Behavior and Human Decision Processes*, 1989, and in B. M. Bass and B. J. Avolio's "OD and Transformational Leadership: Organizational and Individual Applications" in *Research in Organizational Change and Development*, edited by R. W. Woodman and R. Passmore (Greenwich: JAI Press, 1990).

[31]W. A. Kahn, "Toward an Agenda for Business Ethics Research," *Academy of Management Review*, 1990, *15*, 311–328.

In conclusion, building internal ethical standards in leaders is a challenging undertaking which requires formal codes of ethical conduct, top management who subscribe to and practice ethical behavior, systems that reinforce ethical behavior, and role models who exemplify high moral standards. In fact, our ethical charismatic leaders reported that the most significant factor influencing their development of values and priorities was role models with whom they had very direct personal contact.

A LOOK TOWARDS THE FUTURE

Ethical charismatic leaders in the end deserve this label only if they create transformations in their organizations so that members are motivated to follow them and to seek organization objectives not simply because they are ordered to do so, and not merely because they calculate that such compliance is in their self-interest, but because they voluntarily identify with the organization, its standards of conduct and willingly seek to fulfill its purpose.[32]

In the period of time that we currently operate, and with the values of employees entering our organizations today, the successful organization will be a place where individual needs are recognized and enhanced rather than brought into conformity with the old ways of doing things.[33] Leaders will know that the best form of leadership builds followers into leaders who eventually take responsibility for their own ethical behavior, development, and performance.

ABOUT THE AUTHORS

The authors are indebted to Leanne Atwater, Bernard Bass, Joseph DeStefano, Jeffrey Gandz, two anonymous reviewers, and Associate Editor Kathryn Bartol for their helpful comments.

Jane M. Howell, Ph.D., is assistant professor of organizational behavior at The University of Western Ontario. She has published many articles in the areas of transformational leadership, organizational champions, and technological innovation. She conducts leadership, organizational change, and management skill development programs in Canada and abroad.

Bruce J. Avolio, Ph.D., is a leading expert on the study of transformational leadership. He has published numerous articles on this topic and conducted training and organizational development programs worldwide. He is director of graduate programs in the School of Management at SUNY-Binghamton and associate professor in organizational behavior.

---

[32]See F. Bird and J. Gandz, *Good Management: Business Ethics in Action* (Toronto: Prentice-Hall, 1991) 166.

[33]A discussion of future organizations and their workforce was reported by L. R. Offerman and M. K. Gowing "Organizations of the Future: Challenges and Changes," *American Psychologist,* 1990, *45,* 95–108.

HOW TO BECOME AN INFLUENTIAL MANAGER

Bernard Keys, Georgia Southern University
Thomas Case, Georgia Southern University

Executive Overview

Because of the increasing diversity of the goals and values of employees and their increasing interdependence, the effectiveness of formal authority is diminishing. It must be replaced with influence. In this article, we have summarized our research and that of others which have focused on managerial influence behaviors. Those tactics which are used most frequently and those which are most effective in having an impact on superiors, subordinates, and peers are discussed. Five steps which must be taken to develop and maintain managerial influence are outlined.

ARTICLE

A hospital department head attempted in vain to persuade physicians working in a large metropolitan hospital to bring patient medical records up to date. Although doctors consider this an abhorrent chore, hospitals cannot begin the billing process until each record is completed and signed by the physician. After many frustrating attempts, the department head describes how he proved equal to the challenge.

> *Every month we served the doctors breakfast and lunch and organized games that would allow them to win prizes. Sometimes we would place balloons on a bulletin board and let them throw darts at the balloons. At other times we would do something ridiculously child-like such as hosting a watermelon seed spitting contest or playing pin the tail on the donkey. The sessions worked beautifully because the doctors knew that when they came in someone would be there to help them and they would even have a little fun. Once when we were really desperate we hired a popular entertainer. The room was full that day and we completed over 1,000 charts.*

Influence is simply the process by which people successfully persuade others to follow their advice, suggestion, or order. It can be contrasted with power which is a personal or positional attribute that enables one to influence others and which

---

© *Academy of Management Executive*, 1990, Vol. 4, No. 4.

can be thought of as "continuing or sustained" influence.[1] A number of popular books have suggested that influence must replace the use of formal authority in relationships with subordinates, peers, outside contacts, and others on whom the job makes one dependent.[2] The writers of these books attribute the need for greater influence to the rapidity of change in organizations, the diversity of people, goals and values, increasing interdependence, and the diminishing acceptability of formal authority. Bennis and Nanus have suggested that leaders must empower themselves by empowering their subordinates. Kouzes and Posner agree with this conclusion, explaining that the more people believe they can influence and control the organization, the greater will be the effectiveness of the organization. Tichy and Devanna extend this thought even further by suggesting that today we need transformational leaders who will allow networks that funnel diverse views upward from the lower level of the organization where a need for change is often first detected. Similarly, John Kotter observes that the increasing diversity and interdependence of organizational role players is creating a "power gap" for managers who often have knowledge and good ideas for organizations but who have inadequate authority to implement their ideas.

Recently managers have begun to view leadership as the orchestration of relationships between several different interest groups—superiors, peers, and outsiders, as well as subordinates.[3] Effectiveness at leadership requires balance in terms of efforts spent in building relationships in these four directions. Good

---

[1]These definitions follow those of D. R. Hampton, C. E. Summer, and R. A. Webber, Chapter 3, *Organizational Behavior and the Practice of Management,* (Glenview, Illinois: Scott, Foresman, 1987), Fifth Edition.

[2]See Chapter 1 of A. R. Cohen and C. L. Bradford, *Influence Without Authority,* (New York: John Wiley, 1990). For a review of these thoughts, see W. Bennis and B. Nanus, *Leaders: The Strategies for Taking Charge,* (New York: Harper and Row, 1985) and J. M. Kouzes and B. Z. Posner, *The Leadership Challenge,* (San Francisco: Jossey-Bass, 1988). For a book that relates leadership influence to the way in which change is implemented in the American economy, see N. M. Tichy and M. A. Devanna, *The Transformational Leader,* (New York: John Wiley & Sons, 1986). See also Chapter 2 of J. P. Kotter, *Power and Influence—Beyond Formal Authority,* (New York: The Free Press, 1985).

[3]For the review of literature and our conceptualization of an influence model, see J. B. Keys and R. Bell, "The Four Faces of the Fully Functioning Middle Manager," *California Management Review,* 24 (4), Summer 1982, 59–66; a condensed version of this article can be found in *World Executive's Digest,* 4 (7), 1983, 25–31.

relationships in one direction can often be leveraged to obtain influence in another.

For example, effectiveness with subordinates has been found to depend heavily on the ability to develop upward influence with superiors.[4] Influence with the boss often depends on the ability to accomplish things through one's subordinates.[5] Laterally, managers must spend time in group meetings, interorganizational negotiations, and in bids for departmental resources.[6] This is a role replete with power gaps. Most assuredly lateral relationships require the ability to influence without formal authority representatives with unions, customers, and government,

---

[4]For the original research on the importance of upward influence to supervisory success, see D. C. Pelz, "Influence: Keys to Effective Leadership in the First Level Supervisor," *Personnel*, 29, 1959, 209-217. For a later discussion with case illustrations, see F. Bartolomé and A. Laurent, "The Manager: Master and Servant of Power," *Harvard Business Review*, 64 (6), Nov/Dec. 1986, 77-81. The ways in which managers, especially middle managers, acquire and sustain upward influence are outlined in D. H. Kreger, "Functions and Problems of Middle Management," *Personnel Journal*, 49 (11), November 1970, 935; P. D. Couch, "Learning to Be a Middle Manager," *Business Horizons*, 22 (1), February 1979, 33-41; R. A. Webber, "Career Problems of Young Managers," *California Management Review*, 18 (4), Summer 1976, 19-33; H. E. R. Uyterhoeven, "General Managers in the Middle," *Harvard Business Review*, 50 (2), March—April 1972, 75-85. For an article that has become a best selling classic on the subject, see J. J. Gabarro and J. P. Kotter, "Managing Your Boss," *Harvard Business Review*, 58 (1), January-February, 1980, 92-100. For a recent article on maintaining loyalty and developing an initial relationship with the boss, see R. Vecchio, "Are You In or Out With The Boss," *Business Horizons*, 29 (6), November-December 1986, 76-78.

[5]For the review of the way in which managers create influence downward, see Uyterhoeven Endnote 4 and S. H. Ruello, Transferring Managerial Concepts and Techniques to Operating Management," *Advanced Management Journal*, 38 (3), July 1973, 42-48. For a discussion of the importance of defending and supporting subordinates, see Bartolomé and Laurent Endnote 4.

[6]For a discussion of how managers develop political skills, see Ruello, Endnote 5 and Uyterhoeven, Endnote 4. To review the integrative role of middle managers, see J. L. Hall and J. K. Leidecker, "Lateral Relations: The Impact on the Modern Managerial Role," *Industrial Management*, June 1974, 3.

or highly autonomous professionals such as the physician in our introductory example.[7]

The concept of "linking groups" seems to drive the middle manager's work while both middle management and executive levels are heavily engaged in "coordinating" independent groups. In this latter role, they must persuade other organizational groups to provide information, products, resources needed, and negotiate working agreements with other groups. Additionally, executive levels of management must frequently maintain relationships with management-level vendors, consultants, and other boundary-spanning agents through outside meetings. Recent research suggests that the "ambassador role" of "representing one's staff" is vitally important to all levels of management. It consists of developing relationships with other work groups and negotiating for information and resources on behalf of the manager's own group.[8]

Building on the previous thoughts and the research of others, we conducted field studies to collect incidents, similar to the one describing the hospital department head, and used these to analyze how managers build and sustain influence. This article explains our research findings and those of related studies for managers who wish to become more influential with subordinates, superiors, peers, and other target groups.

INFLUENCE TACTIC RESEARCH

Only a few writers have identified influence tactics from research investigations. David Kipnis and his colleagues asked evening graduate students to describe an incident in which they actually succeeded in getting either their boss, a coworker, or a subordinate to do something they wanted. Their analysis revealed that the tactics of ingratiation (making the supervisor feel important) and developing rational plans were the most frequently used methods to influence superiors. When attempting to influence subordinates, respondents most often used formal authority, training, and explanations. Only one tactic, that of requesting help, was frequently associated with influencing coworkers.

---

[7]For a discussion of external relationships, see D. W. Organ, "Linking Pins Between Organizations and Environment," *Business Horizons*, 14 (6), December 1971, 73–80.

[8]A. I. Kraut, P. R. Pedigo, D. D. McKenna, and M. D. Dunnette, "The Role of the Manager: What's Really Important in Different Management Jobs," *The Academy of Management Executive*, 3(4), 286–293.

Our studies were aimed at strengthening the previous research. Since the studies cited above utilized categories of influence tactics derived from research with MBA students, we developed categories from influence incidents collected from practicing managers. Our three studies used trained students from several universities and structured interview forms to collect a wide geographic dispersion of responses.

Attempts were made to collect one successful incident and one unsuccessful incident from managers in a wide variety of both large and small businesses. One study focused on lateral influence processes, another on upward influence processes, and a third study examined downward influence. The primary question asked of each manager was, "Please think of a time when you successfully/unsuccessfully tried to influence a (superior, peer, or subordinate) toward the attainment of a personal, group, or organizational goal . . . Please tell exactly what happened."[9]

---

[9]For other studies on influence tactics see: D. Kipnis, S. M. Schmidt and I. Wilkinson, "Interorganizational Influence Tactics: Explorations in Getting One's Way," *Journal of Applied Psychology*, 65 (4), August 1980, 440–452. This study differed from our field study in that it surveyed evening MBA students and allowed them to describe any successful influence episode in which they had been involved. W. K. Schilit and E. A. Locke, "A Study of Upward Influence in Organizations," *Administrative Science Quarterly*, 1982, 27 (2), 304–316 found that Kipnis and Schmidt's fourteen tactic categories were not sufficient to categorize upward influence incident accounts collected from undergraduate and graduate business students and full-time employees or supervisors. They found evidence supporting the use of 20 types of upward influence tactics. Because these previous investigations relied so heavily on unchallenged global categories derived from a relatively small sample of evening MBA students which might not be representative of managers, we began our studies from scratch and collected narrative accounts of incidents from practicing managers. Each study focused on only one type of target and at least 250 influence tactics were collected. Flanagan's critical incident method was used to develop categories and to content analyze the responses. (J. C. Flanagan, "Defining the Requirements of the Executive's Job," *Personnel*, 28, July, 1951, 28–35.) Our findings for upward influence were more similar to those of Schilit and Locke than to those of Kipnis et al. Over 46 distinct tactics were observed across the three types of targets. Of course, tactics used to influence some targets are rarely, if ever, used to influence other types of targets. The description of managerial influence tactics which emerges from our three studies is much more detailed and therefore more suited to management applications than that provided by the previous investigations. Of equal importance, unlike the previous studies, our investigations also addressed the use of combinations of tactics vis a vis single tactics, and the long term consequences of the influence attempt for the initiator and the organization.

Exhibit 1 presents the summary of findings from these studies.[10]

	Boss	Peers	Subordinates
Presenting a rational explanation	1	1	3
Telling, arguing, or talking without support	2	0	0
Presenting a complete plan	3	0	0
Using persistence or repetition	4	0	0
Developing and showing support of others (employees, outsiders, etc.)	5	2	12
Using others as a platform to present ideas	6	0	0
Presenting an example of a parallel situation	7	3	5
Threatening	8	4	10
Offering to trade favors or concessions	9	5	0
Using manipulative techniques	10	6	7
Calling on formal authority and policies	0	8	6
Showing confidence and support	0	0	1
Delegating duties, guidelines, or goals	0	0	2
Listening, counseling, or soliciting ideas	0	0	4
Questioning, reviewing, or evaluating	0	0	9
Rewarding with status or salary	0	0	7
Developing friendship or trust	0	7	11

Exhibit 1. Rank of Frequency With Which Each Influence Tactic Was Reported By Target Groups

The numbers to the right of each tactic portray the rank order of the frequency with which influence tactics were reported for each target group.

Influencing Superiors

In influence attempts with superiors and peers, rational explanations were the most frequently used tactic. Often these techniques included the presentation of a complete plan, a comparative or quantitative analysis, or documentation of an idea or plan by way of survey, incidents, or interviews. In a few isolated cases,

---

[10]For a more complete description of the research methods and statistical findings of the three studies reported here, see J. B. Keys, T. Miller, T. Case, K. Curran, and C. Jones, "Lateral Influence Tactics," *International Journal of Management*, 4 (3), 1987, 425–431; L. Dosier, T. Case, J. B. Keys, G. Murkinson, "Upward Influence Tactics," *Leadership and Organizational Development Journal*, 9 (4), 1988, 25–31; T. Case, J. B. Keys, and L. Dosier, "How Managers Influence Subordinates: A Study of Downward Influence Tactics," *Leadership and Organizational Development Journal*, 9 (5), 1988, 22–28.

subordinates challenged their superiors' power, tried to manipulate them, bargained for influence, or threatened to quit. When these more assertive techniques were used, the subordinate was successful about 50 percent of the time—not very good odds for the risks which they were taking. In most narratives we found that the subordinate using these methods had discovered a powerless boss, or had developed an unusual position of power themselves by becoming indispensable. In a few cases they had simply become frustrated and thrown caution to the wind.

Upward influence tactics were characterized by numerous supporting tactics such as mustering the support of a variety of other persons (both internal and external to the organization) or by choosing appropriate timing to approach the boss. Only two tactics appeared with significant enough frequency differential to be clearly distinguished as a successful or unsuccessful tactic. Subordinates using the tactic of "talking to or arguing with the boss without support" were more likely to fail. On the other hand, those who continued persistently or repeated an influence attempt continuously were likely to succeed. Caution is in order, however, in interpreting the use of persistence and repetition; this was usually a secondary tactic used in combination with others such as presenting facts and rational plans.

The rational persuasion technique was used by a plant manager to prevent a cutback in his work force when the army phased out one of its tanks.

First the plant manager sold a new product line to divisional staff who reported to his boss. In the meantime he developed a presentation in the form of a comparative analysis showing the pros and cons of taking on the new product line. Ideas presented included such things as the reduced burden on other products, risk reward factors, and good community relations from the layoff avoided. The presentation was polished, written on viewgraphs, and presented in person. The plant manager made certain that his technical staff would be at the meeting ready to answer any questions that might damage the strength of the presentation.

Not only did the plant manager succeed with this influence attempt, he felt that his boss and peers were easier to convince on subsequent attempts.

Influencing Subordinates

When dealing with subordinates, of course, the manager may simply tell an employee to do something. But our research suggests that managers who rely on formal authority alone are greatly limiting their options. The power gap noted earlier exists with subordinates as well as with other groups. Today more than ever, it must be filled with methods of influence other than authority. The following incident presents an interesting view of a furniture manufacturer trying to persuade his upholstery foreman to accept the position of plant superintendent.

The manager met with Foreman Z in the foreman's office for short periods to talk about the promotion. Anticipating resistance, he covered small increments of the superintendent's responsibilities and allowed the foreman time to think about each session. The manager made sure that each session ended on a positive note. He pointed out the many tasks and skills required of the superintendent's job were already inherent in the foreman position. He downplayed the more complex responsibilities, relying on his commitment to future training to resolve these. Several such meetings took place in a five-day period. On one occasion the foreman alluded to resentment from fellow foremen. This prompted the manager to enlist the help of some of the other foremen—several hunting buddies, to talk favorably about Z taking the position. In the last meeting the manager outlined the responsibilities and cited the salary and prestige. which accompanied the position.

But our research suggests that managers who rely on formal authority alone are greatly limiting their options.

The senior manager in this incident later commented that he had always had success at using this technique—that is, breaking down a complex influence task into incremental steps and attacking each step separately. While there is some merit to this process, most readers would agree that the major reason for success in this case was the persistence exerted by the senior manager to win in his influence attempt. The mild deception in over-simplifying the open position could merit criticism but must be moderated by the manager's willingness to train and support the foreman. In this case, the influence tactic had positive long-term consequences; the foreman became a very successful plant superintendent and later trained his own successor.

As expected, managers often use the tactic of explaining (policies, tasks, benefits) or delegating assignments when attempting to influence subordinates. Frequently they showed confidence, encouragement, or support when trying to win subordinates over. The use of reason or facts often cam in the form of a suggestion of a superior procedure or an example. Managers often counseled with subordinates or solicited their ideas to influence them.

Frequently, subordinates were questioned, reviewed, evaluated, threatened, warned, reprimanded, or embarrassed to change their minds or to solicit compliance with plans of the superior. These more threatening and negative techniques were more frequently associated with failure than success. Occasionally subordinates were transferred or relocated to influence them, but usually with little success. The more assertive tactics were typically used in cases where subordinates were initially reluctant to comply with reasonable requests or had violated policies or procedures.

Influencing Peers

Only one tactic from our lateral influence study was noted significantly more often in successful influence attempts with peers—that of "developing and showing support of others." This tactic was most often used along with others and therefore represented a part of a multiple influence tactic. Often a peer in a staff department or a subordinate is used to support a proposal, as in the influence attempt described by a zone manager with a large tire and rubber company.

During this time I was managing 25 company-owned stores in which I initiated an effective program to control the handling of defective merchandise. I wanted to see the method utilized by the other store managers throughout the country who were supervised by other zone managers, but I felt that they would consider me to be intruding if I approached them directly. Therefore, I asked my store managers to tell the store managers in other zones about the sizeable savings to be had from the use of the method. The other store managers told their zone managers and soon they came to me for information about my program. The new program saved the company $90,000, per year which increased our pay in bonuses at the end of the year.

When dealing with peers, managers made extensive use of rational facts or ideas. They often presented an example of another organization using their idea or proposal. Demonstrating that they had the support of others was a frequently used managerial influence tactic. Occasionally they threatened to go to higher level management or called on formal authority or policies to support their case. Assertive and manipulative tactics were used more often when attempting to influence the boss or subordinates, but less frequently with peers.

INFLUENCE TACTIC EFFECTIVENESS

Our research on individual influence attempts somewhat simplifies the area of influence effectiveness. In the first place, the methods listed in Exhibit 1 are the ones that are most frequently used and not necessarily the ones which are most successful. In all three studies we found that techniques that succeed in some instances fail in others. The few exceptions to this finding are noted in Exhibit 1 when the ranks of tactics are underlined. These represent tactics that were reported significantly more often, for either successful or unsuccessful influence attempts. For example, unsuccessful influence attempts with the boss often consisted of simply telling the boss something, arguing, or presenting an idea or suggestion without support. While this technique occasionally succeeded, it was more likely to be associated with unsuccessful episodes. Similarly, the use of persistence or repetition was reported more often in successful influence attempts with the boss than with unsuccessful ones.

Judging from the incidents collected, subordinate influence tactics of "threatening or questioning, reviewing, or evaluating" are significantly more likely to lead to failure than to success. Consider the experience of a plant operations manager attempting to introduce quality circles in an area to improve productivity.

Judging from the incidents collected, subordinate influence tactics of "threatening or questioning, reviewing, or evaluating" are significantly more likely to lead to failure than to success.

> *The operations manager requested the assistance of the manager of organizational development, who warned that such implementation would take time, patience and the building of trust among his employees. Turnover in the operations area was high and negative attitudes tended to prevail. The operations manager became impatient, viewing QC as a quick fix for morale problems. The QD manager made available several persons who had worked successfully with a QC implementation, but after conversing with them the operations manager elected not to listen. He chose two subordinates to be trained as QC facilitators and immediately upon the completion of their training, began to implement QC. The operations manager and facilitators subtly coerced employees to join the circles and directed them toward the projects that management wanted attacked. After several months employee interest fell sharply and several complaints were filed with employee relations leading to abandonment of the project.*

Contrast this occurrence with a less threatening attempt reported by a manufacturing manager in another part of the country:

> *The manager first read numerous articles about QC programs and learned the pitfalls to avoid, QC information handouts were given to the supervisors over a period of a couple of months. The supervisors were never pressured and gradually they approached their manager, asking how they could get quality circles started in their departments. The program was then implemented using recognized procedures and is still operating successfully several years later.*

The analysis of influence attempts such as the quality circles' incidents demonstrates the need for careful implementation of management processes.

STEPS IN BECOMING AN INFLUENTIAL MANAGER

Power, or sustained influence, may be accumulated and stored by a manager for future use. This allows one to call on existing strength to bolster influence tactics and often affects the future choice of influence tactic. Power may also be provided by the strategic position that one occupies in an organization, but position is often beyond the control of the incumbent. Fortunately, power may also be acquired through the development and exercise of certain skills by the manager within the organization. It is this skill-based power that we discuss throughout the rest of this article.[11]

Our research, and that of other writers reviewed in this article, indicates that there are five key steps to establishing sustained managerial influence.

- Develop a reputation as a knowledgeable person or an expert.

- Balance the time spent in each critical relationship according to the needs of the work rather than on the basis of habit or social preference.

- Develop a network of resource persons who can be called upon for assistance.

- Choose the correct combination of influence tactics for the objective and for the target to be influenced.

- Implement influence tactics with sensitivity, flexibility, and adequate levels of communication.

These steps in developing influence might be compared to the development of a "web of influence" (no negative implication intended). Unlike the web of a spider, the manager's web of influence can be mutually advantageous to all who interact within it. The web is anchored by a bridgeline of knowledge and expertise. The structure of the web is extended when invested time is converted into a network of resource persons who may be called upon for information and special assistance or support with an influence attempt. These persons—superiors, peers, subordinates, outside contacts, and others might be thought of as spokes in the web.

---

[11]For an interesting theoretical discussion of these and other power producing factors see D. Mechanic, "Source of Power on Lower Participants in Complex Organizations," *Administrative Science Quarterly*, 7 (3), 1962, 349-364. For an excellent case study of how a middle manager combines expertise, networking and the other techniques noted see D. Izraeli, "The Middle Manager and the Tactics of Power Expansion: A Case Study," *Sloan Management Review*, 16 (2), 1975, 57-69.

Establishing the web, however, does not insure influence attempts will be successful. An effective combination of influence tactics must be selected for each influence target and influence objective sought. Finally, the tactics chosen must be communicated well within the sector of the web targeted.

Managers who possess expert knowledge in a field and who continually build that knowledge base are in a position to convert successful attempts into sustained power.

Our research suggests that the web of influence is continually in a state of construction. It is often broken or weakened by an ill-chosen influence attempt requiring patch-up work for a portion of the web. Some webs are constructed poorly, haphazardly or incompletely like the tangled web of a common house spider, while others are constructed with a beautiful symmetrical pattern like the one of the orb weaver.

Develop a Reputation as an Expert

Of all the influence tactics mentioned by respondents in our interviews, the use of rational facts and explanations was the most commonly reported—although in isolation this method succeeded no more often than it failed. Managers who possess expert knowledge in a field and who continually build that knowledge base are in a position to convert successful attempts into sustained power. In the early stages of a career (or shortly after a move) power from expertise is usually tentative and fragile like the first strands of a web. Hampton and colleagues explain how expertise is extended to become sustained influence with the following example of Bill, a young staff specialist, hired to provide expertise to a number of production managers:

> *Initially, the only influence process available to the specialist is persuasion—gaining the rational agreement of the managers. To be effective he prepares elaborate, clear presentations (even rehearsing with a colleague to anticipate any questions). By data, logic, and argument, he attempts to gain the agreement of his superiors. After a year of this kind of relationship, he goes one day to talk with Barbara, one of the managers. An hour has been reserved for the presentation. He arrives and begins his pitch. After a couple of minutes, however, the busy manager interrupts: "I'm just too busy to go over this. We'll do whatever you want to do."* [12]

---

[12]See Endnote 1, p. 35.

But enhancing expert-based power involves publicizing one's expertise as well as acquiring it. For example, Kotter contrasts two 35-year-old vice presidents in a large research and development organization, who are considered equally bright and technically competent.

Close friends and associates claim the reason that Randley is so much more powerful is related to a number of tactics that he has used more than Kline has. Randley has published more scientific papers and managerial articles than Kline. Randley has been more selective in the assignments he has worked on, choosing those that are visible and that require his strong suits. He has given more speeches and presentations on projects that are his own achievements. And in meetings in general, he is allegedly forceful in areas where he has expertise and silent in those where he does not. [13]

Balance Time With Each Critical Relationship

Managers who desire to become influential must strike a reasonable balance in the investment of their time. In another study using a questionnaire, we surveyed managers from the United States, Korea, Hong Kong, and the Philippines to learn how they spent their time. These managers say that they spend about 10 percent of their time interacting with the boss, approximately 30 percent interacting with subordinates, and about 20 percent interacting with peers. As one might expect, the pattern of outside relations varies with the job (i.e., sales, engineering, etc.), but the managers report, on the average, spending from 15–20 percent of their time with external contracts. Time spent alone varies from 15–28 percent. [14] Although we cannot argue that this pattern is descriptive of all managers, it is similar to the pattern of communication distribution discovered from a sample of United States managers by Luthans and Larson. [15]

---

[13] See Kotter in Endnote 2, p. 35.

[14] B. Keys, T. Case, and A. Edge, "A Cross-National Study of Differences Between Leadership Relationships of Managers in Hong Kong with those in the Philippines, Korea, and the United States," *International Journal of Management*, 6 (4), 1989, 390–404.

[15] For a look at the pattern of managerial communications and time investment see F. Luthans and J. K. Larson, "How Managers Really Communicate," *Human Relations*, 39 (2), 1986, 161–178.

Some popular writers are calling for a heavy rescheduling of time and communications efforts.[16] Peters argues that 75 percent of a middle manager's time must be spent on horizontal relationships to speed up cross-functional communications in the middle of organizations. Johnson and Frostman see this kind of communication as being so critical that it must be mandated by upper level management. Peters emphasizes the argument that upper level managers spend too little time visiting with customers or in face-to-face relationships with subordinates (management by walking around). The bottom line is that time should be spent where influence is most needed to accomplish organizational goals.[17]

The bottom line is that time should be spent where influence is most needed to accomplish organizational goals.[17]

During our seminars on influence over the years, managers have often told us that they failed to spend enough time with the boss or with peers, or in simply keeping up with organizational happenings. This may be due to the fact that many managers are uncomfortable spending time with those who have more formal power than they, (superiors), or with those with whom they must compete, (peers). Sayles believes that managers' uneasiness with peers grows out of the difference in values across departments and work groups, the ambiguities which exist in cross-organizational relationships, and the conflict often generated in lateral relationships.[18] Other things being equal, realigning from a narrow focus on subordinates to a bigger picture which includes lateral and upward relationships can often yield a stronger web of sustained influence and should provide the supporting spokes needed to launch influence tactics.

A strong web of influence may even be quite desirable from the boss's viewpoint. Schilit found that managers who had been working for the same upper

---

[16]For a discussion of the need for middle managers to spend time in lateral and external relationships, see also T. Peters, *Thriving on Chaos: Handbook for a Management Revolution*, (New York: Harper & Row, 1987), T. Peters and N. Austin, *Passion for Excellence*, (New York: Random House, 1985), and L. Johnson and A. L. Frohman, "Identifying and Closing the Gap in the Middle of Organizations," *The Academy of Management Executive*, 3 (2), 107–114.

[17]R. E. Kaplan, "Trade Routes: The Manager's Network of Relationships," *Organizational Dynamics*, 12 (4), 1984, 37–52 and J. Kotter, The General Managers, (New York: The Free Press, 1983).

[18]For an excellent guide to handling lateral relations complete with case illustrations, see Chapter 5 of L. Sayles, *Leadership: Managing in Real Organizations*, (New York: McGraw Hill), Second Edition.

manager for a long period of time were quite capable of influencing that manager even on strategic issues facing the company. He concludes that: "(Managers) should be encouraged to be assertive in presenting their strategic thoughts because widespread strategic thinking may have a positive impact on their division or organization."[19]

Develop a Network of Resource Persons

Although managers do not use other people in most influence attempts, the more important attempts invariably involve others. For example, in the incident cited earlier about the furniture manufacturer who wanted a foreman to accept the plant manager's job, the assistance of other foremen (fishing buddies) was solicited. Similarly, in the case of the plant manager who tried to avoid a cutback in his work force after the phaseout of a military contract, the manager sold his idea to division staff and ensured that his own technical staff would be in attendance at the meeting in which he was making a presentation to the boss. The ability to establish and exploit a network is clearly demonstrated by a branch manager of a bank who used the following tactic with his superior, a vice president, when he found his operation in need of additional space.

My strategy was to convince my immediate superior that the current facilities were too small to not only handle the current volume of business, but too small to allow us to increase our share of the market in a rapidly growing area. First, I persuaded my superior to visit the branch more often, especially at times when the branch was particularly busy. I also solicited accounting's help to provide statistical reports on a regular basis that communicated the amount of overall growth in the area as well as the growth of our competitors. These reports showed that our market share was increasing. I then asked my superior to visit with me as I called on several customers and prospects in the area to let him know the type of potential business in the area. During this period of time, I kept pushing to increase all levels of business at the branch. Finally, I encouraged key customers in the bank to say favorable things about my branch when they visited with my senior managers. Eventually my superior got behind my proposal

---

[19]For a discussion of why managers should encourage their subordinates to influence them, see W. K. Schilit, "An Examination of Individual Differences as Moderators of Upward Influence Activity in Strategic Decisions," *Human Relations*, 30 (10), 1986, 948. The author's findings from this empirical study lend support to the suggestions about transformational leaders by Tichy and Devanna and Kotter in Endnote 2.

and we were able to build an addition to the building which allowed me to add several new employees.

Such influence attempts clearly illustrate the fact that many managers do not assume that achievement in traditional areas of management—selling, organizing, promoting customers—will inspire sufficient confidence by others. Rather than waiting for good publicity and resources to come to them, they seek them out through influence approaches built on carefully planned networks and persistent effort. The findings of our influence studies are supported by the observations of Luthans and his colleagues who concluded that managers who are both effective (have satisfied and committed subordinates and high performance in their units) and successful (receive relatively rapid promotions) strike a balanced approach between networking, human resource management, communications, and traditional management activities.[20]

To some extent, networking activities may affect the positional strength of managers. The more contracts a manager has with others and the more independent the position relative to others, the more control the manager has over the flow of information. Positions that involve interaction with more influential managers of the organization or control information on which they rely, will typically be ones of power.[21]

The more contacts a manager has with others and the more independent the position relative to others, the more control the manager has over the flow of information.

Kaplan compares the strengthening of lateral relationships in the organization to the establishment of trade routes in international trade. According to this writer, managers, unlike countries which trade products, often trade power and the ability to get things done. Their goal is to build strong reciprocal relationships with other departments so that when the manager has immediate needs sufficient obligation exists to ensure fast cooperation. Often positions on the boundary of an organization can be especially influential. Consider the example referred to by Kaplan when describing a newly appointed manager of corporate employee relations. "I wanted a base that was different from what the groups reporting to me had and also from

---

[20]For a further discussion of the activities of successful and effective managers, see F. Luthans, R. M. Hodgetts, and S. A. Rosenkrantz, *Real Managers*, (Cambridge: Ballenger Publishing Company, 1988).

[21]For a review of network theory, see J. Blau and R. Alba, "Empowering Nets of Participation," *Administrative Science Quarterly*, 27, 1982, 363-379. See also Endnote 18.

what my superiors had, so I established a series of contacts in other American industries until I knew on a first-name basis my counterpart at IBM, TRW, Proctor & Gamble, DuPont, and General Electric, and I could get their input—input which the people in my organization didn't have."[22] Kaplan suggests that networks of trading partners can be built by rotating jobs frequently, establishing strong friendships (and maintaining them), and seeking commonality with other managers, such as a shared work history.

Choose the Correct Combination of Influence Tactics

Influence tactics are the threads that complete a web, hold the spokes of the webbed network in place, and in turn are supported by the network. They must be chosen carefully on the basis of influence targets chosen and objectives sought.[23] One of the studies by Kipnis and colleagues found, as did we, that considerably more approaches were used to influence subordinates than were used to influence superiors or peers. Incidents in our studies suggested that most first influence attempts by managers involved soft approaches such as requests or reason, but later attempts included stronger tactics when the target of influence was reluctant to comply. This notion was confirmed statistically in the Kipnis study. Both superior and subordinate target groups in the Kipnis sample tended to use reason to sell ideas and friendliness to obtain favors. These authors also emphasize that influence tactics must vary with the target and objective of influence attempts: "only the most

---

[22]See Kaplan Endnote 17 above.

[23]For an excellent treatment of the objectives and targets of influence, see D. Kipnis, S. Schmidt, C. Swaffin-Smith, and I. Wilkinson, "Patterns of Managerial Influence: Shotgun Managers, Tacticians, and By Standers." *Organizational Dynamics*, 12(3), 1984, 58–67 and Kipnis, et al., 1980, Endnote 9 above. These studies and the Erez, et al. study noted below also used a common questionnaire and a similar factor analysis to find broader categories of influence in which individual influence tactics (similar to those in exhibit 1) fall. The categories derived include:
Reason: The use of facts & data to support logical arguments.
Manipulation: The use of impression management, flattery, or ingratiation.
Coalitions: Obtaining the support of other people in the organization.
Bargaining: The use of negotiation and exchange of benefits or favors.
Assertiveness: Demanding or acting in a forceful manner.
Upward Appeal: Making an appeal to higher levels of management in the organization to back up requests.
Sanctions: Threatening to withhold pay, advancement or to impose organizational discipline. M. Erez, R. Rim and I. Keider, "The Two Sides of the Tactics of Influence: Agent vs Target," *Journal of Occupational Psychology*, 59, 1986, 25–39.

inflexible of managers can be expected to rely rigidly on a single strategy, say assertiveness, to achieve both personal and organizational objectives. It may be appropriate to 'insist' that one's boss pay more attention to cost overruns; it is less appropriate to 'insist' on time off for a game of golf."[24]

Taking a cue from the fact that few tactics were found to be associated more frequently with success than failure in any of our studies, we began to examine combinations of influence tactics. In each of the three influence studies (upward, downward, and lateral), managers who used a combination of approaches tended more often to be successful than managers who relied on a single tactic.

Complex and vital influence attempts, such as those required for major strategies or new projects, always require multiple influence tactics. A successful attempt is likely to begin with homework to gather facts, a citation of parallel examples (who is doing this?), a marshalling of support of others (perhaps insured by an effective web of influence), precise timing and packaging of a presentation, and, in the case of initial resistance, persistence and repetition over weeks or even months. Less frequently, but sometimes successfully, managers may resort to manipulation, threats, or pulling rank.[25]

We noted that in many incidents short term success seemed to lead to enhanced influence in the long term, therefore, we sought ways to measure sustained influence over time. Consequently, in our downward influence study, we asked managers about the nature of the subordinate-superior relationship that occurred two months following an influence attempt. As we expected, successful influence attempts led the managers to perceive that their relationships had improved and to believe they had expanded their potential for future influence. For example, the bank branch manager, who was able to enlarge his building reported that because of his success with the influence attempt his profile at the bank was raised, that he was given a promotion and a raise, and that he was transferred to the main office.

Although we cannot be certain that the managers experiencing short-term influence success derived power with their boss from these episodes, the fact that managers believed this to be so caused them, in most cases, to plan additional influence attempts. These findings are supported by a study by Kipnis and his colleagues which found that managers who perceive that they have power are more

---

[24]See D. Kipnis, et al., Endnote 23 above, p. 32.

[25]For a discussion of the use of manipulation as an influence, and/or managerial approach, see Erez, Endnote 23 above and A. Zalesnik, "The Leadership Gap," *The Academy of Management Executive*, 4 (1), 1990, 7–22.

likely to select assertive influence tactics.[26] Failures at influence attempts may cause managers to plan fewer future attempts and to experience a period of weakened relationships with the boss. Frequently when a subordinate attempts to influence upper level management in a manner where his or her intention is clearly for the advantage of the organization, failure is not damaging to future influence. When the purpose of an influence attempt is clearly seen as a personal goal, failure may be more serious. Such a case was reported by a supervisor of security services dealing with a vice president of operations:

> *I wanted an assistant so that I could have some help in managing my department and would not have to handle petty problems of my employees. I tried to convince my boss that I was overworked since my staff has almost doubled and I was having a lot of people problems. I failed because I was just trying to make it easier on myself and wanted an assistant to do the job that I was supposed to be doing. I was also asking to increase the payroll of the company with no plans to increase revenue or profits. After my boss turned me down, I pouted for a few weeks and later learned that my boss thought I was immature. I then decided to forget about past disappointments and only worry about the future.*

Communicate Influence Tactics Effectively

It is very difficult to separate influence tactic choice with the communications process itself. Cohen and Bradford stress the importance of knowing the world of potential allies—the needs, values, and organizational forces working on them. For example, they suggest that setting the stage for an influence attempt by wining and dining influence targets at a fancy restaurant may work well for a public relations director, but may appear to be a buy-out attempt when directed toward the head of engineering.[27]

Many of our research participants mentioned the importance of their presentation of their manner of approaching the target. Managers who choose rational ideas based on the needs of the target, wrap them with a blanket of humor or anecdotes, and cast them in the language of the person to be influenced, are much more likely to see their influence objective achieved.

---

[26]See D. Kipnis, et al., in Endnote 23, p. 32.

[27]A. R. Cohen and D. L. Bradford, "Influence Without Authority: The Use of Alliances, Reciprocity, and Exchange to Accomplish Work," *Organizational Dynamics*, 17 (3), 1989, 5-17.

Effective communications become interwoven coils of silk in the web of influence that help ensure the success of tactics. Consider for example the combination of influence tactics and communication used by Iacocca in his turn-a-round strategy of Chrysler. Kotter capsules these as follows: "He developed a bold new vision of what Chrysler should be . . . he (then) attracted, held onto, and elicited cooperation and teamwork from a large network. . . . labor leaders, a whole new management team, dealers, suppliers, some key government officials and many others. He did so by articulating his agenda in emotionally powerful ways ("Remember, folks, we have a responsibility to save 600,000 jobs"), by using the credibility and relationships he had developed after a long and highly successful career in the automotive business, by communicating the new strategies in an intellectually, powerful manner and in still other ways."[28]

Managers who choose rational ideas based on the needs of the target, wrap them with a blanket of humor or anecdotes, and cast them in the language of the person to be influenced, are much more likely to see their influence objective achieved.

Upward and lateral communications require more listening and more appreciation of the ideas and thoughts of others than dictated by subordinate relationships. Laborde suggests that a person who would master the communicator part of influence must see more and hear more than most people and must remain flexible to vary their behavior in response to what they see and hear.[29] Kaplan strongly emphasizes the importance of variation in the arsenal of communications skills—knowing when to meet with a person face-to-face, when to call group meetings, and when to use memos.[30]

Implications of Influence Research For Managers

No research is subtle enough to capture all of the relationships present between managers as they work together as peers, subordinates, and superiors. While incident- or questionnaire-type research may be subject to some self-report bias (if possible managers try to make themselves look rational to the researcher), observers, even if they could remain long enough in an area, could never capture and connect all of the thoughts necessary to precisely determine motives, processes, and outcomes of managers attempting to develop long-term influence relationships.

---

[28]J. P. Kotter, *The Leadership Factor*, (New York: The Free Press, 1988), 18.

[29]G. Laborde, *Influencing Integrity: Management Skills for Communication and Negotiation*, (Palo Alto: Syntony Publishing, 1987).

[30]See Endnote 17 above, p. 32.

We have attempted to capture some of the pieces, reviewed the best of what other experts have said about the subject, and tried to establish some connections. While recognizing these limitations, our influence research over the past ten years leads us to the following conclusions.

- Managers are continually in a state of building and extending webs of influence and repairing damaged threads. With every career change new webs must be built. In the early part of a career or after a career move, a manager must establish a web of influence by developing a reputation as an expert, balancing this with key influence targets, networking to establish resources, and selecting and communicating appropriate influence tactics.

- No one influence tactic can be isolated as being superior to others. Tactics must be chosen on the basis of the influence target and objective sought. For more important influence objectives, a combination of influence tactics will be necessary.

- Frequency of reported tactic usage suggests that most contemporary managers initially try positive techniques with targets, but will quickly resort to threats or manipulation if necessary, especially if the target is a subordinate.

- The variety of approaches used to influence subordinates is wider than suggested by the traditional leadership models and wider than the variety used in upward and lateral influence attempts.[31] This appears to be due not only to the additional power bases available when dealing with subordinates, but also to the growing difficulty of obtaining subordinate compliance through traditional means.

- Contrary to traditional views that networking outside the hierarchy is disruptive, today's leaders must recognize the value of reciprocal influence relationships and must encourage them as long as they can be fruitfully directed toward organizational goals. Webs of influence may provide advantages for all involved.

- For these reasons, we are quite convinced that influential managers are ones who have developed and maintained a balanced web of relationships with the boss, subordinates, peers, and other key players; influence in

---

[31]For a discussion of power and influence as a leadership approach, see G. Yuki, "Managerial Leadership: A Review of Theory and Research," *Journal of Management*, 15 (2), 1989, 251–289.

each of these directions is banked for leverage to accomplish goals in the other directions. If knowledge alone and positional authority alone will not accomplish the manager's job, those who would be influential must fill power gaps with webs of influence.

ABOUT THE AUTHORS

The authors appreciate the helpful suggestions to an earlier draft of this manuscript by W. J. Heisler, manager, Management Development and Salaried Employee Training, Newport News Shipbuilding, and Fred Luthans, George Holmes, professor of management, University of Nebraska. We especially appreciate the work of the anonymous reviewers who assisted us with the paper. Thanks also to the professors who participated in original research studies: Robert Bell, Tennessee Tech University; Lloyd Dosier and Gene Murkinson of Georgia Southern University; Tom Miller and Coy Jones, Memphis State University; Kent Curran, University of North Carolina, Charlotte; and Alfred Edge, University of Hawaii.

J. Bernard Keys is Callaway professor of business at Georgia Southern University and directs the Center for Business Simulation. His Ph.D. in Management is from the University of Oklahoma. He is the North American Editor of the *Journal of Management Development* and Co-Editor of *Executive Development*. In addition to his research on influence methods, he conducts research and serves as a consultant throughout the world in the design of customized executive development programs utilizing simulations. He is the author of six books including three business simulations. He is past chair of the Management Education and Development Division of the Academy of Management and vice president of Southern Management Association.

Thomas L. Case is currently an associate professor and acting head of the Department of Management at Georgia Southern University. He obtained a Ph.D. in social psychology at the University of Georgia and has attended both the basic and advanced MIS Faculty Development Institutes sponsored by the AACSB. In addition to managerial influence tactics, his main research and publications have been in the areas of organization development, R & D information systems, and program evaluation for supported employment and other services for developmentally disabled workers. He has been a member of the Academy of Management and Southern Management Association since 1982. He has been proceedings editor and is currently treasurer for the International Academy for Information Management (IAIM).

BUILDING TRUST THROUGH COMMUNICATION

Joanne C. Preston, Pepperdine University,
400 Corporate Pointe, Culver City, CA 92030

BUILDING TRUST THROUGH COMMUNICATION

Communication is an integral part of building trust in a relationship. As individuals interact with one another, trust is increased or decreased. When the sender communicates the message that the receiver is valued, the level of the receiver's trust increases. As trust increases, the behavior patterns change. The speaker is perceived by the receiver as being more trustworthy, which influences the receiver to change his or her communication behavior. This new behavior increases the speaker's trust. This cyclical relationship develops the climate for trust. As consultant or manager, the goal is to build a positive climate for trust rather than a negative one, and verbal communication is a major influence on that development. This chapter will begin by describing behaviors which encourage a positive versus a negative climate for trust. The second part of the chapter will sensitize the readers towards problems in the English language which can undermine trust, and will conclude with a description of a technique of verbal communication which will increase chances for establishing a positive climate for trust even when the speaker must criticize the receiver.

CHARACTERISTICS WHICH INFLUENCE THE CLIMATE FOR TRUST

Two research programs have examined this aspect of verbal communication: 1) Sieburg & Larson, whose unpublished work is explained in Abler, Rosenfeld & Towne's (1980) *Interplay: The Process of Interpersonal Communication*; and 2) Jack Gibb's work in defensiveness and building trust (Gibb, 1961, 1964, & 1967). Both of these programs look at how the sender can devaluate the receiver through verbal communication by creating a negative climate for trust. Since we control only our own behavior, the emphasis in this paper will be on what you can do to eliminate problems in communication. Throughout this paper, you become the sender and a person with whom you are interacting becomes the receiver. Focus on what the sender does and how this behavior affects the receiver. When you are the sender, you can choose how you are perceived by others.

Sieburg & Larson (Abler et al, 1980, Ch. 7) concentrate on subtle ways the sender can hurt the receiver by his words. One way a person devaluates the

---

Article reprinted from Cole, D., Preston, J. & Finley, *What's new in OD*.

receiver is by ignoring major parts of the message. This uncaring attitude is called a disconfirming response because the sender does not attack the receiver's self-concept, but instead denies that the other person exists. There are seven disconfirming responses: 1) Impervious response, 2) Interrupting response, 3) Irrelevant response, 4) Tangential response, 5) Impersonal response, 6) Ambiguous response, and 7) Incongruous response.

An **impervious response** is when the sender verbally and nonverbally behaves as if the receiver is not present. Basically, any attempt by the receiver to communicate is ignored. The **interrupting response** is when the sender stops the receiver from finishing his or her point by changing the subject or evaluating the statement made by the receiver. The **irrelevant response** is a statement made by the sender which is not related to what the receiver is saying. On the other hand, the **tangential response** does acknowledge the receiver's message, but the sender tries to change the conversation either with an abrupt change or with a subtle one which briefly acknowledges the receiver's message. With the **impersonal response,** the sender uses impersonal, intellectual, and general statements so that he or she does not have to interact on a personal level with the receiver. For example, an employee might say, "I am having difficulties working with George," and the sender would reply, "Working with people is a hard task." The **ambiguous response** is tricky because it carries more than one meaning. An employee could say, "I'd like to meet with you about the Jennings account today," and the sender responds, "Sure, later, but it's hard to say." Lastly, the **incongruous response** gives mixed messages to the receiver. The receiver might say, "We got a lot accomplished today," and the sender says, "Quite a bit (laughs)."

All of these behaviors show a lack of caring for the receiver and affects building a climate of trust. The feedback that the receiver gets devaluates his self-image. According to Jack Gibb (1961, 1964, & 1967), this type of behavior increases defensiveness.

Supportive behaviors from the sender build trust. Gibb has identified twelve behaviors which affect the climate for trust—six defensive behaviors and six supportive ones.

Evaluation vs Description. Evaluation implies that the receiver's behavior is being judged and the receiver perceives this judgment as a criticism. These criticisms can take the form of expressions, manner of speech, tone of voice, or verbal content (Patton & Griffin, 1981, p. 365). The result is defensive behavior.

In contrast to evaluative "you" language, is what Gibb calls describing language or "I" language. Instead of the sender saying something like "you're always late" which puts the emphasis on the receiver, the sender would make a statement like "I am frustrated when I have to wait for you." In the second

Table 1.

The Gibb Categories of Defensive and Supportive Behaviors	
DEFENSIVE BEHAVIORS	SUPPORTIVE BEHAVIORS
1. Evaluations	1. Description
2. Control	2. Problem Orientation
3. Strategy	3. Spontaneity
4. Neutrality	4. Empathy
5. Superiority	5. Equality
6. Certainty	6. Provisionalism

statement the person is not blaming the receiver but describing his or her feeling about being left waiting.

Control versus problem orientation. With control, the speaker tries to control the receiver through communication. This can be done through gestures, tone of voice, or through body language. The result is that the sender implies that he or she knows what's best for the receiver. The receiver's ideas appear worthless and nothing the receiver can say will change the situation. The contrasting approach is that of problem-oriented communication. Instead of the send trying to "win" the situation, the sender sends a message that he or she would like to find a clear solution to the problem that both sides are willing to accept. In this way the needs of both people are being met, and both people's concerns and feelings are respected throughout the process.

Strategy versus Spontaneity. In strategy, the individual sender uses communication to manipulate the receiver with hidden motives. The receiver generally feels like a guinea pig or a sucker in the situation. For example, an individual who constantly does you favors may cause you to wonder when that individual is going to ask for a big favor in return. Spontaneity, on the other hand, is when a person is either honest with behaviors or honest with communications. Real feelings are communicated to the receiver without any indication of manipulation or of hidden motives. This honesty or communication must be matched by honest non-verbal signals or the communication will be perceived as manipulating by the receiver.

Neutrality versus empathy. Neutrality is probably better described as being indifferent. Senders send messages that lack feeling, are detached, and are impersonal. The result is that the receiver feels like he is being treated as an object rather than a human being. The opposite type of communication is showing empathy. Here the sender communicates his or her message in a way that the receiver will feel supported. This is accomplished by the sender placing himself in the receiver's position and phrasing the message in a way that he would like to heart it. Thus, the receiver feels accepted and understood by the sender. The sender doesn't have to agree with the receiver's point of view, just communicate that he understands it.

Superiority versus equality. In superiority communication, the sender implies that he or she does not want to relate on equal terms with the receiver. The sender's behavior reinforces the perception of the inadequacy and inferiority of the receiver. In equality communication, the sender projects both verbally and non-verbally that the receiver is a worthwhile human being, that the receiver has much to give to this relationship, and that the sender is interested in hearing the receiver's point of view.

Certainty versus provisionalism. Certainty communication means the sender communicates that there is no doubt that he or she has the answer to the situation and that the receiver has no additional information to give that will help. Most of the sender's communication is done with an air of certainty that implies finality. On the other hand, provisionalism is a style of communication where the sender may have strong feelings about what is said, may believe he or she is right, but leave room for other people's opinions and are open so that they may be influenced by the receiver.

Not only can the sender affect the climate for trust with his overall style of communication as described in both Gibb and Sieburg and Larson's work; but the English language itself can potentially create a negative climate for trust.

PROBLEMS IN THE LANGUAGE

The English language has inherent problems that cause defensiveness and hurt trust-building. These problems are not only in the language structure, but also in troublesome words which we unknowingly use daily. The sender must be sensitive to these problems. This work is discussed at length in Abler, Rosenfeld, and Towne's (1980) language chapter in their book *Interplay: the process of inner personal communication.*

Interplay described five problems inherent in the language.

The first of these are **intentional style.** Although words are symbols in the English language, people mistake the thing that the word represents as if it really were the thing. For example, one woman experienced difficulty with her parents because her fiancee was a nurse. In this situation, the symbol nurse actually became the real thing and the parents could not accept a man working in the role of a female

Table 2.

PROBLEMS INHERENT IN LANGUAGE
INTENTIONAL STYLE POLARIZATION FACT-INFERENCE CONFUSION STATIC EVALUATION ALLNESS

nurse (Abler et al, 1980). Words are only symbols of communication, not reality. A painful example of this fact occurs when somebody communicates to the receiver, "I love you." The receiver may take this statement as reality when, in fact, these words may not be true.

Polarization is another difficulty inherent in our language. Our language describes things in terms of black versus white, instead of shades of gray. Abler, et al (1980), gives an excellent exercise which clarifies this difficulty. Write down the opposite of the following words:

Opposite   Tall   Heavy   Happy   Strong   Legal

Generally, the opposites can be done very quickly. Now on the second line provided, write a word that represents the mid-point between the two opposites. The second task is far more difficult than the first. The reason is that our language does not provide meaningful mid-points. It is more likely to provide opposites. Generally, the mid-point of adjectives are non-specific and vague.

Fact-interference is another problem inherent in our language. We can make statements about what we observe; i.e., I can say that there is a woman sitting next to a table wearing a red blouse. This is highly observable and can be validated by others. Our language also allows us to make statements that cannot be readily observed. I could say that the woman sitting by the table in the red blouse is very unhappy. The second statement is an inference, which often is confused with facts. When the sender makes a statement that is observable, it is fact oriented. But, when the sender makes a statement that is inference it must be clearly communicated that it is an inference rather than a fact. Our language makes that very difficult. Before stating that the woman was unhappy as a fact, one would have to approach the woman who appears unhappy and check out the inference.

Static evaluation also occurs in our language because of the word "is". The verb "to be" implies things do not change. If one makes the statement that Harry is a poor worker, it implies that he has always been a poor worker, and he'll always be a poor worker in the future. That is not necessarily true. One must verify when was Harry a poor worker; how long has he been a poor worker; does Harry need additional skills in order to change his behavior? Thus, the verb "to be" implies Harry will never change; and unfortunately, we don't have a verb that will help us communicate a changing process in our language. When somebody uses the verb "to be," remember that it is not a static evaluation.

The last problem inherent in our language is that of **Allness**. Again, this stems from the verb "to be." The word "is" seems to make a statement true. If we go back to the earlier example of "Harry is a poor worker," it seems to imply that this is all that Harry is. That is also not true. Harry might be a good father, a successful bowler, and an excellent speaker as well. The statement "Harry is a poor worker" only describes part of who Harry is. Another good example of allness can be seen in how we use the Myers-Briggs typologies. We can make the statement that Susan is an INTJ, and we are implying that is all that Susan is. Again, this is not true, but it is part of the problem inherent in our language related to allness.

The language also has words that cause extreme difficulty when we use them.

The first of these troublesome words are called **equivocal words**. These are words that can be interpreted many ways. Alder, et al (1980), gave a wonderful example of a person in the hospital who asked the nurse for things like shaving materials, a robe, and possibly magazines to read. The nurse's reply was, "Oh you won't be needing those items." The nurse may have felt that she was comforting the individual as she made this statement. Unfortunately, the person misinterpreted her communication by thinking that she meant he was going to die soon and these items would not be needed. The reason the nurse made the statement was that the doctor had already signed this patient's release, and he would leave the hospital that afternoon. Equivocal words which can be interpreted in many ways cause serious problems in building trust.

Table 3.

TROUBLESOME WORDS
EQUIVOCAL WORDS
RELATIVE WORDS
EMOTIVE WORDS
INDISCRIMINATE TERMS
FICTIONS WORDS
ABSTRACT WORDS

Another problem in our language is **relative words.** If you use the word, slow—"My car is very slow," this is a relative statement. Is it slow compared to a Lamborghini or slow compared to walking? When we use such words as large, small, fast, and hassle, we must define what we actually mean in order to make the communication clear. "This is a large university of 15,000 students" or "This is a small university of 3,000 students." Being specific clarifies relative words.

A third problem is **emotive words** which imply the sender's attitude about something. You can repeat the same message, but by the words that you choose, you imply your attitude. Abler, et al (1980), gives a list of how emotive words work.

If you approve, say:	If you disapprove, say:
thrifty	cheap
traditional	old-fashioned
cautious	coward
information	propaganda
eccentric	crazy

Thus, you can say something like "I have good self-esteem; you're a little too sure of yourself; he's conceited." By your choice of vocabulary, you imply the attitude that you have toward that individual.

Indiscriminate terms are the way we lump things together in order to make generalizations. An example might be the statement, "This is a book." What type of book is it? Is it a non-fiction book? Is it a fiction book? Is it pornography? Is it excellent writing? Is it poor writing? Indiscriminate terms lump things together so that we can easily classify things. In doing so we create a program. The sender needs to be specific and describe clearly what is meant by a particular term.

Fiction words create problems because they are words that have strong emotional reactions which have little to do with the dictionary's meaning. Examples are democracy, truth, and justice. The sender could be talking about "repressive governments" while the receiver may have a different perception from the sender concerning what is repressive. It may sound like we are speaking the same language, but we are not. "Repressive governments" means different things to different people, and each person has their own emotional feeling about the expression.

Finally, there are **Abstract words.** These are words which have a number of levels to them. If you traveled to the moon and had a bad experience with the people who lived on the moon, you might come back and say, "Well, all those moon people are a bunch of thieves." This kind of abstraction is really an extensive generalization. There are probably only one or two people whom you experienced negatively, but you classified all of the people as being the same. Abstraction ignores the possibilities of individual differences. Many times what we expect of people become self-fulfilling prophesies. If we expect people to be lazy or thieves, then we see behavior that proves that is correct. The way to get around abstract words is to be specific.

The first two sections of this chapter examined the numerous problems associated with communication that builds barriers to developing trust. Now, how can we build trust through communication?

FEEDBACK GUIDELINES

The way to build trust through communication is to be aware of these barriers and develop a style of communication which promotes trust and decreases defensiveness. The first part of this paper has increased your awareness. The following communication styles has been tested in a variety of personal and work situations and has shown a high level of effectiveness. People who use this style of communication, even if they are criticizing the receiver, are seen as supportive, and concerned about the welfare of the receiver (Preston, 1987). Before communicating an important message, the sender must quickly think about six feedback guidelines. The six feedback guidelines (Preston & Guernsey, 1982) can be remembered by the following words:

1. EMPATHY
2. "I"
3. FEELINGS
4. SPECIFIC
5. UNDERLYING POSITIVES
6. INTERPERSONAL MESSAGE

I will explain the concepts behind each of the six guidelines and for clarification, I will give an example.

In the example, you have been asked to provide your superiors with a comprehensive study of your level of the organization. You have worked with several managers in other departments who are peers to gather the information that you need. Recently, you requested additional information from one of these managers and this person has not supplied the requested data. Because the information is essential, you confront the individual.

The first guideline is EMPATHY. Before you express you own point of view, show understanding for the other person's situation by openly acknowledging their point of view to the best of your ability. This compassion may be difficult especially in intense emotional situations. If you can let the other person see that you appreciate his or her feelings, views, and circumstances in the beginning of your message, then that will give the receiver of the request with enough psychological space that they are less likely to become defensive. It is important to choose your words carefully so that you are accurate and truthful. Any flattery or lies will be easily recognized by the receiver, and defense building will begin. Take the time to see the situation from the other person's point of view, and add it to your message. It doesn't cost you anything, and makes the other person feel like you understand and care about their difficulties. For the example, one might say, "I view your job as a high-pressure one with lots of demands. A few days ago, I added one more." This does not take a long time to say, but it can make a big difference to the receiver of the message.

The second guideline is "I." State your ideas from your point of view only. Claim your thoughts, values, and perceptions by using the words: "I," "my," and "mine." Avoid the word "you" as the subject of the sentence. Consider what would happen if the speaker says, "You promised to give me the data yesterday." Immediately the receiver begins to defend himself by hiding behind company rules, creating a diversion by starting an argument over another issue, or counter-attacking. By saying that it is your problem, there is a better chance that the listener will at least hear you out. This guideline will be applied to the example after I explain the next guideline.

FEELINGS is the third guideline in creating a positive climate for trust. State your past, present or anticipated feelings as they relate to this issue. Keep in mind that it is how you feel about something which helps to make the message legitimate for the other person. For example, for some organizations, dress code may or may not be all that important for producing and marketing a product, but if the CEO feels strongly that the employees must present an image of neatness, than a dress code will be instituted. Many of the employees will accept this standard, if it is explained that the dress reflects the image of the over-all organization, and the CEO is pleased when his company is perceived as neat and orderly.

Using the last two guidelines in the example, the speaker might say, "The information that I requested from you is crucial to me, and I am worried that I will not be able to include it in the final report." The receiver will hear this message because the speaker has avoided laying blame.

The fourth guideline is to be SPECIFIC. Be sure to include behavioral descriptions, times, occasions, places, and frequencies. The more specific that you can be the less room there is for an argument. Avoid generalizations such as "always, never, everyone, and nobody." People are not that consistent. When one uses these words, the listener will defend by pointing out examples that show different behavior. All of this defending causes a diversion, which delays the goal of requesting the change in behavior and adds to a negative climate for trust. Also, watch generalizations tied to personality or to motive such as "you're inconsiderate" or "you did that deliberately." These have a tendency to be accusatory, which doesn't aid in solving the problem either and promotes defensiveness.

In the example, one might say, "On Monday, I requested some data; and, I believe, I said that I wanted it by Wednesday afternoon. It is now Friday and to my knowledge I haven't received it." Notice that this statement is specific. It tells the person when you believe that you made the request. Also notice that it keeps the emphasis on the speaker's point of view by saying that "I believe that I said that I wanted it by Wednesday afternoon." This allows the receiver some psychological space especially if they don't remember the request or forgot the request because of other commitments. At the same time, the receiver will listen because you have told them as specifically as possible what you believe the situation is. It is important to say "that to my knowledge I have not received it," because it is not only true, but it can be very face-saving if the person has already given it to your secretary or placed it on your desk without your knowledge.

The fifth guideline is UNDERLYING POSITIVES. When you want to change another person's views or behavior, at the earliest feasible time, state your positive assumptions, attitudes, expectations, and feelings about the other person which are related to the issue. For every negative feeling that we have, there is an underlying positive one. If we did not have this positive feeling, the other person's behavior would not bother us. Again, when the speaker is emotionally intense about an issue, it is hard to remember the underlying positives. If time is taken to sort this out, these underlying positives can be identified and used in the message effectively. These statements must be true for the speaker, or the receiver will easily see through the falseness of the statement.

For our example, the speaker could say, "One thing that I admire about you is your accuracy. I asked you for this information because I know with your help, I can produce a better product."

The last guideline is the INTERPERSONAL MESSAGE. When you desire a change in behavior, you need to specifically state your request making sure to identify the following.

1.   What I desire this person to do in the future.

2.   How it would make me *feel* if he did what I want.

3.   What will my wishes *cost* the listener if he changes his behavior.

4.   What will *he get* from me in return if he cooperates.

This is the goal of the entire message or feedback, and unless this is heard by the receiver the speaker has wasted his or her time. This part of the message must be stated specifically so that the receiver knows exactly what the speaker wishes him/her to do. It is not only important to give the directions specifically and clearly, but also the listener must know exactly "What's in it for them if they comply with request." Whenever a person is asked to change, they will weigh the costs and benefits of this request unconsciously to determine if it is worth it to them to make this change. Therefore, if the person requesting the change deals with these costs and benefits up front and identifies them in the interpersonal message, it will increase the chance for successful change.

The interpersonal message in the example could be stated, "I want to write the first draft of this report this afternoon, and I would appreciate the information I requested by 1:00 today. I realize that this request might be disrupting your priorities; and if you wish, I am willing to have my secretary work with yours for the morning." The speaker must be honest in what they are willing to pay for this cooperation, and the evaluation of this cost ought to be done before confronting the individual.

The actual message would read like this:

"I view your job as a high pressure one with many demands, and a few days ago, I added one more. The information that I requested from you is crucial to me, and I am worried that I will not be able to include it in the final report. On Monday, I requested some data; and, I believe, I said that I wanted it by Wednesday afternoon. It is now Friday and to my knowledge I haven't received it. One thing that I admire about you is your accuracy. I asked you for this information because I know with your help I can produce a better product. I want to write the first draft of this report this afternoon, and I would appreciate the information I requested by 1:00 today. I realize that this request might be disrupting your priorities and if you wish, I am willing to have my secretary work with yours for the morning."

This message takes a little longer than "Hey, where's the data that you promised me," but the results will be more beneficial to building trust. In addition, over many interactions, this approach will strengthen the working relationship and not tear it down because of the cyclical nature of building trust.

Defensive interactions can stifle initiative, productivity, and creativity, because when a person becomes defensive, he or she stops listening and spends energy in building a barrier between you. It is worth the 5–10 minutes it takes to remind yourself of these guidelines and to briefly plan out what you might say in difficult situations. The result will be obtaining your goal of a behavior change, and building a trusting relationship.

Building trust through communication is accomplished by being sensitive to the problems and using a style of communication that produces a positive climate for trust. This chapter has addressed both these issues. If, as sender, you take the time to incorporate this information in your important communication interactions, the result is cost effective and definitely worth the time and effort.

References

Alder, R. B., Rosenfeld, L. B. & Towne, L. (1980). *Interplay: The process of interpersonal communication.* New York: Holt, Rinehart & Winston.

Gibb, J. R. (1961, Sept.). Defensive Communication. *Journal of Communication,* 11, pp. 141–148.

Gibb, J. R. (1964). Climate for trust formation in L. P. Bradford et. al. (eds.) *T-group theory and laboratory method.* New York: Wiley, pp. 279–309.

Gibb, J. R. (1967). Dynamics of leadership. *Current issues of higher education.* Washington, D.C.: American Association for Higher Education.

Patton, B. R. & Griffin, K. (1981). *Interpersonal communication in action* (3rd ed.). NY: Harper & Row.

Preston, J. C. (1987). Changing people's behavior: Try a new way of asking. *Organization Development Journal,* 5(4), 38–42.

Preston, J. D. & Gurney, B. G., Jr. (1982). Relationship enhancement skills training. State College, PA: The Pennsylvania State University Press.

THE DEVELOPMENT AND ENFORCEMENT OF GROUP NORMS

Daniel C. Feldman

This paper examines why group norms are enforced and how group norms develop. It is argued here that groups are likely to bring under normative control only those behaviors that ensure group survival, increase the predictability of group members' behavior, avoid embarrassing interpersonal situations, or give expression to the group's central values. Group norms develop through explicit statements by supervisors or co-workers, critical events in the group's history, primacy, or carry-over behaviors from past situations.

Group norms are the informal rules that groups adopt to regulate and regularize group members' behavior. Although these norms are infrequently written down or openly discussed, they often have a powerful, and consistent, influence on group members' behavior (Hackman, 1976).

Most of the theoretical work on group norms has focused on identifying the types of group norms (March, 1954) or on describing their structural characteristics (Jackson, 1966). Empirically, most of the focus has been on examining the impact that norms have on other social phenomena. For example, Seashore (1954) and Schachter, Ellertson, McBride, and Gregory (1951) use the concept of group norms to discuss group cohesiveness; Trist and Bamforth (1951) and Whyte (1955a) use norms to examine production restriction; Janis (1972) and Longley and Pruitt (1980) use norms to illuminate group decision making; and Asch (1951) and Sherif (1936) use norms to examine conformity.

This paper focuses on two frequently overlooked aspects of the group norms literature. First, it examines *why* group norms are enforced. Why do groups desire conformity to these informal rules? Second, it examines how group norms develop. Why do some norms develop in one group but not in another? Much of what is known about group norms comes from post hoc examination of their impact on outcome variables; much less has been written about how these norms actually develop and why they regulate behavior so strongly.

Understanding how group norms develop and why they are enforced is important for two reasons. First, group norms can play a large role in determining whether the group will be productive or not. If the work group feels that

Reprinted with permission of Publisher from *Academy of Management Review*, 1984, Vol. 4, No. 1, pp. 47–53.

management is supportive, group norms will develop that facilitate—in fact, enhance—group productivity. In contrast, if the work group feels that management is antagonistic, group norms that inhibit and impair group performance are much more likely to develop. Second, managers can play a major role in setting and changing group norms. They can use their influence to set task-facilitative norms; they can monitor whether the group's norms are functional; they can explicitly address counterproductive norms with subordinates. By understanding how norms develop and why norms are enforced, managers can better diagnose the underlying tensions and problems their groups are facing, and they can help the group develop more effective behavior patterns.

Why Norms Are Enforced

As Shaw (1981) suggests, a group does not establish or enforce norms about every conceivable situation. Norms are formed and enforced only with respect to behaviors that have some significance for the group. The frequent distinction between task maintenance duties and social maintenance duties helps explain why groups bring selected behaviors under normative control.

Groups, like individuals, try to operate in such a way that they maximize their chances for task success and minimize their chances of task failure. First of all, a group will enforce norms that facilitate its very survival. It will try to protect itself from interference from groups external to the organization or harassment from groups internal to the organization. Second, the group will want to increase the predictability of group members' behaviors. Norms provide a basis for predicting the behavior of others, thus enabling group members to anticipate each other's actions and to prepare quick and appropriate responses (Shaw, 1981; Kiesler & Kiesler, 1970).

In addition, groups want to ensure the satisfaction of the members and prevent as much interpersonal discomfort as possible. Thus, groups also will enforce norms that help the group avoid embarrassing interpersonal problems. Certain topics of conversation might be sanctioned, and certain types of social interaction might be openly discouraged. Moreover, norms serve an expressive function for groups (Katz & Kahn, 1978). Enforcing group norms gives group members a chance to express what their central values are, and to clarify what is distinctive about the group and central to its identity (Hackman, 1976).

Each of these four conditions under which group norms are most likely to be enforced is discussed in more detail below.

(1) *Norms are likely to be enforced if they facilitate group survival.* A group will enforce norms that protect it from interference or harassment by members of

other groups. For instance, a group might develop a norm not to discuss its salaries with members of other groups in the organization, so that attention will not be brought to pay inequities in its favor. Groups might also have norms about not discussing internal problems with members of other units. Such discussions might boomerang at a later date if other groups use the information to develop a better competitive strategy against the group.

Enforcing group norms also makes clear what the "boundaries" of the group are. As a result of observation of deviant behavior and the consequences that ensue, other group members are reminded of the *range* of behavior that is acceptable to the group (Dentler & Erikson, 1959). The norms about productivity that frequently develop among piecerate workers are illustrative here. By observing a series of incidents (a person produces 50 widgets and is praised; a person produces 60 widgets and receives sharp teasing; a person produces 70 widgets and is ostracized), group members learn the limits of the group's patience: "This far, and no further." The group is less likely to be "successful" (i.e., continue to sustain the low productivity expectations of management) if it allows its jobs to be reevaluated.

The literature on conformity and deviance is consistent with this observation. The group is more likely to reject the person who violates group norms when the deviant has not been a "good" group member previously (Hollander, 1958, 1964). Individuals can generate "idiosyncrasy credits" with other group members by contributing effectively to the attainment of group goals. Individuals expend these credits when they perform poorly or dysfunctionally at work. When a group member no longer has a positive "balance" of credits to draw on when he or she deviates, the group is much more likely to reject that deviant (Hollander, 1961).

Moreover, the group is more likely to reject the deviant when the group is failing in meeting its goals successfully. When the group is successful, it can afford to be charitable or tolerant towards deviant behavior. The group may disapprove, but it has some margin for error. When the group is faced with failure, the deviance is much more sharply punished. Any behavior that negatively influences the success of the group becomes much more salient and threatening to group members (Alvarez, 1968; Wiggins, Dill, & Schwartz, 1965).

(2) *Norms are likely to be enforced if they simplify, or make predictable, what behavior is expected of group members.* If each member of the group had to decide individually how to behave in each interaction, much time would be lost performing routine activities. Moreover, individuals would have more trouble predicting the behaviors of others and responding correctly. Norms enable group members to anticipate each other's actions and to prepare the most appropriate response in the most timely manner (Hackman, 1976; Shaw, 1981).

For instance, when attending group meetings in which proposals are presented and suggestions are requested, do the presenters really want feedback or are they simply going through the motions? Groups may develop norms that reduce this uncertainty and provide a clearer course of action; for example, make suggestions in small, informal meetings but not in large, formal meetings.

Another example comes from norms that regulate social behavior. For instance, when colleagues go out for lunch together, there can be some awkwardness about how to split the bill at the end of the meal. A group may develop a norm that gives some highly predictable or simple way of behaving, for example, split evenly, take turns picking up the tab, or pay for what each ordered.

Norms also may reinforce specific individual members' roles. A number of different roles might emerge in groups. These roles are simply expectations that are shared by group members regarding who is to carry out what types of activities under what circumstances (Bales & Slater, 1955). Although groups obviously create pressure toward uniformity among members, there also is a tendency for groups to create and maintain diversity among members (Hackman, 1976). For instance, a group might have one person whom others expect to break the tension when tempers become too hot. Another group member might be expected to keep track of what is going on in other parts of the organization. A third member might be expected to take care of the "creature" needs of the group—making the coffee, making dinner reservations, and so on. A fourth member might be expected by others to take notes, keep minutes, or maintain files.

None of these roles are *formal* duties, but they are activities that the group needs accomplished and has somehow parcelled out among members. If the role expectations are not met, some important jobs might not get done, or other group members might have to take on additional responsibilities. Moreover, such role assignments reduce individual members' ambiguities about what is expected specifically of them. It is important to note, though, that who takes what role in a group also is highly influenced by individuals' personal needs. The person with a high need for structure often wants to be in the note-taking role to control the structuring activity in the group; the person who breaks the tension might dislike conflict and uses the role to circumvent it.

(3) *Norms are likely to be enforced if they help the group avoid embarrassing interpersonal problems.* Goffman's work on "facework" gives some insight on this point. Goffman (1955) argues that each person in a group has a "face" he or she presents to other members of a group. This "face" is analogous to what one would call "self-image," the person's perceptions of himself or herself and how he or she would like to be seen by others. Groups want to insure that no one's self-image is damaged, called into question, or embarrassed. Consequently, the group will establish norms that discourage topics of conversation or situations in which face is

too likely to be inadvertently broken. For instance, groups might develop norms about not discussing romantic involvements (so that differences in moral values do not become salient) or about not getting together socially in people's homes (so that differences in taste or income do not become salient).

A good illustration of Goffman's facework occurs in the classroom. There is always palpable tension in a room when either a class is totally unprepared to discuss a case or a professor is totally unprepared to lecture or lead the discussion. One part of the awkwardness stems from the inability of the other partner in the interaction to behave as he or she is prepared to or would like to behave. The professor cannot teach if the students are not prepared, and the students cannot learn if the professors are not teaching. Another part of the awkwardness, though, stems from self-images being called into question. Although faculty are aware that not all students are serious scholars, the situation is difficult to handle if the class as a group does not even show a pretense of wanting to learn. Although students are aware that many faculty are mainly interested in research and consulting, there is a problem if the professor does not even show a pretense of caring to teach. Norms almost always develop between professor and students about what level of preparation and interest is expected by the other because both parties want to avoid awkward confrontations.

(4) *Norms are likely to be enforced if they express the central values of the group and clarify what is distinctive about the group's identity.* Norms can provide the social justification for group activities to its members (Katz & Kahn, 1978). When the production group labels rate-busting deviant, it says: "We care more about maximizing group security than about individual profits." Group norms also convey what is distinctive about the group to outsiders. When an advertising agency labels unstylish clothes deviant, it says: "We think of ourselves, personally and professionally, as trend-setters, and being fashionably dressed conveys that to our clients and our public."

One of the key expressive functions of group norms is to define and legitimate the power of the group itself over individual members (Katz & Kahn, 1978). When groups punish norm infraction, they reinforce in the minds of group members the authority of the group. Here, too, the literature on group deviance sheds some light on the issue at hand.

It has been noted frequently that the amount of deviance in a group is rather small (Erikson, 1966; Schur, 1965). The group uses norm enforcement to show the *strength* of the group. However, if a behavior becomes so widespread that it becomes impossible to control, then the labeling of the widespread behavior as deviance becomes problematic. It simply reminds members of the *weakness* of the group. At this point, the group will redefine what is deviant more narrowly, or it will define its job as that of keeping deviants *within bounds* rather than that of obliterating it altogether. For example, though drug use is and always has been illegal, the widespread use of drugs has led to changes in law enforcement over time. A greater distinction now is made between "hard" drugs and other controlled substances; less penalty is given to those apprehended with small amounts than large amounts; greater attention is focused on capturing large scale smugglers and traffickers than the occasional user. A group, unconsciously if not consciously, learns how much behavior it is capable of labeling deviant *and* punishing effectively.

Finally, this expressive function of group norms can be seen nicely in circumstances in which there is an inconsistency between what group members *say* is the group norm and how people actually *behave*. For instance, sometimes groups will engage in a lot of rhetoric about how much independence its managers are allowed and how much it values entrepreneurial effort; yet the harder data suggest that the more conservative, deferring, or dependent managers get rewarded. Such an inconsistency can reflect conflicts among the group's expressed values. First, the group can be ambivalent about independence; the group knows it needs to encourage more entrepreneurial efforts to flourish, but such efforts create competition and threaten the status quo. Second, the inconsistency can reveal major subgroup differences. Some people may value and encourage entrepreneurial behavior, but others do not—and the latter may control the group's rewards. Third, the inconsistency can reveal a source of the group's self-consciousness, a dichotomy between what the group is really like and how it would like to be perceived. The group may realize that it is too conservative, yet be unable or too frightened to address its problem. The expressed group norm allows the group members a chance to present a "face" to each other and to outsiders that is more socially desirable than reality.

How Group Norms Develop

Norms usually develop gradually and informally as group members learn what behaviors are necessary for the group to function more effectively. However, it also is possible for the norm development process to be short-cut by a critical event in the group or by conscious group decision (Hackman, 1976).

Most norms develop in one or more of the following four ways: explicit statements by supervisors or co-workers; critical events in the group's history; primacy; and carry-over behaviors from past situations.

(1) *Explicit statements by supervisors or co-workers.* Norms that facilitate group survival or task success often are set by the leader of the group or powerful members (Whyte, 1955b). For instance, a group leader might explicitly set norms about not drinking at lunch because subordinates who have been drinking are more likely to have problems dealing competently with clients and top management or

they are more likely to have accidents at work. The group leader might also set norms about lateness, personal phone calls, and long coffee breaks if too much productivity is lost as a result of time away from the work place.

Explicit statements by supervisors also can increase the predictability of group members' behaviors. For instance, supervisors might have particular preferences for a way of analyzing problems or presenting reports. Strong norms will be set to ensure compliance with these preferences. Consequently, supervisors will have increased certainty about receiving work in the format requested, so they can plan accordingly; workers will have increased certainty about what is expected, so they will not have to outguess their boss or redo their projects.

Managers or important group members also can define the specific role expectations of individual group members. For instance, a supervisor or a co-worker might go up to a new recruit after a meeting to give the proverbial advice: "New recruits should be seen and not heard." The senior group member might be trying to prevent the new recruit from appearing brash or incompetent or from embarrassing other group members. Such interventions set specific role expectations for the new group member.

Norms that cater to supervisor preferences also are frequently established even if they are not objectively necessary to task accomplishment. For example, although organizational norms may be very democratic in terms of everybody calling each other by their first names, some managers have strong preferences about being called Mr., Ms., or Mrs. Although the form of address used in the work group does not influence group effectiveness, complying with the norm bears little cost to the group member, whereas noncompliance could cause daily friction with the supervisor. Such norms help group members avoid embarrassing interpersonal interactions with their managers.

Fourth, norms set explicitly by the supervisor frequently express the central values of the group. For instance, a dean can set very strong norms about faculty keeping office hours and being on campus daily. Such norms reaffirm to members of the academic community their teaching and service obligations, and they send signals to individuals outside the college about what is valued in faculty behavior or distinctive about the school. A dean also could set norms that allow faculty to consult or do executive development two or three days a week. Such norms, too, legitimate other types of faculty behavior and send signals to both insiders and outsiders about some central values of the college.

(2) *Critical events in the group's history.* At times there is a critical event in the group's history that established an important precedent. For instance, a group member might have discussed hiring plans with members of other units in the organization, and as a result new positions were lost or there was increased

competition for good applicants. Such indiscretion can substantially hinder the survival and task success of the group; very likely the offender will be either formally censured or informally rebuked. As a result of such an incident, norms about secrecy might develop that will protect the group in similar situations in the future.

An example from Janis's *Victims of Groupthink* (1972) also illustrates this point nicely. One of President Kennedy's closest advisors, Arthur Schlesinger, Jr., had serious reservations about the Bay of Pigs invasion and presented his strong objections to the Bay of Pigs plan in a memorandum to Kennedy and Secretary of State Dean Rusk. However, Schlesinger was pressured by the President's brother, Attorney General Robert Kennedy, to keep his objections to himself. Remarked Robert Kennedy to Schlesinger: "You may be right or you may be wrong, but the President has made his mind up. Don't push it any further. Now is the time for everyone to help him all they can." Such critical events led group members to silence their views and set up group norms about the bounds of disagreeing with the president.

Sometimes group norms can be set by a conscious decision of a group after a particularly good or bad experience the group has had. To illustrate, a group might have had a particularly constructive meeting and be very pleased with how much it accomplished. Several people might say, "I think the reason we got so much accomplished today is that we met really early in the morning before the rest of the staff showed up and the phone started ringing. Let's try to continue to meet at 7:30 a.m." Others might agree, and the norm is set. On the other hand, if a group notices it accomplished way too little in a meeting, it might openly discuss setting norms to cut down on ineffective behavior (e.g., having an agenda, not interrupting others while they are talking). Such norms develop to facilitate task success and to reduce uncertainty about what is expected from each individual in the group.

Critical events also can identify awkward interpersonal situations that need to be avoided in the future. For instance, a divorce between two people working in the same group might have caused a lot of acrimony and hard feeling in a unit, not only between the husband and wife but also among various other group members who got involved in marital problems. After the unpleasant divorce, a group might develop a norm about not hiring spouses to avoid having to deal with such interpersonal problems in the future.

Finally, critical events also can give rise to norms that express the central, or distinctive, values of the group. When a peer review panel finds a physician or lawyer guilty of malpractice or malfeasance, first it establishes (or reaffirms) the rights of professionals to evaluate and criticize the professional behavior of their colleagues. Moreover, it clarifies what behaviors are inconsistent with the group's self-image or its values. When a faculty committee votes on a candidate's tenure, it, too, asserts the legitimacy of influence of senior faculty over junior faculty. In addition, it sends (hopefully) clear messages to junior faculty about its values in terms of quality of research, teaching, and service. There are important "announcement effects" of peer reviews; internal group members carefully reexamine the group's values, and outsiders draw inferences about the character of the group from such critical decisions.

(3) *Primacy.* The first behavior pattern that emerges in a group often sets group expectations. If the first group meeting is marked by very formal interaction between supervisors and subordinates, then the group often expects future meetings to be conducted in the same way. Where people sit in meetings or rooms frequently is developed through primacy. People generally continue to sit in the same seats they sat in at their first meeting, even though those original seats are not assigned and people could change where they sit at every meeting. Most friendship groups of students develop their own "turf" in a lecture hall and are surprised/dismayed when an interloper takes "their" seats.

Norms that develop through primacy often do so to simplify, or make predictable, what behavior is expected of group members. There may be very little task impact from where people sit in meetings or how formal interactions are. However, norms develop about such behaviors to make life much more routine and predictable. Every time a group member enters a room, he or she does not have to "decide" where to sit or how formally to behave. Moreover, he or she also is much more certain about how other group members will behave.

(4) *Carry-over behaviors from past situations.* Many group norms in organizations emerge because individual group members bring set expectations with them from other work groups in other organizations. Lawyers expect to behave towards clients in Organization I (e.g., confidentiality, setting fees) as they behaved towards those in Organization II. Doctors expect to behave toward patients in Hospital I (e.g., "bedside manner," professional distance) as they behaved in Hospital II. Accountants expect to behave towards colleagues at Firm I (e.g., dress code, adherence to statutes) as they behaved towards those at Firm II. In fact, much of what goes on in professional schools is giving new members of the profession the same standards and norms of behavior that practitioners in the field hold.

Such carry-over of individual behaviors from past situations can increase the predictability of group members' behaviors in new settings and facilitate task accomplishment. For instance, students and professors bring with them fairly constant sets of expectations from class to class. As a result, students do not have to relearn continually their roles from class to class; they know, for instance, if they come in late to take a seat quietly at the back of the room without being told. Professors also do not have to relearn continually their roles; they know, for instance, not to mumble, scribble in small print on the blackboard, or be vague when making course assignments. In addition, presumably the most task successful norms will be the ones carried over from organization to organization.

Moreover, such carry-over norms help avoid embarrassing interpersonal situations. Individuals are more likely to know which conversations and actions provoke annoyance, irritation, or embarrassment to their colleagues. Finally, when groups carry-over norms from one organization to another, they also clarify what is distinctive about the occupational or professional role. When lawyers maintain strict rules of confidentiality, when doctors maintain a consistent professional distance with patients, when accountants present a very formal physical appearance, they all assert": "These are the standards we sustain *independent* of what we could 'get away with' in this organization. This is *our* self-concept."

Summary

Norms generally are enforced only for behaviors that are viewed as important by most group members. Groups do not have the time or energy to regulate each and every action of individual members. Only those behaviors that ensure group survival, facilitate task accomplishment, contribute to group morale, or express the group's central values are likely to be brought under normative control. Norms that reflect these group needs will develop through explicit statements of supervisors, critical events in the group's history, primacy, or carry-over behaviors from past situations.

Empirical research on norm development and enforcement has substantially lagged descriptive and theoretical work. In large part, this may be due to the methodological problems of measuring norms and getting enough data points either across time or across groups. Until such time as empirical work progresses, however, the usefulness of group norms as a predictive concept, rather than as a post hoc explanatory device, will be severely limited. Moreover, until it is known more concretely why norms develop and why they are strongly enforced, attempts to *change* group norms will remain haphazard and difficult to accomplish.

References

Alvarez, R. Informal reactions to deviance in simulated work organizations: A laboratory experiment. *American Sociological Review*, 1968, 33, 895–912.

Asch, S. Effects of group pressure upon the modification and distortion of judgment. In M. H. Guetzkow (Ed.), *Groups, Leadership, and Men.* Pittsburg: Carnegie, 1951, 117–190.

Bales, R. F. and Slater, P. E. Role differentiation in small groups. In T. Parsons, R. F. Bales, J. Olds, M. Zelditch, and P. E. Slater (Eds.), *Family, Socialization, and Interaction Process.* Glencoe, Ill.: Free Press, 1955, 35-131.

Dentler, R. A. and Erikson, K. T. The functions of deviance in groups. *Social Problems,* 1959, 7, 98-107.

Erikson, K. T. *Wayward Puritans,* New York: Wiley, 1966.

Hackman, J. R. Group influences on individuals. In M. Dunnette (Ed.), *Handbook of Industrial and Organizational Psychology.* Chicago: Rand McNally, 1976, 1455-1525.

Hollander, E. P. Conformity, status, and idiosyncrasy credit. *Psychological Review,* 1958, 65, 117-127.

Hollander, E. P. Some effects of perceived status on responses to innovative behavior. *Journal of Abnormal and Social Psychology,* 1961, 63, 247-250.

Hollander, E. P. *Leaders, Groups, and Influence.* New York: Oxford University Press, 1964.

Jackson, J. A conceptual and measurement model for norms and roles. *Pacific Sociological Review,* 1955, 9, 35-47.

Janis, I. *Victims of Groupthink: A Psychological Study of Foreign Policy Decisions and Fiascos.* New York: Houghton-Mifflin, 1972.

Katz, D. and Kahn, R. L. *The Social Psychology of Organizations.* 2nd ed. New York: Wiley, 1978.

Kiesler, C. A. and Kiesler, S. B. *Conformity.* Reading, Mass.: Addison-Wesley, 1970.

Longley, J. and Pruitt, D. C. Groupthink: A critique of Janis' theory. In Ladd Wheeler (Ed.), *Review of Personality and Social Psychology.* Beverly Hills: Sage, 1980, 74-93.

March, J. Group norms and the active minority. *American Sociological Review,* 1954, 19, 733-741.

Schachter, S., Ellertson, N., McBride, D. and Gregory, D. An experimental study of cohesiveness and productivity. *Human Relations,* 1951, 4, 229-238.

Schur, E. M. *Crimes Without Victims.* Englewood Cliffs, N. J.: Prentice-Hall, 1965.

Seashore, S. *Group Cohesiveness in the Industrial Work Group.* Ann Arbor: Institute for Social Research, University of Michigan, 1954.

Shaw, M. *Group Dynamics.* 3rd ed. New York: Harper, 1936.

Trist, E. L. and Bamforth, K. W. Some social and psychological consequences of the longwall method of coal-getting. *Human Relations,* 1951, 4, 1–38.

Whyte, W. F. *Money and Motivation.* New York: Harper, 1955a.

Whyte, W. F. *Street Corner Society.* Chicago: University of Chicago Press, 1955b.

Wiggins, J. A., Dill, F. and Schwartz, R. D. On status-liability. *Sociometry,* 1965, 28, 197–209.

MAKING MANAGEMENT DECISIONS: THE ROLE OF INTUITION AND EMOTION

Herbert A. Simon, Carnegie-Mellon University

The work of a manager includes making decisions (or participating in their making), communicating them to others, and monitoring how they are carried out. Managers must know a great deal about the industry and social environment in which they work and the decision-making process itself to make decisions well. Over the past 40 years, the technique of decision making has been greatly advanced by the development of a wide range of tools—in particular, the tools of operations research and management science, and the technology of expert systems.

But these advances have not applied to the entire domain of decision making. They have had their greatest impact on decision making that is well-structured, deliberative, and quantitative; they have had less impact on decision making that is loosely structured, intuitive, and qualitative; and they have had the least impact on face-to-face interactions between a manager and his or her coworkers—the give and take of everyday work.

In this article, I will discuss these two relatively neglected types of decision making: "intuitive" decision making and decision making that involves interpersonal interaction. What, if anything, do we know about how judgmental and intuitive processes work and how they can be made to work better? And why do managers often fail to do what they know they should do—even what they have decided to do? What can be done to bring action into closer accord with intention?

My article will therefore have the form of a diptych, with one-half devoted to each of these topics. First, I will discuss judgmental and intuitive decision making; then I will turn to the subject of the manager's behavior and the influence of emotions on that behavior.

Sometimes the term rational (or logical) is applied to decision making that is consciously analytic, the term nonrational to decision making that is intuitive and judgmental, and the term irrational to decision making and behavior that responds to the emotions or that deviates from action chosen "rationally." We will be concerned, then, with the nonrational and the irrational components of managerial decision making and behavior. Our task, you might say, is to discover the reason that underlies unreason.

From *Academy of Management EXECUTIVE,* February 1987.

INTUITION AND JUDGEMENT

As an appendix to the *Functions of the Executive* (Harvard University Press, 1938), Chester I. Barnard published an essay, based on a talk he had given in 1936 at Princeton, entitled "Mind in Everyday Affairs."[1] The central motif of that essay was a contrast between what Barnard called "logical" and "nonlogical" processes for making decisions. He speaks of "the wide divergence of opinion . . . as to what constitutes a proper intellectual basis for opinion or deliberate action." And he continues:

> By "logical processes" I mean conscious thinking which could be expressed in words or by other symbols, that is, reasoning. By "nonlogical processes" I mean those not capable of being expressed in words or as reasoning, which are only made known by a judgment, decision or action.

Barnard's thesis was that executives, as contrasted, say, with scientists, do not often enjoy the luxury of making their decisions on the basis of orderly rational analysis, but depend largely on intuitive or judgmental responses to decision-demanding situations.

Although Barnard did not provide a set of formal criteria for distinguishing between logical and judgmental decision making, he did provide a phenomenological characterization of the two styles that make them easily recognizable, at least in their more extreme forms. In logical decision making, goals and alternatives are made explicit, the consequences of pursuing different alternatives are calculated, and these consequences are evaluated in terms of how close they are to the goals.

In judgmental decision making, the response to the need for a decision is usually rapid, too rapid to allow for an orderly sequential analysis of the situation, and the decision maker cannot usually give a veridical account of either the process by which the decision was reached or the grounds for judging it correct. Nevertheless, decision makers may have great confidence in the correctness of their intuitive decisions and are likely to attribute their ability to make them rapidly to their experience.

Most executives probably find Barnard's account of their decision processes persuasive; it captures their own feelings of how processes work. On the other hand, some students of management, especially those whose goal is to improve

---

[1]Chester I. Barnard's (1938) *The Functions of the Executive* (Cambridge, Mass.: Harvard University Press), contains the essay on the contrast between logical and nonlogical processes as bases for decision making.

management-decision processes, have felt less comfortable with it. It appears to vindicate snap judgments and to cast doubt on the relevance of management-science tools, which almost all involve deliberation and calculation in decision making.

Barnard did not regard the nonlogical processes of decision as magical in any sense. On the contrary, he felt they were grounded in knowledge and experience:

> *The sources of these non-logical processes lie in physiological conditions or factors, or in the physical and social environment, mostly impressed upon us unconsciously or without conscious effort on our part. They also consist of the mass of facts, patterns, concepts, techniques, abstractions, and generally what we call formal knowledge or beliefs, which are impressed upon our minds more or less by conscious effort and study. This second source of non-logical mental processes greatly increases with directed experience, study and education.* (p. 302)

At the time I wrote *Administrative Behavior* (1941–42), I was troubled by Barnard's account of intuitive judgment (see the footnote on p. 51 of *AB*), largely, I think, because he left no clues as to what subconscious processes go on while judgments are being made.[2] I was wholly persuaded, however, that a theory of decision making had to give an account of both conscious and subconscious processes (see the end of p. 75 to the top of p. 76). I finessed the issue by assuming that both the conscious and the unconscious parts of the process were the same, that they involve drawing on factual premises and value premises, and operating on them to form conclusions that became the decisions.

Because I used logic (drawing conclusions from premises) as a central metaphor to describe the decision-making process, many readers of *Administrative Behavior* have concluded that the theory advanced there applies only to "logical" decision making, not to decisions that involve intuition and judgment. That was certainly not my intent. But now, after nearly 50 years, the ambiguity can be resolved because we have acquired a solid understanding of what the judgmental and intuitive processes are. I will take up the new evidence in a moment; but first, a word must be said about the "two brains" hypothesis, which argues that rational and intuitive processes are so different that they are carried out in different parts of the brain.

---

[2]Simon, H. A. (1978) *Administrative Behavior*, 2nd ed. New York: Free Press. For a review of the artificial intelligence research on expert systems, see A. Barr and E. A. Figenbaum's (eds.) *The Handbook of Artificial Intelligence*, Vol. 2, Los Alamos, Cal.: William Kaufmann, 1982, pp. 77–294.

Split Brains and Forms of Thought

Physiological research on "split brains"—brains in which the corpus callosum, which connects the two hemispheres of the cerebrum, has been severed—has provided encouragement to the idea of two qualitatively different kinds of decision making—the analytical, corresponding to Barnard's "logical," and the intuitive or creative, corresponding to his "non-logical." The primary evidence behind this dichotomy is that the two hemispheres exhibit a division of labor: in right-handed people, the right hemisphere plays a special role in the recognition of visual patterns, and the left hemisphere in analytical processes and the use of language.

Other evidence in addition to the split-brain research suggests some measure of hemispheric specialization. Electrical activity in the intact brain can be measured by EEG techniques. Activity in a brain hemisphere is generally associated with partial or total suppression in the hemisphere of the alpha system, a salient brain wave with a frequency of about ten vibrations per second. When a hemisphere is inactive, the alpha rhythm in that hemisphere becomes strong. For most right-handed subjects, when the brain is engaged in a task involving recognition of visual pattern, the alpha rhythm is relatively stronger in the left than in the right hemisphere; with more analytical tasks, the alpha rhythm is relatively stronger in the right hemisphere. (See Doktor and Hamilton, 1973, and Doktor, 1975, for some experiments and a review of the evidence.[3])

The more romantic versions of the split-brain doctrine extrapolate this evidence into the two polar forms of thought labeled above as analytical and creative. As any easy next step, evaluative nuances creep into the discussion. The opposite of "creative," after all, is "pedestrian." The analytical left hemisphere, so this story goes, carries on the humdrum, practical, everyday work of the brain, while the creative right hemisphere is responsible for those flights of imagination that produce great music, great literature, great art, great science, and great management. The evidence for this romantic extrapolation does not derive from the physiological research. As I indicated above, that research has provided evidence only for some measure of specialization between the hemispheres. It does not in any way imply that either hemisphere (especially the right hemisphere) is capable of problem solving, decision making, or discovery independent of the other. The real evidence for two different forms of thought is essentially that on which Barnard relied: the observation that, in everyday affairs, men and women often make competent judgments or reach reasonable decisions rapidly—without evidence indicating that they have engaged in systematic reasoning, and without their being able to report the thought processes that took them to their conclusion.

There is also some evidence for the very plausible hypothesis that some people, confronted with a particular problem, make more use of intuitive processes in solving it, while other people make relatively more use of analytical processes (Doktor, 1978).[3]

For our purposes, it is the differences in behavior, and not the differences in the hemispheres, that are important. Reference to the two hemispheres is a read herring that can only impede our understanding of intuitive, "non-logical" thought. The important questions for us are "What is intuition?" and "How is it accomplished?" not "In which cubic centimeters of the brain tissue does it take place?"

New Evidence on the Processes of Intuition

In the 50 years since Barnard talked about the mind in everyday affairs, we have learned a great deal about the processes human beings use to solve problems, to make decisions, and even to create works of art and science. Some of this new knowledge has been gained in the psychological laboratory; some has been gained through observation of the behavior of people who are demonstrably creative in some realm of human endeavor; and a great deal has been gained through the use of the modern digital computer to model human thought processes and perform problem-solving and decision-making functions at expert levels.

I should like to examine this body of research, which falls under the labels of "cognitive science" and "artificial intelligence," to see what light it casts on intuitive, judgmental decision making in management. We will see that a rather detailed account can be given of the processes that underlie judgment, even though most of these processes are not within the conscious awareness of the actor using them.

THE EXPERT'S INTUITION

In recent years, the disciplines of cognitive science and artificial intelligence have devoted a great deal of attention to the nature of expert problem solving and decision making in professional-level tasks. The goal of the cognitive science research has been to gain an understanding of the differences between the behavior

---

[3]Two works that examine the split brain theory and forms of thought are R. H. Doktor's "Problem Solving Styles of Executives and Management Scientists," in A. Charnes, W. W. Cooper, and R. J. Niehaus's (eds.) *Management Science Approaches to Manpower Planning and Organization Design* (Amsterdam: North-Holland, 1978); and R. H. Doktor and W. F. Hamilton's "Cognitive Style and the Acceptance of Management Science Recommendations" (*Management Science,* 19:884–894, 1973).

of experts and novices, and possibly to learn more about how novices can become experts. The goal of the artificial intelligence research has been to build computer systems that can perform professional tasks as competently as human experts can. Both lines of research have greatly deepened our understanding of expertise.[4]

Intuition in Chessplaying

One much studied class of experts is the grandmasters in the game of chess. Chess is usually believed to require a high level of intellect, and grandmasters are normally full-time professionals who have devoted many years to acquiring their mastery of the game. From a research standpoint, the advantage of the game is that the level of skill of players can be calibrated accurately from their official ratings, based on their tournament success.

From the standpoint of studying intuitive thinking, chess might seem (at least to outsiders) an unpromising research domain. Chess playing is thought to involve a highly analytical approach, with players working out systematically the consequences of moves and countermoves, so that a single move may take as much as a half hour's thought, or more. On the other hand, chess professionals can play simultaneous games, sometimes against as many as 50 opponents, and exhibit only a moderately lower level of skill than in games playing under tournament conditions. In simultaneous play, the professional takes much less than a minute, often only a few seconds, for each move. There is no time for careful analysis.

When we ask the grandmaster or master how he or she is able to find good moves under these circumstances, we get the same answer that we get from other professionals who are questioned about rapid decisions: It is done by "intuition," by applying one's professional "judgment" to the situation. A few seconds' glance at the position suggests a good move, although the player has no awareness of how the judgment was evoked.

Even under tournament conditions, good moves usually come to a player's mind after only a few seconds' consideration of the board. The remainder of the analysis time is generally spent verifying that a move appearing plausible does not have a hidden weakness. We encounter this same kind of behavior in other professional domains where intuitive judgments are usually subjected to tests of various kinds before they are actually implemented. The main exceptions are situations where the decision has to be made before a deadline or almost instantly.

---

[4]For a survey of cognitive science research on problem solving and decision making, see Simon, H. A. (1979) *The Sciences of the Artificial*, 2nd ed., Cambridge, Mass.: The MIT Press, Chapters 3 and 4.

Of course we know that under these circumstances (as in professional chess when the allowed time is nearly exhausted), mistakes are sometimes made.

How do we account for the judgment or intuition that allows the chess grandmaster usually to find good moves in a few seconds? A good deal of the answer can be derived from an experiment that is easily repeated. First, present a grandmaster and a novice with a position from an actual, but unfamiliar, chess game (with about 25 pieces on the board). After five or ten seconds, remove the board and pieces and ask the subjects to reproduce it. The grandmaster will usually reconstruct the whole position correctly, and on average will place 23 or 24 pieces on their correct squares. The novice will only be able to replace, on average, about 6 pieces.

It might seem that we are witnessing remarkable skill in visual imagery and visual memory, but we can easily dismiss that possibility by carrying out a second experiment. The conditions are exactly the same as in the first experiment, except that now the 25 pieces are placed on the board at random. The novice can still replace about 6 pieces and the grandmaster—about 6! The difference between them in the first experiment does not lie in the grandmaster's eyes or imagery, but in his knowledge, acquired by long experience, of the kinds of patterns and clusters of pieces that occur on chessboards in the course of games. For the expert, such a chess board is not an arrangement of 25 pieces but an arrangement of a half dozen familiar patterns, recognizable old friends. On the random board there are no such patterns, only the 25 individual pieces in an unfamiliar arrangement.

The grandmaster's memory holds more than a set of patterns. Associated with each pattern in his or her memory is information about the significance of that pattern—what dangers it holds, and what offensive or defensive moves it suggests. Recognizing the pattern brings to the grandmaster's mind at once moves that may be appropriate to the situation. It is this recognition that enables the professional to play very strong chess at a rapid rate. Previous learning that has stored the patterns and the information associated with them in memory makes this performance possible. This, then, is the secret of the grandmaster's intuition or judgment.

Estimates have been made, in a variety of ways, of the number of familiar patterns (which psychologists now call chunks) that the master or grandmaster must be able to recognize. These estimates fall in the neighborhood of 50,000, give or take a factor of two. Is this a large number? Perhaps not. The natural language vocabularies of college graduates have been estimated to be in the range of 50,000 to 200,000 words, nearly the same range as the chess expert's vocabularies of patterns of pieces. Moreover, when we recognize a word, we also get access to information in our memories about the meaning of the word and to other information associated with it as well. So our ability to speak and understand language has the same intuitive or judgmental flavor as the grandmaster's ability to play chess rapidly.

Intuition in Computerized Expert Systems

A growing body of evidence from artificial intelligence research indicates that expert computer systems, capable of matching human performance in some limited domain, can be built by storing in computer memory tens of thousands of *productions*. Productions are computer instructions that take the form of "if-then" pairs. The "if" is a set of conditions or patterns to be recognized; the "then" is a body of information associated with the "if" and evoked from memory whenever the pattern is recognized in the current situation.

Some of our best data about this organization of expert knowledge come from the areas of medical diagnosis. Systems like CADUCEUS and MYCIN consist of a large number of such if-then pairs, together with an inference machine of modest powers. These systems are capable of medical diagnosis at a competent clinical level within their respective limited domains. Their recognition capabilities, the if-then pairs, represent their intuitive or judgmental ability; their inferencing powers represent their analytical ability.

Medical diagnosis is just one of a number of domains for which expert systems have been built. For many years, electric motors, generators, and transformers have been designed by expert systems developed by large electrical manufacturers. These computer programs have taken over from professional engineers many standards and relatively routine design tasks. They imitate fairly closely the rule-of-thumb procedures that human designers have used, the result of a large stock of theoretical and practical information about electrical machinery. Recognition also plays a large role in these systems. For example, examination of the customer's specifications "reminds" the program of a particular class of devices, which is then used as the basis for the design. Parameters for the design are then selected to meet the performance requirements of the device.

In chemistry, reaction paths for synthesizing organic molecules can be designed by expert systems. In these systems, the process appears relatively analytic, for it is guided by reasoning in the form of means-ends analyses, which work backward from the desired molecule, via a sequence of reactions, to available raw materials. But the reasoning scheme depends on a large store of knowledge of chemical reactions and the ability of the system to recognize rapidly that a particular substance can be obtained as the output of one or more familiar reactions. Thus, these chemical synthesis programs employ the same kind of mixture of intuition and analysis that is used in the other expert systems, and by human experts as well.

Other examples of expert systems can be cited, and all of them exhibit reasoning or analytic processes combined with processes for accessing knowledge banks with the help of recognition cues. This appears to be a universal scheme for the organization of expert systems—and of expert human problem solving as well.

Notice that there is nothing "irrational" about intuitive or judgmental reasoning based on productions. The conditions in a production constitute a set of premises. Whenever these conditions are satisfied, the production draws the appropriate conclusion—it evokes from memory information implied by these conditions or even initiates motor responses. A person learning to drive a car may notice a red light, be aware that a red light calls for a stop, and be aware that stopping requires applying the brakes. For an experienced driver, the sight of the red light simply evokes the application of brakes. How conscious the actor is of the process inversely, how automatic the response is, may differ, but there is no difference in the logic being applied.

Intuition in Management

Some direct evidence also suggests that the intuitive skills of managers depend on the same kinds of mechanisms as the intuitive skills of chessmasters or physicians. It would be surprising if it were otherwise. The experienced manager, too, has in his or her memory a large amount of knowledge, gained from training and experience and organized in terms of recognizable chunks and associated information.

Marius J. Bouwman has constructed a computer program capable of detecting company problems from an examination of accounting statements.[5] The program was modeled on detailed thinking-aloud protocols of experienced financial analysts interpreting such statements, and it captures the knowledge that enables analysts to spot problems intuitively, usually at a very rapid rate. When a comparison is made between the responses of the program and the responses of an expert human financial analyst, a close match is usually found.

In another study, R. Bhaskar gathered thinking-aloud protocols from business school students and experienced businessmen, who were all asked to analyze a

---

[5]Marius J. Bouwman's doctoral dissertation, *Financial Diagnosis* (Graduate School of Industrial Administration, Carnegie-Mellon University, 1978).

business policy case.[6] The final analyses produced by the students and the businessmen were quite similar. What most sharply discriminated between the novices and the experts was the time required to identify the key features of the case. This was done very rapidly, with the usual appearances of intuition, by the experts; it was done slowly, with much conscious and explicit analysis, by the novices.

These two pieces of research are just drops of water in a large bucket that needs filling. The description, in detail, of the use of judgmental and analytical processes in expert problem solving and decision making deserves a high priority in the agenda of management research.

Can Judgment Be Improved?

From this and other research on expert problem solving and decision making, we can draw two main conclusions. *First,* experts often arrive at problem diagnoses and solutions rapidly and intuitively without being able to report how they attained the result. *Second,* this ability is best explained by postulating a recognition and retrieval process that employs a large number—generally tens of thousands or even hundreds of thousands—of chunks or patterns stored in long term memory.

When the problems to be solved are more than trivial, the recognition processes have to be organized in a coherent way and they must be supplied with reasoning capabilities that allow inferences to be drawn from the information retrieved, and numerous chunks of information to be combined. Hence intuition is not a process that operates independently of analysis; rather, the two processes are essential complementary components of effective decision-making systems. When the expert is solving a difficult problem or making a complex decision, much conscious deliberation may be involved. But each conscious step may itself constitute a considerable leap, with a whole sequence of automated productions building the bridge from the premises to the conclusions. Hence the expert appears to take giant intuitive steps in reasoning, as compared with the tiny steps of the novice.

It is doubtful that we will find two types of managers (at least, of good managers), one of whom relies almost exclusively on intuition, the other on analytic techniques. More likely, we will find a continuum of decision-making styles involving an intimate combination of the two kinds of skill. We will likely also find

---

[6]R. Bhaskar's doctoral dissertation, *Problem Solving in Semantically Rich Domains* (Graduate School of Industrial Administration, Carnegie-Mellon University, 1978).

that the nature of the problem to be solved will be a principal determinant of the mix.

With our growing understanding of the organization of judgmental and intuitive processes, of the specific knowledge that is required to perform particular judgmental tasks, and of the cues that evoke such knowledge in situations in which it is relevant, we have a powerful new tool for improving expert judgment. We can specify the knowledge and the recognition capabilities that experts in a domain need to acquire as a basis for designing appropriate learning procedures.

We can also, in more and more situations, design expert systems capable of automating the expertise, or alternatively, of providing the human decision maker with an expert consultant. Increasingly, we will see decision aids for managers that will be highly interactive, with both knowledge and intelligence being shared between the human and the automated components of the system.

A vast research and development task of extracting and cataloging the knowledge and cues used by experts in different kinds of managerial tasks lies ahead. Much has been learned in the past few years about how to do this. More needs to be learned about how to update and improve the knowledge sources of expert systems as new knowledge becomes available.

Progress will be most rapid with expert systems that have a substantial technical component. It is no accident that the earliest expert systems were built for such tasks as designing motors, making medical diagnoses, playing chess, and finding chemical synthesis paths. In the area of management, the analysis of company financial statements is a domain where some progress has been made in constructing expert systems. The areas of corporate policy and strategy are excellent candidates for early development of such systems.

What about the aspects of executive work that involve the managing of people? What help can we expect in improving this crucial component of the management task?

KNOWLEDGE AND BEHAVIOR

What managers know they should do—whether by analysis or intuitively—is very often different from what they actually do. A common failure of managers, which all of us have observed, is the postponement of difficult decisions. What is it that makes decisions difficult and hence tends to cause postponement? Often, the problem is that all of the alternatives have undesired consequences. When people have to choose the lesser of two evils, they do not simply behave like Bayesian statisticians, weighing the bad against the worse in the light of their respective possibilities. Instead, they avoid the decision, searching for alternatives that do not have negative outcomes. If such alternatives are not available, they are likely to continue to postpone making a choice. A choice between undesirables is a dilemma, something to be avoided or evaded.

Often, uncertainty is the source of the difficulty. Each choice may have a good outcome under one set of environmental contingencies, but a bad outcome under another. When this occurs, we also do not usually observe Bayesian behavior; the situation is again treated as a dilemma.

The bad consequences of a manger's decision are often bad for other people. Managers sometimes have to dismiss employees or, even more frequently, have to speak to them about unsatisfactory work. Dealing with such matters face to face is stressful to many, perhaps most, executives. The stress is magnified if the employee is a close associate or friend. If the unpleasant task cannot be delegated, it may be postponed.

The manager who has made a mistake (that is to say, all of us at one time or another) also finds himself or herself in a stressful situation. The matter must be dealt with sooner or later, but why not later instead of sooner? Moreover, when it is addressed, it can be approached in different ways. A manager may try to avoid blame—"It wasn't my fault!" A different way is to propose a remedy to the situation. I know of no systematic data on how often the one or the other course is taken, but most of us could probably agree that blame-avoiding behavior is far more common than problem-solving behavior after a serious error has been made.

The Consequences of Stress

What all of these decision-making situations have in common is stress, a powerful force that can divert behavior from the urgings of reason. They are examples of a much broader class of situations in which managers frequently behave in clearly nonproductive ways. Nonproductive responses are especially common when actions have to be made under time pressure. The need to allay feelings of guilt, anxiety, and embarrassment may lead to behavior that produces temporary personal comfort at the expense of bad long-run consequences for the organization.

Behavior of this kind is "intuitive" in the sense that it represents response without careful analysis and calculation. Lying, for example, is much more often the result of panic than of Machiavellian scheming. The intuition of the emotion-driven manager is very different from the intuition of the expert whom we discussed earlier. The latter's behavior is the product of learning and experience, and is largely adaptive; the former's behavior is a response to more primitive urges, and is more often than not inappropriate. We must not confuse the "nonrational" decisions of the experts—the decisions that derive from expert intuition and judgment—with the irrational decisions that stressful emotions may produce.

I have made no attempt here to produce a comprehensive taxonomy of the pathologies of organizational decision making, but simply have given some examples of the ways that stress interacts with cognition to elicit counterproductive behavior. Such responses can become so habitual for individuals or even for organizations that they represent a recognizable managerial "style."

Organizational psychologists have a great deal to say about ways of motivating workers and executives to direct their efforts toward organizational goals. They have said less about ways of molding habits so that executives can handle situations in a goal-directed manner. When it comes to handling situations, two dimensions of behavior deserve particular attention: the response to problems that arise, and the initiation of activity that looks to the future.

Responding to Problems

The response of an organization to a problem or difficulty, whether it results from a mistake or some other cause, is generally one that looks both backward and forward. It looks backward to establish responsibility for the difficulty and to diagnose it, and forward to find a course of action to deal with it.

The backward look is an essential part of the organization's reward system. The actions that have led to difficulties, and the people responsible for those actions, need to be identified. But the backward look can also be a source of serious pathologies. Anticipation of it—particularly anticipation that it will be acted on in a punitive way—is a major cause for the concealment of problems until they can no longer be hidden. It can also be highly divisive, as individuals point fingers to transfer blame to others. Such outcomes can hardly be eliminated, but an organization's internal reputation for fairness and objectivity can mitigate them. So can a practice of subordinating the blame finding to a diagnosis of causes as a first step toward remedial action.

Most important of all, however, is the forward look: the process of defining the problem and identifying courses of action that may solve it. Here also the reward system is critically important. Readiness to search for problem situations and effectiveness in finding them need to be recognized and rewarded.

Perhaps the greatest influence a manager can have on the problem-solving style of the organization as a role model is making the best responses to problems. The style the manager should aim for rests on the following principles:

1. Solving the problem takes priority over looking backward to its causes. Initially, backward looks should be limited to diagnosing causes; fixing responsibility for mistakes should be postponed until a solution is being implemented.

2. The manager accepts personal responsibility for finding and proposing solutions instead of seeking to shift that responsibility either to superiors or to subordinates, although the search for solutions may, of course, be a collaborative effort involving many people.

3. The manager accepts personal responsibility for implementing action solutions, including securing the necessary authority from above if required.

4. When it is time to look backward, fixing blame may be an essential part of the process, but the primary focus of attention should be on what can be learned to prevent similar problems from arising in the future.

These principles are as obvious as the Ten Commandments and perhaps not quite as difficult to obey. Earlier, I indicated that stress might cause departures from them, but failure to respond effectively to problems probably derives more from a lack of attention and an earlier failure to cultivate the appropriate habits. The military makes much use of a procedure called "Estimate of the Situation." Its value is not that it teaches anything esoteric, but that through continual training in its use, commanders become habituated to approaching situations in orderly ways, using the checklists provided by the formal procedure.

Habits of response to problems are taught and learned both in the manager's one-on-one conversations with subordinates and in staff meetings. Is attention brought back repeatedly to defining the problems until everyone is agreed on just what the problem is? Is attention then directed toward generating possible solutions and evaluating their consequences? The least often challenged and most reliable base of managerial influence is the power to set the agenda, to focus attention. It is one of the most effective tools the manager has for training organization members to approach problems constructively by shaping their own habits of attention.

The perceptive reader will have discerned that "shaping habits of attention" is identical to "acquiring intuitions." The habit of responding to problems by looking for solutions can and must become intuitive—cued by the presence of the problem itself. A problem-solving style is a component of the set of intuitions that the manager acquires, one of the key components of effective managerial behavior.

Looking to the Future

With respect to the initiation of activity, the organizational habit we would like to instil is responsiveness to cues that signal future difficulties as well as to those that call attention to the problems of the moment. Failure to give sufficient attention to the future most often stems from two causes. The first is interruption by current problems that have more proximate deadlines and hence seem more urgent; the second is the absence of sufficient "scanning" activity that can pick up cues from the environment that long-run forces not impinging immediately on the organization have importance for it in the future.

In neither case is the need for sensitivity to the future likely to be met simply by strengthening intuitions. Rather, what is called for is deliberate and systematic allocation of organizational resources to deal with long-range problems, access for these resources to appropriate input from the environment that will attract their attention to new prospects, and protection of these planning resources from absorption in current problems, however urgent they may be. Attention to the future must be institutionalized; there is no simpler way to incorporate it into managerial "style" or habit.

It is a fallacy to contrast "analytic" and "intuitive" styles of management. Intuition and judgment—at least good judgment—are simply analyses frozen into habit and into the capacity for rapid response through recognition. Every manager needs to be able to analyze problems systematically (and with the aid of the modern arsenal of analytical tools provided by management science and operations research). Every manager needs also to be able to respond to situations rapidly, a skill that requires the cultivation of intuition and judgment over many years of experience and training. The effective manager does not have the luxury of choosing between "analytic" and "intuitive" approaches to problems. Behaving like a manager means having command of the whole range of management skills and applying them as they become appropriate.

Herbert A. Simon is Richard King Mellon University Professor of computer science and psychology at Carnegie-Mellon University, where he has taught since 1949. For the past 30 years he has been studying decision-making and problem-solving processes, using computers to simulate human thinking.

Dr. Simon was educated at the University of Chicago (where he received his Ph.D.). He was elected to the National Academy of Sciences in 1967, and has received awards for his research from the American Psychological Association, the American Economic Association, and the Institute of Electrical and Electronic Engineers, among others. He received the Alfred Nobel Memorial Prize in Economics in 1978 and the National Medal of Science in 1986. Dr. Simon has been Chairman of the Board of Directors of the Social Science Research Council and of the Behavioral Science Division of the National Research Council, and was a member of the President's Science Advisory Committee.

Dr. Simon has published over 600 papers and 20 books and monographs.

THE BEHAVIORAL ASPECTS OF GROUP TECHNOLOGY

Mary L. Bertrand   and   Charles T. Mosier
Jefferson Community College   Clarkson University

This paper surveys the major research findings to date in the area of the human aspects of Group Technology (GT). From its onset, it has been claimed that GT would increase worker's satisfaction in their jobs as well as increasing the interest workers take in the quality of their work by providing increased job variety, increased responsibility and immediate feedback concerning performance. Research findings which both support and contradict this claim are presented. Also, a look is taken at GT as it relates to current literature on worker satisfaction and productivity and group theory.

1. Introduction

As manufacturing trends have moved toward small-batch production of parts,[1] efforts have been made to develop more efficient methods of batch manufacturing so that the increased costs for setups[2] and material handling[3]

---

[1]The production batch size to be considered "small" is not well determined. Small batch production runs range from "ones and twos" up to 5,000 or more parts. A more useful notion is to consider manufacturing where a significant number of set-ups (or changeovers) are required to be "small-batch." Examples of industries producing primarily in small-batches include "fabrication and assembly of automobiles, aircraft, computers and the microelectronic components of computers, furniture, appliances, foods, clothing, packaging, building materials and machine tools."[10]

[2]Here a *set-up* is all activity associated with changing the production equipment over to begin the manufacture of a different part. This includes (a.) tearing down current fixturing and tooling and replacing it with that required for the new part, (b.) downloading computer code required to process the new part, (c.) moving the part "stock" from inventory to the work site, and (d.) possibly processing and inspection of the initial units produced from the new batch. *Set-up* may also be used to describe the condition of the equipment, e.g., the *set-up* on the Lathe 12 is that required for part AB-2343.

[3]Theoretically, the frequency of material movement, e.g., to and from inventory, within the small-batch context is significantly higher than in other production configurations. In practice it is even worse; material handling is by far the most difficult aspect of production to control in small-batch manufacturing.

traditionally associated with small-batch production would be eliminated.[3] Group technology (GT), with origins in the Soviet Union during the second world war, was originally thought to be the answer to many of the problems involved in the small-batch production of parts.

There are many definitions of GT. One of the most useful defines GT as a method of production planning and plant layout which groups components into *families* based upon the processing they require and arranges machines into *cells* such that a machine cell is able to perform (or as nearly as possible) required processing of a given family of parts.[15] See Figures 1 and 2 for an example of the difference between a process layout and a cellular layout.

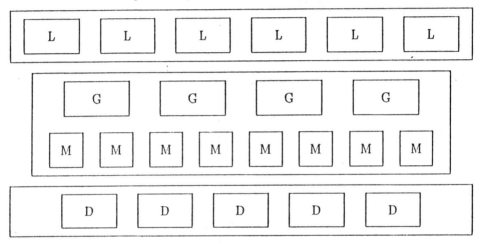

Figure 1. A Process Layout

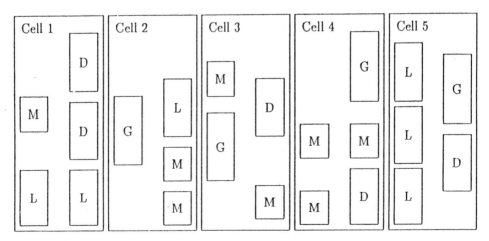

Figure 2. A GT Cellular Layout.

Reduced throughput and materials handling times, decreased work-in-process and finished goods inventory, and increased flexibility to handle forecast errors are some of the technical advantages claimed by proponents.[16] Several studies have been conducted to validate these claims. GT proponents also claim that GT not only lowers the costs associated with small-batch manufacturing but provides many social benefits (increased worker and foreman responsibility, job enrichment and enlargement, to name a few). These claims of social benefits imply a productivity increase beyond that induced by the technical advantages. A few scattered studies have been conducted to validate their claims.

This paper summarizes much of the research that has been conducted to date concerning the human aspects of GT and will address the ability of GT to meet the claims of increased social benefits.

2. Research to Date

Much of the early work examining the human aspects of Group Technology (GT) was conducted at the Universities of Birmingham, Bradford and Stanford and at the London Business School and was subsequently reported by G. Margaret Fazakerly.[7] The researchers used information obtained through interviews, questionnaires, and observation to examine worker flexibility, group social importance, frustration reduction, improvements in physical working conditions, and status and security. The dimensions of human interaction with GT examined in this report include these dimensions expanded as follows:

- *Employee Motivation, Job Variety, and Worker Flexibility*—The characteristics of an employee who is motivated are outlined as well as the factors necessary for the prevalence of employee motivation. Also, characteristics necessary for a worker to do well in a job which provides a high level of motivation are examined. Flexibility is addressed as it pertains to the job in terms of job variety, enlargement, and enrichment and as it pertains to the worker in terms of their ability to adapt to change.

- *Status and Security*—Worker status, job security, and task security are addressed as they relate to the success of GT. Their effect on employee motivation is also discussed.

- *Group Social Importance*—This topic includes the following: group formation, and the physical and psychological factors that effect the ease in which groups come to be formed and the requirements for efficient group performance, the significance of the group to its members (often referred to as group cohesiveness) or the importance each member places on being a part of the group, and the power of groups to meet their objectives, including the influence that clarity of objectives, delegation of responsibility, and management-worker relations have on this power.

- *Frustration Reduction*—Worker frustration is defined in relation to any conditions that prevent workers from achieving their objectives or cause them to feel their efforts have been rendered worthless. Here, frustration is addressed as it pertains to what the worker is supposed to accomplish and how it is to be accomplished.

- *Improvements in Physical Working Conditions*—Physical working conditions are characterized by the environment. GT's ability to improve physical working conditions, such as reduce stock pile-ups (clutter) and the relationship of improved physical working conditions to the elimination of worker dissatisfaction is addressed.

The following describes the results of GT research conducted to date concerning these dimensions and relates the current available knowledge on worker satisfaction, productivity, and group theory to the proposed success of GT.

2.1 *Employee Motivation, Job Variety, and Worker Flexibility*

Much of today's literature addressed employee motivation and its effects on production. When employees are motivated, both the quantity and quality of their work is said to improve. According to Hackman and Oldham,[11] internal motivation occurs when the following conditions exist:

- A person has knowledge of the results of their work.

- A person experiences responsibility for the results of their work.

- A person experiences the work as meaningful.

In order for a person to have knowledge of the results of their work, a feedback system must be present. Job feedback can be defined as the degree to which carrying out the work activities required by the job provides the individual with direct and clear information about the effectiveness of their performance.[11]

In a GT situation, the worker passes a part which they have completed to someone in their own cell. Thus they become immediately aware of any errors made and of the consequences of these errors.

A study conducted by B. G. Dale[4] supports the notion that GT provides immediate feedback. Eight foremen from three companies employing GT were interviewed concerning their views on how GT affected their jobs. In terms of feedback, all eight foremen said that faster feedback was provided for operators after implementation.

In order for workers to feel directly responsible for the results of their work, their jobs must be high in autonomy. Autonomy may be defined as the degree to which the job provides freedom, independence, and discretion to the individual in scheduling the work and determining the processes to be used in carrying it out.[11]

Though not a primary objective of most companies employing GT, many delegate lower level management tasks to machine operator.[5, 6, 7] These tasks can provide the autonomy needed to ensure worker motivation.

According to Hackman and Oldham,[11] a job may be considered meaningful when it provides the chance to use and test personal skills and abilities. They further state that meaningfulness can be provided by any one of the following factors:

- *Skill Variety*—The degree to which a job requires a variety of different activities in carrying out the work, involving the use of a number of different talents and skills.

- *Task Identity*—The degree to which a job requires completion of a whole and identifiable piece of work, doing a job from beginning to end with a visible outcome.

- *Task Significance*—The degree to which the job has a substantial impact on the lives of other people.

According to Fazakerly,[7] because of restrictions imposed by trade unions and because most workers' skills are highly specialized, the notion that GT provides for the full utilization of man-hours and job variety (enlargement) in the traditional sense could not be supported in full. In actuality, flexibility occurs in only two ways. First, workers run additional machinery of similar types, and second, operators are shifted between cells as required.

Because families of components were manufactured or processed in one cell, the worker's horizontal variety (the number of different components a worker sees) was seen to decrease. However, an increase was seen in the "sense" of variety for the worker.

*The operator is exposed to a mixed environment, sees a wide range
of activities, can relate to other kinds of tasks and is more aware of
his/her contributions to schedules, quality and the overall work
environment.[7]*

Task identity is inherent in GT on a cellular basis. Each cell completely produces one part, therefore, each worker although not singly producing a complete part is assured task identity in that their cell completely produces parts.

Task significance can vary depending upon the parts being produced. For example, a cell producing brakes for cars will provide its employees with a higher level of task significance than a cell producing lawn furniture, because peoples' lives may well depend on the quality of their car brakes, but a poorly assembled lawn chair will likely cause little injury.

A job that is high in motivational potential might be high on at least one of the factors that induce meaningfulness as well as high on autonomy and job feedback.[11] As illustrated above, GT provides high levels of task identity, autonomy, and job feedback, and at least moderate levels of task variety. Thus, it appears that GT may be able to provide employees with a sense of internal motivation.

This notion was supported in a report directed toward the future of advanced technology in Norway by Astrop.[1] The report related the beliefs of Oyvend Bjorke of Norway's NTH Institute of Production Engineering, a major contributor to the report, concerning the effects of advanced technology on society. Bjorke believed that as a result of the growing concern for workers' rights and job satisfaction, and of the awareness that industrialization can bring harm as well as good; advances in industry must be evaluated in terms of their holistic effects on workers and society. Bjorke saw motivation as a key factor in the improvement of production. Because financial motivators were seen to be decreasing in strength, Bjorke asserted that it was of prime importance to provide a sense of personal satisfaction and fulfillment for workers. He felt that this could best be accomplished in Norway through the use of vertical job enlargement as it related to GT. Bjorke elaborated that job enlargement would be met by delegating to workers a wide variety of different functions including operations planning, part programming, work scheduling, machine loading, and quality control. Thus flexibility, as defined by Fazakerly, would be provided through what Bjorke and Astrop termed job enlargement. It should be noted that when Astrop's paper was published, the NTH-SINT F cell concept as presented by Bjorke was still in the developmental stage.

Hackman and Oldham[11] provided information on the characteristics they considered essential for a worker to succeed in a job that is structured to provide high levels of employee motivation. These characteristics are:

- The workers should possess good task-relevant knowledge and skills.

- The workers should have strong growth needs (e.g., the desire to get ahead or expand their knowledge).

- The workers must be relatively satisfied with their job context (e.g., pay, job security, supervisor).

While the effect of growth needs and worker knowledge on the success of GT has not yet been studied, the effect of status and security has been addressed and is discussed in a later section of this paper.

A later report[15] addressed flexibility of the labor force as it pertained to the success of GT. The report linked lessons and information obtained from past experience with GT. McManus defines worker flexibility as having two forms: flexibility within groups and flexibility between groups.

Flexibility within groups is deemed necessary for the manufacturing systems to operate, and flexibility between groups allowed manufacturing flexibility and greater utilization of labor skills.[15] In simpler terms, flexibility (both within and between groups) is deemed desirable because with a flexible labor force, workers can alternate between key machines as needed to keep the plant functioning.

2.2 Status and Security

With the surge of recent research on increasing job satisfaction and employee motivation through techniques such as job redesign, the importance of factors such as job security and status has been downplayed. However, most psychologists agree that these factors are essential for employees to achieve job satisfaction. For example, F. Herzberg's two factor theory terms job security and status as hygiene factors whose presence does not lead to job satisfaction but whose absence leads to job dissatisfaction.[12]

Although this theory has received much criticism,[14] some psychologists argue that factors such as status and security are essential and should be present before job redesign, such as with GT, takes place.

The three main points made by Fazakerly,[7] in her report outlined earlier, which are listed below, coincide with current thinking concerning status and security.

- The work force will be unwilling to accept change unless status and security, which they sometimes associate with pay increases, are retained. Since GT usually results in higher productivity, higher pay rates can be established which will aid in assuring workers that their job status and security will not be threatened.

- GT, to date, had been applied in an expanding economy where reducing the work force was not its goal. If job security were to be threatened, such as in a stagnant economy where the aim would be to cut production costs by cutting workers, resistance should be expected.

- In a narrow sense, some workers may feel that their task security is threatened. Fazakerly stated that the workers who feel most threatened may be the most reliable workers. Most recent articles advise that when setting up an experimental cell, flexible workers should be chosen. That is, workers chosen should have the ability to move between and within cells and should not be wary of change.

2.3 *The Importance of the Social Group*

GT involves the grouping of machines and people into cells, with each cell producing one part or a group of similar parts. Thus workers are arranged far differently than in traditional manufacturing settings and are expected to interact with co-workers in an attempt to achieve a common objective. In other words, cells are expected to demonstrate cohesiveness. They are expected to demonstrate teamwork, high morale, and group spirit[17] so that they may achieve their objective of increased, high-quality production.

Because of the importance of group cohesiveness to the success of GT, Fazakerly[7] believed that group behavior should be considered in a situation where Group Technology is employed, and attention, although it is often not, should be given to the following factors:

- The processes by which groups come to be formed.

- The significance of the group to its members.

- The power groups have to pursue their objectives.

The ease of which groups come to be formed depends, according to Fazakerly, on both physical factors (such as factory layout) and psychological factors (such as failure to explain changes which are being implemented) which may hinder their formation. When developing cells, attention should be paid to the minimization of these barriers or cohesive groups will not be formed.

In terms of the physical factors that affect group formation, a factory layout should be developed with thought given to how to best encourage communication where it is needed. That is, if it is desirable for two machinists to be in constant communication over tolerance requirements and/or quality control, their machines must be positioned in a manner to facilitate this communication.

R. A. Baron[2] illustrated the importance of factory layout by relating a study conducted in a research and development firm. It was found that employees located more than 25 feet apart, on the same floor, rarely had any significant communication.

In terms of psychological barriers, workers should be informed of any company changes that will affect them and of the consequences of these changes. That is, if workers are being grouped into cells they should be told why they are being grouped as such, how the grouping will affect them and what will be expected of them in this new formation.

Task interdependence was seen to be prevalent in companies employing GT and also was seen to be a psychological factor that promoted the formation of cohesive groups. Task interdependence was seen to promote immediate feedback and to provide the workers with a better understanding of the importance of quality and of tolerance requirements.[7] As mentioned earlier, in a GT situation, the worker passes a part which they have completed to someone in their own cell; they become immediately aware of any mistakes they may have made and of the consequences of these mistakes.

A previously mentioned study,[4] in which eight foremen from three companies employing GT were interviewed, illustrates the effect of task interdependence on quality. In the area of quality attainment, all eight supervisors said they have better control and that quality levels in their departments had improved for the following reasons:

- Workers were more knowledgeable after the implementation of GT and tended not to repeat their mistakes.

- Faster feedback was provided from other operators than before GT was implemented.

- Workers seemed generally more aware of quality issues.

- There was better intergroup communication and better general knowledge (awareness) on the part of workers concerning problems in their group.

- Quality problems were easier (after GT) to identify, isolate, and rectify.

Dale's findings in this study seemed to concur with Fazakerly's results.

According to Hackman and Oldham,[11] how a group is composed should not be overlooked, because it directly affects the amount of knowledge and skill that can be applied to work on a group task. To obtain maximum knowledge and skills, they recommend groups be composed keeping the following aspects in mind:

- Groups should include members who have high levels of task-relevant expertise.

- The group should be large enough to do the work but not much larger.

- Group members should possess at least a moderate level of interpersonal skills.

- Groups should be composed to provide a balance between the homogeneity and heterogeneity of membership.

One can easily grasp the importance of these aspects in a GT setting. If the group is going to increase productivity and assume the responsibility traditionally assigned foremen, group members must possess the skills necessary to function effectively in their cell.

Concerning group size: Hackman and Oldham's rule of thumb allows groups to vary in size depending on the amount and difficulty of the work to be performed in each cell.

In plants employing GT, cell members are in constant communication with each other and frequent communication with management. Research indicates that with GT an increase in communication can be expected.[4] By choosing group members with sound interpersonal skills, this increase can be seen as positive. This is especially true where job feedback is concerned, because negative feedback can be detrimental to employee motivation.

Concerning homogeneity/heterogeneity: If group members are too much alike, there may not be enough variance in expertise to keep the cell functioning effectively and to handle any problems that may arise in the cell. If group members have too little in common, the group may lack cohesiveness.

Hackman and Oldham's ideas have been tested in a situation similar to GT.[11] The Butler Manufacturing Company worked with groups arranged in a way similar to a GT configuration. Evidence indicates that the groups' productivity and group members' satisfaction were high. While this is only indicative of what may happen in a GT situation, further research may well be warranted concerning the effect of Hackman and Oldham's aspects of group structure on GT cells.

Fazakerly also addressed the significance of the group to its members and found this significance to vary across applications of GT. Factors which affect it were outlined as group size, shared values, and common goals and interests.

The report by McManus,[15] outlined earlier, stated that nominal group size should be between six and ten people and that larger groups would be less effective.

Other researchers seem to agree that the ideal group size was under ten people and that groups should not be any larger than 15 people.[7] Increasing group size beyond that point was thought to decrease morale and cohesiveness.

Fazakerly, however, related a case where, when group size was increased beyond 15 people, absenteeism and turnover rate both decreased, thus indicating an increase in job satisfaction and morale.[7] When group size was reduced, absenteeism and turnover rate increased. It was believed that with the increase in group size, members could find other members who shared their values, goals and interests, and avoid members whom they disliked. As the group grew smaller they could not avoid unpleasant encounters with the coworkers they disliked, thus reducing their job satisfaction.

B. R. Patton and K. Giffen[17] provided evidence to support this theory. The authors cited a study in which the actions of members of small groups were compared to those of members of larger groups. It was noted that members felt less inhibited in large groups than in small groups and that the chances of individual group members being alienated from the group for expressing their opinions lessened as the group grew in size.

Thus, it could be concluded that when forming groups, attention should be paid to group members' personalities and traits. Forced interaction among individuals who do not "get along" can decrease the cohesiveness of small groups.

Perhaps Hackman and Oldham's rule of thumb: *The group should be large enough to do the work but not much larger,* is better suited to GT than limiting group size to a specific number. This, as mentioned earlier, would allow groups to vary in size depending on the amount and difficulty of the work to be performed in each cell.

Shared values and common goals and interests are factors prevalent in cohesive groups. Webster defines cohesiveness as the tendency to stick together. A group that is attractive to its individual members will be cohesive.[9]

McManus pointed out that group cohesiveness is a factor which increases the ease of the achievement of technological innovations. This was seen to be because group members tend to have a greater sense of identification with common aims and objectives than individual production workers. While the traditional production worker only sees what they do and not what the completed part looks like or how it performs, the GT cell members manufacture completely their assigned part(s) and are thus able to comprehend the importance of technical innovations as they are introduced. Thus, while the traditional production workers may be wary of technical change that they cannot understand, the GT workers will understand the importance of technical changes and therefore provide less resistance to these changes.

R. A. Baron[2] cautioned, however, that while cohesiveness is important, groups should not be so cohesive that they isolate themselves from outside correcting influences.

Fazakerly[7] elaborated that although group cohesiveness is important, it should not be strong enough to prevent the acceptance of new group members and transfer of group members to other cells.

The power which groups have to pursue assigned objectives, according to Fazakerly, depends on three variables:

- Clarity of objectives.

- Delegation of responsibility.

- Relations with management.

Fazakerly claimed that it is most important that objectives be clearly stated. In other words, the requirements of the group's tasks should be known to all group members.[18] This is essential, because a vital element for group cohesiveness is a sense of purpose, and a sense of purpose cannot be achieved unless objectives are clearly stated and known to all workers. GT, with its production scheduling on a cell by cell basis, provides the objective to each cell of completely manufacturing a part, and thus provides the sense of purpose needed for group cohesiveness. Once objectives are clearly stated and a cohesive work group is formed, improved work scheduling, production control, and upward and downward communication are claimed, by Fazakerly, to follow.

B. G. Dale's[4] study conducted with foremen, mentioned earlier, supported this notion. All eight foremen said that their control had improved with the onset of GT, and five foremen said that their upward and downward communication had improved. When, in the study, the workers were polled concerning communication, 50 percent said that communication had improved. While these results are not dramatic, they are indicative of the improvements that can be achieved as an indirect result of objective clarity and group cohesiveness.

As mentioned earlier, most companies employing GT take advantage of the opportunity to delegate responsibility and lower level management tasks to the worker. This is seen as a factor which increases worker satisfaction.[5,6,15] However, it can be either a threat or an opportunity for the foreman, in that it will either mean that the foreman's responsibility is limited and possibly the elimination of the job, or the foreman may face new and challenging responsibilities.

One of the studies conducted by Dale[5] supported the notion that companies often increase the responsibilities of the foremen. Eight foremen from three different companies were interviewed and all stated that with GT their responsibility and prestige had increased, and seven of the eight stated that their morale and satisfaction had increased. Only three claimed that their workers' responsibilities and participation in decision making had increased, although all indicated their workload had increased.

The increase in foremen responsibility reported by Dale caused the need to retrain two of the foremen questioned, and problems for four of them in terms of gaining the respect of workers who operated machines on which the foremen were inexperienced. Three foremen said, however, that their jobs were made easier in the sense that workers were more self-motivated.

Fazakerly, in her report,[7] outlined the benefits from this delegation of responsibility to be as follows:

- Problems would be more effectively dealt with because the responsibility would lie where the problems arose.

- The work that would be considered boring or routine at one level would be delegated to a level where it would be seen as interesting and challenging.

- Upper management would be freed from routine tasks so that they would be able to devote their time to planning and more important management functions.

These proposed benefits seem to align with the information reported by Dale. Dale's study also revealed, however, that in general, the foremen initially resisted GT. Fazakerly cautioned that this may happen if lower management saw GT as a threat to their security, or if their tasks were delegated to operators and they were given no new responsibilities.

Hackman and Oldham[11] predicted this when they stated that the worker (the foreman in this case) must be relatively satisfied with the job context to succeed in a job requiring employee motivation. It should be noted that this could be prevented by enriching the foreman's position and by providing the foreman with a thorough explanation of the program at its onset with assurances that the job would not be eliminated.

Fazakerly proposed that with GT, relations with management would improve because contact between management and workers would be constant and meaningful. Later research,[4,19] although supporting an increase in communications between workers and managers, did not address worker-manager relations.

2.4 Reduction in Frustration

Any condition(s) that prevent workers from achieving an objective or render their efforts as worthless causes frustration or low worker morale. Improving the work environment and clearly defining worker job objectives can have a positive impact on worker morale.[3] According to Fazakerly,[7] in the typical production situation, the major sources of frustration for workers, as seen by management, are shortages of materials and machine breakdowns. These are perceived to be the main obstacles that prevent workers from successfully performing their tasks. GT, by its very nature, prevents at least the shortage of materials by reducing work in process and ordering the work flow.

Another sense of frustration for the workers was determined to be *not seeing what the job is*.[7] In other words, in traditional batch production the workers do not know what goes on before they get a part, or what happens to the part when they are finished with it. In a GT situation, each product is completely manufactured in one cell providing the task interdependence and clarity necessary to give the workers a true definition of what their job is. Although later reports[4,21,19] indicated that jobs are more clearly defined with GT, and most material shortages are reduced, these factors have not been clearly linked to a reduction in frustration. Fazakerly conceded that reduction in frustration from these factors themselves may be peripheral.

2.5 *Improvement in Material Working Conditions*

As mentioned earlier, with the surge of recent research on increasing employee motivation and job satisfaction through techniques such as job redesign, the importance of factors such as good working conditions has been downplayed. Most psychologists agree, however, that without these factors it is impossible to design a job that will motivate employees and provide them with high levels of job satisfaction.[8]

Changing from traditional batch production to GT eliminates stock pile ups (cluttered work areas) by reducing work in process and ordering the work flow, thus improving material working conditions. While this in itself will not eliminate concerns over improving working conditions, it will allow attention to be centered on the generation of more significant improvements.[7] Further, the elimination of job dissatisfaction will allow attention to be focused on the area of increased job satisfaction.

2.6 *Other Research Findings*

Additional research has been conducted that does not directly tie in with the dimensions detailed above but is nonetheless related to the human aspects of GT. One such report, written by B. G. Dale,[4] compared two departments in one company; one which had successfully implemented GT, and one which was unsuccessful in its attempted implementation. What were seen, in part, as the reasons for failure of GT in one department are listed below:

- The cells did not identify types of work so there were duplicate facilities producing a wide variety of work.

- Work flow between cells was high.

- Conflict arose concerning responsibility.

- A high level of work in process existed.

- The labor force was not flexible.

The converse seemed to be true of the facility that had successfully implemented GT.

In another report,[5,6] data was collected on several different factors from 35 companies that had implemented GT. The data was obtained on conditions noted before and after GT was introduced. Although there was a decrease in worker absenteeism and turnover rate, factors often associated with job satisfaction, after GT was implemented, the decrease was not thought to be significant. Furthermore, in a later article, he related a procedure he had devised for predicting the success of GT.[5,6] This was done by comparing data from a company interested in GT with data from 35 companies previously interviewed that had successfully implemented GT. Of the seven companies that had requested a prediction of their success with GT, as of March 1980 none had requested predictions concerning absenteeism and/or turnover rates.

3. Summary

While the quantity of research necessary to validate the claims made by GT proponents in the human factors area does not yet exist, it can be concluded that GT generally seems to increase worker satisfaction and has other positive effects. Specifically, GT will increase or improve the following areas:

- *Employee Motivation.* GT provides workers with the knowledge of the results of their work through job feedback, the responsibility for the results of their work through autonomy, and a sense of meaningfulness concerning their work through skill variety, task identity, and, in some cases, task significance.

- *Task Interdependence.* This, in turn, will aid in the formation of cohesive groups. Task interdependence was also seen as a factor which increases job feedback, quality, and communication, and decreases worker errors.

- *Resistance to Change.* Because GT workers tend to have a greater sense of identity with common aims and objectives than traditional production workers, their resistance to technical changes will decrease.

- *Responsibility.* GT provides the opportunity for the delegation of much of what is traditionally the foremen's responsibilities to the workers and allows the foremen to assume new and challenging responsibilities.

- *Material Working Conditions.* GT reduces work in process and orders the work flow, thus improving material working conditions.

GT does not seem to produce a significant decrease in absenteeism, worker turnover rate, or worker frustration.

Much can be said concerning the proper implementation of a GT program. The following are the major areas to which attention should be given:

- *Cell Worker Characteristics.* Workers should possess good knowledge and skills, strong growth needs, and be satisfied with their job context (status, security, etc.). Foremen should also possess these characteristics.

- *Worker Flexibility.* Workers should be able and willing to move both within and between cells.

- *Cell structure.* To insure cohesiveness the following should be accomplished:

  1. Physical barriers (such as factory layout) and psychological barriers (such as failure to explain changes being implemented) should be eliminated.

  2. To obtain maximum knowledge and skills when composing groups, the following aspects should be considered:

     - Groups should include members who have high levels of task relevant expertise.

     - The group should be large enough to do the work but not much larger.

     - Group members should possess at least a moderate level of interpersonal skills.

     - Groups should be composed to provide a balance between the homogeneity and heterogeneity of its membership.

  3. While some researchers contend that cell size should be between six and ten people, perhaps the size should be governed by the amount and difficulty of the tasks to be accomplished.

  4. A sense of purpose should be provided workers by assuring that objectives are clearly stated.

  5. An increase in worker responsibility is inherent in GT. Attention should also be paid to providing new responsibilities and adequate training to foremen.

- *Work Flow.* Work flow between cells, as well as work in process, should be kept to a minimum.

It is clear that more empirical research is needed, not only to determine the exact effects of GT on the worker but to examine the success of GT implementation.

References

1. Astrop, A. (1979). "Preserving the Man in Manufacturing," *Machinery and Production Engineering,* (December 5), 26–28.

2. Baron, R. A. (1983). *Behavior in Organizations,* Allyn and Bacon, Boston.

3. Blumberg, M., and Alber, A. (1983). "The Human Element: Its Impact on the Productivity of Advanced Batch Manufacturing Systems," *Journal of Manufacturing Systems,* Vol. i, Number 1, 43–52.

4. Dale, B. G. (1979). "Group Technology 2: Effect on Shop Floor Supervisors," *Work Study,* (November), 22–27.

5. Dale, B. G., and Wiley, P. C. T. (1980). "Group Technology: Predicting Its Benefits," *Work Study,* (February), 14–23.

6. Dale, B. G., and Wiley, P. C. T. (1980). "How to Predict the Benefits of Group Technology," *The Production Engineer,* (February), 51–55.

7. Fazakerly, G. M. (1976). "A research report on the human aspects of group technology and cellular manufacture," *International Journal of Production Research,* Vol. 14, No. 1, 123–134.

8. Gruneberg, M. M. (1979). *Understanding Job Satisfaction,* John Wiley and Sons, New York.

9. Gruneberg, M. M., and Oborne, D. J. (1982). *Industrial Productivity,* John Wiley and Sons, New York.

10. Gunn, T. G. (1982). "The Mechanization of Design and Manufacturing," *Scientific American,* Vol. 247, No. 3, 114–131.

11. Hackman, J. R., and Oldham, G. R. (1980). *Work Redesign,* Addison-Wesley, Reading, Mass.

12. Herzberg, F. (1968). "One More Time: How Do You Motivate Employees?" *Harvard Business Review,* Vol. XLIV.

13. Hyer, N. J., and Huber, V. L. (1984). "The human factor in group technology: an analysis of the effects of job redesign," *Academy of Management Proceedings '84.*

14. King, N. (1970). "Clarification and Evaluation of the Two-Factor Theory of Job Satisfaction," *Psychological Bulletin,* Vol. LXXIV.

15. McManus, J. (1985). "Some Lessons From a Decade of Group Technology," *The Production Engineer,* (November), 40–42.

16. Mosier, C. T., and Taube, L. (1985). "The Facets of Group Technology and Their Impacts on Implementation: A State of the Art Survey," *OMEGA: The International Journal of Management Science,* Vol. 13, No. 5, 381–391.

17. Patton, B. R., and Giffen, K. (1978). *Decision-Making Group Interaction,* Harper and Row, New York.

18. Shaw, M. E. (1981). *Group Dynamics,* McGraw-Hill, New York.

19. Sinha, R. K., Hollier, R. H., and Grayson, I. F. (1980). "Cellular Manufacturing Systems," CME, (December), 39–41.

20. Wemmerlov, U., and Hyer, N. L. (1987). "Research issues in cellular manufacturing," *International Journal of Production Research,* Vol. 25, No. 3, 413–431.

21. Whitehead, W., and Rathmill, K. (1979). "Group Technology: The Good and the Bad," *Machinery and Production Engineering,* (December 12), 34–36.

PART IV
ORGANIZATION STRUCTURE AND INFLUENCE

In this part, the readings are concerned with approaches to organizational behavior which are oriented toward the entire organization. The first article, by Likert, reports on work growing out of the activity at the University of Michigan. Likert's article is concerned with the importance of applying measures of an organization's human assets and the importance of the concept of time. The article by Sorensen and Baum reports on activities directed toward measuring the amount and distribution of power in an organization.

The next three articles represent important works which moved organization theory toward a contingency orientation. The articles by Burns and Lawrence and Lorsch report on the implications of rate of change in the environment for organization structure. The article by Sayles discusses the relationship of technology and organization structure. Each of these three articles contributed to the currently popular differentiation between "mechanistic" and "organic" organizations and to the current reevaluation of the appropriateness of more traditional or bureaucratic structures under certain conditions.

MANAGEMENT STYLES AND THE HUMAN COMPONENT

Rensis Likert
Rensis Likert Associates, Inc.

Production Data, the profit-and-loss statement, and similar measures are often used as performance criteria to assess the relative effectiveness of different management systems and leadership styles. But studies using these criteria have yielded conflicting results

A major reason for the conflict is a serious inadequacy in the choice of criteria. Measurements of current earnings, production, and similar variables all ignore any changes that may have occurred in the human component of a department or firm and the subsequent impact these changes will have on the firm's performance and profitability.

When human component changes are taken into consideration, relatively consistent patterns of relationships generally emerge. Until investigators pay attention to these changes, their studies will continue to lead to erroneous conclusions on the best style of leadership or management.

"Quick and Dirty" Approach

Let's look at some data from a continuous approach plant with about 600 employees. Top management was not satisfied with the productivity of the plant and brought in one of the best known management consulting firms to improve performance. This firm used what management consultants call the "quick and dirty" method. It analyzed the staffing of each department in the plant against standards the consultants themselves established and found about a third of the departments appreciably overstaffed.

Teams made up of persons from other departments, corporate or division staff, and the consulting firm were assigned to study each of these departments and recommend ways to reorganize the work to make excessive labor unnecessary. No one from the department being studied was a member of the team that developed the plan for that department.

Reprinted by permission of the publisher, from Rensis Likert, "Management styles and the human component," from *Management Review,* ©1977. American Management Association, New York. All rights reserved.

After the plan for reorganizing the work of the department was prepared and approved, the department manager was ordered to introduce it and to eliminate the excess labor. This was done for each of the departments involved. The resulting savings in direct labor costs totaled approximately $250,000.

This highly authoritarian behavior by management was perceived as such by the employees. This is seen in Figure 1, which shows the profile of the key dimensions of the human component obtained *before* the cost reduction program started, compared with the profile one year later, *after* the program was completed.

The employees in the departments affected saw all four measurements of supervisory leadership as even more authoritarian (lower scores on the profile) than they had been before the cost reduction effort was started. In terms of Systems 1, 2, 3, and 4, the management system and leadership style of the affected departments shifted closer to System 1. (System 1 is punitive authoritarian; System 2, benevolent authoritarian; System 3, consultative management; and System 4, a participative group model.)

Looking only at costs and earnings, the results show that the shift toward System 1 brought improved productivity. The employees in the affected departments also perceived that peer help with work (the extent to which employees help each other in getting the work done) and peer interaction (team building and teamwork) improved.

However, a careful look at Figure 1 shows that this increase in teamwork and cooperation among the employees was accompanied by a substantial drop in their motivation to produce. These employees also felt that after the cost control steps were imposed, the company had less capacity to exercise influence (control) on what occurred in the departments (relating to such matters as productivity and scrap loss) than previously. They also were less satisfied with company, job, and pay.

These changes in perceptions and reactions caused by the authoritarian cost reduction program were not limited to the employees in the affected departments. They spread to all employees, as shown by the profiles in Figure 2. The differences in scores between people when the cost reduction program started and *after* it was over are significant at the 0.01 level or less for the following variables: peer help with work, peer interaction, motivation, control, and satisfaction with company, job, and pay.

Note the pattern: As the total group of employees became less satisfied with the company, their job, and their pay, they became less motivated to produce and their teamwork and group loyalty increased. This pattern of alienation among the employees restricts output. The workers evidently felt that the company would be unable to stop the restriction of output because management had lost some of its

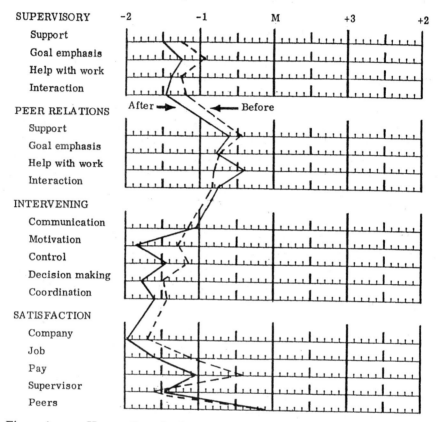

Before and After Cost Reduction Effort
Major Indexes Profile

Figure 1. Human Organization Variables in Departments Where High Cost Reduction Effort Was Applied.

control. The human component of the plant had become less productive than before the cost reduction effort was undertaken and management had less power to manage.

Time Lag in Manifestation of Adverse Data

Managers and researchers misinterpret cause-and-effect relationships because of the lag in time between changes in the human component variables and changes in the productivity and financial variables. Research shows that any deterioration in the human component, such as occurred in this plant, is not likely to manifest

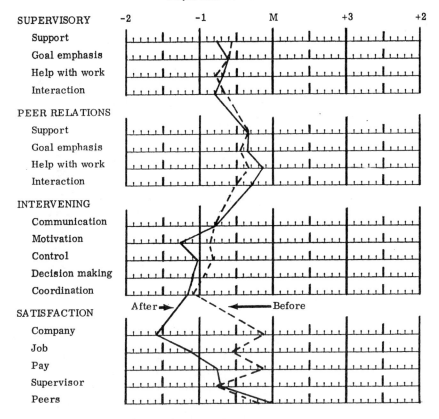

Figure 2. Human Organization Variables For Entire Plant.

itself in performance data until several months, or even years, have elapsed. Consequently, the management of this plant had no immediate evidence of the adverse changes that had occurred in the production capability of the plant's human component.

As soon as an analysis of the measurements of the human component of the plant revealed these changes, the results were reported to the plant manager and his staff and to the corporate executive vice president and divisional staff in charge of the division of which the plant was a part. They were interested in the results, but apart from the director of industrial relations, they treated the human organization measurements as of little consequence. From their point of view, the important fact was the $250,000 in labor savings that had been achieved.

A general feeling prevailed that the measurements of the human component had to be incorrect since they were getting higher productivity and lower costs from the plant's personnel. Even if the measurements were correct, management felt that the deterioration in the human component of the plant did not affect—and was not likely to affect—productivity and costs. As a consequence, it took no action.

The management of the division overseeing this plant was under considerable pressure from top corporate executives to improve earnings. To achieve that goal rapidly, it applied the same pressure-oriented cost-reduction program used in the first plant to two other plants. Again, there were immediate labor savings and cost improvement. And again, the human component scores showed a sizable adverse shift.

In all three plants, however, after the short-range improvement in costs, the firm experienced serious and costly consequences. These became painfully evident three to five years after the cost reduction program was completed. They included such developments as a decrease in productivity (due to a restriction to output), failure to meet delivery dates, a decrease in quality and problems with customers because of lack of quality control, work stoppages, excessive grievances, and other labor relations difficulties.

Measuring Human-Component Changes in Dollars

Sometime after the adverse shift in the attitude of the first plant's personnel had been reported to the plant and division management, a method was developed for computing the value of the change in the productive capability of its personnel in dollars. These computations revealed that worker negativism would increase manufacturing costs by at least $450,000 annually. That is, the cost reduction program, with its shift toward System 1 management, had produced an immediate annual labor savings of $250,000, but at an unrecognized annual cost of $450,000 because of the less motivated, more hostile, and less productive human component.

The unfavorable developments in this and the other plants in productivity, quality, grievances, work stoppages, and other labor problems in the five years after the cost reduction program was completed confirm the validity of the human component measurements and the dollar estimate of the change in the productivity of the plant's human component.

An increasing number of chief executive officers of corporations appear to be recognizing that it is highly profitable to build and maintain the human components of their firms. A number of years ago, I told a corporate executive vice president about our findings of the adverse effect on a firm's personnel in the kind of cost reduction programs described above. He told me his firm had been acquiring smaller companies. In every case, he said, the companies were found to be overstaffed by about 15 to 25 percent according to work standards established by industrial engineers timing the jobs or using standard times for each part of the job. According to him, his corporation was finding it very profitable to send direct orders from the corporate management to the management of the newly acquired firm to reduce personnel by the amount of overstaffing.

About five years after this initial discussion, and after the man had become president and chief officer of his corporation, he surprised me by saying:

> "You'll be interested to know how we are handling an overstaffing problem in a firm we recently acquired. The payroll is about $1.5 million more than it should be, based on work standards. In the past, we would have moved immediately to remove this excess by ordering the designated reductions in staff.

> "This time, however, we are not going to do that. We have found from previous experience that when corporate headquarters orders a newly acquired firm to cut staff to the level called for by work standards, we encounter numerous serious problems caused by alienated personnel in the five years or so after the reduction in staff. These problems increase costs far above the initial savings we achieved by reducing the staff. We are worse off, not better off, when we cut costs the way we have in the past."

This time, he said, his company intended to improve the management and supervision in the newly acquired firm and gradually move toward a more efficient operation.

This company president is providing help to his divisional and plant managers, including the manager of the new division, to enable them to move closer to System 4. He now sees this as much more profitable than using System 1 pressure-oriented cost reduction programs. Each organizational unit will increase its productivity and profitability as it moves toward System 4 management. Excessive costs and waste will be reduced.

Engineered work standards and low morale. IBM conducted a major research project that yielded conclusions confirming the pattern described above. It found that when engineered work standards were imposed on manufacturing plant managers and supervisors, the employees in these plants resented the pressure and the same kinds of adverse trends followed. It also found that employees whose supervisors were closer to the System 4 style in their behavior showed less resentment of the work standards than employees whose supervisors were closer to the System 1 style. (The IBM investigators did not use the System 1-4 labels but used measurements that gave similar parameters.)

The reason employees working for supervisors who managed closer to the System 4 style resented the work standards less was that their supervisors actually changed the way the standards were used. If an employee felt a work standard was unreasonable or had another complaint, these supervisors did something about it. They softened the blow. The impact was much less of a superimposed System 1 "do it or else" approach. Their responsiveness to complaints made a sizable difference in employee attitudes.

A key factor that kept the pressure-imposed work measurement program from having as much long-range negative impact at IBM as usual was the concern by the firm's top corporate management that high employee morale be maintained. These top managers " . . . started asking questions as to why work measurement generally produced low morale and why something wasn't being done about modifying the program to get higher morale."

High productivity and high morale. Another major finding of the IBM project dealt with a manufacturing plant (Plant A) whose manager had flatly refused to introduce work standards in spite of orders from corporate management and top divisional management to do so. He had tried standards years before and knew of their negative side effects.

This manager used other principles and methods to achieve efficient performance. For example, the plant had been using work simplification for years. It was also making effective plantwide use of procedures that the plant manager had developed for rewarding high production with salary increases and promotions.

In addition, interviews with small samples of employees were conducted regularly. If a problem was revealed, it was promptly and constructively resolved. Group problem solving involving both supervisors and workers was used in setting production and quality goals.

The introduction of work standards in the IBM plants increased productivity, and a much larger proportion of the employees began producing at levels close to standard. But even with these short-run improvements in productivity, the plants using this program failed to exceed Plant A in performance. Plant A still had productivity equal to or greater than that achieved by the best of the work measurement plants. Moreover, employee satisfaction in Plant A was substantially better than in the plants that used work standards.

The plant A results were highly important. They demonstrated that an IBM plant with a management style that made no use of engineered work measurement achieved higher productivity than any plant using work measurement and had much higher morale besides.

These findings, combined with top management's desire to maintain employee morale (favorable employee attitudes and motivation) at a high level, led to a plan for a change in the way work measurement was used. The control that had been in the hands of the industrial engineers was returned to the manufacturing departments. Each first-line manager was given "the authority to remove any individual from measurement or change any prescribed method if, in his judgment, the standard or the method was inappropriate."

As might be expected, when the management style of the Plant A's manager was measured, the data revealed that, as seen by middle and upper-level managers, he was a System 4 manager.

An important aspect of the behavior of the Plant A manager was his refusal to pass on to his subordinate managers the pressure put on him to use work measurements and to push employees to produce at the level set by standards. He knew from experience that such pressure would yield short-range increases, but result in power performance over the long run. He sought to get high productivity over both the short and the long range by holding high performance goals himself, by rewarding high performance, and by using other principles of System 4 management.

This refusal to pass pressure on to their subordinate managers seems to be characteristic of System 4 managers. A recent study of a federal agency revealed that of nine district managers of that agency in the United States, the two managers who were seen by their subordinates as System 4 in their management style did not pass on to their subordinate managers the pressure their chief put on them for high performance. The other managers, especially the five whose management system was closest to System 1, appear to have put on their subordinate managers as much or more than the pressure they themselves experienced. The System 4 managers got results without putting direct hierarchical pressure on their organization.

Many other studies have yielded the same findings as those reported here. The introduction of work measurement and the putting of pressure on personnel to produce at the level called for by work standards almost always result in an immediate increase in productivity. Personnel limitations, budget cuts, and requirements to achieve earnings at a specified level are other ways of putting pressure on people to produce. They also yield immediate improvement.

All of these procedures, however, are accompanied by long-range adverse effects. These include less favorable attitudes and covert efforts to defeat the organization in its attempts to obtain high productivity by restriction of output and other evidences of poor labor relations, including slowdowns, excessive grievances, and wildcat and other strikes.

With all of the pressure procedures, there is a shift in management style toward System 1. Investigators have noted that such a shift is accompanied by an increase in productivity. When they compare a System 1 or 2 organization after hierarchical pressure has increased its productivity with an organization that has just started to shift to System 4, they may conclude that System 1 or 2 is more effective than System 4. The rapid short-run increase in productivity that Systems 1 or 2 can bring about leads to this erroneous conclusion. The longer lasting productivity improvement of System 4 does not manifest itself immediately. The lag between the introduction of System 4 and an increase in productivity may be one to three years and, in large organizations, even longer.

An example of this lag occurred in an automotive assembly plant. After a substantial improvement in the human component was shown by measurements (Figure 3), it took one and a half years for direct labor costs to show an improvement and two and a half years for indirect labor costs to begin improving (Figure 4). Costs were still showing an unfavorable trend even after the human component of the plant started to improve.

Evaluating Your Findings

An investigator, therefore, can find evidence that an organization closer to System 1 is more productive than an organization closer to System 4 or the converse, depending on whether or not he ignores the changes in the human component. The results he obtains depend also on whether he picks System 1 or 2 organizations at the peak of their short-run spurt in productivity in response to hierarchical pressure or at their long-run lower productivity level.

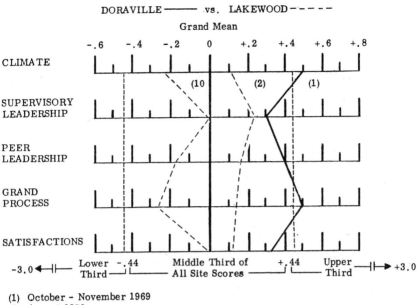

(1) October - November 1969
(2) August 1970

Figure 3. Interplant Salaries Scores Compared With ISR Grand Mean.

From "At General Motors: System 4 Builds Performance and Profits," Organizational Dynamics, Winter 1975, pp. 29-30.

Whether the System 4 organizations selected for comparison are at their lower productivity level as their managements are starting to shift to System 4 or at their long-run high productivity level after the system is well established will affect the findings too.

As long as investigators ignore what happens in the productive capability of the human component of an organization when changes are made in the management system, they will reach the wrong conclusions. They will continue to believe that in some situations management systems closer to System 1 yield the best performance, and that in others, managements closer to System 4 come out ahead. However, if changes in the human component are taken into consideration along with the current data on productivity or earnings, a consistent pattern of findings will emerge. This consistency will also be obtained if the long-run shifts in productivity and earnings, and not just the short-run results, are measured.

In assessing different management systems, there are two ways of evaluating the effect of the improvement or deterioration in the human component measurements. One way is to compute in dollars the gain or loss resulting from this improvement or deterioration. The gain or loss is then added to or subtracted from

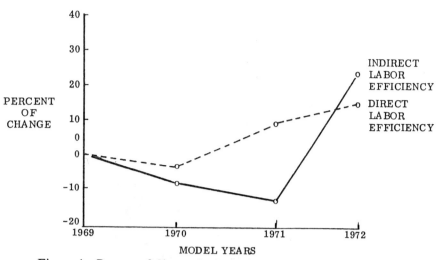

Figure 4. Percent of Change in Operating Efficiency at Lakewood.

From "At General Motors: System 4 Builds Performance and Profits," Organizational Dynamics, Winter 1975, pp. 29-30.

the earnings, costs, or profit-and-loss statement to arrive at a net figure showing total gain or loss.

The second way to take the changes in the human component scores into consideration is to recognize that when these scores have undergone a favorable change, the productivity or financial statement represents an understatement of actual performance. When an unfavorable shift has occurred, the productivity or financial report overstates the true performance. The current productivity or financial statement, consequently, needs to be interpreted in relation to the changes that have occurred in the human component scores. Trends in performance measurements over five or more years often give us some clues to the effect of the changes in the human component upon performance.

Valid conclusions, therefore, cannot be drawn about the relative productivity and superiority of different management systems and leadership styles unless measurements of the changes in the productive capability of the human organization are examined along with the productivity and earnings data.

When the human organizational measurements show an improvement or no change, the productivity and earning data can be considered to be correct or even an understatement of actual performance.

When the human organizational measurements show a significant adverse shift, the productivity and earnings results overstate true performance and must be discounted by the amount of overstatement. When this methodology is used, consistent findings are obtained on the relative effectiveness of different management systems and leadership styles.

In any specific situation, it obviously is necessary to consider the basic principles or system being used and not just the particular procedures employed. Management systems and leadership principles must always be applied in a culturally relevant manner. That is, in each situation, the manager should apply the principles that he or she is seeking to use in ways that fit the work situation and the characteristics, traditions, skills, and expectations of the labor force or work group involved. In comparing performance in one situation with that in another, the focus should be on the principles or management systems being used and how well they fit the culture, traditions, and environment of the organization rather than on the specific procedures alone.

I have examined data from several hundred published and unpublished studies in business, government, schools, hospitals, universities, the military, and voluntary and other kinds of organizations. I am greatly impressed by the extent to which these studies show a consistent pattern of findings when all the relevant organizational variables are taken into account. The studies find the probabilities very high that the closer the management system and leadership style are to System 4, the better the overall performance of the unit is; the closer the management system and leadership behavior are to System 1, the poorer the performance. Summaries of these studies are being prepared for publication.

THE CONTROL GRAPH: A TWENTY YEAR REVIEW

Peter F. Sorensen, Jr. and Bernard H. Baum

The Control Graph has been used in the study of organizations for approximately twenty years, the first application being made in the study of unions in 1956. In a recent review of the literature, we were able to identify over fifty studies which have employed this technique for the measurement of some aspect of organizational control. Although it was first employed in the middle fifties, almost half of the studies were reported in the seventies indicating increased use and acceptance. We have been able to identify at least fifteen different variables which have been reported on, including: total amount and distribution of control within an organization, actual vs. desired control, passive vs. active control. Independent variables have included: participation, ideology, conflict, satisfaction, member attitudes, technology and consensus.

Description

The Control Graph represents a technique for both the conceptualization and measurement of control in organizations. It consists basically of a graph which consists of defining the vertical axis of the graph in terms of the degree of influence (control) exercised and the horizontal axis in terms of an organization's hierarchical levels. Respondent perceptions of the distribution of influence are then plotted from responses to the control questionnaire.

Although a number of concepts have been explored using the Control Graph, two have been the focus for most of the investigative effort. These are total control and distribution of control. Distribution of control refers to the relative amount of control exercised by each organizational level and is reflected in the shape or slope of the curve. The total amount of control, refers to the aggregate control by all levels and is reflected in the height of the curve. These concepts are illustrated by the Control Graphs in Figures 1 and 2.

Relationship to Other Perspectives

One of the basic propositions that has been associated with the Control Graph is the notion that the amount of control which exists in an organization is variable

---

A somewhat modified version of this paper was initially presented at the 1975 Annual Meeting of the Illinois Sociological Association.

rather than fixed, that the size of the influence pie, so to speak, can be expanded. The amount of organizational control can be expanded or contracted based on the management philosophy and strategy adopted. Strategies associated with increased control include such management techniques as participation, delegation, decentralization, MBO, etc.

There are, we suggest, a number of parallels between Tannenbaum's concept of variable control and a number of other organization theories. For example, in Likert's Systems, a System 1 would be a system characterized by low total control while a System 4 would be one with high total control. Similarly, Burns and Stalker's Organic organization would be high in total control while a Mechanistic organization would be low in total control. Blake and Mouton's 9.9 is another example of a high total control organization while 1.1, 9.1 and 1.9 organizations would be lower in total control.

There is clearly, also, a relationship between individual need satisfaction and control. For example, Maslow's need theory has been related to the concept of total control in recent work with the Porter-Lawler needs questionnaire.

Historical Overview

The first eight to ten years of Control Graph work were characterized by a number of large surveys undertaken primarily by the University of Michigan Survey Research Center and included a range of organizations, unions, voluntary organizations, business and industrial firms. This was a period of initial conceptualization and included the introduction of a number of concepts and the identification of potential areas of investigation, as illustrated in the discussion by Tannenbaum and Kahn (1956). Findings from this period were generally supportive of the relationship between total control, member satisfaction and organizational effectiveness.

In a comparative analysis published in 1963 reviewing most of the studies undertaken during this early period, Smith and Tannenbaum state:

> The relevance of total control for organizational effectiveness and positive member attitudes seems especially noteworthy. Substantial control exercised by both leaders and members appears to be a correlate of high organizational performance in the majority of organizations examined. This apparently occurs because the motivations and contributions of the rank and file members are utilized, as well as those of the leaders. This conclusion is substantiated by the positive relationships obtained between the amount of total control and member loyalty or morale.

A similar observation was made by Tannenbaum in 1964:

Patterns of control—as they are perceived by organizational members, at least—are tied significantly to the performance of the organization and to the adjustments and satisfactions of members. If our research leads are correct, the more significant improvements in the "human side of enterprise" are going to come through changes in the way organizations are controlled and particularly through changes in the size of the "influence pie." This "middle way" leans on the assumption that influential workers do not imply uninfluential supervisors or managers. This is a relatively novel assumption for many managers who have been weaned on the all-or-none law of power: One either leads or is led, is strong or is weak, controls or is controlled.

Our "middle way" assumes further that the worker, or supervisor, or manager, who exercises some influence over matters of interest to him in the work situation acquires a sense of self-respect which the powerless individual may lack, and, what is more, he can elicit the respect and high regard of others. This is the key to good human relations practice.

While almost all of the early work with the Control Graph was confined to the work of investigators associated with the Survey Research Center, i.e., Tannenbaum and others, more recent work has been characterized by increased use of the Control Graph by a number of independent researchers.

More recent work has also been characterized by its extension to additional types of organizations, e.g., academic institutions, banks, social service institutions, etc., and the introduction of contingency considerations.

Findings

A review of 232 studies which include the concept of total control or distribution of control and their relationship to member satisfaction or organizational effectiveness indicates the following:

1.   Of the 22 studies which related total control to effectiveness, 75% reported a positive relationship between total control and effectiveness. Twenty-five percent reported a slight negative or no relationship. These latter studies included auto sales, black colleges, container manufacturers, voluntary associations located in the far east and state liquor agencies.

2. Of the 14 studies which related distribution of control to effectiveness, two-thirds reported a positive relationship between distribution and effectiveness. The exceptions included auto sales, a school of nursing, voluntary associations located in the far east and the state liquor agencies.

3. All eight of the studies which examined total control and member satisfaction report a positive relationship.

4. Three of the four studies reporting on distribution and member satisfaction indicate a positive relationship. The one exception is auto sales.

Contingencies: Three Examples

1. Contingencies—uncertainty

One of the more important recent studies reported by Lawrence and Lorsch (1969) in the last half of the sixties indicates that certainty of the environment is a variable which modifies the relationship between total control and effectiveness. The central proposition set forth by Lawrence and Lorsch and for which they provided empirical support is that:

> . . . in general, the effects of total influence (or control) will be moderated by the uncertainty of the organization's environment. When uncertainty is high, total control will be high; when low, total control will be low. As the situation becomes increasingly unpredictable, decision-making is forced further down into the organization where the requisite expertise for daily decisions resides. Control will be more evenly distributed under environments of uncertainty and relatively less democratic under more certain environments. If, then, greater participation and total influence are widely distributed throughout the organization in a relatively "certain" environment, role ambiguity, frustration, and confusion would be expected.

Two of the six exceptions to the positive relationship between total control and effectiveness, the container manufacturer and the state liquor agency, were characterized as having highly certain environments.

2. Contingencies—culture

Another exception was the result reported for voluntary organization in the far east. Similar findings have been reported by Mouton and Blake (1968) relating findings pertaining to the Managerial Grid. Mouton and Blake report that "based on self descriptions, the largest percentage of 9.9 managers are in the English speaking countries, with 9.1 more characteristic of Japan and South America."

3. *Contingencies—type of organization (academic)*

Studies of academic institutions represent two of the other exceptions. A study by Gerald Oncken (1971) of control structures in 37 academic departments at the University of Illinois we feel is of particular interest.

Oncken reports that in relating total control to professional production (measured by number and quality of publications), production was greater for those departments with low total control. These findings are at least partially explained by Oncken's description of members of high producing departments:

> Faculty members in departments with low control were found to have more doctorates and thereby would probably have a greater "cosmopolitan" or professional orientation than faculty members in departments with high total control. Furthermore, in departments with low total control, faculty placed high value on research than did faculty members in departments with high total control. Thus it appears that departments with research-oriented faculty members organize themselves so that overall faculty participation in departmental administration is minimized, and this in turn optimizes conditions which facilitate productive individual endeavor in research.

Studies of Impact of Change on Control Structures

Technology

The first study of which we know that focused on change was the Hoffman and Mann study of industrial change and is the only study that we know which focuses on technology. Mann and Hoffman (1960) applied the control questions to the study of technological change relating to the effects of automation in a power plant. In a comparison of the control structure in a new, highly automated plant with an older, less automated one, responses to the questionnaire showed that the new plant was characterized by a higher level of total control than the old. In terms of changes in the distribution of control, the overall slope of the line comparing all levels in the organization was less negatively sloped in the new than in the old. In terms of the specific influence relationship between foremen the their subordinates, their relationship was reversed, that is, foremen had more influence than their subordinates while in the old plant, the reverse was true.

There have been three attempts reported in Control Graph literature to measure changes in control through the introduction of various management techniques. The first was reported by Seashore and Bowers (1970). In this study, the introduction of a number of management techniques designed to increase participation resulted in increases in the total amount of control and improved organizational effectiveness.

The second study by Baum, Sorensen, and Place (1970) reported on changes in control as a consequence of a management training and development program oriented toward improved participation and redistribution of control. In an experimental design using groups which had, and had not, been in training— questionnaires were distributed before and six months following training. Results indicated movement in the redistribution toward more participatory organization and increases in the total amount of control in the experimental as compared with the control group. Changes in the experimental group are presented in Figure 1.

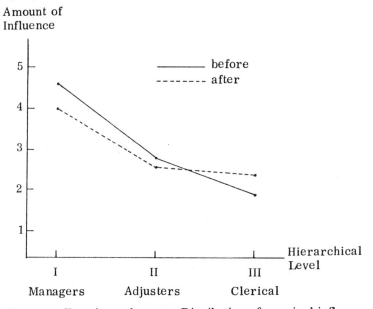

Figure 1. Experimental group: Distribution of exercised influence.

More recently attempts have been made to track the organizational impact of MBO using the Control Graph. In a study of change in a community social service organization, Babcock, Timm, and Sorensen report changes in both the distribution and total amount of control following introduction of MBO. These findings are illustrated in Figure 2. Similar results have been found in an extension of this study to another service organization also working with MBO (Sorensen, Czerniak, and Babcock, 1975).

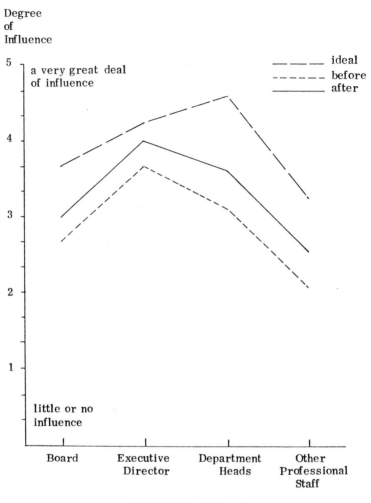

Figure 2.   Changes in Control Structure.

It should also be noted that in the above studies, changes in need satisfaction were measured and increases in satisfaction for Maslow's high level needs (autonomy, esteem, self-realization) paralleled change in the control structure. Similar findings have also been reported by Ivancevich (1970). Changes in need levels following MBO are shown in Figure 3.

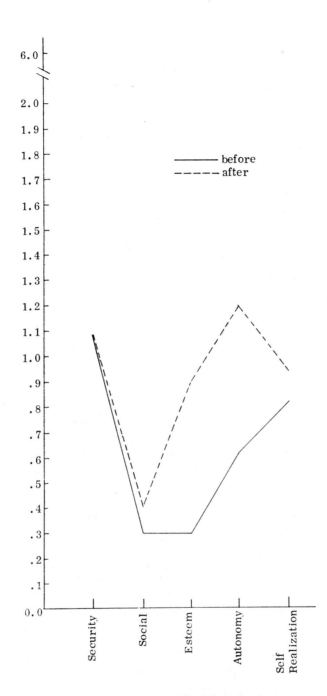

Figure 3. Changes in Need Deprivation.

Discussion and Conclusion

The following are some of our observations relating to some of the advantages in Control Graph analysis:

1. We believe that the systematic tracking of employee attitudes and the use of survey feedback is an important technique for effective organizational improvement—the Control Graph provides one such technique.

2. The Control Graph has the advantage of being closely linked to an explicit theory of management and organizational effectiveness.

3. It is well received (at least in our experience) by line managers—perhaps too well received, in that we find ourselves in a position of frequently cautioning against uncritical acceptance of Control Graph results.

4. It has some advantages in implementation when compared with other more specific questionnaires since it is generally briefer and simpler, less demanding of respondent's time and demands less knowledge of the organization in its construction.

We would also like to make the following, final observations. Little attention has been given to the fact that the questionnaire needs to be tailored carefully to each organization in terms of its hierarchical structure—in our experience it has frequently been necessary to deal with subunits of the organization rather than the organization in total in order to acquire meaningful employee responses.

We believe that the Control Graph has potential not only as a research instrument but as an applied technique for survey feedback—yet little information exists as to the specific applicability of the Control Graph for this purpose.

The Control Graph is primarily subjective in nature and although there is some consensus that it has worth or perhaps even greater worth because of its subjective nature, it would probably still be to our advantage to determine its relationship to some more objective measure of control (this was done to some extent in an article published jointly with Thomas Whisler in the *Journal of Business*, 1967).

Continued attention has to be given to clarifying the conditions under which high total control systems are most appropriate and more careful consideration of these conditions in organizational change projects. Although we concur regarding the validity of a contingency approach to the application of Control Graph Theory, we also believe that the number of organizations that are confronted with increasingly uncertain environments will continue to increase so that the principle of increased total control will continue to find greater applicability. Future work will require accounting for "odd" exceptions cited earlier.

Bibliography

Babcock, R., Sorensen, P. F., Jr., and Timm, D. "MBO: A study in organizational change," in *Dimensions in Organizational Behavior.* Champaign, Illinois: Stipes, 1975, 222-231.

Bachman, J. "Faculty satisfaction and the Dean's influence: An organizational study of twelve liberal arts colleges." *Journal of Applied Psychology,* 52, 1968, 55-81.

Baum, B., and Sorensen, P. F., Jr. "Contemporary student attitudes and the future of management." *Academy of Management Proceedings,* 1970, 162-165.

Baum, B., and Sorensen, P. F., Jr. "Influence Relationships as Administrative Organizational Data." *Journal of Risk and Insurance,* March, 1966, 63-71.

Baum, B., Sorensen, P. F., Jr., and Czerniack, S. "Participation in three organizational settings: Implications for emergent organizational models." *Atlanta Economic Review,* 25, 1975, 46-50.

Baum, B., Sorensen, P. F., Jr., Morrow, J. C., and Kuraitis, C. "Student authoritarian attitudes and perspectives on university power structures." *Psychological Reports,* 36, 1975, 13-14.

Baum, B., Sorensen, P. F., Jr., and Place, W. "The effect of managerial training on organizational control: An experimental study." *Organizational Behavior and Human Performance,* 5, 1970, 170-182.

Baum, B., Sorensen, P. F., Jr., and Place, W. "Patterns of consensus in the perception of organizational control." *Sociological Quarterly,* 10, 1969, 335-340.

Bowers, D. "Organizational Control in an Insurance Company." *Sociometry,* 27, 1964, 230-244.

Domer, F., Sorensen, P. F., Jr., Place, W., and Baum, B. "Control, Communication and Organizational Effectiveness: An Empirical Examination." *Psychological Reports,* 35, 1974, 950.

Dressler, G., Kerr, S., Schiffman, L., and Turner, J. Review of A. S. Tannenbaum, *Control in Organizations. Administrative Science Quarterly,* 11, 1967, 548-574.

Hage, J. Review of A. S. Tannenbaum, *Control in Organizations. American Sociological Review,* 34, 1969, 586-587.

Hill and French. "Perceptions of the power of department chairman by professors." *Administrative Science Quarterly,* 11, 1967, 548-574.

Ivencevich, J. "An Analysis of Control, Bases of Control and Satisfaction in an Organizational Setting." *Academy of Management,* 13, 1970.

Kevcic, Rus, and Tannenbaum. "Control, Participation, and Effectiveness in Four Yugoslav Industrial Organizations," *Administrative Science Quarterly,* 16, 1971, 74-87.

Lawrence and Lorsch. *Organization and Environment.* Boston: Division of Research, Harvard Business School, 1967.

Likert, R. "Influence and national sovereignty," Peatman and Hartley (ed.). *Festschrift for Gardner Murphy.* New York: Harper, 1960, 214-227.

Litterer. *The Analysis of Organization.* New York: Wiley, 1973, 412-44.

Mann, F., and Hoffman, R. *Automation and the Worker.* New York: Holt, 1960.

Marcus, P., and Marcus, D. "Control in Modern Organizations." *Public Administration Review,* 25, 1965, 121-127.

McMahon, T. "Management control structure and organizational effectiveness." *Annual Meeting of the Academy of Management,* 1972.

McMahon and Perritt. "The control structure of organizations: An empirical examination." *Academy of Management Journal,* 14, 1971, 544-546.

McMahon and Perritt. "Toward a contingency theory of organizational control." *Academy of Management Journal,* 16, 1973, 624-635.

Oncken. *The Relationship of Control Structure to Faculty Productivity and Satisfaction in University Departments.* University of Illinois, 1971.

Patchen, M. "Alternative Questionnaire Approaches to the Measurement of Influence in Organizations." *American Journal of Sociology,* 68, 1963.

Patchen, M., Seashore, S., and Eckerman, W. *Some Dealership Characteristics Related to Change in New Car Sales Volume.* Ann Arbor, Michigan: Institute for Social Research.

Perrow, C. *Complex Organizations: A Critical Essay.* Glenview, Ill.: Scott, Foresman, 1972.

Place, W., and Sorensen, P. F., Jr. "An Examination of the Relationship Between Influence Relationships and Faculty Morale." Paper delivered at the 1972 Annual Meeting of the Illinois Sociological Association.

Place, W., and Sorensen, P. F., Jr. "Perceptions of Influence Relationships and Faculty Satisfaction: A Study in Organizational Control." *Psychological Reports,* 35, 1974.

Price, Jr., *Handbook of Organizational Measurement.* Lexington, Mass.: Heath, 1972.

Rus. "Influence Structure in Yugoslav Enterprise." *Industrial Relations,* 9, 1970, 148–160.

Seashore, S., and Bowers, D. *Changing the Structure and Functioning of an Organization: Report of a Field Experiment.* Ann Arbor, Michigan: Institute for Social Research, 1963.

Seashore, S., and Bowers, D. "Durability of Organizational Change." *American Psychologist,* 25, 1970, 227–233.

Smith and Ari. "Organizational Control Structure and Member Consensus." *American Journal of Sociology,* 69, 1964, 623–638.

Smith and Brown. "Communication Structure and Control Structure in a Voluntary Association." *Sociometry,* 27, 1964.

Smith and Jones. "The Role of the Interaction-Influence System in a Planned Organizational Change," in A. Tannenbaum, *Control in Organizations.* New York: McGraw-Hill, 1968.

Smith and Tannenbaum. "Organization Control Structures: A Comparative Analysis." *Human Relations,* 16, 1963, 299–316.

Sorensen, P. F., Jr. "Control and Effectiveness in Twenty-seven Scandinavian Voluntary Organizations." *Journal of Management Studies* (in press).

Sorensen, P. F., Jr., and Babcock, R. "The Application of a Sociological Perspective to the Appraisal of Organizational Change." Paper delivered at the 1974 Annual Meeting of the Illinois Sociological Association.

Sorensen, P. F., Jr., and Baum, B. "Organizational Control and Effectiveness in a Voluntary Association." *The Journal of Social Psychology*, 95, 1975, 125–126.

Sorensen, P. F., Jr., Baum, B., Domer, M., and Mann, F. "Student Perceptions of University Power Structures." *Journal of Educational Research*, 6, 1973.

Sorensen, P. F., Jr., and Place, W. "Preliminary Findings on Cross Cultural Differences in Organizational Control." Paper delivered at the 1972 Annual Meeting of the Illinois Sociological Association.

Strauss, J., Timm, D., and Sorensen, P. F., Jr. "Authoritarian Attitudes and Control in a Social Service Organization." *Psychological Reports* (in press).

Tannenbaum, A. "Communications, Control in Organizations: Comment." *Academy of Management Journal*, 15, 1972, 543–544.

Tannenbaum, A. *Control in Organizations*. New York: McGraw-Hill, 1968.

Tannenbaum, A. "Control Structure and Union Functions." *American Sociological Review*, 61, 1956, 127–140.

Tannenbaum, A. "Unions" in J. March (ed.), *Handbook of Organizations*. Rand McNally, 1965.

Tannenbaum, A., and Cooke, R. "Control and Participation." *Journal of Contemporary Business*, 4, 1974.

Tannenbaum, A., and Georgopoulos, B. "The Distribution of Control in Formal Organizations." *Social Forces*, 36, 1957.

Tannenbaum, A., and Kahn, R. "Organizational Control Structure: A General Descriptive Technique as Applied to Four Local Unions." *Human Relations*, 10, 1957, 127–140.

Tannenbaum, A., and Kahn, R. *Participation in Union Locals*. Evanston, Ill.: Row-Peterson, 1958.

Tannenbaum, A. "Control and Effectiveness in a Voluntary Organization." *American Journal of Sociology*, 67, 1961, 33–36.

Tannenbaum, A. "Control in Organizations: Individual Adjustment and Organizational Performance." *Administrative Science Quarterly*, 7, 1962, 236–257.

Timm, D., and Sorensen, P. F., Jr. "Recent Findings on Control in Organizations: Implications for Effective Management." *Perspectives*, 1, 1975, 12–14.

Whisler, T., Meyer, H., Baum, B., and Sorensen, P. F., Jr. "Centralization of Organizational Control: An Empirical Study of its Meaning and Measurement." *Journal of Business*, 40, 1967, 10–26.

Williams, L., Hoffman, R., and Mann, F. "An Investigation of the Control Graph: Influence in a Staff Organization." *Social Forces*, 37, 1957, 189–195.

Yuchtman. "Control in an Insurance Company: Cause or Effect," in A. Tannenbaum (ed.), *Control in Organizations*. New York: McGraw-Hill, 1968.

Zupanov and Tannenbaum. "The Distribution of Control in Some Yugoslav Industrial Organizations as Perceived by Members," in A. Tannenbaum (ed.), *Control in Organizations*. New York: McGraw-Hill, 1968.

INDUSTRY IN A NEW AGE

T. Burns

Industry has a long past. We are now near the end of the second century of industrialism in its recognizably modern form. To be conscious of the history of an institution like the industrial concern is to become alive to two essential considerations. First, that like any other institution—government, the church, the family, military forces, for example—industry has undergone substantial changes in its organizational form as well as in the activity or task or objectives it performs. Secondly, and in consequence, unless we realize that industrial organization is still in the process of development, we are liable to be trapped into trying to use out-of-date organizational systems for coping with entirely new situations.

A sense of the past—and the very recent past—is essential to anyone who is trying to perceive the here-and-now of industrial organization. What is happening now is part of a continuing development. A study of this process will at least help firms avoid the traps they often fall into when they try to confront a situation of the newest kind with an organizational system appropriate to an earlier phase of industrial development. Adaptation to new challenge is not an automatic process: there are many factors against it.

What we recognize as industrialism is the product of two technologies, material and social. It has developed in spasmodic fashion from the rudimentary forms of the eighteenth century by alternate advances in first one technology and then the other.

The elementary form of industrialism is Adam Smith's conjunction of the division of labour traditional in advanced society with the extension of its advantages by 'those machines by which labour is so much facilitated and enlarged.'

The modern industrial system was founded at a time when the perception by early mechanical scientists that natural events 'obeyed' certain laws became widely diffused—in the eighteenth century. Samuel Smiles' legend that Arkwright was first struck by the feasibility of mechanical spinning 'by accidentally observing a hot piece of iron become elongated by passing between iron rollers' may be fiction, but it reflects truly the commonplace terms in which the new habits of scientific thought could be used by craftsmen-inventors, who saw not just an interesting analogy but

From *New Society,* January 1963, pp. 17-20. Used by permission of the publisher.

one process obeying a law which might also apply to a different and entirely new process.

At the same time that Adam Smith was observing the archetypal form of the two technologies, a third step was being taken: the creation of the first successful factory by Strutt and Arkwright. By 1835, Ure could already discount the basic principles of division of labour as outdated and misleading. The industrial system was simply the factory system as developed by Arkwright: the term, factory, meaning 'the combined operation of many work people, adult and young, in tending with assiduous skill a system of productive machines continuously impelled by a central power. It is the constant aim and tendency of every improvement in machinery to supersede human labour altogether.'

Factory organization stayed for three generations at the point at which Arkwright had left it. Marx's account contains the same essentials: a collection of machines in a building all driven by one prime mover, and preferably, of the same type and engaged on the same process. Attending the machines were men and women who themselves were attended by 'feeders,' most of them children, who fetched and carried away materials. There was also a 'superior but numerically unimportant' class of maintenance and repair workers. All of these worked under a master, with perhaps a chief workman or foreman. The primitive social technology of the factory system still confined it, even by the 1850s, largely to the mass production of textiles.

Technical developments in transport and communications, the impact of the international exhibitions in London and Paris, free trade, the armaments revolutions supported by the development of machine tools and of steel, and chemical technology (in Germany first) all combined during the 1850s and 1860s to form the springboard, in material technology, of the next advance in the social techniques of industrial organization.

As yet, there is no account of how that advance took place. All that can be said is that with the extension of the factory system into engineering and chemicals, iron and steel processing, food manufacture and clothing, an organizational development took place which provided for the conduct and control of many complex series of production processes within the same plant. One overt sign of this development is the increase in the number of salaried officials employed in industry. The proportion of 'administrative employees' to 'production employees' in British manufacturing industry had risen to 8.6 percent by 1907 and to 20 percent by 1948. Similar increases took place in western Europe and the United States.

The growth in the numbers of industrial administrative officials, or managers, reflects the growth of organizational structure. Production department managers, sales managers, accountants, cashiers, inspectors, training officers, publicity managers, and the rest emerged as specialized parts of the general management function as industrial concerns increased in size. Their jobs were created, in fact, out of the eighteenth-century master's either directly or at one or two removes. This gives them and the whole social structure which contains their newly created roles its hierarchical character. It is indeed a patrimonial structure. All rights and powers at every level derive from the boss; fealty, or 'responsibility,' is owed to him; all benefits are 'as if' dispensed by him. The bond is more easily and more often broken than in pre-feudal policies, but loyalty to the concern, to employers, is still regarded not only as proper, but as essential to the preservation of the system.

Chester Barnard makes this point with unusual emphasis: 'The most important single contribution required of the executive, certainly the most universal qualification, is loyalty, domination by the organization personality.' More recently, A. W. Gouldner has pointed out 'much of W. H. Whyte's recent study of Organization Man is a discussion of the efforts by industry to attach managerial loyalty to the corporation.'

The development of the bureaucratic system made possible the increase in scale of undertakings characteristic of the first part of this century. It had other aspects. The divorce of ownership and management, although by no means absolute, went far enough to render survival of the enterprise (and the survival of the existing management) as least as important a consideration as making the best profit. Profit itself wears a different aspect in the large-scale corporation.

More important, the growth of bureaucracy—the social technology which made possible the second state of industrialism—was only feasible because the development of material technology was held relatively steady. An industry based on major technological advances shows a high death rate among enterprises in its early years; growth occurs when the rate of technical advance slows down. What happens is that consumer demand tends to be standardized through publicity and price reductions, and technical progress is consequently restrained. This enables companies to maintain relatively stable conditions, in which large scale production is built up by converting manufacturing processes into routine cycles of activity for machines or semi-skilled assembly hands.

Under such conditions, not only could a given industrial company grow in size, not only could the actual manufacturing processes be routinized, mechanized and quickened, but the various management functions also could be broken down into specialisms and routines. Thus developed specialized management tasks: those of ensuring employee cooperation, of coordinating different departments, of planning and monitoring.

It is this second phase of industrialism which now dominates the institutional life of western societies. But while the greater part of the industrial system is in this second, bureaucratic phase of the historical development (and some older and smaller establishments remain in the first), it is now becoming clear that we have entered a third phase during the past two or three decades. J. K. Galbraith, in his *Affluent Society*, has described the new, more insecure relationship with the consumer that appears as production catches up and overtakes spontaneous domestic demand. The 'propensity to consume' has had to be stimulated by advertising, by styling, and by marketing promotions guided by research into the habits, motives, and potential 'needs' of consumers. At the same time, partly in an effort to maintain expansion, partly because of the stimulus of government spending on new military equipment, industry has admitted a sizeable influx of new technical developments.

There are signs that industry organized according to principles of bureaucracy—by now traditional—is no longer able to accommodate the new elements of industrial life in the affluent second half of the twentieth century. These new demands are made by large-scale research and development and by industry's new relationship with its markets. Both demand a much greater flexibility in internal organization, much higher levels of commitment to the commercial aims of the company from all its members, and an even higher proportion of administrators, controllers and monitors to operatives.

Recently, with G. M. Stalker, I made an attempt to elucidate the situation of concerns in the electronics industry that were confronted with rapidly changing commercial circumstances and a much faster rate of technical progress. I found it necessary to posit two 'ideal types' of working organizations, the one mechanistic, adapted to relatively stable conditions, the other, 'organismic,' adapted to conditions of change.

In mechanistic systems, the problems and tasks which face the concern as a whole are, typically, broken down into specialisms. Each individual carries out his assigned task as something apart from the overall purpose of the company as a whole. 'Somebody at the top' is responsible for seeing that his work is relevant to that of others. The technical methods, duties, and powers attached to each post are precisely defined, and a high value is placed on precision and demarcation. Interaction within the working organization follows vertical lines—i.e., between superiors and subordinates. How a man operates and what he does is prescribed by his functional role and governed by instructions and decisions issued by superiors. This hierarchy of command is maintained by the assumption that the only man who knows—or should know—all about the company is the man at the top. He is the only one, therefore, who knows exactly how the human resources should be properly disposed. The management system, usually visualized as the complex hierarchy familiar in organization charts, operates as a simple control system, with information flowing upwards through a succession of filters, and decisions and instructions flowing downwards through a succession of amplifiers.

Mechanistic systems are, in fact, the 'rational bureaucracy' of an earlier generation of students of organization. For the individual, it provides an ordered world of work. His own decisions and actions occur within a stable constellation of jobs, skills, specialized knowledge, and sectional responsibilities. In a textile mill, or any factory which sees itself turning out any standardized product for a familiar and steady market, one finds decision-making at all levels prescribed by the familiar.

As one descends through the levels of management, one finds more limited information and less understanding of the human capacities of other members of the firm. One also finds each person's task more and more clearly defined by his superior. Beyond a certain limit, he has insufficient authority, insufficient information, and usually insufficient technical ability to be able to make decisions. He is informed quite clearly when this limit occurs; beyond it, he has one course open—to report to his superior.

Organismic systems are adapted to unstable conditions when new and unfamiliar problems and requirements continually arise which cannot be broken down and distributed among specialist roles within a hierarchy. Jobs lose much of their formal definition. The definitive and enduring demarcation of functions becomes impossible. Responsibilities and functions, and even methods and powers, have to be constantly redefined through interaction with others participating in common tasks or in the solution of common problems. Each individual has to do his job with knowledge of overall purpose and situation of the company as a whole. Interaction runs laterally as much as vertically, and communication between people of different rank tends to resemble 'lateral' consultation rather than 'vertical' command. Omniscience can no longer be imputed to the boss at the top.

The head of one successful electronics concern, at the very beginning of the first interview of the whole study, attacked the idea of the organization chart as inapplicable in his concern and as a dangerous method of thinking. The first requirement of a management, according to him, was that it should make the fullest use of the capacities of its members; any individual's job should be as little defined as possible, so that it would 'shape itself' to his special abilities and initiative.

In this company, insistence on the last possible specification for managerial positions was much more in evidence than any devices for ensuring adequate interaction within the system. This did occur, but it was often due to physical conditions rather than to order by top management. A single-storeyed building housed the entire company, two thousand strong, from laboratories to canteen. Access to anyone was, therefore, physically simple and direct; it was easier to walk across to the laboratory door, the office door, or the factory door, and look about for the person one wanted, than even to telephone. Written communication inside the factory was actively discouraged. More important than the physical set up, however, was the need of each individual manager for interaction with others, in order to get his own functions defined, since these were not specified from above.

For the individual, the important part of the difference between the mechanistic and the organismic is in the degree of his commitment to the working organization. Mechanistic systems tell him what he has to attend to, and how, and also tell him what he does *not* have to bother with, what is *not* his affair, what is *not* expected of him—what he can post elsewhere as the responsibility of others. In organismic systems, such boundaries disappear. The individual is expected to regard himself as fully implicated in the discharge of any task appearing over his horizon. He has not merely to exercise a special competence, but to commit himself to the success of the concern's undertakings as a whole.

Mechanistic and Organismic Systems of Management[1]

A mechanistic management system is appropriate to stable conditions. It is characterized by:

1. The *specialized differentiation* of functional tasks into which the problems and tasks facing the concern as a whole are broken down.

2. The *abstract nature* of each individual task, which is pursued with techniques and purposes more or less distinct from those of the concern as a whole.

3. The reconciliation, for each level in the hierarchy, of these distinct performances by the *immediate superiors.*

4. The *precise definition* of rights and obligations and technical methods attached to each functional role.

5. The *translation of rights* and obligations and methods into the responsibilities of a functional position.

6. *Hierarchic structure* of control, authority and communication.

7. A reinforcement of the hierarchic structure by the location of *knowledge* of actualities exclusively *at the top* of the hierarchy.

---

[1]Burns, T. and Stalker, G. M. (1966). *The Management of Innovation,* Tavistock.

8.   A tendency for *vertical interaction* between members of the concern, i.e., between superior and subordinate.

9.   A tendency for operations and working behaviour to be *governed by superiors.*

10. *Insistence on loyalty* to the concern and obedience to superiors as a condition of membership.

11. A greater importance and prestige attaching to *internal* (local) than to general (cosmopolitan) knowledge, experience, and skill.

The organismic form is appropriate to changing conditions, which give rise constantly to fresh problems and unforeseen requirements for action which cannot be broken down or distributed automatically, arising from the functional roles defined within a hierarchic structure. It is characterized by:

1.   The *contributive nature* of special knowledge and experience to the common task of the concern.

2.   The *realistic* nature of the individual task, which is seen as set by the total situation of the concern.

3.   The adjustment and *continual redefinition* of individual tasks through interaction with others.

4.   The *shedding of responsibility* as a limited field of rights, obligations and methods. (Problems may not be posted upwards, downwards or sideways).

5.   The *spread of commitment* to the concern beyond any technical definition.

6.   A *network structure* of control, authority, and communication.

7.   Omniscience no longer imputed to the head of the concern; *knowledge* may be located anywhere in the network; this location becoming the center of authority.

8.   A *lateral* rather than a vertical direction of communication through the organization.

9.   A content of communication which consists of *information and advice* rather than instructions and decisions.

10. *Commitment* to the concern's tasks and to the 'technological ethos' of material progress and expansion is more highly valued than loyalty.

11. Importance and prestige attach to *affiliations* and *expertise* valid in the industrial and technical and commercial milieux external to the firm.

In studying the electronics industry in Britain, we were occupied for the most part with companies which had been started a generation or more ago, well within the time period of the second phase of industrialization. They were equipped at the outset with working organizations designed by mechanistic principles. The ideology of formal bureaucracy seemed so deeply ingrained in industrial management that the common reaction to unfamiliar and novel conditions was to redefine, in more precise and rigorous terms, the roles and working relationships obtaining within management, along orthodox lines of organization charts and organization manuals. The formal structure was reinforced, not adapted. In these concerns the effort to make the orthodox bureaucratic system work produced what can best be described as pathological forms of the mechanistic system.

Three of these pathological systems are described below. All three were responses to the need for finding answers to new and unfamiliar problems and for making decisions in new circumstances of uncertainty.

First, there is the *ambiguous figure* system. In a mechanistic organization, the normal procedure for dealing with any matter lying outside the boundaries of one individual's functional responsibility is to refer it to the point in the system where such responsibility is known to reside, or, failing that, to lay it before one's superior. If conditions are changing rapidly such episodes occur frequently; in many instances, the immediate superior has to put such matters higher up still. A sizeable volume of matters for solution and decision can thus find their way to the head of the concern. There can, and frequently does, develop a system by which a large number of executives find—or claim—that they can only get matters settled by going to the top man.

So, in some places we studied, an ambiguous system developed of an official hierarchy and a clandestine or open system of pair relationships between the head of the concern and some dozens of persons at different positions below him in the management. The head of the concern was overloaded with work, and senior managers whose standing depended on the mechanistic formal system felt aggrieved at being bypassed. The managing director told himself—or brought in consultants to tell him—to delegate responsibility and decision-making. The organization chart would be redrawn. But inevitably, this strategy promoted its own counter measures from the beneficiaries of the old, latent system as the stream of novel and unfamiliar problems built up anew.

The conflict between managers who saw their standing and prospects depending on the ascendancy of the old system or the new deflected attention and effort into internal politics. All of this bore heavily on the time and effective effort the head of the company was free to apply to his proper function, the more so because political moves focused on controlling access to him.

Secondly, the *mechanistic jungle.* Some companies simply grew more branches of the bureaucratic hierarchy. Most of the problems which appeared in all these firms with pathological mechanisms manifested themselves as difficulties in communications. These were met, typically, by creating special intermediaries and interpreters: methods engineers, standardization groups, contract managers, post design engineers. Underlying this familiar strategy were two equally familiar cliches of managerial thinking. The first is to look for the solution of a problem, especially a problem of communication in 'bringing somebody in' to deal with it. A new job, or possibly a whole new department, may then be created, which depends for its survival on the perpetuation of the difficulty. The second attitude probably comes from the traditions of productive management: a development engineer is not doing the job he is paid for unless he is at his drawing board, drawing, and so on. Higher management has the same instinctive reaction when it finds people moving about the works, when individuals it wants are not 'in their place.' These managers cannot trust subordinates when they are not demonstrably and physically 'on the job.' Their response, therefore, when there was an admitted need for 'better communication' was to tether functionaries to their posts and to appoint persons who would specialize in 'liaison.'

The third kind of pathological response is the *super-personal* or committee system. It was encountered only rarely in the electronics firms we studied; it appeared sporadically in many of them, but it was feared as the characteristic disease of government administration. The committee is a traditional device whereby *temporary* commitments over and above those encapsulated in a single functional role may be contained within the system and discharged without enlarging the demands on individual functionaries, or upsetting the balance of power.

Committees are often set up where new kinds of work and/or unfamiliar problems seems to involve decisions, responsibilities and powers beyond the capabilities or deserts of any one man or department. Bureaucratic hierarchies are most prone to this defect. Here most considerations, most of the time, are subordinated to the career structure afforded by the concern (a situation by no means confined to the civil service or even to universities). The difficulty of filling a job calling for unfamiliar responsibility is overcome by creating a super-person—a committee.

Why do companies not adapt to new situations by changing their working organization from mechanistic to organismic? The answer seems to lie in the fact that the individual member of the concern is not only committed to the working organization as a whole. In addition, he is a member of a group or a department with sectional interests in conflict with those of other groups, and all of these individuals are deeply concerned with the position they occupy, relative to others, and their future security or betterment are matters of deep concern.

In regard to sectional commitments, he may be, and usually is, concerned to extend the control he has over his own situation, to increase the value of his personal contribution, and to have his resources possibly more thoroughly exploited and certainly more highly rewarded. He often tries to increase his personal power by attaching himself to parties of people who represent the same kind of ability and wish to enhance its exchange value, or to cabals who seek to control or influence the exercise of patronage in the firm. The interest groups so formed are quite often identical with a department, or the dominant groups in it, and their political leaders are heads of departments, or accepted activist leaders, or elected representatives (e.g., shop stewards). They become involved in issues of internal politics arising from the conflicting demands, such as those on allocation of capital, on direction of others, and on patronage.

Apart from this sectional loyalty, an individual usually considers his own career at least as important as the well being of the firm, and while there may be little incompatibility in his serving the ends of both, occasions do arise when personal interests outweigh the firm's interests, or even a clear conflict arises.

If we accept the notion that a large number, if not all, of the members of a firm have commitments of this kind to themselves, then it is apparent that the resulting relationships and conduct are adjusted to other self-motivated relationships and conduct throughout the concern. We can, therefore, speak of the new career structure of the concern, as well as of its working organization and political system. Any concern will contain these three systems. All three will interact: particularly, the political system and career structure will influence the constitution and operation of the working organization.

(There are two qualifications to be made here. The tripartite system of commitments is not exhaustive, and is not necessarily self-balancing. Besides commitments to the concern, to 'political' groups, and to his own career prospects, each member of a concern is involved in a multiplicity of relationships. Some arise out of social origin and culture. Others are generated by the encounters which are governed, or seem to be governed, by a desire for the comfort of friendship, or the satisfactions which come from popularity and personal esteem, or those other rewards of inspiring respect, apprehension or alarm. All relationships of this sociable kind, since they represent social values, involve the parties in commitments.)

Neither political nor career preoccupations operate overtly, or even, in some cases, consciously. They give rise to intricate maneuvers and counter moves, all of them expressed through decisions, or in discussions about decisions, concerning the organization and the policies of the firm. Since sectional interests and preoccupations with advancement only display themselves in terms of the working organization, that organization becomes more or less adjusted to serving the ends of the political and career system rather than those of the concern. Interlocking systems of commitments—to sectional interests and to individual status—generate strong forces. These divert organizations from purposive adaptation. Out-of-date mechanistic organizations are perpetuated and pathological systems develop, usually because of one or the other of two things: internal politics and the career structure.

Reference

Burns, T. and Stalker, G.M. (1966). *The Management of Innovation*. Tavistock.

HIGH-PERFORMING ORGANIZATIONS IN THREE ENVIRON-MENTS

Paul R. Lawrence and Jay W. Lorsch

In this chapter, we shall summarize and amplify the answers we have found to the major question of this study—What types of organizations are most effective under different environmental conditions? By comparing three high-performing organizations we can arrive at a more concise understanding of how their internal differences were related to their ability to deal effectively with different sets of environmental conditions.[*] This comparison also provides a more complete picture of each organization to allow the reader to move beyond the numerical measures and gain a fuller appreciation of the distinct characters of these three effective organizations. While our focus will be on the high performers, we shall draw occasionally on our findings about the other organizations for help in clarifying our conclusions.

It may seem, in this summary, that we are describing "ideal types" of organizations, which can cope effectively with different environmental conditions. This inference is not valid for two reasons. First, we believe that the major contribution of this study is not the identification of any "type" of organization that seems to be effective under a particular set of conditions. Rather, it is the increased understanding of a complex set of interrelationships among internal organizational states and processes and external environmental demands. It is these relationships that we shall explicate further in this chapter. Second, although all three high-performing organizations were effective in dealing with their particular environments, it would be naive to assume that they were ideal. Each one had problems. One characteristic that the top managers in these organizations seemed to have in common was a constant search for ways to improve their organization's functioning.

From *Organization and Environment,* Boston: Division of Research, Harvard Business School, 1967, Chapter 6. Used by permission of the publisher.

[*]We shall continue to use organization A as our example of a high-performing plastics organization, but the reader should be reminded that the other high-performing plastics organization was in all important features quite similar to organization A.

Organizational States and Environmental Demands

In each industry, as we have seen, the high-performing organization came nearer meeting the demands of its environment than its less effective competitors. The most successful organizations tended to maintain states of differentiation and integration consistent with the diversity of the parts of the environment and the required interdependence of these parts. As we indicated in Chapter 4, the differences in the demands of these three environments meant that the high-performing plastics organization was more highly differentiated than the high-performing food organization, which, in turn, was more differentiated than the high-performing container organization. Simultaneously, all three high-performing organizations were achieving approximately the same degree of integration.

To illustrate the varying states of differentiation among these three organizations, we can use hypothetical encounters among managers in both the plastics and the container high-performing organizations. In the plastics organization we might find a sales manager discussing a potential new product with a fundamental research scientist and an integrator. In this discussion, the sales manager is concerned with the needs of the customer. What performance characteristics must a new product have to perform in the customer's machinery? How much can the customer afford to pay? How long can the material be stored without deteriorating? Further, our sales manager, while talking about these matters, may be thinking about more pressing current problems. Should he lower the price on an existing product? Did the material shipped to another customer meet his specifications? Is he going to meet this quarter's sales targets?

In contrast, our fundamental scientist is concerned about a different order of problems. Will this new project provide a scientific challenge? To get the desired result, could he change the molecular structure of a known material without affecting its stability? What difficulties will he encounter in solving these problems? Will this be a more interesting project to work on than another he heard about last week? Will he receive some professional recognition if he is successful in solving the problem? Thus our sales manager and our fundamental scientist not only have quite different goal orientations, but they are thinking about different time dimensions—the sales manager about what's going on today and in the next few months; the scientist, how he will spend the next few years.

But these are not the only ways in which these two specialists are different. The sales manager may be outgoing and concerned with maintaining a warm, friendly relationship with the scientist. He may be put off because the scientist seems withdrawn and disinclined to talk about anything other than the problems in which he is interested. He may also be annoyed that the scientist seems to have such freedom in choosing what he will work on. Furthermore, the scientist is probably often late for appointments, which, from the salesman's point of view, is no way to run a business. Our scientist, for his part, may feel uncomfortable because the salesman seems to be pressing for immediate answers to technical questions that will take a long time to investigate. All these discomforts are concrete manifestations of the relatively wide differences between these two men in respect to their working and thinking styles and the departmental structures to which each is accustomed.

Between these different points of view stands our integrator. If he is effective, he will understand and to some extent share the viewpoints of both specialists and will be working to help them communicate with each other. We do not want to dwell on his role at this point, but the mere fact that he is present is a result of the great differences among specialists in his organization.

In the high-performing container organization we might find a research scientist meeting with a plant manager to determine how to solve a quality problem. The plant manager talks about getting the problem solved as quickly as possible, in order to reduce the spoilage rate. He is probably thinking about how this problem will affect his ability to meet the current production schedule and to operate within cost constraints. The researcher is also seeking an immediate answer to the problem. He is concerned not with its theoretical niceties, but with how he can find an immediate applied solution. What adjustments in materials or machine procedures can he suggest to get the desired effect? In fact, these specialists may share a concern with finding the most feasible solution. They also operate in a similar, short-term time dimension. The differences in their interpersonal style are also not too large. Both are primarily concerned with getting the job done, and neither finds the other's style of behavior strange. They are also accustomed to quite similar organizational practices. Both see that they are rewarded for quite specific short-run accomplishments, and both might be feeling similar pressures from their superiors to get the job done. In essence, these two specialists, while somewhat different in their thinking and behavior patterns, would not find it uncomfortable or difficult to work together in seeking a joint solution to a problem. Thus they would need no integrator.

These two hypothetical examples show clearly that the differentiation in the plastics organization is much greater than in the equally effective container concern. The high-performing food organization fell between the extremes of differentiation represented by the other two organizations. These examples illustrate another important point stressed earlier—that the states of differentiation and integration within any organization are antagonistic. Other things (such as the determinants of conflict resolution) being equal, the more highly differentiated the units of an organization are, the more difficult it will be to achieve integration among them. The implications of this finding for our comparisons of these three high-performing organizations should be clear. Achieving integration becomes more problematic as we move from the relatively undifferentiated container organization, past the moderately differentiated food organization, to the highly differentiated plastics organization. The organizational problems of achieving the required state of both differentiation and integration are more difficult for a firm in the plastics industry than for one in the container industry. The next issue on which we shall compare these three organizations, then, is the devices they use to resolve conflict and achieve effective integration in the face of the varying degrees of differentiation.

Integrative Devices

Each of these high-performing organizations used a different combination of devices for achieving integration. As the reader will recall, the plastics organization had established a special department, one of whose primary activities was the integration of effort among the basic functional units (Table 1). In addition, this organization had an elaborate set of permanent integrating teams, each made up of members from the various functional units and the integrating department. The purpose of these teams was to provide a formal setting in which interdepartmental conflicts could be resolved and decisions reached. Finally, this organization also placed a great deal of reliance on direct contact among managers at all levels, whether or not they were on a formal team, as a further means of reaching joint decisions. As Table 1 suggests, this organization, the most highly differentiated of the three high performers, had the most elaborate set of formal mechanisms for achieving integration and in addition also relied heavily on direct contact between managers.

Table 1.   Comparison of Integrative Devices in Three High-performing Organizations

	Plastics	Food	Container
Degree of differentiation[a]	10.7	8.0	5.7
Major integrative devices	(1) Integrative department	(1) Individual integrators	(1) Direct managerial contact
	(2) Permanent cross-functional teams at three levels of management	(2) Temporary cross-functional teams	(2) Managerial hierarchy
	(3) Direct managerial contact	(3) Direct managerial contact	(3) Paper system
	(4) Managerial hierarchy	(4) Managerial hierarchy	
	(5) Paper system	(5) Paper system	

[a] High score means greater actual differentiation.

The food organization had somewhat less complex formal integrative devices. Managers within the various functional departments were assigned integrating roles. Occasionally, when the need for collaboration became especially urgent around a particular issue, temporary teams, made up of specialists from the various units involved, were formed. Managers in this organization also relied heavily on direct contact with their colleagues in other units. In this organization, the managerial manpower devoted to integration was less than that in the plastics organization. Yet, compared with the container firm, the food organization was devoting a large amount of managerial time and effort to this activity.

Integration in the container organization was achieved primarily through the managerial hierarchy, with some reliance on direct contact among functional managers and on paperwork systems that helped to resolve the more routine scheduling question. Having little differentiation, this organization was able to achieve integration by relying largely on the formal chain of command. We are not implying that the other two organizations did not use this method at all. As Table 1 suggests, some integration did occur through the hierarchy as well as through paper systems in both of these organizations. But the great differences among functional managers seemed to necessitate the use of additional integrating devices in these two organizations.

From this discussion we can see another partial determinant of effective conflict resolution. This is the appropriateness of the choice that management makes about formal integrating devices. The comparison of these devices in these three high-performing organizations indicates that, if they are going to facilitate the process of conflict resolution, they should be fairly elaborate when the organization is highly differentiated and integration is thus more difficult. But when the units in the organization are not highly differentiated, simpler devices seem to work quite effectively. As we have already seen, however, the appropriate choice of an integrating device is not by itself sufficient to assure effective settlement of differences. All of the plastics and food organizations, regardless of performance level, had some type of integrating device besides the managerial hierarchy. These devices were not equally helpful in interdepartmental decision-making because, as we have pointed out, some of the organizations did not meet many of the other partial determinants of effective conflict resolution. However, there was evidence in all organizations that these devices did serve some useful purpose. To at least a minimal extent, they helped to bridge the gap between highly differentiated functional departments. By contrast, in the low-performing container organization there was no evidence that the integrating unit was serving a useful purpose. Given the low differentiation within the organization, there seemed to be no necessity for an integrating department.

This comparison of the integrating devices in the three high-performing organizations points up the relationship between the types of integrating mechanisms and the other partial determinants of effective conflict resolution. We have stressed earlier that these determinants are interdependent. Even though we have not been able to trace the relationship systematically, this statement seems to include the final partial determinant, the choice of integrative devices. In all these organizations, the choice of integrative devices clearly affected the level at which decisions were made as well as the relative influence of the various basic units.

We should also remember that any one of these determinants is only partial and that they should be seen as immediate determinants only. We have not explored the causes underlying them.

Comparison of Effective Conflict-Resolving Practices

Because of differences in the demands of each environment and the related differences in integrative devices, each of these high-performing organizations had developed some different procedures and practices for resolving interdepartmental conflict. However, certain important determinants of effective conflict resolution prevailed in all three organizations. We shall first examine the differences, then explore the similarities.

Differences in Conflict Resolution

The three effective companies differed in the relative influence of the various departments in reaching interdepartmental decisions. In the plastics organization, it was the integrating department that had the highest influence. This was consistent with the conditions in that organization's environment. The high degree of differentiation and the complexity of problems made it necessary for the members of the integrating unit to have a strong voice in interdepartmental decisions. Their great influence meant that they could work effectively among the specialist managers in resolving interdepartmental issues.

In the food organization, the research and marketing units had the highest influence. This, too, was in line with environmental demands and with the type of integrating device employed. Since there was no integrating unit, the two departments dealing with the important market and scientific sectors of the environment needed high influence if they were effectively to resolve conflicts around issues of innovation. However, as we also indicated earlier, there was ample evidence that within these two units the individuals who were formally designated as integrators did have much influence on decisions.

The pattern of departmental influence in the container organization contributed to the effective resolution of conflict for similar reasons. Here the members of the sales and production department had the highest influence. This was appropriate, since the top managers in these two departments had to settle differences over scheduling and customer service problems. If these managers or their subordinates had felt that the views of their departments were not being given adequate consideration, they would have been less effective in solving problems and implementing decisions.

Here again, we have been restating comparatively the findings reported. Such reiteration helps us to understand how this factor of relative departmental influence contributes to performance in different environments. Each high-performing organization had its own pattern, but each of these was consistent with the demands of the most critical competitive issues.

A second important difference among these three organizations in respect to conflict resolution lay in the pattern of total and hierarchical influence. The food and plastics organizations had higher total influence than their less effective competitors, and, related to this, the influence on decisions was distributed fairly evenly through several levels (Figure 1). The lower level and middle-level managers who had the necessary detailed knowledge also had the influence necessary to make relevant decisions. In fact, they seemed to have as much influence on decisions as their top-level superiors. In the container industry, on the other hand, total influence in the higher performer was lower than in the low performer, and the decision-making influence was significantly more concentrated at the upper management levels. This was consistent with the conditions in this environment. Since the information required to make decisions (especially the crucial scheduling decisions) was available at the top of the organization, it made sense for many decisions to be reached at this level, where the positional authority also resided.

The importance of the differences in these influence lines can be better understood if we let some of the managers in each organization speak for themselves. In the plastics organization, lower and middle managers described their involvement in decisions in this way:

When we have a disagreement, ninety-nine times out of a hundred we argue it out and decide ourselves. We never go up above except in extreme cases.

* * *

We have disagreements, but they don't block progress, and they do get resolved by us. I would say on our team, we have never had a problem which had to be taken up with somebody above us.

* * *

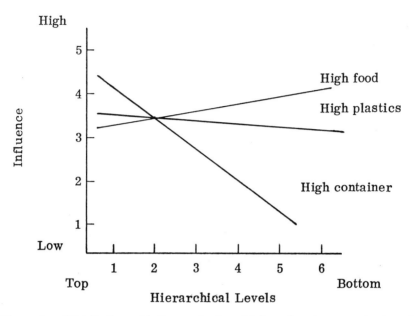

Figure 1.   Distribution of influence in three high-performing organizations.[a]

[a]Lines fitted by least square method. The difference in the slope of the lines between the high-performing food and the high-performing container organization was significant at .001. This difference between the high-performing plastics and the high-performing container organization was significant at .005. There was no significant difference between the food and plastics organizations.

We could use these teams to buck it up to the higher management, but I think this would be a weak committee and a weak individual, and I am not willing to give my freedom up. They give you all the rope you need. If you need their help, they are there; if you don't need them, don't bother them.

The last manager quoted went on to substantiate a point made by many of his colleagues: While lower and middle managers made most decisions at their own level, they also recognized that major issues, which might have implications for products other than their own, should be discussed with higher management. But this discussion always took place *after* they had agreed on the best course of action for their own products.

Over and over, these lower and middle managers indicated their own responsibility for decisions and their feeling that to ask their superior to resolve conflicts would be to acknowledge their own inadequacy. A higher-level manager stressed that this was also the view at his level:

Top management has told these fellows, "We want you to decide what is best for your business, and we want you to run it. We don't want to tell you how to run it." We assume that nobody in the company knows as much about a business as the men on that team.

This same flavor was evident in remarks gathered in the food organization. Here, too, middle and lower managers stressed their own involvement in decisions.

Given these facts, the reader may be wondering about the activities of the upper echelons of management in the plastics and food organizations. If they were not involved in these decisions, what were they doing? While we made no detailed study of their activity, the data collected in interviews indicated clearly that they had plenty to keep them busy. First, they had the problems of administering their respective functional units. Second, they reviewed decisions made by their subordinates to make certain that the specialists working on one part of the product line were not doing anything that would adversely affect another part. In addition, in their dynamic environments, they were constantly concerned with the search for new and longer range opportunities, which would fall outside the purview of any of their subordinates. In this regard, we found in all the effective organizations the managers' time horizons became longer ranged as one moved up the hierarchy. This tendency was particularly marked in the plastics and food organizations. This, too, suggested that top executives in the food and plastics organizations were heavily involved in longer range issues and problems.

The tone of comments by managers in the container organization about who made decisions was dramatically different from that in the other two organizations. We cited some examples, but a few more at this juncture may emphasize the contrast. The middle and lower managers in the container organization emphasized the chief executive's and the other officers' roles in decision-making:

> My primary contact is with [sales vice president and the chief executive]. This contact is around who we are going to give the containers to, because of our oversold position. They will determine which ones we are going to take care of. . . . Actually, what you really need, though, is [the chief executive's] decision. I usually start out these kinds of conflicts with [the production scheduling manager], but when somebody has to get heard, it ends up with [the chief executive]. Usually I am in contact with him three or four times a day.

* * *

> When there is a problem, I try to tell [production vice president] the facts and make some recommendations. He makes the decisions or

takes it up to [the chief executive]. He doesn't get reversed very often. Sometimes he may say to me, "I agree with you, go ahead and do it," and then [the chief executive] will change it.

The sales vice president explained his own involvement, emphasizing application of the available facts:

[The chief executive] holds a weekly scheduling meeting on Monday, which includes him, myself, the scheduling manager, and a couple of the sales managers, depending upon what the crucial problems are. The scheduling manager has prepared the schedule on Friday. On Monday we tear it apart. This business is like playing an organ. You've got to hit the right keys, or it just doesn't sound right. The keys we play with are on the production schedule. In these meetings, though, the final decision rests with [the chief executive]. He gets the facts from us, and we influence the decision, but if there is any doubt, he decides.

All these comments serve to underline the differences in the distribution of influence between plastics and foods, on the one hand, and containers, on the other. These differences directly reflect differences in their respective environments.

Similarities in Conflict Resolution

So far, we have accentuated the important differences in these organizations in terms of the determinants of conflict resolution. Let us now look at some similarities. First, however, we should stress again that the differences actually stemmed from a fundamental similarity: Each of these organizations had developed conflict-resolving practices consistent with its environment.

The first major similarity among these organizations is in the basis of influence of the managers most centrally involved in achieving integration and resolving conflict. In all three organizations, these managers, whatever their level, had reputations in the company for being highly competent and knowledgeable. Their large voice in interdepartmental decision was seen as legitimate by other managers because of this competence. To return to the point made earlier, the positional influence of the managers assigned the task of helping to resolve interdepartmental conflict was consistent with their influence based on competence. Unlike the situation in some of the low-performing organizations, these two important sources of influence coincided in all these effective organizations. This point is illustrated by comments about the competence of the managers centrally concerned with conflict resolution in each organization.

In the container company, as we indicated earlier, the chief executive was regarded as extremely knowledgeable about the various facets of the business. As one manager expressed it:

The fact is, as I understand it, that he is almost a legend in the industry. He knows every function in this company better than any of the people who are supposed to be handling that function.

But the chief executive was not the only one who had this respect. Managers in this organization also emphasized the knowledge and ability of the other top executives. A research engineer described the competence of the research director:

I think another thing related to the close supervision I receive is the nature of the [research director]. He is an exceptional kind of guy, and he seems to know all the details and everything going on in the plant, and in the lab. He is continually amazing people in this regard.

A similar point was made about the production vice president by one of his plant managers:

Oh yes, I hear from [the production vice president], but if he wants you, you are in trouble. You hear from him for sure, if your figures are too far off. He is pretty understanding. If you can explain, he understands. He also can really help you out on a serious production problem. He can tell you what to do. He knows just how far a job should be run before it should be pulled off.

In this organization, as these comments suggest, the knowledge and expertise of the top managers gained them respect from their subordinates and legitimated their strong influence over decisions. In the food and plastics organizations, the knowledged-based influence worked in a similar manner to justify the high influence of the middle managers centrally involved in helping to resolve interdepartmental conflict. Comments similar to those cited may help to highlight this point. An integrator in the food organization explained the importance of expertise in his job.

Generally, the way I solve these problems is through man-to-man contact. I think face-to-face contact is the very best thing. Also, what we [the integrators] find is that most people develop a heavy respect for expertise, and this is what we turn to when we need to work out an issue with the fellows in other departments.

Similarly, a fundamental research scientist in the plastics organization indicated (as did many others in this organization) that he believed the members of the integrating unit to be competent, which helped them to achieve collaboration:

> I believe we have a good setup in [the integrating unit]. They do an excellent job of bringing the industry problems back to somebody who can do something about them. They do an excellent job of taking the projects out and finding uses for them. In recent years I think it has been staffed with competent men.

In all three high-performing organizations, then, our data suggest a consistency in three factors that helped those primarily responsible for achieving integration to settle interdepartmental disputes. The managers who were assigned the responsibility for resolving conflict were at a level in the organization where they had the knowledge and information required to reach interdepartmental decisions, and they were regarded as competent by their associates. Thus (1) *positional influence,* (2) *influence based on competence,* and (3) *the actual knowledge and information required to make decisions* all coincided. While there was this similarity, as we pointed out above, the level at which influence and knowledge were concentrated varied among the organizations because of differences in the certainty of their respective environments.

A second important similarity in these three organizations lay in the mode of behavior employed to resolve conflict. All three, as we have seen, relied heavily on open confrontation. The managers involved in settling conflicts were accustomed to open discussion of all related issues and to working through differences until they found what appeared to be an optimal solution. This was so regardless of the level at which the conflicts were handled. Typical comments from managers in each of the three organizations illustrate this point more vividly than the numerical data reported earlier. A researcher in the plastics organization described how he and his colleagues resolved conflicts:

> I haven't gotten into any disagreements yet where we let emotions stand in the way. We just go to the data and prove out which is right. If there is still some question about it, somebody can do the work to reexamine it. Emotions come up now and then. However, we usually have group decisions, so if I am not getting anywhere, I have to work it out with the others.

A production engineer in the food organization expressed a similar viewpoint:

> We often will disagree as to basic equipment. When we can't agree on what equipment to use, we will collaborate on some tests [with research], and sometimes we will run it both ways to find out what is the best way. Actually, the way this works out, one of their fellows and I will be at each other's desk doing a lot of scratching with a pencil trying to figure out the best answer and to support our point of view. We will finally agree on what is the best way to go. It is a decision we reach together.

The direction of research in the container organization discussed his role in the resolution of conflict with the chief executive:

> I am sure a lot of people would say this is a one-man company. Sure, [the chief executive] keeps close tabs on the dollars, and I must keep good score for him in regard to everything we spend. He is pretty gentle with me, and I have no run-ins with him. He talked to me this morning about a problem, and I knew that regardless of whether I said yes or disagreed with him, he would have gone along and taken my advice. He likes to complain a lot, and holler and bellow and be like a wild bull, but he gives up when he sees a good case. He'll ask for a real good story, and we have to give it to him, but if it *is* a good story, he will go along with us.

We should emphasize several important points about this comment. It and similar remarks from the major executives in the container organization indicated that while the chief executive was strong and dominant, he expected to have all points of view and pertinent information discussed before making a decision. These responses likewise indicated that there was give and take in these discussions and that the other major executives often influence the outcome, if the facts supported their point of view. It is also worth noting, as a comment from a plant manager in this organization suggests, that lower managers used the same method to resolve conflicts:

> I'm an easygoing sort of fellow, but I get mad sometimes. When we get something to fight about, we just say it, face the problem, and it is over. We get the issue out on the table and solve it. It has to be done that way. [The production vice president] does it that way. We all follow his lead.

While these statements all deal with technical issues, we could cite similar comments concerning marketing problems. The important fact to emphasize is that these three organizations relied on confrontation as a mode for resolving interdepartmental conflict to a greater extent than all but one of the other organizations (the low-performing food organization). This fact does not seem unrelated to the importance of competence and knowledge as a basis of influence for the managers primarily responsible for resolving conflicts. High value was traditionally placed on knowledge and expertise in all three organizations. Consequently, managers were very willing to see disagreements settled on this basis.

This reliance on confrontation suggests another important characteristic of all three organizations: Managers must have had sufficient trust in their colleagues and, particularly in the case of the container organization, in their superiors to discuss openly their own points of view as they related to the issues at hand. They seemed to feel no great concern that expressing disagreement with someone else's position (even a superior's) would be damaging to their careers. This feeling of trust apparently fostered effective problem-solving and decision-making.

Summary Comparison of the High-Performing Organizations

The plastics organization, which functioned in the most dynamic and diverse of the three environments, was consequently most highly differentiated of the three high-performing organizations. Since this condition could create major problems in maintaining the required state of integration, this organization, as we have seen, had developed an elaborate set of formal devices (both an integrating unit and cross-functional teams) to facilitate the resolution of conflict and the achievement of integration. Because market and scientific factors were uncertain and complex, the lower and middle echelons of management had to be involved in reaching joint departmental decisions; these managers were centrally involved in the resolution of conflict. This organization also met all the determinants of effective conflict resolution. The integrators had balanced orientations and felt that they were being rewarded for the total performance of their product group. Relative to the functional managers, they had high influence, which was based on their competence and knowledge. In resolving conflict all the managers relied heavily on open confrontation.

In contrast to the plastics organization, the container organization was in a relatively stable and homogeneous environment. Thus its functional units were not highly differentiated, which meant that the only formal integrating device required was the managerial hierarchy. But in using this device this organization also met the determinants of effective conflict resolution. The sales and production units, which were centrally involved in the crucial decisions related to scheduling and delivery, both felt that they had much influence over decisions. Around these issues influence was concentrated at the top of the organization, where top managers could centrally collect the relevant information to reach decisions. Middle managers, particularly those dealing with technical matters, did have some influence. The great influence of the top managers stemmed not only from their position, but also from their competence and knowledge. Finally, conflicts between departments were resolved and decisions reached through problem-solving behavior.

In these two paragraphs, we have described two quite different organizations, each of which is well-equipped to deal with its own external environment. Another way to understand the contrasts between them is to examine the major sources of satisfaction and of stress for the executives in each. While we made no systematic effort to collect such data in the plastics organization, the contrast between the two organizations can be clearly seen from interview comments of the managers in each organization. Managers in both organizations were generally quite well satisfied with their situations, but they were finding satisfaction for some quite different reasons. In the plastics organization an important source of satisfaction was the active involvement in decisions. Middle managers often expressed the feeling that they were running their own firms. One product manager in the sales department put it this way:

> Our present organization allows us as individuals to more formally play a role in decision-making, which we didn't do before. Now, with the teams, we can make a decision which will affect the profit. We can see the results of our efforts more realistically than we could before. Now that it has management approval, it has a nice flavor. It's nice to be doing something they approve of. The product manager has no formal authority. But putting him on the team gives him some sort of authority. I'm not sure what kind of authority it is, but it makes my job more meaningful. . . . Of course, we all recognize that the other guys on the team are depending upon our effort, so we make an effort to produce.

Managers in the container organization, however, indicated that they liked their jobs for quite a different reason—because they knew where to get a decision made. One manager expressed it in this manner:

> He [the chief executive] does all the scheduling himself, and in essence what you have is a large organization run by one man. This is a refreshing switch from the organization where I had previously worked. I find this very beneficial. If I want something decided, I can go right to him and get a direct decision. You tell him what you want to do, and he will tell you right then and there whether he will let you do it or whether he won't.

The sources of dissatisfaction and stress in the two organizations were also different. A manager in the plastics organization described some of the points of concern to him:

> I worked for another company which was different, where there were fairly definite lines of authority. This place was quite a revelation to me. In my old company we always knew whose jobs things were. Occasionally here we run into situations where we don't know whose jobs things are. . . . All of these meetings take a lot of time. I used to spend eight hours by myself, and I thought I could get more things done. I feel now that I spend time on committees instead of making autocratic decisions, but this isn't really a disadvantage, as we do get better solutions. . . . Also, there can be conflict between your position as a team member. The more empathy with others you have, the worse it gets.

What disturbed this manager and a few others was the ambiguity of responsibility and relationships in this organization. Many managers often had dual loyalties—to their functional superiors and to their team colleagues. They had to decide themselves what needed to be done. The involvement of many managers in interdepartmental decision-making made these difficulties unavoidable, and it also meant that managers who had a low tolerance for ambiguity and uncertainty did not always enjoy their work.

In contrast, the few managers in the container organization who expressed dissatisfaction were most concerned because upper managers seemed to be so involved in their activities. As one man said:

> Your boss is telling you to check something, and then he jumps down your throat five minutes later. They should know what you are doing and try to give you some answers, or else they should let you do it. . . . I know this job involves a lot of pressure, particularly because at first you are just getting ignored around here and then they are jumping on you, and the pressure is really acute. Somebody has to be the whipping boy around here, and that is just part of this job.

These data suggest two things. The first is quite obvious—that these two organizations were quite different places in which to work. The second inference is more speculative. There is some suggestion, from the tone of the interviews, that the managers in the two organizations had somewhat different personality needs. Those in the plastics organization seemed to prefer more independence and had a greater tolerance for ambiguity, while those in the container company were perhaps better satisfied with greater dependence upon authority and were more bothered by ambiguity. While there may have been these differences in personality needs, each organization (as well as the food organization) seemed to provide a setting in which many members could gain a sense of competence in their jobs. This provided them with important sources of satisfaction. The fact that so few managers in either organization did express any dissatisfaction with such different organizational climates would suggest that this is so. While we have no way to confirm this speculation, it does raise again the importance of the point made earlier, that the organization must fit not only the demands of the environment, but also the needs of its members.

In any case, the contrast between the plastics and the container organizations is very sharp. In a sense, they represent opposite ends on a continuum, one dealing with a very dynamic and diverse environment, where innovation is the dominant issue, while the other is dealing with a very stable and homogeneous environment, where regularity and consistency of operations were important. The food organization, as our discussion has suggested, was in many ways like the plastics organization. The differences between them seemed to be more of degree than of kind. While the food environment was not so dynamic and diverse as that of plastics, it seemed to be toward that end of the continuum. The integrating devices, although not so elaborate as those in the plastics organization, were of the same nature, designed to provide linkage at the middle and lower managerial levels. The two organizations met most of the same determinants of effective conflict resolution. The major difference between them was that the plastics organization appeared to be devoting more of its managerial manpower to devices that facilitated the resolution of conflict. The important point, however, is that the food organization, like the other effective organizations, had developed a set of internal states and characteristics consistent with the demands of its particular environment.

We should, however, recognize one limit to this conclusion. Each of these organizations had developed characteristics that were in tune with the demands of its *present* environment. Whether these same characteristics will provide long-run viability depends, of course, on whether the environmental demands change in the future. Given the widely observed tendency toward greater scientific, technological, and market change, the plastics and food organizations would seem to be in a more favorable position to maintain their high performance. Major technological or market changes in the container industry would almost certainly create serious problems for the high-performing container organization. This suggests that the managements in stable industries must develop within their organizations some capabilities for watching for environmental changes and preparing to adapt to them. It also suggests that in the future more and more organizations may resemble the high-performing plastics and food organizations.

A Contingency Theory of Organizations

From this comparison we have seen that it is possible to understand the differences in the internal states and processes of these three effective organizations on the basis of the differences in their external environments. This, along with the comparison between the high performers and the other organizations in each environment, has provided us with some important leads as to what characteristics organizations must have in order to cope effectively with different environmental demands. These findings suggest a contingency theory of organization which recognizes their systemic nature. The basic assumption underlying such a theory, which the findings of this study strongly support, is that organization variables are in a complex interrelationship with one another and with conditions in the environment.

In this study we have found an important relationship among external variables (the certainty and diversity of the environment, and the strategic environmental issue), internal states of differentiation and integration, and the process of conflict resolution. If an organization's internal states and processes are consistent with external demands, the findings of this study suggest that it will be effective in dealing with its environment.

More specifically, we have found that the state of differentiation in the effective organization was consistent with the diversity of the parts of the environment, while the state of integration achieved was consistent with the environmental demand for interdependence. But our findings have also indicated that the states of differentiation and integration are inversely related. The more differentiated an organization, the more difficult it is to achieve integration. To overcome this problem, the effective organization has integrating devices consistent with the diversity of the environment. The more diverse the environment, and the more differentiated the organization, the more elaborate the integrating devices.

The process of conflict resolution in the effective organization is also related to these organizational and environmental variables. The locus of influence to resolve conflict is at a level where the required knowledge about the environment is available. The more unpredictable and uncertain the parts of the environment, the lower in the organizational hierarchy this tends to be. Similarly, the relative influence of the various functional departments varies, depending on which of them is vitally involved in the dominant issues posed by the environment. These are the ways in which the determinants of effective conflict resolution are contingent on variation in the environment. Four other determinants, however, seem to be interrelated only with other organizational variables and are present in effective organizations in all environments. Two of these are the confrontation of conflict and influence based on competence and expertise. The other two factors are only present in those effective organizations that have established special integrating roles outside the managerial hierarchy—a balanced orientation for the integrators and a feeling on their part that they are rewarded for achieving an effectively unified effort. Our findings indicate that when an organization meets most of these determinants of effective conflict resolution, both the general ones and those specific to its environment, it will be able to maintain the required state of differentiation and integration.

This contingency theory of organizations suggests the major relationships that managers should think about as they design and plan organizations to deal with specific environmental conditions. It clearly indicates that managers can no longer be concerned about the one best way to organize. Rather, . . . this contingency theory, as supported and supplemented by the findings of other recent research studies, provides at least the beginning of a conceptual framework with which to design organizations according to the tasks they are trying to perform.

MANAGING ORGANIZATIONS: OLD TEXTBOOKS DO DIE!

Leonard R. Sayles

When it is said that a field of study is changing, one usually thinks of the old saw about economics: Students think it hasn't changed because the examinations look the same; they don't realize it's the answers that are different. Or worse yet, change is associated with fads (and the foibles of the academic mind), bandwagons, and obeisance to public opinion or foundation largesse.

Cynicism aside, there can be real change; it is possible to learn more about a subject and to revise and update one's knowledge. It's my conviction that this is happening in what used to be called human relations in industry—the application of social science theory and research method to the people problems of business—and exciting new ideas are appearing in numerous parts of the world.

If we are right about this, and there are many who will disagree with the viewpoints that follow, it becomes increasingly desirable to communicate without delay with countries where fresh thought is occurring. Every day one sees course descriptions for business schools and management development programs in this country as well as in, say, Britain, Denmark, and India that are copies of the pre-1960s work done in the U.S. Just possibly this could represent the same type of waste as building a textile mill based on our old New England models.

The hallmark of the change is the growing emphasis on the impact of the organizational environment on the behavior of an individual in the work situation. This contrasts sharply with the traditional approaches, embodied in the work of the human relationists and their predecessors, the exponents of scientific management, or Taylorism, as it was called after its principal founder.

The field of human relations in industry, which had its meteoric rise in the United States during the 1940s and 1950s, is often seen as a reaction to the inhuman or ahuman developments of scientific management. In a sense, human relations was thought of as the antidote, the putting back of the human element into the study and understanding of work organizations. Unfortunately, a large share of human relations writing for (and preaching to) management copied more than it diverged from scientific management. Both were essentially a priori approaches. They started with certain postulates or "givens" and superimposed them upon the

---

organizational setting. The basic difference between the two schools is that while the scientific management group stressed the rational and unemotional application of certain elemental managerial principles, the human relations school urged consideration of how these principles are modified by the actions of people. Both were "hooked" on the problems of authority. For the scientific management people, it was the problem of getting standard job descriptions, uncluttered tables of organization and the like. Nor did the human relationists disagree, except that their primary focus was on improving the style of supervision. Both would urge careful watching of the S's:

> *Single supervision*—Make sure each man has one and only one boss, thus eliminating, so it was thought, overlapping lines of authority. (Unfortunately, as we shall see, no longer a tenable objective.)

> *Spans* of control must be limited (but not too limited) so that the supervisor can make his orders effective (but not oppressive).

> *Staff* has no authority.

This conception of administration and the manager's role produces the neat organization pyramids with their unquestioned hierarchical characteristics and, in the process, deludes many observers into condemning the monolithic structure. The dichotomy between those who make decisions and those who carry them out is a concession—or rather a capitulation—to the desire for orderly relationships. Unfortunately, it is a most distorted picture of the real world. More realistically, we are coming to understand that decision-making is an organizational process. It is shaped as much by the pattern of interaction of managers as it is by the solitary ruminations of the rational individual.

Myth of the Isolated Thinker

Various special-interest groups converge or intersect at the point at which the decision must be made, namely, the manager. Most of the external groups to which the manager is exposed provide him with the intensely specialized point of view of the expert. But since many, if not most, questions to which he must find solutions are composite generalist problems (e.g., production *and* personnel, product reliability *and* cost, etc.), he cannot rely on only one view, nor does top management want this parochialism to exist.

Observation suggests that the manager accomplishes his objectives by moving about the organization and persuading people with special knowledge and points of view to agree with him against those who seek an alternative objective. Thus, those who design the structure of the organization must arrange for such contacts in the organizational location and in the job description of those who are supposed to impinge on the thinking of the manager.

Dean Acheson perceived this in commenting[1] on the naiveté of the then new Secretary of State Dulles' expectations concerning his job:

"He told me that he was not going to work as I had done, but would free himself from involvement with what he referred to as personnel and administrative problems, in order to have more time to think."

"I did not comment, but was much struck by the conjunction of ideas. I wondered how it would turn out. For it had been my experience that thought was not of much use without knowledge and guidance, and that who should give me both and how competent they would be must depend on who chose, dealt with, assigned and promoted these people and established the forms or organization within which they worked."

Later in this same essay, Acheson expressed criticism of the view that even the President (Eisenhower at that time) needs more time for isolated contemplation:

"This absorption with the Executive as Emerson's 'Man Thinking,' surrounded by a Cabinet of Rodin statues, bound in an oblivion of thought . . . seemed to me unnatural. Surely thinking is not so difficult, so hard to come by, so solemn as all this."

Just as the human relations and the scientific management schools tended to view decision-making in the abstract, so too did they conceive of attitude formation as occurring independent of an organizational setting. Thus, for each, management problems are the result of unthinking or unpleasant people—either recalcitrant employees who could not or would not see the logic of necessary decisions, or authoritarian and overbearing managers who ignored the basic human need of employees to become involved in the decision process. Staff-line conflicts are usually viewed as arising from the inability of the man of thought to work successfully with the man of action; the latter has the responsibility and the former the ideas. The professional is too interested in his colleagues outside the firm and in discovering new knowledge, not ways to make a profit.

Today American and Canadian businessmen in particular are spending great sums of money to change the attitudes of their executives toward other people and toward their jobs. In what is one of the most expensive and controversial types of education, managers are endeavoring to become more self-aware and rid themselves of their imperfections in what is variously called sensitivity, T-group or grid training.

Leaving aside the substantial question of whether people can actually be changed by these techniques, many would argue all of this puts the proverbial cart before the horse. There is a growing body of evidence that attitudes, like decisions, are not independent, autonomously determined variables. Position in a network of pressures and relationships determines attitudes and for many purposes it is easier to change the constraints (the organizational framework) than the people. If Manager X and Y are no longer required by their organizational positions to compete for the same scarce resources, they are more likely to develop satisfactory means of dealing with each other than if they are active competitors for objectives that seem mutually incompatible. Just as historically the "flag followed trade," attitudes most often follow and do not lead changes in objective conditions.

A corollary proposition is that management is not an activity that is applied, full blown, to an organization. Rather the management process grows out of and is integral to the basic technology and operations of the enterprise; change one and the other changes. It is the division of labor particularly which determines where and how department lines should be drawn and who should be supervised by whom and how. But this can best be illustrated from current research findings.

The Woodward Work

In the middle 1950s, Professor Joan Woodward (Production Engineering and Management Studies, Imperial College of Science and Technology) conducted a thorough investigation of the organization and management problems of 100 British manufacturing companies.[2] The work of her team, just recently published in the United States, is receiving more attention than almost any comparable research since the Western Electric studies. One of the major conclusions of this extensive field study is that organization and supervisory problems are a function of technology. The major categories of difference in technology that were most predictive of management response were the following:

Unit Production: Production of single non-standardized units to customer order; prototypes or very massive "one of a kind" items of mechanical or electronic equipment.

Mass and batch production: Standardized parts and products produced in large batches and on assembly lines.

Process production: Continuous flow production, largely of liquids, gases and crystalline substances.

These technological differences produced significant variations in organization. In the unit-production firms sampled, the first-line supervisor had an average span of control of between 21 and 30 employees, but in the process-production concerns his span declined to between 11 and 20, while in batch-or-mass-production companies it went as high as 41 to 50. Similarly the number of people reporting to the top executive varied from a median of four in unit production, to seven in mass production, to 10 in process firms. The average number of levels of management used by the sampled firms ranged from three in unit-production to six in process companies; mass-production firms typically used four. Also, 12% of the unit-production firms used a top-management committee rather than a single executive head, but this percentage rose to 33 in batch and mass production and as high as 80 in process-production.

These structural differences could hardly have been accounted for by difference in management philosophy, the advice of consultants, or trial and error. As Woodward and her colleagues show later in case studies of technological change, as a firm shifts its basic technology, it either changes its organization form or begins to experience serious management problems.

Not only the form but the substance follows from technology. A number of years ago, we showed in a study of 300 work groups that the relative aggressiveness and quantity of antimanagement activity was directly related to the technology (and not as popular preconception would have it, to management skills, supervisory behavior or union orientation). Woodward, building on this research, goes many steps beyond in demonstrating that the character of human relationships throughout the enterprise is a product of technology.

1. Unit production firms, dominated by a sense of product quality, for the most part practice more delegation within their management, are most permissive and more flexible in job interrelationships.

2. Mass-production firms have the most elaborate organization formats and the most complex staff arrangements. This leads to widespread staff-line conflict. At the worker level there is usually comparable bad feeling as management seeks to push up production levels, save motions and reduce waste, essentially because labor costs are so significant.

3. Process-production firms exhibit strikingly good interpersonal relations. Management is largely functional or a line organization with little staff proliferation. Employees feel little pressure from management in that there is little relation between effort by line workers and productivity or efficiency. The ability to see and identify with a total process, the technologically

imposed requirement for repeated management investment in training and upgrading, and the sense of a team effort—all combine to produce these good human relations.

. . . As Well as Status Differences

Even prestige and status among the major functional subdivisions of a business have a technological basis. While traditional management ignored status differences within management (all were equal, of course!) and human relations saw it as a change variable (luck, whim, personality differences, top management bias, historical accident and the like), the Woodward study discloses:

> In unit production, the development people get the greatest attention—again because of the emphasis on quality and uniqueness of product.

> In mass production, it is production personnel who usually win.

> And in process-production, since plant efficiency depends more on uninterrupted demand than in the other two types of companies (products being difficult or impossible to store), the marketing function is key, and sales tends to have the most status.

Though the results of the Woodward research do not appear startling, they are outside the mainstream of findings in this area—and little wonder. Many behavioral scientists still refuse to study the organization as a total entity, preferring to concentrate on closed or partial systems. Generally, the focus of study has been a group of problem solvers in a room, say, a foreman and his workers or an isolated decision maker (at times college sophomores rather than executives were used). And not only are the components regarded in isolation, but structural factors like management controls, technology, and departmentation are treated as independent elements.

A specific example may help to clarify some of the difficulties occasioned by this closed-system approach. Here is a commonplace incident that recurs in almost every large organization which employs engineers and purchasing agents.

The engineer requests that Purchasing order a supply of parts from a particular vendor. Purchasing questions the request on the grounds that the specifications are too "tight," that is, the engineer is "gold plating" his product, perhaps favoring a particular vendor. Purchasing wants an order that can be put up for bid, specifications that can be met by a variety of outside sources of supply or even be consistent with standard parts that are usually inventoried or readily available. The engineer insists that he needs exactly these high quality parts and perhaps it is true that only one vendor can meet his quality standards.

Both Sides Wade In . . .

Who is right and what is the problem? Traditional management texts might ask who has the authority. Since the engineer is "responsible" for the product he is designing he must have the authority to order the parts he desires. (Of course, management also gives Purchasing certain authority to control the variety of different parts that are used, to minimize the costs of acquisition, etc.).

Human relations experts might seek out *motives.* Why are the two conflicting, what is the hidden motive? Perhaps the engineer is anxious to assert his status, is insecure or aggressive, or Purchasing is guilty of harboring distrust or hostility toward the "know-it-all" engineers with their technical degrees.

. . . But Is the Problem Soluble?

The solution for scientific management is to clarify once and for all jurisdictions, authority and responsibility. For human relations the answer is to improve mutual understanding, trust and self-awareness, to root out hidden feelings. Both might recommend a coordinating committee or problem-solving conference or discipline of the guilty party who broke the rules, or at least reeducation. And both may be dead wrong. It may simply be that this conflict is representative of a type of friction that is endemic to the modern organization and typically is not a result of undesirable or unsocial motives or the absence of "table-of-organization" clarity. The organization intends these groups to have somewhat conflicting objectives, and, in fact, establishes countless other specialist groups whose conflicting interests must be reconciled. Union and management don't conflict because of misunderstanding as much as because they understand each other only too well. We have long since learned it is futile to look for bogeymen.

Thus organization analysis must be suitable to dealing with open systems involving a variety of dynamic relationships that are much more complex and subtle than the simple boss-subordinate relationships of more primitive organizations. Similarly, methods of evaluating and controlling organizational behavior must go beyond the simplistic "one best way of managing" to a view of the individual as a participant in a network of relationships, each strand of which may require different behavior in response to different cues and signals.

A modern view of the relationship problems of the organization is very close to the method and approach that has developed over many years in the industrial relations field.   Industrial relations long ago saw the impact of structure (for example, of the grievance procedure and of the union) on relationships.   It considered the impact of technology on human behavior as it discovered that relationships differed in mines as compared to auto plants.   Collective bargaining took distinctive forms in various industries as the so-called industrial relations system adapted itself to the peculiar problems growing out of the nature of work and its dangers.   Also, industrial relations concentrated on behavior and the impact of various patterns of interaction on the attitudes of the parties toward one another, rather than on the reverse (the impact of attitudes on behavior).   Finally, industrial relations saw that one could understand structure by looking at process, i.e., the sequence of actions and interactions over time, rather than simply looking at static correlations, motivation, or finding the guilty party.   To the degree that the new field of organization behavior follows this lead, to that degree will it contribute to an understanding of the complex and varied clusters of relationships that characterize flesh-and-blood organizations.

References

1.   Acheson, Dean. "Thoughts About Thoughts in High Places." *The New York Times Magazine,* October 11, 1959, p. 20.

2.   Woodward, Joan. *Industrial Organization: Theory and Practice.* New York: Oxford University Press, 1965.

PART V

ORGANIZATION DEVELOPMENT

This section presents material pertaining to strategies for organizational change. Two articles, by Larsen and Woodman, respectively, present the authors' opinions on O.D. as it currently exists and where it is headed.

The third and fourth articles provide a detailed description of two specific techniques. Richard Babcock discusses one of the classic interventions, Management By Objectives. The article by Baburoglu and Garr describe a new, innovative, intervention: the search conference strategy.

The final two articles are case studies of highly successful OD programs. The first describes a four year quality of work life program that took place at a small community organization, a YMCA. The second describes how a cultural change aided in the turnaround of SAS, one of the most successful international airlines.

OD IN THE 90'S:
DON'T WORRY, BE HAPPY—OR . . . ?

Henrick Holt Larsen, Institute For Organization And Social Sciences, Blagardsgade 23B, 2200 Copenhagen N, Denmark

OD has been with us for just as long as plastic bags, refrigerators, ball points and LP records. With the exception of LP records, which have been replaced by compact discs, we are still quite happy with—and dependent on—the other inventions. This is also the case with OD, which—despite all accusations about being outdated—still is a recognized method to carry out fairly fundamental changes in the life of organizations.

Nevertheless, there are clouds on the horizon, caused by the radical changes in our understanding of organizations as well as changes in the conditions under which organizations (in both the private and public sector) operate. This paper deals with four dilemmas, reflecting the clash between the traditional definition of OD and the actual circumstances, under which OD unfolds. The paper suggests, on the basis of this, a revised definition of OD.

DILEMMA NO. 1: OD IS GOAL-DIRECTED BEHAVIOR, BUT ORGANIZATIONAL GOALS ARE "MOVING TARGETS"

Traditionally, OD is defined as a rational, well-planned process of intervention, initiated by a carefully diagnosed point of departure and with clearly stated long-range goals.

The rationale for this is understandable. A collaborative diagnosis of strengths and weaknesses of the organization creates a (more or less) unanimous perception of the need for intervention as well as commitment to the change process. Also, clearly stated goals or objectives not only helps the development process to stay on track, but also facilitates a balanced consideration for organizational and individual goals.

As it is expressed by French & Bell:

Both organizations and individuals need to manage their affairs against goals—explicit, measurable, obtainable goals. To help achieve this for

Organization Development Journal, 25th Anniversary Issue, Volume 11, Number 2, Summer 1993.

the organization, OD interventions may be directed toward examination of the planning function, strategy-making processes, and goal-setting processes at the individual, group, and organizational levels. (1990, p. 91)

The goal-setting procedure does not involve just the top echelons of the organization. By involving the lower levels in setting goals, these goals become more realistic and likely to be achieved, as the commitment at all levels is likely to increase.

However, in a turbulent environment it is not easy to live up to the statement that "healthy organizations tend to have goal-setting at all levels" (Beckhard, 1969, p. 35). To push it to extremes, the question is whether some of the most thought-provoking and instructive examples of OD were lacking goals in the first place or had to redefine the goals radically in the course of the intervention process. An example illustrates this: A public agency with highly complicated technical and legal tasks initiated, in the mid 80's, an intensive OD process, involving the establishment of autonomous working groups with collective leadership. If a group decided to select a leader, it was welcome to do so, but the leader had to exert leadership according to principles of leadership ("code of conduct") laid down by the group. Alternatively, the group could exert the leadership function collectively.

Failures are an important stimulus (prerequisite?) for organizational renewal.

After approximately six years of fairly successful operation, the organization decided to start up a management development program. The objective of this was to intensify the democratization and collective responsibility of the organization. As the organization had only few formally appointed managers, the target group for this program was "anybody who wanted to and had the organization." Hence, the program actually had overlapping elements of management development, OD, personnel development and career planning.

Due to external circumstances not related to this program, a survey was done in the organization. As a surprise to most people, the results indicated that most major groups in the organization wanted to abandon the collective leadership, have appointed leaders, introduced a performance appraisal system for non-managerial staff and have formalized assessments of leadership competence of present (and future) managers. After a fairly short decision-making process, these changes were actually implemented. In a sense, the long tradition of democratization and employee involvement was replaced overnight by a much more traditional, hierarchical leadership philosophy.

This cognitive and emotional turnaround was definitely not anticipated, but had a dramatic impact on the organization. The case illustrates how risky it can be to restrict OD to interventions which correspond with predetermined goals. It might be more realistic to base the OD process on an expectation of "moving targets."

Usually, redefining goals is a result of an ongoing trial-and-error process with failures and unanticipated problems serving as catalysts for reassessing the current situation and redirecting the perception and behavior of the people involved. In other words, failures are an important stimulus (prerequisite?) for organizational renewal. Recent research (Sitkin, 1992; Wildavsky, 1988) has revealed that certain characteristics of failures can foster organizational learning and adaptation. Thus, Sitkin claims that "failure enhances adaptation to changing environmental conditions and systemic resilience to unknown future changes, both of which enhance long-term performance" (1992, p. 260). As OD is an organizational learning process, it is a serious shortcoming of most traditional definitions of OD that they do not incorporate the impact of constructive, "strategic" failure.

DILEMMA NO. 2: THE PRECONDITION OF RATIONALITY IN OD—IS IT REALISTIC?

Related to the issue of goal-directed behavior is the question whether OD interventions have to be well planned and rational. Certainly, much of the literature an OD claims this, and it is very much part of the "heritage" of the phenomenon. Thus, one of the pioneers, Richard Beckhard, defined OD as "planned interventions in the organization's processes using behavioral science knowledge" (1969, p. 9).

The perception of rationality is a frequent ingredient in the various phase models of OD interventions, like the one proposed by Harvey & Brown (1988, p. 43) which consists of the following stages:

- awareness of need for change

- entry and intervention

- development of a client/consultant relationship

- data collection intervention

- diagnosis of specific problems

- intervention with OD techniques

- monitor, review and stabilize

- termination of client/consultant relationship

A rational plan for the change process might be a good mental exercise from the outset—and a basis for negotiating the legal and psychological contract with the client—but is not necessarily a realistic picture of what is going to happen.

This flow is rather similar to models of rational decision-making theory, emphasizing the initial diagnosis of the problem, analysis of various alternative solutions, decision-making, implementation and evaluation. However, over the last decade or so these rational preconditions have been questioned to an increasing extent. One has become aware of the element of irrationality, subjectivity and symbolism in organizations. This is very much similar to what characterizes most OD interventions. A rational plan for the change process might be a good mental exercise from the outset—and a basis for negotiating the legal and psychological contract with the client—but is not necessarily a realistic picture of what is going to happen. A dramatic example illustrates this:

A medium-sized paint company was characterized by a very intensive, well-designed ongoing OD process. The catalyst for this was the very idealistic, humanistic and charismatic owner and CEO of the company. Despite his very powerful position, he was able to make room for a genuine involvement of managerial and non-managerial staff in this continuous development process. By accident, suddenly the entire plant burned down. In order to preserve (as much as possible) the market position, it was urgent to establish temporary production facilities as well as more permanent premises. In three weeks, the production was resumed, and a year later a brand new building with a very unusual lay-out was inaugurated. The physical layout was an authentic mirror of the culture of the organization. The building contained more or less just one hall, hosting the production, the administration, the top management team—even the canteen! There weren't separate entrances to the building for the production and the administration. In principle, there was only one door, for which all the employees had the key. In other words, the layout of the building was a mirror of the egalitarian culture, collaborative leadership style, etc., of this company. Thus, setting the company on its feet again and the design of the new plant in itself intensified the OD process.

Obviously, the fire was not a planned or even desired intervention strategy. Nevertheless, it served as such—even a very successful one. The example is very unusual, but any organization is regularly exposed to major changes which are not anticipated or taken into account, but which nevertheless serve as "OD boosters."

DILEMMA NO. 3: IN OD, WE FOCUS ON CHANGING BEHAVIORAL PATTERNS (THE HUMAN OR SOCIAL ENVIRONMENT), BUT FREQUENTLY SUCH CHANGES ARE BEST OBTAINED BY CHANGING *OTHER* SUBSYSTEMS.

It is a well-recognized fact that OD interventions often aim at improving the "human and social competence" of the organization. This is very understandable, as OD as a theoretical concept and a practical tool was invented at a time where the human factor in organizations was fairly neglected. Typically, there was a preoccupation with financial or technical resources, and human resources were mostly regarded as a means to an end. In other words, a cost factor which could and should be minimized. To establish a somewhat more balanced picture, the OD advocates had to push hard on the "OB accelerator."

Today, the situation is different, as more and more organizations are dependent on the human factor and see human resource development as a strategic investment in organizational survival. This is especially the case in knowledge-based and service oriented organizations. The production has got an immaterial nature, and the development and selling of these "products" requires an intensive use of high level human competence. This explains why not only functional expertise, but also personality characteristics become vital in any future-oriented organization. The personnel strategy is no longer merely a passive reflection of and an adjustment to the business strategy. On the contrary, the personnel strategy has got a proactive role and might in fact be the factor determining the business strategy rather than solely being the consequence of the strategy: "Our field of business (and corporate strategy) is the one within which we do have or can develop human competence and professionalism." Each line manager is given a visible, explicit, and unconditional responsibility for the motivation and development of the immediate subordinates.

What this means is that even though the objective of an OD intervention usually is to change to social and human environment, the method used might be of a different nature. Strategic interventions (in terms of new technology, new products, new markets, etc.) are often very effective "detours" in the attempt to change the human subsystem. "Detours" become "short cuts," as human resources are upgraded to a strategic factor and are directly affected by other strategic interventions. In this way, one can also short-circuit the resistance to invest time and money in OD efforts per se, which is quite often found in organizations. The OD results become a spin-off effect of (other) strategic moves.

In order for an OD intervention to be successful, it has to reflect—and contribute to—the synergy between human resources, the organizational characteristics and the technology.

In order for an OD intervention to be successful, it has to reflect—and contribute to—the synergy between human resources, the organizational characteristics and the technology.

DILEMMA NO. 4: WE FOCUS ON FORMALIZED TRAINING ACTIVITIES, ALTHOUGH MOST LEARNING OCCURS SPONTANEOUSLY AND INFORMALLY ON THE JOB

Traditionally, it is believed that the development of skills, knowledge and attitudes is best obtained by formalized training activities (educational programs and training courses). These are often physically isolated from the job environment and with clearly distinguished learner and teacher roles.

This fairly mechanistic and rational perspective of learning is in conflict with the still more widespread belief that learning is an informal, unsystematic and often unplanned process of an organic nature:

> Learning is rarely identified beforehand as an opportunity and, only slightly more frequently, identified afterwards as something that happened. (Mumford, 1982, p. 55)

Performing a job automatically exposes the person to a number of problems, choices and experiences. Acting in a specific situation, observing the consequences of this piece of action and receiving support or sanctions from the environment is a learning process.

This stronger emphasis on organic, experientially-based learning processes is in harmony with recent trends in the concept of organizations. Rather than being perceived as rational, formal and structurally-oriented entities, organizations are, to an increasing extent, perceived as organic, irrational, informal bodies, characterized by symbolic action, culture, values, ideologies and emotions. Even leadership has got a cultural "flavor": "Leaders create cultures, but cultures, in turn, create their next generation of leaders" (Schein, 1985, p. 313).

The line manager has a crucial role in providing the conditions for experiential learning processes within his or her part of the organization. The allocation of tasks to each individual subordinate is—indirectly—providing extensive or restricted learning potential. Job design is a clear-cut example of how a managerial decision determines not only what gets done by whom, but also **who learns what**. Special tasks, involvement in cross-organizational tasks, project teams or working parties as well as expatriation are all examples of potential learning situations.

DISCUSSION

The discussion in the previous sections opens up for a redefinition of the concept of OD. Hence, the question is whether it is more realistic to define OD as **any organic process** (not necessarily only intervention, which has a touch of conscious, external manipulation of a system) **which improves the survival capability** (problem-solving capacity, fitness, effectiveness, socio-technical interplay) of the organization. This development process can be called OD, regardless of whether this change process was deliberately initiated or "just" happened incidentally.

OD is a significant, lasting, deliberate or accidental, rational or irrational, change of the pattern of behavior of the members on an organization.

Along these lines, a coherent definition of OD looks like this:

OD is a significant, lasting, deliberate or accidental, rational or irrational, change of the pattern of behavior of the members on an organization. This process is often facilitated by formal training or experiential learning, resulting in change of the functional flexibility and culture of the organization. The change process is usually facilitated by diagnostic activities and involves a considerable number of key persons in the organization.

This definition takes into consideration the dilemmas mentioned above. However, there are other areas which represent important and challenging research needs for the future:

- OD is conceptually and operationally a very collective process, based on notions like common interests, shared beliefs, collective behavior, etc. How does one tackle the increasing individualism characterizing private and public organizations in these years? The organizational climate has become more competitive, with heavy emphasis on personal goals, achievement and visibility. The budget cut-downs and staff reductions found in many organizations in many countries tend to individualize organizational behavior. "If I don't show the surroundings how productive and competent I am, I might be one of the groups being sacked next month!"

- The concept of OD has been invented in the U.S., but seems to fit better with national cultural characteristics of other countries. Thus, Jaeger (1986), in his study of the underlying values of the OD concept, found that they were more compatible with Scandinavian national cultural values than those of the U.S.

- OD is quite often looked upon as being a generic concept, one whose basic ingredients are "undisturbed" by the actual nature of the society, the business community or even the organizational structure. However, due to the somewhat "whole" nature of the OD concept, it does, in fact, take color from situational factors. This is very evident when looking at the last decade, and the influence of concepts like organizational culture, management development and total quality management (TQM). When one is trying to implement organizational adaptation and learning programs, OD is frequently a Trojan horse in management development. Some TQM programs have OD as an invisible, inherent Trojan horse. The more we develop alternative methods of developing social systems, the more difficult it is to maintain OD as a generic concept.

Regularly, the question is raised whether OD is a fad. This question was raised 30, 20 and 10 years ago. Ironically, the longer we keep asking this question, the more OD becomes "the grey panther" of organizational behavior. Why not conclude that OD has come to stay and still has a tremendous impact on organizational adaptation, learning of flexibility?

However, it is increasingly difficult to distinguish OD from other organic change processes. The challenge for the future is to assess professionally where, how and how much OD can contribute to develop organizations—and where not to use OD because other methods are superior.

References

Beckhard, R. (1969). *Organization Development: Strategies and models.* Reading, MA: Addison-Wesley.

French, W. L., & Bell, C. H., Jr. (1990). *Organization development.* (4th ed.). Englewood Cliffs, NJ: Prentice-Hall.

Harvey, D. F., & Brown, D. R. (1988). *An experiential approach to organization development.* (3rd ed.). Englewood Cliffs, NJ: Prentice-Hall.

Jaeger, A. (1986). Organizational development and national culture: Where's the fit? *Academy of Management Review, 11,* 178–90.

Mumford, A. C. (1982). Learning style and learning skills. *Journal of Management Development, 1,* 2.

Schein, E. H. (1985). *Organizational culture and leadership.* San Francisco, CA: Jossey-Bass.

Sitkin, S. B. (1992). Learning through failure: The strategy of small losses. In B. M. Staw & L. L. Cummings (Eds.). *Research in Organizational Behavior*, 14, 23–266. Greenwich, CT: JAI Press.

Wildavsky, A. (1988). *Searching for safety*. New Brunswick, NJ: Transaction Books.

OBSERVATIONS ON THE FIELD OF ORGANIZATIONAL CHANGE AND DEVELOPMENT FROM THE LUNATIC FRINGE

Richard W. Woodman, Department of Management, Texas A & M University, College Station, TX 77843

I am delighted to have this opportunity to offer my observations on the field of OD. I'm particularly pleased because (1) as a card-carrying member of the "lunatic fringe," I don't often communicate directly with the mainstream of OD, and (2) it's fun to write something without having to look up a bunch of references. (I am grateful to the editors for relieving me of the burden of identifying people who agree with me. That could be a difficult task.)

Before venturing on, a few comments about the paranoiac title for this article. Within some academic circles, serious scholarship and OD have sometimes been considered mutually contradictory labels. Curiously, being an outcast from some portions of the organizational science arena has not necessarily meant a wider acceptance by the practitioner community for the OD scholar/researcher. Putting these observations together, I define the lunatic fringe of the change and development field as consisting (largely) of people who research more than they consult, write more than they speak, and are more often found teaching university students than conducting industry workshops or executive development programs. On the other hand, and unlike some of their academic colleagues, OD scholars have not forgotten that theirs is an *applied* behavioral science. It is from this twilight world on the lunatic fringe of OD—a world too practical for the scientist, too scientific for the practitioner—that the following observations come.

OBSERVATION #1: THERE IS A MAJOR SCHISM BETWEEN THE PRACTITIONER AND ACADEMIC WORLDS OF OD

This dilemma is not unique to the organizational change and development field. To a certain extent the business school in general suffers from a similar schism, as do other applied areas such as industrial/organizational psychology. It does seem, however, that the OD profession epitomizes the tensions that arise when a field is both an applied behavioral science and a field of managerial action. This observation is hardly new. (If I were using references there would be a lot of them here.) Still, the schism is so crucial that it deserves repeated attention.

Organization Development Journal, 25th Anniversary Issue, Volume 11, Number 2, Summer 1993.

Elsewhere I have written that the schism between the science of organizational change and the art of changing organizations represents the single greatest impediment to progress in OD. The dangers of failing to address the schism are very real. Isolated from their science, OD practitioners might find themselves increasingly out-of-date as knowledge of human behavior in complex social settings continues to grow. Isolated from the application of this knowledge, OD researchers might find themselves addressing organizational issues less and less relevant for the design and management of real organizations. It is difficult to see how either the science or the action side of the field could benefit from such isolation.

The schism between the science of organizational change and the art of changing organizations represents the single greatest impediment to progress in OD.

It is hard to make suggestions here without sounding simplistic. Clearly, we need more bridges between our applied and academic sides. It would be quite useful if more change programs involved a research or evaluation component and if these results were more widely shared. Equally valuable, more academics need to get their hands dirty by actually trying to change organizations. Perhaps more members of the OD Institute should be active in the organization development and change division of the Academy of Management. Perhaps more Academy members should join the OD Institute. And so on.

OBSERVATION #2: MANY OF US TALK BIG OD
BUT PRACTICE SMALL OD

BIG OD is what the founders of the field thought they were doing. BIG OD involves second-order transformations of organizational strategy, structure, and culture (however, see observation #4 below). BIG OD is system-wide change. BIG OD has no beginning and no end—it is a way of managing complex organizations so that they are able to survive in a world of constant change. Small od is a variety of techniques and interventions, often done in isolation, having no congruent linkage with the strategy and goals of the firm. Small od is counting how many workshops we did last year. Small od is what the detractors of the field think OD is.

For a portion of our history, the field lost its way (pardon the anthropomorphic imagery). Our energies got lured away into doing micro-interventions where the activities became ends in themselves. Our objective as OD professionals should be to do BIG OD. "Stamp out small od" should be our battle cry. Every intervention, every change effort, needs to be harnessed to a vision of what the organization needs to be doing.

OBSERVATION #3: ORGANIZATIONS MUST BE
CHANGED SYSTEMICALLY

This is a corollary to observation number two. It is not possible, really, to engage in meaningful organizational change in a piece-meal fashion. We can make the inhabitants momentarily more comfortable. We can even do a few things to make more money for awhile. But, to move a system toward greater *sustained* effectiveness requires congruent changes in management practices, organizational group structures, participation levels, commitment levels, reward systems, the design of work, and on and on. Almost everyone seems to know this—academic types teach it, OD consultants certainly know it in their hearts, even some managers know this.

With this knowledge so widely shared, why doesn't anybody do it? The answer is because it's damn difficult and results tend not to be immediately obvious. It is probably not fair to say that no one is engaging in systemic, system-wide change. However, for each effort that is truly system-wide or transformational, there are many-fold more that just piddle around the edges of organizational problems. I do not have any great insight as to why this occurs. However, I suspect that the conventional criticism that American managers (and by extension, people like myself who teach future American managers) are entirely too short-run profit-oriented at the expense of long-range developmental strategies is probably not too far off the mark. The solution, of course, is not to be that way. Good luck.

OBSERVATION #4: ORGANIZATIONAL CULTURE CONTINUES
TO BE ONE OF THE HOTTEST CONSTRUCTS IN TOWN

Never one to pass on a good fad, American management has leapt eagerly on the culture bandwagon and the desire to assess their organization's culture is feverish. However, a lot of what passes for "cultural audits" is simply 1930's attitude surveys, or 1970's survey feedback dressed up in new clothes. This statement is not necessarily intended as a criticism. Knowing who we are and what we believe in seems a valuable precursor for organizational change. Research issues aside, the greatest value of the culture construct is to provide some terminology that captures people's imaginations and calls attention to their commonalities. Culture is the basis for the shared vision that drives effective organizational behavior.

Knowing who we are and what we believe in seems a valuable precursor for organizational change.

On the other hand, the greatest weakness of this term is the temptation to make it a change target. Peter Drucker says that organizational cultures cannot be changed. He is wrong. However, it takes an incredibly long time. (An exception is perhaps the circumstance when there is massive turnover in personnel within a very short period of time.) Cultural change typically takes so long, in fact, that for all practical purposes Dr. Drucker is right. Sometimes, when the most effective remedy would seem to be a major transformation in culture, management might be well advised to close the business down and start over.

My belief is that the most effective use of the culture construct occurs when we restrict our focus on it to the earliest diagnostic phases of an improvement program. Then, the discovery and sharing of the culture can provide a framework for discussion as the action focus shifts to changing jobs, behaviors, rewards, and so on.

OBSERVATION #5: PROCESS INTERVENTIONS ARE OF VALUE, BUT THEY ARE THE MEAN, NOT THE END RESULT, WHEREBY ORGANIZATIONS BECOME MORE EFFECTIVE

Recent surveys of both the Fortune 500 Industrials and the Fortune 500 Service firms indicate that process interventions (such as team building, survey feedback, process consultation, conflict resolution workshops, and so on) continue to be a large part of the activities engaged in by internal OD professionals.

Traditionally, a major expertise that OD change agents bring to the table is their process skills. In a very real sense, these process skills provide much of the OD consultant's competitive advantage. We don't want to lose this—it is important and will always be of great value. However, process-based change efforts must be utilized in the service of system-wide change. Process interventions serve the sociotechnical—the blending and balancing of social and technical aspects of the system. These interventions are way-stations, not the destination. For example, the goal of the organization is not to have effective teams; rather, effective teams are needed in order for the organization to attain its goals. This distinction is subtle, but crucial, for effective change agentry.

OBSERVATION #6: I HAVE SEEN THE FUTURE AND IT IS ALPHABETIZED

TQM.CIP.HP-HC worksystems. This is the current language of system-wide change. Bizarre as it seems to some of us, one can actually find people who believe that these improvement strategies have nothing to do with OD. Somewhere along the line we lost the squirrel on this one—OD ought to own these terms, since they embody what the field has always been about. In the earliest writings of the field, one discovers that OD was intended to be a way of managing complex social systems faced with the reality of constant change. The focus of OD efforts was never intended to be short-term problem solving or incremental change. Nor was changing individual and group behavior considered an end in itself. Rather, Organization Development meant (and still means) creating adaptive organizations capable of repeatedly transforming and reinventing themselves as needed to remain effective.

Certainly one thing that separates OD approaches from other perspectives on organizational change is the field's dual focus on organizational effectiveness and human fulfillment through the work experience. Rather that dismissing the human fulfillment goal as 1960s idealism that is out of place in 1993, the total quality management movement, continuous improvement philosophies, and high performance-high commitment work systems have all reaffirmed the central role of committed human actors in organizational performance. In addition, these approaches have refocused managerial attention on the importance of groups and teamwork within the organization. With the popularity of these system-wide improvement and effectiveness strategies, the field of OD has come full circle and returned to its roots. So, be proud of what you do. OD had it right all along.

OBSERVATION #7: [CONCERNING] SOME COMMENTS ON THE FUTURE OF THE ORGANIZATIONAL CHANGE AND DEVELOPMENT FIELD

. . . There was no 'one, two, three, and away,' but they began running when they liked, and left off when they liked, so that it was not easy to know when the race was over. However, when they had been running half an hour or so, and were quite dry again, the Dodo suddenly called out, 'The race is over!' and they all crowded round it, panting, and asking, 'But who has won?'
—Lewis Carroll, Alice's Adventures in Wonderland

Organization Development means (and still means) creating adaptive organizations capable of repeatedly transforming and reinventing themselves as needed to remain effective.

How will we know if we have won the hearts and minds of management? Theories of organizational change and ideas and approaches for changing organizations exist in a competitive arena. Which perspectives and ideas will last is determined quite simply. Over time, theories that provide insight and approaches that work will continue to be used; ideas and theories that fail this market test will be discarded. So—what is the future of OD?

My answer to this question is decidedly upbeat. My view of the effectiveness of North American organizations is quite the opposite. These two observations are directly related. They can call it anything they want, but organizations need OD, or at least, they need something much like it.

There are a number of "core" issues in organizing human endeavors; examples include organizational structure and role differentiation, participation and commitment, work process and system design, resource and reward allocation, and the like. These issues are so fundamental to effective organization that all social systems must come to grips with them. Complex social systems are, by definition, characterized by constant change. As such, we can regard the management of organizational change as a core issue of organizing.

Problems associated with the core issues of organizing have a nasty habit of not remaining solved. We find that organizations must repeatedly readdress problems associated with these core issues. A fundamental premise underlying my assessment of the future of OD is that effectively managing change is a core issue that organizations must continually resolve. It is my belief that the change approaches and philosophies that comprise the field of OD offer organizations a way of managing change that is robust across time and settings.

In short, for an organization to function effectively, the processes and dynamics of organizational change must be understood and managed. The field of organizational change and development provides managers, change agents, and organizational scientists with a framework for inquiry into these dynamics and a framework for action to manage them.

To avoid sounding completely Pollyannaish, let me, however, offer some cautionary comments as well. The above observations are based on *potential* fit between organizational needs and OD contributions, given the tremendous challenges currently facing our organizations. In order to maximize this potential fit, many issues need to be addressed. For example, the dual nature of the field, while potentially a source of strength, seems problematic currently. Our science and action sides could benefit greatly from wider use of change management teams comprised of both OD practitioners and researchers. Our science and action sides could benefit even more from finding ways to talk to each other on a regular basis.

System-wide change—BIG OD—is where the action is. In my opinion, OD has been broadening its focus considerably from the micro to the macro, from a focus on process to a greater focus on structure and strategy, from a focus exclusively at the individual and group level to a focus which encompasses the organization as a system. This trend must continue if OD is to meet the challenges of the future. To the extent that OD fails to become more systemic and fails to like appropriately with firm strategy, it will, as some critics currently contend, become increasingly irrelevant to the world of organizational change.

I would like to thank Lynda Kilbourne and Gary McMahan for helpful comments on this article.

MBO: AN ADVANCED MANAGEMENT TECHNIQUE

Richard Babcock

The management by objectives technique can serve as a powerful tool for structuring an effective and efficient system of control (and planning, of course) within an enterprise environment. But MBO is not a cure-all for all enterprises—it is only one of the alternative techniques for achieving organizational change and improvement. The purpose of this article is to clarify the dynamics of MBO (how and why it works), to compare the feasibility of choosing MBO as compared with alternate change agents and management programs, and to set down some generalizations about the MBO process.

The conclusions and generalizations reported in this summary article are drawn primarily from a research study by this author reported elsewhere[1] and secondarily on his observation of other successful and unsuccessful MBO programs and published reports of MBO. Using questionnaire, interview, observation, and record analysis techniques, divergent MBO programs were studied in 3 companies, these firms being referenced by their respective industries. One large national firm (labeled the utility firm for purposes of identification) had an operational MBO program for over fifteen years; another large firm (referred to as the aerospace firm) had just completed its first year of MBO at the beginning of the study. The third company (called the consumer firm) was regional in scope and had 3½ years experience with its version of the MBO technique.

The Nature and Dynamics of MBO

The clarification of the dynamics and the fundamental nature of the MBO concept is the first task at hand. MBO is a technique for implementing control and planning which can take on different formats but which basically falls within the parameters of the following definition: A management program that systematically establishes verifiable unit and/or manager objectives in either a quantitative or qualitative sense, including both budgetary and non-budgetary goals, and appraises performance against these goals.

MBO is more than an advanced budgetary control system. If MBO merely formalizes budgets and assesses whether subordinate managers stay within the

---

[1]See R. Babcock, "An Analysis of Management by Objectives in Different Enterprise Environments." (Unpublished Ph.D. dissertation, University of California, Los Angeles, 1970.)

constraints of their budgets, the purpose of MBO is missed. Managers must perform activities not directly related to budgets, and a measure of whether a firm has really implemented MBO is the percentage of non-budgetary goals in a network of derivative subunit and manager objectives.

MBO is also more than the substitution of results appraisals for the more traditional trait appraisal systems. Because development of the MBO concept has taken the results-appraisals path and because there may be a natural bias to think of MBO only in its comprehensive format, MBO is usually seen as revolving around a joint goal-setting and appraisal process, and thereby around the superior-subordinate relationship. The results of the author's study on which this summary report is based demonstrate that the basic change of the MBO process is the development of legitimate and meaningful objectives. Letting the manager participate in the setting of these goals is only one way of making them legitimate or meaningful (see the following paragraphs).

As MBO acts by working directly on the job of the individual manager, the basic change associated with MBO is an alteration in the feelings, conscious and possibly unconscious, of the manager about his job. By prescribing the legitimate and meaningful areas, as defined by his individual or unit objectives, within which the manager is allowed to operate, the manager is freed to concentrate on finding methods of improving activities within these predetermined boundaries, and he is freed from worrying about activities outside these boundaries. The job of the manager has stabilized, being fixed by the end points prescribed by his objectives, and the manager does not have to be concerned about arbitrary changes. Changes, or a movement to a new equilibrium, are signaled by the rewriting of a manager's objectives, and this is a process that each manager must be involved in.

Thus created is a stability in his role (managerial role stability), a psychological state which induces an increased propensity of attacking directly the activities prescribed by his objectives. Consequently, through acquiring managerial role stability, the manager is given a positive impetus to make more focused, clear-cut decisions; to more aggressively coordinate his activities with other personnel; and to introduce changes, new methods and programs, and innovations when warranted. He does so to achieve his prescribed, written objectives.

As such, MBO is a formalized change agent that both limits and adds to a manager's freedom. By prescribing the legitimate areas, as defined by his individual or unit objectives, within which the manager is allowed to operate, the manager is freed to concentrate on finding methods of improving activities within these predetermined boundaries, and he is freed from worrying about activities outside these boundaries. MBO does not give the manager an unlimited amount of freedom, but rather MBO increases his effective freedom to act within predetermined dimensions. As such, MBO channels this freedom without its degenerating into random behavior. A successful MBO program avoids the danger of participation for the sake of participation. It focuses behavior in the direction of predetermined ends.

Common to all MBO approaches, or, to be more exact, all successful MBO programs, is a change process or a restructuring of the distribution of influence, which sometimes includes a redistribution of formal authority, within the enterprise. The change may be in the way formal authority is dispersed throughout the levels in an enterprise hierarchy, as in a comprehensive application of MBO, or in the way superiors and subordinates relate to each other, as in a results-oriented appraisal approach. The change may be obvious in a participative program or subtle in a non-participative format. In a participative program, the subordinate manager has an input in the determination of his or his unit's objectives, so the restructuring of the influence process is direct. In a non-participative program, the specification of derivative objectives mean that the subordinate manager has been delegated the authority to achieve these derivative objectives and has the incentive to act to achieve prescribed defined end points. The change is subtle but just as real.

Manager participation in goal setting, while certainly important, may well have been overemphasized in the MBO literature. The manager or subunit goals also will become meaningful and legitimate if they are related to enterprise objectives, if they are set as fair and achievable levels, if they are verifiable, if managers are rewarded for achieving these goals, if there is an indication of the more important goals, and if top and superior managers give continuing evidence of the importance of these goals. Therefore, giving the subordinate manager an input in the determination of goals is only one of many possible ways of bringing about the fundamental change of a successful MBO program. A manager can feel differently about his job, without actively participating or interacting with his superior in shaping his goals, as long as he sees that these goals are meaningful and legitimate. For example, in the utility firm managerial role stability was achieved without a corresponding improvement in superior-subordinate relationships; in other words, this fundamental change did not take place through the superior interacting with his subordinate.

In fact, in both aerospace and utility firms, MBO acted as a substitute for a subordinate's reliance on his superior—and the subordinate manager gained some of his role stability not from relying on his superior but from having a legitimate and meaningful set of goals. Of course, in the more participative aerospace firm MBO program, the subordinate manager has to interact closely with his superior in the establishment of these goals, but, once set, the dependency relationship was significantly reduced. Consequently, the subordinate manager was more self-reliant and confident in his role.

Of course, to gain the full potential of MBO, the superior must take an active part in the process—especially in regard to establishing qualitative verifiable goals and assessing the achievement of these goals. But it certainly is possible for a firm to derive tangible benefits from MBO without superiors in conjunction with their subordinate taking an active part in bringing about the improvements. Such a case was demonstrated by the utility firm where the emphasis was on handed down quantitative, statistical goals. The conclusion is that managers can gain role stability without materially affecting the interaction process and the relationships between superiors and subordinates.

MBO and Alternative Change Agents: A Comparison

MBO in its comprehensive format can be viewed as just one of the alternative strategies for introducing increased participation, or more freedom, for subordinate managers within the firm. Other strategies include Likert's System 4, Argyris' reality-centered leadership, McGregor's Theory Y, and the emphasis on the group as evidenced by these and other authors.[2]

As a strategy for change, MBO appears to have some advantages over other approaches. The fundamental concept is easy to understand and intuitively appealing, so the initial reaction of subordinate managers to MBO is likely to be positive. The philosophy of MBO can be taught—the majority of the aerospace firm managers were initially enthusiastic about MBO and almost all were willing to give it a chance during the initial training session.

MBO is an active change agent. It relates directly to and involves a restructuring of the manager's job. Consequently, managers with positive reactions to MBO can see a direct and connected payoff from MBO.

The concept of MBO also has serious disadvantages, as compared to the other comprehensive change strategies. There is a continuing discipline associated with an MBO program, especially one of a comprehensive nature, as derivative goals must be rewritten and often adjusted in response to changing or new conditions; progress toward achieving these goals must be monitored; and achievement of derivative goals must be verified. This includes the sometimes difficult tasks of assessing qualitative goals and maintaining a lateral consistency among objectives. A continuing commitment by superior and subordinate managers to MBO is needed

---

[2]See R. Likert, *The Human Organization.* (New York: McGraw-Hill Book Co., Inc., 1967), C. Argyris, *Integrating the Individual and the Organization.* (New York: John Wiley & Sons, Inc., 1964), and D. McGregor, *The Human Side of Enterprise.* (New York: McGraw-Hill Book Co., Inc., 1960).

if a program is to remain viable. Managers need to remain diligent and attentive to the paperwork burden and procedural requirements of MBO. It should be remembered that MBO is a net addition to the manager's job.

Other change strategies are more general in makeup, relying on the manager to implement the specifics, and using the elements of MBO could be one way of implementing these strategies. In the case of Likert's linking pin committees, which is a part of his System 4, a discipline also is involved, but the requirements of setting up and maintaining overlapping committees throughout the levels in an enterprise are certainly less demanding than the requirements of a comprehensive, participative MBO program. The change agents attempt to change attitudes more directly and consequently avoid the direct and continuing discipline implied by MBO.

MBO also is a surer route to the improvement of enterprise efficiency and performance than a firm can obtain by using more limited techniques and methods, provided that top and superior managers make a continuing commitment to the program. For example, a firm might choose to utilize such limited techniques as sensitivity training, company training programs, university tuition refund programs, or executive development programs rather than MBO. These programs involve off-site or off-the-job training and may not relate directly to the work environment. Because MBO works directly on the manager's job, and the MBO process induces the manager to change his job attitudes, decision making processes, and interactions with other personnel, there is a direct link between the success of an MBO program and improvement in enterprise performance. For example, in the case studies of three successful MBO programs reported in this author's background study, there were improvements in manager attitudes and decision making, organizational processes, and enterprise performance. Another company program can itself be successful but this success may still not be transferred to the enterprise. Of course, MBO should not be viewed as a total substitute for other company programs but rather should prove valuable when used in conjunction with other management systems. MBO can be combined or integrated, given proper planning, with other company programs.

MBO Implementation: Impressions

Based on the author's research effects, it becomes possible to make some generalizations about the process of MBO implementation. The first is that an MBO program can have an almost immediately favorable effect on enterprise effectiveness and efficiency, provided that the implementation process is preceded by careful planning. Projecting from the aerospace firm data, the basic change of providing subordinate managers with role stability transpired in the first year of the program; this means that the manager is able to make more rational decisions almost from the beginning of the MBO program. During the latter part of the first year, the aerospace firm managers began to coordinate their tasks more closely with managers at different organizational levels and with managers in lateral functional subunits. In addition, many managers who did not change their methods and ways of interacting now for the first time saw the need or importance of doing so. In the consumer firm, improvements also dated from the first year of the program. Thus, the projection can be made that important improvements in the coordination of enterprise purpose can be made in the first year and significant changes as early as the second year of an MBO program. To contrast this projection with other predictions of the amount of time involved in introducing change, Likert[3] projects up to nine years for a firm to adopt his System 4 in order to reap the full benefits. Howell[4] and Wickstrom[5] predict that MBO will take up to five years to be effective and to complete the process of implementation. The projection set forth here, based on data from this study, is much more optimistic.

Second, the MBO technique is a durable and continuing way of assuring organization effectiveness and efficiency, assuming continued attention is paid to its implementation and administration and provided the environment remains favorable. The example of the utility firm MBO program, which has remained a viable management system for over fifteen years, is direct evidence of durability of the concept, especially with the continuing support and attention of top and superior managers—which certainly is one of the critical factors in the continuing success of MBO. The consumer firm MBO program also adds evidence to the durability of the concept. A relatively mature 3½-year-old MBO program continued to be successful in improving enterprise performance, provided that top and superior managers maintained their support of the program and in spite of the paperwork burden it generated for subordinate regional managers. Managers in both these firms remained favorably disposed toward MBO even though they disagreed with the administration of the respective programs. The aging process, which Tosi and Carroll[6] refer to in their observation of one MBO program, more properly should be referred to as a laxness on the part of top and superior managers. Assuming that there is the continuing existence of sound management, the background research for

---

[3]Likert, *The Human Organization.*

[4]R. Howell, "Managing by Objectives," *Business Horizons,* Vol. 13, No. 1, pp. 41–46 (February, 1970).

[5]W. Wickstrom, *Managing by—and with—Objectives.* (New York: National Industrial Conference Board, Inc., 1968).

[6]H. Tosi and J. Carroll, "Management Reaction to Management by Objectives," *Academy of Management Journal,* Vol. 11, No. 4, pp. 415–426 (December, 1968).

this paper does not support the thesis that there is an aging process in an MBO program. On the contrary, the more logical and proper conclusion is that MBO is an agent, when used properly and especially in its more comprehensive form, that will insure organizational renewal and continued vitality.

MBO also has virtually untapped potential for improving the relationships, interactions, and communications among managers in lateral functional areas. By building interlocking and/or group goals and a visible network of goals (i.e., known goals) into the design of an MBO program, MBO can expand the horizons of subordinate managers beyond their narrowly defined areas of specialization. Managers with interlocking and/or group objectives are dependent on one another for goal achievement, and cooperation among them is given a positive impetus. If managers know the content or the result areas in which other men have set objectives, cooperation is given yet another push. Referring to the author's research, managers who had these goals saw it was to their advantage to cooperate actively with other managers and personnel and did so automatically. Managers without such goals did not. The implications are great indeed, especially for government enterprises or agencies or for non-competitive industries, where goals do not need to be concealed because of competitive pressures or reasons.

MBO Implementation: Guidelines

The findings of the author's research provide some guidelines for firms implementing MBO programs. It appears that an interrelated network of goals and manager participation in goal setting are counterbalancing factors. That is, managers are willing to forego participation in setting goals if they perceive their objectives as being closely related to higher order enterprise objectives. Likewise, if managers have a hand in setting their own goals, they will accept a wide discrepancy between their goals and enterprise objectives—and function effectively. In the aerospace firm, where derivative manager goals were sometimes not closely integrated with enterprise objectives, the bulk of such managers still performed effectively and at higher levels under MBO, provided they felt free to influence the content of their own goals. Utility and consumer firm managers functioned well without participating actively in the goal setting process, given that their goals were clearly related to enterprise objectives. In the absence of both conditions, managers from all firms performed poorly.

A participative program is more essential for the success of MBO when a firm faces a dynamic and changing exterior environment—in such an environment it is difficult to structure an internally interrelated and consistent network of derivative goals. A firm in a stable environment could more easily choose to forego participation and still maintain a successful MBO program. Forces in the exterior firm environment influence the internal goal setting process.

Another implication, drawn from the experience of the aerospace firm, is that the first year of an MBO program is too soon to attempt to structure a highly integrated and consistent network of derivative objectives. The vertical integration of derivative goals among organizational levels represents a major accomplishment: adding the task of horizontal integration and adjusting the derivative goals among lateral subunits makes the process too cumbersome and time consuming for managers just learning the process and philosophy of MBO. By living with inconsistent goals, the subordinate managers learn the need for the horizontal consistency in the network of objectives. The very fact that managers start to see some inconsistencies in the goals of managers in lateral subunits is positive impetus for the horizontal integration of goals in the second year of the program.

The practice of MBO in the respective firms in the author's background study evidenced some deficiencies which reduced the potential benefits of their programs. These weaknesses are pointed out as possible pitfalls that should be watched in introducing MBO.

1. The weaknesses of the utility firm in not emphasizing verifiable qualitative goals. Besides limiting the potential of managerial role stability of subordinate managers within the firm, the main effect was in curtailing the development of healthy superior-subordinate relations. Interestingly enough, in some districts where managers are starting to develop qualitative goals, which are super-imposed on the standardized company-wide MBO program, the early results in facilitating an improvement in superior-subordinate relationships are quite promising.

    There were two factors which partly compensated for this shortcoming in the utility firm MBO program. Therefore, the utility firm MBO program did not become a numbers game, as Raia[7] found in his follow-up study. The reasons seem to lie (a) in the care that goes into devising and continually reviewing the standards that measure goal achievement and (b) in the relatively stable environment and the basic unchanging nature of the firm's product.

2. The weakness of the utility firm in using national standards to evaluate performance. The main effect here was the encouragement among subordinate managers of a feeling that their goals were not related to enterprise objectives and thereby a reduction of the validity they attached to some tasks in their jobs. Regional differences made the national standards invalid for validating performance in each of the regional areas.

---

[7]T. Raia, "A Second Look at Goals and Controls," *California Management Review,* Vol. 9, No. 2, pp. 49–58 (Summer, 1966).

3. The weakness of the consumer firm in paying on one or two goals and leading people through the motions on others. In other words, the payoff in monetary terms was in achieving the sales and new-customers objectives—not in achieving the qualitative goals. This practice was a major factor in the failure to develop qualitative goals at the lower organizational levels and for an increasing difficulty of administering the MBO program.

4. The weakness of the aerospace firm in not initially making sure subordinate managers understood the nature and philosophy of MBO. This factor is emphasized because even though the results of the aerospace MBO program were impressive, the full potential of the program was not realized because of a failure of top and superior managers to communicate the importance of the program to subordinate managers. An important contributing factor was the overselling of MBO by the consultants who assisted in implementing the program. Their attitude was contrary to the top and superior managers' downward communication about the importance and implications of MBO. This aerospace firm experience shows that it is critically important that top and superior managers make every effort to demonstrate their support for the MBO program.

The major consideration in MBO implementation is to make sure that the managers in the program have legitimate and meaningful sets of goals, for themselves or their organizational units. MBO is the type of program which requires diligent and constant attention to insure its continued success and vitality.

MBO: An Overview

By implementing an MBO program, a firm can expect to derive predictable improvements in several critical areas which are at the heart of organized effort and successful enterprise. By introducing an MBO program, as the managers acquire legitimate goals and role stability, the firm can expect (a) improved managerial decision making; (b) better communication of enterprise goals, policies, and procedures; (c) a more meaningful information system; and (d) healthier and more supportive informal communication channels. A firm can also expect (a) a greater assurance that managers will not neglect some aspects of their jobs as these men now have specific goals in more performance areas, (b) the building-in of an organized way of promoting change and innovation within the firm if managers write and achieve innovative goals, and (c) increased communication and coordination among personnel at different organizational levels and in lateral subunits if managers establish and work to achieve interlocking and group goals (especially if such goals are known).

MBO is a method of operationalizing a comprehensive control (and planning) system in an enterprise. For those firms able to manipulate the environment and to build certain factors into the process of implementing MBO, predictable benefits can be derived from an MBO process. These benefits will vary according to the format of MBO that is chosen. A successful MBO program has the potential of affecting the job of the manager, change and innovation in the firm, and the processes of communication and coordination.

INTRODUCTION TO SEARCH CONFERENCE METHODOLOGY FOR PRACTITIONERS

Oguz N. Baburoglu
Clarkson University

and

Andy Garr
Georgia State Senate

Abstract

A macro-rationale for a participative planning and design methodology called "The Search Conference" is provided. This rationale is rooted in adaptation principles to turbulent environments. The adaptation principles covered are flexibility, social responsibility, innovation, and participation. The second half of the paper describes the search conference event and process in detail. A list of helpful decision guides for managing the conference is provided in the conclusion.

Overview

The search conference is a methodology of participatory planning introduced by the Australian systems thinker Fred Emery (Emery and Emery, 1978) that has been applied in the U.S.A., Canada, Mexico, U.K., Norway, India, Sweden, and Turkey for a wide range of purposes. Among situations where the authors were involved, the methodology has been used by large and small businesses to compose a mission statement and to formulate competitive strategy, by the executive and legislative branches of State Government to formulate state policies in various issue areas and to design structures to implement the policies, by governments to rethink national strategies, by social service agencies and grass roots organizations to reconfigure the focus of their organization and to improve the quality of their work lives, and by universities to manage the long range planning process.

The Search Conference is a structured process whereby groups can search future possibilities to select the future they want and design strategies for achieving it. The "search" is for an achievable future. This may be a future that is more desirable than the one which is likely to unfold if no action is taken, or a future that is totally unexpected. The group approach unleashes a creative way of producing organizational philosophy, mission, goals, and objectives enriched by shared values and beliefs of the participants.

Furthermore, the emphasis of the participation is on face-to-face interaction and the positive oriented socio-dynamics that it produces.

The Search Conference Event

The 35–40 participants over two or three days collectively design the organization's most desired future and formulate creative strategies to bring that future about. The process moves from the most general to the most specific within an agreed upon "conference task." The conference task is basically the purpose for which the stakeholders are brought together and a broad guideline for the duration of the conference. The activities in the diagram below represent one such guideline. Every question about the conference task must be discussed in detail and any necessary changes must be introduced in the schedule of activities. The significance of negotiation and mutual agreement regarding the conference task becomes more pertinent when the group enters into a regressive period in the course of the process.

Upon the completion of the conference task, the results are distributed to the extended stakeholders and a follow-up mechanism is designed based on the action plans. Special action implementation groups are formed at the end of the two or three days and at an agreed upon time. It is also beneficial to bring the entire group together to compare the progress made on the implementation of the action plans.

The search conference is staffed by at least two facilitators who are expected to have group process skills and who have been trained in an apprenticeship position by more experienced search conference facilitators. The facilitators must be especially sensitive to recognize group emotional states (Bion, 1961) in order to help the group to self-manage getting in and out of these emotional states such as dependency, fight-flight, or pairing. Having two facilitators is very helpful in discussing the observations of the group dynamics that each facilitator has in order to diagnose the group emotional state and to intervene in ways that continue to empower the group. The other major benefit of having two facilitators is to assure equal attention to both process and content. The facilitators can alternate the responsibility for monitoring process and content.

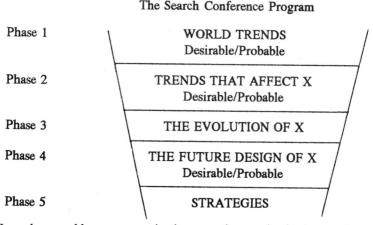

The Search Conference Program

Phase 1	WORLD TRENDS Desirable/Probable
Phase 2	TRENDS THAT AFFECT X Desirable/Probable
Phase 3	THE EVOLUTION OF X
Phase 4	THE FUTURE DESIGN OF X Desirable/Probable
Phase 5	STRATEGIES

X can be a problem, an organization, a nation, an institution, an inter-organizational system.

X is the system that comes into organizational existence during the search conference. The stakeholders who individually would be engaged in a planning or a problem-solving effort in their individual departments or organizations can now plan in the most relevant context. This context is constructed by intra- and extra-system stakeholders—that is by the organization and its environment. Therefore, the planning or the problem-solving effort is always context-full.

Phase 1:

The process starts with a scan of what's happening in the world surrounding the participants. This phase is best introduced to the participants using a metaphor such as "waves washing over you," to indicate that the observed trends are like waves which originate somewhere before one is washed over and do continue onwards to another point past the point of encounter or merge into other waves.

The brainstorming mode of operation of the group suspends judgement and evaluation by any member and allows for conflictual observations to be expressed. The emphasis is not on spontaneous appraisal of what has been offered but on spontaneous sharing of mutual perceptions. As the first activity, the scanning of the environment sets the tone of the conference. This kind of a start demonstrates to the participants that their ideas will be registered without discrimination stemming from status or affiliation. An atmosphere of trust can thus be built which yields a deeper and non-superficial search of the trends in the environment.

All inputs are recorded on a flip chart and hung on the walls of the room. This simple technology assists in the symbolic representation of the shared world of the participants. They can see that their perception is legitimately a part of the whole group. The entire group embarks on this part of the activity and it is recommended that this activity be scheduled in an evening when the participants are in a more reflective mood. Furthermore, this phase is by far the least demanding activity and hence is much easier to facilitate since most people are affected in some way or another by the environment they live in.

Upon the completion of the scanning activity and endowed with a shared appreciation of the contextual nature of the broadest possible environments, the participants are now ready to appraise the trends. The participants are divided into four groups, each expected to elect their own recorder and presenter. The groups sort the trends out into desirable and probable trends. The desirable trends are those trends that they wish to see continue and want to support from a policy standpoint. The probable trends are the ones that will extend into the future regardless of whether they are desirable or not. As such, the groups place a value on the trends and inevitably bring national, regional or organizational assumptions into their judgements. The scenarios of the small groups are then presented to the large group and the most pressing common themes are combined to compose the large group's most desirable and most probable scenarios of the future.

The first phase therefore accomplishes: 1. The creation of shared context, 2. The expression of values on the context, and 3. The realization of collective action and decision making as a group.

Phase 2:

The conference works in the same manner in the second phase. Through a brainstorming exercise the group generates the trends that are washing this time over the focal system—X. The group then moves to sort these trends into desirable and probable categories. This phase is characterized by more detailed knowledge and would correspond to defining the operating environment of the system. There is sometimes a tendency to merge into phase two without searching into the broader environments which the facilitators should steer the group away from. If the conference rushes into the second phase, the opportunity to search the environment extensively is done away with and hence significant trends that might be relevant to the formulation or the implementation of strategies might not be identified. Secondly, the opportunity to develop a shared perception and belonging to the same context—hence the development of the group—is missed. Therefore both content and process suffer.

Phase 3:

In this phase attention is drawn to the evolution of the organization in question. Answers to questions such as why and how it came into being, what kinds of functions it had and has, what its current character is, are sought. Another appraisal that can be pursued is the identification of the strengths and weaknesses of the organization. The purpose at this phase is to consciously share the current configuration and situation of the organization and to appreciate the antecedents of this configuration. Participants usually find this phase particularly engaging, especially when certain constraints have inhibited the sharing of such information. A simple time line drawn on the flip chart sometimes helps to map the events that have shaped the evolution of the system chronologically.

Phase 4:

This phase explicitly calls for creativity and innovation. The future of the organization can now be designed using ideal characteristics to reflect the values of the participants. The resource constraint is an omnipresent deterrent for the participants to really engage in a joyful and hopeful mood and hence to release their creative imagination. The participants must be explicitly forewarned of this tendency and be asked to stress creativity and innovation, rather than focus on the feasibility of proposed changes to the system. This phase is not directed to produce concrete strategies or solutions, although they might well be suggested in the course of brainstorming. On the contrary, it is directed to breed creative, unconventional and surprising conceptions of what the system ought to be. This kind of activity is best performed in small groups. When a small group generates enough design characteristics, they switch their work with another group. Thus, the selection and sorting of the most creative ideas is done by other groups. By introducing stakeholder scrutiny, ideas that would be supported quickly emerge and those stakeholders who have selected the ideas are more likely to be committed to devise implementation strategies. Finally, in the same manner with other phases, the work of each group is merged through a discussion of differences and similarities and a consensus scenario is passed on to the next stage.

Phase 5:

The formulation of strategies follows the same mode as the previous phase, that is to break up into four small groups, to generate the means by which the idealized future can be attained, and to develop a list of strategies that the group endorses. A copy of the idealized future document is supplied to each work group so that the targeted future is the same negotiated future they can all strive for. Creative ways of bringing about the desired future are expected to be produced in the brainstorming mode. The sorting out of all the suggested strategies are done by other small groups. At this phase, more specific strategies or solutions are offered and this reflects the progression of the search conference process.

Once the strategies are articulated, the participants can then self-select themselves into action plan groups to design the implementation plans. The self selection is another sorting mechanism for some of the unpopular strategies to drop out of the agenda or to be reserved for another planning event. The products of the action groups are presented to the large group to be followed by a debate and a discussion of the desirability or the feasibility of these plans. It works much better to send the same work groups back to consider the viability of their implementation plans given the contextual and operating environment trends that they have earlier identified.

Finally, each participant is asked—if they haven't already volunteered—how they would be integrating the plans into their day-to-day operations when they return to work the following day. A mutually agreed upon follow-up program provides a tracking system for the whole group.

Conclusion: Some Directions for the Practitioner

Who to Choose as the Participants

- The stakeholders who are affected or who affect the planning or the problem-solving situation.

- The stakeholders who have a special interest in probable outcomes.

- Decision makers, implementers, responsible or relevant people in private sector or in government.

- Participants do not have to be experts in the planning situation.

- People who would be comfortable without their ranks and status and be able to work with "short sleeves."

- Search conference process works best with stakeholders who volunteer to attend.

Conditions of Participation:

- Participants must attend all the activities. Since the phases are interrelated, partial attendance is not generally permitted.

- Search Conference is not a conventional conference or a special hearing, there are no speeches or testimonies.

- Participants should not be disturbed throughout the conference. They should not be receiving telephone calls, should not be leaving to go home or meet with people other than the search conference participants.

- The conference should take place in a "social island," and the participants should be taken to a resort-like location away from daily disturbances of work or family.

- All opinions and perspectives must be respected by all the participants.

What Can be Expected as the Outcomes of a Search Conference:

- Creative and achievable strategies.

- Collaborative and participative approaches.

- Consensus generation.

- Shared values.

- Commitment to strategies formulated.

- The combination of formulation and implementation.

- Learning from each other and educating members new to the situation.

- The integration of cultural, regional or value differences.

- To complete a task in two or three days that would take months if left to the specialized analysts and experts.

References

Bion, W. R. 1961. *Experience in Groups.* London: Tavistock.

Emery, M., and Emery, F. E. 1978. "Searching," in J. W. Sutherland (ed.), *Management Handbook for Administrators.* New York: Van Nostrand Reinhold.

Emery, F. E., and Trist, E. L. 1965. "The Causal Texture of Organizational Environments." *Human Relations, 18,* 1, pp. 21–32.

Mintzberg, H. 1985. "Of Strategies, Deliberate and Emergent," *Strategic Management Journal,* pp. 257–272.

Trist, E. L. 1983. "Referent Organizations and Development of Inter-organizational Domains," *Human Relations, 36,* 3, pp. 269–284.

IMPROVING THE QUALITY OF WORK LIFE
AT A COMMUNITY SERVICE ORGANIZATION:
A FOUR YEAR PROJECT

Thomas C. Head, Peter F. Sorensen, Jr. and Richard A. Stotz

Interest in Quality of Work Life (QWL) programs as a method for improving organizational effectiveness has increased significantly over the last several years. QWL is not a new concept, though, for organization theorists have been heralding its merits since the Hawthorne studies in the 1930s. This recent gain in popularity is partly due to the great success the Japanese have had with QWL (Takeuchi, 1981). Other reasons for the increase in interest are the quickly changing economic conditions, government legislation, and the more mature, better educated work force.

Quality of work life is basically permitting ". . . every employee to develop himself through his work and to take on responsibility" (Gulowsen, 1971). This development may come in the form of job enrichment, participatory management, quality work circles, and other such organization development interventions.

This heightened awareness in QWL has resulted in a refining of the art. Three items in particular have been found necessary for a successful QWL program. They are (1) knowledge of QWL techniques, (2) proper implementation of these techniques, and (3) knowledge of assessment techniques for determining the effectiveness of the QWL program. This paper reports on a successful QWL program implemented by the authors. The description of this program, now in its fifth year, will provide the reader with an idea of what can be accomplished through directing attention to the human resources of the organization.

The study site involved a community service organization in a midwestern community with a population of 17,000. The organization was comprised of forty-two employees and served approximately 1,000 clients. It had experienced three consecutive deficit years prior to the initiation of the QWL program, which was undertaken at the request of the Chief Executive.

QWL Program

The QWL strategy adopted was primarily a participatory management program directed toward increasing employee satisfaction, the more effective use of the organization's human resources, and increased organization effectiveness. The specific areas of increased involvement and employee participation were determined by data collected from employees regarding their perception of the organization.

Change Strategy

The primary vehicle for the change effort was the survey feedback process following the action research model. Briefly, action research is a collaborative-participatory technique which consists of a cooperative effort between change agents and members of the organization in problem identification, the development and implementation of strategies for resolving identified problems, and the ongoing monitoring of change activities for the purpose of assessing the effectiveness of these changes.

The change model underlying the project was the three variable model set forth by Likert. The three variables comprising the model are causal, intervening, and end result variables. Causal variables include the structure of the organization and management style and behavior. The two basic causal variables, organization structure and managerial behavior, of which participatory management is an important factor, combine to influence employee behavior. This combination sets the "tone," the climate of the organization, or, in Likert's terms, it establishes the nature of the variables characterizing the internal health of the human organization—intervening variables. End result variables pertain to measures of organization effectiveness—productivity, etc.

An important aspect of the Likert model is that these three variables influence each other in a sequential manner—changes in causal variables impact on intervening variables which, in turn, influence end-result variables. A lag time occurs from one set of variables to another. The importance of the lag time phenomenon is that measures of intervening variables can be used to predict the nature of changes in end-result variables.

Assessment Design and Data

The preferred method for assessing the results of an organizational change effort is a classical experimental design. However, the difficulties in implementing and sustaining true experimental designs in organizational settings has led to modifications known as quasi-experimental approaches. These innovative research designs allow the researcher to assess the impact of complex organization development interventions with a good degree of validity, without the use of true control groups or random selection. Three quasi-experimental designs were employed initially as part of the study: a matched external control group; a time series design in which the experimental organization itself acts as its own control group; and third, a design in which level of treatment (intervention) varies with different groups within the same organization. (Although data was collected in the initial phase of the study from the external control group, difficulties within that organization precluded the continued collection of data so that the study is based on the use of time series and internal control group designs.)

Five types of data were collected at various stages of the project. First, questionnaire data in the form of Likert's Organizational Profile was employed to determine the nature and extent of participation in the organization in terms of leadership, motivation, communication, decisions, goals and controls. A second measure was the Control Graph Questionnaire which is designed to determine the levels of participation by level of the organization. Third, data was collected in terms of changes in program income as a measure of end result variables (program income was chosen as that information which would most closely reflect changes in employee attitudes, motivation and commitment). Fourth, data was collected through interviews regarding employee attitudes. Finally, data was collected by the parent organization of all like organizations in that metropolitan area (this data was not part of the original design but became available in the fourth year of the change effort and serves as an independent source of information regarding changes in end result variables and provides a comparison with other comparable organizations).

Intervention Activities

The intervention consistent with the action research model is an ongoing process which had by 1981 evolved through four cycles. Each cycle was characterized by the use of survey feedback consisting of the following steps: the collection and feeding back of organizational data to organizational units, unit analysis of the data for problem identification, development and implementation of action plans. As part of the first cycle, the survey feedback procedure was systematically varied by department in order to evaluate the impact of the process. The intensity of the feedback activity varied from involvement in the complete process including a number of problem solving sessions with department A to a low level involvement limited to data feedback for department F. (See Table 1). Following the first cycle, all units were equally involved.

An overview of the intervention cycles are presented in Figure 1. Cycle one identified the following major problems—lack of cohesive organization, lack of input opportunities for lower level employees and problems with hygiene factors (salaries). Action plans which were developed and implemented during this cycle included the restructuring of the organization, communication of structure to all employees, implementation of team meetings, expanded involvement of lower level employees and changes in the salary structure.

Cycle two was designed to monitor the effectiveness of the actions taken in the first cycle and led to the following additional actions—introduction of an employee orientation program and employee involvement in selection and hiring.

Table 1. Rank Ordering of Departments by Amount of Intervention

	Degree of Feedback	Organizational Profile		Control Graph	
		Mean	Difference Between Means	Mean	Difference Between Means
Department A	1.0	pre 8.10 post 10.66	2.56	pre 2.4 post 3.2	.8
Department B	2.5	pre 8.27 post 12.37	4.10	pre 2.9 post 3.5	.6
Department C	2.5	pre 10.59 post 11.49	.90	pre 3.0 post 3.1	.1
Department D	4.0	pre 9.53 post 11.13	1.60	pre 3.1 post 3.0	−.1
Department E	5.5	pre 13.04 post 14.45	1.36	pre 3.0 post 3.2	.2
Department F	5.5	pre 12.28 post 11.18	−1.10	pre 2.9 post 3.0	.1

The third cycle consisted of again monitoring progress and maintenance and reinforcement of the new management system. The fourth cycle consisted of sharing the parent organization survey with employees.

The following hypotheses guided the study:

1. That employee participation and involvement can be increased using survey feedback;

2. That degree of change will be associated with the intensity of the survey feedback experience;

3. That time lags exist between changes in intervening variables and end result variables;

4. That increased participation will lead to improvement in end result variables.

```
SURVEY 1
     PROBLEM IDENTIFICATION
        • LACK OF COHESIVE ORGANIZATION
        • LACK OF INPUT OPPORTUNITIES FOR LOWER LEVEL
          EMPLOYEES
        • PROBLEMS WITH HYGIENE FACTORS

     ACTION
        • RESTRUCTURING OF ORGANIZATION
        • COMMUNICATION OF STRUCTURE TO ALL EMPLOYEES
        • IMPLEMENTATION OF TEAM MEETINGS
        • EXPANDED INVOLVEMENT OF LOWER LEVEL
          EMPLOYEES
        • CHANGES IN SALARY STRUCTURE

SURVEY 2
     MONITORING OF PROGRESS

     ACTION
        • NEW EMPLOYEE ORIENTATION PROGRAM
        • EMPLOYEE INVOLVEMENT IN SELECTION AND HIRING
        • TRAINING AND DEVELOPMENT PROGRAM

SURVEY 3
     MONITORING OF PROGRESS

     ACTION
        • ORGANIZATION CHANGES COMPLETED
        • MAINTENANCE AND REINFORCEMENT OF NEW
          MANAGEMENT SYSTEM

SURVEY 4
     PARENT ORGANIZATION SURVEY

     ACTION
        • FEEDBACK TO EMPLOYEES
```

Figure 1. Organization Change

Results

Hypothesis 1—Increased Employee Participation

The results to date of the change process are presented in Figures 2 and 3. Figure 2 presents the results of the organizational profile reflecting movement toward a more participatory system. Positive movement is reported for all of the eighteen items measured, with the greatest improvement for the extent to which subordinates' ideas are sought and used constructively, how free do subordinates feel to talk to supervisors about their job, how well do superiors know problems faced by subordinates, and the use of participation in organizational goal setting. See Figure 2.

The results for the control graph are presented in Figure 3. These findings are consistent with, and more striking than, the findings presented for the organizational profile. Here it seems quite clear that the organization has moved toward more participatory management. It is interesting to note that the amount of influence increased for *all* levels. Also of interest, during the second cycle-the height of the transition period when the director was attempting to increase the involvement and participation of others in the decision making—that his influence is perceived as decreasing modestly but increasing again once the transition period has been completed.

Hypothesis 2—Degree of Change will be Associated with the Degree of Intensity of the Survey Feedback Process

Table 1 presents the rank order results pertaining to the intensity of feedback process and degree of change. Here again the hypothesis is supported. The rank order correlation (rho) for the relationship between degree of intervention and increased scores on both the organizational profile and the control graph is .78. It should be noted that unexpected decrease occurred for two departments receiving limited feedback sessions.

Hypothesis 3—The Existence of a Time Lag Between the Introduction of Change, Changes in Intervening Variables and End-Result Variables

The results of changes in end-result variables over the various intervention cycles are presented in Table 2 and Figure 4. During the first cycle there was actually a modest decrease in the end results as measured by program income. As the program developed, there was an increase of 23% in program income over the preceding year, followed by sharp increases in program income as the strategies for dealing with identified problems became institutionalized and the transition to a more participatory organization was finalized.

	SYSTEM 1	SYSTEM 2	SYSTEM 3	SYSTEM 4

Organizational variables

LEADERSHIP

How much confidence and trust is shown in subordinates?
Virtually None — Some — Substantial amount — A great deal

How free do they feel to talk to superiors about job?
Not very free — Somewhat free — Quite free — Very free

How often are subordinate's ideas sought and used constructively?
Seldom — Sometimes — Often — Very frequently

MOTIVATION

Is predominant use made of 1 fear, 2 threats, 3 punishment, 4 rewards, 5 involvements?
1, 2, 3, occasionally 4 — 4, some 3 — some 3 and 5 — 5, 4, based on group

Where is responsibility felt for achieving organization's goals?
Mostly at top — Top and middle — Fairly general — At all levels

How much cooperative teamwork exists?
Very little — Relatively little — Moderate amount — Great deal

COMMUNICATIONS

What is the usual direction of information flow?
Downward — Mostly downward — Down and up — Down, up and sideways

How is downward communication accepted?
With suspicion — Possibly with suspicion — With caution — With a receptive mind

How accurate is upward communication?
Usually inaccurate — Often inaccurate — Often accurate — Almost always accurate

How well do superiors know problems faced by subordinates?
Not very well — Rather well — Quite well — Very well

DECISIONS

At what level are decisions made?
Mostly at top — Policy at top, some delegation — Broad policy at top, more delegation — Throughout but well integrated

Are subordinates involved in decisions related to their work?
Almost never — Occasionally consulted — Generally consulted — Fully involved

What does decision-making process contribute to motivation?
Not very much — Relatively little — Some contribution — Substantial contribution

GOALS

How are organizational goals established?
Orders issued — Orders, some comments invited — After discussion, by orders — By group action (except in crisis)

How much covert resistance to goals is present?
Strong resistance — Moderate resistance — Some resistance at times — Little or none

CONTROL

How concentrated are review and control functions?
Very highly at top — Quite highly at top — Moderate delegation to lower levels — Widely shared

Is there an informal organization resisting the formal one?
Yes — Usually — Sometimes — No--some goals as formal

What are cost, productivity, and other control data used for?
Policing, punishment — Reward and punishment — Reward, some self-guidance — Self-guidance, problem-solving

———— 1978 - - - - - 1979 · · · · · 1980

Figure 2. Profile of Organizational Characteristics

- 406 -

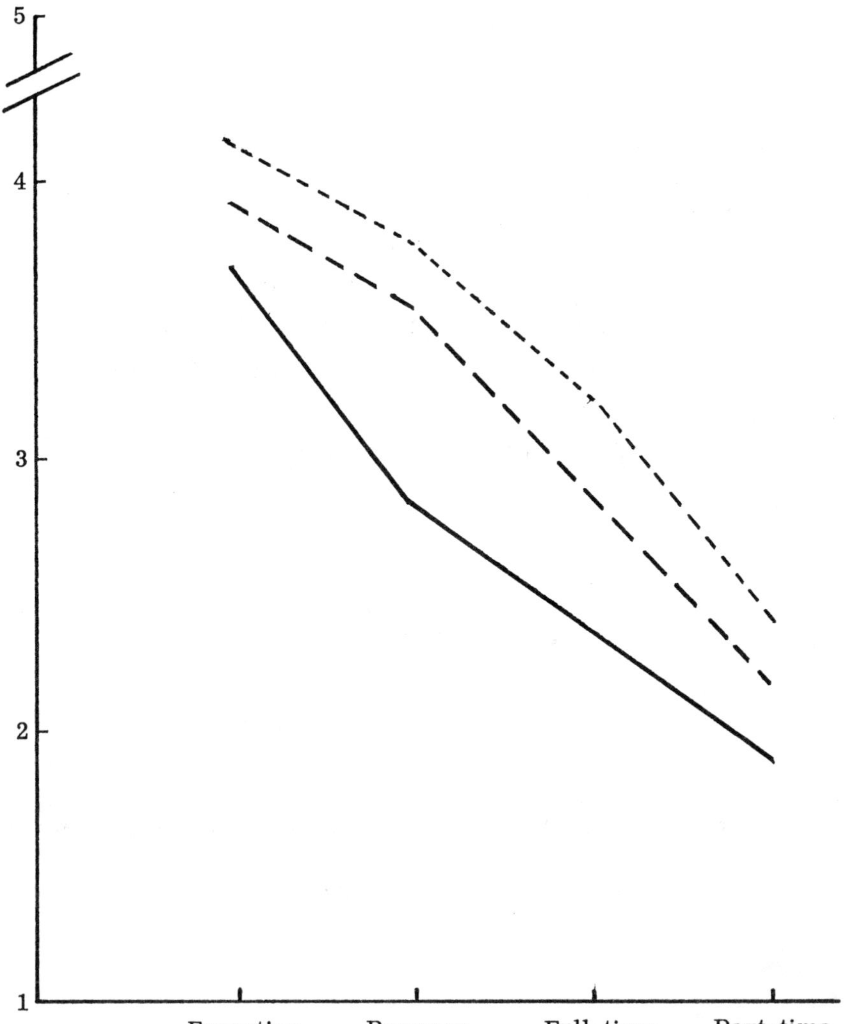

	Executive Director	Program Director	Full-time Employees	Part-time Employees
1980 -----	4.1	3.7	3.1	2.1
1979 ----	3.9	3.6	2.7	2.0
1978 ———	3.7	2.8	2.3	1.6

Figure 3. Total Organization Actual Influence

Table 2.

PROGRAM INCOME

Change in Program Income
over 1977.

SURVEY)
FEEDBACK)
PROGRAM)
STARTS) ⟶ FIRST QUARTER - 7%

SECOND QUARTER + 5%

THIRD QUARTER + 23%

FOURTH QUARTER + 25%

SPECIAL COURSE & PROGRAM INCOME

1974-75	$ 120,000
1975-76	$ 121,000
1976-77	$ 125,000
1977-78	$ 140,000
1978-79	$ 150,000
1979-80	$ 202,000
1980-81	$ 251,000

SURVEY)
FEEDBACK)
PROGRAM)
STARTS) ⟶

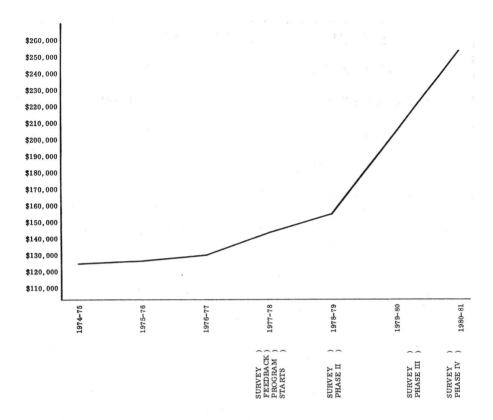

Figure 4. Special Course and Program Income

In Figure 5, data is reported for the independent survey undertaken in 1981 by the parent organization used in the fourth cycle of the intervention. This last set of data provides an independent source of information indicating that the organization has moved from an organization in "trouble" to one which has acquired increased internal health in terms of employee attitudes and productivity reflected in a positive evaluation by its clients—an evaluation which places it at the forefront among 173 comparable units. Within a four year period, a period characterized by intensive collaborative efforts to increase employee involvement and participation, a "troubled" organization characterized by financial deficits, lack of cohesiveness and input opportunities for lower level employees evolved to one which is evaluated by its clients as one which is ranked first of 173 in terms of community respect and among the top three in terms of management, progressiveness and health environment.

PERFORMANCE OF DOWNERS GROVE YMCA	
PROGRESSIVENESS	TOP THREE
WELL MANAGED	TOP TWO
WELL MAINTAINED	FIRST
HEALTH ENVIRONMENT	TOP THREE
RESPECTED IN COMMUNITY	FIRST

Figure 5.   Independent Survey by the Department of Marketing Membership Society of 173 Centers, February 1981.

Summary and Implications

Support for the hypotheses of the study, we feel, has important implications for the Organization Development Change Agent.

First it documents the relationship of QWL programs, specifically employee participation, to increases in organizational effectiveness and productivity. Second, increases in participation and influence on the part of lower level employees do not necessarily mean a decrease in the influence of managers, a phenomenon long recognized by advocates of participation but of which many managers have been skeptical. Third, changes in the level of participation and movement toward a more participatory system are measurable and can be linked to productivity.

Fourth, the finding that more intensive efforts at change lead to greater change is not a surprising finding, but the finding that marginal efforts may result in negative change was not anticipated. This later finding highlights the importance of monitoring change efforts and employing the action research model which focuses on the need for ongoing assessment and modification of change strategies. It reinforces the importance of thorough and sustained commitment to QWL efforts once they are uncertain and underscores the importance of sensitivity to the possibility of unanticipated and certainly unintended negative consequences of these efforts.

Finally, the existence of the lag time phenomena suggests that the OD practitioner should take care to incorporate into the strategy the adequate preparation of line managers that, even with improvements in employee attitudes, changes in end results variables will not be immediate. In the effort reported here, the lag time consisted of several months for a relatively small organization. The lag time in a larger organization could be expected to be considerably longer. The adequate education and preparation of line managers concerning lag time phenomena should serve to increase the credibility of Organization Development Practitioners and help avoid the early abortion of projects before their full potential is realized.

References

Gulowsen, J. *A Measure of Work Group Autonomy.* Oslo: Tanum Press, 1971.

Likert, R. "Management Styles and the Human Component." *Management Review,* *23* October 1977, pp. 23-45.

Morrison, P. "Evaluation in OD: A Review and Assessment." *Group and Organization Studies,* March 1978, pp. 42-70.

Takeuchi, H. "Productivity: Learning from the Japanese." *California Management Review,* Summer 1981, pp. 5-19.

Tannenbaum, A. *Control in Organizations.* New York: McGraw-Hill Publishing Company, 1968.

THE TURNAROUND OF SCANDINAVIAN AIRLINES:
AN OD INTERPRETATION[1]

Peter F. Sorensen, Jr.
Thomas C. Head
Helen Scoggins
Henrick Holt Larsen

This paper reviews, from an OD perspective, the actions and events associated with the turnaround at Scandinavian Airline Systems (SAS) in the early '80s. The dynamics of this turnaround lend themselves to such an interpretation in terms of both the overall process and specific techniques used. It is a case study which identifies the strategies employed to move SAS from an $8 million loss to a $71 million profit position within a period of only twelve months.

Although references to the SAS story are appearing in the popular management literature, i.e., *Passion for Excellence* (Peters and Austin, 1985); *Creating Excellence* (Hickman and Silva, 1986); *Moment of Truth* (Carlson, 1987), there has been no systematic examination of this turnaround in the organization science literature. The SAS case is particularly relevant to OD for several reasons. First, the case takes place in a Scandinavian organization. This is of special interest since the Scandinavian countries have been identified as having cultural values most compatible with, and supportive of, the values behind OD (Jaeger, 1986). This case also provides an excellent illustration of integrating OD activities with, and in support of, strategic corporate changes. The final reason this case is of interest is that it is a dramatic success story, but one that has not received just attention.

Background

Scandinavian Airlines Systems (SAS) was founded on August 1, 1946, in an agreement among the three national airlines of Denmark, Norway and Sweden. In its first year of operation, SAS carried some 21,000 passengers and 300 tons of

---

[1]We would like to express our appreciation for the hospitality, time and assistance from personnel at SAS and the Scandinavian Service School, particularly Goren Noesman, Manager, Finance and Administration, SAS; Jim Marnos, Account Executive, SAS; Neils Sorensen, Copenhagen Handelsbank; Ulrick Sort, President, Scandinavian Service School; and Bo Arnell, Director of Research and Development, Scandinavian Service School. An earlier draft of this paper was presented at the 1988 Eastern Academy of Management Conference in Arlington, Virginia.

cargo and mail with a fleet of seven DC-4's and a staff of 1,100. In 1985, SAS was flying more than ten million passengers and some 150,000 tons of cargo and mail a year and had an operating network covering ninety-one cities in thirty-six countries, with eighty-one jetliners and 17,700 employees. Eleven additional jetliners were purchased to cover expansion in 1986, and $420 million has just been appropriated to purchase 14 new DC-9 aircraft.

SAS is still a cooperative venture, owned 2/7ths by Danish Airlines, 2/7ths by Norwegian Airlines, and 3/7ths by Swedish Airlines. Each parent company is owned 50/50 by government and private interests. Unlike the other European airlines, SAS is not government subsidized.

The SAS group includes twenty travel-related companies with subsidiaries and affiliates in flight catering, restaurants, offshore catering, a chain of twenty hotels, tour producers and operators, charter and domestic airlines, a cargo forwarder, and an insurance company.

The environment for the airlines industry following World War II through the middle '70s was characterized by stability and growth with slowly rising oil prices, protectionist aviation policies, stable profits, cartels, and controlled markets. By the middle '70s, the environment had become considerably more turbulent and uncertain. The world market was stagnating and the market for air travel had not grown for four or five years. Oil prices were rising rapidly. Deregulation had been introduced under the Carter administration in the U.S., and first England, followed by the Common Market, were also moving toward more liberal aviation policies. Competition between carriers increased significantly. Between 1975 and 1980 SAS market share went from 6 to 5.2 percent.

In 1981 SAS experienced a loss of $8 million dollars. A new CEO, Jan Carlzon, was hired to turn the organization around. In little over a year, SAS went from an $8 million loss to a gross profit of $71 million from sales of $2 billion and was voted "Airline of the Year"—at a time when the airline industry in general was losing $11.7 billion a year. These profits were not a onetime fluke. In the following three years, SAS's full-fare traffic increased between 15 and 25 percent, and profits increased to approximately $136 million. This turnaround, as will be seen, was accomplished by integrating a major strategic change with an organizational cultural revolution.

Data Collection

Data on the SAS turnaround were collected primarily through interviews with SAS personnel in Denmark and the U.S., as well as the president and personnel of the SAS subsidiary, Service Management. Service Management, located in

Copenhagen, is responsible for the development of the human resource training events which played a major role in the turnaround.

Data were also collected through the review of a number of in-house documents including the SAS Annual Reports, lectures and speeches by Jan Carlzon, publications by the Stockholm Industrial Council for Social and Economic Studies, various trade journal articles, employee communications, training texts and training tapes.

Turnaround Strategy

The SAS turnaround required simultaneous objectives for its new corporate strategy: (1) developing a particular market niche and (2) the establishment of a service oriented culture in support of this marketing strategy.

The niche that was selected by SAS stressed having a service, rather than production, orientation. Under the new strategy, marketing was directed at attracting and keeping the full fare business passengers. To accomplish this, in Europe, SAS introduced the "Euroclass." This included:

1. Altered physical accommodations in the aircraft, such as more seat space;
2. Providing on-flight shopping services and other additional amenities;
3. Developing "Scanorama" airport lounges for all full-fare passengers; and especially
4. Establishing itself as the "on time" airline.

There were also several secondary strategies adopted. One such strategy was concentration, aimed at increasing cost-efficiency through creating a compatible fleet of aircraft. Another was designed to secure a market advantage for SAS where the airline did not have, or could not develop, its own resources through interorganizational "trading." A third secondary strategy was to sell on the leisure/vacation travel market whatever capacity the business traveler could not use. Thus, by differentiating service levels, SAS launched an aggressive pricing strategy that attracted many new customers in the leisure market. Also the secondary strategies were designed specifically not to require new or separate resources. Their goals were to contribute either to overall improvement in revenue or to aid the central strategy.

Organizational-Culture Change

The marketing aspects of the SAS turnaround have received most of the media attention, but it is the second component of the strategy which provides the focus for this paper; the process of changing the organization from a traditional bureaucratic, hierarchical organization to an organic, service oriented one. A number of different OD perspectives may be used to interpret the events as SAS. This paper will primarily utilize Lewin's three stage process (Burke, 1982). This process is characterized by first unfreezing the organization in order to prepare it for the changes. The actual change process constitutes the second stage, when the interventions are actually implemented. Finally, refreezing occurs, which is the stabilizing of the organization and its people to the new norms, structures, and practices.

Stage One: Unfreezing

The primary goal of the unfreezing stage at SAS was to increase employee sensitivity to the economic difficulties which the company was experiencing and consequently understand the need for change. Hopefully, through these efforts employee resistance to the company changes would be minimal.

Three factors were central to the unfreezing process. The first was the obvious, and highly visible, need for change signalled dramatically by the $8 million loss. Second was the selection of a new president for SAS, Jan Carlzon. The final factor was the replacement of thirteen out of the fifteen top managers. Carlzon described his perceptions of the preconditions for the cultural change at SAS as follows:

> "I think there are two things which, sadly enough, are necessary. One is that you are in a real crisis. And the second is that you select somebody from outside the company. I don't think you can be a prophet in your own organization, and I don't think you can change tradition, history, all manners and all management thinking with a company, if a company is well off and if you have always been successful with what you used to do. . . . I am happy I didn't enter this company three years before, because I don't think I would have been able to make a change at that stage. When I came into the picture, everybody had started to realize that something had to happen; otherwise our jobs were in real danger, and even the airline itself was in real danger. I mean, a crisis is the biggest asset. If you don't use it, you missed the train, passed up your chance to catch it again."

It is interesting to note that Carlzon chose to implement his change strategy by going directly to the line personnel. Standard implementation procedures using the management hierarchy was perceived as being too slow a process for the critical nature of the situation. Middle management played a secondary role in both their involvement in the sequencing of change and in the modification of their role. Middle management's tasks changed from a supervisory-controlling role to more of a support role.

Stage Two: Culture Change

The turnaround at SAS was accomplished by a series of highly diverse interventions, ranging from change strategies aimed at the individual to macro changes involving the organization structure. From an organization development perspective, a useful way of looking at the events at SAS is to describe them as cultural change—a description consistent with the earliest and perhaps most enduring definition of OD (Burke, 1982). The management of cultural change is a perspective developed in *Managing Organization Cultures* (1983), which involves the use of management change levers, those activities and events over which management has control in changing organizational culture. These levers include leadership behavior, strategic definition, structure and human resource systems. The overall change process at SAS is represented in Figure 1.

Leadership behavior. It is clear when investigating the SAS turnaround that it is perceived to a very great extent as Carlzon's success, similar to Lee Iacocca and Chrysler. As the new president, Carlzon played a highly visible and direct role in all aspects of the reorientation of SAS. Carlzon is fairly young, presents a good appearance, is articulate and an excellent spokesperson for SAS. He is considered to be a highly charismatic leader both internally and externally. Carlzon is a citizen of Sweden, and earned an M.B.A. from the Stockholm School of Economics. In 1967 he joined Vingresor, Sweden's largest tour operator as product manager, later being made head of marketing. In 1974 he was named managing director of Vingresor and reversed that company's economic decline. In 1978, he became managing director of Linjeflyg, Sweden's major domestic airline, where again he turned heavy economic losses into healthy profits. Before taking the position at SAS Carlzon definitely had demonstrated an ability to achieve results in turnaround situations.

It is clear that Carlzon believes in the articulation of strategy, ". . . how the leader states the strategy and puts it into words, how value related issues are verbalized" (*Managing Organizational Cultures,* 1983, p. 11), as an important component of his culture shaping activities. For example he often stressed the importance of "the moment of truth," any interface between the customer and an SAS employee. Additional illustrations include: "The only thing that counts in the

ENVIRONMENT

- Deregulation
- Increased Competition
- Increased Costs, Especially Fuel

- Business Passengers Preferred
- Other Carriers
- Loss of Passenger Business

STRATEGY

- Primary Business Strategy:
  Development and implementation
  of business class concept

- Move from asset orientation to
  service orientation

- Human Resources Strategy:
  Development of human resources
  supportive of and capable of
  implementing business strategy

CHANGE PROCESS

- Unfreezing
  $8 million loss
  Change in top management
  Program to increase employee sensitivity
  to need for change

- Change
  Directed and mandated by top management
  Directed toward "Front Line" employees
  Cultural change
  Culture shapers:
  Leadership
  Strategic definition
  Structure
  Human Resources

- Refreezing
  The Second Wave Program

Figure 1. The Cultural Change Process at SAS.

new SAS is a satisfied customer"; "We can have as many aircraft as you like and still not survive if we don't have passengers who would rather fly with SAS than with our competitors"; "SAS treats people as individuals, not as a collective. This applies to both customers and employees" (Carlzon and Hubendick, 1983). These statements were very different from the previous management's attitudes with its traditional production orientation. Carlzon made sure that the employees knew exactly what the new philosophy involved.

Carlzon also demonstrated that he believed in utilizing corporate symbolism to assist with the cultural change. The best known, and perhaps best illustration, of Carlzon's use of symbolic behavior-specific behaviors that have symbolic value in sending messages about values and behavior is his use of the T.V. scheduling monitor placed in his private office. He perceived that a central component in the strategy of capturing the business travels market was on-time departures and arrivals, which he dubbed "operation punctuality." Carlzon had a schedule monitoring screen placed in his office indicating SAS departure and arrival times. He would personally contact flight and airport personnel immediately in the event of a delayed flight, sometimes talking to the pilot while the plane was still in the air, to ascertain the reason for the delay. Carlzon's relationship with the director of Kalstrop Airport (the SAS hub) can be considered as another technique for change, modeling. This is a procedure in which a top manager provides a visible model of the desirable traits and/or behaviors. Carlzon guided the director through the use of controlled delegation in achieving superior performance in the refurbishing and advantageous scheduling of the airport.

How the leader uses his/her personal behavior, recognition, and resources as rewards for traits or behavior that are consistent with the new culture can be extremely important. How Carlzon effectively used personal rewards can be illustrated by the Christmas party at which the success was celebrated by giving each employee a solid gold watch with the SAS logo, symbolizing the success of "Operation Punctuality."

Structure. The culture shapers which effect organizational structure focus on the organization design, rewards/measures, and physical arrangements. One objective of the new SAS strategy was to alter the organization from a hierarchically oriented, traditional organization to an organic, adaptive and service oriented one. Central to making the organization more responsive to the customer was the change of job roles at the interface with the customer. This was accomplished by a concept entitled "The Inverted Pyramid," which actually dispersed authority throughout the organization. The philosophy behind the inverted pyramid was described by Carlzon: "Make decisions so that the customer's needs are satisfied immediately. Do not refer the matter to your superior."

In addition over 50 project groups were formed among the employees. These groups function much like the Quality Circle concept. The groups are charged with reviewing procedures and processes and making improvements where possible, emphasizing the "businessperson's airline" goal.

A third aspect of the structural changes made to support the new strategy is reflected in the appraisal process, specifically in determining which behaviors are to be rewarded in the new organization. Innovation and success were both stressed, as opposed to the previous "good soldier" emphasis. The new norm became "Managers should show results rather than follow instructions," (Carlzon and Hubendick, 1984). Important rewards also came from colleagues and friends outside of SAS as the programs and changes at SAS received increased publicity. SAS, and its employees, represented a new source of national pride. They were no longer the old, rigid, unattractive airline, but an exciting success story in international commerce.

The specific physical and locational aspects of the organization, including layout, office design, physical symbols, etc., also played a role as SAS implemented a $14 million corporate identity program which included refurbishing planes and offices with "SAS" colors and furniture. For example, the lounge at New York's Kennedy Airport was given a new, elegant Scandinavian design, offering the passengers a feeling of peace, while making check-in and seat assignment more efficient. Attention was paid to every detail. A world leader in fashion design, Calvin Klein, was commissioned to design (with input from SAS personnel) new uniforms for the flight crew. The SAS technicians were even given a distinctive overall appearance, so that they could be easily identified.

Human Resources. A final cultural aspect of the turnaround strategy was the concept of "service management." This was implemented through extensive employee development, undertaken by the Scandinavian Service School through intensive two-day seminars. These seminars focused on the development of positive self-concept and were based upon the assumption that a positive self-image is a prerequisite for effective management of the interface with passengers and customers. The objective of these programs was described (SAS Training Document):

> "To encourage people at all levels to make the fullest possible use of their personal skills and talents in providing service. Research indicates that customers really are influenced far more by the personal aspects of service than by material or technical features."

The particular relevance of the training programs is that they represented a systematic effort at reinforcing and assisting the cultural change at SAS and as such made one component of the multilevered approach to change undertaken by SAS.

It is interesting to note that later a similar program was undertaken at British Airways, under the guidance of SAS, which afterwards received the "Airline of the Year" award.

SAS also made several changes in the level of employment. Unlike most corporations faced with large losses, SAS chose not to resort to layoffs. In fact overall employment was increased. What SAS actually did was to change the location of the employees. General administration was reduced by 25 percent, and the people shifted to the service areas involving visible customer relations.

Stage Three: Refreezing

These Second Wave activities stressed the recognition that the initial change efforts had been highly successful and dramatized the need for sustaining the new norms and structures. They primarily took the form of employee group study programs. The nature of these programs is reflected in the following illustrative titles and brief descriptions:

"The Challenge" Reviews the history of SAS from the forties to the present, reviews the situational demands leading to the turnaround and the strategies developed.

"The Businessman's Airline" Purpose is for the participants to learn the SAS strategy and standards so they become live instruments in daily work.

"A Functional Organization" The purpose is to encourage people to experiment with new ways of working. This includes finding ways to decentralize responsibility and decision making power as close to the customer as possible and working across divisional boundaries at the local level in order to solve problems at the source of origin.

"An Introduction to Systems Development" The purpose is to start systems development within the organizational units which support the main business strategy.

"A Personal Concept" Group studies involving identifying behaviors and situations which are no longer compatible with SAS's new strategy or culture.

Carlzon also created an internal consulting group to strengthen the changes. The members of this group work directly with line managers to overcome any obstacles with new projects. This group also insures proper follow-through by monitoring for any unexpected occurrences.

Conclusion

The turnaround at SAS was truly dramatic. While it has received much attention, little of it has been in the organization sciences. It is most often treated as a marketing or strategy success story. While the turnaround was initiated by a strategic change of the marketing focus, it was accomplished by a total cultural innovation, and therefore can be analyzed from an OD perspective.

The change was initiated by a new Chief Executive Officer who perceived an $8 million loss as a signal that the airline environment had significantly changed, and the company required a complete restructuring. The business strategy was changed from a production to a service orientation. However, in order to make the strategic change work, Carlzon realized that the corporate culture must also be totally revised.

This paper, through extensive interviews and reviewing SAS literature, has reviewed SAS's series of interventions which led to the most difficult of OD goals, a successful cultural transformation. By the process of unfreezing, intervention change, and refreezing, Carlzon and his executives made simultaneous changes in structure, rewards, and leadership styles. Frequent use of symbols were used to reinforce, rather than substitute for, the actual changes.

The turnaround at SAS was successful because of the way strategy, structure and culture were all treated synergistically, rather than separately. This is illustrated by the following (SAS Training Document):

"The way we interact with people has become a question of business strategy: It is reflected in our organization and our working methods. It is reflected in our management and control systems and it is reflected in the way we treat our customers and how we treat each other.

It is seen in our management system.

It is seen in the participation, loyalty, motivation and efficiency of our staff. It decides how our everyday relationships will be. . . .

It decides how successful we shall be!"

References and Resources

Airline Executive. SAS Document, June, 1986, p. 56.

"Airline of the Year—Scandinavian Airlines System." *Air Transport World,* January, 1984, p. 62.

Burke, W. W. *Organization Development.* Boston: Little, Brown Company, 1982.

"Business-Class Flyers Lift SAS Over the Clouds." *Business Week,* December 13, 1982, p. 38.

Carlzon, J., and Hubendick. "The Cultural Revolution in SAS." Report of the Industrial Council for Social and Economic Studies, Stockholm, 1983.

Christensen, S., Jakobsen, P., Larsen, H. H., and Molin, J. *Carlzona Klister.* Kopenhagen: Forlaget Valmuen, 1984.

Cowie, P. (ed.). *The Scandinavian Guide: 1986.* London: The Tantivy Press, 1986.

Hickman, C. R., and Silva, M. A. *Creating Excellence.* London: Unwin Paperbacks, 1986.

"How the Business Traveller Changed the Economics and the Bottom Line at SAS." *International Management,* February, 1985, pp. 61-68.

"Inspiration." *SAS Training Document.*

Jaeger, A. M. "Organization Development and National Culture: Where's the Fit?" *Academy of Management Review, 11,* 1986, pp. 178-182.

Larsen, H. H. *Virksomhedskultur og Erferingslasring.* Kopenhagen: Forlaget Valmuen, 1984.

Managing a Corporate Recovery. Lecture by Jan Carlzon. London: September 20, 1983.

Managing Organizational Cultures. New York: Organizational Research and Consultation, Inc., 1983.

"New SAS Management Trying to Return Airline to Profitability." *Air Transport World,* May, 1983, pp. 38-44.

Norman, R. *Service Management.* Chichester: John Wiley and Sons, 1984.

"Our Businessman of the Year: Jan Carlzon, President of SAS." *The Scandinavian Guide.* London: Unwin Paperbacks, 1984.

"People Spell Success." *SAS Training Document.*

Peters, T., and Austin, N. *Passion for Excellence.* Glasgow: Williams Collins and Son, 1985.

"SAS, Crossair and Boeing Win Top Awards." *Air Transport World*, January, 1984, p. 62.

"SAS Makes Progress Towards Recovery." *Intervavia*, May, 1982, p. 458.

SASsy Business. *Economist*, June 5, 1982, p. 74.

"SAS to Stress Discounts in Economy Class." *Aviation Week and Space Technology*, May 3, 1982, p. 34.

"SAS Will Emphasize Business Travel." *Aviation Week and Space Technology*, November 9, 1981, pp. 102–106.

Scandinavian Airlines System Annual Report, 1984–1985.

Tichy, N., and Devanna, M. A. *The Transformational Leader: Molding Tomorrow's Corporate Winners.* New York: Wiley, 1986.

PART VI
CURRENT ISSUES IN MANAGEMENT AND
ORGANIZATIONAL BEHAVIOR

All the topics covered in the book are current issues in that they will always be central to understanding behavior which leads to high organization performance. Yet there are certain issues which hold a particular interest for managers today. These interests include the role of Culture in Management, Total Quality, Empowerment, downsizing and ethical behavior.

The first article in this section, by Hofstede, reviews and discusses differences in the management process as influenced by differences in national culture. The article makes a strong call for the internationalization of management theories.

The second article focuses on one of the most popular recent approaches to management—Total Quality. Here attention is given to the importance of organization culture and the development of a new Total Quality paradigm—a paradigm based on the philosophy and practices presented in this book. "Choosing an Involvement Strategy" by Edward Lawler, the third reading focuses on a topic related to total quality but more comprehensive in application. Again, the article deals with one of the major themes of the book—the movement away from control-oriented to commitment-oriented management practices. It sets forth three approaches to empowerment or involvement: (1) parallel suggestion involvement, (2) job involvement, and (3) high involvement.

The Cascio article reviews the short- and long-term consequences of downsizing. Here we see the reaffirmation of Likert's argument that traditional, old paradigm (systems 1 & 2) organization's may achieve apparent short-term benefits from downsizing but long-term benefits are achieved through new paradigms (systems 3 & 4) designs.

The final article, "Changing Unethical Organizational Behavior", raises probably one of the most fundamental questions in organizational behavior—"What Does it Mean to be Ethical in an Organizational Context?". The author, Richard Nielsen, discusses strategies for intervening to change unethical behavior. In a way, this last article brings us full circle—a return to our preface in this book where we first raise the issue of human dignity and organizational effectiveness.

CULTURAL CONSTRAINTS IN
MANAGEMENT THEORIES

**Geert Hofstede, University of Limburg,
Maastricht, the Netherlands**

Executive Overview

Management *as the word is presently used is an American invention. In other parts of the world not only the practices but the entire concept of management may differ, and the theories needed to understand it, may deviate considerably from what is considered normal and desirable in the USA. The reader is invited on a trip around the world, and both local management practices and theories are explained from the different contexts and histories of the places visited: Germany, Japan, France, Holland, the countries of the overseas Chinese, South-East Asia, Africa, Russia, and finally mainland China.*

A model in which worldwide differences in national cultures are categorized according to five independent dimensions helps in explaining the differences in management found; although the situation in each country or region has unique characteristics that no model can account for. One practical application of the model is in demonstrating the relative position of the U.S. versus other parts of the world. In a global perspective, U.S. management theories contain a number of idiosyncrasies not necessarily shared by management elsewhere. Three such idiosyncrasies are mentioned: a stress on market processes, a stress on the individual, and a focus on managers rather than on workers. A plea is made for an internationalization not only of business, but also of management theories, as a way of enriching theories at the national level.

IN MY VIEW

Lewis Carroll's *Alice in Wonderland* contains the famous story of Alice's croquet game with the Queen of Hearts.

> *Alice thought she had never seen such a curious croquet-ground in all her life; it was all ridges and furrows; the balls were live hedgehogs, the mallets live flamingoes, and the soldiers had to double themselves up and to stand on their hands and feet, to make the arches.*

© *Academy of Management Executive*, 1993, Vol. 7, No. 1.

You probably know how the story goes: Alice's flamingo mallet turns its head whenever she wants to strike with it; her hedgehog ball runs away; and the doubled-up soldier arches walk around all the time. The only rule seems to be that the Queen of Hearts always wins.

Alice's croquet playing problems are good analogies to attempts to build culture-free theories of management. Concepts available for this purpose are themselves alive with culture, having been developed within a particular cultural context. They have a tendency to guide our thinking toward our desired conclusion.

As the same reasoning may also be applied to the arguments in this article, I better tell you my conclusion before I continue—so that the rules of my game are understood. In this article we take a trip around the world to demonstrate that there are no such things as universal management theories.

Diversity in management *practices* as we go around the world has been recognized in U.S. management literature for more than thirty years. The term "comparative management" has been used since the 1960s. However, it has taken much longer for the U.S. academic community to accept that not only practices but also the validity of *theories* may stop at national borders, and I wonder whether even today everybody would agree with this statement.

An article I published in *Organizational Dynamics* in 1980 entitled "Do American Theories Apply Abroad?" created more controversy than I expected. The article argued, with empirical support, that generally accepted U.S. theories like those of Maslow, Merzberg, McClelland, Vroom, McGregor, Likert, Blake and Mouton may not or only very partly apply outside the borders of their country of origin—assuming they do apply within those borders. Among the requests for reprints, a larger number were from Canada than from the United States.

MANAGEMENT THEORISTS ARE HUMAN

Employees and managers are human. Employees as humans was "discovered" in the 1930s, with the Human Relations school, Managers as humans, was introduced in the late 40s by Herbert Simon's "bounded rationality" and elaborated in Richard Cyert and James March's *Behavioral Theory of the Firm* (1963, and recently re-published in a second edition). My argument is that management scientists, theorists, and writers are human too: they grew up in a particular society in a particular period, and their ideas cannot help but reflect the constraints of their environment.

The idea that the validity of a theory is constrained by national borders is more obvious in Europe, with all its borders, than in a huge borderless country like the U.S. Already in the sixteenth century Michel de Montaigne, a Frenchman, wrote a statement which was made famous by Blaise Pascal about a century later: *"Vérite en-deça des Pyrenées, erreur au-delà"*—There are truths on this side of the Pyrenées which are falsehoods on the other.

FROM DON ARMADO'S LOVE TO TAYLOR'S SCIENCE

According to the comprehensive ten-volume Oxford English Dictionary (1971), the words "manage," "management," and "manager" appeared in the English language in the 16th century. The oldest recorded use of the word "manager" is in Shakespeare's "Love's Labour's Lost," dating from 1588, in which Don Adriano de Armado, "a fantastical Spaniard," exclaims (Act I, scene ii, 188):

> *"Adieu, valour! rust, rapier! be still, drum! for your manager is in love; yea, he loveth".*

The linguistic origin of the word is from Latin *manus*, hand, via the Italian *maneggiare*, which is the training of horses in the *manege*; subsequently its meaning was extended to skillful handling in general, like of arms and musical instruments, as Don Armado illustrates. However, the word also became associated with the French *menage*, household, as an equivalent of "husbandry" in its sense of the art of running a household. The theatre of present-day management contains elements of both *manege* and *menage* and different managers and cultures may use different accents.

The founder of the science of economics, the Scot Adam Smith, in his 1776 book *The Wealth of Nations*, used "manage," "management" (even "bad management") and "manager" when dealing with the process and the persons involved in operating joint stock companies (Smith, V.i.e.). British economist John Stuart Mill (1806–1873) followed Smith in this use and clearly expressed his distrust of such hired people who were not driven by ownership. Since the 1880s the word "management" appeared occasionally in writings by American engineers, until it was canonized as a modern science by Frederick W. Taylor in *Shop Management* in 1903 and in *The Principles of Scientific Management* in 1911.

While Smith and Mill used "management" to describe a process and "managers" for the persons involved, "management" in the American sense—which has since been taken back by the British—refers not only to the process but also to the managers as a class of people. This class (1) does not own a business but sells its skills to act on behalf of the owners and (2) does not produce personally but is indispensable for making others produce, through motivation. Members of this class carry a high status and many American boys and girls aspire to the role. In the U.S., the manager is a cultural hero.

Let us know turn to other parts of the world. We will look at management in its context in other successful modern economies: Germany, Japan, France, Holland, and among the Overseas Chinese. Then we will examine management in the much larger part of the world that is still poor, especially South-East Asia and Africa, and in the new political configurations of Eastern Europe, and Russia in particular. We will then return to the U.S. via mainland China.

Germany

The manager is not a cultural hero in Germany. If anybody, it is the engineer who fills the hero role. Frederick Taylor's *Scientific Management* was conceived in a society of immigrants—where large number of workers with diverse backgrounds and skills had to work together. In Germany this heterogeneity never existed.

Elements of the medieval guild system have survived in historical continuity in Germany until the present day. In particular, a very effective apprenticeship system exists both on the shop floor and in the office, which alternates practical work and classroom courses. At the end of the apprenticeship the worker receives a certificate, the *Facharbeiterbrief*, which is recognized throughout the country. About two thirds of the German worker population holds such a certificate and a corresponding occupational pride. In fact, quite a few German company presidents have worked their way up from the ranks through an apprenticeship. In comparison, two thirds of the worker population in Britain have no occupational qualification at all.

The highly skilled and responsible German workers do not necessarily need a manager, American-style, to "motivate" them. They expect their boss or *Meister* to assign their tasks and to be the expert in resolving technical problems. Comparisons of similar German, British, and French organizations show the Germans as having the highest rate of personnel in productive roles and the lowest both in leadership and staff roles.

Business schools are virtually unknown in Germany. Native German management theories concentrate on formal systems. The inapplicability of American concepts of management was quite apparent in 1973 when the U.S. consulting firm of Booz, Allen and Hamilton, commissioned by the German Ministry of Economic Affairs, wrote a study of German management from an American view point. The report is highly critical and writes among other things that "Germans simply do not have a very strong concept of management." Since 1973, from my personal experience, the situation has not changed much. However, during this period the German economy has performed in a superior fashion to the

U.S. in virtually all respects, so a strong concept of management might have been a liability rather than an asset.

Japan

The American type of manager is also missing in Japan. In the United States, the core of the enterprise is the managerial class. The core of the Japanese enterprise is the permanent worker group; workers who for all practical purposes are tenured and who aspire at life-long employment. They are distinct from the non-permanent employees—most women and subcontracted teams led by gang bosses, to be laid off in slack periods. University graduates in Japan first join the permanent worker group and subsequently fill various positions, moving from line to staff as the need occurs while paid according to seniority rather than position. They take part in Japanese-style group consultation sessions for important decisions, which extend the decision-making period but guarantee fast implementation afterwards. Japanese are to a large extent controlled by their peer group rather than by their manager.

Japanese are to a large extent controlled by their peer group rather than by their manager.

Three researchers from the East-West Center of the University of Hawaii, Joseph Tobin, David Wu, and Dana Danielson, did an observation study of typical preschools in three countries: China, Japan, and the United States. Their results have been published both as a book and as a video. In the Japanese preschool, one teacher handled twenty-eight four-year olds. The video shows one particularly obnoxious boy, Hiroki, who fights with other children and throws teaching materials down from the balcony. When a little girl tries to alarm the teacher, the latter answers "what are you calling me for? Do something about it!" In the U.S. preschool, there is one adult for every nine children. This class has its problem child too, Glen, who refuses to clear away his toys. One of the teachers has a long talk with him and isolates him in a corner, until he changes his mind. It doesn't take much imagination to realize that managing Hiroki thirty years later will be a different process from managing Glen.

American theories of leadership are ill-suited for the Japanese group-controlled situation. During the past two decades, the Japanese have developed their own "PM" theory of leadership, in which P stands for performance and M for maintenance. The latter is less a concern for individual employees than for maintaining social stability. In view of the amazing success of the Japanese economy in the past thirty years, many Americans have sought for the secrets of Japanese management hoping to copy them.

There are no secrets of Japanese management, however; it is even doubtful whether there is such a thing as management, in the American sense, in Japan at all. The secret is in Japanese society; and if any group in society should be singled out as carriers of the secret, it is the workers, not the managers.

France

The manager, U.S. style, does not exist in France either. In a very enlightening book, unfortunately not yet translated into English, the French researcher Philippe d'Iribarne (1989) describes the results of in-depth observation and interview studies of management methods in three subsidiary plants of the same French multinational: in France, the United States, and Holland. He relates what he finds to information about the three societies in general. Where necessary, he goes back in history to trace the roots of the strikingly different behaviors in the completion of the same tasks. He identifies three kinds of basic principles *(logiques)* of management. In the USA, the principle is the *fair contract* between employer and employee, which gives the manager considerable prerogatives, but within its limits. This is really a labor *market* in which the worker sells his or her labor for a price. In France, the principle is the *honor* of each class in a society which has always been and remains extremely stratified, in which superiors behave as superior beings and subordinates accept and expect this, conscious of their own lower level in the national hierarchy but also of the honor of their own class. The French do not think in terms of managers versus nonmanagers but in terms of *cadres* versus *non-cadres;* one becomes cadre by attending the proper schools and one remains it forever; regardless of their actual task, cadres have the privileges of a higher social class, and it is very rare for a non-cadre to cross the ranks.

The conflict between French and American theories of management became apparent in the beginning of the twentieth century, in a criticism by the great French management pioneer Henri Fayol (1841-1925) on his U.S. colleague and contemporary Frederick W. Taylor (1856-1915). The difference in career paths of the two men is striking. Fayol was a French engineer whose career as a *cadre supérieur* culminated in the position of Président-Directeur-Général of a mining company. After his retirement he formulated his experiences in a pathbreaking text on organization: *Administration industrielle et générale*, in which he focussed on the sources of authority. Taylor was an American engineer who started his career in industry as a worker and attained his academic qualifications through evening studies. From chief engineer in a steel company he became one of the first management consultants. Taylor was not really concerned with the issue of authority at all; his focus was on efficiency. He proposed to split the task of the first-line boss into eight specialisms, each exercised by a different person; an idea which eventually led to the idea of a matrix organization.

Taylor's work appeared in a French translation in 1913, and Fayol read it and showed himself generally impressed but shocked by Taylor's "denial of the principle of the Unity of Command" in the case of the eight-boss-system.

Seventy years later André Laurent, another of Fayol's compatriots, found that French managers in a survey reacted very strongly against a suggestion that one employee could report to two different bosses, while U.S. managers in the same survey showed fewer misgivings. Matrix organization has never become popular in France as it has in the United States.

Holland

In my own country, Holland or as it is officially called, the Netherlands, the study by Philippe d'Iribarne found the management principle to be a need for *consensus* among all parties, neither predetermined by a contractual relationship nor by class distinctions, but based on an open-ended exchange of views and a balancing of interests. In terms of the different origins of the word "manager," the organization in Holland is more *menage* (household) while in the United States it is more *manege* (horse drill).

At my university, the University of Limburg at Maastricht, every semester we receive a class of American business students who take a program in European Studies. We asked both the Americans and a matched group of Dutch students to describe their ideal job after graduation, using a list of twenty-two job characteristics. The Americans attached significantly more importance than the Dutch to earnings, advancement, benefits, a good working relationship with their boss, and security of employment. The Dutch attached more importance to freedom to adopt their own approach to the job, being consulted by their boss in his or her decisions, training opportunities, contributing to the success of their organization, fully using their skills and abilities, and helping others. This list confirms d'Iribarne's findings of a contractual employment relationship in the United States, based on earnings and career opportunities, against a consensual relationship in Holland. The latter has centuries-old roots; the Netherlands were the first republic in Western Europe (1609–1810), and a model for the American republic. The country has been and still is governed by a careful balancing of interests in a multi-party system.

In terms of management theories, both motivation and leadership in Holland are different from what they are in the United States. Leadership in Holland presupposes modesty, as opposed to assertiveness in the United States. No U.S. leadership theory has room for that. Working in Holland is not a constant feast, however. There is a built-in premium on mediocrity and jealousy, as well as time-consuming ritual consultations to maintain the appearance of consensus and the pretense of modesty. There is unfortunately another side to every coin.

The overseas Chinese

Among the champions of economic development in the past thirty years we find three countries mainly populated by Chinese living outside the Chinese mainland: Taiwan, Hong Kong and Singapore. Moreover, overseas Chinese play a very important role in the economies of Indonesia, Malaysia, the Philippines and Thailand, where they form an ethnic minority. If anything, the little dragons—Taiwan, Hong Kong and Singapore—have been more economically successful than Japan, moving from rags to riches and now counted among the world's wealthy industrial countries. Yet very little attention has been paid to the way in which their enterprises have been managed. *The Spirit of Chinese Capitalism* by Gordon Redding (1990), the British dean of the Hong Kong Business School, is an excellent book about Chinese business. He bases his insights on personal acquaintance and in-depth discussions with a large number of overseas Chinese businesspeople.

Overseas Chinese American enterprises lack almost all characteristics of modern management. They tend to be small, cooperating for essential functions with other small organizations through networks based on personal relations. They are family-owned, without the separation between ownership and management typical in the West, or even in Japan and Korea. They normally focus on one product or market, with growth by opportunistic diversification; in this, they are extremely flexible. Decision making is centralized in the hands of one dominant family member, but other family members may be given new ventures to try their skills on. They are low-profile and extremely cost-conscious, applying Confucian virtues of thrift and persistence. Their size is kept small by the assumed lack of loyalty of non-family employees, who, if they are any good, will just wait and save until they can start their own family business.

If nothing else, the general lack of success in economic development of other countries should be sufficient argument to doubt the validity of Western management theories in non-Western environments.

Overseas Chinese prefer economic activities in which great gains can be made with little manpower, like commodity trading and real estate. They employ few professional managers, except their sons and sometimes daughters who have been sent to prestigious business schools abroad, but who upon return continue to run the family business the Chinese way.

The origin of this system, or—in the Western view—this lack of system, is found in the history of Chinese society, in which there were no formal laws, only formal networks of powerful people guided by general principles of Confucian virtue. The favors of the authorities could change daily, so nobody could be trusted except one's kinfolk—of whom, fortunately, there used to be many, in an extended family structure. The overseas Chinese way of doing business is also very well adapted to their position in the countries in which they form ethnic minorities, often envied and threatened by ethnic violence.

Overseas Chinese businesses following this unprofessional approach command a collective gross national product of some 200 to 300 billion US dollars, exceeding the GNP of Australia. There is no denying that it works.

MANAGEMENT TRANSFER TO POOR COUNTRIES

Four-fifths of the world population live in countries that are not rich but poor. After World War II and decolonization, the stated purpose of the United Nations and the World Bank has been to promote the development of all the world's countries in a war on poverty. After forty years it looks very much like we are losing this war. If one thing has become clear, it is that the export of Western—mostly American—management practices *and* theories to poor countries has contributed little to nothing to their development. There has been no lack of effort and money spent for this purpose: students from poor countries have been trained in this country, and teachers and Peace Corps workers have been sent to the poor countries. If nothing else, the general lack of success in economic development of other countries should be sufficient argument to doubt the validity of Western management theories in non-Western environments.

Assuming that with so-called modern management techniques and theories outsiders can develop a country has proven a deplorable arrogance.

If we examine different parts of the world, the development picture is not equally bleak, and history is often a better predictor than economic factors for what happens today. There is a broad regional pecking order with East Asia leading. The little dragons have passed into the camp of the wealthy; then follow South-East Asia (with its overseas Chinese minorities), Latin America (in spite of the debt crisis), South Asia, and Africa always trails behind. Several African countries have only become poorer since decolonization.

Regions of the world with a history of large-scale political integration and civilization generally have done better than regions in which no large-scale political and cultural infrastructure existed, even if the old civilizations had decayed or been suppressed by colonizers. It has become painfully clear that development cannot be pressure-cooked; it presumes a cultural infrastructure that takes time to grow. Local management is part of this infrastructure; it cannot be imported in package form. Assuming that with so-called modern management techniques and theories outsiders can develop a country has proven a deplorable arrogance. At best, one can hope for a dialogue between equals with the locals, in which the Western partner acts as the expert in Western technology and the local partner as the expert in local culture, habits, and feelings.

Russia and China

The crumbling of the former Eastern bloc has left us with a scattering of states and would-be states of which the political and economic future is extremely uncertain. The best predictions are those based on a knowledge of history, because historical trends have taken revenge on the arrogance of the Soviet rulers who believed they could turn them around by brute power. One obvious fact is that the former bloc is extremely heterogeneous, including countries traditionally closely linked with the West by trade and travel, like Czechia, Hungary, Slovenia, and the Baltic states, as well as others with a Byzantine or Turkish past; some having been prosperous, others always extremely poor.

The industrialized Western world and the World Bank seem committed to helping the ex-Eastern bloc countries develop, but with the same technocratic neglect for local cultural factors that proved so unsuccessful in the development assistance to other poor countries. Free market capitalism, introduced by Western-style management, is supposed to be the answer from Albania to Russia.

Let me limit myself to the Russian republic, a huge territory with some 140 million inhabitants, mainly Russians. We know quite a bit about the Russians as their country was a world power for several hundreds of years before communism, and in the nineteenth century it has produced some of the greatest writers in world literature. If I want to understand the Russians—including how they could so long support the Soviet regime—I tend to re-read Lev Nikolayevich Tolstoy. In his most famous novel *Anna Karenina* (1876) one of the main characters is a landowner. Levin, whom Tolstoy uses to express his own views and convictions about his people. Russian peasants used to be serfs; serfdom had been abolished in 1861, but the peasants, now tenants, remained as passive as before. Levin wanted to break this passivity by dividing the land among his peasants in exchange for a share of the crops; but the peasants only let the land deteriorate further. Here follows a quote:

> *"(Levin) read political economy and socialistic works . . . but, as he had expected, found nothing in them related to his undertaking. In the political economy books—in (John Stuart) Mill, for instance, whom he studied first and with great ardour, hoping every minute to find an answer to the questions that were engrossing him—he found only certain laws deduced from the state of agriculture in Europe; but he could not for the life of him see why these laws, which did not apply to Russia, should be considered universal. . . . Political economy told*

him that the laws by which Europe had developed and was developing her wealth were universal and absolute. Socialist teaching told him that development along those lines leads to ruin. And neither of them offered the smallest enlightenment as to what he, Levin, and all the Russian peasants and landowners were to do with their millions of hands and millions of acres, to make them as productive as possible for the common good. "

In the summer of 1991, the Russian lands yielded a record harvest, but a large share of it rotted in the fields because no people were to be found for harvesting. The passivity is still there, and not only among the peasants. And the heirs of John Stuart Mill (whom we met before as one of the early analysis of "management") again present their universal recipes which simply do not apply.

Citing Tolstoy, I implicitly suggest that management theorists cannot neglect the great literature of the countries they want their ideas to apply to. The greatest novel in the Chinese literature is considered Cao Xueqin's *The Story of the Stone*, also known as *The Dream of the Red Chamber* which appeared around 1760. It describes the rise and fall of two branches of an aristocratic family in Beijing, who live in adjacent plots in the capital. Their plots are joined by a magnificent garden with several pavilions in it, and the young, mostly female members of both families are allowed to live in them. One day the management of the garden is taken over by a young woman, Tan-Chun, who states:

"I think we ought to pick out a few experienced trust-worthy old women from among the ones who work in the Garden—women who know something about gardening already—and put the upkeep of the Garden into their hands. We needn't ask them to pay us rent; all we need ask them for is an annual share of the produce. There would be four advantages in this arrangement. In the first place, if we have people whose sole occupation is to look after trees and flowers and so on, the condition of the Garden will improve gradually year after year and there will be no more of those long periods of neglect followed by bursts of feverish activity when things have been allowed to get out of hand. Secondly there won't be the spoiling and wastage we get at present. Thirdly the women themselves will gain a little extra to add to their incomes which will compensate them for the hard work they put in throughout the year. And fourthly, there's no reason why we shouldn't use the money we should otherwise have spent on nursery-men, rockery specialists, horticultural cleaners and so on for other purposes. "

As the story goes on, the capitalist privatization—because that is what it is—of the Garden is carried through, and it works. When in the 1980s Deng Xiaoping allowed privatization in the Chinese villages, it also worked. It worked so well that its effects started to be felt in politics and threatened the existing political order; hence the knockdown at Tienanmen Square of June 1989. But it seems that the forces of privatization are getting the upper hand again in China. If we remember what Chinese entrepreneurs are able to do once they have become Overseas Chinese, we shouldn't be too surprised. But what works in China—and worked two centuries ago—does not have to work in Russia, not in Tolstoy's days and not today. I am not offering a solution; I only protest against a naive universalism that knows only one recipe for development, the one supposed to have worked in the United States.

A THEORY OF CULTURE IN MANAGEMENT

Our trip around the world is over and we are back in the United States. What have we learned? There is something in all countries called "management," but its meaning differs to a larger or smaller extent from one country to the other, and it takes considerable historical and cultural insight into local conditions to understand its processes, philosophies, and problems. If already the word may mean so many different things, how can we expect one country's theories of management to apply abroad? One should be extremely careful in making this assumption, and test it before considering it proven. Management is not a phenomenon that can be isolated from other processes taking place in a society. During our trip around the world we saw that it interacts with what happens in the family, at school, in politics, and government. It is obviously also related to religion and to beliefs about science. Theories of management always had to be interdisciplinary, but if we cross national borders they should become more interdisciplinary than ever.

Cultural differences between nations can be, to some extent, described using first four, and now five, bipolar *dimensions*. The position of a country on these dimensions allows us to make some predictions on the way their society operates, including their management processes and the kind of theories applicable to their management.

As the word culture plays such an important role in my theory, let me give you my definition, which differs from some other very respectable definitions. Culture to me is *the collective programming of the mind which distinguishes one group or category of people from another*. In the part of my work I am referring to now, the category of people is the nation.

Culture is a *construct*, that means it is "not directly accessible to observation but inferable from verbal statements and other behaviors and useful in predicting still other observable and measurable verbal and nonverbal behavior." It should not be reified; it is an auxiliary concept that should be used as long as it proves useful but bypassed where we can predict behaviors without it.

The same applies to the *dimensions* I introduced. They are constructs too that should not be reified. They do not "exist"; they are tools for analysis which may or may not clarify a situation. In my statistical analysis of empirical data the first four dimensions together explain forty-nine percent of the variance in the data. The other fifty-one percent remain specific to individual countries.

The first four dimensions were initially detected through a comparison of the values of similar people (employees and managers) in sixty-four national subsidiaries of the IBM Corporation. People working for the same multinational, but in different countries, represent very well-matched samples from the populations of their countries, similar in all respects except nationality.

The first dimension is labelled *Power Distance*, and it can be defined as the degree of inequality among people which the population of a country considers as normal: from relatively equal (that is, small power distance) to extremely unequal (large power distance). All societies are unequal, but some are more unequal than others.

The second dimension is labelled *Individualism*, and it is the degree to which people in a country prefer to act as individuals rather than as members of groups. The opposite of individualism can be called *Collectivism*, so collectivism is low individualism. The way I use the word it has no political connotations. In collectivist societies a child learns to respect the group to which it belongs, usually the family, and to differentiate between in-group members and out-group members (that is, all other people). When children grow up they remain members of their group, and they expect the group to protect them when they are in trouble. In return, they have to remain loyal to their group throughout life. In individualist societies, a child learns very early to think of itself as "I" instead of as part of "we." It expects one day to have to stand on its own feet and not to get protection from its group any more; and therefore it also does not feel a need for strong loyalty.

The third dimension is called *Masculinity* and its opposite pole *Femininity*. It is the degree to which tough values like assertiveness, performance, success and competition, which in nearly all societies are associated with the role of men, prevail over tender values like the quality of life, maintaining warm personal relationships, service, care for the weak, and solidarity, which in nearly all societies are more associated with women's roles. Women's roles differ from men's roles in all countries; but in tough societies, the differences are larger than in tender ones.

The fourth dimension is labelled *Uncertainty Avoidance*, and it can be defined as the degree to which people in a country prefer structured over unstructured situations. Structured situations are those in which there are clear rules as to how one should behave. These rules can be written down, but they can also be unwritten and imposed by tradition. In countries which score high on uncertainty avoidance, people tend to show more nervous energy, while in countries which score low, people are more easy-going. A (national) society with strong uncertainty avoidance can be called rigid; one with weak uncertainty avoidance, flexible. In countries where uncertainty avoidance is strong a feeling prevails of "what is different, is dangerous." In weak uncertainty avoidance societies, the feeling would rather be "what is different, is curious."

The fifth dimension was added on the basis of a study of the values of students in twenty-three countries carried out by Michael Harris Bond, a Canadian working in Hong Kong. He and I had cooperated in another study of students' values which had yielded the same four dimensions as the IBM data. However, we wondered to what extent our common findings in two studies could be the effect of a Western bias introduced by the common Western background of the researchers: remember Alice's croquet game. Michael Bond resolved this dilemma by deliberately introducing an Eastern bias. He used a questionnaire prepared at his request by his Chinese colleagues, the *Chinese Value Survey* (CVS), which was translated from Chinese into different languages and answered by fifty male and fifty female students in each of twenty-three countries in all five continents. Analysis of the CVS data produced three dimensions significantly correlated with the three IBM dimensions of power distance, individualism, and masculinity. There was also a fourth dimension, but it did not resemble uncertainty avoidance. It was composed, both on the positive and on the negative side, from items that had not been included in the IBM studies but were present in the Chinese Value Survey because they were rooted in the teachings of Confucius. I labelled this dimension: *Long-term* versus *Short-term Orientation*. On the long-term side one finds values oriented towards the future, like thrift (saving) and persistence. On the short-term side one finds values rather oriented towards the past and present, like respect for tradition and fulfilling social obligations.

Table 1 lists the scores on all five dimensions for the United States and for the other countries we just discussed. The table shows that each country has its own configuration on the four dimensions. Some of the values in the table have been estimated based on imperfect replications of personal impressions. The different dimension scores do not "explain" all the differences in management I described earlier. To understand management in a country, one should have both knowledge of and empathy with the entire local scene. However, the scores should make us aware that people in other countries may think, feel, and act very differently from us when confronted with basic problems of society.

IDIOSYNCRACIES OF AMERICAN MANAGEMENT THEORIES

In comparison to other countries, the U.S. culture profile presents itself as below average on power distance and uncertainty avoidance, highly individualistic,

Table 1
Culture Dimensions Scores for Ten Countries
(PD = Power Distance; ID = Individualism; MA = Masculinity;
UA = Uncertainty Avoidance; LT = Long Term Orientation)
H = top third, M = medium third, L = bottom third (among 53
countries and regions for the first four dimensions;
among 23 countries for the fifth)

	PD	ID	MA	UA	LT
USA	40 L	91 H	62 H	46 L	29 L
Germany	35 L	67 H	66 H	65 M	31 M
Japan	54 M	46 M	95 H	92 H	80 H
France	68 H	71 H	43 M	86 H	30*L
Netherlands	38 L	80 H	14 L	53 M	44 M
Hong Kong	68 H	25 L	57 H	29 L	96 H
Indonesia	78 H	14 L	46 M	48 L	25*L
West Africa	77 H	20 L	46 M	54 M	16 L
Russia	95*H	50*M	40*L	90*H	10*L
China	80*H	20*L	50*M	60*M	118 H

*estimated

fairly masculine, and short-term oriented. The Germans show a stronger uncertainty avoidance and less extreme individualism; the Japanese are different on all dimensions, least on power distance; the French show larger power distance and uncertainty avoidance, but are less individualistic and somewhat feminine; the Dutch resemble the Americans on the first three dimensions, but score extremely feminine and relatively long-term oriented; Hong Kong Chinese combine large power distance with weak uncertainty avoidance, collectivism, and are very long-term oriented; and so on.

The ideal principle of control in organizations in the market philosophy is competition between individuals.

The American culture profile is reflected in American management theories. I will just mention three elements not necessarily present in other countries; the stress on market processes, the stress on the individual, and the focus on managers rather than on workers.

The Stress on Market Processes

During the 1970s and 80s it has become fashionable in the United States to look at organizations from a "transaction costs" viewpoint. Economist Oliver Williamson has opposed "hierarchies" to "markets." The reasoning is that human social life consists of economic transactions between individuals. We found the same in d'Iribarne's description of the U.S. principle of the contract between employer and employee, the labor market in which the worker sells his or her labor for a price. These individuals will form hierarchical organizations when the cost of the economic transactions (such as getting information, finding out whom to trust etc.) is lower in a hierarchy than when all transactions would take place on a free market.

From a cultural perspective the important point is that *the "market" is the point of departure or base model*, and the organization is explained from market failure. A culture that produces such a theory is likely to prefer organizations that internally resemble markets to organizations that internally resemble more structured models, like those in Germany or France. The ideal principle of control in organizations in the market philosophy is *competition* between individuals. This philosophy fits a society that combines a not-too-large power distance with a not-too-strong uncertainty avoidance and individualism; besides the USA, it will fit all other Anglo countries.

The Stress on the Individual

I find this constantly in the design of research projects and hypotheses; also in the fact that in the U.S. psychology is clearly a more respectable discipline in management circles than sociology. Culture however is a collective phenomenon. Although we may get our information about culture from individuals, we have to interpret it at the level of collectivities. There are snags here known as the "ecological fallacy" and the "reverse ecological fallacy." None of the U.S. college textbooks on methodology I know deals sufficiently with the problem of multilevel analysis.

Culture can be compared to a forest, while individuals are trees. A forest is not just a bunch of trees; it is a symbiosis of different trees, bushes, plants, insects, animals and micro-organisms, and we miss the essence of the forest if we only describe its most typical trees. In the same way, a culture cannot be satisfactorily described in terms of the characteristics of a typical individual. There is a tendency in the U.S. management literature to overlook the forest for the trees and to ascribe cultural differences to interactions among individuals.

A striking example is found in the otherwise excellent book *Organizational Culture and Leadership* by Edgar H. Schein (1985). On the basis of his consulting experience he compares two large companies, nicknamed "Action" and "Multi." He explains the differences in culture between these companies by the group dynamics in their respective boardrooms. Nowhere in the book are any conclusions drawn from the fact that the first company is an American-based computer firm, and the second a Swiss-based pharmaceutics firm. This information is not even mentioned. A stress on interactions among individuals obviously fits a culture identified as the most individualistic in the world, but it will not be so well understood by the four-fifths of the world population for whom the group prevails over the individual.

One of the conclusions of my own multilevel research has been that culture at the national level and culture at the organizational level—corporate culture—are two very different phenomena and that the use of a common term for both is confusing. If we do use the common term, we should also pay attention to the occupational and the gender level of culture. National cultures differ primarily in the fundamental, invisible values held by a majority of their members, acquired in early childhood, whereas organizational cultures are a much more superficial phenomenon residing mainly in the visible practices of the organization, acquired by socialization of the new members who join as young adults. National cultures change only very slowly if at all; organizational cultures may be consciously changed, although this isn't necessarily easy. This difference between the two types of culture is the secret of the existence of multinational corporations that employ, as I showed in the IBM case, employees with extremely different national cultural values. What keeps them together is a corporation culture based on common practices.

Managers are much more involved in maintaining networks; if anything, it is the rank-and-file worker who can really make decisions on his or her own, albeit on a relatively simple level.

The Stress on Managers Rather than Workers

The core element of a work organization around the world is the people who do the work. All the rest is superstructure, and I hope to have demonstrated to you that it may take many different shapes. In the U.S. literature on work organization, however, the core element, if not explicitly then implicitly, is considered the manager. This may well be the result of the combination of extreme individualism with fairly strong masculinity, which has turned the manager into a culture hero of almost mythical proportions. For example, he—not really she—is supposed to make decisions all the time. Those of you who are or have been managers must know that this is a fable. Very few management decisions are just "made" as the myth suggests it. Managers are much more involved in maintaining networks; if anything, it is the rank-and-file worker who can really make decisions on his or her own, albeit on a relatively simple level.

An amusing effect of the U.S. focus on managers is that in at least ten American books and articles on management I have been misquoted as having studied IBM *managers* in my research, whereas the book clearly describes that the answers were from IBM *employees*. My observation may be biased, but I get the impression that compared to twenty or thirty years ago less research in this country is done among employees and more on managers. But managers derive their *raison d'être* from the people managed: culturally, they are the followers of the people they lead, and their effectiveness depends on the latter. In other parts of the world, this exclusive focus on the manager is less strong, with Japan as the supreme example.

CONCLUSION

This article started with *Alice in Wonderland*. In fact, the management theorist who ventures outside his or her own country into other parts of the world is like Alice in Wonderland. He or she will meet strange beings, customs, ways of organizing or disorganizing and theories that are clearly stupid, oldfashioned or even immoral—yet they may work, or at least they may not fail more frequently than corresponding theories do at home. Then, after the first culture shock, the traveller to Wonderland will feel enlightened, and may be able to take his or her experiences home and use them advantageously. All great ideas in science, politics and management have travelled from one country to another, and been enriched by foreign influences. The roots of American management theories are mainly in Europe: with Adam Smith, John Stuart Mill, Lev Tolstoy, Max Weber, Henri Fayol, Sigmund Freud, Kurt Lewin and many others. These theories were re-planted here and they developed and bore fruit. The same may happen again. The last thing we need is a Monroe doctrine for management ideas.

The issues explored here were presented by Dr. Hofstede, the Foundation for Administrative Research Distinguished International Scholar, at the 1992 Annual Meeting of the Academy of Management, Las Vegas, Nevada, August 11, 1992.

ABOUT THE AUTHOR

Geert Hofstede is a professor of organizational anthropology and international management at the University of Limburg at Maastricht, the Netherlands. He holds a M.Sc. degree in Mechanical Engineering from Delft Technical University, and a Ph.D. in Social Psychology from Groningen University, both in his native Netherlands.

He worked in Dutch as well as international business companies in roles varying from production worker to director of Human Resources. From 1965–1971, he founded and managed the Personnel Research department of IBM Europe. Since then, he has been teaching and researching at various international management institutes in four different European countries. In 1991 he held a Visiting Research Fellowship at the East-West Center, Honolulu, while simultaneously teaching at the College of Business Administration, University of Hawaii. He is a honorary professor of the University of Hong Kong.

Geert Hofstede is the founder and first director of the Institute for Research on Intercultural Cooperation (IRIC) at the University of Limburg, and an internationally recognized expert in the field of national and organizational culture research and theory. He has been a consultant to national and international business and government organizations. He wrote a pathbreaking book *Culture's Consequences* (Sage, 1980). A more popular book *Cultures and Organizations: Software of the Mind* appeared in 1991; translations have appeared or are under way into ten other languages. His articles—more than a hundred—have been published in the journals and readers of different countries of Europe, Asia, and North America.

TOTAL QUALITY AND HUMAN RESOURCES MANAGEMENT: LESSONS LEARNED FROM BALDRIGE AWARD-WINNING COMPANIES

Richard Blackburn, Benson Rosen

Executive Overview

Moving from business as usual to a Total Quality Management (TQM) culture demands much from an organization. Nowhere in the organization is the demand more apparent or more important than in the human resource management function. Interviews with human resource professionals employed by winners of the Malcolm Baldrige National Quality Award provide insights into how HRM "best practices" support TQM cultures in these firms.

Baldrige Award-winning companies have developed "portfolios" of human resource management policies to complement strategic TQM objectives. Aligning human resource practices with quality initiatives requires revolutionary changes in the way organizations train, empower, evaluate, and reward individuals and teams. However, the revolution is far from over. Even among organizations recognized for their TQM achievements, there is still a need for continuous improvement with respect to HR practices governing the selection, promotion, and development of future leaders.

A profile of fourteen "ideal" human resource practices is derived from the interview data. The best practices profile provides a useful benchmark for organizations to assess their own HR activities. Bottom-line payoffs for successful integration of HRM practices and TQM goals show up in reduced costs, increased product reliability, greater customer satisfaction, and shorter product development cycles.

Which human resource management (HRM) practices most effectively support a total quality culture? Where might a manager look to find the answer to this question? One source should be the HRM practices employed by winners of the Malcolm Baldrige National Quality Award.

Established in 1987, the Baldrige Award recognizes U.S. organizations that excel in quality management. The application process requires evidence of major shifts in management philosophy, practices, and policies related to the pursuit of

---

improved quality. If winning the Malcolm Baldrige National Quality Award is an indication of excellence in quality management, then the HRM policies found in these organizations should be those that support and sustain a total quality culture. What follows is the result of an attempt to codify the HR policies and practices of these Baldrige Award-winning organizations.[1]

Table 1
Participating Baldrige Award-winning Companies

Company	Title of Interviewee	Supporting Documents
Federal Express	Managing Director of HR Development	
General Motors— Cadillac Car Division	Director of Organizational Development	
Globe Metallurgical	No Interview Conducted	The Evolution of Quality at Globe Metallurgical
IBM Rochester	Personnel Advisor	
Motorola	Vice President—Quality	
Wallace Company	District Manager	Mission Statement Quality Guide Baldrige Application (Condensed Version)
Westinghouse—Commercial Nuclear Fuel Division	Manager of Human Resources	Total Quality Guide
Xerox Business Products/Systems	No Interview Conducted	Mission Statement Quality Tool Training Guide Leadership Through Quality Benchmarking Guide Baldrige Application

[1]We developed a clear picture of HR policies and practices by interviewing key human resource professionals in a sample of Baldrige-winning companies. Interviews with representatives from six of these firms covered thirteen broad areas of HRM policy (e.g., training, employee involvement, performance evaluation systems). These areas reflect the Human Resource Development and Management Category on the Baldrige application. In addition, we examined company documents, mission statements, and training materials. Using interview data or company documents, we developed profiles of the HRM policies in eight Baldrige Award-winning companies. Table 1 shows the participating organizations, interviewee titles, and supporting materials.

A PARADIGM SHIFT IN HR PRACTICES

Our interviews provide evidence of a paradigm shift in the HR policies adopted by those organizations who have claimed the Baldrige Award. Traditional HR policies conceived in command and control cultures have given way to new HR policies supportive of cultures characterized by employee commitment, cooperation, and communication. Equally striking is the evidence that Baldrige Award-winning organizations have revolutionized all (or nearly all) of their major HR policies and procedures. HR policies were mutually interdependent, congruent, and directed at supporting a total quality management perspective throughout the corporation. Although individual policies and practices varied across organizations, within organizations the internal consistency of "portfolios" of policies and procedures was impressive. Collectively, the HRM policies in these organizations work to accomplish the following tasks:

1. Communicate the importance of each employee's contribution to total quality;

2. Stress quality-related synergies available through teamwork;

3. Empower employees to "make a difference"; and

4. Reinforce individual and team commitment to quality with a wide range of rewards and reinforcements.

Table 2 contrasts "traditional" HRM policies with those policies found in companies recognized for successfully implementing a total quality effort. The evolution from traditional HRM practices to "new" HRM policies also illustrates the evolving role of HRM; from a support function to a leadership function in the enterprise. In traditional organizations, HRM functions identify, prepare, direct, and reward organizational actors to follow rather narrow organizational and job scripts. In TQM organizations, HRM units develop policies and procedures to insure that employees can perform multiple roles (as the result of cross-training and membership on cross-functional work teams), improvise when necessary, and direct themselves in the continuous improvement of product quality and customer service.

THE TQM CONTEXT—CORPORATE CULTURE

HRM practices in TQM organizations must be congruent with a corporate culture built on the shared assumptions of employee dedication to quality and customer service. Pauline Brody, chairwoman of Xerox's Quality Forum, described the need for such a cultural transformation as follows:

Table 2
The Evolution of a Total Quality HR Paradigm

Corporate Context Dimension	Traditional Paradigm	Total Quality Paradigm
Corporate Culture	Individualism	Collective efforts
	Differentiation	Cross-functional work
	Autocratic leadership	Coaching/enabling
	Profits	Customer satisfaction
	Productivity	Quality

Human Resource Characteristics	Traditional Paradigm	Total Quality Paradigm
Communications	Top-down	Top-down
		Horizontal, lateral
		Multidirectional
Voice and involvement	Employment-at-will	Due process
	Suggestion systems	Quality circles
		Attitude surveys
Job Design	Efficiency	Quality
	Productivity	Customization
	Standard procedures	Innovation
	Narrow span of control	Wide span of control
	Specific job descriptions	Autonomous work teams
		Empowerment
Training	Job related skills	Broad range of skills
	Functional, technical	Cross-functional
		Diagnostic, problem solving
	Productivity	Productivity and quality
Performance	Individual goals	Team goals
Measurement and Evaluation	Supervisory review	Customer, peer and supervisory review
	Emphasize financial performance	Emphasize quality and service
Rewards	Competition for individual merit increases and benefits	Team/group based rewards Financial rewards, financial and nonfinancial recognition
Health and Safety	Treat problems	Prevent problems
		Safety Programs
		Wellness Programs
		Employee assistance
Selection/Promotion	Selected by manager	Selected by peers
Career Development	Narrow job skills	Problem-solving skills
	Promotion based on individual accomplishment	Promotion based on group facilitation
	Linear career path	Horizontal career path

TQM requires a change in organizational culture, a fundamental change in the way individuals and groups approach their work and their roles in the organization, that is, from an environment of distrust and fear of reprisal to one of openness and trust where creativity can flourish; from working as individuals to working as teams; from protection of organizational turfs to the breakdown of departmental barriers; from an autocratic management style of direction and control to a softer style of team leader and coach; from power concentrated at the top to power shared with employees; from a focus on results to a focus on continuous improvement of the processes that deliver the results; and finally a change from making decisions based on gut-feel to an analytic, fact-based approach to management.[2]

Motorola echoes Brody's position that cultural changes are critical to attaining corporate quality objectives. The cultures at both Motorola and Xerox's Business Products and Systems unit (BP&S) value the inherent worth and contribution of the individual employee. At Motorola, the significance of the individual employee to building a "total quality" culture is communicated by the company's perspective on job security. Employees who establish a ten-year record of successful performance become "Service Club" members. Membership virtually guarantees future job security. According to Motorola, job security and the freedom it affords employees contribute to a culture that supports innovation, flexibility, and acceptance of change—important elements in achieving a commitment to total quality.

Mission statements in Baldrige Award-winning companies emphasize the achievement of quality goals through committed, empowered employees. However, words alone will not transform well-entrenched corporate cultures. As noted by Xerox's Brody, successful cultural change requires modification of human resource strategies to support total quality management. Policies with respect to communication, job design, conditions of employment, training, evaluation systems, and reward systems must be congruent with TQM objectives.

HR PROCESSES AT THE BALDRIGE WINNERS

Communication—The Corporate Message

Once top management had established a corporate vision to pursue a TQM culture, each Baldrige winner developed strategies for communicating the new

---

[2]Pauline N. Brody, "Introduction to Total Quality Management," in *Total Quality Management: A report of proceedings from the Xerox Quality Forum II*, August 1990.

mission throughout the organization. The cultural shift toward TQM requires top management to share ownership of all relevant organizational information. While sometimes threatening to those who perceive information as power, Baldrige firms believe that frequent, honest, and open communication with employees is needed to reinforce the quality culture realignment.

Executive actions speak louder than executive words. Clear and consistent communication is achieved only when managers act on their quality pronouncements. Others in an organization observe carefully how top managers allocate their time and attention. Xerox BP&S uses the expression "walk the talk" to emphasize the importance of consistency between the words and deeds of company leaders relative to TQM activities.

To keep employees up to date on the organization's performance in general, and its quality activities and objectives in particular, communication must be timely, clear, and comprehensive. Large, multinational organizations must communicate the mission across time zones and in many languages. Fortunately, communication technologies provide organizations with a rich variety of channels and media with which to accomplish this task.

Federal Express, Cadillac, and IBM Rochester use their own in-house television networks to broadcast "live" to their employees on a wide range of quality issues. On FXTV, Federal Express uses a call-in format where key managers respond to employee questions and problems. Motorola and Westinghouse CNFD prepare TQM-related video tapes for viewing by employees at their convenience. Senior leadership at Wallace holds biweekly teleconferences to acknowledge "quality wins" and associate (no employees at Wallace) suggestions. Voice-mail and E-mail represent additional strategies for communicating rapidly with employees about the continuing corporate emphasis on quality. During the Baldrige application process, Cadillac employees got updates and answers to oft-asked questions via "The Baldrige Minute" on the company's voice-mail system. In addition, all of the individuals we talked to described a variety of corporate newspapers, site-based newsletters, and weekly news bulletins that reported on quality initiatives, tracked TQM and Baldrige progress, and recognized excellent quality performance.

Electronic and print media supplement, but by no means replace, face-to-face meetings on important quality topics. Cadillac management conducts an "Annual State of the Business Meeting," attended by all employees, to share quality victories and future quality objectives. Motorola management hosts quarterly town meetings at every site, supplemented by "rap sessions" between top managers and smaller groups of employees. At Xerox BP&S employees may interview their manager's manager to broaden their perspectives on quality issues.

Formal top-down communication channels keep employees abreast of corporate quality initiatives, progress, and problems. However, top-down communication represents only one direction for important information flow. The Baldrige Award-winning companies encourage bottom-up communication to insure that employee voices are heard in the managerial and executive suites.

These Baldrige winners implemented a variety of systems to facilitate upward communication. Round-table meetings with top managers, open-door policies, and suggestion systems encourage employees to share their insights on improving quality and customer service. In many of the companies, corporate policy requires top managers to quickly acknowledge and reinforce these efforts. IBM Rochester's "Speak Up" program requires responses from responsible parties within ten days. Federal Express has an open-door policy that requires management response to employee concerns within eleven days. Wallace Company's suggestion system requires a twenty-four-hour response to a suggestion or complaint.

Annual employee attitude and satisfaction surveys represent another mechanism for upward communications. Motorola, Federal Express, IBM Rochester and Wallace all use comprehensive employee attitude surveys to monitor employee satisfaction and identify problem areas. These surveys typically ask employees to rate their supervisors on such dimensions as leadership, communication, and support. In the 1991 employee attitude survey, IBM Rochester received and analyzed more than 35,000 written comments. Survey data and written comments are summarized and fed back to supervisors and work units. Managers develop action plans to address employee concerns. The Baldrige companies believe that survey findings help management remove barriers and disincentives that adversely affect employee performance.

Baldrige Award-winning companies go far beyond simply asking for employee ideas. In each of the companies we examined, employees also participate on advisory groups, task forces, and cross-functional teams to solve problems and improve systems. For example, across the corporation, Federal Express has 4,000 Quality Action teams, and Motorola has 2,200 Total Customer Satisfaction teams. Westinghouse CNFD has 200 self-formed and self-managed problem-solving teams, and Cadillac has rationalized its product development process to the point where fifty-five teams now direct the entire process. More than sixty percent of Cadillac's employees are members of some type of team. Xerox BP&S estimates that at any given time seventy-six percent of all employees serve on some type of task force or advisory team. Similarly, IBM Rochester and Wallace create site-wide problem-solving teams on an as needed basis.

While traditional companies rely on suggestion systems and quality circles to solicit employee ideas, the Baldrige-winning companies go much further. Employees are encouraged to ask tough questions, challenge inefficient policies, and stay informed on business strategy. Xerox BP&S, Wallace and IBM Rochester adhere to open-door policies that allow employees at any level to bring quality concerns directly to top management. Moreover, employees are delegated the power and authority to pursue their ideas, work with others to solve problems that they have identified, and improve work systems. In so doing, employees gain greater control over the quality of their work and their work lives.

Job Design

At the operational level, changes in the way jobs are carried out serve as the catalyst forcing revolutionary changes in many HR processes. In the past, work was organized to maximize efficiency. Supervisors narrowly defined jobs and closely monitored both quality and productivity. In a TQM company the focus of jobs must be on quality. This radical shift requires that job design emphasize innovation, creativity, and problem solving aimed at maximizing the quality and not only the quantity of output. Individual jobs may be combined into cross-functional work teams that can operate permanently or be formed on an *ad hoc* basis to deal with short-term quality problems.

Interview data indicate that Baldrige companies have embraced empowerment as an underlying framework that enables individual employees to solve problems and satisfy customers without time-consuming action approvals. Where Motorola once required upper management approval for replacement of defective products, the corporation now gives sales representatives the authority to replace products up to six years after purchase. IBM Rochester has decentralized decision making to lower levels at the site and given employees greater autonomy in how they do their jobs.

At Wallace, associates receive assertiveness training so they will feel comfortable making important decisions, and the company saw a 600 percent increase in associate participation in various quality team activities between 1985 and 1990. In addition, to help associates better appreciate the impact of their jobs on customer satisfaction, each Wallace associate visits one customer one day a year. Similarly, large numbers of Globe Metallurgical employees tour facilities of major customers to gain an understanding of how Globe's products are used. Employees at Globe also have been "given responsibilities unheard of in the old days. Now, no supervisors are needed at (the) Beverly (plant site) on the . . . weekends, as hourly group leaders take care of business."[3] Westinghouse CNFD increased levels

---

[3]From "The Evolution of Quality at Globe Metallurgical," 1989.

of employee autonomy, giving employees greater freedom to plan and execute their job responsibilities. Some of this "empowerment" was necessitated by staff reductions in managerial positions. Fewer managers resulted in broader spans of control and greater pressure to allow employees to manage themselves. Federal Express empowers employees to "do everything humanly possible to get the job done and to satisfy customers."

While empowerment programs are underway in each of the Baldrige companies, only a few of the companies interviewed have attempted to harness and coordinate this individual commitment into permanent autonomous or self-managed work teams. Motorola is moving in the direction of structuring the firm around the self-managed work team. At Westinghouse CNFD team members review peer performance and administer a peer discipline review process. Cadillac has created semi-autonomous work teams, with supervisors retaining authority to deal with scheduling and disciplinary problems. Each of these companies anticipates that creating opportunities for teams to take responsibility for and control of their own work will generate employee pride, commitment, and task ownership.

Training

Redesigned jobs make new demands on the knowledge, skills, and abilities required of employees in a TQM organization. In addition, multiple communication efforts heighten employee awareness about and motivation towards a company's quality objectives. But motivation to pursue quality objectives without the requisite abilities can frustrate even the most conscientious employee.

Once employees understand the corporate mission and quality objectives, they must have or be allowed to develop the skills and abilities necessary to carry out the quality mandate. The firms represented here view training as a crucial step toward TQM. While most organizations train employees in functional and managerial skills, the Baldrige companies focus their training efforts on quality. Their quality training programs are comprehensive, well funded, and fully supported by top management.

While most organizations train employees in functional and managerial skills, the Baldrige companies focus their training efforts on quality.

Each of the companies requires all employees to learn the fundamentals of TQM. For example, every Xerox BP&S employee receives twenty-eight hours of training on a range of quality tools including benchmarking. At Federal Express, all employees attend two programs, "Quality Advantage" and "Quality Action Teams" where they receive instruction on the basics of quality management and quality team development. Similarly, Wallace sends its associates through training it dubs "Quality Awareness Programs." Wallace also requires forty hours of training on "The People Side of Quality." IBM Rochester employees focus on "Market Driven Quality" in their training, and Motorola employees master the fundamentals of statistical process control, cycle time, and six sigma (defect reduction) programs. All Westinghouse CNFD employees receive one week a year of quality training. Among other topics, Westinghouse CNFD employees learn how to empower others to make decisions.

At Cadillac, a union-management team recommended that *skilled* hourly workers receive eighty hours of quality training during 1990. This training included not only statistical quality methods, but also instruction in health and safety issues and leadership skills. And all *supervisory* employees were offered three- or four-day courses based on Deming's leadership and quality models.

Quality training doesn't come cheap. Xerox BP&S estimates that it has invested more than $125 million in quality training.

To reinforce top management commitment to the importance of TQM and quality training, top executives at Wallace take the courses with their associates. Both IBM Rochester and Cadillac require top-level managers to attend quality courses first. These managers then teach the courses to the next level of managers. This strategy builds top-level ownership of the quality message while reinforcing the importance of the training to lower-level employees. Similarly, while Globe Metallurgical sought outside assistance to train personnel at its headquarters, members of the corporate Quality-Efficiency-Cost Committee trained the remaining employees at other sites.

Quality training doesn't come cheap. Xerox BP&S estimates that it has invested more than $125 million in quality training. Federal Express employs more than 650 full-time trainers at sites around the world. Cadillac sent over 1400 employees to a four-day W. Edwards Deming quality training program at a cost of $650 per employee. Wallace has invested nearly $750,000 and over 19,000 hours of training in its associates since 1988. IBM Rochester provides about 45,000 student-days of training a year to its nearly 8,000 employees. Nevertheless, these "best" quality companies view these expenditures not as costs but as investments.

Of course, such a belief brings up the question of how well companies can assess the payback from this quality training. Wallace associates are evaluated on fifty quality-related skills as part of their annual performance appraisal. This enables supervisors to track performance changes attributable to quality training and to report improvements in each of the evaluated skills. Cadillac conducts a careful evaluation of training by comparing employees who have attended programs with a control group of employees who have not yet attended training. Cadillac reports significant improvements for the groups of employees trained in quality management. The most dramatic data on the impact of training come from Motorola. Based on two systematic studies, Motorola estimates that it earns $30 for every $1 invested in quality training.

Interestingly, the training functions in some of the Baldrige companies have taken a TQM perspective on the provision of education by treating other units in their organizations as customers. At IBM Rochester the education department no longer tells senior management what should be provided. Rather, managers tell the education department what is needed and programs are designed to provide that training. By doing so, the time taken to deliver such training programs has been reduced from five days to two.

The most dramatic data on the impact of training come from Motorola. Based on two systematic studies, Motorola estimates that it earns $30 for every $1 invested in quality training.

Similarly, for each Cadillac plant and staff unit, a training priorities committee determines the specific knowledge, skills, and abilities employees need to meet their organization's quality goals. Training programs are then customized to meet those needs at the individual, work unit, and divisional levels, as appropriate.

Training in quality provides employees at every organizational level with the tools needed to recognize faulty processes, identify problems, and evaluate and implement alternative solutions. However, employees must also be afforded the opportunity to use these new skills and to be recognized and rewarded for their actions. The companies in our sample have created human resource policies and practices that permit employees to apply their quality skills, to assume ownership for solving quality problems, and to receive appropriate rewards and recognition for their accomplishments.

Performance Review Systems

In any organization, what gets measured is what gets done! Not surprisingly, the Baldrige Award winners incorporate quality dimensions into their performance review systems. Additionally, individual performance reviews reflected the input of customers, both internal and external, as appropriate.

Westinghouse CNFD uses a management by objectives performance review system with quality improvement representing one of the major objectives against which employees are evaluated. Similarly, Federal Express rates employees on both "quality of work" and "customer service" dimensions in the context of performance reviews. Xerox BP&S made an even more fundamental change in its performance review system. Rather than evaluate employees on such traditional dimensions as "meets standards" or "follows procedures," Xerox BP&S now rates employees on such quality-based dimensions as "continuous improvement," "problem-solving," and "team contributions."

Frequently, managers have only partial information with which to evaluate employee contributions to quality and customer service. For example, when teamwork is required, an employee is regularly off-site, or a supervisor's span of control is extremely large (as may be the case in a team-based structure), co-workers may provide the best knowledge of who has been the most effective team player. To help managers develop a more complete picture of each employee's accomplishments, IBM Rochester, Cadillac, and Federal Express routinely consider peer reviews as a part of performance evaluations, and all of the companies in the sample gather information from both internal and external customers and suppliers to round out the performance assessment.

W. Edwards Deming, one of the founders of the quality movement, argues that evaluating past performance can be destructive and unrelated to future improvement. He argues that a TQM culture requires fundamental changes in the way performance review systems operate. Rather than focus on past mistakes, managers should help employees solve performance problems and reward continuous improvements. Consistent with Deming's philosophy, several Baldrige companies replaced backward-looking performance evaluation systems with forward-looking personal planning and development systems.

Cadillac replaced their traditional performance "review" system with a Personnel Development Planning Process. Managers meet with employees to set future expectations, identify training needs, provide coaching, and reward continuous improvement. Similarly, Motorola uses a Performance and Career Planning System to emphasize progress and coaching in its employee reviews. Wallace has replaced its performance appraisal program with a Performance Enhancement Program.

At Wallace, supervisors *and* associates each complete separate evaluations of the associate's quality-related job skills. Computer-generated profiles highlight areas of agreement and difference. It is the associate's responsibility to schedule a meeting with his or her supervisor to discuss the results of this analysis. Once in the meeting, the associate has complete control of the meeting agenda. The emphasis in the Performance Enhancement Program is on non-threatening discussions of the quality process and the employee's contribution to that process.

These companies have thoroughly revised their performance review systems to make them supportive of TQM objectives. Revisions include incorporating quality dimensions into the review process, using data from customers, peers, and self-assessment, and in several cases, changing the focus from past performance to future-oriented development and continuous improvement. Consistent with the TQM philosophy, these companies are continuously working hard to improve the performance review system and the quality and timeliness of feedback to their employees.

Reward Systems and Recognition Programs

Maintaining a TQM culture requires recognizing and rewarding continuous quality improvement and quality customer service. Examination of the Baldrige Award winners reveals a variety of formal and informal, financial and non-financial rewards for individuals and teams who contribute to the total quality effort.

All of the companies strive for balance between recognizing individual and team performance. At Xerox BP&S, individuals may be nominated for the President's Award or the Xerox Achievement Award. Teams compete for the Team Excellence Award and the Excellence in Customer Satisfaction Award. Motorola also recognizes both individual and team contributions. Motorola sponsors a Team Quality Olympics where teams make formal presentations about their quality successes and receive gold, silver, or bronze medals based on their contributions. At the corporate level, the Motorola CEO Quality Award can go to either individuals or small groups. It is a distinct accomplishment to win such an award, as only seventy of them have been given in nine years. One such award went to an employee who submitted nearly 300 quality suggestions in one year, more than 200 of which were implemented. IBM Rochester presents the Market Driven Quality Award for outstanding individual and team achievements in quality improvement.

Westinghouse CNFD has an elaborate peer review model for determining Quality Achievement winners. The process begins with peer nominations. An employee panel reviews and selects winners from among the nominations. Recipients of these awards are then recognized at a formal dinner. Federal Express and Cadillac empower managers to immediately recognize exceptional performance with cash or other awards. Federal Express managers can make instant awards of cash and pins for meritorious efforts. The Bravo Zulu award is one form of such recognition. Its name comes from the U.S. Navy flags for BZ, meaning "Well done!". The Golden Falcon award is provided for outstanding examples of customer service. These awards can be worth up to $500, and some twenty of them are made each year. Cadillac managers can give up to $500 instantly under their Spontaneous Recognition Award program.

Profit sharing and gainsharing programs allow employees to share in the financial benefits the organization reaps from their quality efforts.

- 457 -

These awards provide immediate feedback to all employees for outstanding quality efforts. Such awards also communicate to employees that the organization values their efforts to improve quality and customer service. In addition to monetary awards, the organizations also highlight excellence through the publication of success stories in company newsletters, through spontaneous celebration of special accomplishments, and through the awarding of plaques and prizes. For instance, at Wallace, the CEO sends congratulatory letters for outstanding quality performance to associates' homes, and high-performing quality teams are rewarded with dinners and picnics.

Building a total quality management culture requires the dedication and cooperation of all employees. Profit sharing and gainsharing programs allow employees to share in the financial benefits the organization reaps from their quality efforts. Xerox BP&S has implemented both a gainsharing and a profit sharing plan. Wallace has implemented a gainsharing plan where bonus money is awarded based on the achievement of specific corporate goals. Cadillac also has a profit sharing plan in place. At Federal Express, performance is heavily weighted with quality measures and key executives can earn up to forty percent of their salaries in performance-based bonuses. Eighty-five percent of other Federal Express employees also participate in some type of incentive program.

IBM has recently moved to a variable pay system which will eventually cover ninety percent of its exempt and non-exempt employees. Employee compensation will soon be influenced by IBM's overall corporate pay position relative to its competitors, an individual's contribution to unit performance, and the unit's actual business performance.

Health and Safety

Companies reaffirm the value of their employees in creating a TQM culture by providing a safe and healthy work environment. In consort with the policies discussed previously, the Baldrige companies emphasize a prevention-oriented approach to health and safety. With respect to building a healthy work force, the companies have all developed wellness programs. Components of these programs range from in-house spas and weight rooms, through seminars and personal advice on nutrition, diet, and stress management, to providing reimbursement for employees who require such assistance from outside professionals. More than 1000 employees at Cadillac take advantage of the company-sponsored health spa. Federal Express sponsors a Weight Watchers program on site, while IBM Rochester provides each employee with a $500 health account to be used for preventive care as the employee sees fit. In addition to providing recreation and health management programs, Xerox BP&S provides confidential family and personal assistance on a variety of issues.

Safety is also a major concern at each of the companies we examined. Xerox BP&S's Office of Environmental Health and Safety coordinates fire protection, toxicology, product safety, and environmental issues. The firm works to eliminate the root causes of safety problems, not just mitigate the symptoms. Similarly, one of Cadillac's People Strategy Teams strives to find ways of making the work environment safer and more enjoyable. Westinghouse CNFD has initiated a safety observer program in which a core of specially trained employees report to their supervisors on safety problems. Supervisors must follow up on each safety report with a recommended course of action to eliminate the problem. Wallace uses safety coordinators and safety committees to identify and respond to potential safety hazards, as part of its "Safety First-Family First" safety assurance program.

The Baldrige Award-winning companies monitor health and safety continuously and systematically. Their dedication to continuous quality improvement includes creating a positive work environment and high quality of life for their employees. The companies work hard to create safe and healthy working conditions, attack these problems proactively, track the progress of remedial actions, and reward improvements.

Selection, Promotion and Career Development

Surprisingly, for many of the Baldrige Award-winning companies, selection, promotion, and career development processes remained relatively unchanged in the shift from a traditional HR perspective to a TQM-based HR perspective. When asked to describe changes in selection processes as a result of their organization's TQM emphasis, most of our respondents indicated that the same processes remained in place—find the best available applicant and assume that he or she can be socialized and trained to function effectively in a TQM environment. The underlying assumption for many of these firms is that individuals with the requisite skills can readily be taught to produce quality work. The only creative modification of the typical recruitment and selection process reported among these companies came from Federal Express. FedEx established eighteen recruitment centers where applicants are screened by possible peers. Employees rotate into and out of these centers and assist in making entry level selection decisions.

None of the other Baldrige firms has yet moved to selecting employees based directly on their motivation and ability to perform effectively in a TQM company. However, traditional selection procedures may need rethinking given the demands of a TQM culture. For example, under the new operating paradigm, employees will be expected to exhibit competencies in customer service, in self-direction and self-development, and in team-development skills. The relatively narrow job descriptions currently in place in most organizations (as the result of legal mandates) must give way to broader descriptions that will include requirements for problem solving and continuous improvements in both functional and cross-functional work teams. Selection methods must enable employees and managers to assess or predict aptitude and ability to adapt to constantly changing job and customer requirements as well as applicant compatibility with an existing or new work team.

If new job requirements demand these competencies, then new selection procedures will have to be developed. For instance, how does one assess an applicant's ability or willingness to provide good customer service or the aptitude for learning multiple skills over time? Will these changing job demands suggest that in the future each semi-autonomous team will be responsible for the recruitment and hiring of new team members? And if this becomes the case, then how can organizations assure that relevant legal constraints have been observed? How does the organization assure that certain groups do not systematically exclude women and minorities from group membership because the applicant fails to "fit" the current group profile? These are issues still waiting to be explored in those firms moving toward a TQM culture.

Accordingly, career development in TQM organizations must deemphasize promotions as symbols of corporate achievement.

TQM companies must also reconsider their promotion criteria. In the past, many organizations relied on assessment centers for evaluating future managers and administrators. The assessment center provided data on managerial candidates' abilities to take charge of leaderless groups, make persuasive presentations, delegate, and work under stressful conditions. In the TQM environment, a complementary set of leadership skills will be needed. Promotion criteria and corresponding assessment center tasks will need to evaluate an individual's potential to help teams clarify goals, set expectations for team excellence, empower others to solve cross-functional problems, encourage innovation, and reward outstanding accomplishments. The transformation of managerial roles from director, controller, and inspector to coach, facilitator, and team manager requires parallel changes in selection and promotion criteria.

Under the traditional paradigm, career development was frequently synonymous with preparation for upward mobility. TQM organizations are flatter, limiting promotion opportunities. Accordingly, career development in TQM organizations must deemphasize promotions as symbols of corporate achievement. In TQM organizations, career paths will include many horizontal moves to prepare managers for solving cross-functional problems and provide them with a more holistic view of organizational issues. In years to come, we might expect a much greater emphasis on career development strategies such as job rotation, liaison assignments, and task force leadership. In addition, career development must emphasize opportunities for continuous learning and challenging entrepreneurial assignments.

The data suggest that the Baldrige Award-winning organizations have not fully considered the implications of TQM for selection, promotion, and career management. Our interviewees are the first to acknowledge that they have much to learn about revising selection and promotion criteria and designing career paths to develop future leaders for TQM organizations.

Organizational Outcomes

What are the tangible outcomes of building a TQM culture and supporting it with appropriate HR practices? A quick look at the bottom line for these award-winning companies suggests that measurable results have been generally impressive. Despite recent setbacks, the Wallace Company did increase on-time deliveries from 75 to 92 percent, sales by 69 percent, and operating profits by 740 percent in three years. Globe Metallurgical reduced customer complaints by 91 percent and increased manpower efficiency in certain areas by more than 50 percent during the same period of time. The firm eliminated $11.3 million in operating costs between 1986 and 1988, a 367 percent cost reduction. IBM Rochester increased revenue per employee 35 percent from 1986 to 1989, and the site was able to reduce new product development cycle time to eighteen months from the previous three to five years. Cadillac reduced reliability problems in its vehicles by as much as 71 percent since 1986 and increased customer satisfaction by 19 percent from 1985 to 1989.

As a result of efforts undertaken by the Baldrige companies regarding the work environment, improvements occurred in many important health and safety areas. While hard data are difficult to obtain, a GAO study of twenty companies that were among the highest scoring applicants for the Baldrige Award in 1988 and 1989 (including some of the companies we examined) found that safety and health rates, measured by work days lost to occupational injury and illness, improved in twelve of fourteen companies with available data.[4] For instance, the accident rate at Globe Metallurgical, which had been near the industry average in 1985, has since fallen, even though there has been an overall increase in accident rate in their industry. In 1987, Wallace's accident record placed them in the state's high-risk insurance pool with a corresponding increase in worker-compensation premiums from $250,000 to as much as $700,000. Intensive job-specific safety training as well as training in general safety such as proper lifting, fire hazards, and CPR reduced the accident rate substantially and lifted the company out of the high-risk pool, creating sizable savings in premiums.

---

[4]"U.S. Companies Improve Performance Through Quality Efforts," United States General Accounting Office, 1991.

Each firm suggested that without the appropriate changes in HRM practices and policies, the TQM culture at least partially responsible for these impressive results would never have become a reality. Top management could provide vision, tools, and communications, but unless systems were in place to support the basic changes in how the organization conducted its business. TQM as an all-pervasive way of doing business would never have survived.

Granted, not all of these Baldrige stories close on a positive note. Like some of Peters and Waterman's excellent companies that over time turned out to be not so excellent, some Baldrige winners also have faced performance problems. For instance, Wallace Company customers eventually rebelled at paying higher prices to fund the costs of the company's quality program. The company lost money, laid off employees, and was forced to operate in Chapter 11. Federal Express's decision to curtail its operation in Europe also was a major setback for the firm. And the larger corporate parents of both IBM Rochester and Cadillac have suffered well-documented reverses in their respective industries. In these latter cases, however, the learnings gleaned from the Baldrige competition may provide a partial basis for the larger organization's recovery. Each of these companies would likely argue, and with some justification, that things would have been much worse much sooner without their TQM efforts. To date, not one of these firms has blamed their Baldrige application efforts for their performance problems. To the contrary, IBM is pushing its Market Driven Quality program throughout the company and using the Baldrige framework for assessment of this effort.

Nevertheless, for many of these organizations, winning the Baldrige Award was the pinnacle of an exhaustive effort. A frequent refrain among those we interviewed suggested that "Getting there was half the fun." But getting there was also an arduous and time-consuming process. None of the firms made these changes overnight. Individuals talked in terms of evolution not revolution; years and not weeks of efforts. In fact, the GAO study alluded to earlier found that most of the positive results reported took an average of two and a half years to materialize.

Can this "ramp up" time be reduced? Can these changes be made incrementally, or must they all be made simultaneously? In the GAO study, some positive results surfaced within one year of the initiation of TQM efforts. It is clear from talking with the HR professionals in these firms that they believe *all* of the new processes must eventually be put in place to support the total quality effort. They also realize that given the resource constraints confronting most organizations, attempting instantaneous transformation to a TQM culture is not only unlikely to succeed but could be detrimental to the health of the firm. What remains unknown, however, is which of the processes discussed above makes the largest or most immediate contribution to a total quality culture. Absent systematic study of this issue, most of the Baldrige winners opted to upgrade quickly those systems already in place (training, communications, etc.), while saving the more substantial and more costly changes (self-managed work teams, team-based compensation, etc.) until such time as acceptance and resources are at sufficient levels.

Without dissent, these Baldrige winners suggested that the effort to win the award was worth it. And without dissent, interviewees also indicated that there will be life after the Baldrige. Some intend to continue the same type of quality self-assessment program in the future, using the Baldrige application as a framework. Westinghouse CNFD has developed its own in-house quality competition culminating in presentation of two George Westinghouse Total Quality Awards, one for the best division and one for the most improved division in the corporation with regard to TQM performance. The winning divisions get $200,000 to spend on their employees and become the prime corporate candidates for the next Baldrige competition.

Others see their firms energized anew, with empowered employees working in autonomous work teams striving to provide 100 percent customer satisfaction. Motorola has gone to its suppliers and asked them if they would be willing to apply for the award within five years. Motorola furnishes some of its quality training to the suppliers that accept this challenge, and those who do not consider the Baldrige challenge are dropped as suppliers. Motorola, IBM, and Xerox, via the Quality Forum, have become major contributors to efforts directed at increasing the level of TQM-related instruction in the nation's business and engineering schools.

Some respondents indicated that there was much work still to be done in the HR function itself. A movement was underway to reorganize the HR function beyond simply providing staff support to the TQM effort at the corporate level. These HR professionals appreciated the necessity of viewing functional areas within their firms as customers and insuring that quality HR services are being provided both inside and outside the organization.

HR Professionals and Total Quality

What should the role of the HR professional be as organizations evolve toward a total quality culture? HR professionals have seen their stock rise in the corporate setting during the last decade. Once viewed by top management as a necessary appendage to getting the work done, HR executives now find themselves welcomed to positions on strategic policy committees. Changing workforce demographics and, more importantly, a fast-changing legal climate have opened executive boardrooms to HR professionals.

To become full partners in the operation of a TQM organization, HR professionals must become experts on their function's contribution to quality. This means they may have to work with or become the change agents who lead the reassessment of current practices. In most cases this will require that functional boundaries be breached and partnerships established with other functional areas in the firm. These partnerships must consider what HRM can do in the areas of selection, training, development, communication, and reward systems pertinent to their various partners within the context of a total quality culture.

As important, in the heat of organizational efforts to implement a total quality culture, the HR professional must look internally at the HR function itself and determine to what extent that unit is employing the same TQM techniques and ideas being pursued by the remainder of the organization. For instance, can the HR function determine how satisfied internal and external customers are with its products and services? To what extent have cross-functional or autonomous work teams been formed within HR as a way of reducing cycle time and increasing the quality of service provided? Has the function made any efforts to benchmark its important activities against accepted "best practices"? To what extent is the HR function designed for continuous learning and continuous improvement? Efforts at helping others develop their quality cultures should not preclude similar efforts directed at the HR function.

HRM in Support of TQM

Critics and supporters alike can and have argued about the relative benefits or liabilities associated with the Baldrige Award. This is not the place to revisit that debate. Rather, we take the position that, despite its possible flaws (that time may correct), the Baldrige Award is the only systematic national framework for assessing quality levels in U.S. companies. It is also one of the few detailed frameworks that organizations can use to model and evaluate their efforts in the direction of total quality management.

The results of this examination suggest that HR policies to support a total quality culture tend to form a constellation of mutually supportive and interdependent processes. Our analyses of the information provided by our interview respondents and gleaned from company documents yielded the following checklist of what we see as an "ideal" profile of human resource strategies in support of total quality management. Like Deming's "Fourteen Commandments" of total quality, these fourteen checkpoints provide HR professionals with a chance to evaluate their own HR organization and its contribution to TQM.

- Top management is responsible for initiating and supporting a vision of a total quality culture.

- This vision is clarified and communicated to the remainder of the firm in a variety of ways.

- Systems that allow upward and lateral communications are developed, implemented, and reinforced.

- TQM training is provided to all employees, and top management shows active support for such training.

- Employee involvement or participation programs are in place.

- Autonomous work groups are not required, but processes that bring multiple perspectives to bear on quality issues are imperative.

- Employees are empowered to make quality-based decisions at their discretion. Job design should make this apparent.

- Performance reviews are refocused from an evaluation of past performance only, to an emphasis on what management can do to assist employees in their future job-related quality efforts.

- Compensation systems reflect team-related quality contributions, including mastery of additional skills.

- Non-financial recognition systems at both the individual and work group levels reinforce both small wins and big victories in the quest for total quality.

- Systems allow employees at all levels of the organization to make known their concerns, ideas, and reactions to quality initiatives. These systems might include suggestion opportunities with rapid response, open-door policies, skip-level policies, attitude surveys, etc.

- Safety and health issues are addressed proactively not reactively. Employee participation in the development of programs in both areas improves acceptance of these programs.

- Employee recruitment, selection, promotion, and career development programs reflect the new realities of managing and working in a TQM environment.

- While assisting others to implement processes in support of TQM, the HR professional does not lose sight of the necessity to manage the HR function under the same precepts.

Though the phrase has been overworked, we know of no better term than "paradigm shift" to describe the changes HR professionals and HR functions will face if they are to contribute to the development of a total quality culture.

We would like to thank Professors Tom Bateman, Jack Evans, and Sara Rynes for their thoughtful comments on an earlier version of this article. They along with two anonymous AME reviewers and Editor Jack Veiga provided helpful comments as this manuscript was being prepared.

ABOUT THE AUTHORS

Richard Blackburn is an associate professor of organizational behavior at the Kenan-Flagler Business School at the University of North Carolina. His research interests include the causes and consequences of service quality in professional organizations, the relationship between HR practices and total quality management, and the impact of corporate design and identity on corporate performance. His research work has appeared in both professional and academic journals, and he has served on several editorial review boards. He is co-author of *Managing Organizational Behavior*, published by the Richard D. Irwin Company. Professor Blackburn earned his M.B.A. and Ph.D. in organizational behavior from the University of Wisconsin-Madison. He is a member of the American Psychological Association and the Academy of Management.

Benson Rosen is Hanes Professor of business administration and chairman of the management area at the Kenan-Flagler Business School at the University of North Carolina. Professor Rosen conducts research on a variety of human resources management issues, including managing diversity, career management, expatriate assignments, and total quality management. He is the coauthor of two books, *Becoming Aware and Older Employees: New Roles for Valued Resources.* He has written more than sixty articles which have been published in both professional and academic journals, including the *Harvard Business Review*, the *Academy of Management Journal*, and the *Journal of Applied Psychology*. Professor Rosen received his Ph.D. in social and industrial psychology from Wayne State University. He is a Fellow of the American Psychological Association and a member of the Academy of Management.

CHOOSING AN INVOLVEMENT STRATEGY

Edward E. Lawler III, Center for Effective Organizations,
University of Southern California

The most prevalent approach to designing work organizations calls for such features as hierarchical decision making, simple repetitive jobs at the lowest level, and rewards based on carefully measured individual job performance. But this "control" approach appears to be losing favor. Numerous articles and books have recently argued that work organizations need to move toward an "involvement" or "commitment" approach to the design and management of work organizations.[1] The advantages of the involvement approach are said to include higher quality products and services, less absenteeism, less turnover, better decision making, and better problem solving—in short, greater organizational effectiveness.[2]

Careful examination of the suggested ways to increase involvement reveals not one but at least three approaches to managing organizations. All three encourage employee participation in decision making. These three approaches, however, have different histories, advocates, advantages, and disadvantages. An organization interested in adopting an involvement-oriented approach needs to be aware of the differences among these approaches and strategically choose the approach that is best for it.

The three approaches to involvement are (1) parallel suggestion involvement, (2) job involvement, and (3) high involvement. They differ in the degree to which they direct that four key features should be moved to the lowest level of an organization. Briefly, the features are: (1) information about the performance of the organization, (2) rewards that are based on the performance of the organization, (3)

© *The Academy of Management Executive*, 1988, Vol. II, No. 3, pp. 197–204.

[1]See, for example, E. E. Lawler, "High Involvement Management," Jossey-Bass: San Francisco, 1986; E. E. Lawler, "Transformation from Control to Involvement," chapter in R. Kilmann, J. Covin and Associates' (Eds.) *Corporate Transformation*, San Francisco: Jossey-Bass, 1987, pp. 46–65; R. E. Walton, "From Control to Commitment in the Workplace," *Harvard Business Review*, 1985, 63(2), 76–84.

[2]Some interesting but limited data are provided by D. Dennison in "Bringing Corporate Culture to the Bottom Line," *Organizational Dynamics*, 1984, 13(2), 4–22.

knowledge that enables employees to understand and contribute to organizational performance, and (4) power to make decisions that influence organizational direction and performance.

Information, rewards, knowledge, and power are the central issues for all organizations. How they are positioned in an organization determines the core management style of the organization. When they are concentrated at the top, traditional control-oriented management exists; when they are moved downward, some form of participative management is being practiced.

The parallel suggestion approach does the least to move power, knowledge, information, and rewards downward, while the high involvement approach does the most. Because they position power, information, knowledge, and rewards differently, these approaches tend to fit different situations and to produce different results. It is not that one is always better than another, but that they are different and, to some degree, competing. Let us consider how these three approaches operate, and the results they produce. Once we have reviewed them, we can discuss when and how they are best used.

Parallel Suggestion Involvement

Probably the oldest approach to employee involvement is suggestion involvement. Formal suggestion programs are perhaps the original way of establishing a problem-solving relationship between lower-level employees and their work. In suggestion involvement, the employees are asked—probably for the first time—to problem solve and produce ideas that will influence how the organization operates. Traditional suggestion programs often include the implementation of a supportive reward system as well. For example, an individual who is not in a management position may be given a reward based on one year's estimated savings from the suggestions he or she produces. Interestingly, managers typically are not rewarded for suggestions because developing workplace improvements is considered "part of their job."

A much more extensive reward system is involved in gainsharing plans.[3] The oldest and best known gainsharing plan is the Scanlon Plan. Other gainsharing plans include the Improshare Plan and the Rucker Plan. Unlike traditional suggestion programs, gainsharing plans offer employees a share in gains for as long as the gains are realized by the organization. In the typical gainsharing plan, employees are asked to suggest improvements, and they share in any performance

---

[3]A good overview is provided by B. Graham-Moore and T. Ross, *Productivity Gainsharing*, Englewood Cliffs, NJ: Prentice-Hall, 1983.

improvement the organization makes. Some gainsharing plans also move new information downward because they focus on organizational performance. In some cases, gainsharing plans go beyond suggestion involvement by creating a joint union/management committee structure that decides on the implementation of suggestions, designs and alters the plan, and makes other policy decisions.

Recently quality circles have become an extremely popular approach to suggestion involvement. At this point, quite a bit is known about the effectiveness of quality circles and how they operate.[4] Like written suggestion programs and Scanlon Plan suggestion programs, they encourage employees to recommend ways that the operations of the organization can be improved. The traditional quality circle approach uses groups, or quality circles, rather than individual written suggestions. According to quality circle advocates, the group process typically leads to better suggestions—and better developed suggestions—than the written suggestion process does. In addition, in quality circles, considerable training is done to enable the group to function effectively and to help individuals become efficient problem solvers. In the more advanced programs, employees are trained in problem analysis and statistical quality control.

As is true with written suggestion programs, quality circle programs provide participants only with recommendation power; they do not have the power to implement and decide on the installation of their suggestions. In this sense, they are a parallel structure because they take people out of their regular organizations and put them in a separate new structure that operates differently than the traditional organization does. Quality circles and other parallel structures are often easy to install, and they start quickly. The problem-solving groups can be small and need not be disruptive to the organization. They can easily be installed in a single plant or in a department of a larger organization. However, they do not change the existing organization structure, and they usually affect only a small percentage of the workforce.

Exhibit 1 summarizes the general characteristics of suggestion involvement plans. As the exhibit shows, these types of plans do not represent a major shift in the way control-oriented organizations deal with most issues. Instead, they rely on a special parallel structure to change the relationship between individuals and their work. This structure gives people the chance to influence decisions that they would not normally influence and, in some cases, to share in the financial results of their new role. It also usually leads to the communication of some additional information

---

[4]E. E. Lawler and S. A. Mohrman, "Quality Circles After the Fad," *Harvard Business Review*, 1985, 85(1), 64-71: E. E. Lawler and S. A. Mohrman, "Quality Circles: After the Honeymoon," *Organizational Dynamics*, 1987, 15(4), 42-54.

Exhibit 1
Suggestion Involvement

Job Design:	Traditional, simple, specialized, focused on the individual
Organizational Structure:	Functional organization
Parallel Structures:	Quality circles; written suggestions; screening or review committees
Performance Information:	Focused on the value of savings from suggestions
Knowledge:	Group skills and problem solving
Decision Power:	Traditional top-down; suggestions decided upon by hierarchy
Rewards:	Traditional job-based with merit pay; possible awards for value of suggestion
Personnel Policies:	Traditional

and to greater knowledge on the part of employees. However, this change in knowledge, information, and rewards often is limited to a small percentage of the workforce. In addition, the change is contained because individuals are asked to use this new knowledge and information only when they are operating inn special suggestion-type activities. During their regular work activities, it is very much work as usual.

Research on the parallel structure or suggestion involvement approach suggests that it can lead to an improvement in organizational performance. Case after case shows that individuals and groups often come up with suggestions that save the company a considerable amount of money.[5] There also seems to be no question that employees enjoy the opportunity to participate in problem solving. As

---

[5]See the following for examples: Carl F. Frost, John H. Wakeley, and Robert A. Ruh, *The Scanlon Plan for Organizational Development: Identity, Participation, and Equity*, East Lansing: Michigan State University Press, 1974; Tom Peters, *Thriving on Chaos*, New York: Knopf, 1987; M. H. Schuster, *Union-Management Cooperation*, Kalamazoo, Mich.: W. E. Upjohn Institute, 1984.

a result, they are often more satisfied with their work situation, are absent less, and are less likely to leave the company.

The parallel suggestion involvement approach however, has a number of well-documented limitations. First, it tends to have a "program character" about it, which often makes it a temporary system in an organization. In addition, parallel structures are expensive and difficult to maintain. In some situations, they run out of suggestions because individuals do not have enough expertise to solve the more complex problems in an organization. They also often are resisted by middle-level managers because parallel structures threaten their power and put them in the position of having to do extra work. Conflict can develop between those who are in parallel structures and those who are not. Nonparticipants can come to resent being left out. Sometimes parallel structures can lead to a call for a systematic restructuring of the organization for greater involvement. In essence, employees like the taste of involvement they have gotten and want more.

Finally, over time suggestion involvement approaches that are not supported by reward system changes may lose their momentum and disappear. This comes about because they do not systematically change an organization's way of operating or the way the total workforce relates to the organization and its performance. Gainsharing plans, because they affect the way everyone is rewarded, typically do not suffer from this limitation. Gainsharing companies like Herman Miller and Donnelley Mirrors have maintained gainsharing plans for decades.

Job Involvement Approaches

Job involvement approaches focus on enriching work to motivate employees to achieve better job performance. One strategy, job enrichment, focuses on creating individual jobs that give people feedback, increases their influence over how the work is done, requires them to use a variety of skills, and gives them a whole piece of work.[6] This approach has an extensive research history going back to the 1950s, when behavioral scientists tried to design alternatives to traditional, standardized, simplified work. Perhaps the most visible champion of this approach has been Herzberg.

---

[6]Three seminal writings in this area are J. R. Hackman and E. E. Lawler's "Employee Reactions to Job Characteristics," *Journal of Applied Psychology*, 1971, 55, 259–286: J. R. Hackman and G. R. Oldham's *Work Redesign*, Reading, Mass.: Addison-Wesley, 1980; F. Herzberg's *Work and the Nature of Man*, New York: World, 1969.

A second strategy for job involvement creates work groups or teams. This approach, too, has an extensive research history going back to the 1940s and the pioneering work of Trist, Emery, and Thorsrud.[7] It differs from individual enrichment in that it considers the work group as the primary unit of involvement. It creates group goals, tasks, and control with the objective of making all group members feel responsible for the group's performance. Groups designed according to this approach are often called autonomous work groups, self-managing groups, semi-autonomous work groups, or work teams.

As Exhibit 2 shows, the job involvement approach does have significant implications for how an organization is structured and managed. In essence, individuals are given new skills and knowledge, new feedback, an additional set of decisions to make, and they may be rewarded differently. Both the individual and the team approach have these effects, although the team approach carried to its fullest extent has them to a greater degree.

Exhibit 2
Job Involvement

Job Design:	Job enrichment or teams
Organizational Structure:	Traditional, functional
Parallel Structures:	None
Performance Information:	Focused on job and/or team performance
Knowledge:	Job specific, team skills
Decision Power:	Performers control how work is done
Rewards:	Traditional for job enrichment; skill-based pay possible for teams
Personnel Policies:	Traditional; some team-based decision making

---

With the team approach, interpersonal skills and group decision making skills are needed in addition to those that are needed for individual enrichment. The

---

[7]T. G. Cumming's "Self-Regulating Work Groups: A Socio-Technical Synthesis," *Academy of Management Review*, 1978, 3, 625–633; F. Emery and E. Thorsrud's *Industrial Democracy*, London: Tavistock, 1969.

reward system also is changed more with groups or teams than with individual job enrichment, since skill-based pay is often used. Finally, teams can make certain decisions that individuals usually cannot. Both individuals and teams can control the way the work is done, performing quality-management, inventory, and other task-related activities, but teams can also decide personnel-management issues. Teams, for example, can make decisions about hiring and firing, and may select their own supervisors. Perhaps the most successful examples of teams are found in the new plants built by Procter and Gamble, Mead, and a host of other manufacturing companies during the last 20 years.[8]

Overall, job involvement represents a significant change in the fundamental operations of an organization. Individuals at the lowest levels get new information, power, and skills, and they may be rewarded differently. The new information, power, knowledge, and rewards correspond to their particular work tasks, and typically do not have to do with the structuring and operating of the whole organization or the development of its strategic direction. Unlike parallel suggestion approaches, job-involvement affects the day-to-day work activities of all individuals. Involvement is not an occasional thing, it is the standard way in which business is done.

Theoretically, the decision to use either teams or individual job enrichment should be based on the technology of the workplace. Teams are more complicated to build and maintain, but may be necessary if the work is such that no one individual could do a whole part of it and get feedback about it. Teams are often appropriate, for example, in process production facilities such as chemical plants and oil refineries, and in complex service organizations such as banks and airlines. Where the technology allows an individual to do a whole task or offer a whole service, individual designs are preferred because they are simpler to install and give the individual more direct feedback.

Studies of job involvement approaches show improvements in productivity, quality, absenteeism, and turnover among individuals working in enriched jobs and in teams.[9] The net result for the organization is usually significant performance improvement over that found with traditional job structures. Unlike suggestion programs, job involvement structures seem to be reasonably stable. This is particularly true of teams, since they represent cohesive organizational units that are difficult to dissolve.

---

[8]An overview of how these plants operate is provided in E. E. Lawler's "The New Plant Revolution," *Organizational Dynamics*, 1978, 6(3), 2–12.

[9]See Endnote 6.

The limitations of the job involvement approach are primarily those of lost opportunities. Because they limit employee involvement to immediate work decisions, they often fail to capture the contributions that individuals can make to strategic decisions and to higher-level management work. As a result, individuals in work teams may tend to optimize their own performance without paying a great deal of attention to overall organization performance.

Work involvement efforts do entail some significant start-up costs because they require considerable training. Often overlooked is the need to train the supervisor and dramatically change the supervisor's job. Some evidence exists that many supervisors have difficulty moving from a traditional management environment to one characterized by job involvement.[10] In some cases, job involvement efforts call for an extensive and expensive physical reconfiguration of the workplace to allow for team interaction and control of a whole piece of work by individuals. Also, these efforts are often resisted by middle managers because they feel threatened by the new power that others have.

Finally, job involvement approaches may be subject to cancellation if they do not influence higher-level strategic decisions concerning organization structure, power, and the allocation of rewards. This is particularly true with individual job enrichment. Unless major restructuring is done to support the program, supervisors are often able unilaterally to change jobs in ways that take away the decision-making power that is critical to enrichment. Job involvement efforts are particularly likely to be cancelled when they affect small parts of an organization. Like parallel structures, they can be installed only on a limited basis and, as a result, create friction between participants and nonparticipants. This friction can, in turn, lead to pressures to eliminate the job involvement program.[11]

High Involvement Approach

The high involvement approach has also been called the commitment approach or, perhaps more descriptively, the business involvement approach. It is relatively new although it has roots in the early work of Likert on System X management,

---

[10]R. E. Walton and L. A. Schlesinger, "Do Supervisors Thrive in Participative Work Systems?", *Organizational Dynamics*, 1979, 8(3), 25–38.

[11]E. Trist and C. Dwyer, *The Limits of Laissez-Faire as a Sociotechnical Change Strategy*, in R. Zager and M. Rosow (Eds.), *The Innovative Organization*, New York: Pergamon, 1982, pp. 149–183.

McGregor on Theory Y, and Trist and others on sociotechnical systems.[12] In many respects, it also builds on what has been learned from the suggestion involvement and job involvement approaches. It tends to structure an organization so that people at the lowest level will have a sense of involvement not just in how they do their jobs or how effectively their group performs, but in the performance of the total organization. It goes considerably farther than either of the other two approaches toward moving power, information, knowledge, and rewards to the lowest organizational level. It is based on the argument that if individuals are going to care about the performance of the organization, they need to know about it, be able to influence it, be rewarded for it, and have the knowledge and skills to contribute to it.

Exhibit 3
High Involvement

Job Design:	Work teams and job enrichment
Organizational Structure:	Business or customer focused
Parallel Structures:	Task forces for major business issues
Performance Information:	Focused on business performance
Knowledge:	Team skills; business economics; problem solving
Decision Power:	Performers make work-method and work-unit management decisions, have input to strategic decisions
Rewards:	Egalitarian; skill-based pay; gain-sharing and/or profit sharing; employee ownership
Personnel Policies:	Employment stability; equality of treatment; participatively developed and administered policies

---

As Exhibit 3 shows, in order to have high involvement management, virtually every major feature of the organization needs to be designed differently than it is

---

[12]See, for example, R. Likert's *The Human Organization*, New York: McGraw-Hill, 1967, and D. McGregor's *The Human Side of Enterprise*, New York: McGraw-Hill, 1960.

with the control approach. The high involvement approach builds upon what is done in the job involvement and the suggestion involvement approaches: Parallel structures are used for certain kinds of problem solving and policy setting, and work is designed according to the principles of individual enrichment and work teams. High involvement is different, however, in the kind of information that is shared, and in the decision-power and reward systems areas. In the case of decision power, employees are not only asked to make decisions about their work activities, they are also asked to play a role in organizational decisions having to do with strategy, investment, and other major areas. Rewards are based on the performance of the organization; hence, profit sharing, gainsharing, and some type of employee ownership are appropriate.

Creating a high involvement organization is clearly a much different and more complex task than implementing job involvement or parallel suggestion involvement is. Virtually every feature of a control-oriented organization has to be redesigned and, in some cases, innovation in design is necessary. Many of the methodologies and approaches for such policies as pay, selection, and training are readily available and well developed for control-oriented management; installing them is simply a matter of taking established systems "off the shelf" and making them operational. On the other hand, there is a relative paucity of technology to support the development of high involvement organizations. This is largely due to the fact that this approach to management is new and the technology has not yet been fully developed. Therefore, those organizations that adopt it are forced into somewhat of a research and development mode with respect to the technology of management.

This point is well illustrated by the now defunct airline, People Express. It had to invent new work scheduling approaches, pay structures, training programs, and a new organization design in order to operate in a high involvement mode. Because no airline had ever operated as a high involvement organization, there simply were no examples around. Not surprisingly, the need for so much invention and system debugging contributed to some operating problems.

There are relatively little data on the effectiveness of high involvement organizations. Indeed, there are few examples to study. The closest examples of organizations using this approach would appear to be the many new team-based plants that have been started around the world. The data on the plants are largely favorable, but limited. In addition, there are some new organizations that have started with this approach and some employee-owned companies that are moving toward operating in a high involvement mode.[13]

---

[13]C. Rosen, K. Klein, and K. Young's *Employee Ownership in America*, Lexington, Mass: Lexington, 1986.

It is hardly surprising that the best examples of high involvement organizations are new start-ups. The high involvement approach represents such an extensive change from the control approach to management that the difficulties in making a conversion are enormous. It is much easier to start with a clean sheet of paper and design the organization from the ground up.[14] This is in notable contrast to job involvement and suggestion involvement approaches, which are often put in place in existing organizations.

The admittedly sketchy, testimonial-type evidence that does exist on high involvement organizations generally shows superior operating results.[15] They tend to be low-cost, relatively flexible, adaptive organizations that are very quality and customer oriented. However, this approach is not cheap to use, since it requires a large initial investment in selection, training, and system development. In addition, as we will discuss, it does not fit every person, situation, and business.

The Strategic Choice

Decisions about which approach an organization should adopt ought to be guided by a number of factors. The different approaches to involvement fit different types of businesses, situations, and individuals. The key to effective utilization of any of them is installing them in conditions to which they are suited. Three major factors need to be examined in deciding which approach to pick: (1) the nature of the work and technology, (2) values of the key participants, and (3) the organization's current management approach.

Work and Technology

Perhaps the overriding determinant of how an organization should approach involvement is the kind of work it does and the technology it uses. Managers' values and attitudes can be changed over time, and the traditional practices of older, control-oriented organizations can evolve into high involvement policies, but

---

[14]See D. Perkins, V. Nieva, and E. E. Lawler, *Managing Creation: The Challenge of Building a New Organization*, New York: Wiley, 1983.

[15]See, for example, Endnotes 1 and 5, as well as *Fortune* (Eds.) *Working Smarter*, New York: Viking, 1982.

organizations cannot necessarily change the kind of technology they use or the kind of jobs that the technology dictates.[16]

Admittedly, technology is only partly driven by the products and services an organization offers. As many advocates of the work redesign approach have pointed out, there is some flexibility in the technology an organization chooses to use. In addition, the technology does not completely dictate the nature of the jobs an organization has. Some technologies can be modified to produce the types of jobs that are congruent with the desired form of involvement. An example of this is Volvo's heroic effort to alter its auto assembly technology to make it congruent with work teams. But in many cases the control of a single organization is limited. There is, for example, little flexibility when it comes to refining oil and generating electricity. It is very difficult to change the telephone operator's job, given the way telephone equipment has been designed. As a result, there are some situations in which the technology is not amenable to any of the involvement approaches, with the possible exception of suggestion involvement.

Two aspects of technology are particularly critical influences on the appropriateness of different involvement approaches: (1) the degree of interdependence and (2) the degree of complexity. Interdependence refers to the extent to which individuals need to coordinate, cooperate, and relate to others to produce the product or services the organization offers. Organizations vary on this dimension from very high interdependence to low interdependence. For example, university professors and insurance salespeople are typically in a low interdependence situation, while chemical plant operators and computer design engineers are in high interdependence situations.

High interdependence argues for teams and against individual approaches to work design. Low interdependence favors maximizing individual performance through job enrichment or well-structured individual tasks that offer large amounts of incentive pay.

A crucial issue in determining which way to go with low interdependence jobs is the complexity of the work involved: High complexity calls for job enrichment, while low complexity calls for simple jobs and incentive pay.

Technology, to a substantial degree, tends to influence the complexity of the work. Complexity can vary from the repetitive jobs associated with assembly lines to the highly complex knowledge-based work required by professional jobs and jobs

---

[16]The following stress the importance of technology: J. Thompson's *Organizations in Action*, New York: McGraw-Hill, 1967, and J. Woodward's *Management and Technology*, London: Her Majesty's Stationery Office, 1958.

in state-of-the-art manufacturing facilities. Where the work is simple and repetitive by necessity, it is hard to put in place a high involvement or even a job involvement approach (unless the technology can be changed). These situations are often limited to parallel suggestion involvement approaches, as they can operate with most approaches to work design and most types of technology.

With complex knowledge work, the clear choice is one of the involvement approaches. At the very least, job involvement is called for—job enrichment in the case of independent work and teams in the case of interdependent work. If other conditions are right, high involvement would seem to be the best choice. High involvement flourishes where complex knowledge work exists because individuals who do this kind of work possess the ability to participate in a wide range of decisions, and they often expect and want this approach to management.

Values and Beliefs

The values and beliefs that key participants in an organization need to have vary widely among the involvement approaches. If the values do not match the chosen approach, the approach is unlikely to be fully implemented and effectively operated.

In the case of the suggestion approach, key managers do not need to have a profound belief that employees can and will exercise self-control, manage themselves, and be able to contribute to major organizational decisions; they simply need to believe that employees have useful ideas about how things can be improved.

The high involvement approach, on the other hand, requires that managers believe in the capabilities, sense of responsibility, and commitment of people throughout the organization. In short, they need to believe that people not only are a key organization resource, but that people can and will behave responsibly if given the opportunity.

The beliefs of management are often captured in the philosophical statements they endorse and write. High involvement organizations typically have clearly stated, widely circulated management philosophy statements that highlight their commitment to employee involvement and their desire to push decision making and information to the lowest levels of the organization. On the other hand, managers who feel most comfortable with suggestion involvement usually make no such statements. If they say anything, it is that employees are an important asset of the organization and know how to do their jobs best.

The values of the employees are also important to consider. For any form of involvement to work, most employees have to want to learn, grow, develop, contribute, and take on new responsibilities. Most researchers have argued that the vast majority of American workers do want to be involved in their work, but few argue it is universally true. Particularly where there has been a long history of autocratic management, the majority of the workforce may not want to be more involved. They may have become conditioned to the control-oriented approach and appreciate the fact that they can just put in their eight hours and not have to take the job home with them. In addition, self-selection may have taken place so that those who most value involvement quit long ago, leaving behind those who are less attracted to it.

Societal values can also come into play in determining the appropriate approach to involvement. Democratic societies provide much more supportive environments for the high involvement approach than do traditional autocratic societies. The United States, with its long democratic tradition and commitment to individual rights, appears to provide the ideal setting for involvement-oriented management. Historically, our society has exempted the workplace from our commitment to democracy and individual rights, but there are many signs that this is breaking down in the area of individual rights and it seems inevitable that the exemption will also disappear as far as participation and involvement are concerned.[17]

Organizational Starting Point

In considering employee involvement strategies, organizations need to assess their current operating approach. As noted earlier, it is hardly surprising that many job involvement and high involvement organizations start as "green field" operations. Without question, it is easier to install involvement-oriented management where no management system currently exists. Not only is it possible to select managers who have values that are supportive of involvement, but it is not necessary to overcome all the traditions, practices, and policies that are inconsistent with it. This is not to say that it is impossible for an organization to evolve toward high involvement; if it seems to be called for because of the kind of work and technology the organization has, and if the values of managers support it, it certainly is possible. However, it may not be feasible to change immediately to a high involvement approach.

In starting a change process toward high involvement, it is critical to see where the organization is and then map out a long-term strategy. If the organization

---

[17]D. W. Ewing, *Freedom Inside the Organization*, New York: Dutton, 1977, and M. Sashkin, "Participative Management is an Ethical Imperative." *Organizational Dynamics*, Spring 1984, 5-22.

is currently operating in an extremely traditional way, the best first step may be to move to quality circles or another suggestion involvement approach. This approach should be structured in ways that make movement to job involvement relatively easy. Quality circles, for example, can be converted into work teams if they are led by a supervisor and organized around natural work units. As noted earlier, work teams are an important part of the high involvement approach, and getting them in place is an important step toward high involvement management. Thus, there can be a natural transition from the parallel structure approach to job involvement and finally to high involvement.

If an organization is already relatively participative in a number of its personnel policies, its work structure, and managerial behaviors, it may not be necessary to start with a suggestion involvement program. The organization can immediately start with the job involvement approach. On the other hand, if an organization is very traditional in the way it operates, and managers are very hesitant to give up decision-making power, then the only way to start involvement is often with a parallel suggestion approach. Quality circles or Scanlon written suggestion programs are particularly appropriate, since they present a minimal threat to existing management prerogatives and power. Sometimes their success can convince management to move ahead to other forms of involvement. As noted earlier, however, suggestion programs are limited in what they can accomplish because they do little to share power, knowledge, rewards, and information among all levels of the organization.

The presence of a union organization can make a significant difference in which approach to involvement is most appropriate. Many unions have been willing to create jointly sponsored parallel structure approaches to involvement. Scanlon plans, for example, have been widely used in unionized workplaces, as have quality-of-work-life programs. The latter usually create a hierarchical structure of joint union/management committees.[18] These committees are involvement devices in their own right, and they typically sponsor problem-solving groups and other participative activities for rank-and-file union members. A common problem with quality-of-work-life programs is that they end up dealing with a very limited set of issues, including primarily those related to workplace hygiene. In a few instances, this type of parallel structure involvement has led to the creation of high involvement efforts. A good example of this is the General Motors Saturn project. General Motors had quality-of-work-life projects for years before it decided to ask the United Auto Workers to create jointly a new company called Saturn, which is to be developed and run in a high involvement manner.

---

[18]E. E. Lawler and L. Ozley's "Winning Union-Management Cooperation on Quality of Work Like Projects," *Management Review*, 1979, 68(3), 19–24.

Our argument so far suggests that there is no one right approach to involvement. The approach needs to be dictated by a number of situational factors. At the extreme, an organization may be able only to progress from control to suggestion involvement. At one extreme if all of an organization's systems are traditional, well developed, and firmly in place, and its technology leads to relatively independent, simple, repetitive tasks, then suggestion involvement is appropriate. However, if the organization is new, has complex knowledge work, interdependent tasks, and managers who value employee involvement, it is possible to move to high involvement management and reap the rewards it has to offer.

Because involvement is not universally good for all organizations, it is important to take a differentiated view toward it. If organizations carefully analyze where they are and where they want to be, they can lay out a series of steps that will lead to the type of involvement that fits their situation. In the absence of this kind of process, they run the risk of managing in a way that compromises the potential effectiveness of the organization.

Edward E. Lawler III is professor of management and organization in the Business School at the University of Southern California. He joined USC in 1978, and during 1979 founded and became director of the University's Center for Effective Organizations. In 1982 Dr. Lawler was named research professor at USC.

After receiving a B.A. from Brown University and a Ph.D. from the University of California at Berkeley, Dr. Lawler joined the faculty of Yale University. He moved to the University of Michigan in 1972 as professor of psychology and program director in the Survey Research Center at the Institute for Social Research.

Dr. Lawler is a member of many professional organizations in his field and is on the editorial boards of five major journals, including the Academy of Management Executive. *He has consulted with over 100 organizations on employee involvement, organizational change, and compensation, and is the author and coauthor of over 150 articles and 15 books. His most recent books include* Pay and Organization Development *(Addison-Wesley, 1981),* Managing Creation *(Wiley-Interscience, 1983), and* High Involvement Management *(Jossey-Bass, 1986). His works have been translated into 10 languages and he has been honored as a top contributor to the fields of organization development, organizational behavior, and compensation.*

DOWNSIZING: WHAT DO WE KNOW?
WHAT HAVE WE LEARNED?

Wayne F. Cascio, University of Colorado

Executive Overview

Downsizing, the planned elimination of positions or jobs, is a phenomenon that has affected hundreds of companies and millions of workers since the late 1980s. While there is no shortage of articles on "How To" or "How Not To" downsize, the current article attempts to synthesize what is known in terms of the economic and organizational consequences of downsizing. We argue that in many firms anticipated economic benefits fail to materialize, for example, lower expense ratios, higher profits, increased return-on-investment, and boosted stock prices. Likewise, many anticipated organizational benefits do not develop, such as lower overhead, smoother communications, greater entrepreneurship, and increases in productivity.

To a large extent, this is a result of a failure to break out of the traditional approach to organization design and management—an approach founded on the principles of command, control, and compartmentalization. For long-term, sustained improvements in efficiency, reductions in headcount need to be viewed as part of a process of continuous improvement that includes organization redesign, along with broad, systemic changes designed to eliminate redundancies, waste, and inefficiency.

IN MY VIEW

American Telephone & Telegraph, Eastman Kodak, Citicorp, Goodyear, Digital Equipment, Amoco, Chevron, Exxon, Black & Decker, CBS, ABC. The list reads like a "who's who" of American business. Is there no end to it? It seems to be endemic to the 1990s. In fact, it's hard to pick up a newspaper on any given day and *not* read about another well-known organization that is announcing a corporate restructuring (a.k.a., cutting workers, and, in some cases, selling off other assets). By the end of 1992, just to cite a few well-known examples, International Business Machines will pare down by another 40,000 workers, and Xerox will cut 2,500 workers from its document-processing division. By mid-1993 the Postal Service will eliminate 30,000 of 130,000 management jobs, and TRW, Inc. will cut its work force by 10,000 people, or fourteen percent. By 1995, General Motors

---

will cut 75,000 workers. More than eighty-five percent of the Fortune 1000 firms downsized their white-collar work forces between 1987 and 1991, affecting more than five million jobs. More than fifty percent downsized in 1990 alone. Across the total economy, counting *only* jobs held for at least three years, 5.6 million people lost permanent jobs from 1987 through 1991.[1] In short, companies large and small are slashing jobs at a pace never before seen in American economic history.

WHAT'S DIFFERENT ABOUT THE CURRENT CUTS?

In previous business downturns, manufacturing has tended to take the big hits. Since 1980, U.S. manufacturing firms have cut more than two million workers. However, the most recent recession has had a decidedly white-collar pattern to it, with more middle managers eliminated during the downturn. For example, while middle managers make up only five to eight percent of the work force, they accounted for seventeen percent of all dismissals from 1989 to 1991. Further evidence comes from the fact that in 1992 white-collar employees constituted thirty-six percent of the unemployed workers in the U.S., compared with twenty-two percent during the 1982 slump. Nearly a million U.S. managers earning more than $40,000 a year lost their jobs in 1991, and, in fact, each year for the past three years, between one and two million middle managers were laid off.[2]

The major reason for this, according to a Boston University survey of manufacturers, is that overhead (which includes staff and white-collar salaries) comprises 26.6% of manufacturing costs in the U.S., compared to 21.6% in Germany, and just 17.9% in Japan. Indeed, after benchmarking its performance against other international chemical companies, DuPont decided to slash $1 billion from its costs. How? Largely by cutting 1,900 white-collar jobs from its fibers business, plus 550, or twenty percent of the total, from in-house engineering.

---

[1]There have been many accounts of such cuts in the business press. Two examples are: "How Jobs Losers Have Been Faring," *Business Week*, September 18, 1992, 16; and A. Murray and D. Wessel, "Swept Away: Torrent of Job Cuts Shows Human Toll of Recession Goes On," *The Wall Street Journal*, December 12, 1991, A1; A9.

[2]A. B. Fisher, "Morale Crisis," *Fortune*, November 28, 1991, 70-72; 76; 80. See also J. Greenwald, "The Great American Layoffs," *Time*, July 20, 1992, 64-65; and S. Overman, "The Layoff Legacy," *HR Magazine*, August 1991, 29-32.

ORIENTATION

Although the subject of downsizing has been addressed from a number of perspectives, this article focuses on just two major issues: (1) What are the economic and human consequences of such massive restructuring? and (2) What have we learned? To provide answers to these questions, I did two things. First, I reviewed more than 500 published articles on the subject of downsizing. Then I conducted semi-structured interviews with twenty-five senior executives—ten who had authorized downsizing actions at their companies, and fifteen who had been laid off as a result of downsizing activities. Let us begin by considering some basic questions: What is downsizing? Who is most likely to downsize, and what do they expect to get out of it?

Definition. Downsizing refers to the planned elimination of positions or jobs. Let us be clear about these terms. While there are as many positions as there are employees, jobs are groups of positions that are similar in their significant duties—such as computer programmers or financial analysts. Downsizing may occur by reducing work (not just employees) as well as by eliminating functions, hierarchical levels, or units. It may also occur by implementing cost containment strategies that streamline activities such as transaction processing, information systems, or sign-off policies.

Debt can be a cruel master, forcing firms to take drastic steps to ensure sufficient cash flow to service it.

Downsizing does not include the discharge of individuals for cause, or individual departures via normal retirement or resignations. The word "normal" is important. Voluntary severance and early retirement packages are commonly used to reduce the size of the work force, especially among firms with traditional "no-layoff" policies. Even if targeted workers are called "redundant," "excessed," or "transitioned," the result is the same—employees are shown the door. It's just called something else.

WHO IS MOST LIKELY TO DOWNSIZE?

The most likely candidates (though by no means the only candidates) are firms that are struggling to get through hard times, saddled with more debt than ever. Over twenty-six percent of corporate cash flow currently goes to meet debt payments, compared with only nine percent at the start of the 1974 recession, and eighteen percent going into the 1982 slump.[3] As an example, consider Marriott Corporation. Marriott eliminated 2,500 jobs at headquarters and also by closing down its hotel construction and development unit. Yet such savings pale against the cost of servicing more than $1 billion in debt taken on in an overly aggressive hotel construction program. Debt can be a cruel master, forcing firms to take drastic steps to ensure sufficient cash flow to service it. In the meantime, companies that didn't take on debt, including foreign competitors, can gain significant market share. Loss of market share, along with a concomitant loss of profitability, stimulates more downsizing.

Anticipated Results

Downsizing is expected to yield economic as well as organizational benefits. Let us consider each of these in turn. In terms of economic benefits, downsizing firms expect to increase value for their shareholders. Executives conclude that future costs are more predictable than future revenues. Thus, cutting costs by cutting people is a safe bet to increase earnings, and, by extension, the price of the company's stock. Judging by the 1,000 companies that the American Management Association follows, downsizing is a popular strategy. From 1989 to 1991 those companies eliminated 212,598 jobs—saving $8 billion per year.[4] Here are some specific company examples.

E. I. du Pont de Nemours took a $125 million, one-time charge against earnings to gain a $230 million recurring, annual, aftertax savings. Union Carbide spent $70 million in up-front charges to obtain $250 million in annual savings subsequently. Consider a third example. An IBM analyst estimated that if 8,000 employees accepted one of IBM's early retirement offers, the company would realize an extra 40 cents per share in earnings the following year, plus a 50-cents-per-share increase in the years afterward. An additional attraction that encourages businesses to consider this retirement cost strategy is the almost $100 billion surplus in overfunded U.S. corporate pension accounts.

---

[3]B. Dumaine, "How To Manage in a Recession," *Fortune*, November 5, 1990, 58–60; 64, 68, 72. See also "All That Lean Isn't Turning Into Green," *Business Week*, November 18, 1991, 39–40.

[4]F. Lalli, "Learn From My Mistake," *Money*, February 1992, 5.

In terms of organizational benefits, proponents of downsizing cite six expected outcomes:[5]

- Lower overhead
- Less bureaucracy
- Faster decision making
- Smoother communications
- Greater entrepreneurship
- Increases in productivity

When coupled with advice from popular business books and journals to "cut out the fat," to get "lean and mean," senior executives might well find the lure of downsizing to be irresistible.

People costs comprise roughly thirty to eighty percent of general and administrative costs in most companies. In capital-intensive industries, such as commercial airlines or oil refining, the cost is about thirty to forty percent. Among savings institutions, that figure is roughly fifty percent, and in highly labor-intensive operations, such as the postal service, the figure may exceed eighty percent.[6] Hence, cutting costs by cutting people appears to be a natural strategy, especially for companies struggling to stay alive in an unprecedented, globally competitive market. Carving out entire echelons of middle-level managers certainly does reduce overhead, and trims the number of layers in the organizational hierarchy. In theory this should lead to less bureaucracy and faster decision making. At Sears, for example, there are only four levels of management from the top to the bottom of the corporation. With fewer layers of middle managers to "filter" information, communications should be smoother and more accurate, entrepreneurship should flourish, and productivity should climb. It all seems so logical.

To be sure, the gains expected to result from downsizing are tantalizing. When coupled with advice from popular business books and journals to "cut out the fat," to get "lean and mean," senior executives might well find the lure of downsizing to be irresistible. Are the proponents of downsizing right? To what

---

[5]D. A. Heenan, "The Downside of Downsizing," *The Journal of Business Strategy*, November–December 1989, 18–23.

[6]There are various sources for these figures. For example, see W. F. Cascio, *Costing Human Resources: The Financial Impact of Behavior in Organizations*, 3rd Ed. (Boston: PWS-Kent, 1991). See also A. R. Karr, "Letter Bomb: Postal Service Again Asks for Rate Increase as Automation Lags," *The Wall Street Journal*, March 7, 1990, A1; A2; and K. Severinsen, "Cost-Cutting Measures Boost the Bottom Line," *Savings Institutions*, February 1989, 50–53.

extent have the economic and organizational benefits actually followed? We will try to provide some answers in the following sections.

ANTICIPATED VERSUS ACTUAL ECONOMIC RESULTS OF DOWNSIZING

A 1991 survey by the Wyatt Company of 1,005 firms suggested that most restructuring efforts fall far short of the objectives originally established for them:[7]

- Only forty-six percent of the companies said their cuts reduced expenses enough over time, in part because four times out of five, managers ended up replacing some of the very people they had dismissed;

- Fewer than one in three and profits increased as much as expected; and

- Only twenty-one percent reported satisfactory improvements in shareholders' return on investment.

What happens to the stock prices of companies that downsize? The answer to that question only makes sense by examining stock prices at different time intervals prior to and subsequent to the initial announcement of downsizing. To provide at least a partial answer to that question, Mitchell & Company, a consulting firm in Weston, Mass., examined what happened to the stock prices of sixteen companies in the Value Line data base that wrote off ten percent or more of their net worth between 1982 and 1988.[8]

In most cases, the stock in question already had lost some ground in the few months before the company announced its decision to downsize. Typically it will have lagged behind the market by twelve percentage points or so. ("The market" in this study was defined as Standard & Poor's 500-stock index for large stocks, and the Nasdaq composite index for small stocks.) On the day that the announcement is made, stock prices generally increase, but then there usually begins a long, slow slide. Two years later, in the Mitchell & Co. study, ten of the sixteen stocks were trading below the market by seventeen to forty-eight percent and, worse, twelve were below comparable firms in their industries by five to forty-five percent. To

---

[7]Lalli, 1992, op. cit.

[8]J. R. Dorfman, "Stocks of Companies Announcing Layoffs Fire Up Investors, But Prices Often Wilt," *The Wall Street Journal*, December 10, 1991, C1; C2.

understand some of the reasons why this is so, we need to examine the impact of downsizing on the day-to-day functioning of organizations.

IMPACT OF DOWNSIZING ON ORGANIZATIONAL FUNCTIONING

One poll of 1,142 companies that recently downsized, conducted by the American Management Association, revealed that nearly half were "badly" or "not well" prepared for the dismantling, and had not anticipated the kinds of problems that developed subsequently. More than half reported that they had begun downsizing with no policies or programs—such as employee retraining or job redeployment—to minimize the negative effects of cutting back. Succumbing to the pressure to produce short-term results, many ignored the massive changes in organizational relationships that result from reorganization. As one observer noted, "In the process, they misused and alienated many middle managers and lower-level employees, sold off solid businesses, shortchanged research and development, and muddled the modernization of their manufacturing floors.[9]

Apparently, a number of top managements have put the concerns of their employees and subordinate managers at the very bottom of their priority lists—and they pay a price for doing so. David Heenan, chief executive officer of Honolulu-based Theo H. Davis and Co. noted, "Corporate America has neglected the downside of downsizing." For just one example of this, consider the impact of extensive reductions of headquarters staffers whose jobs focus on corporate planning.

Once these specialists are gone, operating managers may be expected to fill the void. To do so, however, they need to develop the kinds of skills that will allow them to make groupwide contributions. Yet many line managers have neither the training nor the perspective to see beyond the segment of the business they are assigned to run. Moreover, organizations that employ cut-and-slash tactics are also those least likely to make long-term investments in training and management development. Remaining staff experts who could help subsidiary managers develop a policy-making perspective refuse to plant the seeks of their own destruction.[10] Moreover, they are likely to be demoralized, less productive, and unable to monitor,

---

[9]The source of the quotation is T. J. Murray, "For Downsizers, the Real Misery Is Yet to Come," *Business Month*, February 1989, 71–72; but see also E. R. Greenberg, "The Latest AMA Survey on Downsizing," *Compensation and Benefits Review*, 22, 1990, 66–71.

[10]Heenan, op. cit.

control, and support business units effectively. The result? Strategic planning suffers.

Furthermore, it's unrealistic to ask department or division heads to make long-term decisions about research and development expenditures; capital investments, or work force training when they are paid to attend to short-term profit or production. Last, the loss of staff support means that vital information may not be available to help the chief executive and other top managers make decisions that only they can make. Computer networks and video conferences cannot completely replace the human interaction that is so essential to achieving honest communication.

In summary, managers who remain after a downsizing often find themselves working in new, and not necessarily friendly, environments. These survivors are often stretched think, they manage more people and jobs, and they work longer hours. Many are not willing or able to work under these conditions.[11] More on this shortly, but first let us examine why anticipated cost savings often don't materialize.

WHY ANTICIPATED COST SAVINGS OFTEN DON'T MATERIALIZE

Consider three such reasons: (1) newly lean companies replace staff functions with expensive consultants (as a result of conditions described previously); (2) subsidiary business units recreate the kinds of expertise that headquarters staffers formerly supplied by hiring their own trainers and planners; (3) companies discover that it's expensive to train line managers to handle tasks formerly performed by staff specialists.

The net result of all of this reshuffling is that some severed employees will be hired back permanently, and others will return on a part-time basis as consultants. One executive recruiter estimated that downsizing companies wind up replacing ten to twenty percent of those they dismissed previously.

During an interview, one senior manager of a Fortune 100 company described a situation where a bookkeeper making $9 an hour was let go in a downsizing effort. However, the company later discovered that it lost valuable institutional memory in the process, for the bookkeeper knew "where's, why's, and how-to's" that no one else apparently did. The result? The former bookkeeper was hired back as a consultant for $42 per hour! Another senior manager for a Fortune 500 firm noted that after a downsizing, "Head count went down, but overall human resources

---

[11]R. Zemke, "The Ups and Downs of Downsizing," *Training*, November 1990, 27–34.

expenses went up." How can that be? Because payroll records reflected only the number of full-time employees. Victims of downsizing who were later rehired as part-timers or consultants were paid from subsidiary accounts. Thus, they were not officially listed as part of overall headcount. In other words, an accounting gimmick masked the actual impact of downsizing on labor costs. Now let's consider the impact of downsizing, as usually practiced, on productivity.

IMPACT OF DOWNSIZING ON PRODUCTIVITY

Unfortunately in many companies, downsizing is limited to reductions in headcount (rather than integrated with organization redesign or broad, systemic changes designed to root out redundancies, waste, and inefficiency).[12] Firms take a one-time charge to earnings, their operating margins improve, and the financial markets cheer. In many companies, however, the gains are short-lived, for despite all of the layoffs, automation, and just-in-time inventory management, U.S. nonfarm productivity rose a scant 1.2% a year during the 1980s. That's almost no improvement from the 1970s. In fact, in terms of average productivity growth—a key to future prosperity—the U.S. ranks fifth, behind Japan, Great Britain, France, and Italy.

From a historical perspective, consider what this implies. Beginning in the late nineteenth century the yearly rise in productivity of England, then the world's foremost industrial nation, was just slightly less (one percent) than that of its industrial rivals, mainly the United States and Germany. By the mid-twentieth century that seemingly small difference proved to be enough to tumble England from its previously undisputed industrial prominence.

Now back to the present. More than half the 1,468 restructured companies surveyed by the Society for Human Resource Management reported that employee productivity either stayed the same or deteriorated after the layoffs. Moreover, a four-year study of thirty organizations in the automobile industry revealed that very few of the organizations implemented downsizing in a way that improved their

---

[12]The first large-scale research study to demonstrate this was conducted by K. S. Cameron, S. J. Freeman, and A. K. Mishra, "Best Practices in White-Collar Downsizing: Managing Contradictions," *Academy of Management Executive*, 5(3), 1991, 57–73.

effectiveness. Most deteriorated relative to their "pre-downsizing" levels of quality, productivity, effectiveness, and human relations indicators.[13]

The term productivity is an abstract concept, but the nervousness and gloom that pervaded Bell & Howell during and subsequent to a three-way takeover battle and reports of impending layoffs during a six-month period took a toll on productivity that was very real. Senior executives at the company figured that the drop in productivity may have dragged down the company's profits for the half by as much as eleven percent or $2.1 million.

Study after study shows that following a downsizing, surviving employees become narrow-minded, self-absorbed, and risk averse.

Among firms that execute downsizing well (for example, almost fifty percent of the firms surveyed by the Society for Human Resource Management where productivity went up as a result of downsizing), certain characteristics, each an apparent contradiction, seem to be common. Consider six such characteristics:[14]

- Downsizing is implemented by command from the top, with recommendations from lower-level employees, based on job and task analyses of how work is currently organized.

- Both short-term (workforce reduction) and long-term (organization redesign and systemic change in the organization's culture) strategies are used, together with across-the-board and targeted downsizing.

- Special attention is paid both to those employees who lost their jobs (e.g., through outplacement, generous severance pay, retraining, family counseling), and to those who did not (by increasing information exchange among top managers and employees).

- Through internal data gathering and data monitoring, firms identify precisely where redundancy, excess cost, and inefficiency exist. They then attack those areas specifically. They treat outside agents (suppliers, distributors) as involved partners as well as potential targets of their downsizing efforts.

---

[13]Converging evidence on this point comes from Cameron et al., 1991, op. cit.; A. B. Fisher, "The Downside of Downsizing," *Fortune*, May 23, 1988, 42–52; and R. Henkoff, "Cost Cutting: How To Do It Right," *Fortune*, April 9, 1990, 40–49.

[14]Cameron et al., 1991, op. cit. identified these characteristics.

- Reorganizations often produce small, semi-autonomous organizations within large, integrated ones. However, geographic or product reorganizations often produced larger, more centralized units (e.g., information processing) within decentralized parent companies.

- Downsizing is viewed as a means to an end (that is, as an aggressive strategy designed to enhance competitiveness), as well as the targeted end.

In summary, it seems that the best explanation for the difference between firms that downsized effectively and those that did so ineffectively was the existence of apparent contradictions. Effective downsizing often involves contradictions—that is, processes that are thought to be opposite or incompatible. Organizations that downsized ineffectively generally tried to maintain consistency, harmony, and fit in their downsizing approach. The key seems to be to adapt a "both/and" approach to downsizing, even though this is not consistent with traditional approaches to change.

IMPACT OF DOWNSIZING ON EMPLOYEE MORALE AND MOTIVATION

Study after study shows that following a downsizing, surviving employees become narrow-minded, self-absorbed, and risk averse. Morale sinks, productivity drops, and survivors distrust management. In fact, this constellation of symptoms is so common that it has taken on a name of its own: *survivors' syndrome.*[15]

A survey by Right Associates, a Philadelphia outplacement firm, illustrates these findings. Among senior managers at recently-downsized companies, seventy-four percent said their workers had low morale, feared future cutbacks, and distrusted management. This has a long-term impact that extends far beyond the short-term benefits of reducing headcount. Thus in a survey of about 1,000 readers by *Industry Week* magazine, sixty percent of middle managers said they were less loyal to their employers than they were five years ago. Consider just one indicator of lack of employee involvement. According to Consolidated Edison Co. of New York, the rate of suggestions for improvement per employee is only *one per 25 years* in the electric utility industry, compared to one per seven years for U.S. industry as a whole.

---

[15]A considerable amount of research has been done on this issue. For a summary of it, see J. Brockner, "The Effects of Work Layoffs on Survivors: Research, Theory, and Practice." In B. M. Staw and L. L. Cummings (Eds.), *Research in Organizational Behavior, 10*, (Greenwich, CT: JAI Press, 1988), 213–255. See also D. Rice and C. Dreilinger, "After the Downsizing," *Training and Development*, May 1991, 41–44.

To a large extent, this may be due to lack of communication. Only forty-four percent of companies that downsized in the last five years shared details of their plans with employees, and even fewer (thirty-four percent) told survivors how they would fit into the company's new strategy, according to a 1992 survey of 1,020 directors of human resources.[16] This has a predictable effect on morale. Two-thirds of those polled said that since the restructuring, workers have lost trust in their companies; eighty percent said survivors can't manage their work without stress. The remedy? Plan downsizings *with* employees instead of springing it on them unannounced.

Diminishing expectations. Another survey by the Hay Group reported that in 1979, almost seventy-five percent of middle managers were optimistic about their chances for advancement. Now less than a third still think their futures look sunny. What this implies is a lack of commitment to a given employer, and makes career transitions more frequent. How much more frequent? Twenty years ago a manager worked for only one or two companies in his or her entire career. Even as late as 1981, average job tenure was twelve years. By 1988, that figure had fallen to nine, and by late 1992 it was under seven years. Indeed, workers under age 35 stay on a job a median of only 2.5 years. Soon managers will hold seven to ten jobs in a lifetime. As one observer noted: "People used to be able to count on the organization and its stability. But the myth that institutions will take care of us has been shattered."[17]

A key ingredient that is necessary to sustain programs of total quality management is high morale.

From the perspective of the individual, the implications of all of this can be summarized succinctly: our views of organizational life, managing as a career, hard work, rewards, and loyalty will never be the same. Unfortunately, far too many senior managers in the United States seem to regard employees as "units of production," costs to be cut, rather than as assets to be developed. This is a "plug-in" mentality—that is, like a machine, plug it in when you need it, unplug it when it is no longer needed. Unlike machines, however, employees have values, aspirations, beliefs—and memories.

---

[16]J. E. Rigdon, "Lack of Communication Burdens Restructurings," November 2, 1992, *The Wall Street Journal*, B1.

[17]The source of the quotation is T. F. O'Boyle, "Loyalty Ebbs at Many Companies as Employees Grow Disillusioned," *The Wall Street Journal*, July 11, 1985, 29; but see also E. M. Fowler, "A Good Side to Unwanted Job Changes," *The New York Times*, February 21, 1989, 1H.; also "Labor Letter," *The Wall Street Journal*, October 20, 1992, A1.

From the perspective of organizations, the long-term implications of reduced morale and employee commitment are not pleasant. Consider just one area that is likely to be affected: *efforts to enhance the quality of goods and services.* A key ingredient that is necessary to sustain programs of total quality management is high morale. This is so because employees must "buy in" to the management strategy of improving quality, they must align their interests with those of management, and they must become involved and committed to bring about genuine, lasting improvements in this area.[18] When was the last time you saw an organization try to improve morale and commitment by cutting workers?

Again and again, executives interviewed for this article echoed the same theme: far too often, downsizing is done indiscriminately. The resulting low morale and lack of trust have ripple effects on virtually every people-related aspect of business activity. For firms intent on downsizing or restructuring, is there a better way? In our next section we present one possible alternative.

REDEFINING THE WAY WORK IS ORGANIZED AND EXECUTED

We have already seen the economic and human consequences of simple reductions in headcount without concomitant changes in the reorganization of work. Why do so many organizations seem to be "stuck" in this mode? Perhaps because they operate on the basis of a traditional 3-C system of organization: *command, control,* and *compartmentalization.*[19] In the typical pyramidal hierarchy, senior managers are in command and exercise control through personal supervision, policies, and procedures. Job descriptions compartmentalize specific responsibilities and activities, and, all too often, the larger the organization the more rigid the job descriptions. Organizations that function on 3-C logic are most effective in stable environments. However, they tend to be unresponsive to customers, slow to adapt, and limited in creativity.

Not all large U.S. organizations continue to operate under the 3-C system. General Electric, under the leadership of chief executive officer John F. Welch, exemplifies a different approach. Since 1986 GE's "Work-Out" program has tried to achieve the following objectives: (1) to identify and eliminate sources of

---

[18]See United States General Accounting Office, *Management Practices: U.S. Companies Improve Performance Through Quality Efforts* (Washington, D.C.: USGPO, May 1991).

[19]The 3-C system was pointed out to me by V. Nilakant, "Total-Quality Management: What Is It Really All About?" *Management, Bulletin,* August 1992, No. 1, University of Canterbury, Christchurch, New Zealand, 3.

frustration, bureaucratic inefficiency, and unproductive work to energize employees; (2) to encourage feelings of ownership and self-worth at all levels of the organization; and (3) to overhaul how managers are evaluated and rewarded.

The basic features of the Work-Out system are similar to those that characterize Japanese manufacturing systems: teamwork, communication, efficient use of resources, elimination of waste, and continuous improvement. This is a deceptively simple, yet profound way to view the organization of work. It is based on the assumption that managers are creators of contexts that facilitate the execution of work by other people. One of the important mechanisms that managers can use to do this is to act in ways that add value to others' work.[20]

Perhaps the major advantage of this system is its recognition that continuous improvement eliminates the need for radical "restructurings" whose only outcome is a reduction in headcount. How has GE done? Under Welch's leadership, it has achieved world market-share leadership in nearly all of its fourteen businesses. While GE's approach may someday serve as a model for other firms, for the present and for the immediate future, certain trends seem clear.

Trends

- Downsizing begets more downsizing. Kodak restructured four times between 1982 and 1992. Honeywell is shrinking for the second time in four years. Xerox, Digital Equipment, IBM, and TRW, just to name a few major companies, have announced multiple cutbacks through the 1990s.

- Ongoing staff reductions have become etched into the corporate culture. This is true even among firms with record profits, such as GE Appliance Division, Nordstrom, Saks Fifth Avenue, and Compaq Computer. In late 1992, Compaq announced it would shrink its work force by about 1,000 people, or ten percent of its world-wide total, over several months, despite record revenue and unit shipments. Why? In *anticipation* of a continuing intensely competitive market environment for personal computers.

Conventional wisdom holds that recessions are good opportunities to improve productivity, often by dropping people and putting in automated equipment. However, almost fifty percent of respondents to an American Management Association survey reported that downsizing had nothing to do with the recession.

---

[20]Nilikant, 1992, op. cit.; see also J. P. Womack, D. T. Jones, and D. Roos, *The Machine That Changed the World* (NY: Rawson Associates, 1990).

Mergers and acquisitions, plant obsolescence or newly automated processes, and transfers of operations elsewhere have turned work force reductions into an ongoing activity that continues without regard to current financial performance.

- "Companies are managing their workers as they manage their inventories of unsold goods. They are trying to keep both sets of inventories—employees and merchandise—as low as possible," according to Leslie McNulty, research director of the United Food and Commercial Workers Union. This approach, which may well characterize the 1990s, has been termed "Kanban employment," using the Japanese term for just-in-time delivery and no stockpiling or inventorying of resources.[21]

- Downsize first, ask questions later. Companies often say they turn to layoffs as a last resort. But Right Associates, in polls of 1,204 and 909 companies that had reduced staffing levels, found that only six percent of the employers had tried cutting pay, nine percent had shortened work weeks, nine percent used vacation without pay, and fourteen percent had developed job-sharing plans. Clearly they are not listening to employees, for when a Time/CNN poll asked 1,250 adult Americans "If your company needed to cut expenses in order to stay in business, would you prefer they cut everyone's pay by ten percent or lay off ten percent of the work force?" Eighty percent preferred the pay cut.[22]

- Many unionized blue-collar workers are trading off wage freezes or concessions for job security. White-collar workers in manufacturing and service jobs don't have that security in the lower echelons—and they are being hit hard. Consider the agreement between Uniroyal Goodrich Tire Co. and the United Rubber Workers at the company's 71-year-old Eau Claire, Wisconsin plant. The union agreed to a 63-cent-an-hour reduction in pay, one less vacation week, three fewer annual holidays, no cost-of-living increases, and extensive work-rule changes. In return, Uniroyal guaranteed the jobs of the workers during the life of the contract.

---

[21]E. R. Greenberg, "Downsizing: AMA Survey Results," *Compensation and Benefits Review*, *23*(4), 1991, 33–38.

[22]The term "Kanban employment" comes from A. Freedman, "How the 1980s Have Changed Industrial Relations," *Monthly Labor Review*, May 1988, 35–38. The source of the quotation is L. Uchitelle, "Layoffs Are Rising Even at Companies in Good Condition," *The New York Times*, October 29, 1990, A1; B7.

IMPLICATIONS FOR MANAGERS

The experience of hundreds of downsizings during the late 1980s and early 1990s has spawned a vast literature. Some answers to the questions, "What do we know?" and "What have we learned?" can be summarized in terms of ten key lessons for managers.

1. Downsizing will continue as long as overhead costs remain noncompetitive with domestic and international rivals.

2. Firms with high debt are most likely to downsize by aggressively cutting people.

3. Far too many companies are not well prepared for downsizing, they begin with no retraining or redeployment policies in place, and they fail to anticipate the kinds of human resource problems that develop subsequently.

4. Six months to a year after a downsizing key indicators often do *not* improve: expense ratios, profits, return-on-investment to shareholders, and stock prices.

5. Survivors' syndrome is a common aftermath. Be prepared to manage it. Better yet, try to avoid it by actively involving employees in the planning phase of any downsizing effort.

6. Recognize that downsizing has exploded the myth of job security, and has accelerated employee mobility, especially among white-collar workers. It has fundamentally altered the terms of the psychological contract that binds workers to organizations.

7. Productivity and quality often suffer because there is no change in the *way* work is done. The same amount of work as before a downsizing is simply loaded onto the backs of fewer workers.

8. To downsize effectively, be prepared to manage apparent contradictions—for example, between the use of top-down authority and bottom-up empowerment, between short-term strategies (headcount reduction) and long-term strategies (organization redesign and systemic changes in culture).

9. To bring about sustained improvements in productivity, quality, and effectiveness, integrate reductions in headcount with planned changes in

the way that work is designed. Systematically question the continued appropriateness of 3-C logic.

10. Downsizing is not a one-time, quick-fix solution to enhance competitiveness. Rather, it should be viewed as part of a process of continuous improvement.

ABOUT THE AUTHOR

Wayne F. Cascio received his Ph.D. in industrial and organizational psychology from the University of Rochester in 1973. Currently he is professor of management and director of international programs at the University of Colorado at Denver. He is a past president of the Human Resources Division of the Academy of Management, and currently he is president of the Society for Industrial and Organizational Psychology. He has consulted with firms in North America, Asia, Africa, Europe, New Zealand, and Australia, and has authored or edited five texts in human resource management. His research on staffing, training, performance appraisal, and the economic impact of human resource management activities has appeared in a number of scholarly journals.

CHANGING UNETHICAL ORGANIZATION BEHAVIOR

Richard P. Nielsen, Boston College

"To be, or not to be: that is the question
Whether 'tis nobler in the mind to suffer
The slings and arrows of outrageous fortune,
Or to take arms against a sea of troubles,
And by opposing end them?"

William Shakespeare, *Hamlet*

What are the implications of Hamlet's question in the context of organizational ethics? What does it mean to be ethical in an organizational context? Should one suffer the slings and arrows of unethical organizational behavior? Should one try to take arms against unethical behaviors and by opposing, end them?

The consequences of addressing organizational ethics issues can be unpleasant. One can be punished or fired; one's career can suffer, or one can be disliked, considered an outsider. It may take courage to oppose unethical and lead ethical organizational behavior.

How can one address organizational ethics issues? Paul Tillich, in his book *The Courage to Be*, recognized, as Hamlet did, that dire consequences can result from standing up to and opposing unethical behavior. Tillich identified two approaches: *being* as an individual and *beinig* as a part of a group.[1]

In an organizational context, these two approaches can be interpreted as follows: (1) Being as an individual can mean intervening to end unethical organizational behaviors by working against others and the organizations performing the unethical behaviors; and (2) being as a part can mean leading an ethical organizational change by working with others and the organization. These approaches are not mutually exclusive; rather, depending on the individual, the organization, the relationships, and the situation, one or both of these approaches may be appropriate for addressing ethical issues.

© *The Academy of Management Executive*, 1989, Vol. III, No. 2, pp. 123–130.

[1]Paul Tillich, *The Courage to Be*. New Haven, CT: Yale University Press, 1950.

Being as an Individual

According to Tillich, the courage to be as an individual is the courage to follow one's conscience and defy unethical and/or unreasonable authority. It can even mean staging a revolutionary attack on that authority. Such an act can entail great risk and require great courage. As Tillich explains, "The anxiety conquered in the courage to be . . . in the productive process is considerable, because the threat of being excluded from such a participation by unemployment or the loss of an economic basis is what, above all, fate means today. . . ."[2]

According to David Ewing, retired executive editor of the *Harvard Business Review*, this type of anxiety is not without foundation.

"There is very little protection in industry for employees who object to carrying out immoral, unethical or illegal orders from their superiors. If the employee doesn't like what he or she is asked to do, the remedy is to pack up and leave. This remedy seems to presuppose an ideal economy, where there is another company down the street with openings for jobs just like the one the employee left."[3]

How can one *be* as an individual, intervening against unethical organizational behavior? Intervention strategies an individual can use to change unethical behavior include: (1) secretly blowing the whistle within the organization; (2) quietly blowing the whistle, informing a responsible higher-level manager; (3) secretly threatening the offender with blowing the whistle; (4) secretly threatening a responsible manager with blowing the whistle outside the organization; (5) publicly threatening a responsible manager with blowing the whistle; (6) sabotaging the implementation of the unethical behavior; (7) quietly refraining from implementing an unethical order or policy; (8) publicly blowing the whistle within the organization; (9) conscientiously objecting to an unethical policy or refusing to implement the policy; (10) indicating uncertainty about or refusing to support a cover-up in the event that the individual and/or organization gets caught; (11) secretly blowing the whistle outside the organization; or (12) publicly blowing the whistle outside the organization. Cases of each strategy are considered below.

---

[2]See Endnote 1, page 159.

[3]David Ewing, *Freedom Inside the Organization*. New York: McGraw-Hill, 1977.

Cases

1. *Secretly blowing the whistle within the organization.* A purchasing manager for General Electric secretly wrote a letter to an upper-level manager about his boss, who was soliciting and accepting bribes from subcontractors. The boss was investigated and eventually fired. He was also sentenced to six months' imprisonment for taking $100,000 in bribes, in exchange for which he granted favorable treatment on defense contracts.[4]

2. *Quietly blowing the whistle to a responsible higher-level manager.* When Evelyn Grant was first hired by the company with which she is now a personnel manager, her job included administering a battery of tests that, in part, determined which employees were promoted to supervisory positions. Grant explained:

> *"There have been cases where people will do something wrong because they think they have no choice. Their boss tells them to do it, and so they do it, knowing it's wrong. They don't realize there are ways around the boss. . . . When I went over his [the chief psychologist's] data and analysis. I found errors in assumption as well as actual errors of computation. . . . I had two choices: I could do nothing or I could report my findings to my supervisor. If I did nothing, the only persons probably hurt were the ones who 'failed' the test. To report my findings, on the other hand, could hurt several people, possibly myself."*

She quietly spoke to her boss, who quietly arranged for a meeting to discuss the discrepancies with the chief psychologist. The chief psychologist did not show up for the meeting; however, the test battery was dropped.[5]

3. *Secretly threatening the offender with blowing the whistle.* A salesman for a Boston-area insurance company attended a weekly sales meeting during which the sales manager instructed the salespeople, both verbally and in writing, to use a sales technique that the salesman considered unethical. The salesman anonymously wrote the sales manager a letter threatening to send a copy of the unethical sales instructions to the Massachusetts insurance commissioner and the *Boston Globe* newspaper unless the sales manager retracted his instructions at the next sales

---

[4]The person blowing the whistle in this case wishes to remain anonymous. See also Elizabeth Neuffer, "GE Managers Sentenced for Bribery," *The Boston Globe*, July 26, 1988, p. 67.

[5]Barbara Ley Toffler, *Tough Choices: Managers Talk Ethics.* New York: John Wiley, 1986, pp. 153–169.

meeting. The sales manager did retract the instructions. The salesman still works for the insurance company.[6]

4. Secretly threatening a responsible manager with blowing the whistle outside the organization. A recently hired manager with a San Francisco Real Estate Development Company found that the construction company his firm had contracted with was systematically not giving minorities opportunities to learn construction management. This new manager wrote an anonymous letter to a higher-level real estate manager threatening to blow the whistle to the press and local government about the contractor unless the company corrected the situation. The real estate manager intervened, and the contractor began to hire minorities for foremen-training positions.[7]

5. Publicly threatening a responsible manager with blowing the whistle. A woman in the business office of a large Boston-area university observed that one middle-level male manager was sexually harassing several women in the office. She tried to reason with the office manager to do something about the offensive behavior, but the manager would not do anything. She then told the manager and several other people in the office that if the manager did not do something about the behavior, she would blow the whistle to the personnel office. The manager then told the offender that if he did not stop the harassment, the personnel office would be brought in. He did stop the behavior, but he and several other employees refused to talk to the woman who initiated the actions. She eventually left the university.[8]

6. Sabotaging the implementation of the unethical behavior. A program manager for a Boston-area local social welfare organization was told by her superior to replace a significant percentage of her clients who received disability benefits with refugee Soviet Jews. She wanted to help both the refugees and her current clients; however, she thought it was unethical to drop current clients, in part because she believed such an action could result in unnecessary deaths. Previously, a person who had lost benefits because of what the program manager considered unethical "bumping" had committed suicide: He had not wanted to force his family to sell

---

[6]Richard P. Nielsen, "What Can Managers Do About Unethical Management?" *Journal of Business Ethics*, 6, 1987, 153–161. See also Nielsen's "Limitations of Ethical Reasoning as an Action Strategy," *Journal of Business Ethics*, 7, 1988, pp. 725–733, and "Arendt's Action Philosophy and the Manager as Eichmann, Richard III, Faust or Institution Citizen," *California Management Review*, 26, 3, Spring 1984, pp. 191–201.

[7]The person involved wishes to remain anonymous.

[8]The person involved wishes to remain anonymous.

their home in order to pay for the medical care he needed and qualify for poverty programs. After her attempts to reason with her boss failed, she instituted a paperwork chain with a partially funded federal agency that prevented her own agency from dropping clients for nine months, after which time they would be eligible for a different funding program. Her old clients received benefits and the new refugees also received benefits. In discussion with her boss, she blamed the federal agency for making it impossible to drop people quickly. Her boss, a political appointee who did not understand the system, also blamed the federal agency office.[9]

7. *Publicly blowing the whistle within the organization.* John W. Young, the chief of NASA's astronaut office, wrote a 12-page internal memorandum to 97 people after the Challenger explosion that killed seven crew members. The memo listed a large number of safety-related problems that Young said had endangered crews since October 1984. According to Young, "If the management system is not big enough to stop the space shuttle program whenever necessary to make flight safety corrections, it will not survive and neither will our three space shuttles or their flight crews." The memo was instrumental in the decision to broaden safety investigations throughout the total NASA system.[10]

8. *Quietly refraining from implementing an unethical order/policy.* Frank Ladwig was a top salesman and branch manager with a large computer company for more than 40 years. At times, he had trouble balancing his responsibilities. For instance, he was trained to sell solutions to customer problems, yet he had order and revenue quotas that sometimes made it difficult for him to concentrate on solving problems. He was responsible for signing and keeping important customers with annual revenues of between $250,000 and $500,000 and for aggressively and conscientiously representing new products that had required large R&D investments. He was required to sell the full line of products and services, and sometimes he had sales quotas for products that he believed were not a good match for the customer or appeared to perform marginally. Ladwig would quietly not sell those products, concentrating on selling the products he believed in. He would quietly explain the characteristics of the questionable products to his knowledgeable customers and get their reactions, rather than making an all-out sales effort. When he was asked by his sales manager why a certain product was not moving, he explained what the customers objected to and why. However, Ladwig thought that a salesman or

---

[9]See Endnote 6.

[10]R. Reinhold, "Astronauts Chief Says NASA Risked Life for Schedule," *The New York Times*, 36, 1986, p. 1.

manager with an average or poor performance record would have a difficult time getting away with this type of solution to an ethical dilemma.[11]

9. *Conscientiously objecting to an unethical policy or refusing to implement it.* Francis O'Brien was a research director for the pharmaceutical company Searle & Co. O'Brien conscientiously objected to what he believed were exaggerated claims for the Searle Copper 7 intrauterine contraceptive. When reasoning with upper-level management failed, O'Brien wrote them the following:

> *"Their continued use, in my opinion, is both misleading and a thinly disguised attempt to make claims which are not FDA approved. . . . Because of personal reasons I do not consent to have my name used in any press release or in connection with any press release. In addition, I will not participate in any press conferences."*

O'Brien left the company ten years later. Currently, several lawsuits are pending against Searle, charging that its IUD caused infection and sterility.[12]

10. *Indicating uncertainty about or refusing to support a cover-up in the event that the individual and/or organization gets caught.* In the Boston office of Bear Stearns, four brokers informally work together as a group. One of the brokers had been successfully trading on insider information, and he invited the other three to do the same. One of the three told the others that such trading was not worth the risk of getting caught, and if an investigation ever occurred, he was not sure he would be able to participate in a cover-up. The other two brokers decided not to trade on the insider information, and the first broker stopped at least that type of insider trading.[13]

11. *Secretly blowing the whistle outside the corporation.* William Schwartz-kopf of the Commonwealth Electric Company secretly and anonymously wrote a letter to the Justice Department alleging large-scale, long-time bid rigging among many of the largest U.S. electrical contractors. The secret letter accused the contractors of raising bids and conspiring to divide billions of dollars of contracts. Companies in the industry have already paid more than $20 million in fines to the

---

[11]Personal conversation and letter with Frank Ladwig, 1986. See also Frank Ladwig and Associates' *Advanced Consultative Selling for Professionals.* Stonington, CT.

[12]W. G. Glaberson, "Did Searle Lose Its Eyes to a Health Hazard?" *Business Week*, October 14, 1985, pp. 120–122.

[13]The person involved wishes to remain anonymous.

government in part as a result of this letter, and they face millions of dollars more in losses when the victims sue.[14]

   12. Publicly blowing the whistle outside the organization. A. Ernest Fitzgerald, a former high-level manager in the U.S. Air Force and Lockheed CEO, revealed to Congress and the press that the Air Force and Lockheed systematically practiced a strategy of underbidding in order to gain Air Force contracts for Lockheed, which then billed the Air Force and received payments for cost overruns on the contracts. Fitzgerald was fired for his trouble, but eventually received his job back. The underbidding/cost overruns, on at least the C-5/A cargo plane, were stopped.[15]

Limitations of Intervention

   The intervention strategies described above can be very effective, but they also have some important limitations.

   1. The individual can be wrong aboout the organization's actions. Lower-level employees commonly do not have as much or as good information about ethical situations and issues as higher-level managers. Similarly, they may not be as experienced as higher-level managers in dealing with specific ethical issues. The quality of experience and information an individual has can influence the quality of his or her ethical judgments. To the extent that this is true in any given situation, the use of intervention may or may not be warranted. In Case 9, for example, if Frank Ladwig had had limited computer experience, he could have been wrong about some of the products he thought would not produce the promised results.

   2. Relationships can be damaged. Suppose that instead of identifying with the individuals who want an organization to change its ethical behavior, we look at these situations from another perspective. How do we feel when we are forced to change our behavior? Further, how would we feel if we were forced by a subordinate to change, even though we thought that we had the position, quality of information, and/or quality of experience to make the correct decisions? Relationships would probably be, at the leat, strained, particularly if we made an ethical decision and were nevertheless forced to change. If we are wrong, it may be that we do not recognize it at the time. If we know we are wrong, we still may not like being

---

[14]Andy Pasztor, "Electrical Contractors Reel Under Charges that They Rigged Bids," *The Wall Street Journal*, November 29, 1985, pp. 1, 14.

[15]A. Ernest Fitzgerald, *The High Priests of Waste.* New York: McGraw-Hill, 1977.

forced to change. However, it is possible that the individual forcing us to change may justify his or her behavior to us, and our relationship may actually be strengthened.

3. The organization can be hurt unnecessarily. If an individual is wrong in believing that the organization is unethical, the organization can be hurt unnecessarily by his or her actions. Even if the individual is right, the organization can still be unnecessarily hurt by intervention strategies.

4. Intervention strategies can encourage "might makes right" climates. If we want "wrong" people, who might be more powerful now or in the future than we are, to exercise self-restraint, then we may need to exercise self-restraint even when we are "right." A problem with using force is that the other side may use more powerful or effective force now or later. Many people have been punished for trying to act ethically both when they were right and when they were wrong. By using force, one may also contribute to the belief that the only way to get things done in a particular organization is through force. People who are wrong can and do use force, and win. Do we want to build an organization culture in which force plays an important role? Gandhi's response to "an eye for an eye" was that if we all followed that principle, eventually everyone would be blind.

Being as a Part

While the intervention strategies discussed above can be very effective, they can also be destructive. Therefore, it may be appropriate to consider the advantages of leading an ethical change effort (being as a part) as well as intervening against unethical behaviors (being as an individual).

Tillich maintains that the courage to be as a part is the courage to affirm one's own being through participation with others. He writes,

> *"The self affirms itself as participant in the power of a group, of a movement. . . . Self-affirmation within a group includes the courage to accept guilt and its consequences as public guilt, whether one is oneself responsible or whether somebody else is. It is a problem of the group which has to be expiated for the sake of the group, and the methods of punishment and satisfaction . . . are accepted by the individual. . . . In every human community, there are outstanding members, the bearers of the traditions and leaders of the future. They must have sufficient distance in order to judge and to change. They must take responsibility and ask questions. This unavoidably produces individual doubt and personal guilt. Nevertheless, the predominant pattern is the courage to be a part in all members of the . . . group. . . . The difference*

between the genuine Stoic and the neocollectivist is that the latter is bound in the first place to the collective and in the second place to the universe, while the Stoic was first of all related to the universal Logos and secondly to possible human groups. . . . The democratic-conformist type of the courage to be as a part was in an outspoken way tied up with the idea of progress. The courage to be as a part in the progress of the group to which one belongs. . . .[16]*

Leading Ethical Change

A good cross-cultural conceptualization of leadership is offered by Yoshino and Lifson: "The essence of leadership is the influential increment over and above mechanical compliance with routine directives of the organization."[17] This definition permits comparisons between and facilitates an understanding of different leadership styles through its use of a single variable: created incremental performance. Of course, different types of leadership may be more or less effective in different types of situations; yet, it is helpful to understand the "essence" of leadership in its many different cultural forms as the creation of incremental change beyond the routine.

For example, Yoshino and Lifson compare generalizations (actually overgeneralizations) about Japanese and American leadership styles:

"In the United States, a leader is often thought of as one who blazes new trails, a virtuoso whose example inspires awe, respect, and emulation. If any individual characterizes this pattern, it is surely John Wayne, whose image reached epic proportions in his own lifetime as an embodiment of something uniquely American. A Japanese leader, rather than being an authority, is more of a communications channel, a mediator, a facilitator, and most of all, a symbol and embodiment of group unity. Consensus building is necessary in decision making, and this requires patience and an ability to use carefully cultivated relationships to get all to agree for the good of the unit. A John Wayne in this situation might succeed temporarily by virtue of charisma, but eventually the inability to build strong emotion-laden

---

[16]See Endnote 1, pp. 89, 93.

[17]M. Y. Yoshino and T. B. Lifson, *The Invisible Link: Japan's Saga Shosha and the Organization of Trade*, Cambridge, MA: MIT Press, 1986.

relationships and use these as a tool of motivation and consensus building would prove fatal. "[18]

A charismatic, "John Wayne type" leader can inspire and/or frighten people into diverting from the routine. A consensus-building, Japanese-style leader can get people to agree to divert from the routine. In both cases, the leader creates incremental behavior change beyond the routine. How does leadership (being as a part) in its various cultural forms differ from the various intervention (being as an individual) strategies and cases discussed above? Some case data may be revealing.

Cases

1. Roger Boisjoly and the Challenger launch.[19] In January 1985, after the postflight hardware inspection of Flight 52C, Roger Boisjoly strongly suspected that unusually low temperatures had compromised the performance effectiveness of the O-ring seals on twso field joints. Such a performance compromise could cause an explosion. In March 1985, laboratory tests confirmed that low temperatures did negatively affect the ability of the O-rings to perform this sealing function. In June 1985, the postflight inspection of Flight 51B revealed serious erosion of both primary and backup seals that, had it continued, could have caused an explosion.

These events convinced Boisjoly that a serious and very dangerous problem existed with the O-rings. Instead of acting as an individual against his supervisors and the organization, for example, by blowing the whistle to the press, he tried to lead a change to stop the launching of flights with unsafe O-rings. He worked with his immediate supervisor, the director of engineering, and the organization in leading this change. He wrote a draft of a memo to Bob Lund, viced-president of engineering, which he first showed and discussed with his immediate supervisor to "maintain good relationships." Boisjoly and others developed potential win-win solutions, such as investigating remedies to fix the O-rings and refraining from launching flights at too-low temperatures. He effectively established a team to study the matter, and participated in a teleconference with 130 technical experts.

On the day before the Challenger launch, Boisjoly and other team members were successful in leading company executives to reverse their tentative recommen-

---

[18]See Endnote 17, p. 178.

[19]Roger Boisjoly, address given at Massachusetts Institute of Technology on January 7, 1987. Reprinted in *Books and Religion*, March/April 1987, 3-4, 12-13. See also Caroline Whitbeck, "Moral Responsibility and the Working Engineer," *Books and Religion*, March/April 1987, 3, 22-23.

dation to launch because the overnight temperatures were predicted to be too low. The company recommendation was to launch only when temperatures were above 53 degrees. To this point, Boisjoly was very effective in leading a change toward what he and other engineering and management people believed was a safe and ethical decision.

However, according to testimony from Boisjoly and others to Congress, the top managers of Morton Thiokol, under pressure from NASA, reversed their earlier recommendation not to launch. The next day, Challenger was launched and exploded, causing the deaths of all the crew members. While Boisjoly was very effective in leading a change within his own organization, he was not able to counteract subsequent pressure from the customer, NASA.

2. Dan Phillips and Genco, Inc.[20] Dan Phillips was a paper products group division manager for Genco, whose upper-level management adopted a strategy whereby several mills, including the Elkhorn Mill, would either have to reduce costs or close down. Phillips was concerned that cost cutting at Elkhorn would prevent the mill from meeting government pollution-control requirements, and that closing the mill could seriously hurt the local community. If he reduced costs, he would not meet pollution-control requirements; if he did not reduce costs, the mill would close and the community would suffer.

Phillips did not secretly or publicly blow the whistle, nor did he sabotage, conscientiously object, quietly refrain from implementing the plan, or quit; however, he did lead a change in the organization's ethical behavior. He asked research and development people in his division to investigate how the plant could both become more cost efficient and create less pollution. He then asked operations people in his division to estimate how long it would take to put such a new plant design on line, and how much it would cost. He asked cost accounting and financial people within his division to estimate when such a new operation would achieve a breakeven payback. Once he found a plan that would work, he negotiated a win-win solution with upper-level management: in exchange for not closing the plant and increasing its investment in his division, the organization would over time benefit from lower costs and higher profitability. Phillips thus worked with others and the organization to lead an inquiry and adopt an alternative ethical and cost-effective plan.

---

[20]Personal conversation with Ray Bauer, Harvard Business School, 1975. See also R. Ackerman and Ray Bauer, *Corporate Social Responsiveness*, Reston, VA: Reston Publishing, 1976.

3. Lotus and Brazilian Software Importing.[21] Lotus, a software manufacturer, found that in spite of restrictions on the importing of much of its software to Brazil, many people there were buying and using Lotus software. On further investigation, the company discovered that Brazilian businessmen, in alliance with a Brazilian general, were violating the law by buying Lotus software in Cambridge, Massachusetts and bringing it into Brazil.

Instead of blowing the whistle on the illegal behavior, sabotaging it, or leaving Brazil, Lotus negotiated a solution: In exchange for the Brazilians' agreement to stop illegal importing, Lotus helped set them up as legitimate licensed manufacturers and distributors of Lotus products in Brazil. Instead of working against them and the Lotus salespeople supplying them, the Lotus managers worked with these people to develop an ethical, legal, and economically sound solution to the importing problem.

And in at least a limited sense, the importers may have been transformed into ethical managers and business people. This case may remind you of the legendary "Old West," where government officials sometimes negotiated win-win solutions with "outlaw gunfighters," who agreed to become somewhat more ethical as appointed sheriffs. The gunfighters needed to make a living, and many were not interested in or qualified for such other professions as farming or shopkeeping. In some cases, ethical behavior may take place before ethical beliefs are assumed.

4. Insurance company office/sales manager and discrimination.[22] The sales-office manager of a very large Boston-area insurance company tried to hire female salespeople several times, but his boss refused to permit the hires. The manager could have acted against his boss and the organization by secretly threatening to blow the whistle or actually blowing the whistle, publicly or secretly. Instead, he decided to try to lead a change in the implicit hiring policy of the organization.

The manager asked his boss why he was not permitted to hire a woman. He learned that his boss did not believe women made good salespeople and had never worked with a female salesperson. He found that reasoning with his boss about the capabilities of women and the ethics and legality of refusing to hire women was ineffective.

He inquired within the company about whether being a woman could be an advantage in any insurance sales areas. He negotiated with his boss a six-month experiment whereby he hired on a trial basis one woman to sell life insurance to

---

[21]The person involved wishes to remain anonymous.

[22]The person involved wishes to remain anonymous.

married women who contributed large portions of their salaries to their home mortgages. The woman he hired was not only very successful in selling this type of life insurance, but became one of the office's top salespeople. After this experience, the boss reversed his policy of not hiring female salespeople.

Limitations to Leading Ethical Organizational Change

In the four cases described above, the individuals did not attack the organization or people within the organization, nor did they intervene against individuals and/or the organization to stop an unethical practice. Instead, they worked with people in the organization to build a more ethical organization. As a result of their leadership, the organizations used more ethical behaviors. The strategy of leading an organization toward more ethical behavior, however, does have some limitations. These are described below.

1. In some organizational situations, ethical win-win solutions or compromises may not be possible. For example, in 1975 a pharmaceutical company in Raritan, New Jersey decided to enter a new market with a new product.[23] Grace Pierce, who was then in charge of medical testing of new products, refused to test a new diarrhea drug product on infants and elderly consumers because it contained high levels of saccharin, which was feared by many at the time to be a carcinogen. When Pierce was transferred, she resigned. The drug was tested on infant and elderly consumers. In this case, Pierce may have been faced with an either-or situation that left her little room to lead a change in organizational behavior.

Similarly, Errol Marshall, with Hydraulic Parts and Components, Inc.,[24] helped negotiate the sale of a subcontract to sell heavy equipment to the U.S. Navy while giving $70,000 in kickbacks to two materials managers of Brown & Root, Inc., the project's prime contractor. According to Marshall, the prime contractor "demanded the kickbacks. . . . It was cut and dried. We would not get the business otherwise." While Marshall was not charged with any crime, one of the upper-level Brown & Root managers, William Callan, was convicted in 1985 of extorting kickbacks, and another manager, Frank DiDomenico, pleaded guilty to extorting kickbacks from Hydraulic Parts & Components, Inc. Marshall has left the company. In this case, it seems that Marshall had no win-win alternative to paying

---

[23]David Ewing, *Do It My Way or You're Fired.* New York: John Wiley, 1983.

[24]E. T. Pound, "Investigators Detect Pattern of Kickbacks for Defense Business," *The Wall Street Journal*, November 14, 1985, pp. 1, 25.

the bribe. In some situations it may not be possible to lead a win-win ethical change.

2. Some people do not understand how leadership can be applied to situations that involve organizational-ethics issues. Also, some people—particularly those in analytical or technical professions, which may not offer much opportunity for gaining leadership experience—may not know how to lead very well in any situation. Some people may be good leaders in the course of their normal work lives, but do not try to lead or do not lead very well when ethical issues are involved. Some people avoid discussing ethical, religious, and political issues at work.

For example, John Geary was a salesman for U.S. Steel when the company decided to enter a new market with what he and others considered an unsafe new product.[25] As a leading salesman for U.S. Steel, Geary normally was very good at leading the way toward changes that satisfied customer and organizational needs. A good salesman frequently needs to coordinate and spearhead modifications in operations, engineering, logistics, product design, financing, and billing/payment that are necessary for a company to maintain good customer relationships and sales. Apparently, however, he did not try to lead the organization in developing a win-win solution, such as soliciting current orders for a later delivery of a corrected product. He tried only reasoning against selling the unsafe product and protested its sale to several groups of upper-level engineers and managers. He noted that he believed the product had a failure rate of 3.6% and was therefore both unsafe and potentially damaging to U.S. Steel's longer-term strategy of entering higher technology/profit margin businesses. According to Geary, even though many upper-level managers, engineers, and salesmen understood and believed him, "the only desire of everyone associated with the project was to satisfy the instructions of Henry Wallace [the sales vice-president]. No one was about to buck this man for fear of his job."[26] The sales vice-president fired Geary, apparently because he continued to protest against sale of the product.

Similarly, William Schwartzkopf of Commonwealth Electric Co.[27] did not think he could either ethically reason against or lead an end to the large-scale, long-time bid rigging between his own company and many of the largest U.S. electrical contractors. Even though he was an attorney and had extensive experience in leading organizational changes, he did not try to lead his company toward an ethical

---

[25]See Endnote 23. See also Geary vs. U.S. Steel Corporation, 319 A. 2nd 174, Supreme Court of Pa.

[26]See Endnote 23, p. 86.

[27]See Endnote 14.

solution. He waited until he retired from the company, then wrote a secret letter to the Justice Department accusing the contractors of raising bids and conspiring to divide billions of dollars of contracts among themselves.

Many people—both experienced and inexperienced in leadership—do not try to lead their companies toward developing solutions to ethical problems. Often, they do not understand that it is possible to lead such a change; therefore, they do not try to do so—even though, as the cases here show, many succeed when they do try.

3. Some organizational environments—in both consensus-building and authoritarian types of cultures—discourage leadership that is nonconforming. For example, as Robert E. Wood, former CEO of the giant international retailer Sears, Roebuck, has observed, "We stress the advantages of the free enterprise system, we complain about the totalitarian state, but in our individual organizations we have created more or less a totalitarian system in industry, particularly in large industry."[28] Similarly, Charles W. Summers, in a *Harvard Business Review* article, observes, "Corporate executives may argue that . . . they recognize and protect . . . against arbitrary termination through their own internal procedures. The simple fact is that most companies have not recognized and protected that right."[29]

David Ewing concludes that "It [the pressure to obey unethical and illegal orders] is probably most dangerous, however, as a low-level infection. When it slowly bleeds the individual conscience dry and metastasizes insidiously, it is most difficult to defend against. There are no spectacular firings or purges in the ranks. There are no epic blunders. Under constant and insistent pressure, employees simply give in and conform. They become good 'organization people.'"[30]

Similar pressures can exist in participative, consensus-building types of cultures. For example, as mentioned above, Yoshino and Lifson write, "A Japanese leader, rather than being an authority, is more of a communications channel, a mediator, a facilitator, and most of all, a symbol and embodiment of group unity. Consensus building is necessary to decision making, and this requires patience and

---

[28]See Endnote 3, p. 21.

[29]C. W. Summers, "Protecting All Employees Against Unjust Dismissal," *Harvard Business Review*, 58, 1980, pp. 132–139.

[30]See Endnote 3, pp. 216–217.

an ability to use carefully cultivated relationships to get all to agree for teh good of the unit."[31]

The importance of the group and the position of the group leaders as a symbol of the group are revealed in the very popular true story, "Tale of the Forty-Seven Ronin." The tale is about 47 warriors whose lord is unjustly killed. The Ronin spend years sacrificing everything, including their families, in order to kill the person responsible for their leader's death. Then all those who survive the assault killed themselves.

Just as authoritarian top-down organizational cultures can produce unethical behaviors, so can participative, consensus-building cultures. The Japanese novelist Shusaku Endo, in his *The Sea and Poison*, describes the true story of such a problem.[32] It concersn an experiment cooperatively performed by the Japanese Army, a medical hospital, and a consensus-building team of doctors on American prisoners of war. The purpose of the experiment was to determine scientifically how much blood people can lose before they die.

Endo describes the reasoning and feelings of one of the doctors as he looked back at his behavior:

> *"At the time nothing could be done. . . . If I were caught in the same way, I might, I might just do the same thing again. . . . We feel that getting on good terms ourselves with the Western Command medical people, with whom Second [section] is so cosy, wouldn't be a bad idea at all. Therefore we feel there's no need to ill-temperedly refuse their friendly proposal and hurt their feelings. . . . Five doctors from Kando's section most likely will be glad to get the chance. . . . For me the pangs of conscience . . . were from childhood equivalent to the fear of disapproval in the eyes of others—fear of the punishment which society would bring to bear. . . . To put it quite bluntly, I am able to remain quite undisturbed in the face of someone else's terrible suffering and death. . . . I am not writing about these experiences as one driven to do so by his conscience . . . all these memories are distasteful to me. But looking upon them as distasteful and suffering because of them are two different matters. Then why do I bother writing? Because I'm strangely ill at ease. I, who fear only the eyes of others and the*

---

[31]See Endnote 17, p. 187.

[32]Shusaku Endo, *The Sea and Poison*. New York: Taplinger Publishing Company, 1972. See also Y. Yasuda, *Old Tales of Japan*. Tokyo: Charles Tuttle Company, 1947.

punishment of society, and whose feaers disappear when I am secure from these, am now disturbed. . . . I have no conscience, I suppose. Not just me, though. None of them feel anything at all about what they did here.' The only emotion in his heart was a sense of having fallen as low as one can fall. "[33]

What to Do and How to Be

In light of the discussion of the two approaches to addressing organizational ethics issues and their limitations, what should we do as individuals and members of organizations? To some extent that depends on the circumstances and our own abilities. If we know how to lead, if there's time for it, if the key people in authority are reasonable, and if a win-win solution is possible, one should probably try leading an organizational change.

If, on the other hand, one does not know how to lead, time is limited, the authority figures are unreasonable, a culture of strong conformity exists, and the situation is not likely to produce a win-win outcome, then the chances of success with a leadership approach are much lower. This may leave one with only the choice of using one of the intervention strategies discussed above. If an individual wishes to remain an effective member of the organization, then one of the more secretive strategies may be safer.

But what about the more common, middle range of problems? Here there is no easy prescription. The more win-win potential the situation has, the more time there is, the more leadership skills one has, and the more reasonable the authority figures and organizational cultures are, the more likely a leadership approach is to succeed. If the opposite conditions exist, then forcing change in the organization is the likely alternative.

To a large extent, the choice depends on an individual's courage. In my opinion, in all but the most extreme and unusual circumstances, one should first try to lead a change toward ethical behavior. If that does not succeed, then mustering the courage to act against others and the organization may be necessary. For example, the course of action that might have saved the Challenger crew was for Boisjoly or someone else to act against Morton Thiokol, its top managers, and NASA by blowing the whistle to the press.

If there is an implicitly characteristic American ontology, perhaps it is some version of William James' 1907 *Pragmatism*, which, for better or worse, sees

---

[33]See Endnote 32.

through a lens of interactions the ontologies of being as an individual and being as a part, James explains our situation as follows:

> *"What we were discussing was the idea of a world growing not integrally but piecemeal by the contributions of its several parts. Take the hypothesis seriously and as a live one. Suppose that the world's author put the case to you before creation, saying: 'If I am going to make a world not certain to be savid, a world the perfection of which shall be conditional merely, the condition being that each several agent does its own 'level best.' I offer you the chance of taking part in such a world. Its safety, you see, is unwarranted. It is a real adventure, with real danger, yet it may win through. It is a social scheme of co-operative work genuinely to be done. Will you join the procession? Will you trust yourself and trust the other agents enough to face the risk? . . . Then it is perfectly possible to accept sincerely a drastic kind of a universe from which the element of 'seriousness' is not to be expelled. Who so does so is, it seems to me, a genuine pragmatist. He is willing to live on a scheme of uncertified possibilities which he trusts; willing to pay with his own person, if need be, for the realization of the ideals which he frames. What now actually are the other forces which he trusts to co-operate with him, in a universe of such a type? They are at least his fellow men, in the stage of being which our actual universe has reached."* [34]

In conclusion, there are realistic ethics leadership and intervention action strategies. We can act effectively concerning organizational ethics issues. Depending upon the circumstances including our own courage, we can choose to act and be ethical both as individuals and as leaders. Being as a part and leading ethical change is the more constructive approach generally. However, being as an individual intervening against others and organizations can sometimes be the only short or medium term effective approach.

Acknowledgements

I would like to acknowledge and thank the following people for their help with ideas presented in this article: the members of the Works in Progress Seminar of Boston College particularly Dalmar Fisher, James Gips, John Neuhauser, William Torbert, and the late James Waters; Kenneth Boulding of the University of Colorado; Robert Greenleaf; and, Douglas Steere of Haverford College.

---

[34]William James, *Pragmatism: A New Name for Some Old Ways of Thinking.* New York: Longmans, Green and Co., 1907, p. 290, 297–298.

Richard P. Nielsen is an associate professor in the Department of Organizational Studies, School of Management, Boston College. He has been a faculty member at Boston College since 1980. He has served as a speaker and taught seminars and management development courses in France, Germany, Holland, Indonesia, Mexico, Pakistan, and Switzerland. He has also served as a consultant and presented management development programs to such organizations as Citicorp, GSX/Genstar, IBM, Arthur D. Little, the Society of Friends and the American Friends Service Committee, the United Nations, the U.S. Agency for International Development, the U.S. Office of Education, and the WGBH Educational Foundation.

His research, teaching, and consulting interests are in the areas of ethics practice and cooperative change management. He serves as an editorial board member and referee for the Journal of Business Ethics. *Some of his related recent publications include "Limitations of Reasoning as an Ethics Action Strategy"* (Journal of Business Ethics, *1988),* "Arendt's Action Philosophy and the Manager as Eichmann, Richard III, Faust or Institution Citizen" *(California Management Review, *1984), and* "Cooperative Strategy" *(Strategy Management Journal, *1988).*

PART VII
INSTRUMENTATION

This final section includes eight frequently used instruments in the field of organizational behavior. They represent each of the major orientations to the field. The first instrument focuses on the management assumptions associated with McGregor's Theory X and Theory Y. This is followed by three measures of employee motivation. The first is associated with Maslow's Need Hierarchy and was developed by Porter and Lawler. The Job Diagnostic Survey is next, developed to provide measures for the Hackman-Oldham model. The last measure corresponds to the Expectancy Theory.

The next three instruments are concerned with leadership style: The T-P Questionnaire, which is similar to the Management Grid; the LPC, which serves as a basis for Fiedler's Contingency Theory; and the LEAD Questionnaire, which is related to Life-Cycle Theory. The final instrument represents a modified version of Likert's Systems Questionnaire.

SUPERVISORY ATTITUDES: THE X-Y SCALE

_____

Name

_____

Group

Part I

Directions: The following are various types of behavior which a supervisor (manager, leader) may engage in in relation to subordinates. Read each item carefully and then put a check mark in one of the columns to indicate what you would do.

If I were the supervisor, I would:	Make a Great Effort to Do This	Tend to Do This	Tend to Avoid Doing This	Make a Great Effort to Avoid This
1. Closely supervise my subordinates in order to get better work from them.				
2. Set the goals and objectives for my subordinates and sell them on the merits of my plans.				
3. Set up controls to assure that my subordinates are getting the job done.				
4. Encourage my subordinates to set their own goals and objectives.				
5. Make sure that my subordinates' work is planned out for them.				
6. Check with my subordinates daily to see if they need any help.				
7. Step in as soon as reports indicate that the job is slipping.				
8. Push my people to meet schedules if necessary.				
9. Have frequent meetings to keep in touch with what is going on.				
10. Allow subordinates to make important decisions.				

_____

From _The 1972 Annual Handbook for Group Facilitators_, LaJolla, California: University Associates. Used by permission of the publisher.

7. The feeling of self-fulfillment a person gets from being in my job:
   a) How much is there now?   1   2   3   4   5   6   7
   b) How much should there be?   1   2   3   4   5   6   7
   c) How important is this to me? 1   2   3   4   5   6   7

8. The prestige of my job outside the company:
   a) How much is there now?   1   2   3   4   5   6   7
   b) How much should there be?   1   2   3   4   5   6   7
   c) How important is this to me? 1   2   3   4   5   6   7

9. The feeling of worthwhile accomplishment in my job:
   a) How much is there now?   1   2   3   4   5   6   7
   b) How much should there be?   1   2   3   4   5   6   7
   c) How important is this to me? 1   2   3   4   5   6   7

10. The opportunity, in my job, to give help to other people:
    a) How much is there now?   1   2   3   4   5   6   7
    b) How much should there be?   1   2   3   4   5   6   7
    c) How important is this to me? 1   2   3   4   5   6   7

11. The opportunity, in my job, for participating in the setting of goals:
    a) How much is there now?   1   2   3   4   5   6   7
    b) How much should there be?   1   2   3   4   5   6   7
    c) How important is this to me? 1   2   3   4   5   6   7

12. The opportunity, in my job, for participating in the determination of methods and procedures:
    a) How much is there now?   1   2   3   4   5   6   7
    b) How much should there be?   1   2   3   4   5   6   7
    c) How important is this to me? 1   2   3   4   5   6   7

13. The opportunity to develop close friendships in my job:
    a) How much is there now?   1   2   3   4   5   6   7
    b) How much should there be?   1   2   3   4   5   6   7
    c) How important is this to me? 1   2   3   4   5   6   7

JOB DIAGNOSTIC SURVEY

SHORT FORM

This questionnaire was developed as part of a Yale University study of jobs and how people react to them. The questionnaire helps to determine how jobs can be better designed by obtaining information about how people react to different kinds of jobs.

On the following pages you will find several different kinds of questions about your job. Specific instructions are given at the start of each section. Please read them carefully. It should take no more than 10 minutes to complete the entire questionnaire. Please move through it quickly.

The questions are designed to obtain *your* perceptions of your job and *your* reactions to it.

There are no "trick" questions. Your individual answers will be kept completely confidential. Please answer each item as honestly and frankly as possible.

Thank you for your cooperation.

This part of the questionnaire asks you to describe
your job, as objectively as you can.

Please do not use this part of the questionnaire to show how much you like or dislike
your job. Questions about that will come later. Instead, try to make your descriptions as accurate and as objective as you possibly can.

A sample question is given below.

A.   To what extent does your job require you to work with mechanical
       equipment?

1-----------2-----------3-----------4-----------5--------(6)---------7

Very little; the	Moderately	Very much; the
job requires al-		job requires al-
most no contact		most constant
with mechanical		work with
equipment of		mechanical
any kind.		equipment.

You are to circle the number which is the most accurate description of your job.

If, for example, your job requires you to work with
mechanical equipment a good deal of the time—but also
requires some paperwork—you might circle the number
six, as was done in the example above.

If you do not understand these instructions, please ask for assistance. If you do
understand them, turn the page and begin.

1. To what extent does your job require you to *work closely with other people* (either "clients," or people in related jobs in your own organization)?

```
1-----------2-----------3-----------4-----------5-----------6-----------7
```

Very little; deal- ing with other people is not at all necessary in doing the job.	Moderately; some dealing with others is necessary.	Very much; dealing with other people is an absolutely essential and crucial part of doing the job.

2. How much *autonomy* is there is your job? That is, to what extent does your job permit you to decide *on your own* how to go about doing the work?

```
1-----------2-----------3-----------4-----------5-----------6-----------7
```

Very little; the job gives me almost no per- sonal "say" about how and when the work is done.	Moderate autonomy; many things are standardized and not under my con- trol, but I can make some decisions about the work.	Very much; the job gives me almost complete responsibility for deciding how and when the work is done.

3. To what extent does your job involve doing a *"whole" and identifiable piece of work*? That is, is the job a complete piece of work that has an obvious beginning and end? Or is it only a small *part* of the overall piece of work, which is finished by other people or by automatic machines?

```
1-----------2-----------3-----------4-----------5-----------6-----------7
```

My job is only a tiny part of the overall piece of work; the re- sults of my ac- tivities cannot be seen in the final product or service.	My job is a moderate-sized "chunk" of the overall piece of work; my own contribution can be seen in the final outcome.	My job involves doing the whole piece of work, from start to finish; the re- sults of my ac- tivities are easily seen in the final product or service.

4. How much *variety* is there in your job? That is, to what extent does the job require you to do many different things at work, using a variety of your skills and talents?

```
1-----------2-----------3-----------4-----------5-----------6-----------7
```

Very little; the job requires me to do the same routine things over and over again.	Moderate variety.	Very much; the job requires me to do many differ- ent things, using a number or dif- ferent skills and talents.

5. In general, how *significant or important* is your job? That is, are the results of your work likely to significantly affect the lives or well-being of other people?

1-----------2-----------3-----------4-----------5-----------6-----------7

Not very signifi-
cant; the outcomes
of my work are *not*
likely to have
important effects
on other people.

Moderately
significant.

Highly signifi-
cant; the out-
comes of my
work can affect
other people in
very important
ways.

6. To what extent do *managers or co-workers* let you know how well you are doing on your job?

1-----------2-----------3-----------4-----------5-----------6-----------7

Very little; people
almost never let
me know how well
I am doing.

Moderately;
sometimes people
may give me
"feedback;" other
times they
may not.

Very much;
managers or
co-workers provide
me with almost
constant "feed-
back" as I work
about how well I am
doing.

7. To what extent does *doing the job itself* provide you with information about your work performance? That is, does the actual *work itself* provide clues about how well you are doing—aside from any "feedback" co-workers or supervisors may provide?

1-----------2-----------3-----------4-----------5-----------6-----------7

Very little; the
job itself is set
up so I could
work forever
without finding
out how well I
am doing.

Moderately; some-
times doing the
job provides
"feedback" to me;
sometimes it does
not.

Very much; the
job is set up so
that I get almost
constant "feed-
back" as I work
about how well
I am doing.

Listed below are a number of statements which could be used to describe a job.

You are to indicate whether each statement is an *accurate* or an *inaccurate* description of *your* job.

Once again, please try to be as objective as you can in deciding how accurately each statement describes your job—regardless of whether you like or dislike your job.

Write a number in the blank beside each statement, based on the following scale:

How accurate is the statement in describing your job?

1	2	3	4	5	6	7
Very Inaccurate	Mostly Inaccurate	Slightly Inaccurate	Uncertain	Slightly Accurate	Mostly Accurate	Very Accurate

_____ 1. The job requires me to use a number of complex or high-level skills.

_____ 2. The job requires a lot of cooperative work with other people.

_____ 3. The job is arranged so that I do *not* have the chance to do an entire piece of work from beginning to end.

_____ 4. Just doing the work required by the job provides many chances for me to figure out how well I am doing.

_____ 5. The job is quite simple and repetitive.

_____ 6. The job can be done adequately by a person working alone—without talking or checking with other people.

_____ 7. The supervisors and co-workers on this job almost *never* give me any "feedback" about how well I am doing in my work.

_____ 8. This job is one where a lot of other people can be affected by how well the work gets done.

_____ 9. The job denies me any chance to use my personal initiative or judgment in carrying out the work.

_____ 10. Supervisors often let me know how well they think I am performing the job.

_____ 11. The job provides me the chance to completely finish the pieces of work I begin.

_____ 12. The job itself provides very few clues about whether or not I am performing well.

_____ 13. The job gives me considerable opportunity for independence and freedom in how I do the work.

_____ 14. The job itself is *not* very significant or important in the broader scheme of things.

SECTION THREE

Now please indicate how you personally feel about your job.

Each of the statements below is something that a person might say about his or her job. You are to indicate your own, personal *feelings* about your job by marking how much you agree with each of the statements.

Write a number in the blank for each statement, based on this scale:

How much do you agree with the statement?

1	2	3	4	5	6	7
Disagree Strongly	Disagree	Disagree Slightly	Neutral	Agree Slightly	Agree	Agree Strongly

_____ 1. My opinion of myself goes up when I do this job well.

_____ 2. Generally speaking, I am very satisfied with this job.

_____ 3. I feel a great sense of personal satisfaction when I do this job well.

_____ 4. I frequently think of quitting this job.

_____ 5. I feel bad and unhappy when I discover that I have performed poorly on this job.

_____ 6. I am generally satisfied with the kind of work I do in this job.

_____ 7. My own feelings generally are *not* affected much one way or the other by how well I do on this job.

Now please indicate how *satisfied* you are with each aspect of your job listed below. Once again, write the appropriate number in the blank beside each statement.

1	2	3	4	5	6	7
Extremely Dissatisfied	Dissatisfied	Slightly Dissatisfied	Neutral	Slightly Satisfied	Satisfied	Extremely Satisfied

_____ 1. The amount of job security I have.

_____ 2. The amount of pay and fringe benefits I receive.

_____ 3. The amount of personal growth and development I get in doing my job.

_____ 4. The people I talk to and work with on my job.

_____ 5. The degree of respect and fair treatment I receive from my boss.

_____ 6. The feeling of worthwhile accomplishment I get from doing my job.

_____ 7. The chance to get to know other people while on the job.

_____ 8. The amount of support and guidance I receive from my supervisor.

_____ 9. The degree to which I am fairly paid for what I contribute to this organization.

_____ 10. The amount of independent thought and action I can exercise in my job.

_____ 11. How secure things look for me in the future in this organization.

_____ 12. The chance to help other people while at work.

_____ 13. The amount of challenge in my job.

_____ 14. The overall quality of the supervision I receive in my work.

SECTION FIVE

Listed below are a number of characteristics which could be present on any job. People differ about how much they would like to have each one present in their own jobs. We are interested in learning *how much you personally would like* to have each one present in your job.

Using the scale below, please indicate the *degree* to which you *would like* to have each characteristic present in your job.

NOTE: The numbers on this scale are different from those used in previous scales.

4	5	6	7	8	9	10
Would like having this only a moderate amount (or less).			Would like having this very much.			Would like having this *extremely* much.

_____ 1. High respect and fair treatment from my supervisor.

_____ 2. Stimulating and challenging work.

_____ 3. Chances to exercise independent thought and action in my job.

_____ 4. Great job security.

_____ 5. Very friendly co-workers.

_____ 6. Opportunities to learn new things from my work.

_____ 7. High salary and good fringe benefits.

_____ 8. Opportunities to be creative and imaginative in my work.

_____ 9. Quick promotions.

_____ 10. Opportunities for personal growth and development in my job.

_____ 11. A sense of worthwhile accomplishment in my work.

COMPUTATIONAL GUIDE FOR SELF-SCORING
THE SHORT FORM OF THE JDS

Example: Imagine that your scores were as follows for the 3 items that measure Skill Variety:

Section One, Item #4	6
Section Two, Item #1	5
Section Two, Item #5	2

Here is a worked-out computation of your Skill Variety score, given those item responses.

Section One, Item #4   + *6*

plus Section Two, Item #1   + *5*

minus Section Two, Item #5   - *2*

Sum | *9* |

Adjustment   + 8

Total | *17* | ÷ 3 = | *5.67* |

This is the Skill
Variety Score

I. JOB CHARACTERISTICS

A. Skill Variety

Section One, Item #4   +___

plus Section Two, Item #1   +___

minus Section Two, Item #5   -___

Sum | |

Adjustment   + 8

Total | | ÷ 3 = | |

B. <u>Task Identity</u>

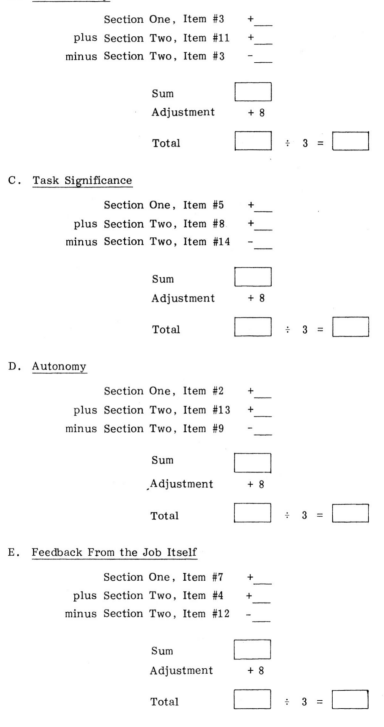

Section One, Item #3   +___

plus Section Two, Item #11   +___

minus Section Two, Item #3   -___

Sum

Adjustment   + 8

Total   ÷ 3 =

C. <u>Task Significance</u>

Section One, Item #5   +___

plus Section Two, Item #8   +___

minus Section Two, Item #14   -___

Sum

Adjustment   + 8

Total   ÷ 3 =

D. <u>Autonomy</u>

Section One, Item #2   +___

plus Section Two, Item #13   +___

minus Section Two, Item #9   -___

Sum

Adjustment   + 8

Total   ÷ 3 =

E. <u>Feedback From the Job Itself</u>

Section One, Item #7   +___

plus Section Two, Item #4   +___

minus Section Two, Item #12   -___

Sum

Adjustment   + 8

Total   ÷ 3 =

F. Feedback From Agents

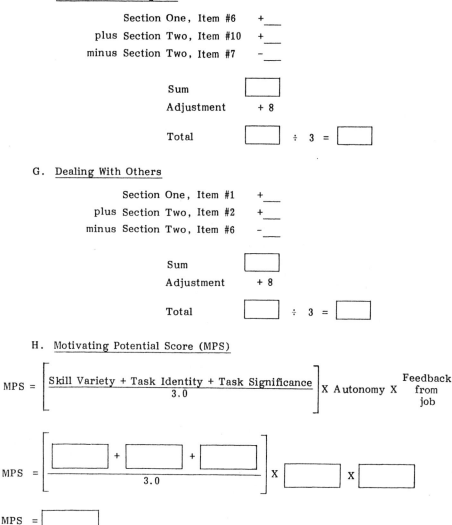

               Section One, Item #6   +___

     plus Section Two, Item #10   +___

  minus Section Two, Item #7   −___

               Sum

               Adjustment   + 8

               Total   ÷ 3 =

G. Dealing With Others

               Section One, Item #1   +___

     plus Section Two, Item #2   +___

  minus Section Two, Item #6   −___

               Sum

               Adjustment   + 8

               Total   ÷ 3 =

H. Motivating Potential Score (MPS)

$$MPS = \left[\frac{\text{Skill Variety} + \text{Task Identity} + \text{Task Significance}}{3.0} \right] \times \text{Autonomy} \times \begin{array}{c}\text{Feedback} \\ \text{from} \\ \text{job}\end{array}$$

$$MPS = \left[\frac{\boxed{} + \boxed{} + \boxed{}}{3.0} \right] \times \boxed{} \times \boxed{}$$

$$MPS = \boxed{}$$

II. AFFECTIVE RESPONSES TO THE JOB

A. General Satisfaction

Section Three, Item #2	+___
plus Section Three, Item #6	+___
minus Section Three, Item #4	−___

Sum   ☐

Adjustment   + 8

Total   ☐ ÷ 3 = ☐

B. Internal Work Motivation

Section Three, Item #1	+___
plus Section Three, Item #3	+___
plus Section Three, Item #5	+___
minus Section Three, Item #7	−___

Sum   ☐

Adjustment   + 8

Total   ☐ ÷ 4 = ☐

C. Specific Satisfactions

1. Pay satisfaction

Section Four, Item #2	+___
plus Section Four, Item #9	+___

Total   ☐ ÷ 2 = ☐

2. Security satisfaction

Section Four, Item #1	+___
plus Section Four, Item #11	+___

Total   ☐ ÷ 2 = ☐

C. Specific Satisfactions (Continued)

3. Social satisfaction

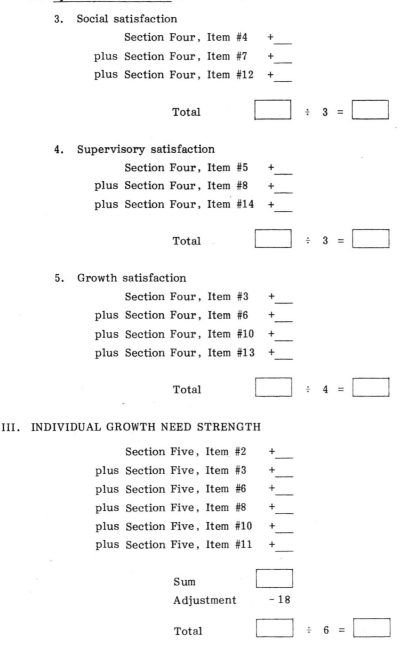

         Section Four, Item #4   +____

plus Section Four, Item #7   +____

plus Section Four, Item #12   +____

Total   [   ] ÷ 3 = [   ]

4. Supervisory satisfaction

         Section Four, Item #5   +____

plus Section Four, Item #8   +____

plus Section Four, Item #14   +____

Total   [   ] ÷ 3 = [   ]

5. Growth satisfaction

         Section Four, Item #3   +____

plus Section Four, Item #6   +____

plus Section Four, Item #10   +____

plus Section Four, Item #13   +____

Total   [   ] ÷ 4 = [   ]

III. INDIVIDUAL GROWTH NEED STRENGTH

         Section Five, Item #2   +____

plus Section Five, Item #3   +____

plus Section Five, Item #6   +____

plus Section Five, Item #8   +____

plus Section Five, Item #10   +____

plus Section Five, Item #11   +____

Sum   [   ]

Adjustment   - 18

Total   [   ] ÷ 6 = [   ]

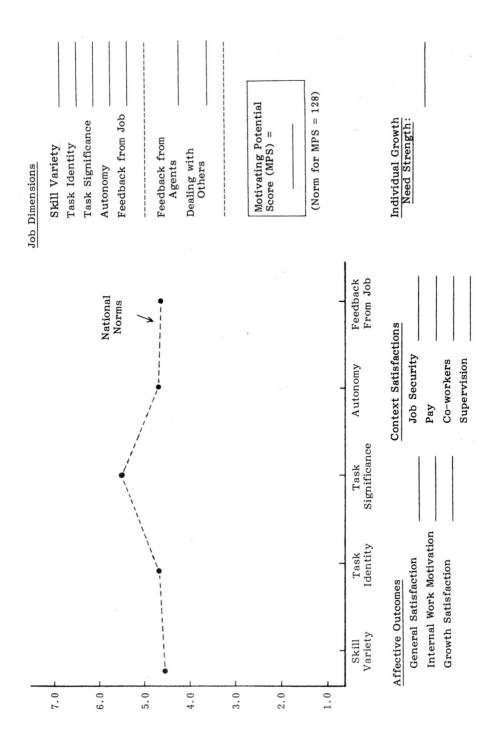

Job Dimensions

Skill Variety _____

Task Identity _____

Task Significance _____

Autonomy _____

Feedback from Job _____

Feedback from Agents _____

Dealing with Others _____

Motivating Potential Score (MPS) = _____

(Norm for MPS = 128)

Individual Growth Need Strength: _____

National Norms

Skill Variety · Task Identity · Task Significance · Autonomy · Feedback From Job

7.0 — 6.0 — 5.0 — 4.0 — 3.0 — 2.0 — 1.0

Affective Outcomes

General Satisfaction _____

Internal Work Motivation _____

Growth Satisfaction _____

Context Satisfactions

Job Security _____

Pay _____

Co-workers _____

Supervision _____

MEASURING MOTIVATION USING EXPECTANCY THEORY[1]

Expectancy theory suggests that it is useful to measure the attitudes individuals have in order to diagnose motivational problems. Such measurement helps the manager to understand why employees are motivated or not, what the strength of motivation is in different parts of the organization, and how effective different rewards are for motivating performance. A short version of a questionnaire used to measure motivation in organizations is included here.[2] Basically, three different questions need to be asked (see Tables 1, 2 and 3).

Using the Questionnaire Results

The results from this questionnaire can be used to calculate a work-motivation score. A score can be calculated for each individual and scores can be combined for groups of individuals. The procedure for obtaining a work-motivation score is as follows:

1. For each of the possible positive outcomes listed in questions 1 and 2, multiply the score for the outcome on question 1 ($P{\to}O$ expectancies) by the corresponding score on question 2 (valences of outcomes). Thus, score 1a would be multiplied by score 2a, score 1b by score 2b, etc.

2. All of the 1 times 2 products should be added together to get a total of all expectancies times valences_____.

3. The total should be divided by the number of pairs (in this case, eleven) to get an average expectancy-times-valence score_____.

4. The scores from question 3 ($E{\to}P$ expectancies) should be added together to get total of all expectancies times valences_____.

---

[1]From D. A. Nadler and E. E. Lawler, "Motivation: A Diagnostic Approach." In *Perspectives on Behavior in Organizations,* edited by J. R. Hackman, E. E. Lawler, and L. W. Porter. New York: McGraw-Hill, 1977.

[2]For a complete version of the questionnaire and supporting documentation, see D. A. Nadler, C. Cammann, G. D. Jenkins, and E. E. Lawler, eds. *The Michigan Organizational Assessment Package* (Progress Report II). Ann Arbor, MI: Survey Research Center, 1975.

5. Multiply the score obtained in step 3 (the average expectancy times valence) by the score obtain in step d (the average $E{\rightarrow}P$ expectancy score) to obtain a total work-motivation score_____.

Table 1

Question 1: Here are some things that could happen to people if they do their jobs *especially well.* How likely is it that each of these things would happen if you performed your job *especially well?*

		Not at all likely	Somewhat likely	Quite likely	Extremely likely			
a	You will get a bonus or pay increase	(1)	(2)	(3)	(4)	(5)	(6)	(7)
b	You will feel better about yourself as a person	(1)	(2)	(3)	(4)	(5)	(6)	(7)
c	You will have an opportunity to develop your skills and abilities	(1)	(2)	(3)	(4)	(5)	(6)	(7)
d	You will have better job security	(1)	(2)	(3)	(4)	(5)	(6)	(7)
e	You will be given chances to learn new things	(1)	(2)	(3)	(4)	(5)	(6)	(7)
f	You will be promoted or get a better job	(1)	(2)	(3)	(4)	(5)	(6)	(7)
g	You will get a feeling that you've accomplished something worthwhile	(1)	(2)	(3)	(4)	(5)	(6)	(7)
h	You will have more freedom on your job	(1)	(2)	(3)	(4)	(5)	(6)	(7)
i	You will be respected by the people you work with	(1)	(2)	(3)	(4)	(5)	(6)	(7)
j	Your supervisor will praise you	(1)	(2)	(3)	(4)	(5)	(6)	(7)
k	The people you work with will be friendly with you	(1)	(2)	(3)	(4)	(5)	(6)	(7)

Table 2.

Question 2: Different people want different things from their work. Here is a list of things a person could have on his or her job. How *important* is each of the following to you?

How important is . . . ?	Moderately important or less		Quite important			Extremely important	
a The amount of pay you get	(1)	(2)	(3)	(4)	(5)	(6)	(7)
b The chances you have to do something that makes you feel good about yourself as a person	(1)	(2)	(3)	(4)	(5)	(6)	(7)
c The opportunity to develop your skills and abilities	(1)	(2)	(3)	(4)	(5)	(6)	(7)
d The amount of job security you have	(1)	(2)	(3)	(4)	(5)	(6)	(7)

How important is . . . ?

	Moderately important or less		Quite important			Extremely important	
e The chances you have to learn new things	(1)	(2)	(3)	(4)	(5)	(6)	(7)
f Your chances for getting a promotion or getting a better job	(1)	(2)	(3)	(4)	(5)	(6)	(7)
g The chances you have to accomplish something worthwhile	(1)	(2)	(3)	(4)	(5)	(6)	(7)
h The amount of freedom you have on your job	(1)	(2)	(3)	(4)	(5)	(6)	(7)

How important is . . . ?

	Moderately important or less		Quite important			Extremely important	
i The respect you receive from the people you work with	(1)	(2)	(3)	(4)	(5)	(6)	(7)
j The praise you get from your supervisor	(1)	(2)	(3)	(4)	(5)	(6)	(7)
k The friendliness of the people you work with	(1)	(2)	(3)	(4)	(5)	(6)	(7)

Table 3.

Question 3: Below, you will see a number of pairs of factors that look like this:

warm weather → sweating   (1) (2) (3) (4) (5) (6) (7)

You are to indicate by checking the appropriate number to the right of each pair how often it is true for *you* personally that the first factor leads to the second on *your job.* Remember, for each pair, indicate how often it is true by checking the box under the response which seems most accurate.

		Never	Sometimes		Often		Almost always
a	Working hard → high productivity	(1) (2)	(3)	(4)	(5)	(6)	(7)
b	Working hard → doing my job well	(1) (2)	(3)	(4)	(5)	(6)	(7)
c	Working hard → good job performance	(1) (2)	(3)	(4)	(5)	(6)	(7)

_____   _____
Name   Group

The following items describe aspects of leadership behavior. Respond to each item according to the way you would be most likely to act if you were the leader of a work group. Circle whether you would be likely to behave in the described way always (A), frequently (F), occasionally (O), seldom (S), or never (N).

A   F   O   S   N   1.   I would most likely act as the spokesman of the group.

A   F   O   S   N   2.   I would allow members complete freedom in their work.

A   F   O   S   N   3.   I would encourage the use of uniform procedures.

A   F   O   S   N   4.   I would permit the members to use their own judgment in solving problems.

A   F   O   S   N   5.   I would needle members for greater effort.

A   F   O   S   N   6.   I would let the members do their work the way they think best.

A   F   O   S   N   7.   I would keep the work moving at a rapid pace.

A   F   O   S   N   8.   I would turn the members loose on a job and let them go to it.

A   F   O   S   N   9.   I would settle conflicts when they occur in the group.

A   F   O   S   N   10.   I would be reluctant to allow the members any freedom of action.

A   F   O   S   N   11.   I would decide what shall be done and how it shall be done.

A   F   O   S   N   12.   I would push for increased production.

A   F   O   S   N   13.   I would assign group members to particular tasks.

A   F   O   S   N   14.   I would be willing to make changes.

A   F   O   S   N   15.   I would schedule the work to be done.

A   F   O   S   N   16.   I would refuse to explain my actions.

A   F   O   S   N   17.   I would persuade others that my ideas are to their advantage.

A   F   O   S   N   18.   I would permit the group to set its own pace.

T_____   P_____

From *A Handbook of Structured Experiences for Human Relations Training*, LaJolla, California: University Associates. Used by permission of the publisher.

Least Preferred Coworker (LPC)

Think of the person with whom you can work least well. He may be someone you work with now, or he may be someone you knew in the past.

He does not have to be the person you like least well, but should be the person with whom you had the most difficulty in getting a job done.

Pleasant	___ ___ ___ ___ / ___ ___ ___ ___	Unpleasant
Friendly	___ ___ ___ ___ / ___ ___ ___ ___	Unfriendly
Rejecting	___ ___ ___ ___ / ___ ___ ___ ___	Accepting
Helpful	___ ___ ___ ___ / ___ ___ ___ ___	Frustrating
Unenthusiastic	___ ___ ___ ___ / ___ ___ ___ ___	Enthusiastic
Tense	___ ___ ___ ___ / ___ ___ ___ ___	Relaxed
Distant	___ ___ ___ ___ / ___ ___ ___ ___	Close
Cold	___ ___ ___ ___ / ___ ___ ___ ___	Warm
Cooperative	___ ___ ___ ___ / ___ ___ ___ ___	Uncooperative
Supportive	___ ___ ___ ___ / ___ ___ ___ ___	Hostile
Boring	___ ___ ___ ___ / ___ ___ ___ ___	Interesting
Quarrelsome	___ ___ ___ ___ / ___ ___ ___ ___	Harmonious
Self-assured	___ ___ ___ ___ / ___ ___ ___ ___	Hesitant
Efficient	___ ___ ___ ___ / ___ ___ ___ ___	Inefficient
Gloomy	___ ___ ___ ___ / ___ ___ ___ ___	Cheerful
Open	___ ___ ___ ___ / ___ ___ ___ ___	Guarded

From *A Theory of Leadership Effectiveness*, New York: Mcgraw-Hill, 1967. Used by permission of the publisher.

LEADER EFFECTIVENESS AND ADAPTABILITY DESCRIPTION (LEAD)

Paul Hersey and Kenneth H. Blanchard

Directions: Assume you are involved in each of the following twelve situations. READ each item carefully and THINK about what you would do in each circumstance. Then CIRCLE the letter of the alternative that you think would most closely describe your behavior in the situation presented. Circle only *one* choice. For each situation, interpret key concepts in terms of the environment or situation in which you most often think of yourself as assuming a leadership role. Say, for example, an item mentions subordinates. If you think that you engage in leadership behavior most often as an industrial manager, then think about your staff as subordinates. If, however, you think of yourself as assuming a leadership role primarily as a parent, think about your children as your subordinates. As a teacher, think about your students as subordinates.

DO NOT change your situational frame of reference from one item to another. Separate LEAD instruments may be used to examine your leadership behavior in as many different settings as you think helpful.

1. Your subordinates have not been responding to your friendly conversation and obvious concern for their welfare. Their performance is in a tailspin.

    A. Emphasize the use of uniform procedures and the necessity for task accomplishment.
    B. Make yourself available for discussion but do not push.
    C. Talk with subordinates and then set goals.
    D. Be careful not to intervene.

2. The observable performance of your group is increasing. You have been making sure that all members are aware of their roles and standards.

    A. Engage in friendly interaction, but continue to make sure that all members are aware of their roles and standards.
    B. Take no definite action.
    C. Do what you can to make the group feel important and involved.
    D. Emphasize the importance of deadlines and tasks.

3. Members of your group are unable to solve a problem themselves. You have normally left them alone. Group performance and interpersonal relations have been good.

   A. Involve the group and together engage in problem solving.
   B. Let the group work it out.
   C. Act quickly and firmly to correct and redirect.
   D. Encourage the group to work on the problem and be available for discussion.

4. You are considering a major change. Your subordinates have a fine record of accomplishment. They respect the need for change.

   A. Allow group involvement in developing the change, but do not push.
   B. Announce changes and then implement them with close supervision.
   C. Allow the group to formulate its own direction.
   D. Incorporate group recommendations, but direct the change.

5. The performance of your group has been dropping during the last few months. Members have been unconcerned with meeting objectives. They have continually needed reminding to do their tasks on time. Redefining roles has helped in the past.

   A. Allow the group to formulate its own direction.
   B. Incorporate group recommendations, but see that objectives are met.
   C. Redefine goals and supervise carefully.
   D. Allow group involvement in setting goals, but do not push.

6. You stepped into an efficiently run situation. The previous administrator ran a tight ship. You want to maintain a productive situation, but would like to begin humanizing the environment.

   A. Do what you can to make the group feel important and involved.
   B. Emphasize the importance of deadlines and tasks.
   C. Be careful not to intervene.
   D. Get the group involved in decision-making, but see that objectives are met.

7. You are considering major changes in your organizational structure. Members of the group have made suggestions about needed change. The group has demonstrated flexibility in its day-to-day operations.

    A.   Define the change and supervise carefully.

    B.   Acquire the group's approval on the change and allow members to organize the implementation.

    C.   Be willing to make changes as recommended, but maintain control of implementation.

    D.   Avoid confrontation; leave things alone.

8. Group performance and interpersonal relations are good. You feel somewhat unsure about your lack of direction of the group.

    A.   Leave the group alone.

    B.   Discuss the situation with the group and then initiate necessary changes.

    C.   Take steps to direct your subordinates toward working in a well-defined manner.

    D.   Be careful of hurting boss-subordinate relations by being too directive.

9. Your superior has appointed you to head a task force that is far overdue in making requested recommendations for change. The group is not clear about its goals. Attendance at sessions has been poor. The meetings have turned into social gatherings. Potentially, the group has the talent necessary to help.

    A.   Let the group work it out.

    B.   Incorporate group recommendations, but see that objectives are met.

    C.   Redefine goals and supervise carefully.

    D.   Allow group involvement in setting goals, but do not push.

10. Your subordinates, usually able to take responsibility, are not responding to your recent redefining of standards.

    A.   Allow group involvement in redefining standards, but do not push.

    B.   Redefine standards and supervise carefully.

    C.   Avoid confrontation by not applying pressure.

    D.   Incorporate group recommendations, but see that new standards are met.

11. You have been promoted to a new position. The previous supervisor was uninvolved in the affairs of the group. The group has adequately handled its tasks and direction. Group interrelations are good.

  A. Take steps to direct subordinates toward working in a well-defined manner.
  B. Involve subordinates in decision-making and reinforce good contributions.
  C. Discuss past performance with the group and then examine the need for new practices.
  D. Continue to leave the group alone.

12. Recent information indicates some internal difficulties among subordinates. The group has a remarkable record of accomplishment. Members have effectively maintained long range goals and have worked in harmony for the past year. All are well-qualified for the task.

  A. Try out your solution with subordinates and examine the need for new practices.
  B. Allow group members to work it out themselves.
  C. Act quickly and firmly to correct and redirect.
  D. Make yourself available for discussion, but be careful of hurting boss-subordinate relations.

		Alternative Actions			
Situations	1	A	C	B	D
	2	D	A	C	B
	3	C	A	D	B
	4	B	D	A	C
	5	C	B	D	A
	6	B	D	A	C
	7	A	C	B	D
	8	C	B	D	A
	9	C	B	D	A
	10	B	D	A	C
	11	A	C	B	D
	12	C	A	D	B
Quadrant		(1)	(2)	(3)	(4)
Quadrant Scores					

Determining Leadership Style and Style Range

Alternative Actions

		A	B	C	D
	1	+2	−1	+1	−2
	2	+2	−2	+1	−1
	3	+1	−1	−2	+2
	4	+1	−2	+2	−1
	5	−2	+1	+2	−1
Situations	6	−1	+1	−2	+2
	7	−2	+2	−1	+1
	8	+2	−1	−2	+1
	9	−2	+1	+2	−1
	10	+1	−2	−1	+2
	11	−2	+2	−1	+1
	12	−1	+2	−2	+1
Sub-Total					

= [Total]

Determining Style Adaptability

PROFILE OF ORGANIZATIONAL CHARACTERISTICS

	Organizational variables	SYSTEM 1	SYSTEM 2	SYSTEM 3	SYSTEM 4	Item No.
LEADERSHIP	How much confidence and trust is shown in subordinates?	Virtually None	Some	Substantial amount	A great deal	1
	How free do they feel to talk to superiors about job?	Not very free	Somewhat free	Quite free	Very free	2
	How often are subordinate's ideas sought and used constructively?	Seldom	Sometimes	Often	Very frequently	3
MOTIVATION	Is predominant use made of 1 fear, 2 threats, 3 punishment, 4 rewards, 5 involvements?	1, 2, 3, occasionally 4	4, some 3	4, some 3 and 5	5, 4, based on group	4
	Where is responsibility felt for achieving organization's goals?	Mostly at top	Top and middle	Fairly general	At all levels	5
	How much cooperative teamwork exists?	Very little	Relatively little	Moderate amount	Great deal	6
COMMUNICATIONS	What is the usual direction of information flow?	Downward	Mostly downward	Down and up	Down, up and sideways	7
	How is downward communication accepted?	With suspicion	Possibly with suspicion	With caution	With a receptive mind	8
	How accurate is upward communication?	Usually inaccurate	Often inaccurate	Often accurate	Almost always accurate	9
	How well do superiors know problems faced by subordinates?	Not very well	Rather well	Quite well	Very well	10
DECISIONS	At what level are decisions made?	Mostly at top	Policy at top, some delegation	Broad policy at top, more delegation	Throughout but well integrated	11
	Are subordinates involved in decisions related to their work?	Almost never	Occasionally consulted	Generally consulted	Fully involved	12
	What does decision-making process contribute to motivation?	Not very much	Relatively little	Some contribution	Substantial contribution	13
GOALS	How are organizational goals established?	Orders issued	Orders, some comments invited	After discussion, by orders	By group action (except in crisis)	14
	How much covert resistance to goals is present?	Strong resistance	Moderate resistance	Some resistance at times	Little or none	15
CONTROL	How concentrated are review and control functions?	Very highly at top	Quite highly at top	Moderate delegation to lower levels	Widely shared	16
	Is there an informal organization resisting the formal one?	Yes	Usually	Sometimes	No—some goals as formal	17
	What are cost, productivity, and other control data used for?	Policing, punishment	Reward and punishment	Reward, some self-guidance	Self-guidance, problem-solving	18